Lecture Notes in Computer Science   10017

Commenced Publication in 1973
Founding and Former Series Editors:
Gerhard Goos, Juris Hartmanis, and Jan van Leeuwen

More information about this series at http://www.springer.com/series/7408

Atsushi Igarashi (Ed.)

Programming Languages and Systems

14th Asian Symposium, APLAS 2016
Hanoi, Vietnam, November 21–23, 2016
Proceedings

 Springer

Editor
Atsushi Igarashi
Kyoto University
Kyoto
Japan

ISSN 0302-9743   ISSN 1611-3349 (electronic)
Lecture Notes in Computer Science
ISBN 978-3-319-47957-6   ISBN 978-3-319-47958-3 (eBook)
DOI 10.1007/978-3-319-47958-3

Library of Congress Control Number: 2016954930

LNCS Sublibrary: SL2 – Programming and Software Engineering

Printed on acid-free paper

This Springer imprint is published by Springer Nature
The registered company is Springer International Publishing AG
The registered company address is: Gewerbestrasse 11, 6330 Cham, Switzerland

Preface

This volume contains the proceedings of the 14th Asian Symposium on Programming Languages and Systems (APLAS 2016), held in Hanoi, Vietnam, during November 21–23, 2016. APLAS aims to stimulate programming language research by providing a forum for the presentation of the latest results and the exchange of ideas in programming languages and systems. APLAS is based in Asia, but is an international forum that serves the worldwide programming language community.

APLAS 2016 solicited submissions in two categories: regular research papers and system and tool presentations. The topics covered in the conference include, but are not limited to: semantics, logics, and foundational theory; design of languages, type systems, and foundational calculi; domain-specific languages; compilers, interpreters, and abstract machines; program derivation, synthesis, and transformation; program analysis, verification, and model-checking; logic, constraint, probabilistic and quantum programming; software security; concurrency and parallelism; and tools for programming and implementation.

This year 53 papers were submitted to APLAS. Each submission was reviewed by three or more Program Committee members with the help of external reviewers. After thoroughly evaluating the relevance and quality of each paper, the Program Committee decided to accept 20 regular research papers and two system and tool presentations. This year's program also continued the APLAS tradition of invited talks by distinguished researchers:

- Kazuaki Ishizaki (IBM Researh – Tokyo) on "Making Hardware Accelerator Easier to Use"
- Frank Pfenning (CMU) on "Substructural Proofs as Automata"
- Adam Chlipala (MIT) on "Fiat: A New Perspective on Compiling Domain-Specific Languages in a Proof Assistant"

This program would not have been possible without the unstinting efforts of several people, whom I would like to thank. First, the Program Committee and subreviewers for the hard work put in towards ensuring the high quality of the proceedings. My thanks also go to the Asian Association for Foundation of Software (AAFS), founded by Asian researchers in cooperation with many researchers from Europe and the USA, for sponsoring and supporting APLAS. I would like to warmly thank the Steering Committee in general and Quyet-Thang Huynh, Hung Nguyen, and Viet-Ha Nguyen for their support in the local organization and for organizing the poster session. Finally, I am grateful to Andrei Voronkov, whose EasyChair system eased the processes of submission, paper selection, and proceedings compilation.

September 2016   Atsushi Igarashi

Organization

General Co-chairs

Quyet-Thang Huynh	Hanoi University of Science and Technology, Vietnam
Viet-Ha Nguyen	Vietnam National University, Vietnam

Program Chair

Atsushi Igarashi	Kyoto University, Japan

Program Committee

Andreas Abel	Gothenburg University, Sweden
Walter Binder	University of Lugano, Switzerland
Sandrine Blazy	University of Rennes 1, IRISA, France
Iliano Cervesato	CMU, Qatar
Bor-Yuh Evan Chang	University of Colorado Boulder, USA
Kung Chen	National Chengchi University, Taipei, Taiwan
Yuxi Fu	Shanghai Jiao Tong University, China
Atsushi Igarashi	Kyoto University, Japan
Oleg Kiselyov	Tohoku University, Japan
Anthony W. Lin	Yale-NUS College, Singapore
David Yu Liu	SUNY Binghamton, USA
Hidehiko Masuhara	Tokyo Institute of Technology, Japan
Bruno C.d.S. Oliveira	The University of Hong Kong, Hong Kong, SAR China
Nadia Polikarpova	MIT, USA
Alex Potanin	Victoria University of Wellington, New Zealand
G. Ramalingam	Microsoft Research, India
Quan-Thanh Tho	Ho Chi Minh City University of Technology, Vietnam
Tamara Rezk	Inria, France
Sukyoung Ryu	KAIST, Korea
Ulrich Schöpp	Ludwig-Maximilians-Universität München, Germany
Éric Tanter	University of Chile, Chile
Tachio Terauchi	JAIST, Japan

Poster Chair

Hung Nguyen	Hanoi University of Science and Technology, Vietnam

Additional Reviewers

Aotani, Tomoyuki
Asakura, Izumi
Bühler, David
Cai, Xiaojuan
Casinghino, Chris
Deng, Yuxin
Grigore, Radu
Groves, Lindsay
Hague, Matthew
Kaki, Gowtham
Kiefer, Stefan
Lam, Edmund Soon Lee
Laporte, Vincent
Le, Xuan Bach
Lengal, Ondrej
Li, Guoqiang
Liu, Annie
Long, Huan
Lu, Tianhan
Madiot, Jean-Marie
Meier, Shawn
Moir, Mark
Mover, Sergio
Ng, Nicholas

Patrignani, Marco
Pearce, David
Pérez, Jorge A.
Rosà, Andrea
Salucci, Luca
Springer, Matthias
Stein, Benno
Streader, David
Suenaga, Kohei
Sun, Haiyang
Swierstra, Doaitse
Tauber, Tomas
Tekle, Tuncay
Trivedi, Ashutosh
Tsukada, Takeshi
Wang, Meng
Weng, Shu-Chun
Wilke, Pierre
Xie, Ningning
Yang, Hongseok
Yang, Yanpeng
Zhang, Haoyuan
Zheng, Yudi

Invited Papers

Making Hardware Accelerator Easier to Use

Kazuaki Ishizaki

IBM Research, Tokyo, Japan
kiszk@acm.org

Hardware accelerators such as general-purpose computing on graphics processing units (GPGPU), field-programmable gate array (FPGA), or application specific integrated circuit (ASIC) are becoming popular for accelerating computation-intensive workloads such as analytics, machine learning, or deep learning. While such a hardware accelerator performs parallel computations faster by an order of magnitude, it is not easy for a non-expert programmer to use the accelerator because it is necessary to explicitly write and optimize low-level operations such as device managements and kernel routines. While some programming languages or frameworks have introduced a set of parallel constructs with a lambda expression to easily describe a parallel program, it is executed on multi-core CPUs or multiple CPU nodes. There are some implementations such as parallel stream APIs in Java 8 or Apache Spark. If a runtime system could automatically convert the parallel program into a set of low-level operations for the accelerator, it would be easy to use the accelerator and achieve high performance.

In this talk, we present our research that transparently exploits a successful hardware accelerator GPGPUs in a programming language or framework. Our approach is to generate GPGPU code from a given program that explicitly expresses parallelism without accelerator-specific code. This approach allows the programmer to avoid explicitly writing low-level operations for a specific accelerator.

First, we describe our compilation technique to generate GPGPU code from a parallel stream in Java 8. We explain how to compile a Java program and what optimizations we apply. It is available in IBM SDK, Java Technology Edition, Version 8. We then describe our compilation technique to generate GPGPU code from a program in Apache Spark. We explain how to compile a program for Apache Spark to generate GPGPU code and how to effectively execute the code.

Fiat: A New Perspective on Compiling Domain-Specific Languages in a Proof Assistant

Adam Chlipala

MIT CSAIL, Cambridge, MA, USA
adamc@csail.mit.edu

Domain-specific programming languages (DSLs) have gone mainstream, and with good reason: they make it easier than ever to choose the right tool for the job. With the proper tool support, large software projects naturally mix several DSLs. Orchestrating such interlanguage cooperation can be difficult: often the choice is between inconvenient tangles of command-line tools and code generators (e.g., calling a Yacc-style parser generator from a Makefile) and more pleasant integration with less specialized compile-time optimization (e.g., a conventional embedded language). At the same time, even a language for a well-defined domain will not cover its every subtlety and use case; programmers want to be able to extend DSLs in the same way as they extend conventional libraries, e.g. writing new classes within existing hierarchies defined by frameworks. It can be taxing to learn a new extension mechanism for each language. Compared to libraries in conventional languages, the original DSLs were difficult enough to learn: they are documented by a combination of prose manuals, which may easily get out of date, and the language implementations themselves, which are usually not written to edify potential users. Implementations are also quite difficult to get right, with the possibility for a malfunctioning DSL compiler to run amok more thoroughly than could any library in a conventional language with good encapsulation features.

In this talk, I will introduce our solution to these problems: Fiat, a new programming approach hosted within the Coq proof assistant. DSLs are libraries that build on the common foundation of Coq's expressive higher-order logic. New programming features are explained via notation desugaring into specifications. Multiple DSLs may be combined to describe a program's full specification by composing different specification ingredients. A DSL's notation implementations are designed to be read by programmers as documentation: they deal solely with functionality and omit any complications associated with quality implementation. The largest advantage comes from the chance to omit performance considerations entirely in the definitions of these macros. A DSL's notation definitions provide its reference manual that is guaranteed to remain up-to-date.

Desugaring of programming constructs to logical specifications allows mixing of many programming features in a common framework. However, the specifications alone are insufficient to let us generate good implementations automatically. Fiat's key technique here is *optimization scripts*, packaged units of automation to build implementations automatically from specifications. These are not all-or-nothing implementation strategies:

each script picks up on specification patterns that it knows how to handle well, with each DSL library combining notations with scripts that know how to compile them effectively. These scripts are implemented in Coq's Turing-complete tactic language Ltac, in such a way that compilations of programs are correct by construction, with the transformation process generating Coq proofs to justify its soundness. As a result, the original notations introduced by DSLs, with their simple desugarings into logic optimized for readability, form a binding contract between DSL authors and their users, with no chance for DSL implementation details to break correctness.

I will explain the foundations of Fiat: key features of Coq we build on, our core language of nondeterministic computations, the module language on top of it that formalizes abstract data types with private state, and design patterns for effective coding and composition of optimization scripts. I will also explain some case studies of the whole framework in action. We have what is, to our knowledge, the first pipeline that automatically compiles relational specifications to optimized assembly code, with proofs of correctness. I will show examples in one promising application domain, network servers, where we combine DSLs for parsing and relational data management.

This is joint work with Benjamin Delaware, Samuel Duchovni, Jason Gross, Clément Pit–Claudel, Sorawit Suriyakarn, Peng Wang, and Katherine Ye.

Contents

Invited Presentations

Substructural Proofs as Automata 3
    Henry DeYoung and Frank Pfenning

Verification and Analysis I

Learning a Strategy for Choosing Widening Thresholds
from a Large Codebase 25
    Sooyoung Cha, Sehun Jeong, and Hakjoo Oh

AUSPICE-R: Automatic Safety-Property Proofs for Realistic Features
in Machine Code 42
    Jiaqi Tan, Hui Jun Tay, Rajeev Gandhi, and Priya Narasimhan

Observation-Based Concurrent Program Logic for Relaxed Memory
Consistency Models 63
    Tatsuya Abe and Toshiyuki Maeda

Process Calculus

SPEC: An Equivalence Checker for Security Protocols 87
    Alwen Tiu, Nam Nguyen, and Ross Horne

Binary Session Types for Psi-Calculi 96
    Hans Hüttel

Static Trace-Based Deadlock Analysis for Synchronous Mini-Go 116
    Kai Stadtmüller, Martin Sulzmann, and Peter Thiemann

Profiling and Debugging

AkkaProf: A Profiler for Akka Actors in Parallel and Distributed
Applications 139
    Andrea Rosà, Lydia Y. Chen, and Walter Binder

A Debugger-Cooperative Higher-Order Contract System in Python 148
    Ryoya Arai, Shigeyuki Sato, and Hideya Iwasaki

λ-Calculus

A Sound and Complete Bisimulation for Contextual Equivalence
in λ-Calculus with Call/cc 171
　Taichi Yachi and Eijiro Sumii

A Realizability Interpretation for Intersection and Union Types........... 187
　Daniel J. Dougherty, Ugo de'Liguoro, Luigi Liquori, and Claude Stolze

Open Call-by-Value... 206
　Beniamino Accattoli and Giulio Guerrieri

Type Theory

Implementing Cantor's Paradise 229
　Furio Honsell, Marina Lenisa, Luigi Liquori, and Ivan Scagnetto

Unified Syntax with Iso-types.................................. 251
　Yanpeng Yang, Xuan Bi, and Bruno C.d.S. Oliveira

Refined Environment Classifiers: Type- and Scope-Safe Code Generation
with Mutable Cells 271
　Oleg Kiselyov, Yukiyoshi Kameyama, and Yuto Sudo

Verification and Analysis II

Higher-Order Model Checking in Direct Style 295
　Taku Terao, Takeshi Tsukada, and Naoki Kobayashi

Verifying Concurrent Graph Algorithms........................... 314
　Azalea Raad, Aquinas Hobor, Jules Villard, and Philippa Gardner

Verification of Higher-Order Concurrent Programs with Dynamic
Resource Creation... 335
　Kazuhide Yasukata, Takeshi Tsukada, and Naoki Kobayashi

Programming Paradigms

Probabilistic Programming Language and its Incremental Evaluation 357
　Oleg Kiselyov

ELIOM: A Core ML Language for Tierless Web Programming............ 377
　Gabriel Radanne, Jérôme Vouillon, and Vincent Balat

Separation Logic

DOM: Specification and Client Reasoning 401
　Azalea Raad, José Fragoso Santos, and Philippa Gardner

Decision Procedure for Separation Logic with Inductive Definitions
and Presburger Arithmetic   423
   Makoto Tatsuta, Quang Loc Le, and Wei-Ngan Chin

Completeness for a First-Order Abstract Separation Logic   444
   Zhé Hóu and Alwen Tiu

Author Index   465

Invited Presentations

Substructural Proofs as Automata

Henry DeYoung and Frank Pfenning[✉]

Carnegie Mellon University, Pittsburgh, PA 15213, USA
{hdeyoung,fp}@cs.cmu.edu

Abstract. We present subsingleton logic as a very small fragment of linear logic containing only $\oplus$, **1**, least fixed points and allowing circular proofs. We show that cut-free proofs in this logic are in a Curry–Howard correspondence with subsequential finite state transducers. Constructions on finite state automata and transducers such as composition, complement, and inverse homomorphism can then be realized uniformly simply by cut and cut elimination. If we freely allow cuts in the proofs, they correspond to a well-typed class of machines we call *linear communicating automata*, which can also be seen as a generalization of Turing machines with multiple, concurrently operating read/write heads.

1 Introduction

In the early days of the study of computation as a discipline, we see fundamentally divergent models. On the one hand, we have Turing machines [16], and on the other we have Church's λ-calculus [4]. Turing machines are based on a finite set of states and an explicit storage medium (the tape) which can be read from, written to, and moved in small steps. The λ-calculus as a pure calculus of functions is founded on the notions of abstraction and composition, not easily available on Turing machines, and relies on the complex operation of substitution. The fact that they define the same set of computable functions, say, over natural numbers, is interesting, but are there deeper connections between Turing-like machine models of computation and Church-like linguistic models?

The discovery of the Curry–Howard isomorphism [5,12] between intuitionistic natural deduction and the *typed* λ-calculus adds a new dimension. It provides a *logical foundation* for computation on λ-terms as a form of proof reduction. This has been tremendously important, as it has led to the development of type theory, the setting for much modern research in programming languages since design of a programming language and a logic for reasoning about its programs go hand in hand. To date, Turing-like machine models have not benefited from these developments since no clear and direct connections to logic along the lines of a Curry–Howard isomorphism were known.

In this paper, we explore several connections between certain kinds of automata and machines in the style of Turing and very weak fragments of linear logic [11] augmented with least fixed points along the lines of Baelde et al. [2] and Fortier and Santocanale [9]. Proofs are allowed to be circular with some conditions that ensure they can be seen as coinductively defined. We collectively

© Springer International Publishing AG 2016
A. Igarashi (Ed.): APLAS 2016, LNCS 10017, pp. 3–22, 2016.
DOI: 10.1007/978-3-319-47958-3_1

refer to these fragments as *subsingleton logic* because the rules naturally enforce that every sequent has at most one antecedent and succedent (Sect. 2).

Our first discovery is a Curry–Howard isomorphism between so-called *fixed-cut* proofs in $\oplus,\mathbf{1},\mu$-subsingleton logic and a slight generalization of deterministic finite-state transducers that also captures deterministic finite automata (Sects. 3 and 4). This isomorphism relates proofs to automata and proof reduction to state transitions of the automata. Constructions on automata such as composition, complement, and inverse homomorphism can then be realized "for free" on the logical side by a process of cut elimination (Sect. 5).

If we make two seemingly small changes – allowing arbitrary cuts instead of just fixed cuts and removing some restrictions on circular proofs – proof reduction already has the computational power of Turing machines. We can interpret proofs as a form of linear communicating automata (LCAs, Sect. 6), where *linear* means that the automata are lined up in a row and each automaton communicates only with its left and right neighbors. Alternatively, we can think of LCAs as a generalization of Turing machines with multiple read/write heads operating concurrently. LCAs can be subject to deadlock and race conditions, but those corresponding to (circular) proofs in $\oplus,\mathbf{1},\mu$-subsingleton logic do not exhibit these anomalies (Sect. 7). Thus, the logical connection defines well-behaved LCAs, analogous to the way natural deduction in intuitionistic implicational logic defines well-behaved λ-terms.

We also illustrate how traditional Turing machines are a simple special case of LCAs with only a single read/write head. Perhaps surprisingly, such LCAs can be typed and are therefore well-behaved by construction: Turing machines do not get stuck, while LCAs in general might (Sect. 7).

We view the results in this paper only as a beginning. Many natural questions remain. For example, can we capture deterministic pushdown automata or other classes of automata as natural fragments of the logic and its proofs? Can we exploit the logical origins beyond constructions by cut elimination to reason about properties of the automata or abstract machines?

2   A Subsingleton Fragment of Intuitionistic Linear Logic

In an intuitionistic linear sequent calculus, sequents consist of at most one conclusion in the context of zero or more hypotheses. To achieve a pleasant symmetry between contexts and conclusions, we can consider restricting contexts to have at most one hypothesis, so that each sequent has one of the forms $\cdot \vdash \gamma$ or $A \vdash \gamma$.

Is there a fragment of intuitionistic linear logic that obeys this rather harsh restriction and yet exists as a well-defined, interesting logic in its own right? Somewhat surprisingly, yes, there is; this section presents such a logic, which we dub $\oplus,\mathbf{1}$-subsingleton logic.

2.1   Propositions, Contexts, and Sequents

The propositions of $\oplus,\mathbf{1}$-subsingleton logic are generated by the grammar

$$A, B, C ::= A_1 \oplus A_2 \mid \mathbf{1},$$

where $\oplus$ is additive disjunction and $\mathbf{1}$ is the unit of linear logic's multiplicative conjunction. Uninterpreted propositional atoms p could be included if desired, but we omit them because they are unnecessary for this paper's results. In Sect. 7, we will see that subsingleton logic can be expanded to include more, but not all, of the linear logical connectives.

Sequents are written $\Delta \vdash \gamma$. For now, we will have only single conclusions and so $\gamma ::= C$, but we will eventually consider empty conclusions in Sect. 7. To move toward a pleasant symmetry between contexts and conclusions, contexts Δ are empty or a single proposition, and so $\Delta ::= \cdot \mid A$. We say that a sequent obeys the *subsingleton context restriction* if its context adheres to this form.

2.2   Deriving the Inference Rules of $\oplus$,$\mathbf{1}$-Subsingleton Logic

To illustrate how the subsingleton inference rules are derived from their counterparts in an intuitionistic linear sequent calculus, let us consider the cut rule. The subsingleton cut rule is derived from the intuitionistic linear cut rule as:

$$\frac{\Delta \vdash A \quad \Delta', A \vdash \gamma}{\Delta, \Delta' \vdash \gamma} \quad \leadsto \quad \frac{\Delta \vdash A \quad A \vdash \gamma}{\Delta \vdash \gamma} \ \text{CUT}$$

In the original rule, the linear contexts Δ and Δ' may each contain zero or more hypotheses. When Δ' is nonempty, the sequent $\Delta', A \vdash \gamma$ fails to obey the subsingleton context restriction by virtue of using more than one hypothesis. But by dropping Δ' altogether, we derive a cut rule that obeys the restriction.

The other subsingleton inference rules are derived from linear counterparts in a similar way – just force each sequent to have a subsingleton context. Figure 1 summarizes the syntax and inference rules of a sequent calculus for $\oplus$,$\mathbf{1}$-subsingleton logic.

2.3   Admissibility of Cut and Identity

From the previous examples, we can see that it is not difficult to derive sequent calculus rules for $A_1 \oplus A_2$ and $\mathbf{1}$ that obey the subsingleton context restriction. But that these rules should constitute a well-defined logic in its own right is quite surprising!

Under the verificationist philosophies of Dummett [8] and Martin-Löf [13], $\oplus$,$\mathbf{1}$-subsingleton logic is indeed well-defined because it satisfies admissibility of CUT and ID, which characterize an internal soundness and completeness:

Theorem 1 (Admissibility of cut). *If there are proofs of $\Delta \vdash A$ and $A \vdash \gamma$, then there is also a cut-free proof of $\Delta \vdash \gamma$.*

Proof. By lexicographic induction, first on the structure of the cut formula A and then on the structures of the given derivations.

Theorem 2 (Admissibility of identity). *For all propositions A, the sequent $A \vdash A$ is derivable without using ID.*

$$\begin{array}{ll}
\text{Propositions} & A, B, C ::= A_1 \oplus A_2 \mid 1 \\
\text{Contexts} & \Delta ::= \cdot \mid A \\
\text{Conclusions} & \gamma ::= C
\end{array}$$

$$\cfrac{}{A \vdash A}\ \text{ID} \qquad\qquad \cfrac{\Delta \vdash A \quad A \vdash \gamma}{\Delta \vdash \gamma}\ \text{CUT}$$

$$\cfrac{\Delta \vdash A_1}{\Delta \vdash A_1 \oplus A_2}\ \oplus\text{R}_1 \qquad\qquad \cfrac{\Delta \vdash A_2}{\Delta \vdash A_1 \oplus A_2}\ \oplus\text{R}_2$$

$$\cfrac{A_1 \vdash \gamma \quad A_2 \vdash \gamma}{A_1 \oplus A_2 \vdash \gamma}\ \oplus\text{L}$$

$$\cfrac{}{\cdot \vdash 1}\ \text{1R} \qquad\qquad \cfrac{\cdot \vdash \gamma}{1 \vdash \gamma}\ \text{1L}$$

Fig. 1. A sequent calculus for $\oplus$,1-subsingleton logic

Proof. By structural induction on A.

Theorem 2 justifies hereafter restricting our attention to a calculus without the ID rule. The resulting proofs are said to be identity-free, or η-long, and are complete for provability. Despite Theorem 1, we do not restrict our attention to cut-free proofs because the CUT rule will prove to be important for composition of machines.

2.4   Extending the Logic with Least Fixed Points

Thus far, we have presented a sequent calculus for $\oplus$,1-subsingleton logic with finite propositions $A_1 \oplus A_2$ and **1**. Now we extend it with least fixed points $\mu\alpha.A$, keeping an eye toward their eventual Curry–Howard interpretation as the types of inductively defined data structures. We dub the extended logic $\oplus$,**1**,μ-subsingleton logic.

Our treatment of least fixed points mostly follows that of Fortier and Santocanale [9] by using circular proofs. Here we review the intuition behind circular proofs; please refer to Fortier and Santocanale's publication for a full, formal description.

Fixed Point Propositions and Sequents. Syntactically, the propositions are extended to include least fixed points $\mu\alpha.A$ and propositional variables α:

$$A, B, C ::= \cdots \mid \mu\alpha.A \mid \alpha$$

Because the logic's propositional connectives – just $\oplus$ and **1** for now – are all covariant, least fixed points necessarily satisfy the usual strict positivity condition that guarantees well-definedness. We also require that least fixed points are contractive [10], ruling out, for example, $\mu\alpha.\alpha$. Finally, we further require that a sequent's hypothesis and conclusion be closed, with no free occurrences of any propositional variables α.

In a slight departure from Fortier and Santocanale, we treat least fixed points *equirecursively*, so that $\mu\alpha.A$ is identified with its unfoldings, $[(\mu\alpha.A)/\alpha]A$ and so on. When combined with contractivity, this means that $\mu\alpha.A$ may be thought of as a kind of infinite proposition. For example, $\mu\alpha.\,1 \oplus \alpha$ is something like $1 \oplus (1 \oplus \cdots)$.

Circular Proofs. Previously, with only finite propositions and inference rules that obeyed a subformula property, proofs in $\oplus,1$-subsingleton logic were the familiar well-founded trees of inferences. Least fixed points could be added to this finitary sequent calculus along the lines of Baelde's μMALL [1], but it will be more convenient and intuitive for us to follow Fortier and Santocanale and use an infinitary sequent calculus of circular proofs.

To illustrate the use of circular proofs, consider the following proof, which has as its computational content the function that doubles a natural number. Natural numbers are represented as proofs of the familiar least fixed point $\text{Nat} = \mu\alpha.\,1 \oplus \alpha$; the unfolding of Nat is thus $1 \oplus \text{Nat}$.

This proof begins by case-analyzing a Nat ($\oplus$L rule). If the number is 0, then the proof's left branch continues by reconstructing 0. Otherwise, if the number is the successor of some natural number N, then the proof's right branch continues by first emitting two successors ($\oplus R_2$ rules) and then making a recursive call to double N, as indicated by the back-edge drawn with an arrow.

In this proof, there are several instances of unfolding Nat to $1 \oplus \text{Nat}$. In general, the principles for unfolding on the right and left of a sequent are

$$\frac{\Delta \vdash [(\mu\alpha.A)/\alpha]}{\Delta \vdash \mu\alpha.A} \quad \text{and} \quad \frac{[(\mu\alpha.A)/\alpha] \vdash \gamma}{\mu\alpha.A \vdash \gamma}$$

Fortier and Santocanale adopt these principles as primitive right and left rules for μ. But because our least fixed points are equirecursive and a fixed point is *equal* to its unfolding, unfolding is not a first-class rule of inference, but rather a principle that is used silently within a proof. It would thus be more accurate, but also more opaque, to write the above proof without those dotted principles.

Is μ Correctly Defined? With proofs being circular and hence coinductively defined, one might question whether $\mu\alpha.A$ really represents a *least* fixed point and not a greatest fixed point. After all, we have no inference rules for μ, only implicit unfolding principles – and those principles could apply to any fixed points, not just least ones.

Stated differently, how do we proscribe the following, which purports to represent the first transfinite ordinal, ω, as a finite natural number?

$$\cfrac{\cfrac{\cdot \vdash \texttt{Nat}}{\cdot \vdash \mathbf{1} \oplus \texttt{Nat}} \oplus R_2}{\cdot \vdash \texttt{Nat}}$$

To ensure that μ is correctly defined, one last requirement is imposed upon valid proofs: that every cycle in a valid proof is a left μ-trace. A left μ-trace (i) contains at least one application of a left rule to the unfolding of a least fixed point hypothesis, and (ii) if the trace contains an application of the CUT rule, then the trace continues along the left premise of the CUT. The above $\texttt{Nat} \vdash \texttt{Nat}$ example is indeed a valid proof because its cycle applies the $\oplus$L rule to $\mathbf{1} \oplus \texttt{Nat}$, the unfolding of a $\texttt{Nat}$ hypothesis. But the attempt at representing ω is correctly proscribed because its cycle contains no least fixed point hypothesis whatsoever, to say nothing of a left rule.

Cut Elimination for Circular Proofs. Fortier and Santocanale [9] present a cut elimination procedure for circular proofs. Because of their infinitary nature, circular proofs give rise to a different procedure than do the familiar finitary proofs.

Call a circular proof a *fixed-cut* proof if no cycle contains the CUT rule. Notice the subtle difference from cut-free circular proofs – a fixed-cut proof may contain the CUT rule, so long as the cut occurs outside of all cycles. Cut elimination on *fixed-cut* circular proofs results in a cut-free circular proof.

Things are not quite so pleasant for cut elimination on arbitrary circular proofs. In general, cut elimination results in an infinite, cut-free proof that is not necessarily circular.

3   Subsequential Finite-State Transducers

Subsequential finite-state transducers (SFTs) were first proposed by Schützenberger [15] as a way to capture a class of functions from finite strings to finite strings that is related to finite automata and regular languages. An SFT T is fed some string w as input and deterministically produces a string v as output.

Here we review one formulation of SFTs. This formulation classifies each SFT state as reading, writing, or halting so that SFT computation occurs in small, single-letter steps. Also, this formulation uses strings over alphabets with (potentially several) endmarker symbols so that a string's end is apparent from its structure and so that SFTs subsume deterministic finite automata (Sect. 3.3). Lastly, this formulation uses string reversal in a few places so that SFT configurations receive their input from the left and produce output to the right.

In later sections, we will see that these SFTs are isomorphic to a class of cut-free proofs in subsingleton logic.

3.1 Definitions

Preliminaries. As usual, the set of all finite strings over an alphabet Σ is written as Σ^*, with ϵ denoting the empty string. In addition, the reversal of a string $w \in \Sigma^*$ is written $w^{\mathcal{R}}$.

An *endmarked alphabet* is a pair $\hat{\Sigma} = (\Sigma_i, \Sigma_e)$, consisting of disjoint finite alphabets Σ_i and Σ_e of internal symbols and endmarkers, respectively, with Σ_e nonempty. Under the endmarked alphabet $\hat{\Sigma}$, the set of finite strings terminated with an endmarker is $\Sigma_i^* \Sigma_e$, which we abbreviate as $\hat{\Sigma}^+$. It will be convenient to also define $\hat{\Sigma}^* = \hat{\Sigma}^+ \cup \{\epsilon\}$ and $\Sigma = \Sigma_i \cup \Sigma_e$.

Subsequential Transducers. A *subsequential finite-state string transducer (SFT)* is a 6-tuple $T = (Q, \hat{\Sigma}, \hat{\Gamma}, \delta, \sigma, q_0)$ where Q is a finite set of states that is partitioned into (possibly empty) sets of read and write states, Q^r and Q^w, and halt states, Q^h; $\hat{\Sigma} = (\Sigma_i, \Sigma_e)$ with $\Sigma_e \neq \emptyset$ is a finite endmarked alphabet for input; $\hat{\Gamma} = (\Gamma_i, \Gamma_e)$ with $\Gamma_e \neq \emptyset$ is a finite endmarked alphabet for output; $\delta \colon \Sigma \times Q^r \to Q$ is a total transition function on read states; $\sigma \colon Q^w \to Q \times \Gamma$ is a total output function on write states; and $q_0 \in Q$ is the initial state.

Configurations $\mathcal{C}$ of the SFT T have one of two forms – either *(i)* $w \, q \, v$, where $w^{\mathcal{R}} \in \hat{\Sigma}^*$ and $q \in Q$ and $v^{\mathcal{R}} \in (\Gamma_i^* \cup \hat{\Gamma}^*)$; or *(ii)* v, where $v^{\mathcal{R}} \in \hat{\Gamma}^+$. Let $\longrightarrow$ be the least binary relation on configurations that satisfies the following conditions.

READ $\qquad w a \, q \, v \longrightarrow w \, q_a \, v$ if $q \in Q^r$ and $\delta(a, q) = q_a$

WRITE $\qquad w \, q \, v \longrightarrow w \, q_b \, bv$ if $q \in Q^w$ and $\sigma(q) = (q_b, b)$ and $v \in \Gamma_i^*$

HALT $\qquad q \, v \longrightarrow v \qquad$ if $q \in Q^h$ and $v^{\mathcal{R}} \in \hat{\Gamma}^+$

The SFT T is said to *transduce input* $w \in \hat{\Sigma}^+$ *to output* $v \in \hat{\Gamma}^+$ if there exists a sequence of configurations $\mathcal{C}_0, \ldots, \mathcal{C}_n$ such that *(i)* $\mathcal{C}_0 = w^{\mathcal{R}} q_0$; *(ii)* $\mathcal{C}_i \longrightarrow \mathcal{C}_{i+1}$ for all $0 \le i < n$; and *(iii)* $\mathcal{C}_n = v^{\mathcal{R}}$.

3.2 Example of a Subsequential Transducer

Figure 2 shows the transition graph for an SFT over $\hat{\Sigma} = (\{a, b\}, \{\$\})$. The edges in this graph are labeled c or $\bar{c}$ to indicate an input or output of symbol c, respectively. This SFT compresses each run of bs into a single b. For instance, the input string $abbaabbb\$$ transduces to the output string $abaab\$$ because $\$bbbaabba \, q_0 \longrightarrow^+ \$baaba$. We could even compose this SFT with itself, but this SFT is an idempotent for composition.

3.3 Discussion

Acceptance and Totality. Notice that, unlike some definitions of SFTs, this definition does not include notions of acceptance or rejection of input strings. This is because we are interested in SFTs that induce a total transduction function, since such transducers turn out to compose more naturally in our proof-theoretic setting.

Normal Form SFTs. The above formulation of SFTs allows the possibility that a read state is reachable even after an endmarker signaling the end of the input has been read. An SFT would necessarily get stuck upon entering such a state because there is no more input to read.

The above formulation also allows the dual possibility that a write state is reachable even after having written an endmarker signaling the end of the output. Again, an SFT would necessarily get stuck upon entering such a state because the side condition of the WRITE rule, $v \in \Gamma_i^*$, would fail to be met.

Lastly, the above formulation allows that a halt state is reachable before an endmarker signaling the end of the input has been read. According to the HALT rule, an SFT would necessarily get stuck upon entering such a state.

Fortunately, we may define *normal-form SFTs* as SFTs for which these cases are impossible. An SFT is in normal form if it obeys three properties:

- For all endmarkers $e \in \Sigma_e$ and read states $q \in Q^r$, no read state is reachable from $\delta(e, q)$.
- For all endmarkers $e \in \Gamma_e$, write states $q \in Q^w$, and states $q_e \in Q$, no write state is reachable from q_e if $\sigma(q) = (q_e, e)$.
- For all halt states $q \in Q^w$, all paths from the initial state q_0 to q pass through $\delta(e, q')$ for some endmarker $e \in \Sigma_e$ and read state $q' \in Q^r$.

Normal-form SFTs and SFTs differ only on stuck computations. Because we are only interested in total transductions, hereafter we assume that all SFTs are normal-form.

Deterministic Finite Automata. By allowing alphabets with more than one endmarker, the above definition of SFTs subsumes deterministic finite automata (DFAs). A DFA is an SFT with an endmarked output alphabet $\hat{\Gamma} = (\emptyset, \{a, r\})$, so that the valid output strings are only a or r; the DFA transduces its input to the output string a or r to indicate acceptance or rejection of the input, respectively.

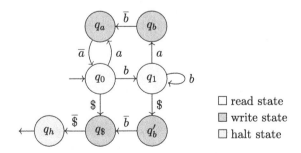

Fig. 2. A subsequential finite-state transducer over the endmarked alphabet $\hat{\Sigma} = (\{a, b\}, \{\$\})$ that compresses each run of bs into a single b

3.4   Composing Subsequential Finite-State String Transducers

Having considered individual subsequential finite-state transducers (SFTs), we may want to compose finitely many SFTs into a linear network that implements a transduction in a modular way. Fortunately, in the above model, SFTs and their configurations compose very naturally into chains.

An SFT chain $(T_i)_{i=1}^n$ is a finite family of SFTs $T_i = (Q_i, \hat{\Sigma}_i, \hat{\Gamma}_i, \delta_i, \sigma_i, q_i)$ such that $\hat{\Gamma}_i = \hat{\Sigma}_{i+1}$ for each $i < n$. Here we give a description of the special case $n = 2$; the general case is notationally cumbersome without providing additional insight.

Let $T_1 = (Q_1, \hat{\Sigma}, \hat{\Gamma}, \delta_1, \sigma_1, i_1)$ and $T_2 = (Q_2, \hat{\Gamma}, \hat{\Omega}, \delta_2, \sigma_2, i_2)$ be two SFTs; let $\hat{\Sigma}_1 = \hat{\Sigma}$ and $\hat{\Gamma}_1 = \hat{\Sigma}_2 = \hat{\Gamma}$ and $\hat{\Gamma}_2 = \hat{\Omega}$. A configuration of the chain $(T_i)_{i=1}^2$ is a string whose reversal is drawn from either $(\Omega_i^* \cup \hat{\Omega}^*) Q_2 (\Gamma_i^* \cup \hat{\Gamma}^*) Q_1 \hat{\Sigma}^*$ or $(\Omega_i^* \cup \hat{\Omega}^*) Q_2 \hat{\Gamma}^*$ or $\hat{\Omega}^+$. Let $\longrightarrow$ be the least binary relation on configurations that satisfies the following conditions.

READ $wa\,q_i\,v \longrightarrow w\,q_i'\,v$ if $\delta_i(a, q_i) = q_i'$

WRITE $w\,q_i\,v \longrightarrow w\,q_i'\,bv$ if $\sigma_i(q_i) = (q_i', b)$

HALT $q_i\,v \longrightarrow v$ if $q_i \in Q_i^{\mathsf{h}}$ and v is a config.

Thus, composition of SFTs is accomplished by concatenating the states of the individual SFTs. The composition of T_1 and T_2 transduces $w \in \hat{\Sigma}^+$ to $v \in \hat{\Omega}^+$ if $w^{\mathcal{R}}\,i_1\,i_2 \longrightarrow^* v^{\mathcal{R}}$.

Notice that an asynchronous, concurrent semantics of transducer composition comes for free with this model. For example, in the transducer chain $w\,q_1\,q_2 \cdots q_n$, the state q_1 can react to the next symbol of input while q_2 is still absorbing q_1's first round of output.

4   Curry–Howard Isomorphism for Subsingleton Proofs

In this section, we turn our attention from a machine model of subsequential finite state transducers (SFTs) to a computational interpretation of the $\oplus, \mathbf{1}, \mu$-subsingleton sequent calculus. We then bridge the two by establishing a Curry–Howard isomorphism between SFTs and a class of cut-free subsingleton proofs – propositions are languages, proofs are SFTs, and cut reductions are SFT computation steps. In this way, the cut-free proofs of subsingleton logic serve as a linguistic model that captures exactly the subsequential functions.

4.1   A Computational Interpretation of $\oplus, \mathbf{1}, \mu$-Subsingleton Logic

Figure 3 summarizes our computational interpretation of the $\oplus, \mathbf{1}, \mu$-subsingleton sequent calculus.

Now that we are emphasizing the logic's computational aspects, it will be convenient to generalize binary additive disjunctions to n-ary, labeled additive disjunctions, $\oplus_{\ell \in L} \{\ell : A_\ell\}$. We require that the set L of labels is nonempty, so that

$$\begin{array}{rl}
\text{Types} & A, B, C ::= \oplus_{\ell \in L}\{\ell{:}A_\ell\} \mid 1 \mid \mu\alpha.A \mid \alpha \\
\text{Contexts} & \Delta ::= \cdot \mid A \\
\text{Conclusions} & \gamma ::= C \\
\text{Proof terms} & P, Q ::= X \mid P \triangleright Q \\
& \qquad\quad \mid \mathsf{writeR}\ k; P \mid \mathsf{readL}_{\ell \in L}(\ell \Rightarrow Q_\ell) \\
& \qquad\quad \mid \mathsf{closeR} \mid \mathsf{waitL}; Q \\
\text{Signatures} & \Theta ::= \cdot \mid \Theta, (\Delta \vdash X = P : \gamma)
\end{array}$$

$$\frac{(\Delta \vdash X = P : \gamma) \in \Theta}{\Delta \vdash_\Theta X : \gamma}\ \text{VAR} \qquad \frac{\Delta \vdash_\Theta P : A \quad A \vdash_\Theta Q : \gamma}{\Delta \vdash_\Theta P \triangleright Q : \gamma}\ \text{CUT} \qquad (\text{no ID rule})$$

$$\frac{\Delta \vdash_\Theta P : A_k \quad (k \in L)}{\Delta \vdash_\Theta \mathsf{writeR}\ k; P : \oplus_{\ell \in L}\{\ell{:}A_\ell\}}\ \oplus\text{R} \qquad \frac{\forall \ell \in L: \ A_\ell \vdash_\Theta Q_\ell : \gamma}{\oplus_{\ell \in L}\{\ell{:}A_\ell\} \vdash_\Theta \mathsf{readL}_{\ell \in L}(\ell \Rightarrow Q_\ell) : \gamma}\ \oplus\text{L}$$

$$\frac{}{\cdot \vdash_\Theta \mathsf{closeR} : 1}\ \text{1R} \qquad\qquad \frac{\cdot \vdash_\Theta Q : \gamma}{1 \vdash_\Theta \mathsf{waitL}; Q : \gamma}\ \text{1L}$$

$$\frac{\Delta \vdash_\Theta P : [(\mu\alpha.A)/\alpha]A}{\Delta \vdash_\Theta P : \mu\alpha.A} \qquad\qquad \frac{[(\mu\alpha.A)/\alpha]A \vdash_\Theta Q : C}{\mu\alpha.A \vdash_\Theta Q : C}$$

$$\frac{}{\vdash_{\Theta'} (\cdot)\ \mathsf{ok}}\ \text{OK-E} \qquad \frac{\vdash_{\Theta'} \Theta\ \mathsf{ok} \quad \Delta \vdash_{\Theta'} P : \gamma}{\vdash_{\Theta'} \Theta, (\Delta \vdash X = P : \gamma)\ \mathsf{ok}}\ \text{OK-VAR}$$

$$(\mathsf{writeR}\ k; P) \triangleright \mathsf{readL}_{\ell \in L}(\ell \Rightarrow Q_\ell) \longrightarrow P \triangleright Q_k$$
$$\mathsf{closeR} \triangleright (\mathsf{waitL}; Q) \longrightarrow Q$$

Fig. 3. A proof term assignment and the principal cut reductions for the $\oplus,1,\mu$-subsingleton sequent calculus

n-ary, labeled additive disjunction does not go beyond what may be expressed (less concisely) with the binary form.[1] Thus, propositions are now generated by the grammar

$$A, B, C ::= \oplus_{\ell \in L}\{\ell{:}A_\ell\} \mid 1 \mid \mu\alpha.A \mid \alpha .$$

Contexts Δ still consist of exactly zero or one proposition and conclusions γ are still single propositions. Each sequent $\Delta \vdash \gamma$ is now annotated with a proof term P and a signature Θ, so that $\Delta \vdash_\Theta P : \gamma$ is read as "Under the definitions of signature Θ, the proof term P consumes input of type Δ to produce output of type γ." Already, the proof term P sounds vaguely like an SFT.

The logic's inference rules now become typing rules for proof terms. The $\oplus$R rule types a write operation, $\mathsf{writeR}\ k; P$, that emits label k and then continues;

---

[1] Notice that the proposition $\oplus\{k{:}A\}$ is distinct from A.

dually, the $\oplus L$ rule types a read operation, $\mathsf{readL}_{\ell \in L}(\ell \Rightarrow Q_\ell)$, that branches on the label that was read. The $1R$ rule types an operation, closeR, that signals the end of the output; the $1L$ rule types an operation, $\mathsf{waitL}; Q$, that waits for the input to end and then continues with Q. The CUT rule types a composition, $P \triangleright Q$, of proof terms P and Q. Lastly, unfolding principles are used silently within a proof and do not affect the proof term.

The circularities inherent to circular proofs are expressed with a finite signature Θ of mutually corecursive definitions. Each definition in Θ has the form $\Delta \vdash X = P : \gamma$, defining the variable X as proof term P with a type declaration of $\Delta \vdash_\Theta X : \gamma$. We rule out definitions of the forms $X = X$ and $X = Y$. To verify that the definitions in Θ are well-typed, we check that $\vdash_\Theta \Theta$ ok according to the rules given in Fig. 3. Note that the same signature Θ' (initially Θ) is used to type all variables, which thereby allows arbitrary mutual recursion.

As an example, here are two well-typed definitions:

$$X_0 = \mathsf{caseL}(a \Rightarrow \mathsf{writeR}\ a; X_0 \qquad\qquad X_1 = \mathsf{caseL}(a \Rightarrow \mathsf{writeR}\ b; \mathsf{writeR}\ a; X_0$$
$$\mid b \Rightarrow X_1 \qquad\qquad\qquad\qquad\qquad \mid b \Rightarrow X_1$$
$$\mid \$ \Rightarrow \mathsf{waitL}; \qquad\qquad\qquad\qquad\qquad \mid \$ \Rightarrow \mathsf{waitL}; \mathsf{writeR}\ b;$$
$$\mathsf{writeR}\ \$; \mathsf{closeR}) \qquad\qquad\qquad\qquad \mathsf{writeR}\ \$; \mathsf{closeR})$$

4.2   Propositions as Languages

Here we show that propositions are languages over finite endmarked alphabets. However, before considering all freely generated propositions, let us look at one in particular: the least fixed point $\mathbf{Str}_{\hat{\Sigma}} = \mu\alpha. \oplus_{\ell \in \Sigma}\{\ell{:}A_\ell\}$ where $A_a = \alpha$ for all $a \in \Sigma_\mathsf{i}$ and $A_e = 1$ for all $e \in \Sigma_\mathsf{e}$. By unfolding,

$$\mathbf{Str}_{\hat{\Sigma}} = \oplus_{\ell \in \Sigma}\{\ell{:}A'_\ell\}, \text{ where } A'_\ell = \begin{cases} \mathbf{Str}_{\hat{\Sigma}} & \text{if } \ell \in \Sigma_\mathsf{i} \\ 1 & \text{if } \ell \in \Sigma_\mathsf{e} \end{cases}$$

The proposition $\mathbf{Str}_{\hat{\Sigma}}$ is a type that describes the language $\hat{\Sigma}^+$ of all finite strings over the endmarked alphabet $\hat{\Sigma}$.

Theorem 3. *Strings from the language $\hat{\Sigma}^+$ are in bijective correspondence with the cut-free proofs of $\cdot \vdash \mathbf{Str}_{\hat{\Sigma}}$.*

A cut-free proof term P of type $\cdot \vdash \mathbf{Str}_{\hat{\Sigma}}$ emits a finite list of symbols from $\hat{\Sigma}$. By inversion on its typing derivation, P is either: $\mathsf{writeR}\ e; \mathsf{closeR}$, which terminates the list by emitting some endmarker $e \in \Sigma_\mathsf{e}$; or $\mathsf{writeR}\ a; P'$, which continues the list by emitting some symbol $a \in \Sigma_\mathsf{i}$ and then behaving as proof term P' of type $\cdot \vdash \mathbf{Str}_{\hat{\Sigma}}$. The above intuition can be made precise by defining a bijection $[\![-]\!]: \hat{\Sigma}^+ \to (\cdot \vdash \mathbf{Str}_{\hat{\Sigma}})$ along these lines. As an example, the string $ab\$ \in \hat{\Sigma}^+$ with $\hat{\Sigma} = (\{a, b\}, \{\$\})$ corresponds to $[\![ab\$]\!] = \mathsf{writeR}\ a; \mathsf{writeR}\ b; \mathsf{writeR}\ \$; \mathsf{closeR}$.

The freely generated propositions correspond to subsets of $\hat{\Sigma}^+$. This can be seen most clearly if we introduce subtyping [10], but we do not do so because we are interested only in $\mathbf{Str}_{\hat{\Sigma}}$ hereafter.

4.3 Encoding SFTs as Cut-Free Proofs

Having now defined a type $\mathtt{Str}_{\hat{\Sigma}}$ and shown that $\hat{\Sigma}^+$ is isomorphic to cut-free proofs of $\cdot \vdash \mathtt{Str}_{\hat{\Sigma}}$, we can now turn to encoding SFTs as proofs. We encode each of the SFT's states as a cut-free proof of $\mathtt{Str}_{\hat{\Sigma}} \vdash \mathtt{Str}_{\hat{\Gamma}}$; this proof captures a (subsequential) function on finite strings.

Let $T = (Q, \hat{\Sigma}, \hat{\Gamma}, \delta, \sigma, q_0)$ be an arbitrary SFT in normal form. Define a mutually corecursive family of definitions $[\![q]\!]_T$, one for each state $q \in Q$. There are three cases according to whether q is a read, a write, or a halt state.

– If q is a read state, then $[\![q]\!] = \mathsf{readL}_{a \in \Sigma}(a \Rightarrow P_a)$, where for each a

$$P_a = \begin{cases} [\![q_a]\!] & \text{if } a \in \Sigma_\mathsf{i} \text{ and } \delta(a, q) = q_a \\ \mathsf{waitL}; [\![q_a]\!] & \text{if } a \in \Sigma_\mathsf{e} \text{ and } \delta(a, q) = q_a \end{cases}$$

When q is reachable from some state q' that writes an endmarker, we declare $[\![q]\!]$ to have type $\mathtt{Str}_{\hat{\Sigma}} \vdash [\![q]\!] : \mathbf{1}$. Otherwise, we declare $[\![q]\!]$ to have type $\mathtt{Str}_{\hat{\Sigma}} \vdash [\![q]\!] : \mathtt{Str}_{\hat{\Gamma}}$.

– If q is a write state such that $\sigma(q) = (q_b, b)$, then $[\![q]\!] = \mathsf{writeR}\ b; [\![q_b]\!]$. When q is reachable from $\delta(e, q')$ for some $e \in \Sigma_\mathsf{e}$ and $q' \in Q^\mathsf{r}$, we declare $[\![q]\!]$ to have type $\cdot \vdash \mathtt{Str}_{\hat{\Gamma}}$. Otherwise, we declare $[\![q]\!]$ to have type $\mathtt{Str}_{\hat{\Sigma}} \vdash \mathtt{Str}_{\hat{\Gamma}}$.

– If q is a halt state, then $[\![q]\!] = \mathsf{closeR}$. This definition has type $\cdot \vdash [\![q]\!] : \mathbf{1}$.

When the SFT is in normal form, these definitions are well-typed. A type declaration with an empty context indicates that an endmarker has already been read. Because the reachability condition on read states in normal-form SFTs proscribes read states from occurring once an endmarker has been read, the type declarations $\mathtt{Str}_{\hat{\Sigma}} \vdash \mathtt{Str}_{\hat{\Gamma}}$ or $\mathtt{Str}_{\hat{\Sigma}} \vdash \mathbf{1}$ for read states is valid. Because normal-form SFTs also ensure that halt states only occur once an endmarker has been read, the type declaration $\cdot \vdash \mathbf{1}$ for halt states is valid.

As an example, the SFT from Fig. 2 can be encoded as follows.

$$\mathtt{Str}_{\hat{\Sigma}} = \oplus\{a{:}\mathtt{Str}_{\hat{\Sigma}}, b{:}\mathtt{Str}_{\hat{\Sigma}}, \${:}\mathbf{1}\}$$

$\mathtt{Str}_{\hat{\Sigma}} \vdash [\![q_0]\!] : \mathtt{Str}_{\hat{\Sigma}}$
$[\![q_0]\!] = \mathsf{readL}(a \Rightarrow [\![q_a]\!] \mid b \Rightarrow [\![q_1]\!]$
$\qquad\qquad \mid \$ \Rightarrow \mathsf{waitL}; [\![q_\$]\!])$

$\mathtt{Str}_{\hat{\Sigma}} \vdash [\![q_1]\!] : \mathtt{Str}_{\hat{\Sigma}}$
$[\![q_1]\!] = \mathsf{readL}(a \Rightarrow [\![q_b]\!] \mid b \Rightarrow [\![q_1]\!]$
$\qquad\qquad \mid \$ \Rightarrow \mathsf{waitL}; [\![q_b']\!])$

$\mathtt{Str}_{\hat{\Sigma}} \vdash [\![q_a]\!], [\![q_b]\!] : \mathtt{Str}_{\hat{\Sigma}}$
$[\![q_a]\!] = \mathsf{writeR}\ a; [\![q_0]\!]$
$[\![q_b]\!] = \mathsf{writeR}\ b; [\![q_a]\!]$

$\cdot \vdash [\![q_b']\!], [\![q_\$]\!] : \mathtt{Str}_{\hat{\Sigma}}$
$[\![q_b']\!] = \mathsf{writeR}\ b; [\![q_\$]\!]$
$[\![q_\$]\!] = \mathsf{writeR}\ \$; [\![q_h]\!]$

$\cdot \vdash [\![q_h]\!] : \mathbf{1}$
$[\![q_h]\!] = \mathsf{closeR}$

If one doesn't care about a bijection between definitions and states, some of these definitions can be folded into $[\![q_0]\!]$ and $[\![q_1]\!]$.

$\mathtt{Str}_{\hat{\Sigma}} \vdash [\![q_0]\!] : \mathtt{Str}_{\hat{\Sigma}}$
$[\![q_0]\!] = \mathsf{caseL}(a \Rightarrow \mathsf{writeR}\ a; [\![q_0]\!]$
$\qquad\qquad \mid b \Rightarrow [\![q_1]\!]$
$\qquad\qquad \mid \$ \Rightarrow \mathsf{waitL};$
$\qquad\qquad\qquad \mathsf{writeR}\ \$; \mathsf{closeR})$

$\mathtt{Str}_{\hat{\Sigma}} \vdash [\![q_1]\!] : \mathtt{Str}_{\hat{\Sigma}}$
$[\![q_1]\!] = \mathsf{caseL}(a \Rightarrow \mathsf{writeR}\ b; \mathsf{writeR}\ a; [\![q_0]\!]$
$\qquad\qquad \mid b \Rightarrow [\![q_1]\!]$
$\qquad\qquad \mid \$ \Rightarrow \mathsf{waitL}; \mathsf{writeR}\ b;$
$\qquad\qquad\qquad \mathsf{writeR}\ \$; \mathsf{closeR})$

This encoding of SFTs as proofs of type $\mathtt{Str}_{\hat{\Sigma}} \vdash \mathtt{Str}_{\hat{\Gamma}}$ is adequate at quite a fine-grained level – each SFT transition is matched by a proof reduction.

Theorem 4. *Let* $T = (Q, \hat{\Sigma}, \hat{\Gamma}, \delta, \sigma, q_0)$ *be a normal-form SFT. For all* $q \in Q^r$, *if* $\Delta \vdash (\mathsf{writeR}\ a; P) : \mathtt{Str}_{\hat{\Sigma}}$ *and* $\delta(a, q) = q_a$, *then* $(\mathsf{writeR}\ a; P) \triangleright [\![q]\!] \longrightarrow P \triangleright [\![q_a]\!]$.

Proof. By straightforward calculation.

Corollary 1. *Let* $T = (Q, \hat{\Sigma}, \hat{\Gamma}, \delta, \sigma, q_0)$ *be a normal-form SFT. For all* $w \in \hat{\Sigma}^+$ *and* $v \in \hat{\Gamma}^+$, *if* $w^{\mathcal{R}} q_0 \longrightarrow^* v^{\mathcal{R}}$, *then* $[\![w]\!] \triangleright [\![q_0]\!] \longrightarrow^* [\![v]\!]$.

With SFTs encoded as cut-free proofs, SFT chains can easily be encoded as fixed-cut proofs – simply use the CUT rule to compose the encodings. For example, an SFT chain $(T_i)_{i=1}^n$ is encoded as $[\![q_1]\!]_{T_1} \triangleright \cdots \triangleright [\![q_n]\!]_{T_n}$. Because these occurrences of CUT do not occur inside any cycle, the encoding of an SFT chain is a fixed-cut proof.

4.4   Completing the Isomorphism: From Cut-Free Proofs to SFTs

In this section, we show that an SFT can be extracted from a cut-free proof of $\mathtt{Str}_{\hat{\Sigma}} \vdash_{\Theta} \mathtt{Str}_{\hat{\Gamma}}$, thereby completing the isomorphism.

We begin by inserting definitions in signature Θ so that each definition of type $\mathtt{Str}_{\hat{\Sigma}} \vdash \mathtt{Str}_{\hat{\Gamma}}$ has one of the forms

$$X = \mathsf{readL}_{a \in \hat{\Sigma}}(a \Rightarrow P_a) \text{ where } P_a = X_a \qquad \text{if } a \in \Sigma_i$$
$$\text{and } P_e = \mathsf{waitL}; Y \text{ if } e \in \Sigma_e$$
$$X = \mathsf{writeR}\ b; X_b \qquad \text{if } b \in \Gamma_i$$
$$X = \mathsf{writeR}\ e; Z \qquad \text{if } e \in \Gamma_e$$

By inserting definitions we also put each Y of type $\cdot \vdash \mathtt{Str}_{\hat{\Gamma}}$ and each Z of type $\mathtt{Str}_{\hat{\Sigma}} \vdash \mathbf{1}$ into one of the forms

$$Y = \mathsf{writeR}\ b; Y_b \qquad \text{if } b \in \Gamma_i$$
$$Y = \mathsf{writeR}\ e; W \qquad \text{if } e \in \Gamma_e$$
$$Z = \mathsf{readL}_{a \in \hat{\Sigma}}(a \Rightarrow Q_a) \text{ where } Q_a = Z_a \qquad \text{if } a \in \Sigma_i$$
$$\text{and } Q_e = \mathsf{waitL}; W \text{ if } e \in \Sigma_e$$

where definitions W of type $\cdot \vdash \mathbf{1}$ have the form $W = \mathsf{closeR}$. All of these forms are forced by the types, except in one case: P_e above has type $\mathbf{1} \vdash \mathtt{Str}_{\hat{\Gamma}}$, which does not immediately force P_e to have the form $\mathsf{waitL}; Y$. However, by inversion on the type $\mathbf{1} \vdash \mathtt{Str}_{\hat{\Gamma}}$, we know that P_e is equivalent to a proof of the form $\mathsf{waitL}; Y$, *up to* commuting the $\mathbf{1}$L rule to the front.

From definitions in the above form, we can read off a normal-form SFT. Each variable becomes a state in the SFT. The normal-form conditions are manifest from the structure of the definitions: no read definition is reachable once an endmarker is read; no write definition is reachable once an endmarker is written; and a halt definition is reachable only by passing through a write of an endmarker.

Thus, cut-free proofs (up to $1L$ commuting conversion) are isomorphic to normal-form SFTs. Fixed-cut proofs are also then isomorphic to SFT chains by directly making the correspondence of fixed-cuts with chain links between neighboring SFTs.

5   SFT Composition by Cut Elimination

Subsequential functions enjoy closure under composition. This property is traditionally established by a direct SFT construction [14]. Having seen that SFTs are isomorphic to proofs of type $\mathtt{Str}_{\hat{\Sigma}} \vdash \mathtt{Str}_{\hat{\Gamma}}$, it's natural to wonder how this construction fits into this pleasing proof-theoretic picture. In this section, we show that, perhaps surprisingly, closure of SFTs under composition can indeed be explained proof-theoretically in terms of cut elimination.

5.1   Closure of SFTs Under Composition

Composing two SFTs $T_1 = (Q_1, \hat{\Sigma}, \hat{\Gamma}, \delta_1, \sigma_1, q_1)$ and $T_2 = (Q_2, \hat{\Gamma}, \hat{\Omega}, \delta_2, \sigma_2, q_2)$ is simple: just compose their encodings. Because $[\![q_1]\!]_{T_1}$ and $[\![q_2]\!]_{T_2}$ have types $\mathtt{Str}_{\hat{\Sigma}} \vdash \mathtt{Str}_{\hat{\Gamma}}$ and $\mathtt{Str}_{\hat{\Gamma}} \vdash \mathtt{Str}_{\hat{\Omega}}$, respectively, the composition is $[\![q_1]\!]_{T_1} \triangleright [\![q_2]\!]_{T_2}$ and is well-typed.

By using an asynchronous, concurrent semantics of proof reduction [7], parallelism in the SFT chain can be exploited. For example, in the transducer chain $[\![w]\!] \triangleright [\![q_1]\!]_{T_1} \triangleright [\![q_2]\!]_{T_2} \triangleright [\![q_3]\!]_{T_3} \triangleright \cdots \triangleright [\![q_n]\!]_{T_n}$, the encoding of T_1 then react to the next symbol of input while T_2 is still absorbing T_1's first round of output.

Simply composing the encodings as the proof $[\![q_1]\!]_{T_1} \triangleright [\![q_2]\!]_{T_2}$ is suitable and very natural. But knowing that subsequential functions are closed under composition, what if we want to construct a single SFT that captures the same function as the composition?

The proof $[\![q_1]\!]_{T_1} \triangleright [\![q_2]\!]_{T_2}$ is a fixed-cut proof of $\mathtt{Str}_{\hat{\Sigma}} \vdash \mathtt{Str}_{\hat{\Omega}}$ because $[\![q_1]\!]_{T_1}$ and $[\![q_2]\!]_{T_2}$ are cut-free. Therefore, we know from Sects. 4.3 and 4.4 that, when applied to this composition, cut elimination will terminate with a cut-free circular proof of $\mathtt{Str}_{\hat{\Sigma}} \vdash \mathtt{Str}_{\hat{\Omega}}$. Because such proofs are isomorphic to SFTs, cut elimination constructs an SFT for the composition of T_1 and T_2. What is interesting, and somewhat surprising, is that a generic logical procedure such as cut elimination suffices for this construction – no extralogical design is necessary!

In fact, cut elimination yields the very same SFT that is traditionally used (see [14]) to realize the composition. We omit those details here.

5.2   DFA Closure Under Complement and Inverse Homomorphism

Recall from Sect. 3.3 that our definition of SFTs subsumes deterministic finite automata (DFAs); an SFT that uses an endmarked output alphabet of $\hat{\Gamma} = (\{\}, \{a, r\})$ is a DFA that indicates acceptance or rejection of the input by producing a or r as its output.

Closure of SFTs under composition therefore implies closure of DFAs under complement and inverse homomorphism: For complement, compose the SFT-encoding of a DFA with an SFT over $\hat{\Gamma}$, *not*, that flips endmarkers. For inverse homomorphism, compose an SFT that captures homomorphism φ with the SFT-encoding of a DFA; the result recognizes $\varphi^{-1}(L) = \{w \mid \varphi(w) \in L\}$ where L is the language recognized by the DFA. (For endmarked strings, a homomorphism φ maps internal symbols to strings and endmarkers to endmarkers.) Thus, we also have cut elimination as a proof-theoretic explanation for the closure of DFAs under complement and inverse homomorphism.

6 Linear Communicating Automata

In the previous sections, we have established an isomorphism between the cut-free proofs of subsingleton logic and subsequential finite-state string transducers. We have so far been careful to avoid mixing circular proofs and general applications of the CUT rule. The reason is that cut elimination in general results in an infinite, but not necessarily circular, proof [9]. Unless the proof is circular, we can make no connection to machines with a finite number of states.

In this section, we consider the effects of incorporating the CUT in its full generality. We show that if we also relax conditions on circular proofs so that μ is a general – not least – fixed point, then proofs have the power of Turing machines. The natural computational interpretation of subsingleton logic with cuts is that of a typed form of communicating automata arranged with a linear network topology; these automata generalize Turing machines in two ways – the ability to insert and delete cells from the tape and the ability to spawn multiple machine heads that operate concurrently.

6.1 A Model of Linear Communicating Automata

First, we present a model of communicating automata arranged with a linear network topology. A *linear communicating automaton (LCA)* is an 8-tuple $M = (Q, \Sigma, \delta^{rL}, \delta^{rR}, \sigma^{wL}, \sigma^{wR}, \rho, q_0)$ where:

- Q is a finite set of states that is partitioned into (possibly empty) sets of left- and right-reading states, Q^{rL} and Q^{rR}; left- and right-writing states, Q^{wL} and Q^{wR}; spawn states, Q^s; and halt states, Q^h;
- Σ is a finite alphabet;
- $\delta^{rL} \colon \Sigma \times Q^{rL} \to Q$ is a total function on left-reading states;
- $\delta^{rR} \colon Q^{rR} \times \Sigma \to Q$ is a total function on right-reading states;
- $\sigma^{wL} \colon Q^{wL} \to \Sigma \times Q$ is a total function on left-writing states;
- $\sigma^{wR} \colon Q^{wR} \to Q \times \Sigma$ is a total function on right-writing states;
- $\rho \colon Q^s \to Q \times Q$ is a total function on spawn states;
- $q_0 \in Q$ is the initial state.

Configurations of the LCA M are strings w and v drawn from the set $(\Sigma^* Q)^* \Sigma^*$. Let $\longrightarrow$ be the least binary relation on configurations that satisfies the following.

READ-L	$wa\,q\,v \longrightarrow w\,q_a\,v$	if $q \in Q^{\mathsf{rL}}$ and $\delta^{\mathsf{L}}(a,q) = q_a$
READ-R	$w\,q\,bv \longrightarrow w\,q_b\,v$	if $q \in Q^{\mathsf{rR}}$ and $\delta^{\mathsf{R}}(q,b) = q_b$
WRITE-L	$w\,q\,v \longrightarrow wa\,q_a\,v$	if $q \in Q^{\mathsf{wL}}$ and $\sigma^{\mathsf{L}}(q) = (a, q_a)$
WRITE-R	$w\,q\,v \longrightarrow w\,q_b\,bv$	if $q \in Q^{\mathsf{wR}}$ and $\sigma^{\mathsf{R}}(q) = (q_b, b)$
SPAWN	$w\,q\,v \longrightarrow w\,q'\,q''\,v$	if $q \in Q^{\mathsf{s}}$ and $\rho(q) = (q', q'')$
HALT	$w\,q\,v \longrightarrow wv$	if $q \in Q^{\mathsf{h}}$

The LCA M is said to *produce output* $v \in \Sigma^*$ *from input* $w \in \Sigma^*$ if there exists a sequence of configurations $u_0, \ldots, u_n$ such that *(i)* $u_0 = w^{\mathcal{R}}\,q_0$; *(ii)* $u_i \longrightarrow u_{i+1}$ for all $0 \le i < n$; and *(iii)* $u_n = v^{\mathcal{R}}$.

Notice that LCAs can certainly deadlock: a read state may wait indefinitely for the next symbol to arrive. LCAs also may exhibit races: two neighboring read states may compete to read the same symbol.

6.2   Comparing LCAs and Turing Machines

This model of LCAs makes their connections to Turing machines apparent. Each state q in the configuration represents a read/write head. Unlike Turing machines, LCAs may create and destroy tape cells as primitive operations (READ and WRITE rules) and create new heads that operate concurrently (SPAWN rule). In addition, LCAs are Turing complete.

Turing Machines. A *Turing machine* is a 4-tuple $M = (Q, \Sigma, \delta, q_0)$ where Q is a finite set of states that is partitioned into (possibly empty) sets of editing states, Q^{e} and halting states, Q^{h}; Σ is a finite alphabet; $\delta \colon (\Sigma \cup \{\epsilon\}) \times Q^{\mathsf{e}} \to Q \times \Sigma \times \{\mathsf{L}, \mathsf{R}\}$ is a function for editing states; and $q_0 \in Q$ is the initial state.

Configurations of the Turing machine M have one of two forms – either *(i)* $w\,q\,v$, where $w, v \in \Sigma^*$ and $q \in Q$; or *(ii)* w, where $w \in \Sigma^*$. In other words, the set of configurations is $\Sigma^* Q \Sigma^* \cup \Sigma^*$. Let $\longrightarrow$ be the least binary relation on configurations that satisfies the following conditions.

EDIT-L	$wa\,q\,v \longrightarrow w\,q_a\,bv$	if $\delta(a,q) = (q_a, b, \mathsf{L})$
	$q\,v \longrightarrow q_\epsilon\,bv$	if $\delta(\epsilon, q) = (q_\epsilon, b, \mathsf{L})$
EDIT-R	$wa\,q\,cv \longrightarrow wbc\,q_a\,v$	if $\delta(a,q) = (q_a, b, \mathsf{R})$
	$wa\,q \longrightarrow wb\,q_a$	if $\delta(a,q) = (q_a, b, \mathsf{R})$
	$q\,cv \longrightarrow bc\,q_\epsilon\,v$	if $\delta(\epsilon, q) = (q_\epsilon, b, \mathsf{R})$
	$q \longrightarrow b\,q_\epsilon$	if $\delta(\epsilon, q) = (q_\epsilon, b, \mathsf{R})$
HALT	$w\,q\,v \longrightarrow wv$	if $q \in Q^{\mathsf{h}}$

LCAs Are Turing Complete. A Turing machine can be simulated in a relatively straightforward way. First, we augment the alphabet with \$ and ^ symbols as endmarkers. Each configuration $w\,q\,v$ becomes an LCA configuration $\$w\,q\,v\hat{}$. Each editing state q becomes a left-reading state in the encoding, and each halting state q becomes a halting state. If q is an editing state, then for each $a \in \Sigma$:

– If $\delta(a, q) = (q_a, b, \mathsf{L})$, introduce a fresh right-writing state q_b and let $\delta^{\mathsf{L}}(a, q) = q_b$ and $\sigma^{\mathsf{R}}(q_b) = (q_a, b)$. In this case, the first EDIT-L rule is simulated by $\$wa\,q\,v\hat{} \longrightarrow \$w\,q_b\,v\hat{} \longrightarrow \$w\,q_a\,bv\hat{}$.

– If $\delta(a, q) = (q_a, b, \mathsf{R})$, introduce fresh left-writing states q_b and q_c for each $c \in \Sigma$, a fresh right-reading state q'_b, and a fresh right-writing state $q\hat{}$. Set $\delta^{\mathsf{L}}(a, q) = q_b$ and $\sigma^{\mathsf{L}}(q_b) = (b, q'_b)$. Also, set $\delta^{\mathsf{R}}(q'_b, c) = q_c$ for each $c \in \Sigma$, and $\delta^{\mathsf{R}}(q'_b, \hat{}) = q\hat{}$. Finally, set $\sigma^{\mathsf{L}}(q_c) = (c, q_a)$ for each $c \in \Sigma$, and set $\sigma^{\mathsf{R}}(q\hat{}) = (q_a, \hat{})$. In this case, the first and second EDIT-L rule are simulated by $\$wa\,q\,cv\hat{} \longrightarrow \$w\,q_b\,cv\hat{} \longrightarrow \$wb\,q'_b\,cv\hat{} \longrightarrow \$wb\,q_c\,v\hat{} \longrightarrow \$wbc\,q_a\,v\hat{}$ and $\$wa\,q\,\hat{} \longrightarrow \$w\,q_b\,\hat{} \longrightarrow \$wb\,q'_b\,\hat{} \longrightarrow \$wb\,q\hat{} \longrightarrow \$wb\,q_a\,\hat{}$.

– The other cases are similar, so we omit them.

7   Extending $\oplus,1,\mu$-Subsingleton Logic

In this section, we explore what happens when the CUT rule is allowed to occur along cycles in circular proofs. But first we extend $\oplus,1,\mu$-subsingleton logic and its computational interpretation with two other connectives: & and $\bot$.

7.1   Including & and $\bot$ in Subsingleton Logic

Figure 4 presents an extension of $\oplus,1,\mu$-subsingleton logic with & and $\bot$.

Once again, it will be convenient to generalize binary additive conjunctions to their n-ary, labeled form: $\&_{\ell \in L}\{\ell{:}A_\ell\}$ where L is nonempty. Contexts Δ still consist of exactly zero or one proposition, but conclusions γ may now be either empty or a single proposition.

The inference rules for & and $\bot$ are dual to those that we had for $\oplus$ and 1; once again, the inference rules become typing rules for proof terms. The &R rule types a read operation, $\mathsf{readR}_{\ell \in L}(\ell \Rightarrow P_\ell)$, that branches on the label that was read; the label is read from the right-hand neighbor. Dually, the &L rule types a write operation, $\mathsf{writeL}\ k; Q$, that emits label k to the left. The $\bot$R rule types an operation, $\mathsf{waitR}; P$, that waits for the right-hand neighbor to end; the $\bot$L rule types an operation, closeL, that signals to the left-hand neighbor. Finally, we restore ID as an inference rule, which types $\leftrightarrow$ as a forwarding operation.

Computational Interpretation: Well-Behaved LCAs. Already, the syntax of our proof terms suggests a computational interpretation of subsingleton logic with general cuts: well-behaved linear communicating automata.

The readL and readR operations, whose principal cut reductions read and consume a symbol from the left- and right-hand neighbors, respectively, become

$$
\begin{array}{rl}
\text{Types} & A, B, C ::= \cdots \mid \&_{\ell \in L}\{\ell{:}A_\ell\} \mid \bot \\
\text{Contexts} & \Delta ::= \cdot \mid A \\
\text{Conclusions} & \gamma ::= C \mid \cdot \\
\text{Proof terms} & P, Q ::= \cdots \mid \leftrightarrow \\
& \quad \mid \mathsf{readR}_{\ell \in L}(\ell \Rightarrow P_\ell) \mid \mathsf{writeL}\ k; Q \\
& \quad \mid \mathsf{waitR}; P \mid \mathsf{closeL} \\
\text{Signatures} & \Theta ::= \cdots
\end{array}
$$

$$
\frac{}{A \vdash_\Theta \leftrightarrow : A}\ \text{ID}
$$

$$
\frac{\forall \ell \in L:\ \Delta \vdash_\Theta P_\ell : A_\ell}{\Delta \vdash_\Theta \mathsf{readR}_{\ell \in L}(\ell \Rightarrow P_\ell) : \&_{\ell \in L}\{\ell{:}A_\ell\}}\ \&\mathrm{R}
\qquad
\frac{A_k \vdash_\Theta Q : \gamma \quad (k \in L)}{\&_{\ell \in L}\{\ell{:}A_\ell\} \vdash_\Theta \mathsf{writeL}\ k; Q : \gamma}\ \&\mathrm{L}
$$

$$
\frac{\Delta \vdash_\Theta P : \cdot}{\Delta \vdash_\Theta \mathsf{waitR}; P : \bot}\ 1\mathrm{R}
\qquad
\frac{}{\bot \vdash_\Theta \mathsf{closeL} : \cdot}\ \bot\mathrm{L}
$$

$$
\leftrightarrow \rhd Q \longrightarrow Q \qquad P \rhd \leftrightarrow \longrightarrow P
$$
$$
\mathsf{readR}_{\ell \in L}(\ell \Rightarrow P_\ell) \rhd (\mathsf{writeL}\ k; Q) \longrightarrow P_k \rhd Q
$$
$$
(\mathsf{waitR}; P) \rhd \mathsf{closeL} \longrightarrow P
$$

Fig. 4. A proof term assignment and principal cut reductions for the subsingleton sequent calculus when extended with $\&$ and $\bot$

left- and right-reading states. Similarly, the writeL and writeR operations that write a symbol to their left- and right-hand neighbors, respectively, become left- and right-writing states. Cuts, represented by the $\rhd$ operation which creates a new read/write head, become spawning states. The ID rule, represented by the $\leftrightarrow$ operation, becomes a halting state.

Just as for SFTs, this interpretation is adequate at a quite fine-grained level in that LCA transitions are matched by proof reductions. Moreover, the types in our interpretation of subsingleton logic ensure that the corresponding LCA is well-behaved. For example, the corresponding LCAs cannot deadlock because cut elimination can always make progress, as proved by Fortier and Santocanale [9]; those LCAs also do not have races in which two neighboring heads compete to read the same symbol because readR and readL have different types and therefore cannot be neighbors. Due to space constraints, we omit a discussion of the details.

7.2 Subsingleton Logic Is Turing Complete

Once we allow general occurrences of CUT, we can in fact simulate Turing machines and show that subsingleton logic is Turing complete. For each state q in the Turing machine, define an encoding $[\![q]\!]$ as follows.

If q is an editing state, let $[\![q]\!] = \mathsf{readL}_{a\in\Sigma}(a \Rightarrow P_{q,a} \mid \$ \Rightarrow P'_q)$ where

$$P_{q,a} = \begin{cases} [\![q_a]\!] \triangleright (\mathsf{writeL}\ b; \leftrightarrow) & \text{if } \delta(a,q) = (q_a, b, \mathsf{L}) \\ \mathsf{readR}_{c\in\Sigma}(c \Rightarrow (\mathsf{writeR}\ c; \mathsf{writeR}\ b; \leftrightarrow) \triangleright [\![q_a]\!] & \text{if } \delta(a,q) = (q_a, b, \mathsf{R}) \\ \quad \mid \hat{\ } \Rightarrow (\mathsf{writeR}\ b; \leftrightarrow) \triangleright [\![q_a]\!]) & \\ \quad\quad \triangleright (\mathsf{writeL}\ \hat{\ }; \leftrightarrow) & \end{cases}$$

and

$$P'_q = \begin{cases} (\mathsf{writeR}\ \$; \leftrightarrow) \triangleright [\![q_\epsilon]\!] \triangleright (\mathsf{writeL}\ b; \leftrightarrow) & \text{if } \delta(\epsilon, q) = (q_\epsilon, b, \mathsf{L}) \\ \mathsf{readR}_{c\in\Sigma}(c \Rightarrow (\mathsf{writeR}\ c; \mathsf{writeR}\ b; \leftrightarrow) \triangleright [\![q_\epsilon]\!] & \text{if } \delta(\epsilon, q) = (q_\epsilon, b, \mathsf{R}) \\ \quad \mid \hat{\ } \Rightarrow (\mathsf{writeR}\ b; \leftrightarrow) \triangleright [\![q_\epsilon]\!] \triangleright (\mathsf{writeL}\ \hat{\ }; \leftrightarrow)) & \end{cases}$$

If q is a halt state, let $[\![q]\!] = \mathsf{readR}_{c\in\Sigma}(c \Rightarrow (\mathsf{writeR}\ c; \leftrightarrow) \triangleright [\![q]\!] \mid \hat{\ } \Rightarrow \leftrightarrow)$. Surprisingly, these definitions $[\![q]\!]$ are in fact well-typed at $\mathsf{Tape} \vdash \mathsf{epaT}$, where

$$\mathsf{Tape} = \mu\alpha.\, \oplus_{a\in\Sigma}\{a{:}\alpha, \${:}\mathbf{1}\}$$
$$\mathsf{epaT} = \mu\alpha.\, \&_{a\in\Sigma}\{a{:}\alpha, \hat{\ }{:}\mathsf{Tape}\}.$$

This means that Turing machines cannot get stuck!

Of course, Turing machines may very well loop indefinitely. And so, for the above circular proof terms to be well-typed, we must give up on μ being an *inductive* type and relax μ to be a *general recursive* type. This amounts to dropping the requirement that every cycle in a circular proof is a left μ-trace.

It is also possible to simulate Turing machines in a well-typed way without using $\&$. Occurrences of $\&$, readR, and writeL are removed by instead using $\oplus$ and its constructs in a continuation-passing style. This means that Turing completeness depends on the interaction of general cuts and general recursion, not on any subtleties of interaction between $\oplus$ and $\&$.

8   Conclusion

We have taken the computational interpretation of linear logic first proposed by Caires et al. [3] and restricted it to a fragment with just $\oplus$ and $\mathbf{1}$, but added least fixed points and circular proofs [9]. Cut-free proofs in this fragment are in an elegant Curry-Howard correspondence with subsequential finite state transducers. Closure under composition, complement, inverse homomorphism, intersection and union can then be realized uniformly by cut elimination. We plan to investigate if closure under concatenation and Kleene star, usually proved via a detour through nondeterministic automata, can be similarly derived.

When we allow arbitrary cuts, we obtain linear communicating automata, which is a Turing-complete class of machines. Some preliminary investigation leads us to the conjecture that we can also obtain deterministic pushdown automata as a naturally defined logical fragment. Conversely, we can ask if the restrictions of the logic to least or greatest fixed points, that is, inductive or coinductive types with corresponding restrictions on the structure of circular proofs yields interesting or known classes of automata.

Our work on communicating automata remains significantly less general than Deniélou and Yoshida's analysis using multiparty session types [6]. Instead of multiparty session types, we use only a small fragment of binary session types; instead of rich networks of automata, we limit ourselves to finite chains of machines. And in our work, machines can terminate and spawn new machines, and both operational and typing aspects of LCAs arise naturally from logical origins.

Finally, in future work we would like to explore if we can design a *subsingleton type theory* and use it to reason intrinsically about properties of automata.

References

1. Baelde, D.: Least and greatest fixed points in linear logic. ACM Trans. Comput. Logic **13**(1) (2012)
2. Baelde, D., Doumane, A., Saurin, A.: Infinitary proof theory: the multiplicative additive case. In: 25th Conference on Computer Science Logic. LIPIcs, vol. 62, pp. 42:1–42:17 (2016)
3. Caires, L., Pfenning, F.: Session types as intuitionistic linear propositions. In: Gastin, P., Laroussinie, F. (eds.) CONCUR 2010. LNCS, vol. 6269, pp. 222–236. Springer, Heidelberg (2010). doi:10.1007/978-3-642-15375-4_16
4. Church, A., Rosser, J.: Some properties of conversion. Trans. Am. Math. Soc. **39**(3), 472–482 (1936)
5. Curry, H.B.: Functionality in combinatory logic. Proc. Nat. Acad. Sci. U.S.A. **20**, 584–590 (1934)
6. Deniélou, P.-M., Yoshida, N.: Multiparty session types meet communicating automata. In: Seidl, H. (ed.) ESOP 2012. LNCS, vol. 7211, pp. 194–213. Springer, Heidelberg (2012). doi:10.1007/978-3-642-28869-2_10
7. DeYoung, H., Caires, L., Pfenning, F., Toninho, B.: Cut reduction in linear logic as asynchronous session-typed communication. In: 21st Conference on Computer Science Logic. LIPIcs, vol. 16, pp. 228–242 (2012)
8. Dummett, M.: The Logical Basis of Metaphysics. Harvard University Press, Cambridge (1991). From the William James Lectures 1976
9. Fortier, J., Santocanale, L.: Cuts for circular proofs: semantics and cut elimination. In: 22nd Conference on Computer Science Logic. LIPIcs, vol. 23, pp. 248–262 (2013)
10. Gay, S., Hole, M.: Subtyping for session types in the pi calculus. Acta Informatica **42**(2), 191–225 (2005)
11. Girard, J.Y.: Linear logic. Theoret. Comput. Sci. **50**(1), 1–102 (1987)
12. Howard, W.A.: The formulae-as-types notion of construction (1969), unpublished note. An annotated version appeared in: To H.B. Curry: Essays on Combinatory Logic, Lambda Calculus and Formalism, pp. 479–490, Academic Press (1980)
13. Martin-Löf, P.: On the meanings of the logical constants and the justifications of the logical laws. Nord. J. Philos. Logic **1**(1), 11–60 (1996)
14. Mohri, M.: Finite-state transducers in language and speech processing. J. Comput. Linguist. **23**(2), 269–311 (1997)
15. Schützenberger, M.P.: Sur une variante des fonctions sequentielles. Theoret. Comput. Sci. **4**(1), 47–57 (1977)
16. Turing, A.M.: On computable numbers, with an application to the Entscheidungsproblem. Proc. Lond. Math. Soc. **42**(2), 230–265 (1937)

Verification and Analysis I

Learning a Strategy for Choosing Widening Thresholds from a Large Codebase

Sooyoung Cha, Sehun Jeong, and Hakjoo Oh$^{(\boxtimes)}$

Korea University, Seoul, South Korea
{sooyoung1990,gifaranga,hakjoo_oh}@korea.ac.kr

Abstract. In numerical static analysis, the technique of widening thresholds is essential for improving the analysis precision, but blind uses of the technique often significantly slow down the analysis. Ideally, an analysis should apply the technique only when it benefits, by carefully choosing thresholds that contribute to the final precision. However, finding the proper widening thresholds is nontrivial and existing syntactic heuristics often produce suboptimal results. In this paper, we present a method that automatically learns a good strategy for choosing widening thresholds from a given codebase. A notable feature of our method is that a good strategy can be learned with analyzing each program in the codebase only once, which allows to use a large codebase as training data. We evaluated our technique with a static analyzer for full C and 100 open-source benchmarks. The experimental results show that the learned widening strategy is highly cost-effective; it achieves 84% of the full precision while increasing the baseline analysis cost only by 1.4×. Our learning algorithm is able to achieve this performance 26 times faster than the previous Bayesian optimization approach.

1 Introduction

In static analysis for discovering numerical program properties, the technique of widening with thresholds is essential for improving the analysis precision [1–4,6–9]. Without the technique, the analysis often fails to establish even simple numerical invariants. For example, suppose we analyze the following code snippet with the interval domain:

```
1   i = 0;
2   while (i != 4) {
3       i = i + 1;
4       assert(i <= 4);
5   }
```

Note that the interval analysis with the standard widening operator cannot prove the safety of the assertion at line 4. The analysis concludes that the interval value of i right after line 2 is $[0, +\infty]$ (hence $[1, +\infty]$ at line 4) because of the widening operation applied at the entry of the loop. A simple way of improving

© Springer International Publishing AG 2016
A. Igarashi (Ed.): APLAS 2016, LNCS 10017, pp. 25–41, 2016.
DOI: 10.1007/978-3-319-47958-3_2

the result is to employ widening thresholds. For example, when an integer 4 is used as a threshold, the widening operation at the loop entry produces the interval $[0, 4]$, instead of $[0, +\infty]$, for the value of i. The loop condition $i \neq 4$ narrows down the value to $[0, 3]$ and therefore we can prove that the assertion holds at line 4.

However, it is a challenge to choose the right set of thresholds that improves the analysis precision with a small extra cost. Simple-minded methods can hardly be cost-effective. For example, simply choosing all integer constants in the program would not scale to large programs. Existing syntactic and semantics heuristics for choosing thresholds (e.g. [3, 6, 8, 9]) are also not satisfactory. For example, the syntactic heuristic used in [3], which is specially designed for the flight control software, is not precision-effective in general [12]. A more sophisticated, semantics-based heuristic sometimes incurs significant cost blow up [8]. No existing techniques are able to prescribe small yet effective set of thresholds for arbitrary programs.

In this paper, we present a technique that automatically learns a good strategy for choosing widening thresholds from a given codebase. The learned strategy is then used for analyzing new, unseen programs. Our technique includes a parameterized strategy for choosing widening thresholds, which decides whether to use each integer constant in the given program as a threshold or not. Following [13], the strategy is parameterized by a vector of real numbers and the effectiveness of the strategy is completely determined by the choice of the parameter. Therefore, in our approach, learning a good strategy corresponds to finding a good parameter from a given codebase.

A salient feature of our method is that a good strategy can be learned by analyzing the codebase only once, which enables us to use a large codebase as a training dataset. In [13], learning a strategy is formulated as a blackbox optimization problem and the Bayesian optimization approach was proposed to efficiently solve the optimization problem. However, we found that this approach is still too costly when the codebase is large, mainly because it requires multiple runs of the static analyzer over the entire codebase. Motivated by this limitation, we designed a new learning algorithm that does not require running the analyzer over the codebase multiple times. The key idea is to use an oracle that quantifies the relative importance of each integer constant in the program with respect to improving the analysis precision. With this oracle, we transform the blackbox optimization problem to a whitebox one that is much easier to solve than the original problem. We show that the oracle can be effectively obtained from a single run of the static analyzer over the codebase.

The experimental results show that our learning algorithm produces a highly cost-effective strategy and is fast enough to be used with a large codebase. We implemented our approach in a static analyzer for real-world C programs and used 100 open-source benchmarks for the evaluation. The learned widening strategy achieves 84 % of the full precision (i.e., the precision of the analysis using all integer constants in the program as widening thresholds) while increasing the cost of the baseline analysis without widening thresholds only by 1.4×. Our learning algorithm is able to achieve this performance 26 times faster than the existing Bayesian optimization approach.

Contributions. This paper makes the following contributions.

- We present a learning-based method for selectively applying the technique of widening thresholds. From a given codebase, our method automatically learns a strategy for choosing widening thresholds.
- We present a new, oracle-guided learning algorithm that is significantly faster than the existing Bayesian optimization approach. Although we use this algorithm for learning widening strategy, our learning algorithm is generally applicable to adaptive static analyses in general provided a suitable oracle is given for each analysis.
- We prove the effectiveness of our method in a realistic setting. Using a large codebase of 100 open-source programs, we experimentally show that our learning strategy is highly cost-effective, achieving the 84 % of the full precision while increasing the cost by 1.4 times.

Outline. We first present our learning algorithm in a general setting; Sect. 2 defines a class of adaptive static analyses and Sect. 3 explains our oracle-guided learning algorithm. Next, in Sect. 4, we describe how to apply the general approach to the problem of learning a widening strategy. Section 5 presents the experimental results, Sect. 6 discusses related work, and Sect. 7 concludes.

2 Adaptive Static Analysis

We use the setting of adaptive static analysis in [13]. Let $P \in \mathbb{P}$ be a program to analyze. Let $\mathbb{J}_P$ be a set of indices that represent parts of P. Indices in $\mathbb{J}_P$ are used as "switches" that determine whether to apply high precision or not. For example, in the partially flow-sensitive analysis in [13], $\mathbb{J}_P$ is the set of program variables and the analysis applies flow-sensitivity only to a selected subset of $\mathbb{J}_P$. In this paper, $\mathbb{J}_P$ denotes the set of constant integers in the program and our aim is to choose a subset of $\mathbb{J}_P$ that will be used as widening thresholds. Once $\mathbb{J}_P$ is chosen, the set $\mathcal{A}_P$ of program abstractions is defined as a set of indices as follows:

$$\mathbf{a} \in \mathcal{A}_P = \wp(\mathbb{J}_P).$$

In the rest of the paper, we omit the subscript P from $\mathbb{J}_P$ and $\mathcal{A}_P$ when there is no confusion.

The program is given together with a set of queries (i.e. assertions) and the goal of the static analysis is to prove as many queries as possible. We suppose that an adaptive static analysis is given with the following type:

$$F : \mathbb{P} \times \mathcal{A} \rightarrow \mathbb{N}.$$

Given a program P and its abstraction $\mathbf{a}$, the analysis $F(P, \mathbf{a})$ analyzes the program P by applying high precision (e.g. widening thresholds) only to the program parts in the abstraction $\mathbf{a}$. For example, $F(P, \emptyset)$ and $F(P, \mathbb{J}_P)$ represent the least and most precise analyses, respectively. The result from $F(P, \mathbf{a})$ indicates the number of queries in P proved by the analysis. We assume that the abstraction correlates the precision and cost of the analysis. That is, if $\mathbf{a}'$ is a more refined abstraction than $\mathbf{a}$ (i.e. $\mathbf{a} \subseteq \mathbf{a}'$), then $F(P, \mathbf{a}')$ proves more queries than $F(P, \mathbf{a})$ does but the former is more expensive to run than the latter. This assumption usually holds in program analyses for C.

In this paper, we are interested in automatically finding an adaptation strategy

$$\mathcal{S} : \mathbb{P} \to \mathcal{A}$$

from a given codebase $\mathbf{P} = \{P_1, \ldots, P_m\}$. Once the strategy is learned, it is used for analyzing unseen program P as follows:

$$F(P, \mathcal{S}(P)).$$

Our goal is to learn a cost-effective strategy $\mathcal{S}^*$ such that $F(P, \mathcal{S}^*(P))$ has precision comparable to that of the most precise analysis $F(P, \mathbb{J}_P)$ while its cost remains close to that of the least precise one $F(P, \emptyset)$.

3   Learning an Adaptation Strategy from a Codebase

In this section, we explain our method for learning a strategy $\mathcal{S} : \mathbb{P} \to \mathcal{A}$ from a codebase $\mathbf{P} = \{P_1, \ldots, P_m\}$. Our method follows the overall structure of the learning approach in [13] but uses a new learning algorithm that is much more efficient than the Bayesian optimization approach in [13].

In Sect. 3.1, we summarize the definition of the adaptation strategy in [13], which is parameterized by a vector $\mathbf{w}$ of real numbers. In Sect. 3.2, the optimization problem of learning is defined. Section 3.3 briefly presents the existing Bayesian optimization method for solving the optimization problem and discusses its limitation in performance. Finally, Sect. 3.4 presents our learning algorithm that avoids the problem of the existing approach.

3.1   Parameterized Adaptation Strategy

In [13], the adaptation strategy is parameterized and the result of the strategy is limited to a particular set of abstractions. That is, the parameterized strategy is defined with the following type:

$$\mathcal{S}_{\mathbf{w}} : \mathbb{P} \to \mathcal{A}^k$$

where $\mathcal{A}^k = \{\mathbf{a} \in \mathcal{A} \mid |\mathbf{a}| = k\}$ is the set of abstractions of size k. The strategy is parameterized by $\mathbf{w} \in \mathbb{R}^n$, a vector of real numbers. In this paper, we assume that k is fixed, which is set to 30 in our experiments, and $\mathbb{R}$ denotes real numbers between -1 and 1, i.e., $\mathbb{R} = [-1, 1]$. The effectiveness of the strategy is solely determined by the parameter $\mathbf{w}$. With a good parameter $\mathbf{w}$, the analysis $F(P, \mathcal{S}_{\mathbf{w}}(P))$ has precision comparable to the most precise analysis $F(P, \mathbb{J}_P)$

while its cost is not far different from the least precise one $F(P, \emptyset)$. Our goal is to learn a good parameter $\mathbf{w}$ from a codebase $\mathbf{P} = \{P_1, P_2, \ldots, P_m\}$.

The parameterized adaptation strategy $\mathcal{S}_\mathbf{w}$ is defined as follows. We assume that a set of program features is given:

$$\mathbf{f}_P = \{f_P^1, f_P^2, \ldots, f_P^n\}$$

where a feature f_P^k is a predicate over the switches $\mathbb{J}_P$:

$$f_P^k : \mathbb{J}_P \to \mathbb{B}.$$

In general, a feature is a function of type $\mathbb{J}_P \to \mathbb{R}$ but we assume that the result is binary for simplicity. Note that the number of features equals to the dimension of $\mathbf{w}$. With the features, a switch j is represented by a feature vector as follows:

$$\mathbf{f}_P(j) = \langle f_P^1(j), f_P^2(j), \ldots, f_P^n(j) \rangle.$$

The strategy $\mathcal{S}_\mathbf{w}$ works in two steps:

1. Compute the scores of switches. The score of switch j is computed by a linear combination of its feature vector and the parameter $\mathbf{w}$:

$$score_P^\mathbf{w}(j) = \mathbf{f}_P(j) \cdot \mathbf{w}. \tag{1}$$

   The score of an abstraction $\mathbf{a}$ is defined by the sum of the scores of elements in $\mathbf{a}$:

$$score_P^\mathbf{w}(\mathbf{a}) = \sum_{j \in \mathbf{a}} score_P^\mathbf{w}(j).$$

2. Select the top-k switches. Our strategy selects top-k switches with highest scores:

$$\mathcal{S}_\mathbf{w}(P) = \underset{\mathbf{a} \in \mathcal{A}_P^k}{\operatorname{argmax}} \, score_P^\mathbf{w}(\mathbf{a}).$$

3.2   The Optimization Problem

Learning a good parameter $\mathbf{w}$ from a codebase $\mathbf{P} = \{P_1, \ldots, P_m\}$ corresponds to solving the following optimization problem:

$$\text{Find } \mathbf{w}^* \in \mathbb{R}^n \text{ that maximizes } obj(\mathbf{w}^*) \tag{2}$$

where the objective function is

$$obj(\mathbf{w}) = \sum_{P_i \in \mathbf{P}} F(P_i, \mathcal{S}_\mathbf{w}(P_i)).$$

That is, we aim to find a parameter $\mathbf{w}^*$ that maximizes the number of queries in the codebase that are proved by the static analysis with $\mathcal{S}_{\mathbf{w}^*}$. Note that it is only possible to solve the optimization problem approximately because the search space is very large. Furthermore, evaluating the objective function is typically very expensive since it involves running the static analysis over the entire codebase.

3.3 Existing Approach

In [13], a learning algorithm based on Bayesian optimization has been proposed. To simply put, this algorithm performs a random sampling guided by a probabilistic model:

1: **repeat**
2:     sample $\mathbf{w}$ from $\mathbb{R}^n$ using probabilistic model $\mathcal{M}$
3:     $s \leftarrow obj(\mathbf{w})$
4:     update the model $\mathcal{M}$ with $(\mathbf{w}, s)$
5: **until** timeout
6: **return** best $\mathbf{w}$ found so far

The algorithm uses a probabilistic model $\mathcal{M}$ that approximates the objective function by a probabilistic distribution on function spaces (using the Gaussian Process [14]). The purpose of the probabilistic model is to pick a next parameter to evaluate that is predicted to work best according the approximation of the objective function (line 2). Next, the algorithm evaluates the objective function with the chosen parameter $\mathbf{w}$ (line 3). The model $\mathcal{M}$ gets updated with the current parameter and its evaluation result (line 4). The algorithm repeats this process until the cost budget is exhausted and returns the best parameter found so far.

Although this algorithm is significantly more efficient than the random sampling [13], it still requires a number of iterations of the loop to learn a good parameter. According to our experience, the algorithm with Bayesian optimization typically requires more than 100 iterations to find good parameters (Sect. 5). Note that even a single iteration of the loop can be very expensive in practice because it involves running the static analyzer over the entire codebase. When the codebase is massive and the static analyzer is costly, evaluating the objective function multiple times is prohibitively expensive.

3.4 Our Oracle-Guided Approach

In this paper, we present a method for learning a good parameter without analyzing the codebase multiple times. By analyzing each program in the codebase only once, our method is able to find a parameter that is as good as the parameter found by the Bayesian optimization method.

We achieve this by applying an *oracle-guided* approach to learning. Our method assumes the presence of an oracle $\mathcal{O}_P$ for each program P, which maps program parts in $\mathbb{J}_P$ to real numbers in $\mathbb{R} = [-1, 1]$:

$$\mathcal{O}_P : \mathbb{J}_P \to \mathbb{R}.$$

For each $j \in \mathbb{J}_P$, the oracle returns a real number that quantifies the relative contribution of j in achieving the precision of $F(P, \mathbb{J}_P)$. That is, $\mathcal{O}(j_1) < \mathcal{O}(j_2)$ means that j_2 contributes more than j_1 to improving the precision during the analysis of $F(P, \mathbb{J}_P)$. We assume that the oracle is given together with the adaptive static analysis. In Sect. 4.3, we show that such an oracle easily results from analyzing the program for interval analysis with widening thresholds.

In the presence of the oracle, we can establish an easy-to-solve optimization problem which serves as a proxy of the original optimization problem in (2). For simplicity, assume that the codebase consists of a single program: $\mathbf{P} = \{P\}$. Shortly, we extend the method to multiple training programs. Let $\mathcal{O}$ be the oracle for program P. Then, the goal of our method is to learn $\mathbf{w}$ such that, for every $j \in \mathbb{J}_P$, the scoring function in (1) instantiated with $\mathbf{w}$ produces a value that is as close to $\mathcal{O}(j)$ as possible. We formalize this optimization problem as follows:

$$\text{Find } \mathbf{w}^* \text{ that minimizes } E(\mathbf{w}^*)$$

where $E(\mathbf{w})$ is defined to be the *mean square error* of $\mathbf{w}$:

$$E(\mathbf{w}) = \sum_{j \in \mathbb{J}_P} (score_P^{\mathbf{w}}(j) - \mathcal{O}(j))^2$$

$$= \sum_{j \in \mathbb{J}_P} (\mathbf{f}_P(j) \cdot \mathbf{w} - \mathcal{O}(j))^2$$

$$= \sum_{j \in \mathbb{J}_P} (\sum_{i=1}^{n} f_P^i(j)\mathbf{w}_i - \mathcal{O}(j))^2.$$

Note that the body of the objective function $E(\mathbf{w})$ is a differentiable, closed-form expression, so we can use the standard gradient decent algorithm to find a minimum of E. The algorithm is simply stated as follows:

1: sample $\mathbf{w}$ from $\mathbb{R}^n$
2: **repeat**
3:     $\mathbf{w} = \mathbf{w} - \alpha \cdot \nabla E(\mathbf{w})$
4: **until** convergence
5: **return** $\mathbf{w}$

Starting from a random parameter $\mathbf{w}$ (line 1), the algorithm keeps going down toward the minimum in the direction against the gradient $\nabla E(\mathbf{w})$. The single step size is determined by the learning rate α. The gradient of E is defined as follows:

$$\nabla E(\mathbf{w}) = (\frac{\partial}{\partial \mathbf{w}_1} E(\mathbf{w}), \frac{\partial}{\partial \mathbf{w}_2} E(\mathbf{w}), \cdots, \frac{\partial}{\partial \mathbf{w}_n} E(\mathbf{w}))$$

where the partial derivatives are

$$\frac{\partial}{\partial \mathbf{w}_k} E(\mathbf{w}) = 2 \sum_{j \in \mathbb{J}_P} (\sum_{i=1}^{n} f_P^i(j)\mathbf{w}_i - \mathcal{O}(j))f_P^k(j)$$

Because the optimization problem does not involve the static analyzer and codebase, learning a parameter $\mathbf{w}$ is done quickly regardless of the cost of the analysis and the size of the codebase, and in the next section, we show that a good-enough oracle can be obtained by analyzing the codebase only once.

It is easy to extend the method to multiple programs. Let $\mathbf{P} = \{P_1, \ldots, P_m\}$ be the codebase. We assume the presence of oracles $\mathcal{O}_{P_1}, \ldots, \mathcal{O}_{P_m}$ for each program $P_i \in \mathbf{P}$. We establish the error function $E_{\mathbf{P}}$ over the entire codebase as follows:

$$E_{\mathbf{P}}(\mathbf{w}) = \sum_{P \in \mathbf{P}} \sum_{j \in \mathbb{J}_P} (\sum_{i=1}^{n} f_P^i(j) \mathbf{w}_i - \mathcal{O}_P(j))^2$$

and now the gradient $\nabla E_{\mathbf{P}}(\mathbf{w})$ is defined with the partial derivatives:

$$\frac{\partial}{\partial \mathbf{w}_k} E_{\mathbf{P}}(\mathbf{w}) = 2 \sum_{P \in \mathbf{P}} \sum_{j \in \mathbb{J}_P} (\sum_{i=1}^{n} f_P^i(j) \mathbf{w}_i - \mathcal{O}(j)) f_P^k(j).$$

Again, we use the gradient decent algorithm to find $\mathbf{w}$ that minimizes $E_{\mathbf{P}}(\mathbf{w})$.

4   Learning a Strategy for Widening Thresholds

In this section, we explain how to employ the oracle-guided method to learn a widening threshold strategy from a codebase. In Sect. 4.1, we define an interval analysis that uses widening with thresholds. Sections 4.2 and 4.3 present the features and oracle that we used for the interval analysis, respectively.

4.1   Interval Analysis with Widening Thresholds

We assume that a program $P \in \mathbb{P}$ is represented by a control flow graph $P = (\mathbb{C}, \hookrightarrow)$, where $\mathbb{C}$ is the set of nodes (i.e. program points) and $(\hookrightarrow) \subseteq \mathbb{C} \times \mathbb{C}$ is a binary relation denoting control-flows of the program; $c' \to c$ means that c is the program point next to c'.

The abstract domain of the analysis maps programs points to abstract states:

$$\mathbb{D} = \mathbb{C} \to \mathbb{S}$$

where $\mathbb{S}$ is a map from program variables to the interval domain:

$$\mathbb{S} = Var \to \mathbb{I}.$$

The abstract semantic function of the analysis is defined as follows:

$$F(X) = \lambda c.\ f_c(\bigsqcup_{c' \to c} X(c'))$$

where we assume that transfer function $f_c : \mathbb{S} \to \mathbb{S}$ is defined for each command c. The goal of the analysis is to compute an upper bound of the least fixed point of F:

$$\mathsf{lfp}F = \bigsqcup_{i \geq 0} F^i(\bot) = F^0(\bot) \sqcup F^1(\bot) \sqcup F^2(\bot) \sqcup \cdots$$

This fixed point iteration may not terminate because the interval domain $\mathbb{I}$ is of infinite height. Therefore, the analysis should use a widening operator for $\mathbb{I}$. A simple widening operator for the interval domain can be defined as follows: (For simplicity, we omit the cases when intervals are bottom).

$$[l_1, u_1] \nabla [l_2, u_2] = [(l_2 < l_1? - \infty : l_1), (u_1 < u_2? + \infty : u_1)] \tag{3}$$

Note that this widening operator is very hasty and immediately replaces unstable bounds by ∞.

The technique of widening with thresholds aims to improve the precision by bounding the extrapolation by widening. Suppose we have a set $T \subseteq \mathbb{Z}$ of thresholds. These thresholds are successively used as a candidate of a fixed point. Formally, the widening operator ∇_T with thresholds is defined as follows:

$$[l_1, u_1] \nabla_T [l_2, u_2] = [(l_2 < l_1 ? glb(T, l_2) : l_1), (u_1 < u_2 ? lub(T, u_2) : u_1)] \quad (4)$$

where $glb(T, i)$ and $lub(T, i)$ are respectively the greatest lower bound and least upper bound of i in thresholds T:

$$glb(T, i) = \max\{n \in T \mid n \leq i\}$$
$$lub(T, i) = \min\{n \in T \mid n \geq i\}$$

The widening operators for $\mathbb{S}$ and $\mathbb{D}$ are defined pointwise.

The precision improvement by widening with thresholds crucially depends on the choice of the set T of thresholds, and our goal is to automatically learn a good strategy for choosing T from a given codebase. In our implementation, the set $\mathbb{J}_P$ in Sect. 5.1 corresponds to the set of all integer constants in program P, and the strategy $\mathcal{S}_{\mathbf{w}}$ chooses top-k integers from P based on the parameter $\mathbf{w}$.

4.2 Features

To use the learning algorithm, we need to design a set of features for integer constants in the program. We have designed 17 syntactic, semantic, and numerical features (Table 1). A feature is a predicate over integers. For example, the first feature in Table 1 indicates whether the number is used as the size of a statically allocated array in the program.

The features have been designed with simplicity and generality in mind. They do not depend on the interval analysis and therefore can be easily reused for other types of numerical analyses. Features 1–12 describe simple syntactic and semantic features for usages of integers in typical C programs. We used a flow-insensitive pre-analysis to extract the semantic features (e.g. feature 7). Features 13–17 describe numerical properties that are commonly found in C programs. We were curious whether these common numerical properties have impacts on the analysis precision when they are used for widening thresholds. Once these features are manually designed, it is the learning algorithm's job to decide how much they are relevant in the given analysis task.

4.3 Oracle

To use our new learning algorithm, we need the oracle:

$$\mathcal{O}_P : \mathbb{Z}_P \to \mathbb{R}$$

Table 1. Features for integer constants in C programs. Each feature represents a predicate over integers.

#	Description
1	Used as The size of a static array
2	The Size of a static array $- 1$
3	Returned By a function (e.g. return 1)
4	Three successive numbers appear in the Program (e.g. $n, n+1, n+2$)
5	Most frequently appeared numbers in The program (i.e. top 10 %)
6	Least frequently appeared numbers in The program (i.e. bottom 10 %)
7	Passed as the size arguments of memory Copy functions (e.g. memcpy)
8	Used as the size of the destination arrays in memoryCopy functions (e.g. memcpy)
9	The null position of a string buffer Involved in some loop condition
10	The null position of a static array of primitive types (e.g., Arrays of int and char)
11	The null position of a static Array of structure fields
12	Constants involved in conditional Expressions (e.g. if (x == 1))
13	Integers Of the form 2^n (e.g. 2, 4, 8, 16)
14	Integers Of the form $2^n - 1$ (e.g., 1, 3, 7, 15)
15	Integers In the range $0 < n \leq 50$
16	Integers In the range $50 < n \leq 100$
17	Integers In the range $n > 1000$

where $\mathbb{Z}_P$ is the set of integer constants that appear in the program P. That is, $\mathcal{O}_P$ maps integer constants in the program into their relative importance when they are used for widening thresholds.

We use a simple heuristic to build the oracle. The idea is to analyze the codebase with full precision and estimate the importance by measuring how many times each integer constant contributes to stabilizing the fixed point computation. The term *full precision* means that the heuristic uses a thresholds set, which includes constant integers of the program's variables, the sizes of static arrays, and the lengths of constant strings. Through relatively cheap analysis (e.g., flow insensitive), we get an abstract memory state which holds the candidate thresholds information we mentioned above.

Let P be a program in the codebase. We analyze the program by using all its integer constants as thresholds. During the fixed point computation of the analysis, we observe each widening operation and maintain a map $\mathcal{C} : \mathbb{Z}_P \to \mathbb{N}$ that counts the integer constants involved in a local fixed point. That is, $\mathcal{C}(n)$ is initially 0 for all n, and whenever we perform the widening operation on intervals:

$$[l_1, u_1] \nabla [l_2, u_2] = [l_3, u_3]$$

we check if the result reaches a local fixed point (i.e. $[l_3, u_3] \sqsubseteq [l_1, u_1]$). If so, we increase the counter values for l_3 and u_3: $\mathcal{C}(l_3) := \mathcal{C}(l_3)+1$ and $\mathcal{C}(u_3) := \mathcal{C}(u_3)+1$. We keep updating the counter $\mathcal{C}$ until a global fixd point is reached. Finally, we normalize the values in $\mathcal{C}$ to obtain the oracle $\mathcal{O}_P$. We repeat this process over the entire codebase and generate a set of oracles.

5   Experiments

In this section, we evaluate our approach with an interval analyzer for C and open-source benchmarks. We organized the experiments to answer the following research questions:

1. **Effectiveness:** How much is the analyzer with the learned strategy better than the baseline analyzers? (Section 5.2)
2. **Comparison:** How much is our learning algorithm better than the existing Bayesian optimization approach? (Section 5.3)
3. **Important Features:** What are the most important features identified by the learning algorithm? (Section 5.4)

5.1   Setting

We implemented our approach in Sparrow, a static buffer-overflow analyzer for real-world C programs [18]. The analysis is based on the interval abstract domain and performs a flow-sensitive and selectively context-sensitive analysis [11]. Along the interval analysis, it also simultaneously performs a flow-sensitive pointer analysis to handle indirect assignments and function pointers in C. The analyzer takes as arguments a set of integers to use for widening thresholds. Our technique automatically generates this input to the analyzer, by choosing a subset of integer constants that appear in the program.

To evaluate our approach, we collected 100 open-source C programs from GNU and Linux packages. The list of programs we used is available in Table 5. We randomly divided the 100 benchmark programs into 70 training programs and 30 testing programs. A strategy for choosing widening threshold is learned from the 70 training programs, and tested on the remaining 30 programs. We iterated this process for five times. Tables 2 and 3 show the result of each trial. In our approach, based on our observation that the number of effective widening thresholds in each program is very small, we set k to 30, which means that the strategy chooses the top 30 integer constants from the program to use for widening thresholds.

In the experiments, we compared the performance of three analyzers.

- NoThld is the baseline Sparrow without widening thresholds. That is, it performs the interval analysis with the basic widening operator in (3).
- FullThld is a variant of Sparrow that uses all the integer constants in the program as widening thresholds. The thresholds set includes constant integers in the program, the sizes of static arrays, and the lengths of constant strings.
- Ours is our analyzer whose threshold strategy is learned from the codebase. That is, the threshold argument of the analyzer is given by the strategy learned from the 70 programs via our oracle-guided learning algorithm.

5.2   Effectiveness

Tables 2 and 3 show the effectiveness of the learned strategy in the training and testing phases, respectively. Table 2 shows the training performance with 70 programs. For the five trials, NOTHLD proved 68,556 buffer-overrun queries. On the other hand, FULLTHLD proved 76,608 queries. For the training programs, our learning algorithm was able to find a strategy that can prove 81.0 % of the FULLTHLD-only provable queries.

Table 3 shows the results on the 30 testing programs. In total, NOTHLD proved the 23,344 queries, while FULLTHLD proved 26,347 queries. Our analysis with the learned strategy (OURS) proved 25,877 queries, achieving 84.3 % of the precision of FULLTHLD. In doing so, OURS increases the analysis time of NOTHLD only 1.4×, while FULLTHLD increases the cost by 4.8×.

5.3   Comparison

We have implemented the previous learning algorithm based on Bayesian optimization [13] and compared its performance with that of our learning algorithm.

Table 2. Performance on the training programs.

Trial	Training			
	NOTHLD	FULLTHLD	OURS	
	prove	prove	prove	quality
1	13,297	14,806	14,518	80.9 %
2	14,251	15,912	15,602	81.3 %
3	14,509	16,285	15,988	83.2 %
4	11,931	13,313	13,020	78.8 %
5	14,568	16,292	15,948	80.0 %
Total	68,556	76,608	75,076	**81.0 %**

Table 3. Performance on the testing programs.

Trial	Testing								
	NOTHLD		FULLTHLD			OURS			
	prove	sec	prove	sec	cost	prove	sec	quality	cost
1	5,083	222	5,785	1,789	8.0×	5,637	361	78.9 %	1.6×
2	4,129	605	4,679	2,645	4.4×	4,623	748	89.8 %	1.2×
3	3,871	397	4,306	1,068	2.7×	4,237	543	84.1 %	1.4×
4	6,449	792	7,278	4,606	5.8×	7,133	1228	82.5 %	1.6×
5	3,812	281	4,299	1,014	3.6×	4,247	389	89.3 %	1.4×
Total	23,344	2,297	26,347	11,122	**4.8×**	25,877	3,269	**84.3 %**	**1.4×**

Table 4. Performance comparison with the Bayesian optimization approach. For Bayesian optimization, we set the maximum number of iterations to 100.

Trial	Learning cost				speedup
	Ours		Bayesian optimization		
	quality	sec	quality	sec	
1	80.9%	6,682	74.3%	185,825	27.8×
2	81.3%	5,971	80.1%	155,438	26.0×
3	83.2%	7,192	77.1%	170,311	23.7×
4	78.8%	3,976	73.7%	113,738	28.6×
5	80.0%	6,947	74.7%	185,375	26.7×
Total	81.0%	30,768	76.0%	810,687	**26.3×**

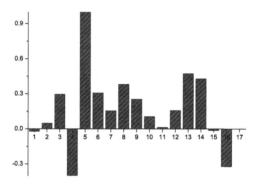

Fig. 1. Relative importance among features

Table 4 shows the results. For the five trials, our approach took on average 6,154 seconds to find a strategy of the average quality 81.0%. On the other hand, the Bayesian optimization approach was able to find a strategy that resulted 76.0% quality on training sets after it exhausted its iteration budget, which took on average 162,137 seconds. The results show that our learning algorithm is able to find a better strategy 26 times faster than the existing algorithm.

The Bayesian optimization approach did not work well with a limited time budget. When we allowed the Bayesian optimization approach to use the same time budget as ours, the existing approach ended up with a strategy of the average quality 57%. Note that our algorithm achieves the quality 81% in the same amount of time.

5.4 Important Features

In our approach, the learned parameter **w** indicates the relative importance of the features in Table 1. To identify the important features for widening thresholds, we performed the training phase ten times and averaged the parameters obtained from each run.

Figure 1 shows the relative feature importance identified by the learning algorithm. During the ten trials, the feature 5 (most frequently appeared numbers in the program) was always the highest ranked feature. Features 13 (numbers of the form 2^n) and 14 (numbers of the form $2^n - 1$) were also consistently listed in the top 5.

These results were not expected from the beginning. At the initial stage of this work, we manually identified important features for widening thresholds and conjectured that the features 9, 10, and 11, which are related to null positions, are the most important ones. Consider the following code:

```
char *text="abcd";
i=0;
while (text[i] != NULL) {
    i++;
    assert(i <= 4);
}
```

When we convert the loop condition into an equivalent one $i \neq 4$ and use the null position 4 as a widening threshold, we can prove the safety of the assertion with the interval domain. We observed the above code pattern multiple times in the target programs being investigated and thought that using null position as thresholds would be one of the most important. However, the learning algorithm let us realize that unexpected features such as 5, 13, and 14 are the most important over the entire codebase, which is an insight hardly obtained manually because it is infeasible for humans to investigate the large codebase.

6   Related Work

Widening with Thresholds. The technique of widening with thresholds has been widely used in numerical program analyses [1–4,6–9]. For example, its effectiveness has been shown with polyhedra [6], octagons [1,3,4], and intervals [7]. However, existing techniques use a fixed strategy for choosing the threshold set. For example, in [1,3,4,7], all the integer constants that appear in conditional statements are used for the candidate of thresholds. In [6], a simple pre-analysis is used to infer a set of thresholds. The main limitation of these approaches is that the strategies are fixed and overfitted to some particular class of programs. For example, the syntactic and semantic heuristics were shown to be not always cost-effective [6,7]. On the other hand, the goal of this paper is not to fix a particular strategy beforehand but to automatically learn a strategy from a given codebase, so that it can be adaptively used in practice.

Learning-Based Program Analysis. Recently, machine learning techniques are increasingly used in the field of program analysis [5,10,13,15–17]. Among them, our work lies in the direction of designing an adaptive static analysis via learning [5,13]. In particular, our work is motivated by [13]'s result, which used

Table 5. Benchmark programs

Programs	LOC	Programs	LOC
wwl-1.3+db.c	474	e2ps-4.34.c	6, 222
gosmore-0.0.0.20100711.c	497	apng2gif-1.5.c	6, 522
ircmarkers-0.14.c	619	isdnutils-3.25+dfsg1.c	6, 609
rovclock-0.6e.c	1, 177	bwm-ng-0.6.c	6, 833
xcircuit-3.7.55.dfsg.c	1, 222	diffstat-1.58.c	7, 077
iputils-20121221.c	1, 311	lgrind-3.67.c	7, 363
confget-1.02.c	1, 393	lacheck-1.26.c	7, 385
codegroup-19981025.c	1, 518	lakai-0.1.c	7, 487
time-1.7.c	1, 759	libdebug-0.4.4.c	7, 645
rexima-1.4.c	1, 843	cmigemo-1.2+gh0.20140306.c	7, 729
xinit-1.3.2.c	1, 893	barcode-0.96.c	7, 901
nlkain-1.3.c	1, 927	apngopt-1.2.c	8, 315
xchain-1.0.1.c	1, 955	makedepf90-2.8.8.c	8, 415
display-dhammapada-1.0.c	2, 007	mpage-2.5.6.c	8, 538
authbind-2.1.1.c	2, 041	stripcc-0.2.0.c	8, 914
unhtml-2.3.9.c	2, 057	photopc-3.05.c	9, 266
elfrc-0.7.c	2, 142	psmisc-22.20.c	9, 624
jbofihe-0.38.c	2, 182	ircd-ircu-2.10.12.10.dfsg1.c	10, 206
delta-2006.08.03.c	2, 273	auto-apt-0.3.23ubuntu0.14.04.1.c	11, 110
petris-1.0.1.c	2, 411	glhack-1.2.c	11, 237
libixp-0.6 20121202+hg148.c	2, 428	sac-1.9b5.c	11, 999
whichman-2.4.c	2, 493	dict-gcide-0.48.1.c	12, 318
acpi-1.7.c	2, 597	gzip-spec2000.c	12, 980
zmakebas-1.2.c	2, 606	cutils-1.6.c	14, 122
forkstat-0.01.04.c	2, 710	mtr-0.85.c	14, 127
setbfree-0.7.5.c	2, 929	rhash-1.3.1.c	14, 352
haskell98-tutorial-200006-2.c	3, 161	gnuspool-1.7ubuntu1.c	16, 665
kcc-2.3.c	3, 429	smp-utils-0.97.c	17, 520
ipip-1.1.9.c	3, 605	ccache-3.1.9.c	17, 536
gif2apng-1.7.c	3, 816	gzip-1.2.4a.c	18, 364
desproxy-0.1.0 pre3.c	3, 841	netkit-ftp-0.17.c	19, 254
magicfilter-1.2.c	3, 856	libchewing-0.3.5.c	19, 262
pgpgpg-0.13.c	3, 908	archimedes.c	19, 559
rsrce-0.2.2.c	3, 956	tcs-1.c	19, 967
rinetd-0.62.c	4, 123	gnuplot-4.6.4.c	20, 306
unsort-1.1.2.c	4, 290	phalanx-22+d051004.c	24, 099
hexdiff-0.0.53.c	4, 334	gnuchess-5.05.c	28, 853
acorn-fdisk-3.0.6.c	4, 450	combine-0.3.3.c	29, 508
pmccabe-2.6.c	4, 920	rtai-3.9.1.c	30, 739
dvbtune-0.5.ds.c	5, 068	gnushogi-1.4.1.c	31, 796
bmf-0.9.4.c	5, 451	tmndec-3.2.0.c	31, 890
libbind-6.0.c	5, 497	fondu-0.0.20060102.c	32, 298
mixal-1.08.c	5, 570	libart-lgpl-2.3.21.c	38, 815
cmdpack-1.03.c	5, 575	flex-2.5.39.c	39, 977
picocom-1.7.c	5, 613	fwlogwatch-1.2.c	46, 601
xdms-1.3.2.c	5, 614	chrony-1.29.c	49, 119
cifs-utils-6.0.c	5, 815	uudeview-0.5.20.c	54, 853
dtaus-0.9.c	6, 018	sn-0.3.8.c	56, 227
device-tree-compiler-1.4.0+dfsg.c	6, 033	shadow-4.1.5.1.c	85, 201
buildtorrent-0.8.c	6, 170	skyeye-1.2.5.c	85, 905

Bayesian optimization to guide the learning process to more promising directions. We followed the general idea of the previous work, but we proposed a more efficient learning algorithm than the Bayesian optimization method. Because Oh et al.'s work uses the number of proven queries to measure quality of the learned strategy, the learning algorithm has to perform full-scale analysis on all training programs repeatedly until the learnt strategy meets a target quality. As we mentioned in Sect. 5.3, its takes too much time to get an acceptably good strategy over the large codebase. By contrast, our method reduces the learning cost by exploiting of the existence of the oracle for a given training program. Since the process of obtaining the oracle requires performing single full-scale analysis per training program, our learning algorithm radically reduced time cost than the existing method.

7 Conclusion

In this paper, we proposed a method that automatically learns a good strategy for choosing widening thresholds from a large codebase. We showed that the learned strategy is highly cost-effective; we can achieve 84 % of the full precision with the 1.4× increase in analysis time.

The success of the method is largely attributed to our new learning algorithm that is significantly faster than the previous Bayesian optimization algorithm. In the presence of a large codebase, the Bayesian optimization approach failed to learn a good strategy in a reasonable amount of time. By contrast, our new learning algorithm is at least 26 times faster and is able to find a better parameter than the previous method.

Our approach is general enough to be used for other types of adaptive static analyses. As future work, we plan to apply our technique to other instances such as selective flow-sensitivity and context-sensitivity.

Acknowledgement. This work was supported by the Institute for Information & communications Technology Promotion (IITP) grant funded by the Korea government (MSIP) (No. R0190-15-2011, Development of Vulnerability Discovery Technologies for IoT Software Security); the Basic Science Research Program through the National Research Foundation of Korea (NRF) funded by the Ministry of Science, ICT & Future Planning (NRF-2016R1C1B2014062); and the MSIP (Ministry of Science, ICT and Future Planning), Korea, under the ITRC (Information Technology Research Center) support program (IITP-2016-H85011610120001002) supervised by the IITP (Institute for Information & communications Technology Promotion).

References

1. Blanchet, B., Cousot, P., Cousot, R., Feret, J., Mauborgne, L., Miné, A., Monniaux, D., Rival, X.: Design and implementation of a special-purpose static program analyzer for safety-critical real-time embedded software. In: Mogensen, T.Æ., Schmidt, D.A., Sudborough, I.H. (eds.) The Essence of Computation. LNCS, vol. 2566, pp. 85–108. Springer, Heidelberg (2002). doi:10.1007/3-540-36377-7_5

2. Bouissou, O., Seladji, Y., Chapoutot, A.: Acceleration of the abstract fixpoint computation in numerical program analysis. J. Symb. Comput. **47**(12), 1479–1511 (2012). International Workshop on Invariant Generation

3. Cousot, P., Cousot, R., Feret, J., Mauborgne, L., Antoine, M., Rival, X.: Why does astrée scale up? Formal Methods Syst. Des. **35**(3), 229–264 (2009)

4. Cousot, P., Cousot, R., Feret, J., Mauborgne, L., Miné, A., Monniaux, D., Rival, X.: Combination of abstractions in the ASTRÉE static analyzer. In: Okada, M., Satoh, I. (eds.) ASIAN 2006. LNCS, vol. 4435, pp. 272–300. Springer, Heidelberg (2007). doi:10.1007/978-3-540-77505-8_23

5. Grigore, R., Yang, H.: Abstraction refinement guided by a learnt probabilistic model. In: POPL (2016)

6. Halbwachs, N., Proy, Y.-E., Roumanoff, P.: Verification of real-time systems using linear relation analysis. In: Formal Methods in System Design, pp. 157–185 (1997)

7. Kim, S., Heo, K., Hakjoo, O., Yi, K.: Widening with thresholds via binary search. Pract. Exp. Softw. **46**, 1317–1328 (2015)

8. Lakhdar-Chaouch, L., Jeannet, B., Girault, A.: Widening with thresholds for programs with complex control graphs. In: Bultan, T., Hsiung, P.-A. (eds.) ATVA 2011. LNCS, vol. 6996, pp. 492–502. Springer, Heidelberg (2011). doi:10.1007/978-3-642-24372-1_38

9. Mihaila, B., Sepp, A., Simon, A.: Widening as abstract domain. In: Brat, G., Rungta, N., Venet, A. (eds.) NFM 2013. LNCS, vol. 7871, pp. 170–184. Springer, Heidelberg (2013). doi:10.1007/978-3-642-38088-4_12

10. Naik, M., Yang, H., Castelnuovo, G., Sagiv, M.: Abstractions from tests. In: POPL (2012)

11. Hakjoo, O., Lee, W., Heo, K., Yang, H., Yi, K.: Selective context-sensitivity guided by impact pre-analysis. In: PLDI (2014)

12. Hakjoo, O., Lee, W., Heo, K., Yang, H., Yi, K.: Selective X-sensitive analysis guided by impact pre-analysis. ACM Trans. Program. Lang. Syst. **38**(2), 6:1–6:45 (2015)

13. Hakjoo, O., Yang, H., Yi, K.: Learning a strategy for adapting a program analysis via Bayesian optimisation. In: OOPSLA (2015)

14. Rasmussen, C.E., Williams, C.K.I.: Gaussian Processes for Machine Learning (Adaptive Computation and Machine Learning). The MIT Press, Cambridge (2005)

15. Sharma, R., Gupta, S., Hariharan, B., Aiken, A., Liang, P., Nori, A.V.: A data driven approach for algebraic loop invariants. In: Felleisen, M., Gardner, P. (eds.) ESOP 2013. LNCS, vol. 7792, pp. 574–592. Springer, Heidelberg (2013). doi:10.1007/978-3-642-37036-6_31

16. Sharma, R., Gupta, S., Hariharan, B., Aiken, A., Nori, A.V.: Verification as learning geometric concepts. In: Logozzo, F., Fähndrich, M. (eds.) SAS 2013. LNCS, vol. 7935, pp. 388–411. Springer, Heidelberg (2013). doi:10.1007/978-3-642-38856-9_21

17. Sharma, R., Nori, A.V., Aiken, A.: Interpolants as classifiers. In: Madhusudan, P., Seshia, S.A. (eds.) CAV 2012. LNCS, vol. 7358, pp. 71–87. Springer, Heidelberg (2012). doi:10.1007/978-3-642-31424-7_11

18. Sparrow. http://ropas.snu.ac.kr/sparrow

AUSPICE-R: Automatic Safety-Property Proofs for Realistic Features in Machine Code

Jiaqi Tan[⊠], Hui Jun Tay, Rajeev Gandhi, and Priya Narasimhan

Department of Electrical and Computer Engineering,
Carnegie Mellon University, Pittsburgh, USA
{jiaqit,htay}@andrew.cmu.edu, rgandhi@ece.cmu.edu, priya@cs.cmu.edu

Abstract. Automatically generating proofs of safety properties for software is important as software becomes safety-critical, e.g., in medical devices and automobiles. While current techniques can automatically prove safety properties for machine code, they either: (i) do not support user-mode programs in an operating system, (ii) do not support realistic program features such as system calls, or (iii) have been demonstrated only on programs of limited sizes. We present AUSPICE-R, which automates safety-property proof generation for user-mode ARM machine code containing system calls, and greatly improves the scalability of automated safety-property proof generation. AUSPICE-R uses an axiomatic approach to model system calls, and leverages idioms in compiled code to optimize its proof automation. We demonstrate AUSPICE-R on (i) simple working versions of common text utilities that perform I/O, and (ii) embedded programs for the Raspberry Pi single-board-computer containing hardware I/O. AUSPICE-R automatically proves safety up to $12\times$ faster, and supports programs $3\times$ larger, than prior techniques.

1 Introduction

Interactive theorem proving (ITP) is a promising approach for reasoning about programs, as it produces succinct proofs. While ITP has required manual user inputs in "heavy-weight" [21] proofs of functional correctness, recent work [24,27] has automated "light-weight" proofs for single classes of safety properties (e.g., Software Fault Isolation (SFI) [25], Control-Flow Integrity (CFI) [6]) using ITP for machine code, eliminating the need for manual user inputs. Reasoning about machine code provides a foundational approach for verification, as machine code proofs are not affected by miscompilation bugs that may cause safety problems [26], as compared to proofs about source-code. However, current approaches for automating safety proofs for machine code are limited: they either target embedded programs running directly on a processor without an operating system (OS) [27], or they do not support proofs for user-mode machine code containing system calls (syscalls) [24]. As embedded systems become more powerful, it is increasingly common for them to run full-fledged OSes. Then, applications run as user-mode programs [17], which need syscalls to perform useful tasks. In addition, current approaches are limited in the scale of programs for which they can feasibly generate safety proofs, due to their long proof times.

© Springer International Publishing AG 2016
A. Igarashi (Ed.): APLAS 2016, LNCS 10017, pp. 42–62, 2016.
DOI: 10.1007/978-3-319-47958-3_3

Modeling and proving safety properties about syscalls in machine code is challenging as syscall behavior occurs in two processor modes: in the user-mode where the syscall is invoked, and in the supervisor mode where the syscall is serviced by an OS kernel. However, our safety properties focus on user-mode behavior, and OS kernels are complex. Hence, we wish to ensure that our safety proofs for user-mode machine code are modular, and avoid needing to prove that syscalls are correctly serviced by the OS kernel. In addition, current approaches for automating safety proofs face scalability challenges, due to the large number of logic terms manipulated. Hence, we wish to improve the scalability of automatically generating safety proofs by reducing the computation required to generate a safety proof.

In this paper, we present AUSPICE-R, an automated safety-property proof-generation framework (for CFI [6]) for user-mode ARM machine code that supports syscalls, and scales up to larger programs than prior techniques. AUSPICE-R extends our earlier work, AUSPICE [24]. First, to ensure modularity in its safety proofs for machine code with syscalls, AUSPICE-R treats syscalls as *black-boxes*: We focus on the inputs to and the user-mode-visible effects of syscalls; we model the effects of syscalls using axioms that capture the specified (e.g., in the syscall API of the OS) behavior of the syscall. This lets us reason about syscalls in user-mode machine code without having to verify the behavior of the underlying OS. Second, we optimize the proof automation in AUSPICE-R to improve the times taken to prove safety, and to increase the size of programs for which safety can be proved. These optimizations leverage common conventions found in gcc-emitted machine code to speed up AUSPICE's analysis.

Our contributions are: (i) an axiomatic approach to modeling syscall behavior with the goal of automating safety property proofs, (ii) a delayed algorithm for performing safety property analysis to support syscalls, (iii) optimizations to AUSPICE-R's analysis that leverage idioms in compiled machine code, and (iv) an evaluation of AUSPICE-R on programs containing syscalls that perform both file and hardware I/O, that are significantly larger than in prior techniques.

2 Problem Statement

Goals. AUSPICE-R's goals are to: (i) fully automate safety property proofs for machine code containing system call (syscall) invocations, (ii) formalize the user-mode-visible effects of a syscall while assuming that the underlying OS services the syscall "correctly" (we discuss "correct" next), (iii) construct a formalization that is sound with respect to the trustworthy Hoare Logic for ARM machine code [18,19] that we build on, and (iv) work with programs compiled by unmodified commodity compilers (e.g., gcc), i.e., we disallow compiler modifications.

Scope. In this work, we target machine code programs for the ARM platform, as ARM is the dominant platform for embedded systems [4]. We consider programs that run in user-mode on the Linux operating system (OS) in this work, and we focus specifically on the safety property of Control-Flow Integrity (CFI) [6].

In this work, we describe how to automate safety proofs for machine code with syscalls; we address how to enforce these safety properties in source-code in [23].

Assumptions. AUSPICE-R extends AUSPICE [24], which builds on the Hoare Logic for ARM machine code developed at Cambridge University [18,19] (which we refer to as the Cambridge ARM model). Hence, safety proofs in AUSPICE-R inherit some of the assumptions and limitations of AUSPICE and the Cambridge ARM model. Specifically, we assume that our target machine code programs:

1. Have behavior that is not affected by hardware exceptions, interrupts, or page-table operations (not modeled by Cambridge ARM model),
2. Do not contain recursive function calls (unsupported by AUSPICE),
3. Have no floating-point instructions (not modeled by Cambridge ARM model),
4. Have no `goto` nor `longjmp` statements (unsupported by AUSPICE),
5. Do not contain explicit function pointers (unsupported by AUSPICE),
6. Contain only sequential execution behavior (multi-threaded behavior and concurrency are not modeled by the Cambridge ARM model),
7. Are statically compiled and linked, so that all executable code is present,
8. Are compiled with an unmodified version of `gcc` at `-O0` optimization, and obey the ARM-THUMB Procedure Call Standard (ATPCS) [3], and
9. Have well-defined function prologues and epilogues.

We also assume that our target programs run in an OS that isolates user processes, preventing attackers from modifying the memory of a process, and that the OS and physical security of the host are not compromised. We assume that the underlying OS (Linux in this paper) "correctly" services syscall invocations by correctly restoring the context (program counter, register, and memory) of the user process at the end of every syscall invocation, and providing its specified (e.g., in Sect. 2 of the Linux Programmer's Manual [2]) functionality. Recent work has verified the functional correctness of microkernels for realistic OSes [11], making this assumption a realistic one. We also assume that each syscall is invoked via an assembly wrapper with a C function prototype that sets up the arguments for the syscall, whose name identifies the invoked syscall. This is the convention by which common C libraries give programmers access to syscalls.

Non-goals. We do not verify that the OS correctly services syscalls. We consider only direct (e.g., register and memory) effects of syscalls on CFI, but not OS state not directly observed by a user-mode process (e.g., file descriptor mappings, user-space memory mappings in `mmap`). We do not verify arbitrary safety properties: we focus on the safety properties in Sect. 3.1 that ensure CFI.

3   Background

We summarize our prior work, AUSPICE [24], before we present AUSPICE-R's extensions. We describe the safety properties proved automatically by AUSPICE (Sect. 3.1) and the Cambridge ARM model which AUSPICE is based on (Sect. 3.2), and AUSPICE's proof rules (Sect. 3.3) and proof automation algorithm (Sect. 3.4).

3.1 Safety Properties of Interest

The main goal of AUSPICE is to prove that a machine code program possesses Control-Flow Integrity (CFI) [6]. CFI requires that the execution of a program follows a path in a Control-flow Graph (CFG) that is "determined ahead of time" [6]. For a program which has CFI with respect to its load-time CFG (i.e., its execution follows the CFG describing the instructions loaded from disk), attackers cannot change the program's execution in unintended ways (e.g., by supplying malformed or malicious inputs), nor inject instructions to be executed.

AUSPICE proves CFI for a program by proving three safety properties: that (1) loaded program instructions in memory cannot be overwritten, (2) function-return addresses saved to the program's stack cannot be overwritten, and (3) only instructions at initially loaded addresses can be executed. AUSPICE instantiates these safety properties as safety assertions at each instruction to be proved.

The above three safety properties are necessary and sufficient (in the absence of goto and longjmp statements in C and explicit function pointers) to ensure CFI holds for an ARM machine code program. To see why this is the case, consider how the three safety properties together prevent a machine code program's CFG from being changed at run-time: Property (1) prevents CFG nodes from being changed by preventing loaded instructions in memory from being modified; Property (2) prevents CFG edges from being changed by preventing function return addresses from being changed; Property (3) prevents CFG nodes from being added by preventing the injection and running of new instructions. Hence, the 3 safety properties that AUSPICE proves for each instruction in a program are sufficient to prove that CFI holds (given our assumptions in Sect. 2).

3.2 Hoare Logic for ARM Machine Code: Cambridge ARM Model

Next, we describe the Hoare Logic we use to reason about ARM machine code. The Cambridge ARM model [18] specializes a Hoare Logic [19] to reason about low-level details of ARM machine code. This model is formalized in higher-order logic and mechanized in the HOL4 [22] proof system, and captures low-level details of processor state as seen by ARM machine code programs, namely: values of registers and status flags, data values stored in memory, and the value of the program counter (pc). The model represents the behavior of each instruction using a Hoare triple theorem:

$$\vdash \text{SPEC } x \text{ \{p\} c \{q\}}$$

"SPEC" indicates the theorem is a Hoare triple; "x" is a tuple that defines the next-step relation and other relations for the instruction set architecture (ISA) modeled in the triple, and is instantiated with the "ARM_MODEL" tuple of relations in the Cambridge ARM model [18] (other ISAs are also supported in the Cambridge model [19], but are beyond the scope of this paper). Informally, the theorem reads: if assertion p holds for the current processor state, and instruction c is executed, then q will hold for the resulting processor state. We refer to p and q as the pre-state and post-state assertions of instruction c.

Processor state assertions p and q either assert the value of a processor state element (namely register values, status flags, memory, and the program counter value), or are pure boolean assertions about logical variables. Pure boolean assertions can be *pre-conditions* (labelled precond($\cdot$)), which are predicates known to hold before an instruction executes (e.g., statements in the body of "if (i == 0) {...}" have the pre-condition "$i = 0$"), or *assumptions* (labelled cond($\cdot$)).

State assertions can assert the values of multiple resources (e.g., multiple registers) using the separating conjunction $*$ [20]. Note that $*$ in the Cambridge ARM model prevents assertions about repeated processor resources (e.g., the same register cannot be asserted about twice), but not memory locations. Instead, processor memory is treated as a single resource in the model. Memory is represented as a map from 32-bit addresses to the bytes stored at each address. AUSPICE uses the following proved rules from the Cambridge ARM model:

$$\frac{\text{SPEC } x \ p \ c_1 \ q \quad \text{SPEC } x \ q \ c_2 \ r}{\text{SPEC } x \ p \ (c_1; c_2) \ r} \text{ COMPOSE} \qquad \frac{\text{SPEC } x \ p \ c \ q}{\text{SPEC } x \ (p * r) \ c \ (q * r)} \text{ FRAME}$$

Note that there are no side-conditions restricting the form of r in the Frame rule above, as machine resource values are asserted using register relations (see Sect. 4.1) rather than variables in the Hoare logic of the Cambridge ARM model [19], effectively turning all symbolic variables into single-static assignment variables.

3.3   AUSPICE: Hoare Logic-Based Safety Property Proofs

Next, we describe AUSPICE's proof rules which enable safety properties to be proved automatically. Then, we describe AUSPICE's abstract interpretation algorithm for automating safety proofs.

AUSPICE defines proof rules to hierarchically build up, in a bottom-up fashion, to a whole-program definition of safety with respect to its 3 safety properties. First, AUSPICE defines proof rules for its safety properties to hold at the single instruction and basic block levels (Fig. 1). The MEM_CFI_SAFE rule constructs a "safe instruction" theorem by requiring each instruction's Hoare triple to be augmented with safety assertions (as assumptions) for AUSPICE's three safety properties. Our three safety properties (Sect. 3.1) are concretely instantiated in the predicates *ms*, cfi_1, cfi_2 respectively with the safe ranges for memory addresses written to, and the value of the program counter after each instruction runs. The code in the MEM_CFI_SAFE rule, "{(*offset, ins*)}", enforces that safe instruction theorems can be constructed only from a Hoare triple for a single instruction with instruction word "*ins*" at address "*offset*" in the program. Then, the MEM_CFI_SAFE_COMPOSE rule builds up to a "safe basic block" theorem by allowing only theorems for safe instructions, and theorems composed from smaller safe basic blocks, to be composed. The MEMCFISAFE_FRAME rule lifts the FRAME rule in the Cambridge ARM model to reason about safe basic blocks.

$$\frac{\text{SPEC } x \ (\text{cond}(ms \wedge cfi_1 \wedge cfi_2) * p) \ \{(\textit{offset}, ins)\} \ q}{\text{MEMCFISAFE } x \ (\text{cond}(ms \wedge cfi_1 \wedge cfi_2) * p) \ \{(\textit{offset}, ins)\} \ q} \quad \text{MEM\_CFI\_SAFE}$$

$$\frac{\text{MEMCFISAFE } x \ p \ c \ q}{\text{MEMCFISAFE } x \ (p * r) \ c \ (q * r)} \quad \text{MEMCFISAFE\_FRAME}$$

$$\frac{\text{MEMCFISAFE } x \ p \ c_1 \ q \quad \text{MEMCFISAFE } x \ q \ c_2 \ r}{\text{MEMCFISAFE } x \ p \ (c_1; c_2) \ r} \quad \text{MEM\_CFI\_SAFE\_COMPOSE}$$

Fig. 1. AUSPICE logic rules for single instruction and basic block level safety.

$\vdash \quad \forall addr, nodes, funcs, cfg_{pred}, cfg_{succ}, assns, postcond, p, q \ \cdot$

$\quad \text{FUN\_SAFE}(addr, nodes, funcs, cfg_{pred}, cfg_{succ}, assns, postcond, p, q)$

$\Leftrightarrow (\forall n \cdot n \in nodes \Rightarrow \min(n, addr) = addr)$

$\wedge \ (\forall min \cdot min \in nodes \Rightarrow (cfg_{pred}(min) = \emptyset) \Rightarrow \exists x, p', q', c' \ \cdot$

$\quad (\text{MEMCFISAFE } x \ (\text{aPC } min * \text{cond}(assns) * p') \ c' \ (q')))$

$\wedge \ (\forall out \cdot out \in nodes \Rightarrow (cfg_{succ}(out) = \emptyset) \Rightarrow \exists x, p', q', c', r' \ \cdot$

$\quad (\text{MEMCFISAFE } x \ (\text{aPC } out * \text{precond}(r') * p') \ c' \ (q')) \wedge (r' \Rightarrow postcond))$

$\wedge \ (\forall n, pred, succ \cdot (\{n, pred\} \subseteq nodes \Rightarrow pred \in cfg_{pred}(n) \Rightarrow n \in cfg_{pred}(succ) \Rightarrow$

$\quad \exists x, r', p', c_1, q', s', c_2, q'', r' \ \cdot$

$\quad (\text{MEMCFISAFE } x \ (\text{aPC } pred * \text{precond}(r') * p') \ c_1 \ (\text{aPC } n * q') \wedge$

$\quad \text{MEMCFISAFE } x \ (\text{aPC } n * \text{cond}(s') * q') \ c_2 \ (\text{aPC } succ * q'') \wedge (r' \Rightarrow s'))))$

$\wedge \ (\forall n, pred \cdot (pred \in nodes \Rightarrow (n \in funcs) \Rightarrow pred \in cfg_{pred}(n) \Rightarrow n \in cfg_{succ}(pred) \Rightarrow$

$\quad \exists x, r', p', q', nodes', funcs', cfg'_p, cfg'_s, s', postcond', q'', c_1 \ \cdot$

$\quad (\text{MEMCFISAFE } x \ (\text{aPC } pred * \text{precond}(r') * p') \ c_1 \ (\text{aPC } n * q') \wedge$

$\quad \text{FUN\_SAFE}(n, nodes', funcs', cfg'_p, cfg'_s, s', postcond', q', q'') \wedge (r' \Rightarrow s'))))$

$\wedge \ (\forall n, pred, succ \cdot (n \in nodes \Rightarrow (pred \in funcs) \Rightarrow pred \in cfg_{pred}(n) \Rightarrow n \in cfg_{pred}(succ) \Rightarrow$

$\quad \exists x, nodes', funcs', cfg'_p, cfg'_s, s', postcond', p', q', s'', q'', c_1 \ \cdot$

$\quad (\text{FUN\_SAFE}(pred, nodes', funcs', cfg'_p, cfg'_s, s', postcond', p', q') \wedge$

$\quad \text{MEMCFISAFE } x \ (\text{aPC } n * \text{cond}(s'') * q') \ c_1 \ (\text{aPC } succ * q'') \wedge (postcond' \Rightarrow s''))))$

Fig. 2. AUSPICE's FUNSAFE rule for function-level and whole-program safety. aPC asserts that the program counter contains the asserted value.

Each MEMCFISAFE (i.e., safe instruction and safe basic block) theorem is also sound with respect to the Cambridge ARM model, as AUSPICE proved:

$$\vdash \forall x \ p \ c \ q \ \cdot \ \text{MEMCFISAFE } x \ p \ c \ q \ \Rightarrow \ \text{SPEC } x \ p \ c \ q$$

Next, AUSPICE defines the FUNSAFE rule (Fig. 2), which enables *local reasoning* about safety properties at the function (and whole-program) levels. AUS-PICE's local reasoning principle [24] states that the safety properties at each instruction depend only on the program state immediately before that instruction runs: thus, for a program to be safe, we only need to ensure that the safety assertions at each instruction hold given the pre-conditions of all its predecessor instructions. Informally, if the FUN_SAFE theorem for a function holds, then the machine code of the function is safe with respect to AUSPICE's three safety properties. The safety of a (machine code) function is defined by the FUN_SAFE relation, with respect to: (i) *addr*, the address of the function, (ii) *nodes*, a set of addresses of the function's CFG nodes (i.e., its basic blocks), (iii) *funcs*, a set of addresses of callee functions, (iv) cfg_{pred}, cfg_{succ}, maps of CFG predecessors/successors of each node, (v) *assns*, the safety assertions of the function's entry node, (vi) *postcond*, the pre-conditions of the function's exit node, and p,q, the pre-state/post-state of the function's entry/exit nodes respectively.

Then, the 6 conjunct clauses of the FUNSAFE rule specify the requirements that need to hold for the function to be safe. The requirements for the function to be safe are instantiated according to the function's CFG. The first 3 conjunct clauses define: (i) the address of the function, as given by its entry node with the smallest address, (ii) the entry node of the function to have no CFG predecessors, and (iii) the exit node of the function to have no CFG successors.

The 4th to 6th conjunct clauses define the requirements for the function to be safe for all control-flow transfers, that are either: (i) intra-procedural, (ii) inter-procedural function calls, or (iii) inter-procedural function returns. The FUNSAFE rule is instantiated with one clause for each CFG edge. Each conjunct clause begins with a description of the CFG predecessor/successor relationships for the kind of control-flow transfer described (e.g., $\forall n, pred, succ \cdot \{n, pred\} \subseteq nodes \Rightarrow pred \in cfg_{pred}(n) \Rightarrow n \in cfg_{pred}(succ)$ for intra-procedural control-flow transfers). In each conjunct clause, the MEMCFISAFE and FUN_SAFE terms describe the behavior of the basic blocks or functions in the clause, and the predicate $r' \Rightarrow s'$ is the requirement for the pre-conditions r' of each predecessor basic block to discharge the safety assertions s' at each basic block. Note also that in each of the first two conjuncts of each requirement, the post-state of the predecessor CFG node's MEMCFISAFE or FUN_SAFE which describes its behavior must match the pre-state of the successor CFG node's MEMCFISAFE or FUN_SAFE. This is in line with the standard COMPOSE rule in Hoare Logic.

Thus, the goal of the FUN_SAFE theorem is to state that the machine code of a function (and all its callee functions) possesses the three AUSPICE safety properties at each instruction, which in turn implies that the program has CFI. The soundness and correctness arguments for our proof rules are in [24].

3.4   Proof Automation in AUSPICE

Next, we describe AUSPICE's proof automation algorithm (Fig. 3). At the top level, AUSPICE calls SAFEFUNCTIONANALYSIS for the entry-function of the program. SAFEFUNCTIONANALYSIS is a context-sensitive inter-procedural analysis which returns a FUN_SAFE theorem for a function proved safe, or terminates with an error message. SAFEFUNCTIONANALYSIS calls the abstract interpretation in SAFETYASSERTIONANALYSIS (Fig. 4). This abstract interpretation is a backwards analysis, whose domain is predicates about processor state. The analysis finds the pre-conditions needed to discharge the safety assertions at each instruction, and its information records undischarged safety assertions. These

```
 1: function SAFEFUNCTIONANALYSIS(instr_thms)
 2:    (cfg, func) ← COMPUTECFGANDCALLEES(instr_thms)
 3:    safe_thms ← ADDSAFETYASSERTIONS(instr_thms)         ▷ Add the ms,cfi₁,cfi₂
    safety assertions to each instruction's Hoare triple.
 4:    bb_safe ← SAFECOMPOSE(safe_thms)        ▷ Use MEM_CFI_SAFE_COMPOSE rule.
 5:    func_safe ← ∀callee ∈ func· SAFEFUNCTIONANALYSIS(callee)
 6:    assertion_info ← SAFETYASSERTIONANALYSIS(bb_safe, func_safe, cfg)
 7:    (bb_safe', func_safe') ← AUGMENTTHEOREMS(bb_safe, func_safe, assertion_info)
 8:    return FUN_SAFE_RULE(bb_safe', func_safe')
 9: end function
10: instr_thms ← ∀instr· CAMBRIDGEARM_GETINSTRUCTIONMODEL(instr)
11: SAFEFUNCTIONANALYSIS(instr_thms)
```

Fig. 3. Safe Function analysis in AUSPICE [24]. Uses single-instruction theorems from the Cambridge ARM model, and returns FUN_SAFE theorem for function. *bb_safe* and *func_safe* contain basic block and callee function safety theorems respectively.

undischarged safety assertions are added as assumptions to predecessor theorems using the Frame rule in Hoare logic in the AUGMENTTHEOREMS function. SAFETYASSERTIONANALYSIS also checks that undischarged assertions are not propagated in a cycle, otherwise the analysis diverges with new undischarged safety assertions continually recorded. Hence the analysis is terminated and fails.

4 Safety Proofs for Machine Code with System Calls

There are two main steps to support safety proofs of machine code with syscalls.

First, we model the supervisor call instruction (svc), whose effects occur in both user-mode, and in supervisor-mode where the OS services the syscall. As we focus on the safety of user-mode programs, we do not wish to fully model the actions of the OS. Instead, we assume that the processor correctly handles the mode-switch from user to supervisor mode, and that the OS correctly services the syscall (Sect. 2). We focus on only the user-mode-observed effects after the syscall has been serviced by the OS. We model syscalls in user-mode in an *axiomatic* manner: we represent the user-mode-observed effects of syscalls as "axiomatized" (rather than proven) Hoare triples, that we introduce as hypotheses in our model.

Second, we need to augment our syscall models to support safety proof automation. AUSPICE's proof automation needs concrete safety assertions for each instruction. For typical instructions in user-mode programs, the proven Hoare triple for each instruction contains enough information for computing concrete safety assertions (Line 3 in Fig. 3). However, the effects of a syscall cannot be determined from the svc instruction alone, and depends on the arguments passed to it. These arguments are set up in the instructions leading to the svc instruction, and in the callers of the syscall. In AUSPICE-R, we use a *delayed* approach to analyze syscalls: We express the effects of syscalls symbolically, and we concretize these symbolic variables later in the analysis when information is available from callers of the syscall.

1: **function** SAFETYASSERTIONANALYSIS(*bb_safe_thms*, *func_safe_thms*, *cfg*)
2:    *info* ← ∅   ▷ Analysis information keyed by CFG node
3:    **procedure** ASSERTIONANALYSISSTEP(*info*, *last_info*, *cfg*)
4:       **for all** *node* ∈ *cfg*, *pred* ∈ FINDPREDS(*cfg*, *node*) **do**
5:          *pred_preconds* ← GETTHMPRECONDS(*pred*) ∪ *last_info*[*pred*]
6:          *node_asserts* ← GETTHMASSERTS(*node*) ∪ *last_info*[*node*]
7:          **for all** *assert* ∈ *node_asserts* **do**
8:             **if** PROVE(*pred_preconds*, *assert*) == **False then**
9:                *info*.term[*pred*] ← *info*.term[*pred*] ∪ *assert*
10:                *a_path* ← FINDASSERTPATH(*last_info*.path[*node*], *assert*)
11:                *info*.path[*pred*] ← *info*.path[*pred*] ∪ *a_path*
12:                ABORTIFASSERTPATHISCYCLE(*a_path*)
13:    **end procedure**
14:    **repeat**
15:       *last_info* ← *info*; *info* ← ASSERTIONANALYSISSTEP(*info*, *last_info*, *cfg*)
16:    **until** *last_info* == *info*
17:    **return** *info*
18: **end function**

Fig. 4. Safety assertion analysis in AUSPICE [24]. FINDPREDS gives the CFG predecessors of a node; GETTHMPRECONDS and GETTHMASSERTS are helper functions that
return the pre-conditions and safety assertions in a given Hoare triple; PROVE invokes
the HOL4 METIS prover to try to discharge a safety assertion given a pre-condition;
FINDASSERTPATH computes the propagation path of an undischarged safety assertion.

4.1   Modeling of System Calls in User-Mode Programs

Rationale Behind Model. First, we focus on the user-mode-visible effects of
syscalls that may affect our safety properties. Our safety properties are affected
by memory addresses that are written to, and by the value of the program
counter. As the processor will restore the program counter to the address of the
instruction immediately following the svc instruction (B1.8.10 in [5]), we need
to focus on only the addresses in the user process's memory that are written to
during the servicing of the syscall. All other processor state (user-mode registers, apart from r0 which stores a return value, and status flag values) remains
unchanged, as user-mode registers are distinct from supervisor-mode registers,
and the processor restores the values of the original status flags (B1.8.10 in [5]).

Second, we need to know the user-mode visible effects of each syscall in user-
mode. We need to: (i) retrieve the number of the syscall invoked (passed in
register r7, based on the Linux Application Binary Interface (ABI) for ARM
[1]), (ii) identify the syscall invoked (e.g., from the Linux kernel's documentation and/or source-code), and (iii) retrieve the arguments passed to the syscall
(via user-mode registers or the user-mode stack). This allows us to identify the
behavior of each invoked syscall from its specification. We can then instantiate
our safety-assertions from the user-mode-observed effects of each syscall invocation.

SPEC ARM_MODEL (aR 0w $r0$ * aR 1w $r1$ * ⊢ SPEC ARM_MODEL (aR 0w $r0$ * aR 1w $r1$ *

  aR 2w $r2$ * aR 7w 4w * aPC p *   aR 2w $r2$ * aR 7w 4w * aPC p *

    aR 14w $r14$ * aMEMORY df f)   aR 14w $r14$ * aMEMORY df f)

$\{(p, \text{0xEF000000})\}$ (aR 0w rv * aR 1w $r1$ * $\{(p, \text{0xEF000000})\}$ (aR 0w rv * aR 1w $r1$ *

  aR 2w $r2$ * aR 7w 4w * aR 14w $r14$ *   aR 2w $r2$ * aR 7w 4w * aR 14w $r14$ *

    aPC $(p + 4w)$ * aMEMORY df f)   aPC $(p + 4w)$ * aMEMORY df f)

Fig. 5. Constructed Hoare triple axiom for the write syscall. 4w is a numerical constant 4, where the suffix w indicates 4 is a fixed-width word.

Axiomatization of System Call Effects. We "axiomatize" the Hoare triples for syscalls by constructing an unproven Hoare triple for each syscall, which we then introduce as an assumption. These unproven Hoare triples are collected as hypotheses of the final safety proof, and they formalize our assumption of each syscall's effects on user-mode state, based on the syscall's specification.

Figure 5 shows an example axiom for the write syscall. 3 kinds of assertion relations are shown: (i) aR asserts the value of the specified register; (ii) aPC asserts the value of the program counter; (iii) aMEMORY asserts the domain (df) and contents of memory (map f from addresses to stored values). The pre-state value of register r7 is asserted to be the literal 4, which is the syscall number for write, while the other pre-state register values are asserted to be symbolic variables ($r0$, $r1$, $r2$, $r14$), as they are unknown when we analyze the svc instruction alone. We instantiate these symbolic variables with concrete values later when analyzing the instructions leading up to the syscall invocation (details in Sect. 4.2). While some of the asserted resources (e.g., register r1) remain unchanged and could be omitted from the Hoare triple, we include this information as it may be required in our analysis for modeling the full behavior of the syscall.

Note that the Hoare triple is repeated on the left-hand-side of the turnstile "⊢", indicating that the Hoare triple is a hypothesis. The post-state of this axiom for write is identical to its pre-state (except for the value of register r0, given by the aR 0w assertion), as write does not modify any user-mode-visible processor state. The value of register r0 in the post-state is given by the symbolic variable rv, which indicates the return value from the syscall, and can represent the return value of both failed and successful syscalls. This axiom is representative of the other syscalls AUSPICE-R supports for which there are no effects that are directly visible in user-mode: open, close, mmap, munmap, nanosleep.

In contrast, consider our constructed axiom for the read syscall in Fig. 6. read has user-mode-visible effects: the bytes that it reads are written to and visible in the process's memory at the supplied address. The condition "cond($addrs \subseteq df$)" asserts that the set of addresses $addrs$ supplied to the syscall are in the domain of the memory map f. Also, the process's memory is updated from map f to $(g\ f)$, where g represents the effects of read on memory. Note that $addrs$ and g are both symbolic. Note also that the value in register r0 (asserted by aR 0w) in

SPEC ARM_MODEL (aR 0w $r0$ * aR 1w $r1$ * ⊢ SPEC ARM_MODEL (aR 0w $r0$ * aR 1w $r1$ *

aR 2w $r2$ * aR 7w 3w * aR 14w $r14$ *   aR 2w $r2$ * aR 7w 3w * aR 14w $r14$ *

aPC p * cond($addrs \subseteq df$) * aMEMORY df f)   aPC p * cond($addrs \subseteq df$) * aMEMORY df f)

{$(p, 0xEF000000)$} (aR 0w rv * aR 1w $r1$ *   {$(p, 0xEF000000)$} (aR 0w rv * aR 1w $r1$ *

aR 2w $r2$ * aR 7w 3w * aR 14w $r14$ *   aR 2w $r2$ * aR 7w 3w * aR 14w $r14$ *

aPC $(p + 4w)$ * aMEMORY df $(g\ f)$))   aPC $(p + 4w)$ * aMEMORY df $(g\ f)$))

Fig. 6. Constructed Hoare triple axiom for the **read** syscall.

the post-state of the axiom is symbolic, and can represent the return values from both successful and failed invocations of the syscall. While the OS may not have written to all the addresses in the set *addrs* when **read** fails or reads fewer than the requested number of bytes, *addrs* conservatively lists the maximum extent of the memory written to by **read**.

```
1: function AUSPICE_R_GetInstructionModel(addr, addr_to_func, instr)
2:     if !(instr = 0xEF000000) then
3:         return CambridgeARM_GetInstructionModel(instr)
4:     else
5:         func_containing_instr ← addr_to_func[addr]
6:         return ConstructSyscallTriple(instr, addr, func_containing_instr)
7: end function
```

Fig. 7. Algorithm for unproven Hoare triple construction for syscalls.

Implementation. The construction of unproven Hoare triples for each syscall (Fig. 7) is implemented as a wrapper around the model construction for individual instructions in the Cambridge ARM model, and replaces Line 10 in Fig. 3. When a **svc** instruction (0xEF000000) is detected, AUSPICE-R constructs an unproven Hoare triple based on the name of the function that the instruction is in. ConstructSyscallTriple implements the unproven Hoare triple construction process described above. We initially support modeling the following syscalls for simple I/O operations: **read**, **write**, **open**, **close**, **mmap**, **munmap**, **nanosleep**.

4.2 Supporting Safety Proof Automation for System Calls

Next, to support automated safety proofs in AUSPICE-R for syscalls, we need to concretize the initially-symbolic effects in the unproven Hoare triples for each syscall, as the safety assertion discharge in SafetyAssertionAnalysis (Fig. 4) reasons about memory addresses individually. To concretize the symbolic effects of a syscall's unproven triple, AUSPICE-R examines the arguments the syscall is invoked with when running SafeFunctionAnalysis (Fig. 3) on the caller of the syscall. We first illustrate how the arguments to system calls are interpreted, using the **read** syscall. Then we discuss how the symbolic effects are concretized, before we describe how these are implemented in AUSPICE-R's analysis.

```
80e4: e3a00000  mov r0, #0
80e8: e59f1098  ldr r1, [pc, #152]
80ec: e3a02003  mov r2, #3
80f0: eb000049  bl 821c <c_read>
...   ...
8188: 00010250
...   ...
0000821c <c_read>:
821c: e92d4880  push {r7, fp, lr}
8220: e28db004  add fp, sp, #4
8224: e24dd000  sub sp, sp, #0
8228: e3a07003  mov r7, #3
822c: ef000000  svc 0x00000000
...   ...
```

Fig. 8. Example ARM machine code invoking the **c_read** wrapper to the **read** syscall.

```
ssize_t read(int fd, void *buf,
             size_t count);
```

Fig. 9. Prototype of C function wrapper to **read** syscall.

System Call Arguments. The Linux Programmer's Manual [2] states that the **read** syscall takes 3 arguments: (i) an integer indicating the file descriptor, (ii) a pointer at which to store bytes that have been read, and (iii) the number of bytes to read. Figure 8 shows a fragment of machine code, where the basic block at address 0x80E4 calls the function **c_read**, which is the assembly-code wrapper that invokes the **read** syscall (at address 0x822C). Figure 9 shows the C prototype of the assembly-code wrapper. For each invocation of the **read** syscall, the values of the arguments to the syscall are loaded to the relevant registers ($r0$, $r1$, $r2$) at the call-site to its wrapper (i.e., at the basic block at 0x80E4). AUSPICE-R extracts these values from the post-state assertions of the Safe Basic Block theorem for the call-site. Concretely, for this example, the values to the arguments are $fd = 0$, $buf = 0x10250$, $count = 3$. Note that the arguments may still be symbolic at this point (e.g., if reading a variable-length number of bytes). However, for AUSPICE to prove our safety properties for the **read** syscall, the pointer to store read bytes and the number of bytes to read must be concrete. This enables AUSPICE-R to update the symbolic safety assertions in the FUN_SAFE theorem of **read**'s syscall wrapper with concrete expressions, thus enabling the safety assertions to be discharged. If the pointer and number of bytes read remain symbolic, SAFETYASSERTIONANALYSIS cannot reason about the symbolic safety assertions, and the safety proof will fail.

Updating of Symbolic Effects. Next, we construct variable substitutions for the initial symbolic effects (written-address set *addrs* and memory-update function g), which we apply to the unproven Hoare triple for the **read** syscall. These substitutions concretize the effects of the syscall on user-mode processor state, so that SAFETYASSERTIONANALYSIS can reason about the safety of these effects. To complete its automated safety-property proofs, AUSPICE needs to enumerate the memory address of each byte written to. While AUSPICE can reason about byte-addresses containing symbolic variables (e.g., when the address written to is a symbolic variable $r3$), it cannot reason about symbolic ranges of addresses where the number of elements in the set is symbolic (even if the elements of the set are drawn from a finite universe, e.g., fixed-width words). This is due to limitations with HOL4's built-in tactics for reasoning about sets (**pred_setLib**). Hence, AUSPICE-R enumerates the byte-addresses written to by the syscall.

For the example in Fig. 8, 3 bytes are written at the address 0x10250. Hence, we substitute *addrs* with {0x10250w; 0x10251w; 0x10252w}, and the update function *g* with the expression shown in Fig. 10. extmem__c_read__0x80E4 is an opaque function that represents the results of external I/O, and it returns the (symbolic) data read given the byte-number read; "=+" is the map update operator, where "$a = +b$" indicates the value b is stored at address a.

$$\lambda f \ . \ ((\text{0x10250w} = + \ (\text{extmem\_\_c\_read\_\_0x80E4 0w}))$$
$$((\text{0x10251w} = + \ (\text{extmem\_\_c\_read\_\_0x80E4 1w}))$$
$$((\text{0x10252w} = + \ (\text{extmem\_\_c\_read\_\_0x80E4 2w})) \ f)))$$

Fig. 10. Concretized memory-update expression for the read syscall in Fig. 8.

After substituting the symbolic effects for concrete values in each syscall's Hoare triple axioms, AUSPICE can automatically discharge the safety assertions for these axioms (if the machine code contains the necessary safety-checks).

Implementation. Figure 11 describes the updated Safe Function analysis algorithm in AUSPICE-R, incorporating the unproven Hoare triple axiomatization (Line 12), and the concretization of symbolic effects (Line 7). In functions that call syscalls, SAFEFUNCTIONANALYSISWITHSYSCALLS is first called on each syscall callee (Line 5). Then, the arguments to the syscall are available in the caller of the syscall, and the FUN_SAFE theorems of syscalls are concretized using information from the caller's basic blocks, *bb_safe* (Line 7). This concretization must take place before SAFETYASSERTIONANALYSIS (Line 8). AUSPICE-R adds 1300 lines of ML proof scripts to AUSPICE's code-base of 11.8 KLOC of ML.

```
 1: function SAFEFUNCTIONANALYSISWITHSYSCALLS(instr_thms)
 2:     (cfg, func) ← COMPUTECFGANDCALLEES(instr_thms)
 3:     safe_thms ← ADDSAFETYASSERTIONS(instr_thms)
 4:     bb_safe ← SAFECOMPOSE(safe_thms)          ▷ Use MEMCFISAFE_COMPOSE rule.
 5:     func_safe ← ∀callee ∈ func· SAFEFUNCTIONANALYSISWITHSYSCALLS(callee)
 6:     syscall_callees ← ∀callee ∈ func | IS_SYSCALL(callee)
 7:     func_safe′ ← ∀c ∈ syscall_callees · CONCRETIZEARGS(func_safe[c], bb_safe)
 8:     assertion_info ← SAFETYASSERTIONANALYSIS(bb_safe, func_safe′, cfg)
 9:     (bb_safe′, func_safe″) ← AUGMENTTHEOREMS(bb_safe, func_safe′, assertion_info)
10:     return FUN_SAFE_RULE(bb_safe′, func_safe″)
11: end function
12: instr_thms ← ∀instr· AUSPICE_R_GETINSTRUCTIONMODEL(instr)
13: SAFEFUNCANALYSISWITHSYSCALLS(instr_thms)
```

Fig. 11. Updated Safe Function analysis in AUSPICE-R with support for safety proofs for machine code with syscalls. Lines 6, 7 and 12 are new to the analysis.

5   Optimizing Safety Proof Automation

AUSPICE-R optimizes SafeFunctionAnalysis (Fig. 3) and SafetyAssertionAnalysis (Fig. 4) to speed up its safety-proof generation, so that larger programs can be verified in less time. AUSPICE-R leverages (i) common patterns in gcc-compiled machine code for local-variable-writes to speed up SafetyAssertionAnalysis, and (ii) the behavior of safety assertions in callee functions in its inter-procedural analysis to speed up SafeFunctionAnalysis.

Common Compiler Conventions. SafetyAssertionAnalysis performs two tasks: (i) it finds pairs of pre-conditions $p \in P$ and safety assertions $a \in A$, such that $p \Rightarrow a$, and (ii) for assertions $a \in A$ for which no p is found, it propagates a to predecessor nodes, and checks if a's propagation path has a cycle. However, computing the propagation path of assertion a is expensive, as it requires symbolic execution along the propagation path.

We leverage two observations in gcc-compiled code: (i) there are two classes of memory-writes: to local variables (i.e., a constant offset from the frame pointer r11 or stack pointer r13), and to arbitrarily-computed addresses (typically stored in registers); (ii) r11 and r13 are generally updated only at the start and end of each function. Thus, safety assertions for writes to local variables will not change during the analysis of function bodies. To speed up SafetyAssertionAnalysis for writes to local variables, AUSPICE-R: (i) reduces the number of assertion terms analyzed, and (ii) skips the propagation-cycle check.

```
 1: procedure AssertionAnalysisStepOpt(info, last_info, cfg)
 2:    for all node ∈ cfg, pred ∈ FindPreds(cfg, node) do
 3:       pred_preconds ← GetThmPreconds(pred) ⋃ last_info[pred]
 4:       node_asserts ← GetThmAsserts(node) ⋃ last_info[node]
 5:       (range_pds, other_pds) ← Partition Is_Range pred_preconds
 6:       (localvar_asserts, other_asserts) ← Partition Is_Localvar node_asserts
 7:       for all assert ∈ localvar_asserts do
 8:          curr_range ← Narrow(Compute_Range_Predicate(assert), range_pds)
 9:          (prev_range, other_terms) ← Partition Is_Range (info.term[pred])
10:          info.term[pred] ← other_terms ⋃ Narrow(curr_range, prev_range)
11:       for all assert ∈ other_asserts do
12:          if Prove(other_pds, assert) == False then
13:             info.term[pred] ← info.term[pred] ⋃ assert
14:             a_path ← FindAssertPath(last_info.path[node], assert)
15:             info.path[pred] ← info.path[pred] ⋃ a_path
16:             AbortIfAssertPathIsCycle(a_path)
17: end procedure
```

Fig. 12. Optimized analysis step for SafetyAssertionAnalysis in AUSPICE-R. Lines 5 to 10 are new to the analysis. Is_Range and Is_Localvar return true for predicates that are ranges and that are about local-variable writes respectively.

Figure 12 describes the optimized version of the inner analysis step in SAFETYASSERTIONANALYSIS, which replaces ASSERTIONANALYSISSTEP in Fig. 4. First, we represent the safety assertions for local-variable writes using range predicates: e.g., for a safety assertion "$\{r13 - 21w;\ r13 - 22w;\ r13 - 23w;\ r13 - 24w\} \subseteq \{addr \mid addr < r11\}$", the addresses that are offset from r13 are where a local variable is stored on the stack; we replace this safety assertion with the range predicate "$24w \leq r13 < r11 + 24w$", which implies the original safety assertion. Thus, for writes to N different local variables in a function, only 2 rather than $2N$ predicates are propagated: one each for Safety Properties 1 and 2 (Sect. 3.1). We also define a narrowing operator for the meet of two range predicates which returns the more restrictive of two predicates to merge terms from multiple CFG paths. Second, since writes to local variables are to fixed offsets from the frame pointer (r11) or stack pointer (r13), which do not change in the function's body, we do not need to compute nor check for cycles in propagation paths.

```
bar() { ... }
baz() { bar();
        ... }
foo() { bar();
        baz();
        bar();
        ... }
```

Fig. 13. Example program for inter-procedural analysis.

Context-Sensitivity of Analysis. SAFEFUNCTION-ANALYSIS (Fig. 3) is an inter-procedural analysis which constructs a distinct Safe Function (FUN_SAFE) theorem for every call to each callee function. We use the program in Fig. 13 to illustrate AUSPICE-R's approach. First, consider the behavior of SAFEFUNCTIONANALYSIS in AUSPICE: in foo(), bar() is called twice, thus one FUN_SAFE theorem is constructed for each of its two call-sites. We call this analysis "call-site context-sensitive", or *CSCS*. CSCS provides the highest level of precision. We would like to reduce the precision of our analysis to reduce the number of iterations of SAFEFUNCTIONANALYSIS (Fig. 3) needed to successfully generate a safety proof.

Context-insensitive inter-procedural analysis provides the lowest level of precision: we analyze each function once for the whole program and generate one FUN_SAFE theorem for it. However, in our example, having only one FUN_SAFE theorem for each function results in imprecise analysis by forcing safety assertions from instructions at different call-tree depths (e.g., foo() vs. baz()) to be framed onto the same theorem (bar()). (We refer to the function-level CFG as a call-tree, whose depth is the number of nested function calls.) This is logically equivalent to different instances of the function's stack overlapping in memory at the same time, although during execution, only one instance of the function's stack exists in memory at any point in time, resulting in imprecise analysis. Hence, the proof generation fails when there are safety assertions from a smaller call-tree depth (e.g., foo()) than the call-tree depth of the currently-analyzed function (e.g., baz()). Having one FUN_SAFE theorem per-function per-call-tree-depth is also insufficient, as two caller functions at the same call-tree depth could have different stack sizes, resulting in the same contradiction as above.

On the other hand, in each function, we need to analyze each callee function only once, regardless of how many times that callee function is called. We call this analysis "single-function context-sensitive" (*SFCS*). When analyzing a function F, we need only one FUN_SAFE theorem for each callee function C, regardless of how many times C is called in F. Then, we can frame the safety assertions from all the return-sites of C in the function F to the single theorem for C, as there would not be any contradiction in the analysis. In our example, we can merge all the safety assertions required at all the return-sites from bar() in foo(), and add them to the FUN_SAFE theorem for bar(). While there is some loss of precision (e.g., the FUN_SAFE theorem for the second call to bar() does not need to consider the safety assertions that need to be discharged when calling baz()), we now need to run SAFEFUNCTIONANALYSIS fewer times.

Limitations. AUSPICE-R continues to analyze syscall wrapper functions using CSCS analysis, as AUSPICE-R needs to generate a unique FUN_SAFE theorem to correctly consider the arguments passed to a syscall at each distinct call-site.

6 Evaluation

First, we evaluate the ability of AUSPICE-R (with Sect. 5 optimizations) to automatically prove safety properties in ARM machine code with syscalls. We picked 2 classes of programs: (i) simple versions of file I/O utilities that we implemented for Linux on the ARM platform; (ii) programs with hardware inputs/outputs on the Raspberry Pi single-board-computer. All our test programs are Linux usermode programs on ARM, and compiled with an unmodified gcc toolchain for ARMv6 with -O0 optimization. All proofs were generated using the HOL4 proof assistant [22] on an Intel Core i7 2.6 GHz with 16 GB RAM. Our test programs are available at http://users.ece.cmu.edu/~jiaqit/aplas16data.

6.1 File-Based I/O

We implemented simple versions of three common file I/O utilities in C for Linux on the ARM platform. These programs contained the read, write, open, and close syscalls. Table 1 summarizes our test programs, their sizes and functionality, and the times taken to automatically prove the safety of each program. Our results show that AUSPICE-R can prove safety automatically in realistic programs with useful I/O functionality, and AUSPICE-R took less than 2 h to automatically prove the safety of each program.

6.2 Embedded Software

We implemented 4 programs containing hardware inputs and outputs on the Raspberry Pi. These programs contained the mmap, munmap, open, close, and nanosleep syscalls. Table 2 describes and summarizes our programs, their sizes, and the times taken to prove safety automatically. The proof times for the blink and light test-programs are under 2 h, and comparable to the proof times for our file I/O examples above. The proof times for the lcd and fall-det test-programs

Table 1. Descriptions and proof times for file-based I/O utilities.

Program	Lines of C	Instructions	Proof time	Description
cat	411	207	26.9 min	Outputs contents of a file
wc	427	641	95.1 min	Counts number of words in a file
grep	428	621	40.2 min	Prints lines containing given string

Table 2. Proof times for hardware I/O programs.

Program	Lines of C	Instructions	Call-tree depth	Proof time	Description
blink	418	619	3	58.7 min	Turn LED repeatedly on/off
light	429	854	4	81.7 min	Use light-sensor to light LED when dark
lcd	559	2229	6	22.2 h	Print string to 16 × 2 monochrome LCD
fall-det	923	3331	6	47.9 h	Detect human falls with accelerometer using algorithm in [13]

are significantly longer, as they are significantly larger, and have much deeper call-trees: the run-time of AUSPICE-R's inter-procedural analysis is exponential in the depth of the call-tree. lcd and fall-det, with 2229 and 3331 instructions respectively are, to the best of our knowledge, the largest programs for which safety properties have been automatically proved using an approach that considers the full semantics of instructions (vs. 1104 instructions using ARMor [27], which also uses the Cambridge ARM model [18]).

6.3   Proof Optimization

We report the proof times for programs that have been evaluated on prior techniques, to evaluate AUSPICE-R's optimizations. Table 3 summarizes our results for our 3 test programs (without syscalls): memcpy, which copies an array of

Table 3. Comparing AUSPICE-R's proof times with AUSPICE [24] and ARMor [27].

Program	Instructions	AUSPICE-R	AUSPICE-R vs. AUSPICE [24]		AUSPICE-R vs. ARMor [27]	
		Proof time	Proof time	AUSPICE-R X % faster	Proof time	AUSPICE-R X % faster
memcpy	116	6.5 min	16.4 min	252 %	-	-
sort	337	9.4 min	122 min	1297 %	-	-
string-search	530	0.76 h	6.05 h	796 %	8 h	1067 %

Table 4. Comparison of number of iterations of analysis of Call-Site Context-Sensitivity (CSCS) vs. Single-Function Context-Sensitivity (SFCS) (Sect. 5).

Program	Instructions	Iterations of analysis		Optimization
		CSCS (AUSPICE)	SFCS (AUSPICE-R)	
lcd	2229	2799	751	73 %
fall-det	3331	5069	845	83 %

integers; **sort**, which implements Insertion Sort; and **string-search**, from the MiBench benchmark suite [12], which implements the Boyer-Moore string-search algorithm. We compared AUSPICE-R's proof times to our prior work, AUS-PICE [24], for all 3 programs: AUSPICE-R's safety proofs were between 252 % to 1297 % faster. Also, AUSPICE-R's proof time for **string-search** was 1067 % faster than ARMor [27] (which used an Intel Core i7 2.7 GHz). AUSPICE-R's proof optimizations significantly improved the times taken for automated safety proofs.

To show the optimization gains from AUSPICE-R's SFCS inter-procedural analysis (Sect. 5), we compared the number of iterations of SAFEFUNCTION-ANALYSIS (Fig. 3) in SFCS to that in CSCS analysis. The optimization gains are greatest in programs with repeated calls to non-syscall-wrapper functions. We simulated the number of iterations the inter-procedural analysis needs to run for **lcd** and **fall-det** by analyzing their function-level call-trees. Table 4 summarizes the results of using SFCS over CSCS. The number of iterations of the inter-procedural analysis for constructing a safety proof reduced by 73 % for **lcd**, and by 83 % for **fall-det**, showing that SFCS made our analysis feasible for large test-programs.

7   Discussion

First, our axioms of syscall behavior provide a formal, succinct expression of our expectations of the behavior of syscalls, as observed in user-mode. We envision that these axioms can be used to empirically validate the behavior of syscalls in future, e.g., through dynamic testing.

Second, we found our requirement of the **read()** syscall to accept only concrete lengths and buffer addresses to not be a significant limitation. To support **read()**s to buffers of variable lengths and symbolic addresses, we implemented a wrapper function that reads to a fixed length/address buffer, and copies its contents to the final destination buffer.

8   Related Work

ARMor [27], and our prior work AUSPICE [24], automatically prove safety properties for ARM machine code using HOL4 [22], and are closest to AUSPICE-R. ARMor supports only "bare-metal" programs running without an OS, while AUSPICE supports user-mode machine code but not syscalls. Goel et al. [21] reason about x86 machine code with syscalls in the ACL2 logic for "heavy-weight", manual proofs of functional-correctness, while AUSPICE-R automates proofs of "light-weight" safety properties. Goel's formalization of x86 syscalls tracks OS-state that may not be user-mode-visible that is needed for functional correctness proofs, while AUSPICE-R focuses only on user-mode-visible state that impacts our safety properties.

Sequoll [9] performs model-checking on ARM machine code using the Cambridge ARM model [18]. Bedrock [10] "mostly-automates" functional correctness proofs for an idealized machine-language, whereas, AUSPICE-R proves safety properties for machine code emitted by standard compilers. CompCert [16] is a compiler that has been formally verified to preserve the semantics of well-behaved C programs during compilation. VST [8] is a program logic for reasoning about programs in Cminor (a CompCert intermediate language), whose claims hold in its compiled machine code due to its use of CompCert. Verasco [14] is a formally verified static-analyzer for Cminor whose guarantees carry over to its compiled code due to CompCert. It checks for the absence of run-time errors that can cause safety violations such as the ones AUSPICE-R proves the absence of, but does not produce proofs for individual programs. SeaHorn [7] and Dafny [15] allow users to specify source-code assertions for checking arbitrary properties, while AUSPICE-R focuses on specific safety properties for CFI [6], without needing user specifications.

9   Conclusion and Future Work

We have presented AUSPICE-R, an extension to AUSPICE [24] that: (i) automates safety-property proofs in ARM machine code containing system calls by axiomatizing their user-mode-visible effects, and (ii) optimizes automated safety-property proofs by leveraging common conventions in compiled code and by providing a more efficient inter-procedural analysis. We have demonstrated AUSPICE-R on simple file I/O utilities implemented for Linux on ARM, and on programs containing hardware I/O on the Raspberry Pi single-board-computer. We showed that AUSPICE-R is up to 12× faster and supports programs up to 3x larger than prior work.

In future, we plan to tackle the challenges associated with more complex syscalls, e.g., for network communications, that may have more complex user-mode effects. We also plan to investigate how our axioms of syscall behavior can be used to aid dynamic testing of syscall-servicing behavior by OS kernels.

References

1. Application Binary Interface for the ARM Architecture. http://bit.ly/22OaMai
2. Linux Programmer's Manual: Syscalls. http://bit.ly/1VChJMY
3. The ARM-THUMB Procedure Call Standard (2000). http://bit.ly/1NbOQhT
4. As Gadgets Shrink, ARM Still Reigns As Processor King, September 2013. http://onforb.es/19LIzgd
5. ARM Architecture Reference Manual: ARMv7-A and ARMv7-R edition (2014)
6. Abadi, M., Budiu, M., Erlingsson, U., Ligatti, J.: Control-flow Integrity. In: ACM CCS (2005)
7. Gurfinkel, A., Kahsai, T., Komuravelli, A., Navas, J.A.: The SeaHorn verification framework. In: Kroening, D., Păsăreanu, C.S. (eds.) CAV 2015. LNCS, vol. 9206, pp. 343–361. Springer, Heidelberg (2015). doi:10.1007/978-3-319-21690-4_20
8. Appel, A.W.: Verified software toolchain. In: Barthe, G. (ed.) ESOP 2011. LNCS, vol. 6602, pp. 1–17. Springer, Heidelberg (2011). doi:10.1007/978-3-642-19718-5_1
9. Blackham, B., Heiser, G.: Sequel: a framework for model checking binaries. In: IEEE RTAS (2013)
10. Chlipala, A.: Mostly-automated verification of low-level programs in computational separation logic. In: PLDI (2011)
11. Klein, G., et al.: seL4: formal verification of an OS kernel. In: SOSP, October 2009
12. Guthaus, M., et al.: MiBench: a free, commercially representative embedded benchmark suite. In: IEEE WWC Workshop (2001)
13. Jia, N.: Detecting human falls with a 3-axis digital accelerometer (2009). http://bit.ly/23fXhFE
14. Jourdan, J.H., Laporte, V., Blazy, S., Leroy, X., Pichardie, D.: A formally-verified C static analyzer. In: POPL (2015)
15. Leino, K.R.M.: Dafny: an automatic program verifier for functional correctness. In: Clarke, E.M., Voronkov, A. (eds.) LPAR 2010. LNCS (LNAI), vol. 6355, pp. 348–370. Springer, Heidelberg (2010). doi:10.1007/978-3-642-17511-4_20
16. Leroy, X.: Formal verification of a realistic compiler. Commun. ACM **52**(7), 107–115 (2009)
17. Miller, C., Valasek, C.: Remote exploitation of an unaltered passenger vehicle. http://bit.ly/1Xk71rn
18. Myreen, M.O., Fox, A.C.J., Gordon, M.J.C.: Hoare logic for ARM machine code. In: Arbab, F., Sirjani, M. (eds.) FSEN 2007. LNCS, vol. 4767, pp. 272–286. Springer, Heidelberg (2007). doi:10.1007/978-3-540-75698-9_18
19. Myreen, M.O., Gordon, M.J.C.: Hoare logic for realistically modelled machine code. In: Grumberg, O., Huth, M. (eds.) TACAS 2007. LNCS, vol. 4424, pp. 568–582. Springer, Heidelberg (2007). doi:10.1007/978-3-540-71209-1_44
20. Reynolds, J.: Separation logic: a logic for shared mutable data structures. In: IEEE LICS (2002)
21. Goel, S., et al.: Simulation and formal verification of x86 machine-code programs that make system calls. In: FMCAD (2014)
22. Slind, K., Norrish, M.: A brief overview of HOL4. In: Mohamed, O.A., Muñoz, C., Tahar, S. (eds.) TPHOLs 2008. LNCS, vol. 5170, pp. 28–32. Springer, Heidelberg (2008). doi:10.1007/978-3-540-71067-7_6
23. Tan, J., Tay, H., Drolia, U., Gandhi, R., Narasimhan, P.: PCFIRE: towards provable preventative control-flow integrity enforcement for realistic embedded software. In: EMSOFT (2016)

24. Tan, J., Tay, H.J., Gandhi, R., Narasimhan, P.: AUSPICE: Automatic Safety Property verification for unmodified Executables. In: Gurfinkel, A., Seshia, S.A. (eds.) VSTTE 2015. LNCS, vol. 9593, pp. 202–222. Springer, Heidelberg (2016). doi:10.1007/978-3-319-29613-5_12

25. Wahbe, R., Lucco, S., Anderson, T., Graham, S.: Efficient software-based fault isolation. In: SOSP (1993)

26. Yang, X., Chen, Y., Eide, E., Regehr, J.: Finding and understanding bugs in C compilers. In: PLDI (2011)

27. Zhao, L., Li, G., Sutter, B.D., Regehr, J.: ARMor: fully verified software fault isolation. In: EMSOFT (2011)

Observation-Based Concurrent Program Logic for Relaxed Memory Consistency Models

Tatsuya Abe[✉] and Toshiyuki Maeda

STAIR Lab, Chiba Institute of Technology,
2-17-1 Tsudanuma, Narashino, Chiba 275-0016, Japan
{abet,tosh}@stair.center

Abstract. Concurrent program logics are frameworks for constructing proofs, which ensure that concurrent programs work correctly. However, most conventional concurrent program logics do not consider the complexities of modern memory structures, and the proofs in the logics do not ensure that programs will work correctly. To the best of our knowledge, Independent Reads Independent Writes (IRIW), which is known to have non-intuitive behavior under relaxed memory consistency models, has not been fully studied under the context of concurrent program logics. One reason is the gap between theoretical memory consistency models that program logics can handle and the realistic memory consistency models adopted by actual computer architectures. In this paper, we propose observation variables and invariants that fill this gap, releasing us from the need to construct operational semantics and logic for each specific memory consistency model. We describe general operational semantics for relaxed memory consistency models, define concurrent program logic sound to the operational semantics, show that observation invariants can be formalized as axioms of the logic, and verify IRIW under an observation invariant. We also obtain a novel insight through constructing the logic. To define logic that is sound to the operational semantics, we dismiss shared variables in programs from assertion languages, and adopt variables observed by threads. This suggests that the so-called bird's-eye view of the whole computing system disturbs the soundness of the logic.

Keywords: Relaxed memory consistency model · Concurrent program logic · Rely/guarantee method · Observation · Independent Reads Independent Writes

1 Introduction

Memory structures are becoming increasingly complicated as computing systems continue to grow. This can be overwhelming when attempting to write programs that work on architectures consisting of complicated memory structures. Since conventional program verification considers architectures with simple memory structures, it struggles to deal with architectures that consist of complicated memory structures.

© Springer International Publishing AG 2016
A. Igarashi (Ed.): APLAS 2016, LNCS 10017, pp. 63–84, 2016.
DOI: 10.1007/978-3-319-47958-3_4

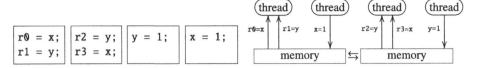

| r0 = x; r1 = y; | r2 = y; r3 = x; | y = 1; | x = 1; |

Fig. 1. Independent Reads Independent Writes

Fig. 2. Non-remote-write-atomic memories

To illustrate the problem, consider an example racy program. Readers may consider that racy programs should be prohibited as their behaviors are specified *undefined* in C++11 [12]. However, in lower-level programming (e.g., on virtual machine or computer architecture), racy programs are necessary to implement register algorithms, which provide mutual exclusion etc. Although such racy programs are not typically large, their non-intuitive behaviors make it difficult to verify them.

Figure 1 shows *Independent Reads Independent Writes (IRIW)* [4]. Variables x and y are shared, and variables r_0, r_1, r_2, and r_3 are thread-local. We assume that all variables are initialized to 0. IRIW consists of four threads. Two threads are *readers*, which read values from the shared variables x and y. The other two threads are *writers*. One writes 1 to x, and the other writes 1 to y. If the write to x is performed before the write to y, then $r_2 \leq r_3$ seems to hold, since $r_2 > r_3$ (i.e., $r_2 = 1$ and $r_3 = 0$) does not hold for the following reason:

1. $r_2 = 1$ implies $y = 1$, and
2. we assume that the write to x is performed before the write to y;
3. therefore, when x is read (to r_3), its value is 1.

Similarly, if the write to y is performed before the write to x, then $r_0 \leq r_1$ seems to hold. Therefore, it would appear that $r_0 \leq r_1 \vee r_2 \leq r_3$.

However, this is not always the case, because an architecture may realize a form of shared memory, as shown in Fig. 2. This means that the first reader and writer share the same physical memory, and the second reader and writer share another physical memory. Shared memory is realized by any mechanism for data transfer (denoted by $\leftrightarrows$) between the physical memories. The architecture that has mechanism for data transfer is sensitive to the so-called *remote-write-atomicity* [11] (also called *multi-copy-atomicity* in [24]). Remote-write-atomicity claims that if two thread write values to (possibly distinct) locations, then the other threads *must* observe the *same* order between the two write operations.

Here, let us assume that physical memories do not enjoy remote-write-atomicity, that is, effects on one memory *cannot* be immediately transferred to the other memory. Under this architecture, while the first reader *may* observe that the write to x is performed before the write to y, the second reader *may* observe that the write to y is performed before the write to x. Therefore, there is no guarantee that $r_0 \leq r_1 \vee r_2 \leq r_3$.

Thus, in modern program verification, we cannot ignore remote-write-atomicity. However, to the best of our knowledge, there exists no concurrent program logic in which remote-write-atomicity can be switched on and off. One reason is the existence of a gap between theoretical memory consistency models, which concurrent program logics can handle, and realistic memory consistency models, which are those adopted by actual computer architectures. While theoretical memory consistency models (axioms written in assertion languages) in concurrent program logics describe relations between expressions, which are often the orders of values that are evaluated by expressions, realistic memory consistency models (which are often written in natural languages rather than formal languages) describe the orders of executions of statements on actual computer architectures. In this paper, we propose *observation variables and invariants* that fill this gap, thus releasing us from the need to construct operational semantics and logic for each specific memory consistency model. We define general operational semantics to consider cases in which threads own their memories, and construct concurrent program logic in which we give proofs that ensure certain properties hold when programs finish. We can control observation invariants as uniform *axioms* of the logic. This enables us to show that a property holds when a program finishes under an observation invariant, whereas the property does not hold when the program finishes without the observation invariant. In Sect. 9, we verify IRIW using this logic under an observation invariant induced by a realistic memory consistency model like SPARC-PSO [27].

To the best of our knowledge, the derivation shown in Sect. 9 is the first to ensure that a property holds in concurrent program logic that handles relaxed memory consistency models like SPARC-PSO, although the behavior of IRIW under more relaxed memory consistency models that refute the property has been discussed several times in the literature (e.g., [4, 22, 24, 25, 31]).

In constructing the concurrent program logic, we obtained a novel insight into the use of shared variables in an assertion language for operational semantics with relaxed memory consistency models. First, we extend an assertion language in the logic by introducing the additional variable x^i to denote x as observed by the i-th thread. The value of x^i is not necessarily the same as that of x. Next, we restrict the assertion language by dismissing shared variables in programs from assertion languages. This prohibits us from describing the value of x. By designing this assertion language, we can construct a concurrent program logic that is *sound* to operational semantics (explained in Sect. 4) with relaxed memory consistency models. This suggests that, in concurrent computation, the so-called bird's-eye view that overlooks the whole does not exist, and that each thread runs according to its own observations, and some (or all) threads sometimes reach a consensus.

The rest of this paper is organized as follows. Section 2 discusses related work, and Sect. 3 presents some definitions that are used throughout this paper. Section 4 gives operational semantics (based on the notion of state transition systems) for relaxed memory consistency models. Section 5 explains our concurrent program logic. Section 6 defines validity of judgments. Section 7 introduces the notion of observation invariants. Section 8 then presents our soundness theorem.

In Sect. 9, we provide example derivations for concurrent programs. Section 10 concludes the paper and discusses ideas for future work.

2   Related Work

Stølen [28] and Xu et al. [35,36] provided concurrent program logics based on rely/guarantee reasoning [13]. However, they did not consider relaxed memory consistency models containing observation invariants, that is, they handle *strict consistency*, the strictest memory consistency model. This paper handles relaxed memory consistency models. The memory consistency models with observation invariants in this paper are more relaxed than those obeying strict consistency.

Ridge [23] developed a concurrent program logic for x86-TSO [26] based on rely/guarantee reasoning by introducing *buffers*. However, buffers to *one* shared memory are known to be insufficient to cause the behavior of IRIW. This paper handles more relaxed memory consistency models than x86-TSO, as threads have their own memories to deal with observation invariants.

Ferreira et al. [7] introduced a concurrent separation logic that is parameterized by invariants, and explained the non-intuitive behavior of IRIW. Their motivation for constructing a parametric logic coincides with ours. However, their logic is based on *command subsumptions*, which describe the execution orders of statements. This is different from our notion of observations; their approach therefore has no direct connection to our logic, and gave no sufficient condition to ensure the correctness of IRIW. Any connection between their logic and ours remains an open question.

Vafeiadis et al. presented concurrent separation logics for restricted C++11 memory models [30,32]. The restricted C++11 semantics are so weak that the property for IRIW (shown in Sect. 1) does not hold without additional assumptions. However, unlike our approach, they did not handle programs that contain write operations to *distinct* locations, such as IRIW. In another paper [15], Lahav and Vafeiadis described an Owicki–Gries style logic and verified a program consisting of multiple reads and writes in the logic. This program is different from IRIW, as the reads/writes are from/to the same location. The essence of IRIW is to write to *distinct* locations x and y. Our paper proposes the notion of observation invariants, constructs a simple concurrent program logic, formalizes the axioms of our logic, and gives a formal proof for IRIW. This simplification provides the insight explained in Sect. 1.

The authors proposed a notion of program graphs, representations of programs with memory consistency models, gave operational semantics and construct program logic for them [1]. However, the semantics and logic cannot handle the non-intuitive behavior of IRIW since remote-write-atomicity is implicitly assumed.

There also exist verification methods that are different from those using concurrent program logics. Model checking based on exhaustive searches is a promising program verification method [2,10,14,17]. Given a program and an assertion, model checking is good at detecting execution traces that violate the assertions, but is less suitable for ensuring that the assertion holds.

Some reduction methods to *Sequential Consistency (SC)* via race-freedom of programs are well-known (e.g., [5,20,21]). However, verification of racy programs like concurrent copying protocols is one of the authors' concerns [3], and programs that have non-SC behaviors are our main targets.

Boudol et al. proposed an operational semantics approach to represent a relaxed memory consistency model [5,6]. They defined a process calculus, equipped with buffers that hold the effects of stores, and its operational semantics to handle the non-intuitive behavior of IRIW. He proved *Data Race Freedom (DRF)* guarantee theorem that DRF programs have the same behaviors as those under SC. However, IRIW is not DRF.

Owens et al. reported that x86-CC [25] allows the non-intuitive behavior of IRIW, and designed x86-TSO [22] that prohibits the behavior. He also extended DRF to *Triangular Race Freedom (TRF)* that TRF programs have the same behaviors under x86-TSO as those under SC [21]. Although IRIW is surely TRF, a slight modification of IRIW in which additional writes to distinct variables at the start on the reader threads are inserted is not TRF. Since the program has a non-SC behavior, verification of the program under SC cannot ensure correctness of the program under x86-TSO. Our verification method to use observation invariants is robust to such slight changes. In addition, our method is not specific to a certain memory consistency model like x86-TSO. An observation invariant introduced in Sect. 7 for IRIW is independent of the slight change, and we can construct a derivation for the program that is similar to the derivation for IRIW explained in Sect. 9.3.

3   Concurrent Programs

In this section, we formally define our target concurrent programs.

Similar to the conventional program logics (e.g., [8]), sequential programs are defined as sequences of statements. Let r denote the thread-local variables that cannot be accessed by other threads, $x, y, \ldots$ denote shared variables, and e denote thread-local expressions (thread-local variables, constant values val, arithmetic operations, and so on). A sequential program can then be defined as follows:

$$S^i ::= \mathsf{SK}^i \mid \mathsf{MV}^i\, r\, e \mid \mathsf{LD}^i\, r\, x \mid \mathsf{ST}^i\, x\, e \mid \mathsf{IF}^i\, \varphi?S^i{:}S^i \mid \mathsf{WL}^i\, \varphi?S^i \mid S^i; S^i$$

$$\varphi ::= e = e \mid e \le e \mid \neg\varphi \mid \varphi \supset \varphi \mid \forall r.\varphi.$$

In the above definition, the superscript i represents (an identifier of) the thread on which the associated statement will be executed. In the rest of this paper, this superscript is often omitted when the context is clear. The SK statement denotes an ordinary no-effect statement (SKip). As in conventional program logics, MV $r\,e$ denotes an ordinary variable substitution (MoVe). The **load** and **store** statements denote read and write operations, respectively, for shared variables (LoaD and STore). The effect of the **store** statement issued by one thread may not be immediately observed by the other threads. The IF and

WL statements denote ordinary conditional branches and iterations, respectively, where we adopt ternary conditional operators (IF-then-else-end and WhiLe-do-end). Finally, $S\,;S$ denotes a sequential composition of statements.

We write $\varphi \vee \psi$, $\varphi \wedge \psi$, $\varphi \leftrightarrow \psi$, and $\exists\, r.\varphi$ as $(\neg \varphi) \supset \psi$, $\neg\,((\neg \varphi) \vee (\neg \psi))$, $(\varphi \supset \psi) \wedge (\psi \supset \varphi)$, and $\neg\, \forall\, r. \neg \varphi$, respectively. In the following, we assume that $\neg$, $\wedge$, $\vee$, and $\supset$ are stronger with respect to their connective powers. In addition to the above definition, $\top$ is defined as the tautology $\forall\, r. r = r$.

A concurrent program with N threads is defined as the composition of sequential programs by parallel connectives $\|$ as follows:

$$P ::= S^0 \parallel S^1 \parallel \dots \parallel S^{N-1}.$$

In this paper, the number of threads N is fixed during program execution. Parentheses are often omitted, and all operators except $\supset$ are assumed to be left associative.

4   Operational Semantics

In this section, we define small-step operational semantics for the programming language defined in Sect. 3. Specifically, the semantics is defined as a standard state transition system, where a *state* (written as st) is represented as a pair of $\langle \sigma, \Sigma \rangle$. The first element of the pair, σ, consists of the values of thread-local variables and shared variables that threads observe on registers and memories; formally, a function from thread identifiers and (thread-local and shared) variables to values. The second element, Σ, represents buffers that temporarily buffer the effects of store operations to shared variables. It may be worth noting that, in the present paper, buffers are not queues, that is, each buffer stores only the latest value written to its associated variable, for simplicity. This is because the present paper focuses on verifying IRIW, and storing the latest value suffices for the purpose. Replacing buffers with queues is straightforward and not shown in the present paper. $\Sigma^{i,j}$ refers to thread j's buffer for effects caused by thread i's statements. If $i \neq j$, then thread j cannot observe the effects that are buffered. If $i = j$, then thread j can observe the effects that are buffered.

Using Fig. 3, we now present an informal explanation of buffers and memories. Thread 0 executes statement $\mathsf{ST}^0 x1$, and buffers $\Sigma^{0,0}$ and $\Sigma^{0,1}$ are updated. Next, thread 1 executes statement $\mathsf{LD}^1 r_1\, x$. If the effect of $\mathsf{ST}^0\, x\, 1$ has not yet reached σ^1, thread 1 cannot observe it, and reads the initialized value 0. If the effect of $\mathsf{ST}^0\, x\, 1$ has already reached σ^1, thread 1 reads 1. Finally, thread 0 executes statement $\mathsf{LD}^0\, r_0\, x$. Whether the effect of $\mathsf{ST}^0\, x\, 1$ has reached σ^1 or not, thread 0 can observe it. Therefore, thread 0 reads a value of 1. Updates from Σ to σ are performed without the need for statements.

Formally, in the following, a function from triples formed of two thread identifiers and shared variables to values is evaluated by *currying* all functions, for the convenience of *partial applications*. We assume that the set of values contains a special constant value udf to represent uninitialized or invalidated buffers. We often write σi, Σi, and Σij as σ^i, Σ^i, and $\Sigma^{i,j}$, respectively, for readability. We

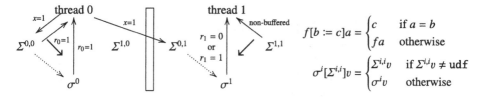

Fig. 3. Buffers and memories

Fig. 4. Update functions

define the following two operations for update functions as in Fig. 4 where f ranges over each among σ, σ^i, Σ, Σ^i, and $\Sigma^{i,j}$.

Figure 5 shows the rules of the operational semantics, where $\langle\!\langle e \rangle\!\rangle_{\sigma^i}$ denotes the valuation of an expression e as follows:

$$\langle\!\langle val \rangle\!\rangle_{\sigma^i} = val \quad \langle\!\langle r \rangle\!\rangle_{\sigma^i} = \sigma^i r \quad \langle\!\langle x \rangle\!\rangle_{\sigma^i} = \sigma^i x \quad \langle\!\langle e_1 + e_2 \rangle\!\rangle_{\sigma^i} = \langle\!\langle e_1 \rangle\!\rangle_{\sigma^i} + \langle\!\langle e_2 \rangle\!\rangle_{\sigma^i} \quad \ldots$$

and $\sigma^i \vDash \varphi$ denotes the satisfiability of φ on σ^i in the standard manner, which is defined as follows:

$$\sigma^i \vDash e_1 = e_2 \Leftrightarrow \langle\!\langle e_1 \rangle\!\rangle_{\sigma^i} = \langle\!\langle e_2 \rangle\!\rangle_{\sigma^i} \quad \sigma^i \vDash e_1 \leq e_2 \Leftrightarrow \langle\!\langle e_1 \rangle\!\rangle_{\sigma^i} \leq \langle\!\langle e_2 \rangle\!\rangle_{\sigma^i} \quad \sigma^i \vDash \neg\varphi \Leftrightarrow \sigma^i \nvDash \varphi$$

$$\sigma^i \vDash \varphi \supset \varphi' \Leftrightarrow \sigma^i \vDash \varphi \text{ implies } \sigma^i \vDash \varphi' \quad \sigma^i \vDash \forall r. \varphi(r) \Leftrightarrow \sigma^i \vDash \varphi(v) \text{ for any } v.$$

$$\frac{}{\langle P, st \rangle \xrightarrow{e} \langle P, st' \rangle} \text{(O-ENV)} \qquad \frac{}{\langle \mathsf{MV}^i\ r\ e, \langle \sigma, \Sigma \rangle \rangle \xrightarrow{c} \langle \mathsf{SK}^i, \langle \sigma[i := \sigma^i[r := \langle\!\langle e \rangle\!\rangle_{\sigma^i}]], \Sigma \rangle \rangle} \text{(O-MV)}$$

$$\frac{}{\langle \mathsf{LD}^i\ r\ x, \langle \sigma, \Sigma \rangle \rangle \xrightarrow{c} \langle \mathsf{SK}^i, \langle \sigma[i := \sigma^i[r := \sigma^i[\Sigma^{i,i}]x]], \Sigma \rangle \rangle} \text{(O-LD)}$$

$$\frac{}{\langle \mathsf{ST}^i\ x\ e, \langle \sigma, \Sigma \rangle \rangle \xrightarrow{c} \langle \mathsf{SK}^i, \langle \sigma, \Sigma[i := \Sigma^i[j := \Sigma^{i,j}[x := \langle\!\langle e \rangle\!\rangle_{\sigma^i}] \mid 0 \leq j < N]] \rangle \rangle} \text{(O-ST)}$$

$$\frac{\sigma^i \vDash \varphi}{\langle \mathsf{IF}^i\ \varphi?P{:}Q, \langle \sigma, \Sigma \rangle \rangle \xrightarrow{c} \langle P, \langle \sigma, \Sigma \rangle \rangle} \text{(O-IT)} \qquad \frac{\sigma^i \nvDash \varphi}{\langle \mathsf{IF}^i\ \varphi?P{:}Q, \langle \sigma, \Sigma \rangle \rangle \xrightarrow{c} \langle Q, \langle \sigma, \Sigma \rangle \rangle} \text{(O-IE)}$$

$$\frac{\sigma^i \vDash \varphi}{\langle \mathsf{WL}^i\ \varphi?P, \langle \sigma, \Sigma \rangle \rangle \xrightarrow{c} \langle P; \mathsf{WL}^i\ \varphi?P, \langle \sigma, \Sigma \rangle \rangle} \text{(O-WT)} \qquad \frac{\sigma^i \nvDash \varphi}{\langle \mathsf{WL}^i\ \varphi?P, \langle \sigma, \Sigma \rangle \rangle \xrightarrow{c} \langle \mathsf{SK}^i, \langle \sigma, \Sigma \rangle \rangle} \text{(O-WE)}$$

$$\frac{\langle P, \langle \sigma, \Sigma \rangle \rangle \xrightarrow{c} \langle \mathsf{SK}, \langle \sigma', \Sigma' \rangle \rangle}{\langle P; Q, \langle \sigma, \Sigma \rangle \rangle \xrightarrow{c} \langle Q, \langle \sigma', \Sigma' \rangle \rangle} \text{(O-SQ}_0\text{)} \qquad \frac{\langle P, \langle \sigma, \Sigma \rangle \rangle \xrightarrow{c} \langle P', \langle \sigma', \Sigma' \rangle \rangle}{\langle P; Q, \langle \sigma, \Sigma \rangle \rangle \xrightarrow{c} \langle P'; Q, \langle \sigma', \Sigma' \rangle \rangle} \text{(O-SQ}_1\text{)}$$

$$\frac{\langle P, \langle \sigma, \Sigma \rangle \rangle \xrightarrow{c} \langle \mathsf{SK}, \langle \sigma', \Sigma' \rangle \rangle}{\langle P \parallel Q, \langle \sigma, \Sigma \rangle \rangle \xrightarrow{c} \langle Q, \langle \sigma', \Sigma' \rangle \rangle} \text{(O-PR}_0\text{)} \qquad \frac{\langle Q, \langle \sigma, \Sigma \rangle \rangle \xrightarrow{c} \langle \mathsf{SK}, \langle \sigma', \Sigma' \rangle \rangle}{\langle P \parallel Q, \langle \sigma, \Sigma \rangle \rangle \xrightarrow{c} \langle P, \langle \sigma', \Sigma' \rangle \rangle} \text{(O-PR}_1\text{)}$$

$$\frac{\langle P, \langle \sigma, \Sigma \rangle \rangle \xrightarrow{c} \langle P', \langle \sigma', \Sigma' \rangle \rangle}{\langle P \parallel Q, \langle \sigma, \Sigma \rangle \rangle \xrightarrow{c} \langle P' \parallel Q, \langle \sigma', \Sigma' \rangle \rangle} \text{(O-PR}_2\text{)} \qquad \frac{\langle Q, \langle \sigma, \Sigma \rangle \rangle \xrightarrow{c} \langle Q', \langle \sigma', \Sigma' \rangle \rangle}{\langle P \parallel Q, \langle \sigma, \Sigma \rangle \rangle \xrightarrow{c} \langle P \parallel Q', \langle \sigma', \Sigma' \rangle \rangle} \text{(O-PR}_3\text{)}$$

Fig. 5. Our operational semantics

A pair of a program and a state is called a *configuration*. Each rule is represented by a one-step transition between configurations $\langle P, st \rangle \xrightarrow{\delta} \langle P', st' \rangle$, which indicates that a statement causes $\langle P, st \rangle$ to transit to $\langle P', st' \rangle$, where δ is c or e.

Specifically, Rule O-ENV denotes a transition that requires no statement in P, which means that other threads are executing statements or memories are being updated from buffers. Although the rule was originally introduced to mean that other threads consume statements in conventional operational semantics for concurrent programming languages (with strict consistency) [35,36], the rule has the additional meaning here that memories are updated from buffers in constructing operational semantics for relaxed memory consistency models.

Readers unfamiliar with operational semantics for an imperative concurrent programming language (and its rely/guarantee reasoning) may consider $\xrightarrow{e}$ to be nonsense because $\xrightarrow{e}$ seems to allow any transitions. However, it is restricted to being admissible under a rely-condition by the notion of *validity* for judgments (called *rely/guarantee specifications*), as defined in Sect. 6. This is similar to the context of Hoare logic, where transitions consuming statements are defined to be large *at first*, and the transitions are restricted to be admissible ones under pre-conditions by the notion of validity for Hoare triples. This is one of the standard methods of defining operational semantics for an imperative concurrent programming language (e.g., as seen in [35,36]), and is not caused by handling relaxed memory consistency models. Here, in accordance with the standard, a transition $\xrightarrow{e}$ that consumes no statements is defined to be the product of states.

Rule O-MV evaluates e and updates σ with respect to r. Rule O-LD evaluates x on $\Sigma^{i,i}$, if $\Sigma^{i,i}x$ is defined (i.e., effects on x by statements on thread i itself are buffered), and on σ^i otherwise, and updates σ^i with respect to r. O-ST evaluates e and updates $\Sigma^{i,j}$ (not σ^i) with respect to x for any j; i.e., the rule indicates that the effect of the store operation is buffered in $\Sigma^{i,j}$. Rule O-IT handles a branch statement by asserting that φ is satisfied under state σ^i, and P is chosen. If σ^i is not satisfied, rule O-IE is applied and Q is chosen. Rule O-WT handles a loop statement by asserting that φ^i is satisfied under state σ, and an iteration is performed. If σ^i is not satisfied, rule O-WE is applied, and the program exits from the loop. Rules O-SQ and O-PR handle sequential and parallel compositions of programs, respectively.

5   Concurrent Program Logic

In this section, we define our concurrent program logic. Our assertion language is defined as follows:

$$\Phi ::= E = E \mid E \leq E \mid \neg \Phi \mid \Phi \supset \Phi \mid \forall v. \Phi \qquad\qquad v ::= r \mid x^i \mid \underline{r} \mid \underline{x}^i$$

where E represents a pseudo-expression denoting thread-local variables r, observation variables x^i, next thread-local variables $\underline{r}$, next observation variables $\underline{x}^i$, constant values val, arithmetic operations, and so on. Our assertion language does not contain a shared variable x that occurs in programs. This means that *nobody* observes the whole system. This novelty is a key point of this paper. We often write r as r^i when referring to r being a thread-local variable on the i-th thread. The observation variable x^i represents the value written to the shared variable x by ST on a thread with identifier i. The next variable $\underline{v}$ represents the value of v on a state to which the current state transits under the operational semantics.

Figure 6 shows the judgment rules. They are defined in the styles of Stølen and Xu's proof systems [28,35,36], which have two kinds of judgments. Each judgment of the form $\vDash \varPhi$ refers to satisfiability in the first-order predicate logic with equations in a standard manner. Each judgment of the form $\{pre, rely\}P\{guar, post\}$ (where pre and $post$ have no next variable) states that, if program P runs under pre-condition pre and rely-condition $rely$ (which are guaranteed by the other threads as well as the *environments*, as explained in Sect. 6) according to the operational semantics of Sect. 4, then the guarantee-condition $guar$ (on which the other threads rely) holds, as in conventional rely/guarantee systems. In the rest of this paper, we write $\vdash \{pre, rely\}\, P\, \{guar, post\}$ if $\{pre, rely\}\, P\, \{guar, post\}$ can be derived from the judgment rules of Fig. 6.

$$\frac{\vDash pre \supset [e/r]post \qquad \vDash pre \supset \lceil \mathrm{MV}^i\ r\ e \rceil^V \supset guar \qquad \vDash pre \perp rely \qquad \vDash post \perp rely}{\{pre, rely\}\ \mathrm{MV}^i\ r\ e\ \{guar, post\}}\ (\text{L-MV})$$

$$\frac{\vDash pre \supset post \qquad \vDash pre \supset \mathrm{I}(V) \supset guar \qquad \vDash pre \perp rely \qquad \vDash post \perp rely}{\{pre, rely\}\ \mathrm{SK}^i\ \{guar, post\}}\ (\text{L-SK})$$

$$\frac{\vDash pre \supset [x^i/r]post \qquad \vDash pre \supset \lceil \mathrm{LD}^i\ r\ x \rceil^V \supset guar \qquad \vDash pre \perp rely \qquad \vDash post \perp rely}{\{pre, rely\}\ \mathrm{LD}^i\ r\ x\ \{guar, post\}}\ (\text{L-LD})$$

$$\frac{\vDash pre \supset [e/x^i]post \qquad \vDash pre \supset \lceil \mathrm{ST}^i\ x\ e \rceil^V \supset guar \qquad \vDash pre \perp rely \qquad \vDash post \perp rely}{\{pre, rely\}\ \mathrm{ST}^i\ x\ e\ \{guar, post\}}\ (\text{L-ST})$$

$$\frac{\vDash \{pre \wedge \varphi, rely\}\, S_0^i\, \{guar, post\} \qquad \vDash \{pre \wedge \neg\varphi, rely\}\, S_1^i\, \{guar, post\} \qquad \vDash pre \supset \mathrm{I}(V) \supset guar \qquad \vDash pre \perp rely}{\{pre, rely\}\ \mathrm{IF}^i\ \varphi ? S_0^i : S_1^i\ \{guar, post\}}\ (\text{L-IF})$$

$$\frac{\vDash pre \supset \neg\varphi \supset post \qquad \vDash \{pre \wedge \varphi, rely\}\, S^i\, \{guar, pre\} \qquad \vDash pre \supset \mathrm{I}(V) \supset guar \qquad \vDash pre \perp rely \qquad \vDash post \perp rely}{\{pre, rely\}\ \mathrm{WL}^i\ \varphi ? S^i\ \{guar, post\}}\ (\text{L-WL})$$

$$\frac{\{pre, rely\}\, S_0^i\, \{guar, \varPhi\} \qquad \{\varPhi, rely\}\, S_1^i\, \{guar, post\}}{\{pre, rely\}\, S_0^i ; S_1^i\, \{guar, post\}}\ (\text{L-SQ})$$

$$\frac{\{pre_0, rely_0\}\, P\, \{guar_0, post_0\} \qquad \vDash pre \supset pre_0 \qquad \vDash rely \supset rely_0 \qquad \vDash guar_0 \supset guar \qquad \vDash post_0 \supset post}{\{pre, rely\}\, P\, \{guar, post\}}\ (\text{L-WK})$$

$$\frac{\{pre_0, rely_0\}\, P_0\, \{guar_0, post_0\} \qquad \{pre_1, rely_1\}\, P_1\, \{guar_1, post_1\} \qquad \vDash rely \vee guar_0 \supset rely_1 \qquad \vDash rely \vee guar_1 \supset rely_0 \qquad \vDash guar_0 \vee guar_1 \supset guar}{\{pre_0 \wedge pre_1, rely\}\, P_0 \parallel P_1\, \{guar, post_0 \wedge post_1\}}\ (\text{L-PR})$$

Fig. 6. Our concurrent program logic

$$\langle\sigma,\Sigma\rangle,\langle\sigma',\Sigma'\rangle \vDash E_0 = E_1 \Leftrightarrow [\![E_0]\!]_{\langle\sigma,\Sigma\rangle,\langle\sigma',\Sigma'\rangle} = [\![E_1]\!]_{\langle\sigma,\Sigma\rangle,\langle\sigma',\Sigma'\rangle}$$

$$\langle\sigma,\Sigma\rangle,\langle\sigma',\Sigma'\rangle \vDash E_0 \le E_1 \Leftrightarrow [\![E_0]\!]_{\langle\sigma,\Sigma\rangle,\langle\sigma',\Sigma'\rangle} \le [\![E_1]\!]_{\langle\sigma,\Sigma\rangle,\langle\sigma',\Sigma'\rangle}$$

$$\langle\sigma,\Sigma\rangle,\langle\sigma',\Sigma'\rangle \vDash \neg\,\Phi \Leftrightarrow \langle\sigma,\Sigma\rangle,\langle\sigma',\Sigma'\rangle \nvDash \Phi$$

$$\langle\sigma,\Sigma\rangle,\langle\sigma',\Sigma'\rangle \vDash \Phi \supset \Phi' \Leftrightarrow \langle\sigma,\Sigma\rangle,\langle\sigma',\Sigma'\rangle \vDash \Phi \text{ implies } \langle\sigma,\Sigma\rangle,\langle\sigma',\Sigma'\rangle \vDash \Phi'$$

$$\langle\sigma,\Sigma\rangle,\langle\sigma',\Sigma'\rangle \vDash \forall\,v.\,\Phi(v) \Leftrightarrow \langle\sigma,\Sigma\rangle,\langle\sigma',\Sigma'\rangle \vDash \Phi(v') \text{ for any } v'$$

where $[\![val]\!]_{\langle\sigma,\Sigma\rangle,\langle\sigma',\Sigma'\rangle} = val$ $[\![r^i]\!]_{\langle\sigma,\Sigma\rangle,\langle\sigma',\Sigma'\rangle} = \sigma^i r$

$[\![\underline{r^i}]\!]_{\langle\sigma,\Sigma\rangle,\langle\sigma',\Sigma'\rangle} = \sigma'^i r$ $[\![x^i]\!]_{\langle\sigma,\Sigma\rangle,\langle\sigma',\Sigma'\rangle} = \sigma^i[\Sigma^{i,i}]x$

$[\![\underline{x^i}]\!]_{\langle\sigma,\Sigma\rangle,\langle\sigma',\Sigma'\rangle} = \sigma'^i[\Sigma'^{i,i}]x$ $[\![E_1 + E_2]\!]_{\langle\sigma,\Sigma\rangle,\langle\sigma',\Sigma'\rangle} = [\![E_1]\!]_{\langle\sigma,\Sigma\rangle,\langle\sigma',\Sigma'\rangle} + [\![E_2]\!]_{\langle\sigma,\Sigma\rangle,\langle\sigma',\Sigma'\rangle} \cdots$

Fig. 7. The interpretation of the assertion language

$$\lceil\mathtt{MV}^i\ r\ e\rceil^V \equiv \underline{r} = e \wedge \bigwedge I(V \setminus \{r\}) \qquad \lceil\mathtt{LD}^i\ r\ x\rceil^V \equiv \underline{r} = x^i \wedge \bigwedge I(V \setminus \{r\})$$

$$\lceil\mathtt{ST}^i\ x\ e\rceil^V \equiv \underline{x^i} = e \wedge \bigwedge I(V \setminus \{x^j \mid 0 \le j < N\})$$

Fig. 8. Invariants about variables before and after assignments

More specifically, rule L-MV of Fig. 6 handles the substitution of thread-local variables with expressions. This is the same as in conventional rely/guarantee proof systems. $[e/v]$ represents the substitution of v with e. The first assumption means that *pre* must be a sufficient condition that implies *post* with respect to the substitution. We define $\vDash \Phi$ as $\langle\sigma,\Sigma\rangle,\langle\sigma',\Sigma'\rangle \vDash \Phi$ for any $\langle\sigma,\Sigma\rangle,\langle\sigma',\Sigma'\rangle$, where $\langle\sigma,\Sigma\rangle,\langle\sigma',\Sigma'\rangle \vDash \Phi$ is defined in a similar manner to a conventional rely/guarantee system, as shown in Fig. 7. In the following, we often write $\langle\sigma,\Sigma\rangle \vDash \Phi$ when Φ has no next variable. The second assumption means that *pre* must be a sufficient condition that implies *guar* under an invariant about V before and after an execution of an assignment C (formally defined as $\lceil C\rceil^V$), where C is MV $r\,e$, LD $r\,x$, or ST $x\,e$, and V is a finite set of non-next variables that occur in *guar*. A formula $\lceil\mathtt{MV}^i\ r\ e\rceil^V$ is defined as $\underline{r} = e \wedge \bigwedge I(V\setminus\{r\})$, which means that the value of $\underline{r}$ is equal to the evaluation of e while the values of variables in $V\setminus\{r\}$ are assignment-invariant, where $I(V)$ is $\{v = \underline{v} \mid v \in V\}$. Its formal definition is shown in Fig. 8. The third assumption means that *pre* and *post* are *stable under* the *rely* condition guaranteed by another thread, where we denote that Φ is *stable under* Ψ (written as $\Phi \perp \Psi$) as $\Phi(v) \wedge \Psi(v,\underline{v}) \supset \Phi(\underline{v})$, where v denotes a sequence of variables.

Rule L-SK states that an ordinary no-effect statement does not affect anything.

Rule L-LD handles the substitution of thread-local variables with shared variables. Note that r is substituted with the observation variables x^i, instead of the shared variables x. Rule L-ST handles the substitution of shared variables with expressions. Note that, as for L-LD, this rule considers the observation variable x^i instead of the shared variable x.

Rules L-IF and L-WL handle branch and loop statements, respectively. Careful readers may have noticed that Xu et al.'s papers [35,36] do not require the third assumption, which is implicitly assumed because these logics adopt the restriction that rely/guarantee-conditions are *reflexive* (as in [19,29]). This restriction often makes it difficult to write down derivations. Therefore, in this paper, we do not adopt the restriction, following van Staden [33]. As suggested by Nieto in [19], reflexivity is used to ensure soundness. However, we do not adopt the reflexivity of rely/guarantee-conditions, but instead use the third assumption regarding L-IF and L-WL, which prohibits the so-called *stuttering transitions* [16], as explained in Sect. 6.

Rule L-SQ handles the sequential composition of programs. Rule L-WK is the so-called consequence rule. L-PR handles parallel compositions of programs in a standard rely/guarantee system. The third assumption means that P_1's rely-condition $rely_1$ must be guaranteed by the global rely-condition $rely$ or P_0's guarantee-condition $guar_0$. The fourth assumption is similar. The fifth assumption means that $guar$ must be guaranteed by either $guar_0$ or $guar_1$.

6   Validity for Judgments

We now define *computations* of programs, and *validity* for judgments.

We define the set of computations $Cmp(P)$ of P as a finite or infinite sequence c of configurations whose adjacent configurations are related by $\xrightarrow{c}$ or $\xrightarrow{e}$ defined in Sect. 4. We write $Cfg(c,i)$, $Prg(c,i)$, and $St(c,i)$ as the i-th configuration, program, and state of c, respectively. By definition, the program $Prg(c,0)$ is P. As mentioned in Sect. 5, we do not assume that the rely/guarantee-conditions are reflexive. Therefore, our logic does not unconditionally ensure that the guarantee conditions hold on computations that contain $\langle P, st \rangle \xrightarrow{e} \langle P, st \rangle$, as Xu et al. noted in [36].

The length of a computation of c is denoted by $|c|$. If c is an infinite sequence, then $|c|$ is the smallest limit ordinal ω. Let c' be a computation that satisfies $St(c', |c'| - 1) = St(c, 0)$. We define $c' \cdot c$ as a concatenation of c' and c. We define $\vDash \{pre, rely\} P \{guar, post\}$ as $Cmp(P) \cap A(pre, rely) \subseteq C(guar, post)$, which means that any computation under pre/rely-conditions satisfies guarantee/post-conditions, as shown in Fig. 9. Thus, this paper does not handle post-conditions in non-terminating computations. This kind of validity is called *partial correctness* [34].

Careful readers may have noticed that the second arguments of Σ and substitutions to $\Sigma^{i,j}$ ($i \neq j$) at rule O-ST are redundant, as $\xrightarrow{e}$, which satisfies a rely-condition, is allowed at any time, and our assertion language cannot describe $\Sigma^{i,j}$ ($i \neq j$). Strictly speaking, although technically unnecessary and redundant, we have adopted these arguments to explain admissible computations more intuitively. A computation that formally represents the non-intuitive behavior of IRIW *without* remote-write-atomicity in Sect. 9.3 may help readers understand how memories are updated by effects from buffers.

$$A(pre, rely) = \left\{ c \,\middle|\, \begin{array}{l} St(c,0) \vDash pre, \text{ and} \\ St(c,i), St(c,i+1) \vDash rely \text{ for any } Cfg(c,i) \xrightarrow{e} Cfg(c,i+1) \end{array} \right\}$$

$$C(guar, post) = \left\{ c \,\middle|\, \begin{array}{l} St(c,i), St(c,i+1) \vDash guar \text{ for any } Cfg(c,i) \xrightarrow{c} Cfg(c,i+1), \text{ and} \\ |c| < \omega \text{ and } Prg(c,|c|-1) = \varnothing \text{ imply } St(c,|c|-1) \vDash post \end{array} \right\}$$

Fig. 9. Computations under pre/rely-conditions satisfies guarantee/post-conditions

7 Observation Invariant

In this section, we propose an *observation invariant*, which is an invariant written by observation variables. Formally, we define an observation invariant as a formula of the first-order predicate logic with the equations of Sect. 5.

We adopt observation invariants as axioms of the logic in Sect. 5. For example, let $x^0 = x^1$ be an observation invariant, which means that the value of x observed by thread 0 coincides with the value of x observed by thread 1. Adopting the observation invariant as an axiom means handling execution traces that always satisfy $\sigma^0[\Sigma^{0,0}]x = \sigma^1[\Sigma^{1,1}]x$.

Let us consider three examples of observation invariants. The program shown in Fig. 10 is called Dependence Cycle (DC). Although we intuitively think that either r_0 or r_1 has an initial value of 0, $r_0 = 1 \wedge r_1 = 1$ may not hold under a relaxed memory consistency model such as C++11 memory models. Memory consistency models for programming languages are often very relaxed in consideration of compiler optimization.

Our intuition that either r_0 or r_1 has an initial value is supported by *no speculation* regarding store statements on distinct threads, which is assumed under SPARC-PSO and similar architectures. For DC, this can be represented as $y^0 = 0 \supset y^1 = 0$, $x^1 \leq \underline{x^1} \supset x^0 \leq \underline{x^0}$, $x^1 = 0 \supset x^0 = 0$, and $y^0 \leq \underline{y^0} \supset y^1 \leq \underline{y^1}$ if the buffers are empty with respect to x and y when DC launches, and a rely-condition ensures no store operation to x and y. The first formula, $y^0 = 0 \supset y^1 = 0$, means that thread 1 observes $y = 0$ as long as thread 0 observes $y = 0$. This is because thread 0 is the only thread that has a store statement to y in DC. The second formula, $x^1 \leq \underline{x^1} \supset x^0 \leq \underline{x^0}$, means that thread 0 observes that x is *monotone* if thread 1 observes x is monotone. Thread 0 cannot observe x is not monotone, because thread 1 (which has a store statement to x and can see its own buffer) observes x is monotone. The third and fourth formulas are similar.

Next, let us consider an observation invariant for the One Reader One Writer (1R1W) program shown in Fig. 11, which consists of one reader thread and one writer thread. The reader thread in 1R1W has no store statement. Therefore, $y^1 \leq x^1 \supset y^0 \leq x^0$ is an observation invariant for 1R1W under x86-TSO [26]. This prohibits the reordering of effects of store statements, where we assume that the buffers are empty with respect to x and y when 1R1W launches, and a rely-condition ensures no store operations to x and y. Note that this is not an invariant under SPARC-PSO, which allows the effects of store statements

```
r0 = x;
y = 1;
```

```
r1 = y;
x = 1;
```

```
r0 = y;
r1 = x;
```

```
x = 1;
y = 1;
```

Fig. 10. Dependence cycle   **Fig. 11.** One reader one writer (1R1W)

to be reordered. The transfer of monotonicity $x^1 \leq \underline{x}^1 \supset x^0 \leq \underline{x}^0$ is also an observation invariant, even under SPARC-PSO, since the reader thread has no store statement to x.

Finally, let us consider an observation invariant for IRIW. Similar to DC, the transfer of monotonicity $(x^2 \leq \underline{x}^2 \supset x^0 \leq \underline{x}^0, x^2 \leq \underline{x}^2 \supset x^1 \leq \underline{x}^1,$ $y^3 \leq \underline{y}^3 \supset y^0 \leq \underline{y}^0,$ and $y^3 \leq \underline{y}^3 \supset y^1 \leq \underline{y}^1)$ holds, because the reader threads in IRIW have no store statement. In addition, $\underline{x}^0 = \underline{x}^1$ and $\underline{y}^0 = \underline{y}^1$ are invariants under remote-write-atomicity (which is assumed under SPARC-PSO and similar architectures), as threads 0 and 1 can detect nothing in their own buffers, and share a common observation of a shared memory. Note that the invariants are properly weaker than the strict consistency assumed by conventional concurrent program logics [13, 28, 35, 36], which forces the variable updates to be immediately observed by all threads, that is, $\underline{x}^0 = \underline{x}^1 = \underline{x}^2 = \underline{x}^3$ and $\underline{y}^0 = \underline{y}^1 = \underline{y}^2 = \underline{y}^3$.

8 Soundness

In this section, we present the soundness of the operational semantics defined in Fig. 5. In Sect. 5, we derived a concurrent program logic that is sound to the operational semantics defined in Fig. 5. However, the logic is actually insufficient to derive some valid judgments.

Auxiliary variables are known to enhance the provability of concurrent program logics [28]. Auxiliary variables are fresh variables that do not occur in the original programs, and are used only for the description of assertions. By using auxiliary variables in assertions, we can describe the progress of thread executions as rely/guarantee-conditions. In Sect. 9.3, we show a typical usage of auxiliary variables.

We extend our logic to contain the following inference rule (called *the auxiliary variables rule* [28, 35]):

$$\frac{\{pre \wedge pre_0, rely \wedge rely_0\} \, P_0 \, \{guar, post\} \qquad \vDash \exists \underline{z}. \, rely_0((\boldsymbol{v}, z), (\underline{\boldsymbol{v}}, \underline{z}))}{\vDash \exists z. \, pre_0(\boldsymbol{v}, z) \qquad z \cap (\mathrm{fv}(pre) \cup \mathrm{fv}(rely) \cup \mathrm{fv}(guar) \cup \mathrm{fv}(post)) = \varnothing}{\{pre, rely\} \, (P_0)_z \, \{guar, post\}} \text{(L-AX)}$$

where $\mathrm{fv}(\varPhi)$ denotes free variables that occur in $\varPhi$ in a standard manner, and $(P_0)_z$ is defined as the program that coincides with P_0, except that an assignment A is removed if

– A is an assignment whose left value belongs to z,

– no variable in z occurs in assignments whose left values do not belong to z, and
– no variable in z freely occurs in conditional statements.

Let c be $\langle P_0, \langle \sigma_0, \Sigma_0 \rangle \rangle \xrightarrow{\delta_0} \cdots \xrightarrow{\delta_{i-1}} \langle P_i, \langle \sigma_i, \Sigma_i \rangle \rangle \xrightarrow{\delta_i} \cdots$ for any $0 \leq i$. We write $tr(c, i)$ as δ_i. Given $c \in Cmp(P_0 \parallel P_1)$, $c_0 \in Cmp(P_0)$, and $c_1 \in Cmp(P_1)$, a ternary relation $c = c_0 \parallel c_1$ is defined if $|c| = |c_0| = |c_1|$ and

1. $St(c, i) = St(c_0, i) = St(c_1, i)$,
2. $tr(c, i) = \text{c}$ implies either of $tr(c_0, i) = \text{c}$ or $tr(c_1, i) = \text{c}$ holds,
3. $tr(c, i) = \text{e}$ implies $tr(c_0, i) = \text{e}$ and $tr(c_1, i) = \text{e}$ hold, and
4. $Prg(c, i) = Prg(c_0, i) \parallel Prg(c_1, i)$

for $0 \leq i < |c|$. We write ci and $\mathrm{postfix}(c, i)$ as the prefix of c with length $i + 1$ and the sequence that is derived from c by removing $ci - 1$, respectively.

Proposition 1. $Cmp(P_0 \parallel P_1) = \{ c_0 \parallel c_1 \mid c_0 \in Cmp(P_0), c_1 \in Cmp(P_1) \}$.

Lemma 2. *Assume* $\vdash \{pre_0 \wedge pre_1, rely\} P_0 \parallel P_1 \{guar, post_0 \wedge post_1\}$ *by* $L\text{-}PR$, $Cmp(P_0) \cap A(pre_0, rely_0) \subseteq C(guar_0, post_0)$, $Cmp(P_1) \cap A(pre_1, rely_1) \subseteq C(guar_1, post_1)$, $\vDash rely \vee guar_0 \supset rely_1$, $\vDash rely \vee guar_1 \supset rely_0$, $\vDash guar_0 \vee guar_1 \supset guar$, *and* $c \in Cmp(P_0 \parallel P_1) \cap A(pre_0 \wedge pre_1, rely)$. *In addition, we take* $c_0 \in Cmp(P_0)$ *and* $c_1 \in Cmp(P_1)$ *such that* $c = c_0 \parallel c_1$ *by Proposition 1.*

1. $St(c, i), St(c, i + 1) \vDash guar_0$ *and* $St(c, i), St(c, i + 1) \vDash guar_1$ *hold for any* $Cfg(c_0, i) \xrightarrow{c} Cfg(c_0, i + 1)$ *and* $Cfg(c_1, i) \xrightarrow{c} Cfg(c_1, i + 1)$, *respectively.*
2. $St(c, i), St(c, i+1) \vDash rely \vee guar_1$ *and* $St(c, i), St(c, i+1) \vDash rely \vee guar_0$ *hold for any* $Cfg(c_0, i) \xrightarrow{e} Cfg(c_0, i + 1)$ *and* $Cfg(c_1, i) \xrightarrow{e} Cfg(c_1, i + 1)$, *respectively.*
3. $St(c, i), St(c, i + 1) \vDash guar$ *for any* $Cfg(c, i) \xrightarrow{c} Cfg(c, i + 1)$ *holds.*
4. *Assume* $|c| < \omega$ *and* $Prg(c, |c| - 1) = \varnothing$. *Then,* $St(c, |c| - 1) \vDash post_0 \wedge post_1$ *holds.*

Proof. 1. Let us consider the former case. Without loss of generality, we can assume that $St(c, i), St(c, i + 1) \not\vDash guar_0$ where $St(c, j), St(c, j + 1) \vDash guar_0$ and $St(c, j), St(c, j + 1) \vDash guar_1$ for any $0 \leq j < i$.

By the definition, there exists $Cfg(c, k) \xrightarrow{e} Cfg(c, k + 1)$ or $Cfg(c_1, k) \xrightarrow{c} Cfg(c_1, k + 1)$ corresponding to $Cfg(c_0, k) \xrightarrow{e} Cfg(c_0, k + 1)$ for any $0 \leq k \leq i$. Therefore, $St(c, k), St(c, k + 1) \vDash rely \vee guar_1$ holds. By $\vDash rely \vee guar_1 \supset rely_0$, $c_0 i + 1 \in A(pre_0, rely_0)$ holds. Since $Cmp(P_0) \cap A(pre_0, rely_0) \subseteq C(guar_0, post_0)$ holds, in particular, $St(c, i), St(c, i + 1) \vDash guar_0$ holds. This contradicts $St(c, i), St(c, i + 1) \not\vDash guar_0$. The latter case is similar.
2. Immediate from the definition of $c = c_0 \parallel c_1$ and 1.
3. Immediate from 1 and $\vDash guar_0 \vee guar_1 \supset guar$.
4. By 2, $\vDash rely \vee guar_0 \supset rely_1$, and $\vDash rely \vee guar_1 \supset rely_0$, $c_0 \in A(pre_0, rely_0)$ and $c_1 \in A(pre_1, rely_1)$ hold.

By $Cmp(P_0) \cap A(pre_0, rely_0) \subseteq C(guar_0, post_0)$ and $Cmp(P_1) \cap A(pre_1, rely_1) \subseteq C(guar_1, post_1)$, $St(c, |c|) \vDash post_0$ and $St(c, |c| - 1) \vDash post_1$ hold. Therefore, $St(c, |c| - 1) \vDash post_0 \wedge post_1$ holds. $\qquad \square$

Theorem 3. $\vdash \{pre, rely\}\, P\, \{guar, post\}$ *implies* $\vDash \{pre, rely\}\, P\, \{guar, post\}$.

Proof. By induction on derivation and case analysis of the last inference rule.

First, assume L-ST. Let $c \in Cmp(\mathtt{ST}^i\, x\, e) \cap A(pre, rely)$. By O-ST, there exist $\sigma_0, \Sigma_0, \ldots$ such that $\langle \sigma_{n+1}, \Sigma_{n+1} \rangle = \langle \sigma_n, \Sigma[i := \Sigma^i[j := \Sigma^{i,j}[x := \langle\!\langle e \rangle\!\rangle_{\sigma^i}]\ |\ 0 \le j < N]] \rangle$,

$$c = \langle \mathtt{ST}^i\, x\, e, \langle \sigma_0, \Sigma_0 \rangle \rangle \xrightarrow{e}{}^* \langle \mathtt{ST}^i\, x\, e, \langle \sigma_n, \Sigma_n \rangle \rangle \xrightarrow{c} \langle \mathtt{SK}^i, \langle \sigma_{n+1}, \Sigma_{n+1} \rangle \rangle \xrightarrow{e} \cdots,$$

$\langle \sigma_0, \Sigma_0 \rangle \vDash pre$, and $\langle \sigma_j, \Sigma_j \rangle, \langle \sigma_{j+1}, \Sigma_{j+1} \rangle \vDash rely$ for any $0 \le j < n$. By $\vDash pre \perp rely$, $\langle \sigma_n, \Sigma_n \rangle \vDash pre$. By the definition, $\langle \sigma_n, \Sigma_n \rangle, \langle \sigma_n, \Sigma[i := \Sigma^i[j := \Sigma^{i,j}[x := \langle\!\langle e \rangle\!\rangle_{\sigma^i}]\ |\ 0 \le j < N]] \rangle \vDash \lceil \mathtt{ST}^i\, x\, e \rceil^V$. By $\vDash pre \supset \lceil \mathtt{ST}^i\, x\, e \rceil^V \supset guar$, $\langle \sigma_n, \Sigma_n \rangle, \langle \sigma_n, \Sigma[i := \Sigma^i[j := \Sigma^{i,j}[x := \langle\!\langle e \rangle\!\rangle_{\sigma^i}]\ |\ 0 \le j < N]] \rangle \vDash guar$, that is, $\langle \sigma_n, \Sigma_n \rangle, \langle \sigma_{n+1}, \Sigma_{n+1} \rangle \vDash guar$. In addition, assume $|c| < \omega$. By $\vDash pre \supset [e/x^i]post$, $\langle \sigma_n, \Sigma_n \rangle \vDash [e/x^i]post$. By the definition, $\langle \sigma_n, \Sigma[i := \Sigma^i[j := \Sigma^{i,j}[x := \langle\!\langle e \rangle\!\rangle_{\sigma^i}]\ |\ 0 \le j < N]] \rangle \vDash post$, that is, $\langle \sigma_{n+1}, \Sigma_{n+1} \rangle \vDash post$. By $\vDash post \perp rely$, $\langle \sigma_{|c|-1}, \Sigma_{|c|-1} \rangle \vDash post$.

Second, assume L-WL. Let $c \in Cmp(\mathtt{WL}^i\, \varphi?S_0^i) \cap A(pre, rely)$, which consists of the following five segments:

- $\langle S^i, \langle \sigma_{k_n}, \Sigma_{k_n} \rangle \rangle \xrightarrow{e}{}^* \langle S^i, \langle \sigma_{k_0}, \Sigma_{k_0} \rangle \rangle$,
- $\langle S^i, \langle \sigma_{k_0}, \Sigma_{k_0} \rangle \rangle \xrightarrow{c} \langle S_0^i; S^i, \langle \sigma_{k_0}, \Sigma_{k_0} \rangle \rangle$ where $\sigma_{k_0} \vDash \varphi$,
- $\langle S^i, \langle \sigma_{k_0}, \Sigma_{k_0} \rangle \rangle \xrightarrow{c} \langle \mathtt{SK}^i, \langle \sigma_{k_0}, \Sigma_{k_0} \rangle \rangle \xrightarrow{e} \cdots$ where $\sigma_{k_0} \not\vDash \varphi$,
- $\langle S_0^i; S^i, \langle \sigma_{k_0}, \Sigma_{k_0} \rangle \rangle \longrightarrow^* \langle S^i, \langle \sigma_{k_n}, \Sigma_{k_n} \rangle \rangle$.
- $\langle S_0^i; S^i, \langle \sigma_{k_0}, \Sigma_{k_0} \rangle \rangle \longrightarrow \cdots$ which does not reach S^i.

where $\langle \sigma', \Sigma' \rangle, \langle \sigma'', \Sigma'' \rangle \vDash rely$ for any $\langle S', \langle \sigma', \Sigma' \rangle \rangle \xrightarrow{e} \langle S'', \langle \sigma'', \Sigma'' \rangle \rangle$ in the five segments. By $\vDash pre \perp rely$, $\langle \sigma_{k_0}, \Sigma_{k_0} \rangle \vDash pre$. Let c' be $\langle S_0^i, \langle \sigma_{k_0}, \Sigma_{k_0} \rangle \rangle \longrightarrow^* \langle \mathtt{SK}^i, \langle \sigma_{k_n}, \Sigma_{k_n} \rangle \rangle$. By induction hypothesis, $\langle \sigma', \Sigma' \rangle, \langle \sigma'', \Sigma'' \rangle \vDash guar$ holds for any $\langle S', \langle \sigma', \Sigma' \rangle \rangle \xrightarrow{c} \langle S'', \langle \sigma'', \Sigma'' \rangle \rangle$ in c' holds. The case that c does not reach S^i is similar. Therefore, since $\vDash pre \supset I(V) \supset guar$ holds, $\langle \sigma', \Sigma' \rangle, \langle \sigma'', \Sigma'' \rangle \vDash guar$ holds for any $\langle S', \langle \sigma', \Sigma' \rangle \rangle \xrightarrow{c} \langle S'', \langle \sigma'', \Sigma'' \rangle \rangle$ in c holds. In addition, assume $|c| < \omega$. By $\vDash pre \perp rely$ and induction hypothesis, $\langle \sigma_{k_0}, \Sigma_{k_0} \rangle \vDash pre$ holds. By $\vDash pre \supset \neg \varphi \supset post$ and $\vDash post \perp rely$, $St(c, |c| - 1) \vDash post$.

Third, assume L-SQ. Let $c \in Cmp(P_0^i; P_1^i) \cap A(pre, rely)$. There exist $st_0, \delta_0, \ldots$ such that

$$c = \langle P_0^i; P_1^i, st_0 \rangle \xrightarrow{\delta_0} \cdots \xrightarrow{\delta_{n-1}} \langle P_1^i, st_n \rangle \xrightarrow{\delta_n} \cdots,$$

$st_0 \vDash pre$, and $st_j, st_{j+1} \vDash rely$ for any $0 \le j < n$. Let c' and c'' be $\langle P_0^i, st_0 \rangle \xrightarrow{\delta_0} \cdots \xrightarrow{\delta_{n-1}} \langle \mathtt{SK}^i, st_n \rangle$ and postfix(c, n), respectively. Obviously, $c' \in Cmp(P_0^i) \cap A(pre, rely)$ holds. By induction hypothesis, $c' \in C(guar, \Phi)$ holds. By the definition, $\langle \sigma_n, \Sigma_n \rangle \vDash \Phi$ holds. Therefore, $c'' \in Cmp(P_1^i) \cap A(\Phi, rely)$ holds. By induction hypothesis, $c'' \in C(guar, post)$ holds. Therefore, $c \in C(guar, post)$ holds.

Fourth, assume L-PR. By Lemmas 2.3 and 2.4.

Fifth, assume L-AX. Let $c \in Cmp(P) \cap A(pre, rely)$. There exist $\sigma_0, \Sigma_0, \delta_0, \ldots$ such that

$$c = \langle (P)_z, \langle \sigma_0, \Sigma_0 \rangle \rangle \xrightarrow{\delta_0} \cdots \xrightarrow{\delta_{n-1}} \langle P_n, \langle \sigma_n, \Sigma_n \rangle \rangle \xrightarrow{\delta_n} \cdots,$$

$$\dfrac{\{pre_0, rely^0\}\, \mathrm{LD}^0\, r_0\, x\, \{guar^0, post_0\} \qquad \{pre_1, rely^0\}\, \mathrm{ST}^0\, y\, 1\, \{guar^0, post_1\}}{\{pre_0, rely^0\}\, \mathrm{LD}^0\, r_0\, x; \mathrm{ST}^0\, y\, 1\, \{guar^0, post_1\}}$$

$$\dfrac{\{pre_2, rely^0\}\, \mathrm{LD}^1\, r_1\, y\, \{guar^1, post_2\} \qquad \{pre_3, rely^1\}\, \mathrm{ST}^1\, x\, 1\, \{guar^1, post_3\}}{\{pre_2, rely^1\}\, \mathrm{LD}^1\, r_1\, y; \mathrm{ST}^1\, x\, 1\, \{guar^1, post_3\}}$$

$$\{pre_0 \wedge pre_2, rely^0 \wedge rely^1\}\, \mathrm{LD}^0\, r_0\, x; \mathrm{ST}^0\, y\, 1 \parallel \mathrm{LD}^1\, r_1\, y; \mathrm{ST}^1\, x\, 1\, \{guar^0 \vee guar^1, post_1 \wedge post_3\}$$

Fig. 12. A essential part of a derivation for DC

$\langle \sigma_0, \Sigma_0 \rangle \vDash pre$, and $\langle \sigma_j, \Sigma_j \rangle, \langle \sigma_{j+1}, \Sigma_{j+1} \rangle \vDash rely$ for any $0 \le j < n$. Since $\vDash$ $\exists z.\, pre_0(\boldsymbol{v}, z)$, $\vDash \exists \underline{z}.\, rely_0((\boldsymbol{v}, z), (\boldsymbol{v}, \underline{z}))$, and $z \cap (\mathrm{fv}(pre) \cup \mathrm{fv}(rely) \cup \mathrm{fv}(guar) \cup \mathrm{fv}(post)) = \varnothing$, there exist $P_0', \sigma_0', \Sigma_0', \ldots$ such that

$$c' = \langle P_0', \langle \sigma_0', \Sigma_0' \rangle \rangle \xrightarrow{\delta_0} \cdots \xrightarrow{\delta_{n-1}} \langle P_n', \langle \sigma_n', \Sigma_n' \rangle \rangle \xrightarrow{\delta_n} \cdots,$$

and $P_0' = P$, $(P_n')_z = P_n$, $\sigma_j'^i v = \sigma_j^i v$, $\Sigma_j'^{i,i'} v = \Sigma_j^{i,i'} v$, $\langle \sigma_0', \Sigma_0' \rangle \vDash pre \wedge pre_0$, and $\langle \sigma_j', \Sigma_j' \rangle, \langle \sigma_{j+1}', \Sigma_{j+1}' \rangle \vDash rely \wedge rely_0$ for any $v \notin z$, $0 \le i, i' < N$ and $0 \le j < n$. Therefore, $c' \in Cmp(P) \cap A(pre \wedge pre_0, rely \wedge rely_0)$ holds. By induction hypothesis, $c' \in C(guar, post)$ holds. Therefore, $c \in C(guar, post)$ holds.

The other cases are similar and omitted due to space limitation.   □

9   Examples

In this section, we verify several example racy programs.

9.1   Verification of DC

The first example program is DC, introduced in Sect. 7. The verification property, a judgment consisting of the post-condition $r_0 = 0 \vee r_1 = 0$ under appropriate pre/rely-conditions, is shown with a derivation for DC.

Figure 12 shows an essential part of a derivation for DC, where

$$pre_0 \equiv y^0 = 0 \wedge ((x^0 = 0 \wedge r_0 = 0) \vee (x^0 = 1 \wedge r_1 = 0))$$

$$pre_1 \equiv post_0 \equiv y^0 = 0 \wedge (r_0 = 0 \vee (x^0 = 1 \wedge r_1 = 0))$$

$$post_1 \equiv y^0 = 1 \wedge (r_0 = 0 \vee (x^0 = 1 \wedge r_1 = 0))$$

$$rely^0 \equiv (y^0 = 0 \vee r_0 = 1 \supset \underline{r_1} = 0) \wedge x^0 \le \underline{x^0} \wedge \mathrm{I}\{y^0, r_1\} \wedge D \wedge \underline{D}$$

$$guar^0 \equiv (x^0 = 0 \vee r_1 = 1 \supset \underline{r_0} = 0) \wedge y^0 \le \underline{y^0} \wedge \mathrm{I}\{x^0, x^1, r_1\} \wedge D \wedge \underline{D}$$

$$pre_2 \equiv x^1 = 0 \wedge ((y^1 = 0 \wedge r_1 = 0) \vee (y^1 = 1 \wedge r_0 = 0))$$

$$pre_3 \equiv post_2 \equiv x^1 = 0 \wedge (r_1 = 0 \vee (y^1 = 1 \wedge r_0 = 0))$$

$$post_3 \equiv x^1 = 1 \wedge (r_1 = 0 \vee (y^1 = 1 \wedge r_0 = 0))$$

$$rely^1 \equiv (x^1 = 0 \vee r_1 = 1 \supset \underline{r_0} = 0) \wedge y^1 \le \underline{y^1} \wedge \mathrm{I}\{x^1, r_1\} \wedge D \wedge \underline{D}$$

$$guar^1 \equiv (y^1 = 0 \vee r_0 = 1 \supset \underline{r_1} = 0) \wedge x^1 \le \underline{x^1} \wedge \mathrm{I}\{y^0, y^1 r_1\} \wedge D \wedge \underline{D}$$

$$\{y^0 \le x^0, rely^0\} \text{ LD}^0 \ r_0 \ y \ \{guar^0, r_0 \le x^0\} \qquad \{x^1 = 0 \wedge y^1 = 0, rely^1\} \text{ ST}^1 \ x \ 1 \ \{guar^1, x^1 = 1\}$$

$$\frac{\{r_0 \le x^0, rely^0\} \text{ LD}^0 \ r_1 \ x \ \{guar^0, r_0 \le r_1\}}{\{y^0 \le x^0, rely^0\} \text{ 1R} \ \{guar^0, r_0 \le r_1\}} \qquad \frac{\{x^1 = 1, rely^1\} \text{ ST}^1 \ y \ 1 \ \{guar^1, \top\}}{\{x^1 = 0 \wedge y^1 = 0, rely^1\} \text{ 1W} \ \{guar^1, \top\}}$$

$$\{y^0 \le x^0 \wedge x^1 = 0 \wedge y^1 = 0, rely\} \text{ 1R} \parallel \text{1W} \ \{guar, r_0 \le r_1 \wedge \top\}$$

Fig. 13. An essential part of a derivation for 1R1W

and D, $\underline{D}$ are $\bigwedge\{(x^i = 0 \vee x^i = 1) \wedge (y^i = 0 \vee y^i = 1) \mid 0 \le i < 4\}$ and $\bigwedge\{(\underline{x^i} = 0 \vee \underline{x^i} = 1) \wedge (\underline{y^i} = 0 \vee \underline{y^i} = 1) \mid 0 \le i < 4\}$, respectively. Some assumptions regarding the inference rules are omitted when the context renders them obvious.

A key point is that $\vDash (rely^0 \wedge rely^1) \vee guar^0 \supset rely^1$ and $\vDash (rely^0 \wedge rely^1) \vee guar^1 \supset rely^0$ are derived from the observation invariants for DC, $y^0 = 0 \supset y^1 = 0$, $x^1 \le \underline{x^1} \supset x^0 \le \underline{x^0}$, $x^1 = 0 \supset x^0 = 0$, and $y^0 \le \underline{y^0} \supset y^1 \le \underline{y^1}$ introduced in Sect. 7 at the final inference by L-PR.

9.2   Verification of 1R1W

Let us consider a relaxed memory consistency model that prohibits the reordering of the effects of store statements. Therefore, we expect $r_0 \le r_1$ under an appropriate condition when the program in Fig. 11 finishes.

Figure 13 shows an essential part of a derivation for 1R1W, where

$$rely^0 \equiv \underline{y^0} \le x^0 \wedge x^0 \le \underline{x^0} \wedge I\{r_0, r_1\} \quad guar^0 \equiv I\{x^1, y^1\}$$

$$rely^1 \equiv I\{x^1, y^1\} \qquad\qquad\qquad\qquad guar^1 \equiv \underline{y^1} \le x^1 \wedge x^1 \le \underline{x^1} \wedge I\{r_0, r_1\}$$

$\text{1R} \equiv \text{LD}^0 \ r_0 \ y; \text{LD}^0 \ r_1 \ x$, $\text{1W} \equiv \text{ST}^1 \ x \ 1; \text{ST}^1 \ y \ 1$, and some assumptions of the inference rules are omitted when the context renders them obvious.

A key point here is that $\vDash (rely^0 \wedge rely^1) \vee guar^0 \supset rely^1$ and $\vDash (rely^0 \wedge rely^1) \vee guar^1 \supset rely^0$ are derived from the observation invariants for 1R1W, $y^1 \le x^1 \supset y^0 \le x^0$ and $x^1 \le \underline{x^1} \supset x^0 \le \underline{x^0}$ introduced in Sect. 7 at the final inference by L-PR.

As explained in Sect. 7, under SPARC-PSO, $\vDash (rely^0 \wedge rely^1) \vee guar^1 \supset rely^0$ is not implied, since $y^1 \le x^1 \supset y^0 \le x^0$ is not an observation invariant.

9.3   Verification of IRIW

Finally, we demonstrate the verification of the program introduced in Sect. 1. The verification property is a judgment consisting of the post-condition $r_0 \le r_1 \vee r_2 \le r_3$ under appropriate pre/rely-conditions, although the judgment is formally shown as (2) in this section since the pre/rely-conditions require some notation.

First, note that the post-condition does not always hold without axioms for remote-write-atomicity. Actually, the following computation:

$$\langle \mathrm{LD}^0\ r_0\ x; \mathrm{LD}^0\ r_1\ y \parallel \mathrm{LD}^1\ r_2\ y; \mathrm{LD}^1\ r_3\ x \parallel \mathrm{ST}^2\ x\ 1 \parallel \mathrm{ST}^3\ y\ 1, \langle \sigma, \Sigma \rangle \rangle$$

$$\xrightarrow{c}{}^* \langle \mathrm{LD}^0\ r_0\ x; \mathrm{LD}^0\ r_1\ y \parallel \mathrm{LD}^1\ r_2\ y; \mathrm{LD}^1\ r_3\ x, \langle \sigma,$$

$$\Sigma[x^{2,0} \mapsto 1, y^{3,0} \mapsto 1, x^{2,1} \mapsto 1, y^{3,1} \mapsto 1, x^{2,2} \mapsto 1, y^{3,2} \mapsto 1, x^{2,3} \mapsto 1, y^{3,3} \mapsto 1] \rangle \rangle$$

$$\xrightarrow{e}{}^* \langle \mathrm{LD}^0\ r_0\ x; \mathrm{LD}^0\ r_1\ y \parallel \mathrm{LD}^1\ r_2\ y; \mathrm{LD}^1\ r_3\ x, \langle \sigma[x^0 \mapsto 1, y^1 \mapsto 1],$$

$$\Sigma[y^{3,0} \mapsto 1, x^{2,1} \mapsto 1, x^{2,2} \mapsto 1, y^{3,2} \mapsto 1, x^{2,3} \mapsto 1, y^{3,3} \mapsto 1] \rangle \rangle$$

$$\xrightarrow{c}{}^* \langle \mathrm{SK}, \langle \sigma[r_0{}^0 \mapsto 1, r_1{}^0 \mapsto 0, r_2{}^1 \mapsto 1, r_3{}^1 \mapsto 0, x^0 \mapsto 1, y^1 \mapsto 1],$$

$$\Sigma[y^{3,0} \mapsto 1, x^{2,1} \mapsto 1, x^{2,2} \mapsto 1, y^{3,2} \mapsto 1, x^{2,3} \mapsto 1, y^{3,3} \mapsto 1] \rangle \rangle$$

implies this fact, where we write the substitutions $[v^i \mapsto n]$ and $[v^{i,j} \mapsto n]$ as $[i := \sigma^i[v := n]]$ and $[i := \Sigma^i[j := \Sigma^{i,j}[v := n]]]$, respectively, for readability. Additionally, σ and Σ are constant functions to 0 and udf, respectively. Note that we must confirm that $\xrightarrow{e}$ satisfies the rely-condition of (2).

Thus, the post-condition does not always hold with no additional axiom. Let us show that the post-condition holds under appropriate pre/rely/guarantee-conditions with axioms for remote-write-atomicity. To construct a derivation, we add the auxiliary variables z_0 and z_1, as shown in Fig. 14.

r0 = x;	r2 = y;	y = 1;	x = 1;
r1 = y;	r3 = x;		
z0 = 1;	z1 = 1;		

Fig. 14. IRIW with auxiliary variables

We construct a derivation on each thread. The following three judgments:

$$\left\{ \begin{array}{l} z_0 = 0 \wedge (x^0 \le y^0 \vee \\ (z_1 = 1 \supset r_2 \le r_3)), rely^0 \end{array} \right\} \mathrm{LD}\ r_0\ x \left\{ \begin{array}{l} guar^0, z_0 = 0 \wedge r_0 \le x^0 \wedge \\ ((x^0 \le y^0 \wedge r_0 \le y^0) \vee (z_1 = 1 \supset r_2 \le r_3)) \end{array} \right\}$$

$$\left\{ \begin{array}{l} z_0 = 0 \wedge r_0 \le x^0 \wedge \\ ((x^0 \le y^0 \wedge r_0 \le y^0) \vee \\ (z_1 = 1 \supset r_2 \le r_3)), rely^0 \end{array} \right\} \mathrm{LD}\ r_1\ y \left\{ \begin{array}{l} guar^0, z_0 = 0 \wedge r_0 \le x^0 \wedge r_1 \le y^0 \wedge \\ ((x^0 \le y^0 \wedge r_0 \le r_1) \vee \\ (z_1 = 1 \supset r_2 \le r_3)) \end{array} \right\}$$

$$\left\{ \begin{array}{l} z_0 = 0 \wedge r_0 \le x^0 \wedge r_1 \le y^0 \wedge \\ ((x^0 \le y^0 \wedge r_0 \le r_1) \vee \\ (z_1 = 1 \supset r_2 \le r_3)), rely^0 \end{array} \right\} z_0 = 1 \left\{ \begin{array}{l} guar^0, z_0 = 1 \wedge r_0 \le x^0 \wedge r_1 \le y^0 \wedge \\ ((x^0 \le y^0 \wedge r_0 \le r_1) \vee \\ (z_1 = 1 \supset r_2 \le r_3)) \end{array} \right\}$$

are derived by L-LD and L-MV, where M(V) is $\bigwedge \{ v \le \underline{v} \mid v \in V \}$, and

$$rely^0 \equiv (\underline{y}^0 < \underline{x}^0 \vee (z_0 = 1 \wedge r_1 < r_0)) \supset \underline{z_1} = 1 \supset \underline{r_2} \le \underline{r_3}) \wedge \mathrm{M}\{x^0, y^0, z_1\} \wedge \mathrm{I}\{z_0, r_0, r_1\}$$

$$guar^0 \equiv (\underline{x}^0 < \underline{y}^0 \vee (z_1 = 1 \wedge r_3 < r_2)) \supset \underline{z_0} = 1 \supset \underline{r_0} \le \underline{r_1}) \wedge$$

$$\mathrm{I}\{z_1, x^1, x^2, x^3, y^1, y^2, y^3, r_2, r_3\}.$$

$$\left\{ \begin{array}{l} z_0 = 0 \wedge (x^0 \leq y^0 \vee \\ (z_1 = 1 \supset r_2 \leq r_3)), rely^0 \end{array} \right\} \begin{array}{c} \text{LD } r_0 \text{ } x; \text{LD } r_1 \text{ } y; \\ z_0 = 1 \end{array} \left\{ \begin{array}{l} guar^0, z_0 = 1 \wedge ((x^0 \leq y^0 \wedge r_0 \leq r_1) \vee \\ (z_1 = 1 \supset r_2 \leq r_3)) \end{array} \right\}$$

is derivable by L-SQ. Similarly, so is

$$\left\{ \begin{array}{l} z_1 = 0 \wedge (x^1 \leq y^1 \vee \\ (z_0 = 1 \supset r_0 \leq r_1)), rely^1 \end{array} \right\} \begin{array}{c} \text{LD } r_2 \text{ } y; \text{LD } r_3 \text{ } x; \\ z_1 = 1 \end{array} \left\{ \begin{array}{l} guar^1, z_1 = 1 \wedge ((x^1 \leq y^1 \wedge r_2 \leq r_3) \vee \\ (z_0 = 1 \supset r_0 \leq r_1)) \end{array} \right\}$$

from symmetricity, where

$$rely^1 \equiv (\underline{x^1} < \underline{y^1} \vee (z_1 = 1 \wedge r_3 < r_2) \supset \underline{z_0} = 1 \supset \underline{r_0} \leq \underline{r_1}) \wedge M\{x^1, y^1, z_0\} \wedge I\{z_1, r_2, r_3\}$$
$$guar^1 \equiv (\underline{y^1} < \underline{x^1} \vee (z_0 = 1 \wedge r_1 < r_0) \supset \underline{z_1} = 1 \supset \underline{r_2} \leq \underline{r_3}) \wedge$$
$$I\{z_0, x^0, x^2, x^3, y^0, y^2, y^3, r_0, r_1\}.$$

Let D and $\underline{D}$ be $\bigwedge\{ (x^i = 0 \vee x^i = 1) \wedge (y^i = 0 \vee y^i = 1) \mid 0 \leq i < 4 \}$ and $\bigwedge\{ (\underline{x^i} = 0 \vee \underline{x^i} = 1) \wedge (\underline{y^i} = 0 \vee \underline{y^i} = 1) \mid 0 \leq i < 4 \}$, respectively. Note that $v < v' \wedge D \wedge \underline{D}$ means $v = 0 \wedge v' = 1$.

By L-ST, $\{D, rely^2\}$ ST y 1 $\{guar^2, \top\}$ and $\{D, rely^3\}$ ST x 1 $\{guar^3, \top\}$ are derivable, where

$$rely^2 \equiv x^2 \leq \underline{x^2} \wedge D \wedge \underline{D} \qquad rely^3 \equiv y^3 \leq \underline{y^3} \wedge D \wedge \underline{D}$$
$$guar^2 \equiv y^2 \leq \underline{y^2} \wedge y^3 \leq \underline{y^3} \wedge I\{x^0, x^1, x^2, x^3, r_0, r_1, r_2, r_3\} \wedge D \wedge \underline{D}$$
$$guar^3 \equiv x^2 \leq \underline{x^2} \wedge x^3 \leq \underline{x^3} \wedge I\{y^0, y^1, y^2, y^3, r_0, r_1, r_2, r_3\} \wedge D \wedge \underline{D}.$$

Let us construct separate derivations corresponding to Independent Reads (IR), Independent Writes (IW), and IRIW. To construct a derivation for IR, it is sufficient that

$$\vDash (rely^0 \wedge rely^1) \vee guar^0 \supset rely^1 \qquad \vDash (rely^0 \wedge rely^1) \vee guar^1 \supset rely^0 \quad (1)$$

is satisfied, as this implies

$$\left\{ \begin{array}{c} z_0 = 0 \wedge z_1 = 0 \wedge \\ pre_{01}, \\ rely^0 \wedge rely^1 \end{array} \right\} \begin{array}{c} \text{LD } r_0 \text{ } x; \text{LD } r_1 \text{ } y; \\ z_0 = 1 \end{array} \bigg\| \begin{array}{c} \text{LD } r_2 \text{ } y; \text{LD } r_3 \text{ } x; \\ z_1 = 1 \end{array} \left\{ \begin{array}{c} guar^0 \vee guar^1, \\ z_0 = 1 \wedge z_1 = 1 \wedge \\ (r_0 \leq r_1 \vee r_2 \leq r_3) \end{array} \right\}$$

under L-PR and L-WK, where $pre_{01} \equiv x^0 = 0 \wedge y^0 = 0 \wedge x^1 = 0 \wedge y^1 = 0$. Therefore, we can deduce

$$\{pre_{01}, rely^{01}\} \text{ LD } r_0 \text{ } x; \text{LD } r_1 \text{ } y \parallel \text{LD } r_2 \text{ } y; \text{LD } r_3 \text{ } x \{guar^0 \vee guar^1, r_0 \leq r_1 \vee r_2 \leq r_3\}$$

by L-AX and L-WK, where $rely^{01} \equiv M\{x^0, y^0, x^1, y^1\} \wedge I\{r_0, r_1, r_2, r_3\}$.

Similarly, to construct a derivation for IW, it is sufficient that

$$\vDash (rely^2 \wedge rely^3) \vee guar^2 \supset rely^3 \qquad \vDash (rely^2 \wedge rely^3) \vee guar^3 \supset rely^2$$

is satisfied, since this allows us to deduce that $\{D, rely^2 \wedge rely^3\}$ $\{$ST y 1 $\parallel$ ST x 1, $guar^2 \vee guar^3\} \top$.

We now construct the following derivation for IRIW

$$\{pre_{01} \wedge D, rely^{01} \wedge rely^2 \wedge rely^3\} \text{ IRIW } \{\bigvee\{guar^i \mid 0 \le i < 4\}, r_0 \le r_1 \vee r_2 \le r_3\} \qquad (2)$$

it is sufficient that the following is satisfied:

$$\vDash guar^0 \vee guar^1 \supset rely^2 \wedge rely^3 \qquad \vDash guar^2 \vee guar^3 \supset rely^{01}. \qquad (3)$$

Let us recall the observation invariants $\underline{x^0} = \underline{x^1}$ and $\underline{y^0} = \underline{y^1}$ under the remote-write-atomicity explained in Sect. 7. Obviously, the observation invariants imply (1). Additionally, the transfer of monotonicity implies (3). Thus, under remote-write-atomicity, which is more relaxed than strict consistency (and therefore under SPARC-PSO), IRIW is guaranteed to work correctly.

10   Conclusion and Future Work

This paper has proposed the notion of observation invariants to fill the gap between theoretical and realistic relaxed memory consistency models. We have derived general small-step operational semantics for relaxed memory consistency models, introduced additional variables x^i to denote a value of x observed by i in an assertion language, and stated a concurrent program logic that is sound with respect to the operational semantics. Our analysis suggests that the non-existence of shared variables without observations by threads in the assertion language ensures the soundness. We have successfully constructed a formal proof for the correctness of IRIW via the notion of observation invariants. To the best of our knowledge, the derivation in this paper is the first to verify IRIW in a logic that handles relaxed memory consistency models like SPARC-PSO.

There are four directions for future work. The first is to invent systematic construction of observation invariants and to find further applications of observation invariants. The observation invariants shown in this paper are given in ad-hoc ways. The example programs that are verified in this paper are small. Systematic construction of observation invariants will tame observation invariants for larger programs, provide further applications of observation invariants, and enable us to compare our method with existing methods. The second is to implement a theorem prover that can verify programs in the logic in this paper. Manual constructions of derivations, which are done in this paper, are tedious and error-prone. The third is to compare our logic with *doxastic logic* [18], which is based on the notion of *belief*. We introduced the additional variable x^i to denote x as observed by thread i, but this variable does not always coincide with x on physical memories. Therefore, x^i may be considered to be x as *believed* by thread i. The fourth is a mathematical formulation of our logic. Although mathematical formulations of rely/guarantee-reasoning have been stated in some studies (e.g., [9]), they assume that (program) shared variables are components in assertion languages (called a *cheat* in [9]). Since the insight provided in this paper dismisses shared variables from assertion languages, the assumption cannot be admissible, and a new mathematical formulation of our logic based on rely/guarantee-reasoning is significant.

Acknowledgments. Some definitions in this paper are inspired by Qiwen Xu's PhD thesis [35]. The authors would like to thank him for answering our questions respectfully. The authors also thank the anonymous reviewers for several comments to improve the paper. This work was supported by JSPS KAKENHI Grant Number 16K21335.

References

1. Abe, T., Maeda, T.: Concurrent program logic for relaxed memory consistency models with dependencies across loop iterations. J. Inf. Process. (2016, to appear)
2. Abe, T., Maeda, T.: A general model checking framework for various memory consistency models. Int. J. Softw. Tools Technol. Transferr (2016, to appear). doi:10.1007/s10009-016-0429-y
3. Abe, T., Ugawa, T., Maeda, T., Matsumoto, K.: Reducing state explosion for software model checking with relaxed memory consistencymodels. In: Proceedings of SETTA. LNCS, vol. 9984 (2016, to appear). doi:10.1007/978-3-319-47677-3_8
4. Boehm, H.J., Adve, S.V.: Foundations of the C++ concurrency memory model. In: Proceedings of PLDI, pp. 68–78 (2008)
5. Boudol, G., Petri, G.: Relaxed memory models: an operational approach. In: Proceedings of POPL, pp. 392–403 (2009)
6. Boudol, G., Petri, G., Serpette, B.P.: Relaxed operational semantics of concurrent programming languages. In: Proceedings of EXPRESS/SOS, pp. 19–33 (2012)
7. Ferreira, R., Feng, X., Shao, Z.: Parameterized memory models and concurrent separation logic. In: Gordon, A.D. (ed.) ESOP 2010. LNCS, vol. 6012, pp. 267–286. Springer, Heidelberg (2010). doi:10.1007/978-3-642-11957-6_15
8. Hoare, C.A.R.: An axiomatic basis for computer programming. Commun. ACM **12**(10), 576–580, 583 (1969)
9. Hoare, T., Möller, B., Struth, G., Wehrman, I.: Concurrent Kleene algebra and its foundations. J. Log. Algebraic Program **80**(6), 266–296 (2011)
10. Holzmann, G.J.: The SPIN Model Checker. Addison-Wesley, Reading (2003)
11. Intel Corporation: A Formal Specification of Intel Itanium Processor Family Memory Ordering (2002)
12. ISO, IEC 14882: 2011: Programming Language C++ (2011)
13. Jones, C.B.: Development methods for computer programs including a notion of interference. Ph.D. thesis, Oxford University (1981)
14. Jonsson, B.: State-space exploration for concurrent algorithms under weak memory orderings: (preliminary version). SIGARCH Comput. Archit. News **36**(5), 65–71 (2008)
15. Lahav, O., Vafeiadis, V.: Owicki-Gries reasoning for weak memory models. In: Halldórsson, M.M., Iwama, K., Kobayashi, N., Speckmann, B. (eds.) ICALP 2015. LNCS, vol. 9135, pp. 311–323. Springer, Heidelberg (2015). doi:10.1007/978-3-662-47666-6_25
16. Lamport, L.: The temporal logic of actions. ACM TOPLAS **16**(3), 872–923 (1994)
17. Linden, A., Wolper, P.: An automata-based symbolic approach for verifying programs on relaxed memory models. In: Pol, J., Weber, M. (eds.) SPIN 2010. LNCS, vol. 6349, pp. 212–226. Springer, Heidelberg (2010). doi:10.1007/978-3-642-16164-3_16
18. Meyer, J.J.C.: Modal epistemic and doxastic logic. In: Gabbay, D.M., Guenthner, F. (eds.) Handbook of Philosophical Logic, vol. 10, 2nd edn, pp. 1–38. Springer, Dordrecht (2004)

19. Nieto, L.P.: The rely-guarantee method in Isabelle/HOL. In: Degano, P. (ed.) ESOP 2003. LNCS, vol. 2618, pp. 348–362. Springer, Heidelberg (2003). doi:10. 1007/3-540-36575-3_24

20. Oracle Corporation: The Java Language Specification. Java SE 8 Edition (2015)

21. Owens, S.: Reasoning about the implementation of concurrency abstractions on x86-TSO. In: D'Hondt, T. (ed.) ECOOP 2010. LNCS, vol. 6183, pp. 478–503. Springer, Heidelberg (2010). doi:10.1007/978-3-642-14107-2_23

22. Owens, S., Sarkar, S., Sewell, P.: A better x86 memory model: x86-TSO. In: Berghofer, S., Nipkow, T., Urban, C., Wenzel, M. (eds.) TPHOLs 2009. LNCS, vol. 5674, pp. 391–407. Springer, Heidelberg (2009). doi:10.1007/978-3-642-03359-9_27

23. Ridge, T.: A rely-guarantee proof system for x86-TSO. In: Leavens, G.T., O'Hearn, P., Rajamani, S.K. (eds.) VSTTE 2010. LNCS, vol. 6217, pp. 55–70. Springer, Heidelberg (2010). doi:10.1007/978-3-642-15057-9_4

24. Sarkar, S., Sewell, P., Alglave, J., Maranget, L., Williams, D.: Understanding POWER multiprocessors. In: Proceedings of PLDI, pp. 175–186 (2011)

25. Sarkar, S., Sewell, P., Nardelli, F.Z., Owens, S., Ridge, T., Braibant, T., Myreen, M.O., Alglave, J.: The semantics of x86-CC multiprocessor machine code. In: Proceedings of POPL, pp. 379–391 (2008)

26. Sewell, P., Sarkar, S., Owens, S., Nardelli, F.Z., Myreen, M.O.: x86-TSO: a rigorous and usable programmer's model for x86 multiprocessors. Commun. ACM **53**(7), 89–97 (2010)

27. SPARC International Inc.: The SPARC Architecture Manual, Version 9 (1994)

28. Stølen, K.: Development of parallel programs on shared data-structures. Technical report UMCS-91-1-1, Department of Computer Science, University of Manchester (1991)

29. Tofan, B., Schellhorn, G., Bäumler, S., Reif, W.: Embedding rely-guarantee reasoning in temporal logic. Technical report, Institut für Informatik, Universität Augsburg (2010)

30. Turon, A., Vafeiadis, V., Dreyer, D.: GPS: Navigating weak memory with ghosts, protocols, and separation. In: Proceedings of OOPSLA. 691–707(2014)

31. Vafeiadis, V.: Formal reasoning about the C11 weak memory model. In: Proceedings of CPP (2015)

32. Vafeiadis, V., Narayan, C.: Relaxed separation logic: a program logic for C11 concurrency. In: Proceedings of OOPSLA, pp. 867–884 (2013)

33. Staden, S.: On rely-guarantee reasoning. In: Hinze, R., Voigtländer, J. (eds.) MPC 2015. LNCS, vol. 9129, pp. 30–49. Springer, Heidelberg (2015). doi:10.1007/978-3-319-19797-5_2

34. Winskel, G.: The Formal Semantics of Programming Languages. MIT Press, Cambridge (1993)

35. Xu, Q.: A theory of state-based parallel programming. Ph.D. thesis, Oxford University Computing Laboratory (1992)

36. Xu, Q., de Roever, W.P., He, J.: The rely-guarantee method for verifying shared variable concurrent programs. Formal Aspects Comput. **9**(2), 149–174 (1997)

Process Calculus

SPEC: An Equivalence Checker for Security Protocols

Alwen Tiu, Nam Nguyen, and Ross Horne[(✉)]

School of Computer Science and Engineering, Nanyang Technological University,
Singapore, Singapore
atiu@ntu.edu.sg, nam4@e.ntu.edu.sg, rhorne@ntu.edu.se

Abstract. SPEC is an automated equivalence checker for security protocols specified in the spi-calculus, an extension of the pi-calculus with
cryptographic primitives. The notion of equivalence considered is a variant of bisimulation, called open bisimulation, that identifies processes
indistinguishable when executed in any context. SPEC produces compact
and independently checkable bisimulations that are useful for automating the process of producing proof-certificates for security protocols. This
paper gives an overview of SPEC and discusses techniques to reduce the
size of bisimulations, utilising up-to techniques developed for the spi-
calculus. SPEC is implemented in the Bedwyr logic programming language that we demonstrate can be adapted to tackle further protocol
analysis problems not limited to bisimulation checking.

1 Introduction

SPEC is a tool for automatically checking the equivalence of processes specified
in the spi-calculus [1], an extension of the π-calculus [11], with operators encoding cryptographic primitives. The spi-calculus can be used to encode security
protocols, and via a notion of *observational equivalence*, security properties such
as secrecy and authentication can be expressed and proved. Intuitively, observational equivalence between two processes means that the (observable) actions
of the processes cannot be distinguished in any execution environment (which
may be hostile, e.g., if it represents an active attacker trying to compromise the
protocol). The formal definition of observational equivalence [1] involves infinite quantification over all such execution environments and is therefore not an
effective definition that can be implemented. SPEC implements a refinement
of observational equivalence, called *open bisimulation* [13,17,18] that respects
the context throughout execution. The decision procedure (for finite processes)
implemented here is derived from earlier work [19].

The current version of SPEC allows modelling of symmetric and asymmetric encryption, digital signatures, cryptographic hash functions, and message
authentication codes (MAC). It is currently suited to work with finite processes,
i.e., those without recursion or replication. SPEC is designed with the goal of
producing explicit witness of equivalence, in the form of a bisimulation set, that
can be verified independently. To reduce the size of the witness, so as to ease

© Springer International Publishing AG 2016
A. Igarashi (Ed.): APLAS 2016, LNCS 10017, pp. 87–95, 2016.
DOI: 10.1007/978-3-319-47958-3_5

verification, we employ a technique known as bisimulation "up-to" [14]. Bisimulation up-to allows one to quotient a bisimulation with another relation, as long as the latter is sound w.r.t. bisimilarity. Section 5 discusses some simple up-to techniques that produce significant reduction in proof size.

The proof engine of SPEC is implemented in the Bedwyr prover [2], with a user interface implemented directly in OCaml utilising a library of functions available from Bedwyr. The user, however, does not need to be aware of the underlying Bedwyr implementation and syntax in order to use the tool. The latest version of SPEC can be downloaded from the project page[1].

This paper gives a high-level overview of SPEC and the theory behind it. For a more detailed hands-on tutorial, the reader is referred to the user manual included in the SPEC distribution. All examples discussed here can also be found in the example directory in the distribution.

SPEC is one of a handful of tools for checking observational equivalence for cryptographic process calculi. We briefly mention the other tools here; Cheval's Ph.D. thesis [8] gives a good overview of the state of the art. Brias and Borgström implemented the SBC tool to check symbolic bisimulation for the spi-calculus [4,5]. SBC does not allow compound keys in encryption, nor does it support asymmetric encryption, so it is strictly less expressive than SPEC (see Sect. 4). Blanchett implements an extension to ProVerif to check observational equivalence of *biprocesses* [3], i.e., pairs of processes which differ only in the structure of the terms, by reducing it to reachability analysis. Other tools such as AKISS [6], Adecs [8] and APTE [9] implement symbolic trace equivalence checking (for bounded processes), which is coarser than bisimulation. However, unlike SPEC, none of these tools currently produce proofs to support the correctness claim for the protocols they verify.

2   The spi-Calculus

The spi-calculus generalises the π-calculus by allowing arbitrary terms (or messages) to be output, instead of just names. The set of messages allowed is defined by the following grammar:

$$M, N ::= x \mid \langle M, N \rangle \mid \mathrm{enc}(M, N) \mid \mathrm{pub}(M) \mid \mathrm{aenc}(M, N) \mid \mathrm{sign}(M, N) \mid \mathrm{h}(M) \mid \mathrm{mac}(M)$$

where x denotes a variable. The message $\langle M, N \rangle$ represents a pair of messages M and N, $\mathrm{enc}(M, N)$ represents a message M encrypted with symmetric key N using a symmetric encryption function, $\mathrm{aenc}(M, N)$ represents a message M encrypted with public key N using an asymmetric encryption function, $\mathrm{pub}(M)$ represents a public key corresponding to secret key M, $\mathrm{sign}(M, N)$ represents a message M signed with secret key N using a digital signature function, $\mathrm{h}(M)$ represents the hash of M and $\mathrm{mac}(M)$ represents the MAC of M.

The language of processes is given by the following grammar:

$$P ::= 0 \mid \tau.P \mid x(y).P \mid \bar{x}\langle M \rangle.P \mid \nu(x_1, \ldots, x_m).P \mid (P \mid P) \mid (P + P) \mid !P \mid$$
$$[M = N]P \mid [\mathrm{checksign}(M, N, L)]P \mid$$
$$\mathrm{let}\ \langle x, y \rangle = M\ \mathrm{in}\ P \mid \mathrm{case}\ M\ \mathrm{of}\ \mathrm{enc}(x, N)\ \mathrm{in}\ P \mid \mathrm{let}\ x = \mathrm{adec}(M, N)\ \mathrm{in}\ P.$$

---

[1]   http://www.ntu.edu.sg/home/atiu/spec-prover/.

The intuitive meaning of each of the process constructs is as follows:

- 0 is a deadlocked process. It cannot perform any action.
- $\tau.P$ performs a silent action then continues as P.
- $x(y).P$ is an input-prefixed process, where y is bound in P. The process accepts a value on channel x, binds it to the variable y and evolves as P.
- $\bar{x}\langle M\rangle.P$ is an output-prefixed process. It outputs a message M on channel x and evolves into P.
- $\nu(x_1,\ldots,x_m).P$ is a process that introduces m fresh names $x_1,\ldots,x_m$ that can be used in the body of P. These fresh names may be used to represent nonces in protocols or (private) encryption keys.
- $P \mid Q$ is the parallel composition of P and Q.
- $P + Q$ represents a non-deterministic choice between P and Q.
- $!P$ is a replicated process representing infinitely many parallel copies of P.
- $[M = N]P$ is a process which behaves like P when M is syntactically equal to N.
- $[\text{checksign}(M, N, L)]P$ is used to check that a signature is valid with respect to a message and public key. This process behaves like P when M is a message, N is message M signed with some secret key K, i.e. $N = \text{sign}(M, K)$, and L is the corresponding public key $\text{pub}(K)$.
- let $\langle x, y\rangle = M$ in P is a deconstructor for pairs. The variables x and y are binders whose scope is P. This process checks that M decomposes to a pair of messages, and binds those messages to x and y, respectively.
- case M of $\text{enc}(x, N)$ in P is a deconstructor for symmetrically encrypted messages. The variable x here is a binder whose scope is P. This process checks that M is a message encrypted with key N, decrypts the encrypted message and binds it to x.
- let $x = \text{adec}(M, N)$ in P is a deconstructor for asymmetrically encrypted messages that binds free occurrences of x in P. This process checks that M is a message encrypted with public key $\text{pub}(N)$, and binds the resulting decrypted message to x.

3   Open Bisimulation

The equivalence checking procedure implemented by SPEC is based on a notion of *open bisimulation* for the spi-calculus developed in [17]. Two processes related by open bisimulation [15] are observationally indistinguishable, and remain so even if they are executed in an arbitrary execution context. Hence open bisimulation is robust in an environment where processes are mobile.

An *open bisimulation* is a relation over processes, parameterised by a representation of the history of messages called a *bitrace*, satisfying some conditions (see [18,19]). The bitrace is a list of *i/o pairs* which are either an *input pair*, written $(M, N)^i$, where M and N are messages, or an *output pair*, written $(M, N)^o$. Note that open bisimulation uses *names*, indicated using boldface, to distinguish extruded private names from free variables. We call these names *rigid names*, to distinguish them from constants.

A bitrace represents the history of messages input and output by a pair of processes. That is, the first (resp. the second) projection of a bitrace represents a trace of the first (resp. the second) process in the pair. In an open bisimulation, a bitrace attached to a pair of processes must be *consistent* [18]. Roughly, consistency here means that the two traces that form the bitrace are indistinguishable to the attacker. One instance where this is the case is if the two traces are syntactically identical. However, we also allow two traces to be indistinguishable if one can be obtained from the other by renaming the rigid names in the traces. The idea is that these rigid names represent nonces (i.e., random numbers) generated during runs of a protocol and should therefore be treated as indistinguishable: a process that outputs a random number and terminates should be considered indistinguishable from another process that also outputs a random number and terminates, although they may output different random numbers. The actual notion of consistency of bitraces extends this further to allow traces that contain different encrypted parts that cannot be decrypted by the attacker to be treated as indistinguishable. The reader is referred to [18] for the formal definition of bitrace consistency.

Two processes P and Q are bisimilar if there exists a bisimulation set containing the triple (H, P, Q), where H is a bitrace consisting of input pairs of identical free variables occurring in P and Q. Intuitively, H makes explicit that free variables in P and Q may be affected by earlier inputs in the context.

SPEC also supports *progressing bisimulation* [12], which is a form of weak bisimulation sensitive to mobile contexts. Simulation is also supported by the keyword `sim` in place of `bisim`.

4   An Example

We show here a simple example to illustrate features of the bisimulation output. The SPEC distribution contains a number of examples, including small tests and full protocols. Consider the following two processes.

$$P := a(x).\nu(k).\bar{a}\langle enc(x, k)\rangle.\nu(m).\bar{a}\langle enc(m, enc(a, k))\rangle.\bar{m}\langle a\rangle$$

$$Q := a(x).\nu(k).\bar{a}\langle enc(x, k)\rangle.\nu(m).\bar{a}\langle enc(m, enc(a, k))\rangle.[x = a]\bar{m}\langle a\rangle$$

This example is taken from [5], where it is used to show the incompleteness of their symbolic bisimulation. The process P inputs a message via channel a, binds it to x and outputs an encrypted message $enc(x, k)$. It then generates a new channel m, sends it off encrypted with the key $enc(a, k)$. Here we assume a is a constant (or a public channel), so it is known to the intruder. The process then sends a message on the newly generated channel m. Although the channel m is a secret generated by P, and it is not explicitly extruded, the intruder can still interact via m if it feeds the name a to P (hence binds x to a). As a result, the (symbolic) output $enc(x, k)$ can be 'concretized' to $enc(a, k)$, which can be used to decrypt $enc(m, enc(a, k))$ to obtain m.

The process Q is very similar, except that it puts a 'guard' on the possibility of interacting on m by insisting that $x = a$. The above informal reasoning about the behaviour of P shows that it should be observationally equivalent to Q. SPEC shows that the two processes are bisimilar, and produces the following bisimulation (up-to) set:

1. Bi-trace: $(?a, ?a)^i$
   First process:
   $?a(n3).\nu(n4).\overline{?a}\langle$ enc$(n3, n4)$ $\rangle.\nu(n5).\overline{?a}\langle$ enc$(n5,$ enc$(?a, n4))$ $\rangle.\overline{n5}\langle$?a $\rangle.0$.
   Second process:
   $?a(n3).\nu(n4).\overline{?a}\langle$ enc$(n3, n4)$ $\rangle.\nu(n5).\overline{?a}\langle$ enc$(n5,$ enc$(?a, n4))$ $\rangle.[n3 = ?a]\overline{n5}\langle$?a $\rangle.0$.

2. Bi-trace: $(?a, ?a)^i.(?n3 , ?n3)^i$.
   First process:
   $\nu(n4).\overline{?a}\langle$ enc$(?n3, n4)$ $\rangle.\nu(n5).\overline{?a}\langle$ enc$(n5,$ enc$(?a, n4))$ $\rangle.\overline{n5}\langle$?a $\rangle.0$
   Second process:
   $\nu(n4).\overline{?a}\langle$ enc$(?n3, n4)$ $\rangle.\nu(n5).\overline{?a}\langle$ enc$(n5,$ enc$(?a, n4))$ $\rangle.[?n3 = ?a]\overline{n5}\langle$?a $\rangle.0$.

3. Bi-trace: $(?a, ?a)^i.(?n3 , ?n3)^i.(enc(?n3, n4) ,$ enc$(?n3, n4))^o$.
   First process: $\nu(n5).\overline{?a}\langle$ enc$(n5,$ enc$(?a, n4))$ $\rangle.\overline{n5}\langle$?a $\rangle.0$
   Second process: $\nu(n5).\overline{?a}\langle$ enc$(n5,$ enc$(?a, n4))$ $\rangle.[?n3 = ?a]\overline{n5}\langle$?a $\rangle.0$.

4. Bi-trace:
   $(?a, ?a)^i.(?n3 , ?n3)^i.(enc(?n3, n4) ,$ enc$(?n3, n4))^o$.
   $\qquad\qquad\qquad ($enc$(n5,$ enc$(?a, n4)) ,$ enc$(n5,$ enc$(?a, n4)))^o$.
   First process: $\overline{n5}\langle$?a $\rangle.0$, and second process: $[?n3 = ?a]\overline{n5}\langle$?a $\rangle.0$.

5. Bi-trace:
   $(?a, ?a)^i.($enc$(?a, n3) ,$ enc$(?a, n3))^o.($enc$(n4,$ enc$(?a, n3)) ,$ enc$(n4,$ enc$(?a, n3)))^o$.
   First process: 0, and second process: 0.

This is more or less the output produced automatically by SPEC, with minor editing to improve presentation. A few notes on this output:

- *Typesetting of names and variables*: Variables are typeset by prefixing the variables with a question mark '?' to distinguish them from private names. Notice how input prefixes are replaced with variables in the bitraces, e.g., when moving from 1 to 2.
- The triples are given in the order of the unfolding of the processes, e.g., the first triple is the original input processes (with a bitrace indicating free variable $?a$) which unfolds to the second triple. Notice that in moving from 4 to 5, the input pair disappears from the bitrace. This is because the variable $?n3$ gets instantiated to $?a$, and is removed from the bitrace by the simplification steps of SPEC.
- *Equivariance of bisimulation*: Notice that in proceeding from 4 to 5 there is an implicit renaming performed by SPEC. It is a by-product of *equivariance tabling* implemented in Bedwyr (see Sect. 5). Each triple in the bisimulation set output by SPEC represents an equivalence class of triples modulo renaming of variables and names (but excluding constants).

5   Implementation

The proof engine of SPEC is implemented on top of the theorem prover/model checker Bedwyr [2]. The logic behind Bedwyr is a variant of the logic Linc [16], which is a first-order intuitionistic logic, extended with fixed points and a name-quantifier ∇. The quantifier ∇ provides a logical notion of fresh names and is crucial to modelling scope extrusion and fresh name generation in bisimulation checking. Propositions are considered equivalent modulo renaming of ∇-variables. This property, called the *equivariance* principle, allows one to support equivariant reasoning in bisimulation checking, by encoding names in the spi-calculus as ∇-quantified variables.

The proof extraction part of SPEC relies on the *tabling* mechanism in Bedwyr. Bedwyr allows one to store previously proved goals in a table, and reuse them in proving a query later. SPEC utilises this to store bisimulation triples in the table. The earlier versions of Bedwyr implement a simple syntactic matching to query a table, which results in too many variants of the same triples to be stored. In the course of SPEC implementation, the tabling mechanism in Bedwyr is modified so as to allow one to match a query with a table entry modulo renaming of ∇-variable. Logically, this is justified by the equivariant principle of the logic underlying Bedwyr. We call this form of tabling *equivariant tabling*.

In the initial version of SPEC, where a naïve version of the bisimulation algorithm from [19] was implemented, the size of the bisimulation sets quickly got out of hand, even for small examples. Several simplifications have then been introduced to reduce the size of the bisimulation sets. However, these simplifications mean that the produced sets are no longer bisimulations; they are, instead, bisimulation up-to sets, in the sense of [14]. The following are among the simplifications done in bisimulation checking:

– Equivariant tabling. The bisimulation set is closed under renaming.
– Reflexivity checking. This says that any process P should be considered bisimilar to itself. However, a simple syntactic check is not enough, and even unsound. This is due to the fact that in a triple (H, P, P), the bitrace H may have different orders of names. For example, if $H = (a, b)^o.(b, a)^o$, then the triple $(H, \bar{c}\langle a \rangle.0, \bar{c}\langle a \rangle.0)$ is not in the largest bisimilarity. One needs to consider equality checking modulo renaming.
– Structural simplification. This is basically applying structural congruences to simplify processes.

These rather straightforward simplifications, especially equivariant tabling, turn out to be effective in reducing the bisimulation set and running time. Table 1 shows the significant effect of equivariant tabling on a selection of example problems. The protocols are single-session authentication protocols, encoded into the spi-calculus by Brias and Borgström in the SBC prover. The table shows the running time (in seconds) and the size of the bisimulation set produced for each example. These examples were tested on a PC with Intel Xeon CPU E5-1650, 16 GB RAM and running Ubuntu 14.04 LTS 64-bit operating system. The descriptions of the protocols can be found in, e.g., the security protocol repository at ENS Cachan.[2] The performance gain seems to increase with larger examples, e.g., the amended version of the Needham-Schroeder symmetric key authentication protocol produced more than ten thousand triples in the earlier unimproved version of SPEC, but has been cut down to 835 triples in the current version.

Note that the running time is still considerably higher than other tools such as ProVerif, which can solve all these problems in a few seconds. However, ProVerif and other tools do not produce symbolic proofs of equivalence, so there is no direct comparison with this proof-producing aspect of SPEC.

Table 1. Running time and bisimulation size for some authentication protocols

Protocol	Equiv. tabling on		Equiv. tabling off	
	Time	Proof size	Time	Proof size
Andrew secure RPC (BAN version)	16 s	98	17 s	108
Denning-Sacco-Lowe	19 s	63	31 s	103
Kao Chow, v.1	140 s	223	215 s	300
Kao Chow, v.2	177 s	259	273 s	352
Needham-Schroeder symm. key	46 s	161	50 s	173
Needham-Schroeder symm. key (amended)	377 s	835	1598 s	2732
Yahalom (BAN version)	268 s	513	281 s	548
Yahalom (Paulson's version)	288 s	513	300 s	548

6 Key Cycles Detection

Bedwyr is suited to protocol analysis problems beyond bisimulation. To illustrate this power, SPEC includes a feature that detects key cycles. Key cycles are formed when a key is directly or indirectly encrypted by itself. The absence of key cycles in possible runs of a protocol is important in relating symbolic approaches and computational approaches to protocol analysis [10]. For example, the process

$$nu(k1, k2).a\langle \text{enc}(k1, k2)\rangle.a\langle \text{enc}(k2, k1)\rangle$$

has a private key $k1$ encrypted with private key $k2$ which is encrypted with $k1$. Key cycles are a security issue, since the computational security of the encryption function is dependent on the assumption there are no such cycles. Thus although both $k1$ and $k2$ are never directly revealed to attackers, we cannot computationally prove that the encryption cannot be broken.

For example, using keyword **keycycle**, SPEC detects that the following generates a key cycle.

$$P := \nu(k1, k2, k3).(a\langle \text{enc}(k1, k3) \mid a(x).\text{case } x \text{ of enc}(y, k3).a\langle \text{enc}(y, k2)\rangle \mid a\langle k2, k1\rangle)$$

---

[2] http://www.lsv.ens-cachan.fr/Software/spore/.

7   Future Work

We are investigating extensions of SPEC to include blind signatures [7], homomorphic encryption and the mismatch operator. Each of these features requires a problem in the theory to be resolved, before an implementation can be proven to be correct. SPEC is intended to be part of a tool chain for machine assisted certification of security protocols. Another part of this tool chain will involve a proof assistant that will be used to independently verify the bisimulation up-to relations generated by SPEC. Independently verifiable bisimulation up-to relations would thereby form dependable proof certificates for security protocols.

Acknowledgements. The authors receive support from MOE Tier 2 grant MOE2014-T2-2-076. The first author receives support from NTU Start Up grant M4081190.020.

References

1. Abadi, M., Gordon, A.D.: A calculus for cryptographic protocols: the spi calculus. Inf. Comput. **148**(1), 1–70 (1999)
2. Baelde, D., Gacek, A., Miller, D., Nadathur, G., Tiu, A.F.: The Bedwyr system for model checking over syntactic expressions. In: Pfenning, F. (ed.) CADE 2007. LNCS (LNAI), vol. 4603, pp. 391–397. Springer, Heidelberg (2007)
3. Blanchet, B., Abadi, M., Fournet, C.: Automated verification of selected equivalences for security protocols. J. Log. Algebr. Program. **75**(1), 3–51 (2008)
4. Borgström, J.: Equivalences and calculi for formal verification of cryptographic protocols. Ph.D. thesis, École Polytechnique Fédérale de Lausanne (2008)
5. Borgström, J., Briais, S., Nestmann, U.: Symbolic bisimulation in the spi calculus. In: Gardner, P., Yoshida, N. (eds.) CONCUR 2004. LNCS, vol. 3170, pp. 161–176. Springer, Heidelberg (2004). doi:10.1007/978-3-540-28644-8_11
6. Chadha, R., Ciobâcă, V., Kremer, S.: Automated verification of equivalence properties of cryptographic protocols. In: Programming Languages and Systems, pp. 108–127 (2012)
7. Chaum, D.: Blind signature system. In: Advances in Cryptology, Proceedings of CRYPTO 1983, Santa Barbara, California, USA, 21–24 August 1983, p. 153. Plenum Press, New York (1984)
8. Cheval, V.: Automatic verification of cryptographic protocols: privacy-type properties. Ph.D. thesis, ENS Cachan, December 2012
9. Cheval, V.: APTE: an algorithm for proving trace equivalence. In: Ábrahám, E., Havelund, K. (eds.) TACAS 2014 (ETAPS). LNCS, vol. 8413, pp. 587–592. Springer, Heidelberg (2014)
10. Comon-Lundh, H., Cortier, V., Zalinescu, E.: Deciding security properties for cryptographic protocols. Application to key cycles. ACM Trans. Comput. Log. **11**(2), 9:1–9:42 (2010). doi:10.1145/1656242.1656244
11. Milner, R., Parrow, J., Walker, D.: A calculus of mobile processes, Part II. In: Information and Computation, pp. 41–77 (1992)
12. Montanari, U., Sassone, V.: Dynamic congruence vs. progressing bisimulation for CCS. Fundamenta Informaticae **16**(2), 171–199 (1992)
13. Sangiorgi, D.: A theory of bisimulation for the pi-calculus. Acta Inf. **33**(1), 69–97 (1996)

14. Sangiorgi, D.: On the bisimulation proof method. Math. Struct. Comput. Sci. **8**, 447–479 (1998)
15. Sangiorgi, D., Walker, D.: π-Calculus: A Theory of Mobile Processes. Cambridge University Press, Cambridge (2001)
16. Tiu, A.: A logical framework for reasoning about logical specifications. Ph.D. thesis, Pennsylvania State University, May 2004
17. Tiu, A.F.: A trace based bisimulation for the spi calculus: an extended abstract. In: Shao, Z. (ed.) APLAS 2007. LNCS, vol. 4807, pp. 367–382. Springer, Heidelberg (2007)
18. Tiu, A.: A trace based bisimulation for the spi calculus. CoRR, abs/0901.2166 (2009)
19. Tiu, A., Dawson, J.E.: Automating open bisimulation checking for the spi calculus. In: Proceedings of the 23rd IEEE Computer Security Foundations Symposium (CSF 2010), pp. 307–321. IEEE Computer Society (2010)

Binary Session Types for Psi-Calculi

Hans Hüttel[(✉)]

Department of Computer Science, Aalborg University, Aalborg, Denmark
hans@cs.aau.dk

Abstract. Binary session types can be used to describe communication protocols, and to ensure a variety of properties, e.g. deadlock freedom, liveness, or secure information flow. Session type systems are often formulated for variants of the π-calculus, and for each such system, the central properties such as session fidelity must be re-established.

The framework of psi-calculi introduced by Bengtson et al. makes it possible to give a general account of variants of the pi-calculus. We use this framework to describe a generic session type system for variants of the π-calculus. In this generic system, standard properties, including fidelity, hold at the level of the framework and are then guaranteed to hold when the generic system is instantiated.

We show that our system can capture existing systems including the session type system due to Gay and Hole, a type system for progress due to Vieira and Vasconcelos and a refinement type system due to Baltazar et al. The standard fidelity property is proved at the level of the generic system, and automatically hold when the system is instantiated.

1 Introduction

Binary session types are a type discipline for concurrent processes that arose in the work of Honda [16] in the setting of the π-calculus; a binary session type describes the protocol followed by the two ends of a communication channel. A well-typed process will not exhibit communication errors, since the endpoints of a channel are then known to follow the dual parts of their protocol. Session types have been used for describing a variety of program properties, including liveness properties. In the setting of sessions, a particularly important property is that of progress [9,24], namely that a session will be never stuck waiting for a message that does not arrive. Binary session type systems have been extended with standard notions of polymorphism [12] and subtyping [13].

Overall, there are now many different session type systems that share certain features and yet are different. For every such system certain properties must be established in order for them to be useful; in particular, one must establish a *fidelity* property: any usage of a channel in a well-typed process will evolve according to the usage of the channel as described by its session type.

An attempt to classify existing type systems for process calculi is that of *generic type systems* that consist of a collection of general type rules that can be instantiated to give a concrete type system for a particular property. This approach was introduced by Igarashi and Kobayashi [21] and continued by König [23].

© Springer International Publishing AG 2016
A. Igarashi (Ed.): APLAS 2016, LNCS 10017, pp. 96–115, 2016.
DOI: 10.1007/978-3-319-47958-3_6

At the level of process calculus semantics one can also formulate *generic process calculi*. The psi-calculus framework of Bengtson et al. [2] uses a generic process syntax and semantics, and concrete π-like process calculi can then be obtained by suitable instantiations of the parameters of the generic calculus. The genericity of psi-calculus comes from having the notion of mobile names with scope together with allowing for channels to be arbitrary terms from a so-called nominal data type.

This paper presents a generic session type system for psi-calculi. Other generic type systems have already been proposed in this setting: A type system generalizing simple type systems [19] and a type system for resource-aware properties [20].

In our generic type system there is no type language for sessions; instead we assume that session types have certain labelled transitions. This is in the tradition of behavioural contracts [6] and the work of [7] that both provide behavioural type disciplines in which types have transitions.

Psi-calculus session channels can be arbitrary terms, so a major challenge is to deal with this. More precisely, we capture the terms-as-channels discipline by introducing a notion of session constructor. Whenever a session is created, private session channels are introduced by means of scoped endpoint constructors that must be applied to an ordinary term in order to create a session channel from the term. The type system keeps track of how the behaviour of a session channel evolves by using the transition relation on types to keep track of the modified behaviour of the endpoint constructors.

The central safety result for a binary session type discipline is that of fidelity. In order to express and prove that fidelity holds for all instances of our generic type system, we give a labelled transition semantics that records the information consumed by each step of a session.

Finally, we describe how existing binary session type systems arise as instances of our general type system. Here, the use of assertions makes it possible to explicitly capture the additional concepts used in some of these systems. The systems that we study are a system for ensuring progress due to Vieira and Vasconcelos [24], a type system for correspondence assertions due to Vasconcelos et al. [1] and the original systems of Gay and Hole [13].

2 Psi-Calculi

In presentations of binary session type systems for process calculi (e.g. [1,14,24]), a common approach taken is to use an untyped syntax of the process calculus along with an untyped semantics. One will then state the fidelity and safety results by suitable annotations of the untyped process expressions and transitions. In this paper we also take this route: We first introduce an untyped syntax of processes and an untyped semantics. In Sect. 4.3 we then present a typed version of the syntax and show how to find typed transitions from the untyped semantics.

2.1 Names, Terms and Assertions

Names are central to psi-calculi; we assume that these form a *nominal set* $\mathcal{N}$ – for the precise definition, see [11]. Informally speaking, a nominal set is a set whose members can be affected by names being bound or swapped. If x is an element of a nominal set and $a \in \mathcal{N}$, we write $a \,\sharp\, x$, to denote that a is fresh for x; the notion extends to sets of names in the expected way.

Psi-calculus processes can contain *terms* $M, N, \ldots$; these must form a *nominal data type* [2] **T** [11] which is a nominal set with internal structure. If Σ is a signature, a nominal data type is then a Σ-algebra, whose carrier set is a nominal set. In the nominal data types of ψ-calculi we use simultaneous term substitution $X[\widetilde{z} := \widetilde{Y}]$ which is to be read as stating that the terms in $\widetilde{Y}$ replace the names in $\widetilde{z}$ in X in a capture-avoiding fashion.

Processes can also contain *assertions* Ψ, that must form a nominal datatype **A**. We require a partial composition operator $\otimes$ on **A**, a symmetric and transitive binary relation $\simeq$ on **A** and a special unit assertion **1** such that

$$\Psi_1 \otimes \Psi_2 \simeq \Psi_2 \otimes \Psi_1 \qquad\qquad \Psi_1 \otimes (\Psi_2 \otimes \Psi_3) \simeq (\Psi_1 \otimes \Psi_2) \otimes \Psi_3$$
$$\Psi \otimes \mathbf{1} \simeq \Psi \qquad\qquad \Psi \simeq \Psi' \Rightarrow \Psi \otimes \Psi_1 \simeq \Psi' \otimes \Psi_1$$

An assertion Ψ is *unlimited* if $\Psi \simeq \Psi \otimes \Psi$. We have a partial order on assertions induced by $\Psi \leq \Psi \otimes \Psi'$, and we write $\Psi < \Psi'$ iff $\Psi \leq \Psi'$ and $\Psi \not\simeq \Psi'$.

2.2 Processes

Unlike the π-calculus, channels can be arbitrary terms in a psi-calculus. We therefore assume a notion of *channel equivalence*; $\Psi \models M \leftrightarrow N$ denotes that terms M and N represent the same channel, given the assertion Ψ. That channel equivalence can in the general case depend on the global knowledge, represented by Ψ, is due to the fact that psi-calculus instances may use assertions that involve identities on names.

We extend psi-calculi with the selection and branching primitives of Honda et al. [18], as these are standard in session calculi. Branching now becomes $M \triangleright \{l_1 : P_1, \ldots, l_k : P_k\}$ and selection is written as $M \triangleleft l.P_1$, where l ranges over a set of selector label names. As in [18], these label names cannot be bound by input or restriction.

We introduce session channels by means of dual endpoints as in Giunti and Vasconcelos [14]. The construct $(\nu c)P$ can be used to set up a new session channel with the session constructor c that can be used to build channels from terms. The notion of session constructor is explained in Sect. 4.1.

All in all, this gives us the untyped formation rules

$$P ::= \underline{M}(\lambda \widetilde{x})X.P \mid \overline{M}N.P \mid P_1 \mid P_2 \mid (\nu c)P \mid \,!P \mid (\!|\Psi|\!) \mid \mathbf{case}\ \varphi_1 : P_1, \ldots, \varphi_k : P_k$$
$$\mid M \triangleleft l.P_1 \mid M \triangleright \{l_1 : P_1, \ldots, l_k : P_k\}$$

Restriction and input are the binding constructs; we use $\mathrm{bn}(P)$ and $\mathrm{n}(P)$ to denote the sets of bound names in P and names in P, respectively.

The input process $\underline{M}(\lambda \widetilde{x})X.P$ contains the *pattern* X; this is to be thought of as a term with free pattern variables $\widetilde{x}$. We allow patterns to be arbitrary and simply require that they form a nominal datatype. The input process can receive a term M if and only if M matches the pattern X. The bound names of this process are $\widetilde{x} \cup \mathrm{bn}(P)$.

The output process $\overline{M}N.P$ sends out the term N on the channel M and continues as P. The selector construct $\mathbf{case}\ \varphi_1 : P_1, \ldots, \varphi_k : P_k$ describes a conditional process that continues as P_i if condition φ_i is true. Any assertion Ψ can be embedded as the process $(\lvert\Psi\rvert)$, and in this way it is possible to express the notion of inaction (a 'nil' process). The remaining process constructs are those of the π-calculus.

Moreover, processes can contain *conditions* φ that are used in the **case**-construct; these are also assumed to form a nominal datatype.

3   An Annotated Semantics

Our labelled transition semantics has transitions are of the form $\Psi \blacktriangleright P \xrightarrow{\alpha} P'$. This is to be read as stating that, given the global knowledge represented by the assertion Ψ, process P can evolve to process P' by performing the action α.

In the semantics, we need to give an account of pattern matching for input processes. Like [5] we assume the existence of a match relation that describes the conditions on pattern variables needed for a term N to match a pattern X. This match relation is particular to the actual psi-calculus instance under consideration. In any case, $\widetilde{L} \in \text{MATCH}(N, \widetilde{y}, X)$ if the term N can match the pattern X with pattern variables $\widetilde{y}$ in such a way that these variables are instantiated with the corresponding subterms of $\widetilde{L}$.

Moreover, the semantics must describe when and how conditions in a **case**-construct hold. We therefore assume the existence of an entailment relation $\Psi \models \varphi$ that describes when a condition φ is true, given an assertion Ψ. This relation is also particular to the actual psi-calculus instance under consideration.

Finally, assertions are important in the semantics. We sometimes need to extract the assertion information of a process P; we call this its *frame* $\mathscr{F}(P) = \Psi_P$, where Ψ_P is the composition of assertions in P. We let

$$\mathscr{F}(P \mid Q) = \mathscr{F}(P) \otimes \mathscr{F}(Q) \qquad\qquad \mathscr{F}((vb)P) = (vb)\mathscr{F}(P)$$
$$\mathscr{F}((\lvert\Psi\rvert)) = \Psi \qquad\qquad\qquad\qquad \mathscr{F}(P) = \mathbf{1} \quad \text{otherwise}$$

The semantics is specially tailored for stating and proving the safety properties of our type system. The structure of actions is given by the formation rules

$$\alpha ::= M \lhd l \mid M \rhd l \mid \overline{M}(v\widetilde{a})N \mid \underline{K}N \mid (v\widetilde{a})\tau@(v\widetilde{b})(\overline{M}\,N\,\underline{K}) \mid (v\widetilde{a})\tau@(M \lhd l \rhd N)$$

The labels for observable actions are as in [2]: $\overline{M}(v\widetilde{a})N$ denotes an output on channel M of N that extrudes the names in $\widetilde{a}$, and $\underline{K}N$ denotes an input on channel K of term N. The transition rules for observable transitions are given in Table 1.

On the other hand, τ-actions now record usage of bound names. This is a major difference from the presentation in [2] and is introduced, since we have to describe how the session type of a bound name that is used as a session constructor will evolve as the result of a τ-action. The rules for τ-transitions are shown in Table 2.

In the label $(v\widetilde{a})\tau@(v\widetilde{b})(\overline{M}\,N\,\underline{K})$ we record the set of private names $\widetilde{a}$ that are used in the channel subject pair (M, K) communication as well as the set of private names $\widetilde{b}$ that are extruded from the output process. This is expressed by the side condition of the rules (COM) and (RES-COM).

In the label $(v\widetilde{a})\tau@(M \lhd l \rhd N)$ we record the set of private names $\widetilde{a}$ that are used to build the selector pair (M, N). This is captured by the side conditions of the rules (CHOOSE) and (RES-CHOOSE). If any of the sets in a label is empty, we omit it.

Table 1. Labelled transition rules for observable transitions. The symmetric versions of COM, CHOOSE and PAR are omitted. In PAR we assume $\mathcal{F}(Q) = (\nu \widetilde{b_Q})\Psi_Q$ where $\widetilde{b_Q} \,\sharp\, \Psi, P$ and α.

$$(\text{SELECT}) \quad \frac{\Psi \models M \leftrightarrow K}{\Psi \blacktriangleright M \triangleleft l.P \xrightarrow{K \triangleleft l} P} \qquad\qquad (\text{REP}) \quad \frac{\Psi \blacktriangleright P \mid !P \xrightarrow{\alpha} P'}{\Psi \blacktriangleright !P \xrightarrow{\alpha} P'}$$

$$(\text{OFFER}) \quad \frac{\Psi \models M \leftrightarrow K}{\Psi \blacktriangleright M \triangleright \{l_1 : P_1, \ldots l_k : P_k\} \xrightarrow{K \triangleright l_i} P_i}$$

$$(\text{IN}) \quad \frac{\Psi \models M \leftrightarrow K \quad \widetilde{L} \in \text{MATCH}(N, \widetilde{x}, X)}{\Psi \blacktriangleright \underline{M}(\lambda \widetilde{x})X.P \xrightarrow{KN} P[\widetilde{x} := \widetilde{L}]} \qquad (\text{OUT}) \quad \frac{\Psi \models M \leftrightarrow K}{\Psi \blacktriangleright \overline{M}N.P \xrightarrow{\overline{K}N} P}$$

$$(\text{PAR}) \quad \frac{\Psi_Q \otimes \Psi \blacktriangleright P \xrightarrow{\alpha} P'}{\Psi \blacktriangleright P \mid Q \xrightarrow{\alpha} P' \mid Q} \quad \text{bn}(\alpha)\#Q \qquad (\text{CASE}) \quad \frac{\Psi \blacktriangleright P_i \xrightarrow{\alpha} P' \quad \Psi \models \varphi_i}{\Psi \blacktriangleright \mathbf{case} \ \widetilde{\varphi} : \widetilde{P} \xrightarrow{\alpha} P'}$$

$$(\text{SCOPE}) \quad \frac{\Psi \blacktriangleright P \xrightarrow{\alpha} P'}{\Psi \blacktriangleright (\nu b)P \xrightarrow{\alpha} (\nu b)P'} \quad b \,\sharp\, \alpha$$

$$(\text{OPEN}) \quad \frac{\Psi \blacktriangleright P \xrightarrow{\overline{M}(\nu \widetilde{a})N} P'}{\Psi \blacktriangleright (\nu b)P \xrightarrow{\overline{M}(\nu \widetilde{a} \cup b)N} P'} \quad \begin{array}{l} b \,\sharp\, M, \widetilde{a} \\ b \in \text{n}(N) \end{array}$$

4   Types in the Generic Type System

In this and the following section we present our generic type system; our account of session types does not rely on a particular type language and is inspired by the transition-based approach of [6].

4.1   Session Types and Endpoint Types

We let T range over the set of types and distinguish between *base types B*, *session types S* and *endpoint types T_E*. An endpoint type T_E describes the behaviour at one end of a channel. A session type S describes the behaviour at both ends of a channel and is a pair (T_1, T_2) of endpoint types.

In psi-calculi channels can be arbitrary terms; in our setting we use special names called *session constructors*; this is a term constructor that can be applied to an appropriate number of terms. The result of this is a term that can be used as session channel. A term M can contain more than one session constructor; if the principal session constructor of the term is c, M will have a type of the form $T @ c$. The type rules for terms depend on the specific psi-calculus instance, and these rules must describe what is meant by the principal session constructor and how the type of a composite term to be used as a session channel is determined.

Table 2. Labelled transition rules for τ-transitions. Symmetric versions of COM and CHOOSE are omitted. In COM and CHOOSE we assume that $\mathscr{F}(P) = (\nu \widetilde{b_P})\Psi_P$ and $\mathscr{F}(Q) = (\nu \widetilde{b_Q})\Psi_Q$ where $\widetilde{b_P} \mathbin{\sharp} \Psi, \widetilde{b_Q}, Q, M$ and P, and $\widetilde{b_Q} \mathbin{\sharp} \Psi, \widetilde{b_P}, P, K$ and Q.

(COM)
$$
\dfrac{
\begin{array}{c}
\Psi \otimes \Psi_Q \blacktriangleright P \xrightarrow{\overline{M}(\nu\widetilde{b})N} P' \\[4pt]
\Psi \otimes \Psi_P \blacktriangleright Q \xrightarrow{KN} Q' \\[4pt]
\Psi \otimes \Psi_P \otimes \Psi_Q \models M \leftrightarrow K
\end{array}
}{
\Psi \blacktriangleright P \mid Q \xrightarrow{(\nu\widetilde{a})\tau@(\nu\widetilde{b})(\overline{M}NK)} (\nu\widetilde{b})(P' \mid Q')
}
\qquad
\begin{array}{l}
\widetilde{b} \mathbin{\sharp} Q, M, K \\[4pt]
\widetilde{a} = (\widetilde{b_Q} \cap \mathrm{n}(M)) \cup (\widetilde{b_P} \cap \mathrm{n}(K))
\end{array}
$$

(CHOOSE)
$$
\dfrac{
\Psi \otimes \Psi_Q \blacktriangleright P \xrightarrow{M \lhd l} P' \quad \Psi \otimes \Psi_P \blacktriangleright Q \xrightarrow{N \rhd l} Q' \quad \Psi \otimes \Psi_P \otimes \Psi_Q \models M \leftrightarrow N
}{
\Psi \blacktriangleright P \mid Q \xrightarrow{\tau@(M \lhd l \rhd N)} P' \mid Q'
}
$$

(RES-COM)
$$
\dfrac{
\Psi \blacktriangleright P \xrightarrow{(\nu\widetilde{a})\tau@(\nu\widetilde{b})(MNK)} P'
}{
\Psi \blacktriangleright (\nu a)P \xrightarrow{(\nu\widetilde{a}\cup a)\tau@(\nu\widetilde{b})(MNK)} (\nu a)P'
}
\qquad
\begin{array}{l}
a \mathbin{\sharp} \widetilde{a}, \widetilde{b} \\[4pt]
a \in \mathrm{n}(M) \cup \mathrm{n}(N) \cup \mathrm{n}(K)
\end{array}
$$

(RES-CHOOSE)
$$
\dfrac{
\Psi \blacktriangleright P \xrightarrow{(\nu\widetilde{a})\tau@(M \lhd l \rhd K)} P'
}{
\Psi \blacktriangleright (\nu a)P \xrightarrow{(\nu\widetilde{a}\cup a)\tau@(M \lhd l \rhd K)} (\nu a)P'
}
\qquad
\begin{array}{l}
a \mathbin{\sharp} \widetilde{a} \\[4pt]
a \in \mathrm{n}(M) \cup \mathrm{n}(K)
\end{array}
$$

Types may contain free names. A type with free names $\widetilde{x}$ is denoted $T(\widetilde{x})$, while a type with names instantiated by the terms $\widetilde{M}$ is denoted $T[\widetilde{M}]$.

We assume an additive structure on types [17].

Definition 1 (Type structure [17]). *A type structure is a triple $(\mathbb{T}, +, \doteq)$ where $\mathbb{T}$ is a set of types, $+$ is a partial binary operation on $\mathbb{T}$ and $\doteq$ is a partial equivalence relation on $\mathbb{T}$ such that $T_1 + T_2 \doteq T_2 + T_1$ and $(T_1 + T_2) + T_3 \doteq T_1 + (T_2 + T_3)$ for all $T_1, T_2, T_3 \in \mathbb{T}$.*

We say that an endpoint type T_E is *unlimited* if $T_E = T_E + T_E$ and assume the existence of a type end; this is the type of a completed session. Following [14], we also assume that the additive structure on types satisfies the axioms

$$(T_1, T_2) \doteq (T_1, T_2) + (\mathrm{end}, \mathrm{end}) \quad \text{if } T_1, T_2 \text{ are not unlimited} \tag{1}$$

$$(T_1, T_2) \doteq T_1 + T_2 \tag{2}$$

In all other cases, summation of session types is undefined.

The summation axiom (2) ensures that a session type can be split into its two endpoints, as will be clear from the type rule for parallel composition. Note that, because of the axiom (2) and the commutativity requirement for structures, we identify the session types (T_1, T_2) and (T_2, T_1).

Definition 2. *Let T_1 and T_2 be types. We write $T_1 \leq T_2$ if either $T_1 = T_2$ or for some T we have $T_1 + T = T_2$. We write $T_1 \leq_{\min} T_2$ if T_1 is a least type T such that $T \leq T_2$.*

Note that the least type defined above need not be unique.

Transitions for Types. We assume a deterministic labelled transition relation defined on the set of endpoint types. Transitions are of the form $T_E \xrightarrow{\lambda} T'$ where

$$\lambda ::= \; !T_1 \mid ?T_1 \mid \triangleleft l \mid \triangleright l$$

If a channel has endpoint type T_E with a transition $T_E \xrightarrow{?T_1} T_E'$, then following an input of a term of type T_1, the channel will now have endpoint type T_E'. For a given type language, we must give transition rules that describe how these transitions arise. The type end has no transitions.

We assume a *duality condition* for labels in labelled type transitions; we define $\overline{!T_1} = ?T_2$ and $\overline{\triangleleft l} = \triangleright l$ and vice versa, and we require that $\overline{\overline{\lambda}} = \lambda$.

We assume an involution $\overline{T}$ on endpoint types. For base types (ranged over by B), duality is not defined. For transitions we require that $T_E \xrightarrow{\lambda} T_E' \iff \overline{T_E} \xrightarrow{\overline{\lambda}} \overline{T_E'}$. Since an unlimited type T satisfies that $T = T + T$, any type of this kind is only allowed to have labelled transitions leading back to itself. That is, if T is unlimited, then whenever $T \xrightarrow{\lambda} T'$ for some λ we require $T' = T$. A session type is balanced if the types of its endpoint are dual to each other.

Definition 3. *A session type S is balanced if $S = (T_E, \overline{T_E})$ for some T_E.*

4.2 Type Environments

A type environment Γ is a finite function from names to types, often written as $\widetilde{x} : \widetilde{T}$. We denote the empty type environment by $\emptyset$. Addition is defined by

Definition 4. *Let Γ_1 and Γ_2 be type environments. The sum of Γ_1 and Γ_2 is defined as the type environment $\Gamma_1 + \Gamma_2$ that is given by*

$$(\Gamma_1 + \Gamma_2)(x) = \begin{cases} \Gamma_1(x) & x \in \mathrm{dom}(\Gamma_1) \setminus \mathrm{dom}(\Gamma_2) \\ \Gamma_2(x) & x \in \mathrm{dom}(\Gamma_2) \setminus \mathrm{dom}(\Gamma_1) \\ \Gamma_1(x) + \Gamma_2(x) & \textit{otherwise, if this sum is defined} \end{cases}$$

We write $\Gamma_1 \leq \Gamma_2$ if there exists a Γ such that $\Gamma_1 + \Gamma = \Gamma_2$.

We write $\Gamma \pm c : T$ to denote $\Gamma + c : T$ if $c \notin \mathrm{dom}(\Gamma)$ and $\Gamma' + c : T$ if $\Gamma = \Gamma' + c : U$ for some type U; this operation is used to denote how the type information for a session constructor c is updated when a session channel built using the session constructor c evolves. If c is already present in Γ, the session behaviour is updated. Otherwise, the behaviour is added to Γ.

A type environment Γ is *balanced* if for every $x \in \mathrm{dom}(\Gamma)$ we have that whenever $\Gamma(x) = S$, then S is balanced. Similarly, Γ is *unlimited* if for every $x \in \mathrm{dom}(\Gamma)$ we have that $\Gamma(x)$ is an unlimited type.

4.3 A Typed Syntax and Its Semantics

From now on we will use a typed syntax for ψ-calculi, where restrictions are of the form $(vx:T)P$ and state that x has type T in P. If P is a process in the untyped syntax with all bound names distinct and Γ is a type environment where $\mathrm{dom}(\Gamma) = \mathrm{bn}(P)$, then P_Γ is the corresponding typed process which has been annotated according to the bindings in Γ. If P_1 and P_2 are typed processes, we write $P_1 \stackrel{\circ}{=} P_2$ if P_1 and P_2 differ only in their type annotations for bound names, i.e. for some P and Γ_1, Γ_2 where $\mathrm{dom}(\Gamma_{P_1}) = \mathrm{dom}(\Gamma_{P_2})$ we have $P_1 = P_{\Gamma_1}$ and $P_2 = P_{\Gamma_2}$.

We extend the semantics to the typed case as follows. For a typed process P we write $\Psi \blacktriangleright P \xrightarrow{\alpha} P'$ if there exists a type environment Γ such that $P = \overline{P}_\Gamma$ where $\overline{P}$ is an untyped process and $\Psi \blacktriangleright \overline{P} \xrightarrow{\alpha} \overline{P'}$ where $P' = \overline{P'}_{\Gamma'}$ for some Γ'. When no confusion arises, we say that a typed transition follows from a given transition rule in the untyped semantics if the corresponding untyped transition was concluded using this rule.

Note that in this typed interpretation we can have that $\Psi \blacktriangleright P \xrightarrow{\alpha} P'$ for more than one P' for any given α, since there can be several different type annotations of the result of a transition in the untyped semantics. All our results on type preservation are therefore stated up to $\stackrel{\circ}{=}$ and must be read as saying that *there exists a type annotation* such that the conclusion holds. We therefore write $\Gamma, \Psi \vdash^{\stackrel{\circ}{=}} P$ if there exists a P_1 where $P_1 \stackrel{\circ}{=} P$ such that $\Gamma, \Psi \vdash P_1$.

5   Type Judgements in the Generic Type System

Since the type system is generic, some parts of the type system depend on the specific psi-calculus instance under consideration. The type rules for processes are common to all instances, since the syntax for processes is always the same. On the other hand, the structure and interpretation of terms, patterns, assertions, and conditions is specific to each psi-calculus instance and must be defined separately. In the following sections we describe the requirements that any such instance of the type system must follow.

The type judgements in any instance of the system are of the form $\Gamma, \Psi \vdash \mathscr{J}$ where $\mathscr{J}$ is built using the formation rules

$$\mathscr{J} ::= M : T \mid X : \widetilde{T} \to U \mid \Psi \mid \varphi \mid P$$

Type judgments must satisfy the standard well-formedness requirement: whenever free names occur, their types must be declared in the type environment. More specifically, we require that judgements $\Gamma, \Psi \vdash \mathscr{J}$ must always be *well-formed*, i.e. that $\mathrm{fn}(\mathscr{J}) \subseteq \mathrm{dom}(\Gamma)$, and that the environment-assertion pair Γ, Ψ must be similarly well-formed, i.e. that $\mathrm{fn}(\Psi) \subseteq \mathrm{dom}(\Gamma)$.

In order for our generic type system to be safe, we must keep track of the resources used in communication and selections to ensure that they are only those needed. We capture this by requiring certain judgements to be *minimal*.

Definition 5. *We write $\Gamma, \Psi \vdash_{\mathrm{min}} \mathscr{J}$ if $\Gamma, \Psi \vdash \mathscr{J}$ and for every $\Gamma' < \Gamma$ and $\Psi' < \Psi$ we have $\Gamma', \Psi' \nvdash \mathscr{J}$.*

We require minimality to be unique up to assertion equivalence.

Requirement 1. *If $\Gamma_1, \Psi_1 \vdash_{\mathrm{min}} \mathscr{J}$ and $\Gamma_2, \Psi_2 \vdash_{\mathrm{min}} \mathscr{J}$ then $\Gamma_1 = \Gamma_2$ and $\Psi_1 \simeq \Psi_2$.*

5.1 Typing Session Channels

Since arbitrary terms can be used as session channels as long as they contain session constructors, we need a special notation for describing that a term is a well-typed session channel. We write $\Gamma, \Psi \vdash M : T @ c$ if the term M has type T when using session constructor c. The rules defining this judgement depend on the instance of the type system but we require that the session constructor must have an endpoint type for the resulting channel to be typeable.

Requirement 2. *If* $\Gamma, \Psi \vdash M : T @ c$ *then* $\Gamma(c) = T_E$ *for some endpoint type* T_E.

5.2 Typing Patterns

For patterns, judgments are of the form

$$\Gamma, \Psi \vdash X : \widetilde{T} \to U$$

The intended interpretation is that the pattern X has type $\widetilde{T} \to U$ if the pattern variables will be bound to terms of types $\widetilde{T}$ whenever the pattern matches a term of type U.

In our treatment of typing patterns we again appeal to the matching predicate. The type rules for patterns must be defined for each instance. However, we require the following application rule which says that if a term N matches a pattern of type $\widetilde{T} \to U$, binding the pattern variables to terms of types $\widetilde{T}$, then N must be of type U.

$$(\text{APP}) \quad \frac{\Gamma, \Psi' \vdash X : \widetilde{T} \to U \quad \widetilde{L} \in \text{MATCH}(N, \widetilde{x}, X) \qquad \Gamma_i, \Psi_i \vdash L_i : T_i \text{ for } 1 \leq i \leq |\widetilde{T}|}{\Gamma + \Sigma_{i=1}^{|\widetilde{T}|} \Gamma_i, \Psi \vdash N : U} \quad \text{where } \Psi = \Psi' \otimes \bigotimes_{1 \leq i \leq |\widetilde{T}|} \Psi_i$$

Moreover, the type rules must satisfy the converse requirement: If a term M matches a pattern X, then all subterms $\widetilde{N}$ that instantiate the pattern variables will have the types required by the type of X. Moreover, the type environments and assertions required to type these subterms are exactly those needed to type the corresponding parts of M.

Requirement 3. *Suppose* $\widetilde{N} \in \text{MATCH}(M, \widetilde{x}, X)$ *and* $\Gamma_1 + \widetilde{x} : \widetilde{T}, \Psi_1 \vdash_{\min} X : \widetilde{T} \to U$. *Then there exist* Γ_{2i}, Ψ_{2i} *such that* $\Gamma_{2i}, \Psi_{2i} \vdash_{\min} N_i : T_i$ *for all* $1 \leq i \leq |\widetilde{x}| = n$.

5.3 Type Rules for Terms, Assertions and Conditions

The sets of terms, assertions and conditions are specific to each psi-calculus instance, so the type rules are also specific for the instance.

The type rules for terms must always satisfy the requirement that equivalent channels either have the same session type (in which case the channels are session channels) or dual endpoint types (in which case the channels are the two endpoints of the same session channel).

Requirement 4. *If* $\Psi \models M \leftrightarrow K$ *and* $\Gamma, \Psi \vdash M : S$ *then* $\Gamma, \Psi \vdash K : S$. *If* $\Psi \models M \leftrightarrow K$ *and* $\Gamma, \Psi \vdash M : T$ *then* $\Gamma, \Psi \vdash K : \overline{T}$.

The unit assertion must be typeable using no assumptions, i.e. we must have $\emptyset, \mathbf{1} \vdash \mathbf{1}$.

5.4   Type Rules for Processes

Type judgements for processes are of the form $\Gamma, \Psi \vdash P$, where Ψ is an assertion. Table 3 contains the type rules for processes. In the type rules, and notably in (PAR), we use a typed notion of frames for processes; the *qualified frame* of a process P is still denoted $\mathscr{F}(P)$ but is now a pair $\langle \Gamma_P, \Psi_P \rangle$, where Ψ_P is the composition of assertions in P and Γ_P records the types of the names local to Ψ_P. We define this as follows

$$\mathscr{F}(P \mid Q) = \langle \Gamma_P + \Gamma_Q, \Psi_P \otimes \Psi_Q \rangle$$
$$\text{where } \mathscr{F}(P) = \langle \Gamma_P, \Psi_P \rangle, \mathscr{F}(Q) = \langle \Gamma_Q, \Psi_Q \rangle$$
$$\mathscr{F}((vb:T)P) = \langle b:T + \Gamma_P, \Psi_P \rangle \text{ where } \mathscr{F}(P) = (\Gamma_P, \Psi_P)$$
$$\mathscr{F}((\lvert \Psi \rvert)) = \langle \emptyset, \Psi \rangle$$
$$\mathscr{F}(P) = \langle \emptyset, \mathbf{1} \rangle \quad \text{otherwise}$$

For patterns, judgments are of the form $\Gamma, \Psi \vdash X : \widetilde{T} \to U$. The intended interpretation is that pattern X has type $\widetilde{T} \to U$ if the pattern variables are bound to terms of types $\widetilde{T}$ whenever the pattern matches a term of type U. An important rule is (PAR); the type addition axiom (2) enables us to split a session type into two endpoint types, one for each parallel component; this follows Giunti and Vasconcelos [14].

The type rules for input and output generalize those of usual session type systems such as [14]. In particular, the subject and the object of the prefix are typed in separate subenvironments and the type of the subject is updated when typing the continuation. As subjects in the psi-calculus setting can be arbitrary terms, one cannot simply update the session type of a channel by updating the type bound to the channel in the type environment. Instead, we update the type of the channel constructor used to construct the channel.

6   A Type Preservation Theorem

We now establish a fidelity result that will ensure that whenever a process P is well-typed in a balanced environment, then in any τ-transition that is the result of a communication or selection on a session channel constructed using session constructor c, the resulting process will also be well-typed in a balanced environment – only now the type of c has evolved according to the protocol specified by the session type.

The *direction* of a visible action α in the labelled semantics is either ! or ? for a communication and $\lhd$ or $\rhd$ for a selection; we denote this by $d(\alpha)$.

Definition 6 (Well-typed label). *Let α be a label. We call $(\alpha, (T, U))$ a typed label if U is either a type or $\bullet$. We define $\Gamma, \Psi \vdash \alpha : (T@c, U)$ as follows:*

1. *If $\Gamma_1, \Psi_1 \vdash M : T@c$ and $\Gamma_2 + \widetilde{a} : \widetilde{T}, \Psi_2 \vdash N : U$ and $T \xrightarrow{!U} T'$ then $\Gamma_1 + \Gamma_2, \Psi_1 \otimes \Psi_2 \vdash \overline{M}(v\widetilde{a})N : (T@c, U)$.*

2. *if $\Gamma_1, \Psi_1 \vdash K : T@c$ and $\Gamma_2, \Psi_2 \vdash N : U$ and $T \xrightarrow{?U} T'$ then $\Gamma_1 + \Gamma_2, \Psi_1 \otimes \Psi_2 \vdash \underline{K}N : (T@c, U)$.*

3. *If $\Gamma, \Psi \vdash M : T@c$ and $T \xrightarrow{\lhd, l} T'$ then $\Gamma, \Psi \vdash M \lhd l : (T@c, \bullet)$.*

Table 3. Psi-calculus type rules

(OUTPUT)
$$\frac{\Gamma_1, \Psi_1 \vdash_{\min} M : T_1 @ c \quad T_1 \xrightarrow{!T_2} T_3 \quad \Gamma_2, \Psi_2 \vdash_{\min} N : T_2 \quad \Gamma_3 \pm c : T_3, \Psi_3 \vdash P}{\Gamma_1 + \Gamma_2 + \Gamma_3, \Psi_1 \otimes \Psi_2 \otimes \Psi_3 \vdash \overline{M}N.P}$$

(INPUT)
$$\frac{\Gamma_1, \Psi_1 \vdash_{\min} M : T_1 @ c \quad T_1 \xrightarrow{?T_2} T_3(\tilde{x}) \quad \Gamma_2, \Psi_2 \vdash_{\min} X : \tilde{U} \to T_2 \quad \Gamma_3 + \tilde{x} : \tilde{U} \pm c : T_3[\tilde{x}], \Psi_3 \vdash P}{\Gamma_1 + \Gamma_2 + \Gamma_3, \Psi_1 \otimes \Psi_2 \otimes \Psi_3 \vdash \underline{M}(\lambda \tilde{x})X.P} \quad \begin{array}{l} \tilde{x} \,\natural\, \text{dom}(\Gamma_1 + \Gamma_2 + \Gamma_3) \\[4pt] \tilde{x} \,\natural\, \Psi_1 \otimes \Psi_2 \otimes \Psi_3 \end{array}$$

(SELECT)
$$\frac{\Gamma_1, \Psi_1 \vdash_{\min} M : T @ c \quad \Gamma_2 \pm c : T_i, \Psi_2 \vdash P \quad T \xrightarrow{\lhd l_i} T_i}{\Gamma_1 + \Gamma_2, \Psi_1 \otimes \Psi_2 \vdash M \lhd l_i.P}$$

(BRANCH)
$$\frac{\Gamma_1, \Psi_1 \vdash_{\min} M : T @ c \quad T \xrightarrow{\rhd l_i} T_i \text{ and } \Gamma_2 \pm c : T_i, \Psi_{2i} \vdash P_i \text{ for } 1 \leq i \leq k}{\Gamma_1 + \Gamma_2, \Psi_1 \otimes \bigotimes_{i=1}^{k} \Psi_{2i} \vdash M \rhd \{l_1 : P_1, \ldots, l_k : P_k\}}$$

(CASE)
$$\frac{\Gamma, \Psi \vdash \varphi_i \quad \Gamma, \Psi \vdash P_i \quad 1 \leq i \leq k}{\Gamma, \Psi \vdash \mathbf{case} \ \varphi_1 : P_1, \ldots, \varphi_k : P_k}$$

(PAR)
$$\frac{\Gamma_1 + \Gamma'_{P_2}, \Psi'_1 \otimes \Psi'_{P_2} \vdash P_1 \quad \Gamma_2 + \Gamma'_{P_1}, \Psi'_2 \otimes \Psi'_{P_1} \vdash P_2}{\Gamma, \Psi \vdash P_1 \mid P_2}$$

where
$$\Gamma = \Gamma_1 + \Gamma_2 \text{ and } \Psi = \Psi_1 \otimes \Psi_2$$
$$\Psi'_1 \leq \Psi_1 \text{ and } \Psi'_2 \leq \Psi_2$$
$$\Psi'_{P_1} \leq \Psi_{P_1} \text{ and } \Psi'_{P_2} \leq \Psi_{P_2}$$
$$\Gamma'_{P_1} \leq \Gamma_1 \text{ and } \Gamma'_{P_2} \leq \Gamma_2$$

(SESSION)
$$\frac{\Gamma + x : T, \Psi \vdash P}{\Gamma, \Psi \vdash (\nu x : T)P} \quad x \,\natural\, \Gamma, \Psi$$

(BANG)
$$\frac{\Gamma, \Psi \vdash P}{\Gamma, \Psi \vdash !P} \quad \Gamma, \Psi \text{ unlimited}$$

(ASSERT)
$$\frac{\Gamma, \Psi \vdash \Psi_1}{\Gamma, \Psi \vdash (\!|\Psi_1|\!)}$$

4. If $\Gamma, \Psi \vdash M : T @ c$ and $T \xrightarrow{\rhd, l} T'$ then $\Gamma, \Psi \vdash M \rhd l : (T @ c, \bullet)$.
5. If $\Gamma_1, \Psi_1, \tilde{b}_1 : \tilde{V}_1 \vdash \overline{M}(\nu \tilde{a})N : (T @ c, U)$ and $\Gamma_2, \Psi_2, \tilde{b}_2 : \tilde{V}_2, \tilde{a} : \tilde{V}_3 \vdash \underline{K}N : (\overline{T @ c}, U)$ then $\Gamma_1 + \Gamma_2, \Psi_1 \otimes \Psi_2 \vdash (\nu \tilde{b}_1 \cup \tilde{b}_2)\tau @ (\nu \tilde{a})(\overline{M} \ N \ \underline{K}) : (T @ c, U)$.
6. If $\Gamma_1 + \Gamma_{11}, \Psi_1 \vdash M \lhd l : (T @ c, \bullet)$ and $\Gamma_2 + \Gamma_{12}, \Psi_2 \vdash K \rhd l : (\overline{T @ c}, \bullet)$ then $\Gamma_1 + \Gamma_2, \Psi_1 \otimes \Psi_2 \vdash \tau @ (\nu \tilde{a})(M \lhd l \rhd K) : (T @ c, \bullet)$, where $\Gamma_{11} + \Gamma_{12} = \tilde{a} : \tilde{T}$.

We write $\Gamma, \Psi \vdash_{\min} \alpha : (T @ c, U)$ if the type judgements involved in the above are all minimal.

For our result, we define session updates for τ-labels. The idea behind the definition is that the behaviour of the session constructor should be updated in the type environment if the τ-label was due to a communication created by a free session constructor. Otherwise, the behaviour is not mentioned in the type environment and not modified.

Definition 7 (Update for unobservable labels). *Let* Γ_1, Γ *be type environments with* $\Gamma_1 \leq \Gamma$. *Then*

1. *If* $\Gamma_1, \Psi_1 \vdash (v\widetilde{a})\tau @ (v\widetilde{b})(\overline{M} \, N \, \underline{K}) : (T @ c, T_1)$ *and* $\Gamma = \Gamma' + c : (T', T'')$ *with* $c \notin \widetilde{b} \cup \mathrm{dom}(\Gamma')$ *and* $T' \xrightarrow{!T_1} T_1'$ *and* $T'' \xrightarrow{?T_1} T_2''$, *we let*

$$\Gamma \pm (v\widetilde{a})\tau @ (v\widetilde{b})(\overline{M} \, N \, \underline{K} : (T @ c, T_1)) \overset{\mathrm{def}}{=} \Gamma' + c : (T_1', T_2'')$$

2. *If* $\Gamma_1, \Psi_1 \vdash \tau @ (v\widetilde{a})(M \lhd l \rhd K) : (T @ c, \bullet)$ *and* $\Gamma = \Gamma' + c : (T', T'')$ *with* $c \notin \widetilde{a}, \mathrm{dom}(\Gamma')$ *and* $T' \xrightarrow{\lhd, l} T_1'$ *and* $T'' \xrightarrow{\rhd, l} T_2''$, *we let*

$$\Gamma \pm \tau @ (v\widetilde{a})(M \lhd l \rhd K) : (T @ c, \bullet) \overset{\mathrm{def}}{=} \Gamma' + c : (T_1', T_2'')$$

Lemma 8 (Well-typed observable actions). *Suppose we have* $\Psi_0 \blacktriangleright P \xrightarrow{\alpha} P'$ *and that* $\Gamma, \Psi \vdash P$ *with* $\Psi \leq \Psi_0$. *Then*

1. *If* $\alpha = M \lhd l$ *there exists a* $\Gamma' \leq \Gamma$ *and a* $\Psi' \leq \Psi$ *such that* $\Gamma', \Psi' \vdash_{\min} \alpha : (T_1 @ c, T_2)$
2. *If* $\alpha = M \rhd l$ *there exists a* $\Gamma' \leq \Gamma$ *and a* $\Psi' \leq \Psi$ *such that* $\Gamma', \Psi' \vdash_{\min} \alpha : (T_1 @ c, T_2)$
3. *If* $\alpha = \overline{M}(v\widetilde{a})N$ *there exists a* $\Gamma' \leq \Gamma$, *a* $\Gamma_P' \leq \Gamma_P$ *and a* $\Psi' \leq \Psi$ *such that* $\Gamma' + \Gamma_P', \Psi' \vdash_{\min} \alpha : (T_1 @ c, T_2)$. *Moreover,* $\mathrm{dom}(\Gamma_P') = \widetilde{a}$.
4. *If* $\alpha = KN$ *there exists a* $\Gamma' \leq \Gamma$ *and a* $\Psi' \leq \Psi$, *a* Γ'' *and a* Ψ'' *such that* $\Gamma' + \Gamma'', \Psi' \otimes \Psi'' \vdash_{\min} \alpha : (T_1 @ c, T_2)$ *with* $\Gamma', \Psi' \vdash_{\min} K : T_1 @ c$ *and* $\Gamma'', \Psi'' \vdash_{\min} N : T_2$.

We can now show that all τ-transitions have a well-typed label. If P is well-typed in a balanced type environment Γ and all type annotations of local names in P are balanced, we write $\Gamma, \Psi \vdash_{\mathrm{bal}} P$,

Note that for τ-labels, the subject types involved have to be dual to each other for the label to be well-typed.

Theorem 9 (Well-typed τ-actions). *Suppose we have* $\Psi_0 \blacktriangleright P \xrightarrow{\alpha} P'$, *where* α *is a* τ-action and that $\Gamma, \Psi \vdash_{\mathrm{bal}} P$ *and* $\Psi \leq \Psi_0$. *Then for some* $\Psi' \leq \Psi$ *and* $\Gamma' \leq \Gamma$ *we have* $\Gamma', \Psi' \vdash_{\min} \alpha : (T @ c, U)$.

If $\Gamma, \Psi \vdash_{\mathrm{bal}} P$ and P performs an internal move to P', the fidelity theorem tells us that P' is also well-typed wrt. a balanced type environment in which the types of the session name involved in the action have evolved according to its protocol.

Theorem 10 (Fidelity). *Suppose we have* $\Psi_0 \blacktriangleright P \xrightarrow{\alpha} P'$, *where* α *is a* τ-action and that $\Gamma, \Psi \vdash_{\mathrm{bal}} P$. *Then for some* $\Gamma' \leq \Gamma$ *and for some* $\Psi' \leq \Psi$ *we have* $\Gamma', \Psi' \vdash_{\min} \alpha : (T @ c, U)$ *and* $\Gamma \pm (\alpha, (T @ c, U)), \Psi' \vdash_{\mathrm{bal}} \overset{\circ}{=} P'$.

Proof. (Outline) By Theorem 9, we know that the label α is minimally well-typed; that is, we have $\Gamma', \Psi' \vdash_{\min} \alpha : (T @ c, U)$ for some $\Gamma' \leq \Gamma, \Psi' \leq \Psi$. The rest of the proof now proceeds by induction in the proof tree for the transition $\Psi_0 \blacktriangleright P \xrightarrow{\alpha} P'$.

7 Instances of the Type System

In this section we describe how existing binary session type systems can be captured within our generic type system. For each instance we represent the process calculus used in the original type system as a psi-calculus and then define the *sets of types*, the *transition rules for session types* and the addition operation on session types. We must then supply type rules for terms, assertions and conditions.

For every existing type system with a typability relation $\vdash'$ we describe a translation $\llbracket \cdot \rrbracket$ of the original type judgements $\Gamma \vdash' P$ into our generic system such that we have

$$\Gamma \vdash' P \iff \llbracket \Gamma \vdash' P \rrbracket$$

In each case we show that the type rules for processes in the definition of $\vdash'$ are instances of our generic type rules for processes together with the new type rules for terms, assertions and conditions for the instance.

7.1 Gay-Hole Sessions

The session type system due to Gay and Hole [13] introduces recursive types and subtyping for a π-calculus; the two ends of a channel c are distinct names, c^+ and c^-. Session types are given by the formation rules

$$S ::= X \mid \text{end} \mid ?T_1.T_2 \mid !T_1.T_2 \mid \&\langle l_1 : S_1, \ldots, l_k : S_k \rangle \mid \oplus\langle l_1 : S_1, \ldots, l_k : S_k \rangle \mid \mu X.S$$

and endpoint types by the formation rules

$$T ::= X \mid S \mid \mu X.T \mid B$$

Base types B are self-dual. For session types we have

$$\overline{\text{end}} \stackrel{\text{def}}{=} \text{end} \qquad\qquad \overline{?T_1.T_2} \stackrel{\text{def}}{=} !T_1.\overline{T_2}$$

$$\overline{!T_1.T_2} \stackrel{\text{def}}{=} ?T_1.\overline{T_2} \qquad\qquad \overline{\&\langle l_1 : S_1, \ldots, l_k : S_k \rangle} \stackrel{\text{def}}{=} \oplus\langle l_1 : \overline{S_1}, \ldots, l_k : \overline{S_k} \rangle$$

$$\overline{\oplus\langle l_1 : S_1, \ldots, l_k : S_k \rangle} \stackrel{\text{def}}{=} \&\langle l_1 : \overline{S_1}, \ldots, l_k : \overline{S_k} \rangle \qquad\qquad \overline{\mu X.S} \stackrel{\text{def}}{=} \mu X.\overline{S}$$

In our representation $\llbracket \rrbracket$ of the π-calculus used by [13] as a psi-calculus we represent restriction $(vc^+, c^- : T)P$ as $(vc : (T, \overline{T}))\llbracket P \rrbracket$ and define addition by $(T, \overline{T}) = T + \overline{T}$. The transition rules for Gay-Hole session types include the following.

$$\text{(S-IN)} \qquad ?T_1.T_2 \xrightarrow{?T_1} T_2 \qquad\qquad \text{(S-OUT)} \qquad !T_1.T_2 \xrightarrow{!T_1} T_2$$

$$\text{(S-BRANCH) } \&\langle l_1 : S_1, \ldots, l_k : S_k \rangle \xrightarrow{\triangleright l_i} S_i \quad \text{(S-SELECT) } \otimes\langle l_1 : S_1, \ldots, l_k : S_k \rangle \xrightarrow{\triangleleft l_i} S_i$$

The corresponding psi-calculus has terms that are names and uses names to which a session constructor has been applied to create the endpoint of a session channel. To this end we introduce two unit new terms $+$ and $-$ and let c be a unary term constructor. We then represent $(vc^+, c^- : T)P$ as $(vc : (\text{Unit} \to T, \text{Unit} \to \overline{T}))P$. The names c^+ and c^- correspond to $c(+)$ and $c(-)$, respectively.

A crucial notion of the type system is that of subtyping. Using our notion of type transitions we can capture this as follows by a coinductive definition.

Definition 11. *A* type simulation *is a binary relation R on types which satisfies that whenever* $(T,U) \in R$ *we have*

1. *If* $T \xrightarrow{!T_1} T_2$ *then* $U \xrightarrow{!U_1} U_2$ *with* $(U_1, T_1) \in R$ *and* $(T_2, U_2) \in R$
2. *If* $T \xrightarrow{?T_1} T_2$ *then* $U \xrightarrow{?U_1} U_2$ *with* $(T_1, U_1) \in R$ *and* $(T_2, U_2) \in R$
3. *If* $U \xrightarrow{\lhd k} U_1$ *then* $T \xrightarrow{\lhd k} T_1$ *with* $(T_1, U_1) \in R$
4. *If* $T \xrightarrow{\rhd k} T_1$ *then* $U \xrightarrow{\rhd k} U_1$ *with* $(T_1, U_1) \in R$

If $(T,U) \in R$ *for some type simulation R we write* $T \leq U$.

The type rules for typing session channels are given below. We only have one assertion **1**, and let $\mathbf{1} \models a \leftrightarrow a$ and $\mathbf{1} \models c(+) \leftrightarrow c(-)$.

$$(\text{SUBSUME}) \quad \frac{\Gamma, \Psi \vdash M : T \quad T \leq T'}{\Gamma, \Psi \vdash M : T'}$$

$$(\text{LOOKUP}) \quad \Gamma, \Psi \vdash n : T \qquad\qquad \text{if } \Gamma(n) = T$$
$$(\text{SESSION+}) \ \Gamma, \Psi \vdash c(+) : T@c \qquad \text{if } \Gamma(c) = \text{Unit} \to T$$
$$(\text{SESSION-}) \ \Gamma, \Psi \vdash c(-) : \overline{T}@c \qquad \text{if } \Gamma(c) = \text{Unit} \to \overline{T}$$

7.2 A Type System for Progress

The type system by Vieira and Vasconcelos [24] captures a liveness property, namely *progress* in a π-calculus: in any session, every communication requesting an input eventually takes part in a synchronization.

Session types T are annotated with events e and multiplicities linear (lin) and shared (un); p denotes polarities and τ describes a synchronization pair.

$$p ::= ! \mid ? \mid \tau \qquad L ::= \text{end} \mid e \,\text{lin}\, p\, T.L \qquad T ::= L \mid e \,\text{un}\, p\, T$$

Type judgements are of the form $\Gamma, \prec \vdash P$ where Γ is a type environment and $\prec$ a strict partial order (spo) on events. Disjoint union of spo's is denoted by $\uplus$ and is only defined when the ordinary union would not introduce cycles in the resulting relation. The spo formed by adding e as new least element to the spo $\prec$ is denoted $e + \prec$. The support $supp(\prec)$ is the set of events occurring in $\prec$. We use $T \downarrow$ to define the sequence of events that occur along the session type T:

$$T \downarrow \overset{\text{def}}{=} \begin{cases} e + (L \downarrow) & \text{if } T = e \,\text{lin}\, p/T_1.L \\ \{(\text{end}, \top)\} & \text{if } T = \text{end} \\ \{(e, \top)\} & \text{if } T = e \,\text{un}\, p\, T_1 \end{cases}$$

A type is matched if it does not contain pending outputs, and we then write matched(T).

When typing a parallel composition, the type environment is split into subenvironments for each parallel component. Two of the rules for splitting types are

$$\frac{L = L_1 \circ L_2}{e \,\text{lin}\, \tau T.L = e \,\text{lin}\, !T.L_1 \circ e \,\text{lin}\, ?T.L_2} \qquad e \,\text{un}\, !T = e \,\text{un}\, !T \circ e \,\text{un}\, !T$$

Thus, a linear synchronized pair can be split into an input type and an output type, while any unlimited output type can be split into arbitrarily many copies.

Two of the type rules are shown below; Γ_{end} denotes any type environment Γ where $\Gamma(x) = \text{end}$ for all $x \in \text{dom}(\Gamma)$.

$$\Gamma_{end}; \{(\text{end}, \bot)\} \vdash \mathbf{0}$$

$$\frac{\Gamma, x:L, y:T; \prec\, \vdash P \quad e \notin supp(\prec)}{\Gamma, x: e\,\text{lin}\,?T.L; e+\, \prec\, \vdash x(y).P}$$

In the representation in our generic type system, names become nullary session constructors: for any name c in the original type system we have that if c has type T, the corresponding c in the representation has type $T@c$. We use events with polarities e^+ and e^- to describe how events are associated with outputs and inputs, respectively, at channel endpoints.

The formation rules for *types* are now

$$L ::= \text{end} \mid e^+ \text{lin}\,!T.L \mid e^- \text{lin}\,?T.L$$
$$T ::= L \mid e^+ \text{un}!T \mid e^- \text{un}?T \mid e\,\text{un}?T \mid e\,\text{un}!T \mid e\,\text{lin}\,T.L$$

The sum operator for types is defined by

$$e^+ \text{lin}\,!T.L_1 + e^- \text{lin}\,?T.L_2 = e\,\text{lin}\,T.L \quad \text{where}\, L = L_1 + L_2$$

The transition relation for types is defined as follows.

$$e^+ \text{lin}\,!T.L \xrightarrow{!T} L \qquad\qquad e^- \text{lin}\,?T.L \xrightarrow{?T} L$$
$$e^+ \text{un}!T \xrightarrow{!T} e^+ \text{un}!T \qquad\qquad e^- \text{un}?T \xrightarrow{?T} e^- \text{un}?T$$

We use assertions to represent strict partial orders and to guide the application of the prefix type rules. The formation rules for assertions are (where $k \geq 0$)

$$\Psi ::= \text{un}\,x\{x_1,\ldots,x_n\}(e^+,T) \mid \text{lin}\,x\{x_1,\ldots,x_n\}(e^+,T) \mid \text{un}\,x\{x_1,\ldots,x_n\}e$$
$$\mid \text{lin}\{x_1,\ldots,x_n\}e \mid \{x_1,\ldots,x_k\} \prec \mid \mathbf{0} \mid \text{matched}(T)$$
$$\prec ::= \{(e_1^1,e_1^2),\ldots,(e_k^1,e_k^2)\} \mid (\text{end},\bot)$$

The assertion (e^+,T) denotes an event as used for typing an output. This is used to ensure that assertion composition is well-defined wrt. the side conditions in the type rules. The assertion $\text{un}\,x\{x_1,\ldots,x_k\}(e^+,T)$ records the set of names $\{x_1,\ldots,x_k\}$ that have already been used as shared channels and requires that the behaviour of the name x that is now to be used as a shared channel must be typed in a type environment in which every names have the following properties: It must be a shared channel, must use event e, must communicate content of type T and cannot be one of the names in $\{x_1,\ldots,x_k\}$. The matched(T) predicate in the type rule for restriction corresponds to a new assertion matched(T).

Composition is defined by a collection of axioms; these include

$$\text{lin } x\{x_1,\ldots,x_k\}e \otimes \{x,x_1,\ldots,x_k\} \prec = \{x_1,\ldots,x_k\}(e+\prec) \quad \text{if } e \notin \prec$$
$$\{x_1,\ldots,x_k\} \prec_1 \otimes \{x_1,\ldots,x_k\} \prec_2 = \{x_1,\ldots,x_k\} \prec_1 \cup \prec_2$$

The representation of *processes* is homomorphic except for restriction, where we must add the condition that the type of x must be matched.

$$[\![(vx : T)P]\!] = (vx : T)(\text{matched}(T) \mid [\![P]\!])$$

In the representation of the type system the type judgements of the original system of the form $\Gamma; \prec \vdash P$ appear as judgments $\Gamma; \Psi_\prec \vdash P$ where $\Psi_\prec$ is the assertion that represents the strict partial order $\prec$.

We here show one of the type rules for typing names; note how assertions are used to guide typability together with the generic rule for typing input processes.

$$(\text{LIN-NAME-IN}) \; x : e\,\text{lin}?T.L, \text{lin } x\{x_1,\ldots,x_k\}e \vdash x : e\,\text{lin}?T.L$$

Vieira and Vasconcelos provide transition relations for type environments and for strict partial ordering. Assuming these, they prove

Theorem 12 ([24]). *If* $\Gamma_1; \prec_1 \vdash P_1$ *and* $P_1 \to P_2$ *then* $\Gamma_1; \prec_1 \to \Gamma_2; \prec_2$ *with* $\Gamma_2; \prec_2 \vdash P_2$

This theorem follows directly from Theorem 10 for our generic type system, since our transition relation on types corresponds to that of the original type system and since the transition relation on spo's is captured by the ordering relation $\leq$ on assertions.

The final theorem guarantees progress: a process P that is well-typed in a matched type environment (i.e. a Γ where matched(T) for every $x \in \text{dom}(\Gamma)$, where $\Gamma(x) = T$) and has a communication prefix available (written active(P)), can always perform a communication. However, the progress result

Theorem 13 ([24]). *If* active(P) *and* $\Gamma; \prec \vdash P$ *and* matched(Γ), $P \to P'$ *for some* P'.

must still be established separately since this is a property of the specific instance.

7.3 Refinement Types

In [1], Baltazar et al. describe a π-calculus with refinement types that generalizes the the correspondence type systems introduced by Gordon and Jeffrey [15] and later extended by Fournet et al. to include formulae in a fragment of first-order logic [10].

The idea is to annotate processes with *correspondence assertions* that are formulae from a multiplicative fragment of linear logic. The syntax of the calculus is given by

$$\varphi ::= A(\tilde{v}) \mid \varphi_1 \otimes \varphi_2 \mid 1$$
$$P ::= x(y).P_1 \mid \bar{x}\langle v \rangle.P_1 \mid P_1 \mid P_2 \mid !P \mid 0 \mid (vxy : T)P_1 \mid (\text{assume } \varphi)P \mid \text{assert } \varphi.P$$

The restriction $(vxy : T)P_1$ declares two endpoints of a session channel whose scope is P_1. Values v can be either names x or the null value ().

assert φ and assume φ are the correspondence assertions. In the reduction semantics, an assert φ can only be passed if the assertion φ has been assumed previously:

$$(\text{assume } \varphi)(\text{assert } \varphi.P \mid Q) \rightarrow P \mid Q$$

A process is *safe* if every assertion will be met by an assumption. Only communications involving bound endpoints are allowed. This can be seen from the following reduction rule that also states how endpoint types evolve. Here the q denotes (as in the previous type system) if a type is linear (lin) or unrestricted (un).

$$(vxy : (q!w : T.U))(\overline{x}\langle v\rangle.P \mid y(z).Q \mid R) \rightarrow (vxy : U[v/w])(P \mid Q[v/z] \mid R) \qquad (3)$$

The types in the system are given by the formation rules

$$T ::= \text{unit} \mid \text{end} \mid q\,p \mid \{x : T \mid \varphi\} \mid \alpha \mid \mu\alpha.T$$
$$q ::= \text{lin} \mid \text{un} \qquad p ::= ?x : T_1.T_2 \mid !x : T_1.T_2$$

A session type p is a dependent type; it can be a refinement type $\{x : T \mid \varphi\}$. Types T can be recursive types of the form $\mu\alpha.T$ where α is a recursion variable.

Type environments may contain formulae:

$$\Gamma ::= \cdot \mid \Gamma, x : T \mid \Gamma, \varphi$$

A formula is well-formed in Γ, written $\Gamma \vdash_{wf} \varphi$ if all its variables belong to $\text{dom}(\Gamma)$. A type environment is *unlimited*, written $\text{un}(\Gamma)$ if for every $x \in \text{dom}(\Gamma)$ we have that $\Gamma(x) = \text{un}\,p$ for some p. The splitting rules for type environments Γ are similar to those of the type system for progress and are omitted here.

Two of the most interesting type rules are given below. In (T-REFE) we type a refinement assertion by adding a type assumption for the name in the abstraction type and instantiating it. (T-OUT) is a rule for name-dependent session types. When typing the suffix of a communication, the remaining session type must be instantiated with the name that was communicated.

$$(\text{T-REFE}) \quad \frac{\Gamma_1, x : T, \varphi[x/y], \Gamma_2 \vdash P}{\Gamma_1, x : \{y : T \mid \varphi\}, \Gamma_2 \vdash P}$$

$$(\text{T-OUT}) \quad \frac{\Gamma_1 \vdash x : (q!y : T.U) \quad \Gamma_2 \vdash v : T \quad \Gamma_3 + x : U[v/y] \vdash P}{\Gamma_1 \circ \Gamma_2 \circ \Gamma_3 \vdash \overline{x}\langle v\rangle.P}$$

Most of the representation of the process calculus as a psi-calculus is straightforward. A restriction $(vxy : T)P_1$ introduces two nullary session constructors x and y for which we have that $x \leftrightarrow y$. We represent assume φ's as assertions; to indicate their scope every assertion is associated with a fresh name as follows.

$$[\![(\text{assume } \varphi)P]\!] = (vc)(\varphi@c \mid [\![P]\!])$$

where $c \notin n(P) \cup n(\varphi)$ and define the satisfaction relation as $\varphi@c \models \varphi$ for any c.

We encode an assert φ using the case construct

$$[\![\text{assert } \varphi.P]\!] \overset{\text{def}}{=} \textbf{case } \varphi \; [\![P]\!]$$

Type judgements $\Gamma \vdash P$ are represented as $\Gamma_{\Gamma}, \Psi_{\Gamma} \vdash P$ where Γ_{Γ} is the collection of type bindings in Γ and Ψ_{Γ} is the composition of the assertions in Γ.

The transition relation for types is defined as follows.

$$q\,?x : T_1.T_2 \xrightarrow{\;?T(y)\;} T_2[y/x] \quad \text{for every } y \qquad q\,!x : T_1.T_2 \xrightarrow{\;!T(y)\;} T_2[y/x] \quad \text{for every } y$$

The original type system satisfies the subject reduction property.

Theorem 14 ([1]). *If $\Gamma \vdash P$ and $P \to P'$ then $\Gamma \vdash P'$.*

It may be surprising that this result is captured by Theorem 10. However, Γ only records the types of free names, and names involved in a reduction are bound according to (3). Moreover, for this particular psi-calculus instance, assertions corresponding to formulae do not disappear along a reduction, so the assertions needed to type the resulting component must be identical for it to be well-typed. On the other hand, the safety result for well-typed processes must be established separately.

8   Conclusions and Future Work

In this paper we have presented a generic type system capable of capturing existing session type systems in the setting of psi-calculi. Our type system satisfies a fidelity property that carries over to specific instances that satisfy certain natural requirements.

A crucial aspect of the generic type system is its ability to use assertions to represent concrete instances. Assertions in the original psi-calculus framework were mostly thought of as related to the operational semantics, but the work in this paper demonstrates that assertions provide us with the necessary means of controlling typability.

A challenge is to be able to give a general account of the safety properties considered in the instances studied in this paper, such that the type safety properties of instances follow from a general theorem about well-typed processes. As the generic type system can be instantiated both to type systems for safety properties such as that of [1] and liveness properties such as that of [24], a general theorem of this kind will probably require a classification of the properties of the assertions that can be used in a particular type system instance.

A future goal is to show how to express the linear type system for psi-calculi of [20] in the session type system and vice versa. In the setting of π-calculus, a translation from session types to linear types was hinted at by Kobayashi and later carried out by Dardha et al. [8]. An encoding along these lines will probably take the form of a translation $[\![P]\!]_{\Psi}$ where Ψ is an assertion that 'renames' the channel object to a fresh name.

Further work involves dealing with behavioural type systems in which the types of an arbitrary number of names are modified as the result of performing a labelled transition. This includes the systems for deadlock prevention due to Kobayashi [22].

In the present work, our notion of duality is the original one from [18]. However, other notions of duality have recently been proposed [4] and a natural next step is to capture these in a general setting. If our treatment is extended to a higher-order setting, a new treatment of duality will also be necessary [3].

Acknowledgements. The author would like to thank Johannes Borgström and Björn Victor for useful comments and suggestions. The work was supported by the COST Action IC1021 BETTY.

References

1. Baltazar, P., Mostrous, D., Vasconcelos, V.T.: Linearly refined session types. In: LINEARITY, pp. 38–49 (2012)
2. Bengtson, J., Johansson, M., Parrow, J., Victor, B.: psi-calculi: a framework for mobile processes with nominal data and logic. Logical Methods Comput. Sci. **7**(1) (2011)
3. Bernardi, G., Hennessy, M.: Using higher-order contracts to model session types (Extended Abstract). In: Baldan, P., Gorla, D. (eds.) CONCUR 2014. LNCS, vol. 8704, pp. 387–401. Springer, Heidelberg (2014). doi:10.1007/978-3-662-44584-6_27
4. Bernardi, G., Dardha, O., Gay, S.J., Kouzapas, D.: On duality relations for session types. In: Maffei, M., Tuosto, E. (eds.) TGC 2014. LNCS, vol. 8902, pp. 51–66. Springer, Heidelberg (2014). doi:10.1007/978-3-662-45917-1_4
5. Borgström, J., Gutkovas, R., Parrow, J., Victor, B., Pohjola, J.Å.: A sorted semantic framework for applied process calculi (Extended Abstract). In: Abadi, M., Lluch Lafuente, A. (eds.) TGC 2013. LNCS, vol. 8358, pp. 103–118. Springer, Heidelberg (2014). doi:10.1007/978-3-319-05119-2_7
6. Castagna, G., Dezani-Ciancaglini, M., Giachino, E., Padovani, L.: Foundations of session types. In: PPDP, pp. 219–230. ACM (2009)
7. Castagna, G., Gesbert, N., Padovani, L.: A theory of contracts for web services. ACM Trans. Program. Lang. Syst. **31**(5), 19: 1–19: 61 (2009)
8. Dardha, O., Giachino, E., Sangiorgi, D.: Session types revisited. In: Proceedings of the 14th Symposium on Principles and Practice of Declarative Programming, PPDP 2012, pp. 139–150. ACM, New York (2012)
9. Dezani-Ciancaglini, M., de'Liguoro, U., Yoshida, N.: On progress for structured communications. In: Barthe, G., Fournet, C. (eds.) TGC 2007. LNCS, vol. 4912, pp. 257–275. Springer, Heidelberg (2008). doi:10.1007/978-3-540-78663-4_18
10. Fournet, C., Gordon, A.D., Maffeis, S.: A type discipline for authorization policies. ACM Trans. Program. Lang. Syst., **29**(5) (2007)
11. Gabbay, M.J., Mathijssen, A.: Nominal (universal) algebra: equational logic with names and binding. J. Log. Comput. **19**(6), 1455–1508 (2009)
12. Gay, S.J.: Bounded polymorphism in session types. Math. Struct. Comput. Sci. **18**(5), 895–930 (2008)
13. Gay, S.J., Hole, M.: Subtyping for session types in the pi calculus. Acta Inf. **42**(2–3), 191–225 (2005)
14. Giunti, M., Vasconcelos, V.T.: A linear account of session types in the pi calculus. In: Gastin, P., Laroussinie, F. (eds.) CONCUR 2010. LNCS, vol. 6269, pp. 432–446. Springer, Heidelberg (2010). doi:10.1007/978-3-642-15375-4_30
15. Gordon, A.D., Jeffrey, A.: Authenticity by typing for security protocols. J. Comput. Secur. **11**(4), 451–519 (2003)
16. Honda, K.: Types for dyadic interaction. In: Best, E. (ed.) CONCUR 1993. LNCS, vol. 715, pp. 509–523. Springer, Heidelberg (1993). doi:10.1007/3-540-57208-2_35

17. Honda, K.: Composing processes. In: POPL, pp. 344–357 (1996)
18. Honda, K., Vasconcelos, V.T., Kubo, M.: Language primitives and type discipline for structured communication-based programming. In: Hankin, C. (ed.) ESOP 1998. LNCS, vol. 1381, pp. 122–138. Springer, Heidelberg (1998). doi:10.1007/BFb0053567
19. Hüttel, H.: Typed π-calculi. In: Katoen, J.-P., König, B. (eds.) CONCUR 2011. LNCS, vol. 6901, pp. 265–279. Springer, Heidelberg (2011). doi:10.1007/978-3-642-23217-6_18
20. Hüttel, H.: Types for resources in ψ-calculi. In: Abadi, M., Lluch Lafuente, A. (eds.) TGC 2013. LNCS, vol. 8358, pp. 83–102. Springer, Heidelberg (2014). doi:10.1007/978-3-319-05119-2_6
21. Igarashi, A., Kobayashi, N.: A generic type system for the Pi-calculus. Theoret. Comput. Sci. **311**(1–3), 121–163 (2004)
22. Kobayashi, N.: A new type system for deadlock-free processes. In: Baier, C., Hermanns, H. (eds.) CONCUR 2006. LNCS, vol. 4137, pp. 233–247. Springer, Heidelberg (2006). doi:10.1007/11817949_16
23. König, B.: Analysing input/output-capabilities of mobile processes with a generic type system. J. Logic Algebraic Program. **63**(1), 35–58 (2005)
24. Torres Vieira, H., Thudichum Vasconcelos, V.: Typing progress in communication-centred systems. In: Nicola, R., Julien, C. (eds.) COORDINATION 2013. LNCS, vol. 7890, pp. 236–250. Springer, Heidelberg (2013). doi:10.1007/978-3-642-38493-6_17

Static Trace-Based Deadlock Analysis for Synchronous Mini-Go

Kai Stadtmüller[1], Martin Sulzmann[1(✉)], and Peter Thiemann[2]

[1] Faculty of Computer Science and Business Information Systems,
Karlsruhe University of Applied Sciences,
Moltkestrasse 30, 76133 Karlsruhe, Germany
kai.stadtmueller@live.de, martin.sulzmann@hs-karlsruhe.de
[2] Faculty of Engineering, University of Freiburg,
Georges-Köhler-Allee 079, 79110 Freiburg, Germany
thiemann@acm.org

Abstract. We consider the problem of static deadlock detection for programs in the Go programming language which make use of synchronous channel communications. In our analysis, regular expressions extended with a fork operator capture the communication behavior of a program. Starting from a simple criterion that characterizes traces of deadlock-free programs, we develop automata-based methods to check for deadlock-freedom. The approach is implemented and evaluated with a series of examples.

1 Introduction

The Go programming language [6] attracts increasing attention because it offers an elegant approach to concurrent programming with message-passing in the style of Communicating Sequential Processes (CSP) [9]. Although message passing avoids many of the pitfalls of concurrent programming with shared state (atomicity violations, order violations, issues with locking, and so on), it still gives rise to problems like deadlock. Hence, the goal of our work is the static detection of deadlocks in Go programs which make use of (synchronous) message-passing using the unbuffered version of Go's channels.

Related Work. Leaving aside data races, deadlocks constitute one of the core problems in concurrent programming. However, most work on static detection of deadlocks on the programming language level deals with shared-memory concurrency.

Boyapati and coworkers [1] define a type-based analysis that relies on a partial order on locks and guarantees that well-typed programs are free of data races and deadlocks. The approaches by Williams and coworkers [22] and Engler and Ashcraft [5] detect cycles in a precomputed static lock-order graph to highlight potential deadlocks. In distributed and database systems, most approaches are dynamic but also involve cycle detection in wait-for graphs (e.g., [10]). In these

© Springer International Publishing AG 2016
A. Igarashi (Ed.): APLAS 2016, LNCS 10017, pp. 116–136, 2016.
DOI: 10.1007/978-3-319-47958-3_7

approaches, the main points of interest are the efficiency of the cycle detection algorithms and the methods employed for the construction and maintenance of the wait-for graph.

Mercouroff [16] employs abstract interpretation for an analysis of CSP programs using an abstract domain that approximates the number of messages sent between processes. Colby [4] presents an analysis that uses control paths to identify threads that may be created at the same point and constructs the communication topology of the program. A more precise control-flow analysis was proposed by Martel and Gengler [15]. Similar to our approach, in their work the accuracy of the analysis is enhanced by analyzing finite automata to eliminate some impossible communication traces.

For message-passing programs, there are elaborate algorithms that attempt accurate matching of communications in process calculi (e.g., the work of Ladkin and Simon [14]). However, they consider messages between fixed partners whereas we consider communication between multiple partners on shared channels.

Further analysis of message passing in the context of Concurrent ML (CML) [20] is based on effect systems that abstract programs into regular-expression-like behaviors with the goal of detecting finiteness of communication topologies [19]. The deadlock detection analysis of Christakis and Sagonas [3] also constructs a static graph and searches it for cycles. Specific to Go, the paper by Ng and Yoshida [18] translates Go programs into a core calculus with session types and then attempts to synthesize a global choreography that subsumes all session. A program is deemed deadlock-free if this synchronization succeeds and satisfies some side condition. Like our work, they consider a fixed number of processes and synchronous communication. Section 6 contains a more detailed comparison with this work.

Kobayashi [13] considers deadlock detection for the π-calculus [17]. His type inference algorithm infers usage constraints among receive and send operations. In essence, the constraints represent a dependency graph where the program is deadlock-free if there are no circular dependencies among send and receive operations. The constraints are solved by reduction to Petri net reachability [12]. A more detailed comparison with Kobayashi's work is given in Sect. 6.

Contributions. Common to all prior work is their reliance on automata-/ graph-based methods. The novelty of our work lies in the use of a symbolic deadlock detection method based on forkable behavior.

Forkable behaviors in the form of regular expressions extended with fork and general recursion were introduced by Nielson and Nielson [19] to analyze the communication topology of CML (which is based on ideas from CSP, just like Go). In our own recent work [21], we establish some important semantic foundations for forkable behaviors such as a compositional trace-based semantics and a symbolic Finite State Automata (FSA) construction method via Brzozowski-style derivatives [2]. In this work, we apply these results to statically detect deadlocks in Go programs.

```
func sel(x, y chan bool) {
        z := make(chan bool)
        go func() { z <- (<-x) }()
        go func() { z <- (<-y) }()
        <-z
}
func main() {
        x := make(chan bool)
        y := make(chan bool)
        go func() { x <- true }()
        go func() { y <- false }()
        sel(x,y)
        sel(x,y)
}
```

Listing 1.1. Message passing in Go

Specifically, we make the following contributions:

- We formalize Mini-Go, a fragment of the Go programming language which is restricted to synchronous message-passing (Sect. 3).
- We approximate the communication behavior of Mini-Go programs with forkable behaviors (Sect. 4).
- We define a criterion for deadlock-freedom in terms of the traces resulting from forkable behaviors. We give a decidable check for deadlock-freedom for a large class of forkable behaviors by applying the FSA construction method developed in prior work [21]. We also consider improvements to eliminate false positives (Sect. 5).
- We evaluate our approach with examples and conduct a comparison with closely related work (Sect. 6).

For further details such as proofs we refer to the online version of this paper[1].

2 Highlights

Before we delve into deadlocks and deadlock detection, we first illustrate the message passing concepts found in Go with the example program in Listing 1.1. The **main** function creates two synchronous channels x and y that transport Boolean values. Go supports (a limited form of) type inference and therefore no type annotations are required. We create two threads using the go *exp* statement. It takes an expression *exp* and executes it in a newly spawned go-routine (a thread). Each of these expressions calls an anonymous function that performs a send operation on one of the channels. In Go, we write x <- **true** to send value **true** via channel x. Then we call the function **sel** twice. This function

---

[1] http://arxiv.org/abs/1608.08330.

creates another Boolean channel **z** locally and starts two threads that "copy" a value from one of the argument channels to **z**. In Go, we write **<-x** to receive a value via channel **x**. Thus, **z <- (<-x)** sends a value received via channel **x** to channel **z**.

So, the purpose of **sel** is to choose a value which can either be received via channel **x** or channel **y**. As each channel is supplied with a value, each of the two calls to **sel** might be able to retrieve a value. While there is a schedule such that the **main** program runs to completion, it is also possible that execution of the second **sel** call will get stuck. Consider the case that in the first call to **sel** both helper threads get to execute the receive operations on **x** and **y** and forward the values to channel **z**. In this case, only one of the values will be picked up by the **<-z** and returned, but the local thread with the other value will be blocked forever waiting for another read on **z**. In the second call to **sel**, none of the local threads can receive a value from **x** or **y**, hence there will be no send operation on **z**, so that the final receive **<-z** remains blocked.

Our approach to detect such devious situations is to express the communication behavior of a program in terms of forkable behaviors. For the **main** function in Listing 1.1, we obtain the following forkable behavior

$$Fork(x!) \cdot Fork(y!) \cdot Fork(x? \cdot z_1!) \cdot Fork(y? \cdot z_1!) \cdot z_1? \cdot Fork(x? \cdot z_2!) \cdot Fork(y? \cdot z_2!) \cdot z_2?$$

We abstract away the actual values sent and write $x!$ to denote sending a message to channel **x** and $x?$ to denote reception via channel **x**. $Fork()$ indicates a forkable (concurrent) behavior which corresponds to **go** statements in the program. The concatenation operator $\cdot$ connects two forkable behaviors in a sequence. The function calls to **sel** are inlined and the local channels renamed to z_1 and z_2, respectively.

The execution schedules of **main** can be described by a matching relation for forkable behaviors where we symbolically rewrite expressions. Formal details follow later. Here are some possible matching steps for our example.

$$
\begin{aligned}
& Fork(x!) \cdot Fork(y!) \cdot Fork(x? \cdot z_1!) \cdot Fork(y? \cdot z_1!) \cdot z_1? \cdot \\
& Fork(x? \cdot z_2!) \cdot Fork(y? \cdot z_2!) \cdot z_2? \\
\Rightarrow \quad & \{\!\{\underline{x!}, y!, \underline{x?} \cdot z_1!, y? \cdot z_1!, z_1? \cdot Fork(x? \cdot z_2!) \cdot Fork(y? \cdot z_2!) \cdot z_2?\}\!\} \\
\xrightarrow{x! \cdot x?} \quad & \{\!\{y!, \underline{z_1!}, y? \cdot z_1!, \underline{z_1?} \cdot Fork(x? \cdot z_2!) \cdot Fork(y? \cdot z_2!) \cdot z_2?\}\!\} \\
\xrightarrow{z_1! \cdot z_1?} \quad & \{\!\{y!, y? \cdot z_1!, Fork(x? \cdot z_2!) \cdot Fork(y? \cdot z_2!) \cdot z_2?\}\!\} \\
\Rightarrow \quad & \{\!\{y!, y? \cdot z_1!, x? \cdot z_2!, y? \cdot z_2!, z_2?\}\!\} \\
\xrightarrow{y! \cdot y? \cdot z_2! \cdot z_2?} \quad & \{\!\{y? \cdot z_1!, x? \cdot z_2!\}\!\}
\end{aligned}
$$

We first break apart the expression into its concurrent parts indicated by the multiset notation $\{\!\{\cdot\}\!\}$. Then, we perform two rendezvous (synchronization) steps where the partners involved are underlined. In essence, the first call to **sel** picks up the value sent via channel **x**. The last step where we combine two synchronization steps (and also omit underline) shows that the second call to **sel** picks up the value sent via channel **y**. Note that the main thread terminates but as for each call to `sel` one of the helper threads is stuck our analysis reports a deadlock.

As mentioned above, another possible schedule is that the first call to `sel` picks up both values sent via channels x and y. In terms of the matching relation, we find the following

$$
\begin{aligned}
&Fork(x!) \cdot Fork(y!) \cdot Fork(x?\cdot z_1!) \cdot Fork(y?\cdot z_1!) \cdot z_1?\cdot \\
&Fork(x?\cdot z_2!) \cdot Fork(y?\cdot z_2!) \cdot z_2?
\end{aligned}
$$

$$
\xrightarrow{x!\cdot x?\cdot y!\cdot y?\cdot z_1!\cdot z_1?} \{\!\{ z_1!, x?\cdot z_2!, y?\cdot z_2!, z_2? \}\!\}
$$

As we can see, the second helper thread of the first call to `sel` is stuck, both helper threads of the second call are stuck as well as the main thread. In fact, this is the deadlock reported by our analysis as we attempt to find minimal deadlock examples.

The issue in the above example can be fixed by making use of *selective* communication to non-deterministically choose among multiple communications.

```
func selFixed(x, y chan bool) {
  select {
    case z = <-x:
    case z = <-y:
  }
}
```

The select statement blocks until one of the cases applies. If there are multiple select cases whose communication is enabled, the Go run-time system 'randomly' selects one of those and proceeds with it. Based on a pseudo-random number the select cases are permuted and tried from top to bottom. Thus, the deadlocking behavior observed above disappears as each call to `selFixed` picks up either a value sent via channel x or channel y but it will never consume values from both channels.

3 Mini-Go

We formalize a simplified fragment of the Go programming language where we only consider a finite set of pre-declared, synchronous channels. For brevity, we also omit procedures and first-class channels and only consider Boolean values.

Definition 1 (Syntax).

$$
\begin{array}{lll}
x, y, \ldots & & \textit{Variables, Channel Names} \\
s & ::= v \mid \textit{Chan} & \textit{Storables} \\
v & ::= \textit{True} \mid \textit{False} & \textit{Values} \\
vs & ::= [\,] \mid v : vs & \textit{Value Queues} \\
b & ::= v \mid x \mid b\&\&b \mid !b & \textit{Expressions} \\
e, f & ::= x \leftarrow y^{\mathsf{r}} \mid y^{\mathsf{s}} \leftarrow b & \textit{Receive/Send} \\
p, q & ::= \mathsf{skip} \mid \mathsf{if}\ b\ \mathsf{then}\ p\ \mathsf{else}\ q \mid \mathsf{while}\ b\ \mathsf{do}\ p \mid p; q & \textit{Commands} \\
& \mid\ \mathsf{select}\ [e_i \Rightarrow p_i]_{i \in I} & \textit{Communications} \\
& \mid\ \mathsf{go}\ p & \textit{Threads}
\end{array}
$$

Variables are either bound to Boolean values or to the symbol *Chan* which denotes a synchronous channel. Like in Go, we use the 'arrow' notation for the send and receive operations on channels. We label the channel name to distinguish receive from send operations. That is, from $x \leftarrow y^{\mathsf{r}}$ we conclude that y is the channel via which we receive a value bound to variable x. From $y^{\mathsf{s}} \leftarrow b$ we conclude that y is the channel to which some Boolean value is sent. Send and receive communications are shorthands for unary selections: $e = \mathsf{select}\ [e \Rightarrow \mathsf{skip}]$.

The semantics of a Mini-Go program is defined with a small-step semantics. The judgment $\langle S, \{\!\{p_1, \ldots, p_n\}\!\} \rangle \xRightarrow{T} \langle S', \{\!\{p'_1, \ldots, p'_m\}\!\} \rangle$ indicates that execution of program threads p_i may evolve into threads p'_j with trace T. The notation $\{\!\{p_1, \ldots, p_n\}\!\}$ represents a multi-set of concurrently executing programs $p_1, \ldots, p_n$. For simplicity, we assume that all threads share a global state S and that distinct threads have only variables bound to channels in common.

Program trace T records the communication behavior as a sequence of symbols where symbol $x!$ represents a send operation on channel x and symbol $x?$ represents a receive operation on channel x. As we assume synchronous communication, each communication step involves exactly two threads as formalized in the judgment $\langle S, \{\!\{p, q\}\!\} \rangle \xRightarrow{T} \langle S', \{\!\{p', q'\}\!\} \rangle$.

The semantics of Boolean expressions is defined with a big-step semantics judgment $S \vdash b \Downarrow v$, where S is the state in which expression b evaluates to value v. For commands, the judgment $S \vdash p \Rightarrow q$ formalizes one (small-) step that executes a single statement. Thus, we are able to switch among different program threads after each statement. Here are the details.

Definition 2 (State). *A state S is either empty, a mapping, or an override a state with a new mapping: $S ::= (\,) \mid (x \mapsto s) \mid S \lhd (x \mapsto s)$*

We write $S(x)$ to denote state lookup. We assume that mappings in the right operand of the map override $\lhd$ take precedence. They overwrite any mappings in the left operand. That is, $(x \mapsto \textit{True}) \lhd (x \mapsto \textit{False}) = (x \mapsto \textit{False})$. We assume that for each channel x the state contains a mapping $x \mapsto \textit{Chan}$.

Definition 3 (Expression Semantics $S \vdash b \Downarrow v$).

$$S \vdash \mathit{True} \Downarrow \mathit{True} \qquad\qquad S \vdash \mathit{False} \Downarrow \mathit{False}$$

$$\frac{S(x) = v}{S \vdash x \Downarrow v} \qquad \frac{S \vdash b_1 \Downarrow \mathit{False}}{S \vdash b_1 \&\& b_2 \Downarrow \mathit{False}} \qquad \frac{S \vdash b_1 \Downarrow \mathit{True} \quad S \vdash b_2 \Downarrow v}{S \vdash b_1 \&\& b_2 \Downarrow v}$$

$$\frac{S \vdash b \Downarrow \mathit{False}}{S \vdash !b \Downarrow \mathit{True}} \qquad\qquad \frac{S \vdash b \Downarrow \mathit{True}}{S \vdash !b \Downarrow \mathit{False}}$$

Definition 4 (Commands $S \vdash p \Rightarrow q$).

$$(\textit{If-T}) \frac{S \vdash b \Downarrow \mathit{True}}{S \vdash \mathsf{if}\ b\ \mathsf{then}\ p\ \mathsf{else}\ q \Rightarrow p} \qquad (\textit{If-F}) \frac{S \vdash b \Downarrow \mathit{False}}{S \vdash \mathsf{if}\ b\ \mathsf{then}\ p\ \mathsf{else}\ q \Rightarrow q}$$

$$(\textit{While-F}) \frac{S \vdash b \Downarrow \mathit{False}}{S \vdash \mathsf{while}\ b\ \mathsf{do}\ p \Rightarrow \mathsf{skip}}$$

$$(\textit{While-T}) \frac{S \vdash b \Downarrow \mathit{True}}{S \vdash \mathsf{while}\ b\ \mathsf{do}\ p \Rightarrow p; \mathsf{while}\ b\ \mathsf{do}\ p} \qquad (\textit{Skip})\ S \vdash \mathsf{skip}; p \Rightarrow p$$

$$(\textit{Reduce}) \frac{S \vdash p \Rightarrow p'}{S \vdash p; q \Rightarrow p'; q} \qquad (\textit{Assoc})\ S \vdash (p_1; p_2); p_3 \Rightarrow p_1; (p_2; p_3)$$

Definition 5 (Communication Traces).

$$
\begin{aligned}
T ::=\ &\epsilon && \textit{empty trace} \\
\mid\ &x! && \textit{send event} \\
\mid\ &x? && \textit{receive event} \\
\mid\ &T \cdot T && \textit{sequence/concatenation}
\end{aligned}
$$

As we will see, the traces obtained by running a program are of a particular 'synchronous' shape.

Definition 6 (Synchronous Traces). *We say T is a* synchronous *trace if T is of the following more restricted form.*

$$T_s ::= \varepsilon \mid \alpha \cdot \bar{\alpha} \mid T_s \cdot T_s$$

where $\bar{\alpha}$ denotes the complement of α and is defined as follows: For any channel y, $\overline{y?} = y!$ and $\overline{y!} = y?$.

We assume common equality laws for traces such as associativity of $\cdot$ and ϵ acts as a neutral element. That is, $\epsilon \cdot T = T$. Further, we consider the two synchronous traces $\alpha_1 \cdot \overline{\alpha_1} \cdot \ldots \cdot \alpha_n \cdot \overline{\alpha_n}$ and $\overline{\alpha_1} \cdot \alpha_1 \cdot \ldots \cdot \overline{\alpha_n} \cdot \alpha_n$ to be equivalent.

Definition 7 (Synchronous Communications $\langle S, \{\!\!\{p, q\}\!\!\}\rangle \overset{T}{\Rightarrow} \langle S', \{\!\!\{p', q'\}\!\!\}\rangle$).

$$(Sync) \quad \frac{\begin{array}{c} for \ k \in I \ \ l \in J \ where \\ e_k = x \leftarrow y^r \ \ f_l = y^s \leftarrow b \\ S_1(y) = Chan \ \ S_1 \vdash b \Downarrow v \ \ S_2 = S_1 \lhd (x \mapsto v) \end{array}}{\langle S_1, \{\!\!\{\mathsf{select} \ [e_i \Rightarrow p_i]_{i \in I}, \mathsf{select} \ [f_j \Rightarrow q_j]_{j \in J}\}\!\!\} \xrightarrow{y! \cdot y?} \langle S_2, \{\!\!\{p_k, q_l\}\!\!\}\rangle}$$

A synchronous communication step non-deterministically selects matching communication partners from two select statements. The sent value v is immediately bound to variable x as we consider unbuffered channels here. Programs p_k and q_l represent continuations for the respective matching cases. The communication effect is recorded in the trace $y! \cdot y?$, which arbitrarily places the send before the receive communication. We just assume this order (as switching the order yields an equivalent, synchronous trace) and use it consistently in our formal development.

In the upcoming definition, we make use of the following helper operation:
$p \fatsemi q = \begin{cases} p & q = \mathsf{skip} \\ p; q & otherwise. \end{cases}$ Thus, one rule can cover the two cases that a **go** statement is final in a sequence or followed by another statement. If the **go** statement is final, the pattern **go** $p \fatsemi q$ implies that q equals skip. See upcoming rule (Fork). Similar cases arise in the synchronous communication step. See upcoming rule (Comm).

Definition 8 (Program Execution $\langle S, \{\!\!\{p_1, \ldots, p_n\}\!\!\}\rangle \overset{T}{\Rightarrow} \langle S', \{\!\!\{p'_1, \ldots, p'_m\}\!\!\}\rangle$).

$$(Comm) \quad \frac{\langle S, \{\!\!\{p_1, p_2\}\!\!\}\rangle \overset{T}{\Rightarrow} \langle S', \{\!\!\{p'_1, p'_2\}\!\!\}\rangle}{\langle S, \{\!\!\{p_1 \fatsemi p''_1, p_2 \fatsemi p''_2, p_3, \ldots, p_n\}\!\!\}\rangle \overset{T}{\Rightarrow} \langle S', \{\!\!\{p'_1 \fatsemi p''_1, p'_2 \fatsemi p''_2, p_3, \ldots, p_n\}\!\!\}\rangle}$$

$$(Step) \quad \frac{S \vdash p_1 \Rightarrow p'_1}{\langle S, \{\!\!\{p_1, \ldots, p_n\}\!\!\}\rangle \overset{\varepsilon}{\Rightarrow} \langle S, \{\!\!\{p'_1, \ldots, p_n\}\!\!\}\rangle}$$

$$(Fork) \quad \langle S, \{\!\!\{\mathbf{go} \ p_1 \fatsemi q_1, p_2, \ldots, p_n\}\!\!\}\rangle \overset{\varepsilon}{\Rightarrow} \langle S, \{\!\!\{p_1, q_1, p_2, \ldots, p_n\}\!\!\}\rangle$$

$$(Stop) \quad \langle S, \{\!\!\{\mathsf{skip}, p_2, \ldots, p_n\}\!\!\}\rangle \overset{\varepsilon}{\Rightarrow} \langle S, \{\!\!\{p_2, \ldots, p_n\}\!\!\}\rangle$$

$$(Closure) \quad \frac{\langle S, P\rangle \overset{T}{\Rightarrow} \langle S', P'\rangle \ \ \langle S', P'\rangle \overset{T'}{\Rightarrow} \langle S'', P''\rangle}{\langle S, P\rangle \xrightarrow{T \cdot T'} \langle S'', P''\rangle}$$

Rule (Comm) performs a synchronous communication step whereas rule (Step) executes a single step in one of the threads. Rule (Fork) creates a new thread. Rule (Stop) removes threads that have terminated. Rule (Closure) executes multiple program steps. It uses P to stand for a multiset of commands.

We are interested in identifying *stuck programs* as characterized by the following definition.

Definition 9 (Stuck Programs). *Let $C = \langle S, \{\!\{p_1, \ldots, p_n\}\!\} \rangle$ where $n > 1$ be some configuration which results from executing some program p. We say that p is* stuck *w.r.t. C if each p_i starts with a select statement[2] and no reduction rules are applicable on C. We say that p is stuck if there exists a configuration C such that p is stuck w.r.t. C.*

A stuck program indicates that *all* threads are *asleep*. This is commonly referred to as a *deadlock*. In our upcoming formal results, we assume that for technical reasons there must be at least two such threads. Hence, a 'stuck' program consisting of a single thread, e.g. $x^s \leftarrow True;\ y \leftarrow x^r$, is not covered by the above definition. Our implementation deals with programs in which only a single or some of the threads are stuck.

Our approach to detect deadlocks is to (1) abstract the communication behavior of programs in terms of forkable behaviors, and then (2) perform some behavioral analysis to uncover deadlocks. The upcoming Sect. 4 considers the abstraction. The deadlock analysis is introduced in Sect. 5.

4   Approximation via Forkable Behaviors

Forkable behaviors extend regular expressions with a fork operator and thus allow for a straightforward and natural approximation of the communication behavior of Mini-Go programs.

Definition 10 (Forkable Behaviors [21]). *The syntax of forkable behaviors (or behaviors for short) is defined as follows:*

$$r, s, t ::= \phi \mid \varepsilon \mid \alpha \mid r + s \mid r \cdot s \mid r^* \mid Fork(r)$$

where α are symbols from a finite alphabet Σ.

We find the common regular expression operators for alternatives ($+$), concatenation ($\cdot$), repetition (*) and a new fork operator $Fork()$. We write ϕ to denote the empty language and ε to denote the empty word.

In our setting, symbols α are send/receive communications of the form $x!$ and $x?$, where x is a channel name (viz. Definition 5). As we assume that there are only finitely many channels, we can guarantee that the set of symbols Σ is finite.

A program p is mapped into a forkable behavior r by making use of judgments $p \rightsquigarrow r$. The mapping rules are defined by structural induction over the input p. Looping constructs are mapped to Kleene star. Conditional statements and select are mapped to alternatives and a sequence of programs is mapped to some concatenated behaviors.

---

[2] Recall that primitive send/receive communications are expressed in terms of select.

Definition 11 (Approximation $p \rightsquigarrow r$).

$$\text{skip} \rightsquigarrow \varepsilon \qquad \frac{p \rightsquigarrow r \quad q \rightsquigarrow s}{\text{if } b \text{ then } p \text{ else } q \rightsquigarrow r + s} \qquad \frac{p \rightsquigarrow r}{\text{while } b \text{ do } p \rightsquigarrow r^*} \qquad \frac{p \rightsquigarrow r \quad q \rightsquigarrow s}{p; q \rightsquigarrow r \cdot s}$$

$$x \leftarrow y^r \rightsquigarrow y? \qquad y^s \leftarrow b \rightsquigarrow y! \qquad \frac{e_i \rightsquigarrow r_i \quad p_i \rightsquigarrow s_i \quad \text{for } i \in I}{\text{select } [e_i \Rightarrow p_i]_{i \in I} \rightsquigarrow \sum_{i \in I} r_i \cdot s_i}$$

$$\frac{p \rightsquigarrow r}{\text{go } p \rightsquigarrow Fork(r)}$$

What remains is to verify that the communication behavior of p is safely approximated by r. That is, we need to show that all traces resulting from executing p are also covered by r.

A similar result appears already in the Nielsons' work [19]. However, there are significant technical differences as we establish connections between the traces resulting from program execution to the trace-based language semantics for forkable behaviors introduced in our prior work [21].

In that work [21], we give a semantic description of forkable behaviors in terms of a language denotation $L(r, K)$. Compared to the standard definition, we find an additional component K which represents a set of traces. Thus, we can elegantly describe the meaning of an expression $Fork(r)$ as the shuffling of the meaning of r with the 'continuation' K. To represent Kleene star in the presence of continuation K, we use a fixpoint operation μF that denotes the least fixpoint of F in the complete lattice formed by the powerset of Σ^*. Here, F must be a monotone function on this lattice, which we prove in prior work.

Definition 12 (Shuffling). *The (asynchronous) shuffle $v \| w \subseteq \Sigma^*$ is the set of all interleavings of words $v, w \in \Sigma^*$. It is defined inductively by*

$$\varepsilon \| w = \{w\} \qquad v \| \varepsilon = \{v\} \qquad xv \| yw = \{x\} \cdot (v \| yw) \cup \{y\} \cdot (xv \| w)$$

The shuffle operation is lifted to languages by $L \| M = \bigcup \{v \| w \mid v \in L, w \in M\}$.

Definition 13 (Forkable Expression Semantics). *For a trace language $K \subseteq \Sigma^*$, the semantics of a forkable expression is defined inductively by*

$$\begin{aligned}
L(\phi, K) &= \emptyset & L(r + s, K) &= L(r, K) \cup L(s, K) \\
L(\varepsilon, K) &= K & L(r \cdot s, K) &= L(r, L(s, K)) \\
L(x, K) &= \{x \cdot w \mid w \in K\} & L(r^*, K) &= \mu \, \lambda X. L(r, X) \cup K \\
& & L(Fork(r), K) &= L(r) \| K
\end{aligned}$$

As a base case, we assume $L(r) = L(r, \{\varepsilon\})$.

Next, we show that when executing some program p under some trace T, the resulting program state can be approximated by the left quotient of r w.r.t. T

where r is the approximation of the initial program p. This result serves two purposes. (1) All communication behaviors found in a program can also be found in its approximation. (2) As left quotients can be computed via Brzozowski's derivatives [2], we can employ his FSA methods for static analysis. We will discuss the first point in the following. The second point is covered in the subsequent section.

If L_1 and L_2 are sets of traces, we write $L_1 \backslash L_2$ to denote the left quotient of L_2 with L_1 where $L_1 \backslash L_2 = \{w \mid \exists v \in L_1.v \cdot w \in L_2\}$. We write $x \backslash L_1$ as a shorthand for $\{x\} \backslash L_1$. For a word w we give the following inductive definition: $\varepsilon \backslash L = L$ and $x \cdot w \backslash L = w \backslash (x \backslash L)$.

To connect approximations of resulting programs to left quotients, we introduce some matching relations which operate on behaviors. To obtain a match we effectively rewrite a behavior into (parts of) some left quotient. Due to the fork operation, we may obtain a multiset of (concurrent) behaviors written $\{\!\{ r_1, ..., r_n \}\!\}$. We sometimes use R as a short-hand for $\{\!\{ r_1, ..., r_n \}\!\}$. As in the case of program execution (Definition 8), we introduce a helper operation

$$r \bullet s = \begin{cases} r & s = \varepsilon \\ r \cdot s & \text{otherwise} \end{cases}$$ to cover cases where a fork expression is either the

final expression, or possibly followed by another expression. We write $\cdot \Rightarrow \cdot$ as a short-hand for $\cdot \overset{\varepsilon}{\Rightarrow} \cdot$. We also treat r and $\{\!\{ r \}\!\}$ as equal.

Definition 14 (Matching Relation).

$$\boxed{r \overset{T}{\Rightarrow} s}$$

$$(L) \; r + s \Rightarrow r \qquad\qquad (R) \; r + s \Rightarrow s$$

$$(K_n) \; r^* \Rightarrow r \cdot r^* \qquad (K_0) \; r^* \Rightarrow \varepsilon \qquad (X) \; \alpha \cdot r \overset{\alpha}{\Rightarrow} r$$

$$(A1) \; \varepsilon \cdot r \Rightarrow r \qquad (A2) \; \frac{r \Rightarrow s}{r \cdot t \Rightarrow s \cdot t} \qquad (A3) \; (r \cdot s) \cdot t \Rightarrow r \cdot (s \cdot t)$$

$$\boxed{\{\!\{ r_1, \dots, r_m \}\!\} \overset{T}{\Rightarrow} \{\!\{ s_1, \dots, s_n \}\!\}}$$

$$(F) \; \{\!\{ Fork(r) \bullet s, r_1, \dots, r_n \}\!\} \overset{\varepsilon}{\Rightarrow} \{\!\{ s, r, r_1, \dots, r_n \}\!\} \qquad (C) \; \frac{R \overset{T}{\Rightarrow} R' \quad R' \overset{T'}{\Rightarrow} R''}{R \overset{T \cdot T'}{\Rightarrow} R''}$$

$$(S1) \; \frac{r \overset{T}{\Rightarrow} s}{\{\!\{ r, r_1, \dots, r_n \}\!\} \overset{T}{\Rightarrow} \{\!\{ s, r_1, \dots, r_n \}\!\}} \qquad (S2) \; \{\!\{ \varepsilon, r_1, \dots, r_n \}\!\} \overset{\varepsilon}{\Rightarrow} \{\!\{ r_1, \dots, r_n \}\!\}$$

We establish some basic results for the approximation and matching relation. The following two results show that matches are indeed left quotients.

Proposition 1. *Let r, s be forkable behaviors and T be a trace such that $r \xRightarrow{T} s$. Then, we find that $L(s) \subseteq T \backslash L(r)$.*

Proposition 2. *Let $r_1,...,r_m$, $s_1,...,s_n$ be forkable behaviors and T be a trace such that $\{\!\{ r_1, \ldots, r_m \}\!\} \xRightarrow{T} \{\!\{ s_1, \ldots, s_n \}\!\}$. Then, we find that $L(s_1) \| ... \| L(s_n) \subseteq T \backslash (L(r_1) \| ... \| L(r_m))$.*

Finally, we establish that all traces resulting during program execution can also be obtained by the match relation. Furthermore, the resulting behaviors are approximations of the resulting programs.

Proposition 3. *If $S \vdash p \Rightarrow q$ and $p \rightsquigarrow r$ then $r \Rightarrow s$ for some s where $q \rightsquigarrow s$.*

Proposition 4. *If $\langle S, \{\!\{ p_1, ..., p_m \}\!\} \rangle \xRightarrow{T} \langle S', \{\!\{ q_1, ..., q_n \}\!\} \rangle$ and $p_i \rightsquigarrow r_i$ for $i = 1, ..., m$ then $\{\!\{ r_1, ..., r_m \}\!\} \xRightarrow{T} \{\!\{ s_1, ..., s_n \}\!\}$ where $q_j \rightsquigarrow s_j$ for $j = 1, .., n$.*

5   Static Analysis

Based on the results of the earlier section, all analysis steps can be carried out on the forkable behavior instead of the program text. In this section, we first develop a 'stuckness' criterion in terms of forkable behaviors to identify programs with a potential deadlock. Then, we consider how to statically check stuckness.

5.1   Forkable Behavior Stuckness Criterion

Definition 15 (Stuck Behavior). *We say that r is* stuck *if and only if there exists $r \xRightarrow{T} \varepsilon$ for some non-synchronous trace T.*

Recall Definition 6 for a description of synchronous traces.

The following result shows that if the stuck condition does *not* apply, we can guarantee the absence of a deadlock. That is, non-stuckness implies deadlock-freedom.

Proposition 5. *Let p be a stuck program and r be a behavior such that $p \rightsquigarrow r$. Then, r is stuck.*

The above result does not apply to stuck programs consisting of a single thread. For example, consider $p = x^s \leftarrow True; y \leftarrow x^r$ and $r = x! \cdot x?$ where $p \rightsquigarrow r$. Program p is obviously stuck, however, r is not stuck because any matching trace for r is synchronous. For example, $r \xRightarrow{x! \cdot x?} \varepsilon$. Hence, Definition 9 assumes that execution of program p leads to some state where all threads are asleep, so that we can construct a non-synchronous trace for the approximation of p.

Clearly, the synchronous trace $x! \cdot x?$ is not observable under any program run of p. Therefore, we will remove such non-observable, synchronous traces from consideration. Before we consider such refinements of our stuckness criterion, we develop static methods to check for stuckness.

5.2   Static Checking of Stuckness

To check for stuckness, we apply an automata-based method where we first translate the forkable behavior into an equivalent finite state machine (FSA) and then analyze the resulting FSA for stuckness. The FSA construction method for forkable behaviors follows the approach described in our prior work [21] where we build a FSA based on Brzozowski's derivative construction method [2].

We say that a forkable behavior r is *well-behaved* if there is no fork inside a Kleene star expression. The restriction to well-behaved behaviors guarantees finiteness (i.e., termination) of the automaton construction.

Proposition 6 (Well-Behaved Forkable FSA [21]). *Let r be a well-behaved behavior. Then, we can construct an $\mathcal{FSA}(r)$ where the alphabet coincides with the alphabet of r and states can be connected to behaviors such that (1) r is the initial state and (2) for each non-empty trace $T = \alpha_1 \cdot \ldots \cdot \alpha_n$ we find a path $r = r_0 \xrightarrow{\alpha_1} r_1 ... r_{n-1} \xrightarrow{\alpha_n} r_n$ in $\mathcal{FSA}(r)$ such that $T \backslash L(r) = L(r_n)$.*

The kind of FSA obtained by our method [21] guarantees that all matching derivations (Definition 14) which yield a non-trivial trace can also be observed in the FSA.

Proposition 7 (FSA covers Matching). *Let r be a well-behaved behavior such that $r \xRightarrow{T} \{\!\!\{ s_1, ..., s_m \}\!\!\}$ for some non-empty trace $T = \alpha_1 \cdot \ldots \cdot \alpha_n$. Then, there exists a path $r = r_0 \xrightarrow{\alpha_1} r_1 ... r_{n-1} \xrightarrow{\alpha_n} r_n$ in $\mathcal{FSA}(r)$ such that $L(s_1) \| ... \| L(s_m) \subseteq L(r_n)$.*

Based on above, we conclude that stuckness of a behavior implies that the FSA is *stuck* as well. That is, we encounter a non-synchronous path.

Proposition 8. *Let r be a well-behaved behavior such that r is stuck. Then, there exists a path $r = r_0 \xrightarrow{\alpha_1} r_1 ... r_{n-1} \xrightarrow{\alpha_n} r_n$ in $\mathcal{FSA}(r)$ such that $L(r_i) \neq \{\}$ for $i = 1, ..., n$ and $\alpha_1 \cdot \ldots \cdot \alpha_n$ is a non-synchronous trace.*

Proposition 9. *Let r be a well-behaved behavior such that $\mathcal{FSA}(r)$ is stuck. Then, any non-synchronous path that exhibits stuckness can be reduced to a non-synchronous path where a state appears at most twice along that path*

Based on the above, it suffices to consider minimal paths. We obtain these paths as follow. We perform a breadth-first traversal of the $\mathcal{FSA}(r)$ starting with the initial state r to build up all paths which satisfy the following criterion: (1) We must reach a final state, and (2) a state may appear at most twice along a path. It is clear that the set of all such paths is finite and their length is finite. If among these paths we find a non-synchronous path, then the $\mathcal{FSA}(r)$ is stuck.

Proposition 10. *Let r be a well-behaved behavior. Then, it is decidable if the $\mathcal{FSA}(r)$ is stuck.*

Based on the above, we obtain a simple and straightforward to implement method for static checking of deadlocks in Mini-Go programs. Any non-synchronous path indicates a potential deadlock and due to the symbolic nature of our approach, erroneous paths can be traced back to the program text for debugging purposes.

5.3   Eliminating False Positives

Naive application of the criterion developed in the previous section yields many false positives. In our setting, a false positive is a non-synchronous path that is present in the automaton $\mathcal{FSA}(r)$, but which cannot be observed in any program run of p. This section introduces an optimization to eliminate many false positives. This optimization is integrated in our implementation.

For example, consider the forkable behavior $r = Fork(x! \cdot y!) \cdot x? \cdot y?$ resulting from the program $p = $ go $(x^s \leftarrow True; y^s \leftarrow False); z \leftarrow x^r; z \leftarrow y^r$. Based on our FSA construction method, we discover the non-synchronous path $r \xrightarrow{x! \cdot y! \cdot x? \cdot y?} \varepsilon$ where ε denotes some accepting state. However, just by looking at this simple program it is easy to see that there is no deadlock. There are two threads and for each thread, each program statement synchronizes with the program statement of the other thread at the respective position. That is, $\langle \_, \{p\}\rangle \xrightarrow{x! \cdot x? \cdot y! \cdot y?} \langle \_, \{\}\rangle$.

So, a possible criterion to 'eliminate' a non-synchronous path from consideration seems to be to check if there exists an alternative synchronous permutation of this path. There are two cases where we need to be careful: (1) Conditional statements and (2) inter-thread synchronous paths.

Conditional Statements. Let us consider the first case. For example, consider the following variant of our example:

$$r = Fork(x! \cdot y!) \cdot (x? \cdot y? + y? \cdot x?)$$

$$p = \text{go } (x^s \leftarrow True; y^s \leftarrow False);$$
$$\text{if } True \text{ then } (z \leftarrow x^r; z \leftarrow y^r) \text{ else } (z \leftarrow y^r; z \leftarrow x^r)$$

By examining the program text, we see that there is no deadlock as the program will always choose the 'if' branch. As our (static) analysis conservatively assumes that both branches may be taken, we can only use a synchronous permutation to eliminate a non-synchronous path if we do not apply any conditional statements along this path. In terms of the matching relation from Definition 14, we can characterize the absence of conditional statements if none of the rules (L), (R), (K_n) and (K_0) has been applied.

Inter-thread Synchronous Paths. The second case concerns synchronization within the same thread. Consider yet another variant of our example:

$$r = Fork(x! \cdot x?) \cdot y! \cdot y?$$

$$p = \text{go } (x^s \leftarrow True; z \leftarrow x^r); y^s \leftarrow False; z \leftarrow y^r$$

The above program will deadlock. However, in terms of the abstraction, i.e. forkable behavior, we find that for the non-synchronous path there exists a synchronous permutation which does not make use of any of the conditional matching rules, e.g. $r \xrightarrow{x! \cdot x? \cdot y! \cdot y?} \{\}$. This is clearly not a valid alternative as for example $x!$ and $x?$ result from the same thread.

To identify the second case, we assume that receive/send symbols α in a trace carry a distinct thread identifier (ID). We can access the thread ID of each symbol α via some operator $\sharp(\cdot)$. Under our assumed restrictions (i.e., no forks inside of loops, which is no go inside a while loop) it is straightforward to obtain this information precisely.

We refine the approximation of a program's communication behavior in terms of a forkable behavior such that communications carry additionally the thread identification number. Recall that we exclude programs where there is a go statement within a while loop. Thus, the number of threads is statically known and thread IDs can be attached to communication symbols via a simple extension $p \overset{i}{\rightsquigarrow} r$ of the relation $p \rightsquigarrow r$. The additional component i represents the identification number of the current thread. We start with $p \overset{0}{\rightsquigarrow} r$ where 0 represents the main thread. We write symbol $x!^i$ to denote a transmission over channel x which takes place in thread i. Similarly, symbol $x?^i$ denotes reception over channel x in thread i. For each symbol, we can access the thread identification number via operator $\sharp(\cdot)$ where $\sharp(x!^i) = i$ and $\sharp(x?^i) = i$.

The necessary adjustments to Definition 11 are as follows.

$$\text{skip} \rightsquigarrow \varepsilon i \qquad \frac{p \rightsquigarrow ri \quad q \rightsquigarrow si}{\text{if } b \text{ then } p \text{ else } q \rightsquigarrow r + si} \qquad \frac{p \rightsquigarrow ri}{\text{while } b \text{ do } p \rightsquigarrow r^*i}$$

$$\frac{p \rightsquigarrow ri \quad q \rightsquigarrow si}{p; q \rightsquigarrow r \cdot si} \qquad x \leftarrow y^{\mathbf{r}} \rightsquigarrow y?^i i \qquad y^{\mathbf{s}} \leftarrow b \rightsquigarrow y!^i i$$

$$\frac{e_i \rightsquigarrow r_i i \quad p_i \rightsquigarrow s_i i \text{ for } i \in I}{\text{select } [e_i \Rightarrow p_i]_{i \in I} \rightsquigarrow \sum_{i \in I} r_i \cdot s_i} i \qquad \frac{p \rightsquigarrow ri + 1}{\text{go } p \rightsquigarrow Fork(r)} i$$

We summarize our observations.

Definition 16 (Concurrent Synchronous Permutation). *Let T_1 and T_2 be two traces. We say that T_1 is a concurrent synchronous permutation of T_2 iff (1) T_1 is a permutation of the symbols in T_2, (2) T_1 is a synchronous trace of the form $\alpha_1 \cdot \overline{\alpha_1} \cdot \ldots \cdot \alpha_n \cdot \overline{\alpha_n}$ where $\sharp(\alpha_i) \neq \sharp(\overline{\alpha_i})$ for $i = 1, \ldots, n$.*

Proposition 11 (Elimination via Concurrent Synchronous Permutation). *Let p be a program. Let r be a well-behaved behavior such that $p \rightsquigarrow r$. For any non-synchronous path T in $\mathcal{FSA}(r)$, there exists a synchronous path T_1, a non-synchronous path T_2 and a concurrent synchronous permutation T_3 of T_2 such that $r \overset{T_1}{\Longrightarrow} \{\!\{r_1, \ldots, r_m\}\!\}$, $\{\!\{r_1, \ldots, r_m\}\!\} \overset{T_2}{\Longrightarrow} \{\!\{\}\!\}$, and $\{\!\{r_1, \ldots, r_m\}\!\} \overset{T_3}{\Longrightarrow} \{\!\{\}\!\}$ where in the last match derivation none of the rules (L), (R), (K_n) and (K_0) have been applied. Then, program p is not stuck.*

The 'elimination' conditions in the above proposition can be directly checked in terms of the $\mathcal{FSA}(r)$. Transitions can be connected to matching rules.

This follows from the derivative-based FSA construction. Hence, for each non-synchronous path in $\mathcal{FSA}(r)$ we can check for a synchronous alternative. We simply consider all (well-formed) concurrent synchronous permutations and verify that there is a path which does not involve conditional transitions.

A further source for eliminating false positives is to distinguish among nondeterminism resulting from selective communication and nondeterminism due to conditional statements. For example, the following programs yield the same (slightly simplified) abstraction

$$r = Fork(x!) \cdot (x? + y?)$$

$$p_1 = \text{go } x^s \leftarrow \textit{True}; \text{select } [z \leftarrow x^r \Rightarrow \text{skip}, z \leftarrow y^r \Rightarrow \text{skip}]$$

$$p_2 = \text{go } x^s \leftarrow \textit{True}; \text{if } \textit{True} \text{ then } z \leftarrow x^r \Rightarrow \text{ else } z \leftarrow y^r$$

It is easy to see that there is a non-synchronous path, e.g. $r \xrightarrow{x!\cdot y?} \varepsilon$. Hence, we indicate that the program from which this forkable behavior resulted may get stuck. In case of p_1 this represents a false positive because the non-synchronous path will not be selected.

The solution is to distinguish between both types of nondeterminism by abstracting the behavior of select via some new operator $\oplus$ instead of $+$. We omit the straightforward extensions to Definition 11. In terms of the matching relation, $+$ and $\oplus$ behave the same. The difference is that for $\oplus$ certain non-synchronous behavior can be safely eliminated.

Briefly, suppose we encounter a non-synchronous path where the (non-synchronous) issue can be reduced to $\{\!\!\{\alpha_1 \oplus ... \oplus \alpha_n, \beta_1 \oplus ... \oplus \beta_m\}\!\!\} \xrightarrow{\alpha_i \cdot \beta_j} \{\!\!\{\}\!\!\}$ for some $i \in \{1, ..., n\}$ and $j \in \{1, ..., m\}$ where $\alpha_i \cdot \beta_j$ is non-synchronous. Suppose there exists $l \in \{1, ..., n\}$ and $k \in \{1, ..., m\}$ such that $\{\!\!\{\alpha_1 \oplus ... \oplus \alpha_n, \beta_1 \oplus ... \oplus \beta_m\}\!\!\} \xrightarrow{\alpha_l \cdot \beta_k} \{\!\!\{\}\!\!\}$ and $\alpha_l \cdot \beta_k$ is synchronous. Then, we can eliminate this non-synchronous path. The reason why this elimination step is safe is due to rule (Sync) in Definition 7. This rule guarantees that we will always synchronize if possible. As in case of the earlier 'elimination' approach, we can directly check the $\mathcal{FSA}(r)$ by appropriately marking transitions due to $\oplus$.

Further note that to be a safe elimination method, we only consider select statements where case bodies are trivial, i.e. equal skip. Hence, we find α_i and β_j in the above instead of arbitrary behaviors. Otherwise, this elimination step may not be safe. For example, consider

$$r = Fork(x! \cdot y!) \cdot (x? \cdot y? \oplus x? \cdot x?)$$

$$p = \text{go } (x^s \leftarrow \textit{True}; y^s \leftarrow \textit{False}); \text{select } [z \leftarrow x^r \Rightarrow z \leftarrow y^r, z \leftarrow x^r \Rightarrow z \leftarrow x^r]$$

Due to the non-trivial case body $z \leftarrow x^r$ we encounter a non-synchronous path which cannot be eliminated.

6   Experimental Results

6.1   Implementation

We have built a prototype of a tool that implements our approach, referred to as gopherlyzer [8]. Our analysis operates on the Go source language where we make use of the oracle tool [7] to obtain (alias) information to identify matching channel names. We currently assume that all channels are statically known and all functions can be inlined. The implementation supports select with default cases, something which we left out in the formal description for brevity. Each default case is treated as an empty trace ε.

Go's API also contains a close operation for channels. Receiving from a closed channel returns a default value whereas sending produces an error. An integration of this feature in our current implementation is not too difficult but left out for the time being. The technical report provides further details.

Gopherlyzer generates the FSA 'on-the-fly' while processing the program. It stops immediately when encountering a deadlock. We also aggressively apply the 'elimination' methods described in Sect. 5.3 to reduce the size of the FSA. When encountering a deadlock, the tool reports a minimal trace to highlight the issue. We can also identify stuck threads by checking if a non-synchronous communication pattern arises for this thread. Thus, we can identify situations where the main thread terminates but some local thread is stuck. The reported trace could also be used to replay the synchronization steps that lead to the deadlock. We plan to integrate extended debugging support in future versions of our tool.

6.2   Examples

For experimentation, we consider the examples deadlock, fanin, and primesieve from Ng and Yoshida [18]. To make primesieve amenable to our tool, we moved the dynamic creation of channels outside of the (bounded) for-loop. Ng and Yoshida consider two further examples: fanin-alt and htcat. We omit fanin-alt because our current implementation does not support closing of channels. To deal with htcat we need to extend our frontend to support certain syntactic cases. In addition, we consider the examples sel and selFixed from Sect. 2 as well as philo which is a simplified implementation of the dining philosophers problem where we assume that all forks are placed in the middle of the table. As in the original version, each philosopher requires two forks for eating. All examples can be found in the gopherlyzer repository [8].

6.3   Experimental Results

Comparison with Dingo-Hunter [18]. For each tool we report analysis results and the overall time used to carry out the analysis. Table 1 summarizes our results which were carried out on some commodity hardware (Intel i7 3770 @ 3.6GHz, 16 GB RAM, Linux Mint 17.3).

Table 1. Experimental results. All times are reported in ms

Example	LoC	Channels	Goroutines	Select	Deadlock	dingo-hunter		gopherlyzer	
						result	time	result	time
deadlock	34	2	5	0	true	true	155	true	21
fanin	37	3	4	1	false	false	107	false	29
primesieve	57	4	5	0	true	true	8000	true	34
philo	34	1	4	0	true	true	480	true	31
sel	25	4	4	0	true	true	860	true	24
selFixed	25	2	2	2	false	false	85	false	30

Our timings for dingo-hunter are similar to the reported results [18], but it takes significantly longer to analyze our variant of `primesieve`, where we have unrolled the loop. There is also significant difference between `sel` and `selFixed` by an order of magnitude. A closer inspection shows that the communicating finite state machines (CFSMs) generated by dingo-hunter can grow dramatically in size with the number of threads and channels used.

The analysis time for our tool is always significantly faster (between $3\times$ and $235\times$ with a geometric mean of $17\times$). Judging from the dingo-hunter paper, the tool requires several transformation steps to carry out the analysis, which seems rather time consuming. In contrast, our analysis requires a single pass over the forkable behavior where we incrementally build up the FSA to search for non-synchronous paths.

Both tools report the same analysis results. We yet need to conduct a more detailed investigation but it seems that both approaches are roughly similar in terms of expressive power. However, there are some corner cases where our approach appears to be superior.

Consider the following (contrived) examples in Mini-Go notation: (go $x^s \leftarrow$ *True*); $y \leftarrow x^r$ and $y \leftarrow x^r$; (go $x^s \leftarrow$ *True*). Our tool reports that the first example is deadlock-free but the second example may have a deadlock. The second example is out of scope of the dingo-hunter because it requires all go-routines to be created before any communication takes place. Presently, dingo-hunter does not seem to check this restriction because it reports the second example as deadlock-free.

Our approximation with forkable behaviors imposes no such restrictions. The first example yields $Fork(x!) \cdot x?$ whereas the second example yields $x? \cdot Fork(x!)$. Thus, our tool is able to detect the deadlock in case of the second example.

Comparison with Kobayashi [13]. We conduct a comparison with the TyPiCal tool [11] which implements Kobayashi's deadlock analysis [13]. As the source language is based on the π-calculus, we manually translated the Go examples to the syntax supported by TyPiCal's Web Demo Interface available from Kobayashi's homepage. The translated examples can be found in the gopherlyzer repository [8].

To the best of our knowledge, TyPiCal does *not* support a form of selective communication. Hence, we need to introduce some helper threads which results in an overapproximation of the original Go program's behavior and potentially introduces a deadlock. Recall the discussion in Sect. 2.

For programs not making use of selective communication (and closing of channels; another feature not supported by TyPiCal), we obtain the same analysis results. Analysis times seem comparable to our tool. The exception being the `primesieve` example which cannot be analyzed within the resource limits imposed by TyPiCal's Web Demo Interface which we used in the experiments. Like our tool, TyPiCal properly maintains the order among threads. Recall the example $y \leftarrow x^r$; (go $x^s \leftarrow True$) from above.

```
// Go program
x := make(chan int)            /*** TyPiCal input ***/
y := make(chan int)            new x in
go func() {                    new y in
  x <- 42                        x!42.y?v1.x!43.y?v2
  v1 := <-y        // P1       | x?v3.x?v4.x?v5.y!42
  x <- 43
  v2 := <-y }()                /*** TyPiCal output ***/
v3 := <-x                      new x in
v4 := <-x          // P2       new y in
v5 := <-x                        x!!42.y?v1.x!!43.y?v2
y <- 42                        | x??v3.x?v4.x?v5.y!!42
```

Analysis report: $x!^1 \cdot x?^2 \cdot \underline{y?^1 \cdot x?^2} \ldots$

Fig. 1. Analysis report: gopherlyzer versus TyPiCal

Finally, gopherlyzer reports the analysis result in a different way than TyPiCal. The left side of Fig. 1 contains a simple Go program and the right side its translation to TyPiCal's source language. TyPiCal reports that the program is unsafe and might deadlock. Annotations ? and ! denote potentially stuck receive and send operations whereas ?? and !! indicate that the operations might succeed. The trace-based analysis (on the left) yields a non-synchronous trace from which we can easily pinpoint the position(s) in the program which are likely to be responsible. In the example, the underlined events are connected to program locations P1 and P2.

7   Conclusion

We have introduced a novel trace-based static deadlock detection method and built a prototype tool to analyze Go programs. Our experiments show that our approach yields good results and its efficiency compares favorably with existing tools of similar scope.

In future work, we intend to lift some of the restrictions of the current approach, for example, supporting programs with dynamically generated goroutines. Such an extension may result in a loss of decidability of our static analysis. Hence, we consider mixing our static analysis with some dynamic methods.

Acknowledgments. We thank the APLAS'16 reviewers for their constructive feedback.

References

1. Boyapati, C., Lee, R., Rinard, M.C.: Ownership types for safe programming: preventing data races and deadlocks. In: Proceedings of OOPSLA 2002, pp. 211–230. ACM (2002)
2. Brzozowski, J.A.: Derivatives of regular expressions. J. ACM **11**(4), 481–494 (1964)
3. Christakis, M., Sagonas, K.: Detection of asynchronous message passing errors using static analysis. In: Rocha, R., Launchbury, J. (eds.) PADL 2011. LNCS, vol. 6539, pp. 5–18. Springer, Heidelberg (2011). doi:10.1007/978-3-642-18378-2_3
4. Colby, C.: Analyzing the communication topology of concurrent programs. In: Proceedings of PEPM 1995, pp. 202–213. ACM (1995)
5. Engler, D.R., Ashcraft, K.: RacerX: effective, static detection of race conditions and deadlocks. In: Proceeding of SOSP 2003, pp. 237–252. ACM (2003)
6. The Go programming language. https://golang.org/
7. Oracle: a tool for answering questions about go source code. https://godoc.org/golang.org/x/tools/cmd/oracle
8. Gopherlyzer: Trace-based deadlock detection for mini-go. https://github.com/KaiSta/gopherlyzer
9. Hoare, C.A.R.: Communicating sequential processes. Commun. ACM **21**(8), 666–677 (1978)
10. Huang, S.T.: A distributed deadlock detection algorithm for CSP-like communication. ACM Trans. Program. Lang. Syst. **12**(1), 102–122 (1990)
11. Kobayashi, N.: TyPiCal: type-based static analyzer for the Pi-Calculus. http://www-kb.is.s.u-tokyo.ac.jp/~koba/typical/
12. Kobayashi, N.: Type-based information flow analysis for the pi-calculus. Acta Inf. **42**(4–5), 291–347 (2005)
13. Kobayashi, N.: A new type system for deadlock-free processes. In: Baier, C., Hermanns, H. (eds.) CONCUR 2006. LNCS, vol. 4137, pp. 233–247. Springer, Heidelberg (2006). doi:10.1007/11817949_16
14. Ladkin, P.B., Simons, B.B.: Static deadlock analysis for CSP-type communications. In: Fussell, D.S., Malek, M. (eds.) Responsive Computer Systems: Steps Toward Fault-Tolerant Real-Time Systems, pp. 89–102. Springer, Boston (1995)
15. Martel, M., Gengler, M.: Communication topology analysis for concurrent programs. In: Havelund, K., Penix, J., Visser, W. (eds.) SPIN 2000. LNCS, vol. 1885, pp. 265–286. Springer, Heidelberg (2000). doi:10.1007/10722468_16
16. Mercouroff, N.: An algorithm for analyzing communicating processes. In: Brookes, S., Main, M., Melton, A., Mislove, M., Schmidt, D. (eds.) MFPS 1991. LNCS, vol. 598, pp. 312–325. Springer, Heidelberg (1992). doi:10.1007/3-540-55511-0_16
17. Milner, R.: Communicating and Mobile Systems: The π-Calculus. Cambridge University Press, New York (1999)

18. Ng, N., Yoshida, N.: Static deadlock detection for concurrent go by global session graph synthesis. In: Proceedings of CC 2016, pp. 174–184. ACM (2016)
19. Nielson, H.R., Nielson, F.: Higher-order concurrent programs with finite communication topology. In: Proceedings of POPL 1994, pp. 84–97. ACM Press, January 1994
20. Reppy, J.H.: Concurrent Programming in ML. Cambridge University Press, New York (1999)
21. Sulzmann, M., Thiemann, P.: Forkable regular expressions. In: Dediu, A.-H., Janoušek, J., Martín-Vide, C., Truthe, B. (eds.) LATA 2016. LNCS, vol. 9618, pp. 194–206. Springer, Heidelberg (2016). doi:10.1007/978-3-319-30000-9_15
22. Williams, A., Thies, W., Ernst, M.D.: Static deadlock detection for Java libraries. In: Black, A.P. (ed.) ECOOP 2005. LNCS, vol. 3586, pp. 602–629. Springer, Heidelberg (2005). doi:10.1007/11531142_26

Profiling and Debugging

AkkaProf: A Profiler for Akka Actors in Parallel and Distributed Applications

Andrea Rosà[1]([⊠]), Lydia Y. Chen[2], and Walter Binder[1]

[1] Faculty of Informatics, Università della Svizzera Italiana (USI),
Lugano, Switzerland
{andrea.rosa,walter.binder}@usi.ch
[2] Cloud Server Technologies Group, IBM Research Zurich, Rüschlikon, Switzerland
yic@zurich.ibm.com

Abstract. Nowadays, numerous programming languages and frameworks offer concurrency based on the actor model. Among the actor libraries for the Java Virtual Machine, Akka is the most used one, as it is employed in various parallel and distributed applications and frameworks. Unfortunately, despite the spread of actors libraries, Akka in particular, existing profiling tools are not very effective at identifying performance drawbacks in applications using actors. In this tool paper, we aim at filling this gap by presenting AkkaProf, a profiling tool for Akka actors. AkkaProf provides detailed metrics on actor utilization and on the communication between them, two fundamental aspects of actor-based applications that are overlooked by other profilers. AkkaProf aids performance analysis in several applications and frameworks in both parallel and distributed environments.

Keywords: Actor model · Concurrent applications · Parallel and distributed frameworks · Profiling tools · Performance evaluation and optimization

1 Introduction

The actor model [1] is being adopted in concurrent applications by an increasing community of developers. Essentially, the model is centered on *actors*, atomic entities relying on message exchange to coordinate between each other and executing computations, and builds on typical characteristics—such as asynchronous communication, location transparent addressing, absence of locks and shared states—that help avoiding deadlocks and data races. As a result, actors are now consistently employed in both parallel and distributed environments, either in isolation or mixed with other concurrent constructs [2].

The interest in adopting the model is confirmed by the large number of programming languages and libraries that implement it for a great variety of platforms. In this paper, we focus on the Java Virtual Machine (JVM). Among the actor libraries targeting the JVM, Akka[1] is the most popular one. As evidence

---

[1] http://akka.io.

© Springer International Publishing AG 2016
A. Igarashi (Ed.): APLAS 2016, LNCS 10017, pp. 139–147, 2016.
DOI: 10.1007/978-3-319-47958-3_8

of its prominence over other actor libraries, Scala includes Akka actors since 2013[2], and numerous applications use Akka, including parallel and distributed computing frameworks such as Signal/Collect [3], Apache Spark [4] and Apache Flink [5].

Despite the spread of actors libraries, particularly Akka, and actor-based applications, existing profiling tools are not very effective at analyzing the performance of actor-based applications. The key properties that characterize actors (i.e., the absence of locks, the large number of messages sent and received, the fact that actors cannot share state between each other, and the actor behavior being strongly dependent to the type of the received message) make actor utilization and the communication between them fundamental metrics for locating key performance drawbacks in such applications (see Sect. 4). Although tools for profiling Akka applications are available [6,7], they focus mainly on mailboxes and errors occurred to actors rather than on their utilization and communication. Moreover, other profilers targeting parallel [8,9] or distributed [10,11] applications lack metrics dedicated to actors. As actors feature unique properties that make them rather different from other concurrency abstractions, investigating performance problems in Akka applications without the support of metrics dedicated to actors is a difficult task.

In this tool paper, we aim at filling this gap by introducing AkkaProf, a profiling tool for Akka actors. AkkaProf is based on bytecode instrumentation making possible to track and collect low-level metrics related to actors. In particular, AkkaProf focuses on actor utilization and on the communication between them. AkkaProf is implemented on top of the DiSL framework for program analysis [12] that ensures full bytecode coverage such that the collected metrics are profiled accurately. AkkaProf can benefit an increasing number of parallel and distributed applications and frameworks relying on Akka, and can aid several tasks, such as analyzing the utilization of each actor, determining whether the load is balanced in computing frameworks, and locating inefficiencies in actor communication. To the best of our knowledge, AkkaProf is the first profiler tracking detailed metrics on the utilization and communication of Akka actors.

2   Motivating Scenarios

We motivate the need for a tool like AkkaProf by describing three scenarios, each focusing on a specific context where our tool can be helpful. These scenarios will guide the evaluation of AkkaProf described in Sect. 4.

In the first scenario, we consider a user who is interested in analyzing how much actors are utilized in an application where concurrency is obtained exclusively by means of Akka actors. In particular, she wants to assess whether the application leverages an adequate number of actors, that is, that enough actors are spawned to execute computations, and that none of them remains idle after creation. AkkaProf can be helpful in reaching her goal, thanks to fine-grained metrics centered on *actor utilization*. On the other hand, profiling tools for

---

[2] Akka actors have replaced Scala actors since Scala 2.10.

Akka [6,7] and object profilers [8,9] lack metrics dedicated to actor utilization, focusing mostly on actor mailboxes, errors occurred, or other CPU- or heap-related metrics that provide little help when investigating actor utilization.

In the second scenario, we consider a user willing to investigate *load balancing* in parallel processing frameworks, i.e., whether the subdivision of computations is balanced between workers. In such frameworks, Akka actors can be used as computing workers; for example, the Signal/Collect framework [3] does so. To reach her goal, she might try to use existing profilers for parallel applications [8,9] or apply existing techniques for load profiling [10,13] to computing workers. Unfortunately, while the former tools are not very helpful when analyzing load balancing, as they keep track neither of the amount of computations processed by actors nor of the amount of messages exchanged, the latter usually center on message latency rather than computations, and consider the latter at a coarse granularity (e.g., the number of tasks), without looking at the size of each task or the amount of computations assigned to tasks, which are very important in the considered scenario. In contrast, AkkaProf collects information on the amount of bytecodes executed per worker, a fine-grained metric that is very effective in analyzing load balancing, in conjunction with metrics related to the message exchange.

In the third use case, we consider a user who wants to analyze *communication* between different workers in a distributed computing framework. In many distributed frameworks such as the popular Apache Spark [4] or Apache Flink [5], endpoints managing communication are implemented as Akka actors. In these frameworks, AkkaProf can track the amount of communication incurred between endpoints, enabling performance evaluation and guiding related optimizations. Alternatively, the user might consider other tools for network [14,15] or communication profiling [11]. However, the former track metrics and information at the granularity of the network stack, being not very useful when analyzing message exchange in applications using actors, while the latter cannot guarantee precise results, and mainly focus on latencies in the communication.

3   Profiler Overview

AkkaProf instruments every Akka actor created during the execution of an actor-based application, collecting detailed metrics on actor utilization and on the communication between them. AkkaProf is implemented on top of DiSL [12], a bytecode instrumentation framework achieving complete bytecode coverage. The integration with DiSL ensures that all actors created (i.e., akka.actor.Actor and all its subtypes) are effectively profiled and that the metrics tracked and collected are accurate. In particular, since an important metric profiled by AkkaProf is the number of executed bytecodes, full bytecode coverage ensures that all bytecode instructions that are executed by Akka actors are counted, including those in core library classes (such as java.lang).

Architecture. Figure 1 illustrates a high-level picture of the AkkaProf architecture. AkkaProf is launched together with the target application. As AkkaProf is

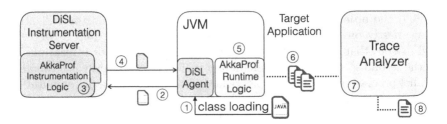

Fig. 1. AkkaProf architecture for applications using a single JVM.

built on top of DiSL, a *DiSL agent* runs in the same JVM process as the target application, while a *DiSL instrumentation server* is spawned in a separate JVM process. The instrumentation performed by AkkaProf is done as follows. The DiSL agent intercepts classes loaded on the target application (1) and forwards them to the instrumentation server (2). Thanks to the *AkkaProf instrumentation logic* running in the server, the latter determines the classes and the methods that shall be instrumented to track the desired metrics (3). Classes are then sent back to the target application (4). During the application execution, *AkkaProf runtime logic* collects several metrics related to the utilization of each actor and the communication occurred (5). Periodically, or at the end of the application, AkkaProf stores collected metrics in *traces* (6). Finally, a *trace analyzer* accumulates all traces (7) and aggregates metrics to compute per-actor data (8). Although Fig. 1 exemplifies the AkkaProf architecture when the application uses a single JVM, AkkaProf can be applied also to applications spawning multiple JVMs or multiple nodes. We do not show the AkkaProf architecture in these configurations due to the lack of space.

Metrics. The AkkaProf instrumentation logic enables the profiling of numerous metrics on actors and messages. For each actor, our tool collects its *creational overhead* and the amount of *executed computations*, both of them expressed as the number of executed bytecodes, a platform-independent metric that makes it possible to quantify computations while being less prone to perturbations arising from the instrumentation code [16]. Specifically, the former metric tracks the number of bytecode instructions executed in the dynamic extent of the constructor of each actor, while the latter captures the number of bytecode instructions executed by actors when they receive a message. AkkaProf stores also other information for each actor, e.g., their ID, class, and other Akka-specific data. Regarding messages, our profiler collects information on every message sent or received by actors, such as the message ID and class, mailbox queue order and direction (i.e., sent or received), sender and receiver actor ID, and the transmission type (i.e., `tell` or `ask`). Additionally, the trace analyzer aggregates traces to derive other per-actor metrics, such as the *actor utilization*, defined as the ratio of the executed computations to the creational overhead of each actor. Small values of actor utilization can be a sign of suboptimal performance, because the system might spend more resources for the creation and initialization of actors rather than for the execution of computations. On the contrary, high values of utilization indicate that the application could be speeded up if more computing actors are added.

4   Evaluation

In this section, we show how AkkaProf is helpful in analyzing the performance of actor-based applications by discussing some profiling results obtained from real-world workloads in the different scenarios introduced in Sect. 2[3].

Scenario 1 (actor utilization). To exemplify actor utilization profiling, we use benchmarks from the Savina suite [17] as target applications. The suite is composed of 30 diverse, CPU-intensive benchmarks implemented in 10 actor frameworks for the Java platform, including Akka. To better highlight profiling results, we categorize each actor spawned by the benchmarks in one of three groups, according to its utilization u, i.e., (1) *highly utilized* ($u >$500k), (2) *well-utilized* ($1 < u \leq$ 500k), and *little utilized* ($0 \leq u \leq 1$). We note that this is an arbitrary classification done for the purpose of this paper.

Table 1. Distribution of actors wrt. their utilization in the Savina benchmark suite. The left (right) side of the table reports five benchmarks with the highest percentage of highly (little) utilized actors.

Benchmark	# actors	% actors			Benchmark	# actors	% actors		
		Highly	Well	Little			Highly	Well	**Little**
bndbuffer	85	**90.6**	7.0	2.4	pingpong	6	0.0	66.7	**33.3**
nqueenk	25	**80.0**	12.0	8.0	count	6	16.7	50.0	**33.3**
piprecision	25	**80.0**	12.0	8.0	sieve	15	0.0	86.7	**13.3**
uct	199977	**77.7**	22.3	0.0	bitonicsort	190525	0.0	91.7	**8.3**
recmatmul	25	**20.0**	72.0	8.0	nqueenk	25	80.0	12.0	**8.0**

Table 1 summarizes the percentage of highly, well, and little utilized Akka actors in selected benchmarks. As shown by the left side of the table, a significant percentage of actors is highly utilized in some benchmarks. Depending on the characteristics of the environment and the available resources, utilization in these benchmarks could be lowered by adding more actors, with the goal of better exploiting resources available in the system. For example, in environments where more cores are available than actors running at the same time, applications

---

[3] All evaluation results are measured on a multicore platform (Intel Xeon E5-2680 2.7 GHz with 16 cores, 128 GB of RAM, CPU frequency scaling and Turbo mode disabled, Oracle JDK 1.8.0_66 b17 Hotspot Server VM 64-bit, Ubuntu Linux Server 64-bit version 14.04.3 64-bit). Each Spark o Flink worker is deployed on one such platform.

might be speeded up by adding more actors, as additional worker actors could be executed by idle cores.

On the other hand, some benchmarks feature little utilized actors. Low utilization might arise from an excessive amount of actors spawned wrt. the amount of computations to be done, or unbalanced assignment of computations to actors. As possible optimizations aimed at improving actor utilization—under the assumption that the amount of computations cannot be altered—developers might, in the first case, remove some actors. This action would avoid creating actors that would be utilized only scarcely. In the latter case, developers could consider redesigning the assignment of computations to worker actors where possible, aiming at improving load balancing. For example, bitonicsort might benefit from such an action, as 15892 actors are underutilized because of bad design rather than due to few computations to be executed.

Overall, AkkaProf is helpful in identifying highly and little utilized actors thanks to dedicated actor-centric metrics.

Scenario 2 (load balancing). We show how AkkaProf helps investigating load balancing with a field analysis on Signal/Collect [3], a parallel framework for computations on large graphs. In Signal/Collect, vertices act as computational entities that interact by means of signals flowing along the edges. Vertices are sharded across Akka worker actors, with each worker managing a whole vertex shard. The framework transforms signals into messages exchanged among Akka actors. AkkaProf can be applied proficiently to frameworks such as Signal/Collect to analyze whether computations are distributed equally between workers. In particular, AkkaProf tracks the amount of computations as bytecodes executed by workers, while signals can be analyzed by inspecting sent and received messages.

Figure 2 shows the results profiled from an 8-worker computation of the PageRank algorithm on a set of 20k webpages.[4] Overall, the subdivision of computations in the framework appears to be rather balanced between worker actors. As shown by Fig. 2(a), all workers execute similar numbers of bytecodes, i.e., around 640M, a sign of good load balancing. This is further confirmed by Figs. 2(b) and (c), revealing that all workers send and receive similar amounts of signals/messages. Overall, the number of executed bytecodes and messages exchanged are two metrics collected by AkkaProf that aid the investigation of load balancing in computing frameworks.

Scenario 3 (communication). Communication is a key activity in computing frameworks as it is involved in many operations, including job scheduling, assignment of tasks to computing workers, logging, and heartbeat signaling. As a result, an adequate knowledge on the communication occurred at runtime is necessary to completely understand the application performance in computing frameworks. Here, we use AkkaProf to compare the amount of messages sent between the master and the worker nodes in the Apache Spark [4] and Apache

---

[4] We applied the algorithm on a reduced set of 20k webpages taken from a public data source [18].

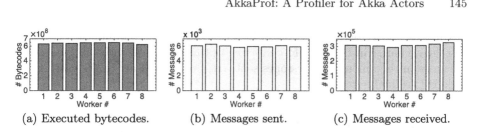

(a) Executed bytecodes.   (b) Messages sent.   (c) Messages received.

Fig. 2. Load balancing in Signal/Collect during an 8-worker PageRank computation. Results are broken down by worker actor. As worker actors can exchange messages with other non-worker actors, the total number of messages sent and received does not coincide.

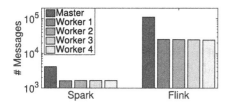

Fig. 3. Messages sent in Spark and Flink during a Kmeans computation on 10M points.

Table 2. Messages sent by the master node in Spark and Flink wrt. different input sizes.

# points	# messages sent	
	Spark	Flink
10k	3645	125005
100k	3651	92162
1M	3774	104878
10M	4088	110337

Flink [5] frameworks wrt. the amount of data processed. For each framework, we set up a small cluster composed of 1 master and 4 worker nodes, and analyze the communication incurred in a Kmeans computation. We repeat the evaluation for different numbers of data points, i.e., 10k, 100k, 1M, and 10M, to relate communication to the data size. We note that the input data set and the parameters of the computation are equal in Spark and Flink.

In Fig. 3, we compare the amount of messages sent by the master and the workers where both frameworks execute a Kmeans computation on an input set of 10M points. As can be seen from the figure, the number of messages sent is overall well distributed among workers of the same computing framework, i.e., ~1.6k messages in Spark and ~25k messages in Flink, while the master node sends many more messages, i.e., 2.5× in Spark and 4.35× in Flink wrt. the worker nodes. Judging from these results, communication in Spark appears to be more optimized than in Flink, since the latter generates 20× more messages than Spark given the same algorithm to be carried out. Exchanging too many messages, as in the case of Flink, could be sign of bad performance. Regarding the correlation between the amount of messages sent and the input data size (see Table 2), Spark shows a strong positive correlation (the correlation coefficient[5] between the two metrics is 0.99), while the correlation is rather weak in Flink (the correlation coefficient is equal to 0.18). From the traces collected by AkkaProf,

---

[5] With this term, we refer to the Pearson product-moment correlation coefficient.

we can observe a good degree of optimization in Spark communication, while message exchange in Flink could be further optimized, given the strong negative difference in the amount of messages sent wrt. Spark (at least in the case of the workload studied here).

5   Concluding Remarks

In this tool paper, we have presented AkkaProf, a profiling tool for Akka actors. To the best of our knowledge, AkkaProf is the first profiler tracking detailed metrics on the utilization and communication of Akka actors. Evaluation results demonstrate that AkkaProf can be used profitably in many scenarios. More information on AkkaProf can be found in [19] and at http://www.inf.usi.ch/phd/rosaa/akkaprof.

Limitations and Future Work. AkkaProf tracks creational overhead and the amount of executed computations as bytecode count. While being less prone to perturbations caused by the instrumentation and being platform-independent, the bytecode count is unable to track code without a bytecode representation (e.g., native methods) and cannot catch optimizations removing bytecode instructions during just-in-time compilation. We are extending AkkaProf to support machine code count profiling, which can be useful in scenarios where higher accuracy is preferred to platform independence. We are also aware that certain attributes related to Akka actors are not tracked by the current version of the tool. For example, profiling of actor hierarchy and supervising strategy, failures, and message flows between actors is currently not supported. We are extending AkkaProf to support these metrics in our ongoing work.

Acknowledgments. This work has been supported by the Swiss National Science Foundation (project 200021_141002) and by the European Commission (contract ACP2-GA-2013-605442).

References

1. Hewitt, C., Bishop, P., Steiger, R.: A universal modular ACTOR formalism for artificial intelligence. In: IJCAI, pp. 235–245 (1973)
2. Tasharofi, S., Dinges, P., Johnson, R.E.: Why do scala developers mix the actor model with other concurrency models? In: Castagna, G. (ed.) ECOOP 2013. LNCS, vol. 7920, pp. 302–326. Springer, Heidelberg (2013). doi:10.1007/978-3-642-39038-8_13
3. Stutz, P., Bernstein, A., Cohen, W.: Signal/collect: graph algorithms for the (semantic) web. In: Patel-Schneider, P.F., Pan, Y., Hitzler, P., Mika, P., Zhang, L., Pan, J.Z., Horrocks, I., Glimm, B. (eds.) ISWC 2010. LNCS, vol. 6496, pp. 764–780. Springer, Heidelberg (2010). doi:10.1007/978-3-642-17746-0_48
4. Zaharia, M., Chowdhury, M., Das, T., Dave, A., Ma, J., McCauley, M., Franklin, M.J., Shenker, S., Stoica, I.: Resilient distributed datasets: a fault-tolerant abstraction for in-memory cluster computing. In: NSDI, pp. 2:1–2:14 (2012)

5. Apache: Flink. https://flink.apache.org
6. Lightbend Monitoring. https://www.lightbend.com/products/monitoring
7. Akka Tracing. https://github.com/levkhomich/akka-tracing
8. YourKit. https://www.yourkit.com
9. VisualVM. https://visualvm.java.net
10. Bestavros, A.: Load profiling in distributed real-time systems. Inf. Sci. **101**, 1–27 (1997)
11. Vetter, J.: Dynamic statistical profiling of communication activity in distributed applications. In: SIGMETRICS, pp. 240–250 (2002)
12. Marek, L., Villazón, A., Zheng, Y., Ansaloni, D., Binder, W., Qi, Z.: DiSL: a domain-specific language for bytecode instrumentation. In: AOSD, pp. 239–250 (2012)
13. Tallent, N.R., Adhianto, L., Mellor-Crummey, J.M.: Scalable identification of load imbalance in parallel executions using call path profiles. In: SC, pp. 1–11 (2010)
14. Yu, M., Greenberg, A., Maltz, D., Rexford, J., Yuan, L., Kandula, S., Kim, C.: Profiling network performance for multi-tier data center applications. In: NSDI, pp. 57–70 (2011)
15. Fonseca, R., Porter, G., Katz, R.H., Shenker, S., Stoica, I.: X-trace: a pervasive network tracing framework. In: NSDI, pp. 271–284 (2007)
16. Binder, W., Hulaas, J.G., Villazón, A.: Portable resource control in java. In: OOPSLA, pp. 139–155 (2001)
17. Imam, S.M., Sarkar, V.: Savina - an actor benchmark suite: enabling empirical evaluation of actor libraries. In: AGERE!, pp. 67–80 (2014)
18. Backstrom, L., Huttenlocher, D., Kleinberg, J., Lan, X.: Group formation in large social networks: membership, growth, and evolution. In: KDD, pp. 44–54 (2006)
19. Rosà, A., Chen, L.Y., Binder, W.: Profiling actor utilization and communication in Akka. In: Erlang, pp. 1–9 (2016)

A Debugger-Cooperative Higher-Order Contract System in Python

Ryoya Arai[1], Shigeyuki Sato[2]($\boxtimes$), and Hideya Iwasaki[1]

[1] The University of Electro-Communications, Tokyo, Japan
`ryoya@ipl.cs.uec.ac.jp, iwasaki@cs.uec.ac.jp`
[2] Kochi University of Technology, Kochi, Japan
`sato.shigeyuki@kochi-tech.ac.jp`

Abstract. Contract programming is one of the most promising ways of enhancing the reliability of Python, which becomes increasingly desired. Higher-order contract systems that support fully specifying the behaviors of iterators and functions are desirable for Python but have not been presented yet. Besides, even with them, debugging with contracts in Python would still be burdensome because of delayed contract checking. To resolve this problem, we present PYBLAME, a higher-order contract system in Python, and ccdb, a source-level debugger equipped with features dedicated to debugging with delayed contract checking. PYBLAME and ccdb are designed on the basis of the standard of Python and thus friendly to many Python programmers. We have experimentally confirmed the advantage and the efficacy of PYBLAME and ccdb through the web framework Bottle.

Keywords: Contracts · Python · Debugging

1 Introduction

Python is a dynamic language used in various areas such as data analytics and web development. Software systems in Python grow increasingly large and complicated and become hard to maintain. For maintaining large and complicated systems, mechanical checking based on API specifications is of high importance. A reasonable and promising approach for Python is "design by contract" [17].

Contracts are assertions of the preconditions and postconditions of functions. They are represented as predicates over given arguments and results and are dynamically checked, usually in debug mode. Because of this dynamic nature, contracts are suited to Python. In addition to the classic work [18] on contracts for Python, PyContracts[1], a contract library of practical design in Python, is now available. It enables us to benefit from "design by contract" in Python.

PyContracts provides first-order contracts in the sense that functions in contracts are limited to unrestricted callable objects and checks contracts eagerly in the sense that contracts are fully evaluated at the entries and exits of target

---

[1] https://github.com/AndreaCensi/contracts.

© Springer International Publishing AG 2016
A. Igarashi (Ed.): APLAS 2016, LNCS 10017, pp. 148–168, 2016.
DOI: 10.1007/978-3-319-47958-3_9

functions. This is sufficient for a certain range of Python applications such as scientific computing and data analytics based on NumPy[2]. However, it misses the higher-order nature of Python and fails to support fully specifying the behaviors of important kinds of Python objects such as iterators and functions. To utilize contracts fully in Python, higher-order contract systems are required.

Higher-order contracts generally necessitate delayed checking [10,14,23], which is to keep checking contracts with values observed in actual use. To understand the necessity of delayed checking, consider function *ints* that returns an iterator that yields integers infinitely. For example, a contract asserting that its resultant iterators yield positive integers is a higher-order contract. At the exit of *ints*, no value to be used for checking a resultant iterator is available. When resultant iterators are used, we can check the contract with actually yielded values. Similar situations come from functions. Consider a contract that asserts two given functions, say f and g, to be behaviorally equivalent, say $\forall x, f(x) = g(x)$. We cannot enumerate this x because of its arbitrariness.

Readers might consider that higher-order contracts can be eagerly checked if values to be used for checking are finite. This is, however, unsafe in Python. Consider function *lines* that returns an iterator that yields the lines of a given file. Although we could enumerate all lines of a given file at the exit of *lines*, lines can be appended to the file afterward. Eager checking misses such appended lines although they can be observed in actual use. In higher-order functions, given/resultant functions may contain side effects. For example, in the context of web frameworks such as Python WSGI [8], given callbacks issue IO operations internally. If we invoke such callbacks eagerly for checking, we will dirty external environment with IO operations different from ones in actual use.

As can be seen from the above, delayed checking is necessary for higher-order contract systems in Python, but unfortunately leaves problems in debugging.

Contract systems *blame* culprits for contract violations: the culprits for the violations of contracts on arguments are callers (i.e., call sites) and those on results are callees (i.e., function definitions). Although this blame information is reasonably helpful for debugging with first-order contracts under eager checking, it is not so helpful for debugging with higher-order contracts under delayed checking. For example, consider assigning to *ints*, a contract that asserts its resultant iterators to yield values greater than a global variable, say n. Even though n is expected to be invariant in the contract, n cannot be guaranteed to be invariant in Python. To figure out violations regarding this contract, we therefore have to examine the value of n at the violation point as well as the violated value yielded from iterators. Because iterators can be used from place to place in the presence of side effects, it is burdensome to track violation situations. Blame information about whether a culprit is a call site of *ints* or its definition does not provide useful information for debugging. We will face a similar situation for contracts on functions because of their closures. Furthermore, if we suppose that contracts are inadequate, we should not trust the whole results of checking in debugging. The standard blame information is therefore not always sufficient.

---

[2] http://www.numpy.org/.

Generally, dealing with the above problems in debugging is part of the role of debuggers rather than contract systems. A reasonable solution is therefore the cooperation of debuggers with delayed contract checking. In this work, we have developed PYBLAME, a higher-order contract system in Python on the basis of the work by Findler and Felleisen [10], and the contract-checking debugger ccdb dedicated to debugging with delayed contract checking of PYBLAME. The contract language of PYBLAME is based on Type Hints [19], ccdb is a domain-specific extension of the Python standard debugger pdb, and the PYBLAME implementation is a pure Python library, like PyContracts. Our PYBLAME system is thus designed to be friendly to many Python programmers.

PYBLAME's higher-order contracts on iterators and functions strongly support web development. Iterators are used extensively in the Python standard library and web frameworks such as Tornado[3] for abstracting IO. Higher-order functions in the forms of callbacks and decorators are utilized in web frameworks such as WSGI, Bottle[4], and Flask[5]. We have experimentally confirmed the practical advantage of PYBLAME in expressiveness through Bottle, and the efficacy of ccdb in debugging Bottle-based applications.

Our work additionally has a notable point. To the best of our knowledge, the cooperation of debuggers with delayed contract checking has not been seriously investigated yet. Even Racket[6], which is a full-blown programming language equipped with a mature higher-order contract system, has excellent functionality of debugging but provides no support dedicated to debugging with contract checking. In this sense, our work is the first to investigate it.

Our main contributions are summarized as follows.

- We have developed PYBLAME, a higher-order contract system in Python, on the basis of the work by Findler and Felleisen [10] and Python Type Hints [19], in the form of a pure Python library (Sects. 3 and 5).
- We have developed the contract-checking debugger ccdb equipped with features dedicated to debugging with the contract checking of PYBLAME by extending the Python standard debugger pdb (Sect. 4). To the best of our knowledge, this is the first to study debuggers cooperating with delayed contract checking.
- We have experimentally demonstrated the practical advantage of PYBLAME over PyContracts in expressiveness by adding contracts into the web framework Bottle, and how effectively ccdb functions in debugging Bottle-based applications (Sect. 6). We also report the overhead of PYBLAME.

2   PyBlame at a Glance

This section briefly describes usage of PYBLAME and ccdb by example.

First, we introduce the following generator ascend with an example contract.

---

[3] http://www.tornadoweb.org/.
[4] http://bottlepy.org/.
[5] http://flask.pocoo.org/.
[6] https://racket-lang.org/.

```
def ascend(i):
    """
contracts:
  i:         int and 'i > 0'
  returns: Iterator[x: int and 'x >= glb']
    """
      i = max(i, glb)
      while True:
          yield i
          i += 1
```

Generators in Python are functions in a form dedicated to producing iterators. ascend returns an iterator that infinitely yields ascending integers starting from a given i, where global variable glb denotes the greatest lower bound of them.

Contracts in PYBLAME are described in docstrings, which are string literals attached to declarations. The contract above denotes that the parameter i of ascend is a positive integer and the result (named returns) is an iterator that yields integers greater than or equal to glb, where x is bound to each yielded value and predicates enclosed in backquotes are Boolean expressions in Python.

Next, we use this ascend as follows.

```
1  glb = 0
2  if wrongApp:
3        it = ascend(0)
4  else:
5        it = ascend(1)
6  fst = next(it)
7  glb = 3
8  snd = next(it)
```

In this example, if wrongApp is true, 0 is passed. This argument violates the contract on i and PYBLAME blames the call site at Line 3 as in common contract systems. Concretely, after printing a stack backtrace from a violation point, PYBLAME shows the following:

```
target   = <function ascend at 0x7f5944275d08>
expected = <0>Callable[[i: <2>int <1>and <3>'i > 0'],
            returns: <4>Iterator[x: <6>int <5>and <7>'x >= glb']]
violated = <3>'i > 0'
actual   = 0
blame    = ctx.
```

Here, target denotes a target function, which is a function having a concerned contract. expected denotes the whole contract assigned to a target function, which we call a *top-level contract* to contrast with its sub-contracts in the rest of this paper. To distinguish sub-contracts, each of them is numbered with a *contract index*, which is enclosed in <> in the above. violated denotes a minimal violated sub-contract. `actual` denotes an actual value that violates a `violated` sub-contract. In this case, it means the value of `i`. `blame` denotes a culprit of the violation, where `ctx` denotes a calling context (i.e., call site). This blame information is sufficient to debug this case, even for users unaware of the implementation of `ascend`.

Letting `wrongApp` be false, we then consider the case where 1 is passed to `ascend`. Since this argument is valid for the contract on `i`, this call of `ascend` (Line 5) passes contract checking. The first value yielded from its resultant iterator is 1 and the contract on `returns`, `<7>'x >= glb'`, holds at the first application of `next` (Line 6) because `glb` is 0 at this point. The definition of `glb`, however, changes to 3 at Line 7 and then `<7>'x >= glb'` does not hold at the second application of `next` (Line 8) because the second yielded value `x` is 2. Since the contract on `returns` is violated, PYBLAME blames the definition of `ascend` by providing the following message:

```
... (the same as above)
violated = <7>'x >= glb'
actual   = 2
blame    = def,
```

where `actual` denotes the value of `x` and the definition (denoted by `def`) of a target function is blamed. This blame information is logically correct. The definition of `ascend` does not guarantee that its resultant iterators always yield integers greater than or equal to `glb`. The definition does not match the contract and hence should be wrong. However, from a practical viewpoint, the definition is not always a true culprit because `glb` can be assumed to be a loop invariant. Culprits in this kind of situations would be certain misunderstandings among uses, definitions, contracts, and environments.

In order to figure out such misunderstandings, it is important for programmers to investigate the whole process of delayed checking and to observe the environment during it. At least in the example above, the concerned call site of `ascend` (Line 5) and all trigger points of its contract checking (Lines 6 and 8) should be investigated. Although the example is so small as to find them quickly, they can be far scattered over different modules in practice. Even finding them is a burdensome task before observing environments.

Our debugger `ccdb` shoulders this burdensome task. It can set breakpoints flexibly at program points concerned with contract checking on the basis of the information logged by PYBLAME. Concretely, PYBLAME generates file `.ccdbrc` when a contract violation occurs at Line 8. We then run `ccdb` with this file in the same manner as `pdb`. `ccdb` automatically sets breakpoints at Lines 5, 6, and 8, where contract checking was actually triggered. Besides, we can set breakpoints at Lines 6 and 8, where the checking of `<7>'x >= glb'` was actually triggered, by using command `ccbreak spam.py:ascend 7`, where `ascend` is assumed to be defined in file `spam.py`, on the `ccdb` prompt. After that, we can investigate the behaviors of the example program at these points with the commands of `pdb` and will identify misunderstandings (e.g., a careless change of `glb`) easily. Note that `pdb`'s command `display` is ready-made for observing the changes of `glb`.

⟨*decl*⟩   ::=   **contracts** : ⟨*var-con*⟩ {\n ⟨*var-con*⟩}

⟨*var-con*⟩   ::=   ⟨*var*⟩ : ⟨*pred*⟩

⟨*pred*⟩   ::=   ⟨*type-con*⟩ | '⟨*python-exp*⟩' | ⟨*pred*⟩ **and** ⟨*pred*⟩ | ⟨*pred*⟩ **or** ⟨*pred*⟩

⟨*type-con*⟩   ::=   ⟨*base-type*⟩ | **Tuple** [⟨*tuple-con*⟩] | **List** [⟨*elm-con*⟩]

    | **Set** [⟨*elm-con*⟩] | **Dict** [⟨*elm-con*⟩ , ⟨*elm-con*⟩]

    | **Iterator** [⟨*elm-con*⟩] | **Iterable** [⟨*elm-con*⟩]

    | **Callable** [⟨*param-con*⟩ , ⟨*elem-con*⟩]

⟨*elm-con*⟩   ::=   ⟨*var*⟩ : ⟨*pred*⟩ | ⟨*pred*⟩

⟨*tuple-con*⟩   ::=   ε | ⟨*elm-con*⟩ {, ⟨*elm-con*⟩}

⟨*param-con*⟩   ::=   ... | [⟨*tuple-con*⟩]

⟨*base-type*⟩   ::=   **Any** | ⟨*class-name*⟩

Fig. 1. Syntax of contract language of PYBLAME, where {*s*} denote 0 or more times repetition of *s*, terms in a type-writer font are terminal, and ε denotes the empty.

The misunderstandings mentioned above can result in inadequate contracts. We sometimes should investigate suspicious contracts. Even if `<7>'x >= glb'` is not actually violated, we could set breakpoints with the same command. We thus can investigate unintentional passing of contract checking. Apart from `ascend`, top-level contracts can be large and complicated. Another additional command `exam` shows actually examined sub-contracts in order to make it easier to find suspicious sub-contracts. `ccdb` thus alleviates the burden of debugging even in the presence of inadequate contracts.

3   Contract Language

This section describes the contract language of PYBLAME. As described in Sect. 2, it is supposed to be used within the docstrings of target functions.

3.1   Syntax

We design our contract language as a mixture of type annotations and Python expressions. We employ the syntax of Type Hints [19] for part of type annotations. Figure 1 shows the syntax of our contract language.

⟨*var-con*⟩ denotes a contract on variables, where ⟨*var*⟩ is a target variable and ⟨*pred*⟩ is the body part. Target variables are either parameters or the special variable `returns`, which is bound to the result of the current call of target functions. ⟨*var-con*⟩ on parameters corresponds to preconditions and the one on `returns` corresponds to postconditions.

⟨*pred*⟩ denotes predicates, where **and** and **or** are logical operators with short-circuit evaluation. ⟨*python-exp*⟩ denotes arbitrary Boolean expressions in Python, which are supposed to have no side effect in user's responsibility. Evaluation rules for them shall be explained in the next subsection.

⟨*type-con*⟩ denotes type-checking predicates. It basically follows the syntax of Type Hints but enables us to describe ⟨*pred*⟩ on elements of data structures as contract ⟨*elem-con*⟩. ⟨*elem-con*⟩ can introduce names, ⟨*var*⟩, bound to element values for enriching the ⟨*pred*⟩ part: e.g., `List[x : int and x > 0]` denotes a contract of positive integer lists. ⟨*type-con*⟩ therefore is more expressive than common type checking.

`Iterator` denotes objects that satisfy the iterator protocol in Python. As in the Python standard library document[7], `Iterable` denotes objects that provide iterators and `Callable` denotes function-like objects. `Tuple`, `List`, `Set`, and `Dict` denote built-in ones in Python. Our system does not capture their subclasses but implementation of capturing subclasses is straightforward.

⟨*param-con*⟩ is also based on Type Hints: e.g., ... denotes unrestricted parameters and `[]` denotes no parameter. Although not described in Fig. 1 for brevity, it can accept arbitrary argument lists and keyword argument dictionaries: e.g., `Callable[[*args: List[int], **kwargs: Dict[str,int]], bool]` denotes a contract on functions that return `bool` by taking an arbitrary number of `int` arguments followed by keyword arguments of `int`. ⟨*base-type*⟩ is either a class name in Python, which can be built-in or user-defined, or `Any`, which denotes any value of any type. Note that the `Any` contract is assigned to all parameters and `returns` by default.

There is a restriction on contracts on `Iterator`, `Iterable`, and `Callable`, i.e., higher-order contracts, which are checked in a delayed manner. The restriction is that at most one higher-order contract is permitted to exist within an `or`-chain of contracts. It is added in order to simplify implementation of delayed checking, as in Racket's contract system[8]. Note that we can remove this restriction, on the basis of the recent work by Keil and Thiemann [14].

3.2 Evaluation

Environments (i.e., evaluation contexts) for ⟨*python-exp*⟩ are based on the ones in which target functions are defined, and augmented with argument environments, which include the entries of `returns` besides parameters if ⟨*python-exp*⟩ is for postconditions. ⟨*elem-con*⟩ performs name binding optionally; it can shadow names: e.g., `x: int or List[x: str and 'len(x) > 0']` of ⟨*var-con*⟩ denotes that parameter `x` is of `int` or is a list of positive-length strings. Environments of ⟨*elem-con*⟩ within ⟨*tuple-con*⟩ are extended with name binding in the left-to-right order. Note that local variables except for parameters in target functions are not visible. The name lookup out of argument environments and ⟨*elem-con*⟩ complies with the semantics of Python; i.e., letting v be a name bound neither in argument environments nor ⟨*elem-con*⟩, v is looked up in the same manner as the target function name; e.g., `glb` in the contract in Sect. 2 is looked up in the same manner as `ascend`. ⟨*class-name*⟩ is looked up in the environments in which target functions are defined, independently of arguments and ⟨*elem-con*⟩.

---

[7] http://docs.python.org/3/.
[8] https://docs.racket-lang.org/reference/data-structure-contracts.html.

Sequences of ⟨*var-con*⟩ are serially evaluated. ⟨*elem-con*⟩ is evaluated in the left-to-right order on argument lists like Scheme. Higher-order sub-contracts are checked in a delayed manner, while first-order (or *flat* in Racket) sub-contracts are fully evaluated in an eager manner. The evaluation order within higher-order sub-contracts and that within first-order ones are preserved. For example, consider the **and**-chains containing higher-order operands and first-order ones. The first-order ones are evaluated from left to right at call/return time and checking on them finishes, while the higher-order ones are checked from left to right in a delayed manner. Higher-order **or**-chains are similar but delayed checking on **or**-chain of higher-order contracts does not arise from them because of the syntactic restriction above. This evaluation strategy is identical to Racket's.

Nested ⟨*type-con*⟩ is evaluated from outermost constructs. This is important for understanding higher-order contracts because they are gradually evaluated in delayed checking. For example, consider `f: <1>Callable[...,` `<2>Iterable[ <3>int]]` of ⟨*var-con*⟩ and the following code:

```
iterable = f ()
iterator = iter ( iterable )
x = next ( iterator ),
```

where the contract on `f` is checked in a delayed manner. Then, the part of `<1>` is checked at the call of `f()`; the part of `<2>` is checked at the call of `iter(iterable)`; the part of `<3>` is checked at the call of `next(iterator)`. Note that checking on Python-level signature matching in `Callable` is always performed in an eager manner regardless of contracts on parameters.

4   Contract-Checking Debugger

This section describes our contract-checking debugger ccdb, which is a domain-specific debugger for delayed contract checking. In the following subsections, we describe domain-specific issues and the basic design of ccdb. We then explain the features and usage of ccdb.

4.1   Motivation and Basic Design

As mentioned in Sects. 1 and 2, an essential issue of debugging on delayed contract checking is that contract checking can occur from place to place and we sometimes have to investigate each result of this checking together with the current environment.

A common way of investigating environments at some points is to use breakpoints of debuggers. With breakpoints at triggers of delayed checking, we would utilize the functionality of debuggers fully for dealing with the issue above. It is, however, difficult to statically determine exact trigger points of delayed checking. With static (may) analysis, we would get too many trigger points to debug without burden. For example, it is even difficult for static analysis to focus on the trigger points of a specific sub-contract. We therefore consider it reasonable to utilize dynamic information for determining breakpoints concerned with contract checking.

Use of complete dynamic information is generally expensive and far from lightweight use because data to be recorded have to be huge. For the simplicity of tooling, we then assume that programmers can reproduce the same behaviors of target programs. Although it is generally nontrivial, it is assumed in common use of traditional debuggers. Under this assumption, we can consider two-phase debugging with contracts: with the first run (called *check-run*) of target programs, we record points concerned with delayed contract checking; in the second run (called *debug-run*), we use debuggers for investigating suspicious code at the recorded points. We have adopted this two-phase approach.

Essentially desired functionality is to set breakpoints at trigger points of delayed contract checking. Because contracts can be large and complicated in practice, it is particularly important for debugging to focus on a specific sub-contract of a top-level contract. The primary domain-specific feature should be to set breakpoints at trigger points of specific sub-contracts.

Note that we could set breakpoints at trigger points of delayed checking by setting breakpoints to predicates in contracts without dedicated commands. In order to focus on specific sub-contracts in such cases, users would manage to introduce dummy predicates only for breakpoints by hand. This is never desirable because it dirties contracts for debugging as well as is error-prone. A command dedicated to this domain-specific feature is therefore desired.

Besides this domain-specific feature, features of matured debuggers are also desired for debugging. It is reasonable to extend existing debuggers so as to avoid reinventing the wheel and imposing on users a cost to learn APIs. The most friendly debugger with Python programmers is the standard debugger pdb, which is a source-level debugger suitable to Python. We therefore have adopted pdb for a base debugger and extended it with domain-specific features.

In summary, the following is the basic design of ccdb.

- It requires users to do the check-run and debug-run of target programs and to reproduce their behaviors.
- It enables us to set breakpoints at trigger points of specific sub-contracts.
- It is based on pdb for becoming friendly with common Python programmers.

4.2   Features and Usage

ccdb provides four domain-specific commands: ccbreak, contract, exam, and blame. We describe their features together with their use cases.

First of all, these domain-specific commands enable us to focus on specific sub-contracts. To enable us to identify sub-contracts, as shown in Sect. 2, PyBlame numbers in preorder all sub-contracts of each top-level contract with contract indices. Index 0 always means a top-level contract. With a triple of a module name, function name, and contract index, we can identify a specific sub-contract globally. Note that contract indices of **and** and **or** used in command arguments have different meanings for usability. They denote all their sub-contracts but not themselves; e.g., in the contract shown in Sect. 2, index 1 denotes the set of indices 2 and 3.

The `ccbreak` command sets breakpoints at the trigger points of a given sub-contract. This is the primary feature of `ccdb`. Breakpoints are set at the trigger points of checking of a violated sub-contract by default but `ccbreak` enables us to set ones at those of non-violated sub-contracts. This is particularly useful for investigating suspicious sub-contracts, where contracts may be inadequate for specifications. With the standard commands to enable/disable breakpoints, we also can focus on specific triggers of delayed checking in debugging.

The `contract` command pretty-prints the top-level contract of a given function. This pretty-print includes contract indices. By using this command, we choose which contract index we focus on, particularly just before debug-run.

The `exam` command displays actually examined sub-contracts in a given sub-contract in the form of contract indices. This is useful for investigating whether contract checking worked expectedly because we can cause unintentional skips of sub-contracts with the short-circuit evaluation of **and** and **or**.

The `blame` command shows the standard blame information of a given contract, i.e., points out a culprit if the contract is violated. This is useful for contracts on higher-order functions because the criteria of blames for them are a bit complicated. PYBLAME follows the basic criterion [10] of blames.

Although these commands take the names of modules and functions but not expressions, we can identify them on `ccdb` owing to Python's reflection.

5   Implementation

This section describes the implementation of our system, assuming some knowledge on the Python standard library[9]. Note that our implementation is a set of pure Python modules based on CPython 3.4 or later.

5.1   Outline

We describe the outline of PYBLAME by following the workflow of our system shown in Fig. 2.

Given a source-code file containing docstrings that declare contracts, first, the main module `pyblame` of PYBLAME parses it into an AST. Next, `pyblame` examines the docstrings of all functions on the AST and attaches to each function having a contract, a decorator that wraps a given function with a proxy object. This proxy object is an object that behaves the same as a wrapped object except for checking the associated contract by intercepting arguments and results. The details of proxy objects shall be explained later. Lastly, `pyblame` compiles this decorator-attached AST to a bytecode object and runs it as a check-run.

---

[9] https://docs.python.org/3/library/index.html.

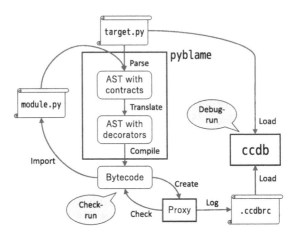

Fig. 2. Workflow of our system, where rectangles denote our system. `pyblame` is the main module of PYBLAME and the proxy is part of it; `target.py` is a main program given to `pyblame` and imports `module.py`; `.ccdbrc` is a configuration file.

To enable PYBLAME in all the modules used from a given program, `pyblame` adds an import hook globally for hijacking the implementation of all import statements so that the compilation above is applied to imported modules. Once modules are imported, their compiled bytecode objects are cached, and will be simply returned in the later imports. This import hook thus enables PYBLAME recursively for all.

To enable `ccdb` to take account of delayed checking and blame, PYBLAME generates configuration files of `ccdb`. Proxy objects record all triggers of delayed checking and log them to files.

5.2   Proxy Objects

Use of proxy objects is a key technique of implementing contract checking as a library like PyContracts and Racket's contract system because contract checking ought to be transparent within target programs.

As described in the previous subsection, proxy objects wrap target functions so as to check their contracts at call/return time. If contracts are first-order, these proxy objects suffice for checking. If they are higher-order, arguments and/or results are also wrapped with other proxy objects that perform delayed checking. Since targets of delayed checking can be passed to functions with contracts, proxy objects for delayed checking can be nested.

The notion above is the same as Racket's contract system, but in Python, functions are merely objects, i.e., stateful and mutable. Any effect on proxy objects such as property access and method invocation has to be bypassed to their wrapped objects. Fortunately, Python provides various hook methods that trap operations on objects, which are just the very thing for proxy objects. Concretely, we have used the `__getattribute__` hook for trapping any property access (including method invocation). In this hook, we can distinguish operations on objects, e.g., __call__, calling as functions, and __next__, extracting the next value as iterators. The __getattribute__ hooks of proxy objects, according to the associated contracts, trap appropriate operations and check arguments and/or results, and bypass the other operations to wrapped objects. The implementation of proxy classes has been based on that in Reticulated Python[10].

Although many operations are successfully trapped in Python hook methods, there are exceptional cases. The first is object identity, which the is operator tests and the built-in function id returns. The second is type extraction with the built-in function type. The third is reflection functionality provided in the inspect module. These are representative. Generally, the functionality implementation at the CPython interpreter level would be untrappable at the Python language level. This is a known issue on the Python language; in fact, PyPy provided to resolve it transparent proxies [1], which have still been experimental[11]. We therefore consider this issue to be beyond the scope of our work.

5.3   Compilation to Proxy Objects

The compilation of our contract language to proxy objects are performed at function definition time by decorators attached to target functions. This compilation is straightforward on the basis of the work [10] of Racket's contract system. Yet, we have simplified implementation by exploiting the Python standard library.

Since contracts in our contract language are designed to inhabit docstrings, target programs of pyblame follow the Python syntax. We have simply employed the standard parser ast module for parsing given source files. We have developed only a parser for docstrings with contracts. Although our contract language has syntactic flexibility derived from Python such as parameter lists of functions, it is basically a simple extension of Python Type Hints. We therefore have been able to employ Python's reflection for parsing; e.g., Signature extracted with inspect is ready-made for parsing parameter lists. Besides, inspect has been useful for constructing environments; we have used run-time stack frames, which inspect provided, in generated decorators for environments on the basis of the fact that they will be called only at the definition positions of target functions. Because our AST transformations are merely to attach decorators to functions, we have been able to use simply the built-in functions compile and exec for bytecode compilation and running.

5.4   Debugger and Debugger Support

ccdb is simply a surface extension of pdb. Proxy objects of PYBLAME record information on delayed checking of each contract in a check-run and logs it in the form of a configuration file of ccdb. Then, ccdb simply loads this configuration

---

[10] https://github.com/mvitousek/reticulated.
[11] http://doc.pypy.org/en/latest/objspace-proxies.html.

file and prepares for the domain-specific commands on the basis of the APIs of pdb. Only this point is the extension of pdb in ccdb.

Configuration files concretely include the following:

- The program point (i.e., file name and line number) and concerned sub-contract of each trigger of the checking of each top-level contract,
- A string representation containing contract indices, of each sub-contract,
- The target of the blame of each sub-contract, and
- A set of examined sub-contracts,

where a sub-contract c in the top-level contract of a function named f in a module (i.e., file) named m is represented as a triple of m, f, and the contract index of c. These data are sufficient to implement the domain-specific commands.

6   Experiments

This section describes experiments that we conducted. All source files are available on http://www.scinfo.kochi-tech.ac.jp/sato-s/pyblame.zip.

6.1   Expressiveness

PYBLAME is a higher-order contract system, which has not ever been developed in Python, while PyContracts is a (matured) first-order contract system. For this difference, PYBLAME is more expressive than PyContracts in principle. However, it does not demonstrate that the expressiveness of PYBLAME is more advantageous in practice. As mentioned in Sect. 1, we observed higher-order programming in Python in web frameworks. We therefore selected Bottle (version 0.13-dev), which is a small yet complete web framework, for a benchmark for evaluating the expressiveness of PYBLAME.

Table 1. Breakdown of contracts assigned to Bottle.

Iterator	Iterable	Callable	Higher-order	Callback	Total
3	2	9	11	14	47

On the basis of the documentation (mostly in docstrings) of Bottle, we assigned contracts to its public methods and top-level functions, which were considered as core APIs. Table 1 shows the breakdown of the contracts assigned, of which the number was 47. Iterator, Iterable, and Callable in Table 1 denote the number of top-level contracts where they were used. The total number of higher-order top-level contracts was 11. It is worth noting that the number of top-level contracts in which callbacks were used was 14 although PYBLAME did not regard them as higher-order. We decided to assign 'callable(c)' to callback c. Callbacks were, in fact, basically like Callable[..., str] but in some cases were not. For example, they can be the instances of template classes, which produce strings via method **render**, not function calling. In redirection, they just raise exceptions without returning values. The documentation of Bottle was not sufficiently clear for us to determine desired specifications. Without the ambiguity of specifications, it would be intuitive to assign higher-order contracts to them. In this sense, the total number of higher-order contracts and potential ones was 25. From these results, we have confirmed that the APIs of Bottle actually had a higher-order nature as we expected and higher-order contracts that PYBLAME supports are practically advantageous to web frameworks like Bottle.

6.2   Overhead

PYBLAME is not offering its run-time performance because it is for debugging programs regarding their behaviors. How much overhead PYBLAME incurs is, however, informative for users to reason practically feasible settings for debugging. We therefore measured the run-time overhead of PYBLAME. We used for a experimental environment, a laptop PC equipped with Intel Core i7 CPU M620 and 8-GB memory of DDR3-1333 running Debian stretch (Linux 4.5.0-2-amd64). All Python programs ran on CPython 3.5.1.

We used for measuring overhead three benchmark programs: empty-bottle, loop-n, and rec-n. empty-bottle is the Bottle having contracts described in the previous subsection without any application so as to end quickly, where its source code was of 4,223 LOC. This is for measuring the overhead of load-time transformation. loop-n is a loop iterating n times with an iterator that yields the same integer as with itertools.repeat and has a type-checking contract that always holds. This indicates the overhead of trapping functions and recording logs. rec-n is a recursive function that corresponds to loop-n. This indicates the worst-case overhead of nesting of proxy objects, where n proxy objects are eventually nested. Note that we do not regard the time for evaluating contracts themselves as overhead because they are part of programs and their practical feasibility relies completely on users. Dumping configuration files are cheap because of their small sizes; its cost is negligible compared to the others.

Table 2. Elapsed time in seconds of benchmarks with/without PYBLAME, where N/A means that it did not finish successfully in realistic time.

	empty-bottle	loop-10^5	loop-$75 \cdot 10^6$	rec-69	rec-997
Without PYBLAME	0.144	0.040	13.876	0.020	0.024
With PYBLAME	1.100	14.072	N/A	2.120	N/A

We measured the elapsed time of each benchmark with/without PYBLAME by using the **time** command. Table 2 shows the results of measurement, where each result was the median of 10 trials. The check-run of empty-bottle was about 7.6× slower than the plain run. The check-run of loop-n was about 750× slower by comparing results at different n. rec-n showed the difference in feasibility as well as time. The check-run exceeded the stack limit of CPython at $n = 70$, while the plain run exceeded the limit at $n = 998$. This was because checking via nesting of proxy objects expended more stack space than rec-n itself. PYBLAME incurs considerable overhead and therefore necessitates small input for debugging.

6.3   Debugging Scenarios

In order to demonstrate how effectively ccdb functions, we explain debugging of a simple yet realistic example based on Bottle, shown in Fig. 3.

```
1   import bottle
2
3   def load_prof_view(must):
4       """
5   contracts:
6     must:    Set[str]
7     returns: Callable[[Callable[..., r: dict and
8                                     'must <= r.keys()']],
9                        Callable[..., str]]
10      """
11      return bottle.view('prof.tpl')
12
13  must_fields = {'name'}
14  prof_view = load_prof_view(must_fields)
15
16  @bottle.route('/spam')
17  @prof_view
18  def spam():
19      return {'name' : 'spam'}
20
21  @bottle.route('/ham')
22  @prof_view
23  def ham():
24      return {'user_id' : 309}
```

Fig. 3. Example application prof.py based on Bottle.

prof.py provides profile pages at paths /spam and /ham. Each profile page is generated from template prof.tpl. Functions spam and ham return dictionaries to be substituted into prof.tpl for generating pages. Two key decorator-based APIs of Bottle are used there. One is bottle.view: it produces a decorator that converts a function returning a dictionary into a function producing a page of string by substituting the dictionary to a given template file. The other is bottle.route: it produces a decorator that associates a function producing a page with a given path. Note that decorator attachment @ corresponds to function composition. By attaching these two decorators to `spam` and `ham`, the corresponding pages are thus respectively provided.

Now, `prof.tpl` is supposed to require the value of `'name'` field for rendering pages. Function `load_prof_view`, which wraps `bottle.view('prof.tpl')`, declares and enforces this requirement by using a contract, where the parameter `must` denotes a set of required field names. `spam` returns a dictionary containing an entry of `'name'`, while `ham` does not, which is a bug. Without the contract, the access to `/ham` simply causes an uninformative internal error. With the contract, it instead causes a contract violation more helpful for debugging.

Then, consider this violation. The point where it occurs is deep in Bottle (i.e., module `bottle`) and far from the point of the root cause (i.e., the definition point of `ham`) because `ham` is part of a callback registered. Its stack backtrace is not informative at all because it does not contain any program point of `prof.py`. From this violation, PYBLAME provides the following blame information:

```
target   = <function load_prof_view at 0x7fcdccced378>
expected = <0>Callable[[must: <1>Set[<2>str]],
  returns: <3>Callable[[<4>Callable[..., r: <6>dict <5>and
                                          <7>'must <= r.keys()']],
                    <8>Callable[..., <9>str]]]
violated = <7>'must <= r.keys()'
actual   = {'user_id': 309}
blame    = ctx,
```

where `actual` denotes the value of `r`. The calling context of `load_prof_view` is blamed but its very call site is not wrong. This blame informs us only that some problem lies around its call site(s). This is not satisfactory for debugging.

`ccdb` enables us to examine programs efficiently by focusing on the violated sub-contract. First, from the violated sub-contract, we notice that `must` and `r` matter. For examining what object `must` is bound to, the trigger point(s) of delayed checking regarding `<1>` is helpful. By using `ccbreak`, we can set a breakpoint at the trigger point (Line 14). From the source code there, we notice that an object to which `must_fields` is bound matters. Assuming that `must_fields` is a correct invariant, the next concern is a function that produces the violation value of `r`. The trigger points of checking regarding `<4>` are helpful for examining it because `load_prof_view` returns a decorator. By using `ccbreak`, we can set breakpoints at the application points of its resultant decorator (Lines 17 and 22). After that, by examining the source code of these suspicious functions, we are eventually able to find a bug of `ham`, whose source code can be shown there by command `source ham.__wrapped__`. This is a typical usage of `ccdb` and useful for common situations.

Next, consider a more complicated situation such that `must_fields` destructively changes to `{'user_id'}` before a web server in Bottle is ready. This is a very hard situation because the access to `/spam` causes a contract violation even though the result of `spam` suffices for rendering a page. Furthermore, the contract is correctly satisfied at the definition point of `spam`. This situation is similar to the example of `ascend` described in Sect. 2. To figure out this problem, we have to monitor the object to which `must` is bound. As mentioned above, we can identify the target object with the one to which `must_fields` is bound at Line 14 in `prof.py`. At this point, we can introduce a fresh global variable, say `__tar`, bound to the target object by executing `__tar = must_fields` on the ccdb prompt. After that, we can keep monitoring the target via `prof.__tar` at arbitrary breakpoints. Although this monitoring would not solve a bug directly, it brings us a better understanding of this very hard situation. It is worth noting that such complicated situations are not artificial in Python programming. Since everything in Python is an object and objects are generally stateful, even contracts in Python easily become stateful. `ccdb` alleviates the burden of debugging complicated situations derived from the stateful nature of Python.

Lastly, consider dealing with inadequate contracts: false-positive ones and false-negative ones. False-positive cases are relatively tractable because wrong sub-contracts are violated. In the same manner as the above, we can examine a wrong sub-contract and the values of its internal expressions at the violation point. False-negative cases are more unclear. For example, assuming that we wrongly write `or` instead of `and`, i.e., `r: dict or 'must <= r.keys()'`, contract violations that depend on the contents of `must_fields` do not occur. We can recognize something wrong from errors caused by the access to `/ham` but obtain no information useful for debugging from contracts themselves. However, by using `exam`, we can immediately find `'must <= r.keys()'` not evaluated and notice that a logical operator around it is wrong.

Through these cases, we have confirmed that `ccdb` are useful for debugging with delayed contract checking.

7 Related Work

This section discusses related work particularly on contract programming and on type checking, and describes the points of our work.

7.1 Contract Programming

Meyer [17] presented the notion of contracts and contract programming (i.e., design by contract). His contract system was implemented as a part of Eiffel, a typed object-oriented language. In the context of object-oriented languages, contract systems were implemented in dynamic languages such as Smalltalk [2] and Python [18]. PyContracts presented a modern and practical design of the classic work [18].

Findler and Felleisen [10] brought contracts into higher-order (functional) languages. This prominent work was followed by various extensions such as contracts for first-class classes [21,22], contracts regarding property access [12], typed lazy contracts [4], option contracts [7], and contracts with union and intersection [14], where several [12,21,22] were particularly for dynamic languages. PyBlame mimics Racket's implementation[12] based on the work [10].

---

[12] https://docs.racket-lang.org/reference/contracts.html.

While contract systems themselves support debugging, several studies utilized contracts for related tasks such as test case generation [13,15] and automatic program repair [25]. Nevertheless, to the best of our knowledge, the cooperation of debuggers has not been well studied. Although IDE integration [9] and automatic program repair [25] could be seen as special forms of debugger cooperation, they did not deal with higher-order contracts. For example, ccdb enables us to set breakpoints around delayed checking of specified sub-contracts. We have not found the same functionality in existing work, while BPGen [26], for example, generated breakpoints automatically on the basis of dynamic fault localization techniques and Chiş et al. [3] pointed out importance of domain-specific debuggers. All in all, we believe that our work on debugger cooperation presents a new point of view in contract programming.

7.2   Type Checking

Although static type checking is the common and standard approach to mechanical checking based on API specifications, standard type systems do not work well for dynamic languages including Python. Many studies dealt with taming their dynamic nature in type systems. Notable work is gradual typing [20], which enables us to specify partially typed programs remaining partially untyped (i.e., dynamic). Static type checking works well for the typed part in gradually typed programs by adding run-time type checking around the boundaries between the typed and the untyped. Gradually typed ones were developed for many dynamic languages: e.g., TypeScript[13] for JavaScript, Hack[14] for PHP, Typed Racket[15] for Racket, and Reticulated Python [24] and mypy[16] for Python. Gradual typing enriches checking merely on static properties of APIs, which are much restrictive and far from dynamic languages, while contracts enrich checking on dynamic properties, which are inherent in dynamic languages.

A *best-effort* approach to static type checking on dynamic properties of programs is hybrid type checking [11,16], which is based on refinement types. Refinement types there are types with arbitrary predicates like contracts. Although static checking of such refinement types is generally undecidable, yet it is feasible for some specific cases. Hybrid type checking employs theorem provers for static type checking in tractable cases and uses dynamic checking for intractable cases. Later developed was a more sophisticated design of refinement types [5,6] dedicated to dynamic languages like JavaScript, where dynamic idioms were statically checked.

These work extended ranges of static checking of contracts but this is orthogonal to dynamic checking, which our work deals with. Besides, the problem setting of our work is different from those of their work. Our setting in use of contracts subsumes the presence of unknown background codebases as in applications based on web frameworks. Backgrounds can be stateful and interaction

---

[13] https://www.typescriptlang.org/.

[14] http://hacklang.org/.

[15] https://docs.racket-lang.org/ts-guide/.

[16] http://mypy-lang.org/.

with them can be implicitly effectful. This setting makes static checking almost infeasible. Rich run-time information, which debuggers provide, on undesired behaviors is still more helpful and important. The presence of static checking does not diminish the significance of our work.

8   Conclusion

In this paper, we have presented PYBLAME, a higher-order contract system in Python, and ccdb, a source-level debugger that takes account of the contract checking of PYBLAME. Delayed contract checking is important for Python contracts but debugging with it is burdensome. The cooperation of debuggers alleviates this burden.

As concluding remarks, we describe two extensions of PYBLAME left for future work. The first is to provide contracts for coroutines. For simplicity, we regarded generators as functions that return iterators. Precisely, their results are not simple iterators but coroutines, which can take values to yield values. Python 3.5 has introduced language constructs dedicated to coroutines and strongly supports asynchronous IO with coroutines. Because we consider coroutine-based APIs of asynchronous IO to be useful partially for web development, coroutines are worth supporting in PYBLAME. The second is to provide contracts on series observed in iterators and coroutines. To describe a contract asserting iterators, for example, to yield monotonically increasing sequences, we have to use two adjacent observations on yielded values. Recording all observations for contracts will incur unacceptable spatial overhead. Moderately expressive contracts with reasonable expense are desirable for observation series.

References

1. D12.1: High-level backends and interpreter feature prototypes. PyPy EU-Report (2007)
2. Carrillo-Castellon, M., Garcia-Molina, J., Pimentel, E., Repiso, I.: Design by contract in smalltalk. J. Object-Oriented Program **7**(9), 23–28 (1996)
3. Chiş, A., Gîrba, T., Nierstrasz, O.: The moldable debugger: a framework for developing domain-specific debuggers. In: Proceedings of the 2015 ACM SIGPLAN International Conference on Software Language Engineering, SLE 2014, pp. 102–121. ACM (2014)
4. Chitil, O.: Practical typed lazy contracts. In: Proceedings of the 17th ACM SIGPLAN International Conference on Functional Programming, ICFP 2012, pp. 67–76. ACM (2012)
5. Chugh, R., Herman, D., Jhala, R.: Dependent types for JavaScript. In: Proceedings of the 2012 ACM International Conference on Object Oriented Programming Systems Languages and Applications, OOPSLA 2012, pp. 587–606. ACM (2012)
6. Chugh, R., Rondon, P.M., Jhala, R.: Nested refinements: a logic for duck typing. In: Proceedings of the 39th Annual ACM SIGPLAN-SIGACT Symposium on Principles of Programming Languages, POPL 2012, pp. 231–244. ACM (2012)

7. Dimoulas, C., Findler, R.B., Felleisen, M.: Option contracts. In: Proceedings of the 2013 ACM SIGPLAN International Conference on Object Oriented Programming Systems Languages and Applications, OOPSLA 2013, pp. 475–494. ACM (2013)
8. Eby, P.J.: PEP 3333 - Python Web Server Gateway Interface v1.0.1 (2010). https://www.python.org/dev/peps/pep-3333/
9. Fähndrich, M., Barnett, M., Leijen, D., Logozzo, F.: Integrating a set of contract checking tools into visual studio. In: Proceedings of the Second International Workshop on Developing Tools as Plug-Ins, TOPI 2012, pp. 43–48. IEEE (2012)
10. Findler, R.B., Felleisen, M.: Contracts for higher-order functions. In: Proceedings of the Seventh ACM SIGPLAN International Conference on Functional Programming, ICFP 2002, pp. 48–59. ACM (2002)
11. Flanagan, C.: Hybrid type checking. In: Conference Record of the 33rd ACM SIGPLAN-SIGACT Symposium on Principles of Programming Languages, POPL 2006, pp. 245–256. ACM (2006)
12. Heidegger, P., Bieniusa, A., Thiemann, P.: Access permission contracts for scripting languages. In: Proceedings of the 39th Annual ACM SIGPLAN-SIGACT Symposium on Principles of Programming Languages, POPL 2012, pp. 111–122. ACM (2012)
13. Heidegger, P., Thiemann, P.: Contract-driven testing of JavaScript code. In: Vitek, J. (ed.) TOOLS 2010. LNCS, vol. 6141, pp. 154–172. Springer, Heidelberg (2010). doi:10.1007/978-3-642-13953-6_9
14. Keil, M., Thiemann, P.: Blame assignment for higher-order contracts with intersection and union. In: Proceedings of the 20th ACM SIGPLAN International Conference on Functional Programming, ICFP 2015, pp. 375–386. ACM (2015)
15. Klein, C., Flatt, M., Findler, R.B.: Random testing for higher-order, stateful programs. In: Proceedings of the 2010 ACM International Conference on Object Oriented Programming Systems Languages and Applications, OOPSLA 2010, pp. 555–566. ACM (2010)
16. Knowles, K., Flanagan, C.: Hybrid type checking. ACM Trans. Program. Lang. Syst. 32(2), 6:1–6:34 (2010)
17. Meyer, B.: Applying "Design by Contract". Computer 25(10), 40–51 (1992)
18. Plösch, R.: Design by contract for Python. In: Proceedings of the Fourth Asia-Pacific Software Engineering and International Computer Science Conference, APSEC 1997, pp. 213–219. IEEE (1997)
19. van Rossum, G., Lehtosalo, J., Langa, Ł.: PEP 484 - Type Hints (2014). https://www.python.org/dev/peps/pep-0484/
20. Siek, J.G., Taha, W.: Gradual typing for functional languages. In: Scheme and Functional Programming 2006. TR-2006-06, University of Chicago (2006)
21. Strickland, T.S., Dimoulas, C., Takikawa, A., Felleisen, M.: Contracts for first-class classes. ACM Trans. Program. Lang. Syst. 35(3), 11:1–11:58 (2013)
22. Strickland, T.S., Felleisen, M.: Contracts for first-class classes. In: Proceedings of the 6th Symposium on Dynamic Languages, DLS 2010, pp. 97–112. ACM (2010)
23. Strickland, T.S., Tobin-Hochstadt, S., Findler, R.B., Flatt, M.: Chaperones and impersonators: run-time support for reasonable interposition. In: Proceedings of the 2012 ACM International Conference on Object Oriented Programming Systems Languages and Applications, OOPSLA 2012, pp. 943–962. ACM (2012)
24. Vitousek, M.M., Kent, A.M., Siek, J.G., Baker, J.: Design and evaluation of gradual typing for Python. In: Proceedings of the 10th ACM Symposium on Dynamic Languages, DLS 2014, pp. 45–56. ACM (2014)

25. Wei, Y., Pei, Y., Furia, C.A., Silva, L.S., Buchholz, S., Meyer, B., Zeller, A.: Automated fixing of programs with contracts. In: Proceedings of the 19th International Symposium on Software Testing and Analysis, ISSTA 2010, pp. 61–72. ACM (2010)
26. Zhang, C., Yan, D., Zhao, J., Chen, Y., Yang, S.: BPGen: an automated breakpoint generator for debugging. In: Proceedings of the 32nd ACM/IEEE International Conference on Software Engineering, ICSE 2010, vol. 2, pp. 271–274. ACM (2010)

λ-Calculus

A Sound and Complete Bisimulation for Contextual Equivalence in λ-Calculus with Call/cc

Taichi Yachi$^{(\boxtimes)}$ and Eijiro Sumii$^{(\boxtimes)}$

Tohoku University, Sendai, Japan
{yachi,sumii}@sf.ecei.tohoku.ac.jp

Abstract. We develop a sound and complete proof method of contextual equivalence in λ-calculus with the abortive control operator call/cc (as opposed to delimited control operators like `shift` and `reset`), and prove the non-trivial equivalence between $\lambda f. f()$ and $\lambda f. f(); f()$ for example, both for the first time to our knowledge. Although our method is based on environmental bisimulations (Sumii et al. 2004-), it makes an essential and general change to their metatheory, which is not only necessary for handling call/cc but is also applicable in other languages with no control operator.

1 Introduction

Background: Continuation and Control Operator. Call-with-current-continuation, or call/cc in short, is a "classical" control operator—in the double sense that it is the most traditional continuation operator and that it corresponds to the classical logic [8]—found in some implementations of functional programming languages such as Scheme and ML (including SML/NJ[1] and OCaml[2]). Simply put, `callcc` f applies the given function f to (a reified copy of) the current *evaluation context* E [7]. It can be formalized by the reduction rule $E[\texttt{callcc } f] \to E[f(\lambda x. \texttt{abort } E[x])]$ that reifies the evaluation context E as $\lambda x. E[x]$ and inserts another control operator `abort` which discards its own evaluation context like $E[\texttt{abort } M] \to M$. For instance, the following pseudo-program, using call/cc for an exception-like global exit,

```
let mul l = callcc(λk. letrec mul' l =
    if null l then 1 else if head l = 0 then k 0 else head l × mul'(tail l)
  in mul' l) in mul [2, 0, 3, 1] + 4
```

reduces roughly as follows:

---

[1] http://www.smlnj.org/doc/SMLofNJ/pages/cont.html
[2] http://pauillac.inria.fr/~xleroy/software.html#callcc

A. Igarashi (Ed.): APLAS 2016, LNCS 10017, pp. 171–186, 2016.
DOI: 10.1007/978-3-319-47958-3_10

$$mul \ [2, 0, 3, 1] + 4 \qquad\qquad\qquad \text{where } mul \ l = \texttt{callcc}(\lambda k. \ldots)$$
$$\rightarrow^* \texttt{callcc}(\lambda k. \ldots) \underline{+ 4} \qquad\qquad \text{where } l = [2, 0, 3, 1]$$
$$\rightarrow^* (\texttt{letrec} \ \ldots \ \texttt{in} \ mul' \ [2, 0, 3, 1]) \underline{+ 4} \quad \text{where } k = \lambda x. \texttt{abort}(x + 4)$$
$$\rightarrow^* 2 \times (\texttt{if} \ head \ [0, 3, 1] = 0 \ \texttt{then} \ k \ 0 \ \texttt{else} \ \ldots) + 4$$
$$\rightarrow^* 2 \times k \ 0 + 4$$
$$\rightarrow \quad \underline{\underline{2 \times}} \, \texttt{abort}(0 + 4) \underline{\underline{+ 4}}$$
$$\rightarrow \quad 0 + 4$$
$$\rightarrow \quad 4$$

Note that the evaluation context $[\,] + 4$ around $\texttt{callcc}(\lambda k. \ldots)$—underlined in the reduction sequence above—is duplicated (not discarded) and remains even after it is reified as $k = \lambda x. \texttt{abort}(x + 4)$, unlike the case of the $\mathscr{C}$ operator [6]. Note also that the context $2 \times [\,] + 4$ around $\texttt{abort}(0 + 4)$—double-underlined above—*is* discarded, hence the epithet of call/cc as an "abortive" control operator (like the $\mathscr{C}$ operator, but unlike the *delimited* continuation operators such as $\texttt{shift}$ and $\texttt{reset}$ [4]).

Background II: Contextual Equivalence in the Presence of Call/cc. Just as equivalence of expressions plays a central role in mathematics, *equivalence of programs* is an essential notion in programming language theory. *Contextual equivalence* [14] (also known as *observational equivalence*) is a general notion of program equivalence, defining that two programs are contextually equivalent when they yield the same result under any context in the language. Contextual equivalence in languages with control operators is known to be tricky because even if $M \rightarrow N$ (that is, a term M reduces in one step to another term N), it may not be the case that $E[M] \rightarrow E[N]$, since the evaluation context E may be captured or discarded by operators like $\texttt{callcc}$ or $\texttt{abort}$ in M. Many theories for program equivalence with continuation operators have been proposed (such as [1–3,5–7,9–11,15,16,18], just to name a few).

However, to our knowledge, there is no proof method that is complete with respect to observational equivalence ("operational semantics") in a language with call/cc (and no state): existing equational theories ("axiomatics semantics") [6, 7,11,15,16] are only complete with respect to $\beta\eta$-equivalence after continuation-passing style (CPS) translation ("denotational semantics"), and no complete logical relations or bisimulations [1–3,5,9,10,18] have been proposed for call/cc without state.

To see the difficulty of program equivalence in the presence of call/cc (but no state), consider the two functions $\lambda f. f()$ and $\lambda f. f(); f()$—where $M; N$ abbreviates $(\lambda z. N)M$ for some z that does not appear free in N—in call-by-value λ-calculus with call/cc (and only pure primitives). Their CPS translations are not $\beta\eta$-equivalent, of course. They are not normal form bisimilar [18], either: normal form bisimilarity coincides with equivalence in the *presence* of state, where $f()$ is of course not equivalent to $f(); f()$ (more syntactically, normal form bisimilarity cannot equate them because the contexts $[\,]$ and $[\,]; f()$ are distinct). Since those existing techniques are incomplete, it is unclear whether $\lambda f. f()$ and $\lambda f. f(); f()$

are contextually equivalent or inequivalent, even though they cannot be proved equivalent by any of the existing methods.

Our Contribution. In this paper, we propose a non-trivial variant of environmental bisimulations [17, 19–21, etc.] for λ-calculus with call/cc, and prove its soundness and completeness with respect to contextual equivalence. Completeness means that all contextually equivalent programs are bisimilar in our theory. By contraposition, it also means that two programs are known to be contextually inequivalent if they are shown to be non-bisimilar. This is useful in practice even though the contextual equivalence, and therefore our bisimilarity, is undecidable. In addition, our bisimulations can actually prove the equivalence of programs like $\lambda f. f()$ and $\lambda f. f(); f()$, which to our knowledge was not possible previously.

Overview. The rest of this paper is structured as follows. After defining the target language in Sect. 2, we define our bisimulations in Sect. 3, for which up-to techniques are developed in Sects. 4 and 5. Section 6 presents examples and Sect. 7 concludes with remarks.

2   The Language

Our target language is untyped call-by-value λ-calculus with tuples and call/cc (but no state) with the following syntax:

$L, M, N, C, D ::=$	term	$E, F, G ::=$	evaluation context
x	variable	$[\,]$	hole
$\lambda x. M$	function	EM	
MN	application	VE	
$\langle M_1, \ldots, M_n \rangle$	tuple $(n \geq 0)$	$\langle V_1, \ldots, V_{m-1}, E, M_{m+1}, \ldots, M_n \rangle$	
$\#_i M$	projection	$\#_i(E)$	
$\texttt{callcc } k. M$	call/cc		
$\texttt{cont}(E)$	continuation		

$T, U, V, W ::=$	value	$I ::=$	redex
x		$(\lambda x. M)V$	
$\lambda x. M$		$\#_i \langle V_1, \ldots, V_i, \ldots, V_n \rangle$	
$\langle V_1, \ldots, V_n \rangle$		$\texttt{callcc } k. M$	
$\texttt{cont}(E)$		$\texttt{cont}(E)V$	

We write $fv(M)$ and $fv(E)$ for the set of free variables (defined as usual) appearing in M and E, respectively, and $[V/x]M$ for the standard capture-avoiding substitution of variable x with value V in term M. We write $E[M]$ for the non-binding hole-filling (that is, capture-avoiding substitution of $[\,]$) of E with M. We use syntactic sugar $\lambda\_. M$ for $\lambda x. M$ with $x \notin fv(M)$, and $M; N$ for $(\lambda\_. N)M$ (with higher precedence than λ-abstraction, that is, $\lambda x. M; N$ stands for $\lambda x. (M; N)$, not $(\lambda x. M); N$).

Although the definition above is standard, a few points deserve mentioning.

- First of all, instead of introducing the second control operator `abort`, we chose to have the reified continuation `cont(E)` directly in the language. For this reason, we needed to define the syntax of evaluation contexts at the same time as the definition of (the syntax of) terms. We also defined (syntactic) values for call-by-value (and left-to-right) evaluation.
- Secondly, we use a term C (or D) with free variables $x_1, \ldots, x_n$ as a (non-binding and) possibly non-evaluation context with possibly multiple holes. For example, term $C = x_1 x_2$ represents context $[]_1[]_2$, with hole-filling $C[V_1, V_2]$ represented by (capture-avoiding) substitution $[V_1, V_2/x_1, x_2]C$.
- We adopt the monolithic syntax `callcc k. M` instead of `callcc(λk. M)` just for the sake of convenience. No expressiveness is lost, since `callcc V` in the latter syntax can be implemented as `callcc k. Vk` in the former.
- Tuples are introduced for studying the treatment of stuck terms such as $\langle\rangle(\lambda x. x)$ in our bisimulation theory.

The operational semantics (the small-step reduction relation $\overset{\text{top}}{\to}$, to be specific) is defined by rules:

$$
\begin{array}{llr}
E[(\lambda x. M)V] & \overset{\text{top}}{\to} E[[V/x]M] & \text{(E-AppAbs)} \\
E[\#_i\langle V_1, \ldots, V_i, \ldots, V_n\rangle] & \overset{\text{top}}{\to} E[V_i] & \text{(E-ProjTuple)} \\
E[\text{callcc } k. M] & \overset{\text{top}}{\to} E[[\text{cont}(E)/k]M] & \text{(E-CallCC)} \\
E[\text{cont}(F)V] & \overset{\text{top}}{\to} F[V] & \text{(E-Throw)}
\end{array}
$$

A term M is called a *normal form* if there is no N such that $M \overset{\text{top}}{\to} N$. A normal form that is not a value is called *stuck*. We write $\overset{\text{top}}{\twoheadrightarrow}$ for the reflexive transitive closure of $\overset{\text{top}}{\to}$. We say that term M *converges* and write $M \downarrow$ if $M \overset{\text{top}}{\twoheadrightarrow} V$ for some value V. Conversely, M *diverges*, written $M \uparrow$, if there is no normal form N such that $M \overset{\text{top}}{\twoheadrightarrow} N$.

Although the definition above is also standard, remember that, because of E-CallCC and E-Throw, $M \overset{\text{top}}{\to} N$ does not generally imply $E[M] \overset{\text{top}}{\to} E[N]$, hence the decoration ^{top} on the arrow $\to$.

In some examples, we will use the syntactic sugar `recfun(f(x) = M)` to denote a value V such that $E[VW] \overset{\text{top}}{\twoheadrightarrow} E[[W/x][V/f]M]$ for any E and W, defined using a (call-by-value) fixed point operator as usual.

We will extensively (though often implicitly) use the following lemmas in our bisimulation proofs. Henceforth, we often use overlines to denote sequences, like $[\overline{V}/\overline{x}]M = [V_1, \ldots, V_n/x_1, \ldots, x_n]M$ for example.

Lemma 2.1 (composition of evaluation contexts). *For any evaluation contexts E_1 and E_2, their composition $E_1[E_2]$ is again an evaluation context.*

Proof. By induction on the syntax of E_1.

Lemma 2.2 (unique decomposition into evaluation context and redex). $E_1[I_1] = E_2[I_2]$ *implies* $E_1 = E_2$ *and* $I_1 = I_2$.

Proof. By induction on the structure of E_1.

Lemma 2.3 (deterministic reduction). $M \overset{\text{top}}{\rightarrow} N$ *and* $M \overset{\text{top}}{\rightarrow} N'$ *imply* $N = N'$.

Proof. By case analysis on the definition of $M \overset{\text{top}}{\rightarrow} N$, with Lemma 2.2.

Definition 2.4 (contextual equivalence). *Closed values V and V' are contextually equivalent, written* $V \equiv V'$, *when* $[V/x]C \downarrow$ *if and only if* $[V'/x]C \downarrow$ *for any C with* $fv(C) = \{x\}$.

Although this definition only considers contextual equivalence of closed values, open terms could also be treated as in previous work [22] by considering the contextual equivalence of closing abstractions $\lambda\overline{x}.\,M$ and $\lambda\overline{x}.\,M'$ for $fv(M, M') \subseteq \{\overline{x}\}$ instead of open terms M and M' (assuming that M and M' are contextually equivalent to $(\lambda\overline{x}.\,M)\overline{x}$ and $(\lambda\overline{x}.\,M')\overline{x}$, respectively).

The definition above does not distinguish stuck and divergent terms, as is often the case with weak bisimulations in general; it would however be straightforward (though slightly cumbersome) to adapt our definition of contextual equivalence and bisimulations to make this distinction.

Definition 2.5. *The* pure reduction $\overset{\text{pure}}{\rightarrow}$ *is defined by the rules* $E[(\lambda x.\,M)V] \overset{\text{pure}}{\rightarrow} E[[V/x]M]$ *and* $E[\#_i\langle V_1, \ldots, V_i, \ldots, V_n\rangle] \overset{\text{pure}}{\rightarrow} E[V_i]$.

Lemma 2.6. *If* $M \overset{\text{pure}}{\rightarrow} N$, *then* $M \overset{\text{top}}{\rightarrow} N$.

Proof. Trivial by definition.

Lemma 2.7. *If* $M \overset{\text{pure}}{\rightarrow} N$, *then* $E[M] \overset{\text{pure}}{\rightarrow} E[N]$ *for any evaluation context E.*

Proof. By Definition 2.5 and Lemma 2.1.

Lemma 2.8 (pure progress). *For any term M, we have either:*

1. *M is a value V,*
2. *M is a type error, that is, has the form $E[\langle V_1, \ldots, V_n\rangle V]$ or $E[\#_i(\lambda x.\,N)]$,*
3. *M makes a pure progress, that is, $M \overset{\text{pure}}{\rightarrow} N$ for some N,*
4. *M captures a continuation, that is, has the form $E[\texttt{callcc}\ k.\,N]$,*
5. *M invokes a continuation, that is, has the form $E[\texttt{cont}(F)V]$,*
6. *M applies a free variable, that is, has the form $E[xV]$, or else*
7. *M projects a free variable, that is, has the form $E[\#_i x]$.*

Proof. By induction on the syntax of M.

Note that all the cases except the last two are preserved by substitution of variables in M with values.

Corollary 2.9 (context reduction). *For any C with $fv(C) \subseteq \{\overline{x}\}$, we have either:*

- *C has one of the forms $E[x_i V]$, $E[\#_j x_i]$, $E[\texttt{callcc}\ k.\,M]$, or $E[\texttt{cont}(F)V]$,*
- *there exists some D such that $[\overline{V}/\overline{x}]C \overset{\text{pure}}{\rightarrow} [\overline{V}/\overline{x}]D$ for any $\overline{V}$, or else*
- *$[\overline{V}/\overline{x}]C$ is a normal form for any $\overline{V}$.*

Proof. By Lemma 2.8.

3   Our Bisimulations

In this section, we define our variant of environmental bisimulations step-by-step.

Definition 3.1. *Value relations* $\mathcal{R}$, $\mathcal{S}$, ... *are binary relations on closed values. Term relations* $\mathcal{X}$, $\mathcal{Y}$, ... *are binary relations on closed terms.*

Definition 3.2. *The* context closure $\mathcal{R}^\star$ *of a value relation* $\mathcal{R}$ *is defined as:*

$$\mathcal{R}^\star = \{([\overline{V}/\overline{x}]C, [\overline{V'}/\overline{x}]C) \mid (\overline{V}, \overline{V'}) \in \mathcal{R}, \, fv(C) \subseteq \{\overline{x}\}\}$$
$$\cup \, \{([\overline{V}/\overline{x}]E, [\overline{V'}/\overline{x}]E) \mid (\overline{V}, \overline{V'}) \in \mathcal{R}, \, fv(E) \subseteq \{\overline{x}\}\}$$

Note our abuse of notation that $\mathcal{R}^\star$ relates both terms and evaluation contexts for the sake of brevity.

Lemma 3.3 (context closure reduction). *Let* $M = [\overline{V}/\overline{x}]C$ *and* $M' = [\overline{V'}/\overline{x}]C$ *with* $\overline{V} \, \mathcal{R}^\star \, \overline{V'}$ *and* $fv(C) \subseteq \{\overline{x}\}$ *(so* $M \, \mathcal{R}^\star \, M'$*). Then we have either:*

- *C has the form* $E[x_i W]$, *hence* $M = F[V_i U]$ *and* $M' = F'[V_i' U']$ *for* $F = [\overline{V}/\overline{x}]E$ *and* $F' = [\overline{V'}/\overline{x}]E$ *(so* $F \, \mathcal{R}^\star \, F'$*) as well as* $U = [\overline{V}/\overline{x}]W$ *and* $U' = [\overline{V'}/\overline{x}]W$ *(so* $U \, \mathcal{R}^\star \, U'$*),*
- *C has the form* $E[\#_j x_i]$, *hence* $M = F[\#_j V_i]$ *and* $M' = F'[\#_j V_i']$ *for* $F = [\overline{V}/\overline{x}]E$ *and* $F' = [\overline{V'}/\overline{x}]E$ *(so* $F \, \mathcal{R}^\star \, F'$*),*
- *there exists some* D *such that* $[\overline{W}/\overline{x}]C \overset{\text{top}}{\to} [\overline{W}/\overline{x}]D$ *for any* $\overline{W}$, *hence* $M \overset{\text{top}}{\to} [\overline{V}/\overline{x}]D$ *and* $M' \overset{\text{top}}{\to} [\overline{V'}/\overline{x}]D$ *(so the reducts are again related by* $\mathcal{R}^\star$*), or else*
- $[\overline{W}/\overline{x}]C$ *is a normal form for any* $\overline{W}$, *hence so are* M *and* M'.

Proof. By Lemma 2.9 with:

- If C has the form $E[\texttt{callcc } k. M]$, we have $[\overline{W}/\overline{x}]C \overset{\text{top}}{\to} [\overline{W}/\overline{x}]D$ for any $\overline{W}$, with $D = E[[\texttt{cont}(E)/k]M]$ in the third case above.
- If C has the form $E[\texttt{cont}(F)V]$, we have $[\overline{W}/\overline{x}]C \overset{\text{top}}{\to} [\overline{W}/\overline{x}]D$ for any $\overline{W}$, with $D = F[V]$ in the third case above.

Definition 3.4. *A term relation* $\mathcal{X}$ *is a* termination simulation *when, for any* $M \, \mathcal{X} \, M'$,

1. *for any* N *with* $M \overset{\text{top}}{\to} N$, *there exists some* N' *such that* $M' \overset{\text{top}}{\twoheadrightarrow} N'$ *with* $N \, \mathcal{X} \, N'$, *and*
2. $M' \downarrow$ *if* M *is a value.*

A termination simulation $\mathcal{X}$ *is called a* termination bisimulation *if* $\mathcal{X}^{-1}$ *is also a termination simulation. The* termination similarity $\prec$ *is the largest termination simulation, and the* termination bisimilarity $\sim$ *is the largest termination bisimulation.*

Although termination (bi)simulations themselves are rather trivial as a proof method, we will later extend them with more up-to techniques.

Lemma 3.5 (soundness and completeness of termination similarity).
If and only if $M \prec M'$, $M \downarrow$ implies $M' \downarrow$.

Since our language is deterministic (Lemma 2.3), simulation equivalence coindices with bisimilarity:

Lemma 3.6. $M \prec M'$ and $M' \prec M$ implies $M \sim M'$ and vice versa.

Proof. For the forward direction, take $\mathcal{X} = \{(N, N') \mid M \prec M', M' \prec M, M \overset{\text{top}}{\twoheadrightarrow} N, M' \overset{\text{top}}{\twoheadrightarrow} N'\}$, which is a termination bisimulation. The converse is trivial.

Definition 3.7. *A value relation $\mathcal{R}$ is adequate if all of the following conditions are satisfied:*

1. *For any $V \mathcal{R} V'$, the top-level types of V and V' match, that is, V is a function if and only if V' is also a function, V is an n-tuple if and only if so is V', and V is a continuation if and only if V' is.*
2. *For any $\lambda x. M \mathcal{R} \lambda x. M'$, we have $E[(\lambda x. M)W] \sim E'[(\lambda x. M')W']$ for any $E \mathcal{R}^\star E'$ and $W \mathcal{R}^\star W'$.*
3. *For any $\langle V_1, \ldots, V_n \rangle \mathcal{R} \langle V_1', \ldots, V_n' \rangle$, we have $V_i \mathcal{R} V_i'$ for $i = 1, \ldots, n$.*
4. *For any $\mathrm{cont}(E) \mathcal{R} \mathrm{cont}(E')$, we have $E[W] \sim E'[W']$ for any $W \mathcal{R}^\star W'$.*

By symmetry, $\mathcal{R}^{-1}$ is also adequate if $\mathcal{R}$ is adequate.

The term "adequate" derives from Koutavas [13] and is not directly related to computational adequacy of denotational semantics.

The most significant difference of Definition 3.7 from previous environmental bisimulations (such as [19]) is the introduction of arbitrary related evaluation contexts $E \mathcal{R}^\star E'$ (in addition to arbitrary related arguments $W \mathcal{R}^\star W'$) in clause 2. They are necessary since we do not always have $E[M] \overset{\text{top}}{\twoheadrightarrow} E[N]$ even if $M \overset{\text{top}}{\twoheadrightarrow} N$ because of call/cc as mentioned in Sect. 1. In return, we no longer need to relate the values resulting from the reductions in Definition 3.4, thereby breaking the mutual (co)induction between the definitions of bisimulations for values and terms. (These features are also shared by some previous work [10].)

In the following sections, we will show that closed values V and V' are contextually equivalent if and only if $V \mathcal{R} V'$ for some adequate $\mathcal{R}$ (using up-to techniques for this proof itself).

4   Up-to Reduction

Generally speaking, *bisimulations up-to* something are a weakened version of bisimulations where the reducts of related terms do not necessarily have to be related themselves, but they instead have only to be related "modulo" that something. In this section we introduce one of such techniques for our bisimulations to omit intermediate reducts.

Definition 4.1. *A term relation $\mathcal{X}$ is a termination simulation up-to reduction when, for any $M \mathcal{X} M'$, either*

- *M is stuck,*
- *M ↑,*
- *M ↓ and M' ↓, or else*
- *there exist some N, L, and L' such that $M \overset{\text{top}}{\twoheadrightarrow} N \overset{\text{top}}{\twoheadrightarrow} L$ and $M' \overset{\text{top}}{\twoheadrightarrow} L'$ with $L \mathcal{X} L'$.*

The termination similarity $\prec^{\rightarrow}$ up-to reduction is the largest of such $\mathcal{X}$. Termination bisimulations and the termination bisimilarity $\sim^{\rightarrow}$ up-to reduction is defined accordingly.

Again, (part of) the definition above may seem redundant, but it is defined as such to allow later extension with another up-to technique.

Lemma 4.2 (soundness and completeness of up-to reduction). $\prec^{\rightarrow}$ *equals $\prec$, that is, $M \prec^{\rightarrow} M'$ if and only if $M \prec M'$.*

Proof. The "if" direction is trivial since Definition 4.1 is weaker than Definition 3.4. The "only if" is proved by checking that $\mathcal{X} = \{(M, M') \mid M \overset{\text{top}}{\twoheadrightarrow} L, L \prec^{\rightarrow} M'\}$ is a termination bisimulation, which is straightforward.

Adequacy up-to reduction is defined by replacing $\prec$ with $\prec^{\rightarrow}$ in Definition 3.7.

5   Up-to Context

We now introduce our bisimulations up-to (reduction and) context, which is the most powerful of up-to techniques in general. Intuitively, it allows one to remove a context that is common to the terms being compared.

Definition 5.1. *A term relation $\mathcal{X}$ is a termination simulation up-to reduction and $\mathcal{R}$-context when, for any $M \mathcal{X} M'$, either*

- *M is stuck,*
- *M ↑,*
- *M ↓ and M' ↓, or else*
- *there exist some N, L, and L' such that $M \overset{\text{top}}{\twoheadrightarrow} N \overset{\text{top}}{\twoheadrightarrow} L$ and $M' \overset{\text{top}}{\twoheadrightarrow} L'$ with $L \mathcal{X} L'$ or $L \mathcal{R}^{\star} L'$.*

The termination similarity $\prec_{\mathcal{R}}$ and bisimilarity $\sim_{\mathcal{R}}$ up-to reduction and $\mathcal{R}$-context are defined as usual.

Adequacy up-to reduction and context is defined accordingly with $\sim_{\mathcal{R}}$ in place of $\sim$ (or $\sim^{\rightarrow}$). We often omit the "reduction and" part in "up-to reduction and context" when it is unimportant.

Note that every adequate $\mathcal{R}$ is also adequate up-to reduction, and every adequate $\mathcal{R}$ up-to reduction is also adequate up-to reduction and context since the latter definitions are weaker than the former.

Lemma 5.2 (adequacy implies bisimulation up-to (reduction and) context). $M \mathcal{R}^\star M'$ implies $M \sim_{\mathcal{R}} M'$ if $\mathcal{R}$ is adequate up-to reduction and context.

Proof. We prove that $\mathcal{R}^\star \cup \sim_{\mathcal{R}}$ is a termination bisimulation up-to reduction and context. The case for $\sim_{\mathcal{R}}$ is trivial. For $\mathcal{R}^\star$, the case follows from Lemma 3.3 and the definition of adequacy up-to reduction and context.

Lemma 5.3 (soundness and completeness of up-to context). $\prec_{\mathcal{R}}$ equals $\prec^\rightarrow$, provided that $\mathcal{R}$ is adequate up-to reduction and context.

Proof. Soundness follows from Definition 5.1 and Lemma 5.2. Completeness is trivial.

The soundness and completeness of our bisimulation proof method are thus obtained:

Theorem 5.4 (soundness and completeness of adequacy). Let V and V' be closed values. Then $V \mathcal{R} V'$ for some adequate $\mathcal{R}$ up-to reduction and context if and only if V and V' are contextually equivalent.

Proof. The "if" part follows by taking $\equiv$ itself as $\mathcal{R}$ and checking its adequacy. The other direction follows from Lemma 5.2.

6   Examples

Example 6.1 (from the Introduction). For the sake of exposition, assume that we have integers and their lists as primitives, and let:

$$mul = \lambda \ell'. \texttt{callcc } k. \, loop_k \, \ell' \qquad\qquad mul' = \lambda \ell'. \, loop' \, \ell'$$
$$loop_k = \texttt{recfun}(f(\ell) = \qquad\qquad\qquad loop' = \texttt{recfun}(f(\ell) =$$
$$\quad\text{if } null \,\, \ell \text{ then } 1 \text{ else} \qquad\qquad\qquad\quad \text{if } null \,\, \ell \text{ then } 1 \text{ else}$$
$$\quad\text{if } head \,\, \ell = 0 \text{ then } k \,\, 0 \text{ else}$$
$$\quad head \,\, \ell \times f(tail \,\, \ell)) \qquad\qquad\qquad\quad head \,\, \ell \times f(tail \,\, \ell))$$

We prove that $\mathcal{R} = \{(mul, mul')\}$ is adequate up-to reduction and context, for which it suffices to show $E[mul \,\, V] \sim_{\mathcal{R}} E'[mul' \,\, V']$ for any $E \mathcal{R}^\star E'$ and $V \mathcal{R}^\star V'$. If neither V nor V' is an integer list, both $E[mul \,\, V]$ and $E'[mul' \,\, V']$ get stuck. Otherwise $V = V'$ since $V \mathcal{R}^\star V'$. If V (as well as V') includes 0 as an element, we have $E[mul \,\, V] \overset{\text{top}}{\twoheadrightarrow} E[\dots \texttt{cont}(E)0\dots] \overset{\text{top}}{\twoheadrightarrow} E[0]$ and $E'[mul' \,\, V'] \overset{\text{top}}{\twoheadrightarrow} E'[\cdots \times 0 \times \dots] \overset{\text{top}}{\twoheadrightarrow} E'[0]$. Otherwise $E[mul \,\, V] \overset{\text{top}}{\twoheadrightarrow} E[i_1 \times \cdots \times i_n \times 1]$ and $E'[mul' \,\, V'] \overset{\text{top}}{\twoheadrightarrow} E'[i_1 \times \cdots \times i_n \times 1]$ for $V = V' = [i_1, \dots, i_n]$. Thus in both cases the reducts are related by $\mathcal{R}^\star$ and we are done with the proof up-to $\mathcal{R}$-context.

Example 6.2 (adapted from Sect. 5 of [23], a contextual equivalence in the presence of continuations and exceptions but no state). Let us fix an arbitrary closed term M and define $\mathcal{R} = \{(\lambda\_.\, M, \lambda\_.\, M; M)\}$. We show that $\mathcal{R}$ is adequate up-to reduction and context as follows. Take arbitrary $E\,\mathcal{R}^\star E'$ and $U\,\mathcal{R}^\star U'$. It suffices to show $E[(\lambda\_.\, M)U] \sim_{\mathcal{R}} E'[(\lambda\_.\, M; M)U']$.

If $E'[M; M] \overset{\text{top}}{\twoheadrightarrow} E'[M]$, then we have $E'[(\lambda\_.\, M; M)U'] \overset{\text{top}}{\twoheadrightarrow} E'[M; M] \overset{\text{top}}{\twoheadrightarrow} E'[M]$. We are done since $E[(\lambda\_.\, M)U] \overset{\text{top}}{\twoheadrightarrow} E[M]$ with $E[M]\,\mathcal{R}^\star E'[M]$.

Thus suppose $E'[M; M] \overset{\text{top}}{\not\twoheadrightarrow} E'[M]$. We define $\mathcal{S}$ by induction with the following rule

$$\frac{E_0\,\mathcal{S}^\star E'_0}{\mathtt{cont}(E[E_0])\,\mathcal{S}\,\mathtt{cont}(E'[E'_0; M])}$$

and then define:

$$\begin{aligned}
\mathcal{X} = \ & \{(E[(\lambda\_.\, M)U], E'[(\lambda\_.\, M; M)U'])\} \\
& \cup \ \{(E[N], E'[N'; M]) \mid E'[N'; M] \overset{\text{top}}{\not\twoheadrightarrow} E'[M],\ N\,\mathcal{S}^\star N'\} \\
& \cup \ \{(N, N') \mid N' \overset{\text{top}}{\not\twoheadrightarrow} E'[M],\ N\,\mathcal{S}^\star N'\}
\end{aligned}$$

Let us check the conditions of a termination bisimulation up-to reduction (and $\mathcal{R}$-context, though the latter up-to technique will not be used here) for each part of the definition of $\mathcal{X}$.

The first part is trivial since $E[(\lambda\_.\, M)U] \overset{\text{top}}{\twoheadrightarrow} E[M]$ and $E'[(\lambda\_.\, M; M)U'] \overset{\text{top}}{\twoheadrightarrow} E'[M; M]$ with $M\,\mathcal{S}^\star M$, where the reducts are related by the second part.

As for the second part, we proceed by case analysis on the reductions of N and N' with $N\,\mathcal{S}^\star N'$. Note that N' (and therefore N) cannot be a value since $E'[M; M] \overset{\text{top}}{\twoheadrightarrow} E'[N'; M] \overset{\text{top}}{\not\twoheadrightarrow} E'[M]$.

- The only non-trivial case is when N and N' invoke continuations, that is, when $N = F[\mathtt{cont}(E_1)W]$ and $N' = F'[\mathtt{cont}(E'_1)W']$ for some $F\,\mathcal{S}^\star F'$, $\mathtt{cont}(E_1)\,\mathcal{S}^\star \mathtt{cont}(E'_1)$, and $W\,\mathcal{S}^\star W'$.
  - If $\mathtt{cont}(E_1)\,\mathcal{S}\,\mathtt{cont}(E'_1)$, then by inversion $E_1 = E[E_0]$ and $E'_1 = E'[E'_0; M]$ for some $E_0\,\mathcal{S}^\star E'_0$, so the reducts $E_1[W] = E[E_0[W]]$ and $E'_1[W'] = E'[E'_0[W']; M]$ with $E_0[W]\,\mathcal{S}^\star E'_0[W']$ are again related by the second part.
  - Otherwise, we have $E_1\,\mathcal{S}^\star E'_1$ and the reducts $E_1[W]$ and $E'_1[W']$ with $E_1[W]\,\mathcal{S}^\star E'_1[W']$ are related by the third part.
- The inductive rule above is applied when N and N' capture their continuations, that is, when $N = E_0[\mathtt{callcc}\ k.\,N_0]$ and $N' = E'_0[\mathtt{callcc}\ k.\,N'_0]$ for some $E_0\,\mathcal{S}^\star E'_0$ and $\mathtt{callcc}\ k.\,N_0\,\mathcal{S}^\star \mathtt{callcc}\ k.\,N'_0$, so that the reducts $E[E_0[[\mathtt{cont}(E[E_0])/k]N_0]]$ and $E'[E'_0[[\mathtt{cont}(E'[E'_0; M])/k]N'_0]; M]$, with $\mathtt{cont}(E[E_0])\,\mathcal{S}\,\mathtt{cont}(E'[E'_0; M])$ by the rule and therefore $E_0[[\mathtt{cont}(E[E_0])/k]N_0]\,\mathcal{S}^\star E'_0[[\mathtt{cont}(E'[E'_0; M])/k]N'_0]$, are again related by the second part.

The proof for the third part is similar.

Example 6.3. We show that $V = \lambda f. f\langle\rangle$ and $V' = \lambda f. f\langle\rangle; f\langle\rangle$ are contextually equivalent. The proof is similar to Example 6.2 but is slightly more complicated because nested calls to V or V' are possible in $f\langle\rangle$. Take

$$\mathcal{X} = \{(N, N') \mid N \, \mathcal{S}^{\star}_{N'} \, N'\}$$
$$\cup \, \{(E[N], E'[N'; W'\langle\rangle]) \mid E'[N'; W'\langle\rangle] \overset{\text{top}}{\not\to} E'[W'\langle\rangle], \, N \, \mathcal{S}^{\star}_{E'[N';W'\langle\rangle]} \, N'\}$$

where:

$$\frac{}{V \, \mathcal{S}_{N'} \, V'} \qquad \frac{N' \overset{\text{top}}{\not\to} E'[W'\langle\rangle] \quad E_0 \, \mathcal{S}^{\star}_{N'} \, E'_0}{\mathrm{cont}(E[E_0]) \, \mathcal{S}_{N'} \, \mathrm{cont}(E'[E'_0; W'\langle\rangle])}$$

Note that $[V/x]C \, \mathcal{X} \, [V'/x]C$ for any C with $fv(C) \subseteq \{x\}$, by the first part of $\mathcal{X}$. Note also that $M' \overset{\text{top}}{\to} N'$ implies $\mathcal{S}_{M'} \subseteq \mathcal{S}_{N'}$. (The latter can be shown from the fact that $M' \overset{\text{top}}{\to} N'$ implies $L \, \mathcal{S}_{M'} \, L' \Rightarrow L \, \mathcal{S}_{N'} \, L'$, for any M', N', L, and L', by induction on the derivation of $L \, \mathcal{S}_{M'} \, L'$.)

We show that $\mathcal{X}$ is a termination bisimulation up-to reduction.

- In the first part,
  - If $N = F[VW]$ and $N' = F'[V'W']$ for some $F \, \mathcal{S}^{\star}_{N'} \, F'$ and $W \, \mathcal{S}^{\star}_{N'} \, W'$, then $N \overset{\text{top}}{\to} F[W\langle\rangle]$ and $N' \overset{\text{top}}{\to} F'[W'\langle\rangle; W'\langle\rangle]$.
    - * If $F'[W'\langle\rangle; W'\langle\rangle] \overset{\text{top}}{\to} F'[W'\langle\rangle]$, then we are done by the first part with $F[W\langle\rangle] \, \mathcal{S}^{\star}_{F'[W'\langle\rangle]} \, F'[W'\langle\rangle]$.
    - * Otherwise, we are done by the second part with $W\langle\rangle \, \mathcal{S}^{\star}_{F'[W'\langle\rangle;W'\langle\rangle]} \, W'\langle\rangle$.
  - If $N = F[\mathrm{cont}(E[E_0])U]$ and $N' = F'[\mathrm{cont}(E'[E'_0; W'\langle\rangle])U']$ for some $F \, \mathcal{S}^{\star}_{N'} \, F'$, $N' \overset{\text{top}}{\not\to} E'[W'\langle\rangle]$, $E_0 \, \mathcal{S}^{\star}_{N'} \, E'_0$, and $U \, \mathcal{S}^{\star}_{N'} \, U'$, then $N \overset{\text{top}}{\to} E[E_0[U]]$ and $N' \overset{\text{top}}{\to} E'[E'_0[U']; W'\langle\rangle]$, so we are done by the second part with $E_0[U] \, \mathcal{S}^{\star}_{E'[E'_0[U'];W'\langle\rangle]} \, E'_0[U']$.
  - If $N = F[\mathrm{cont}(F_0)U]$ and $N' = F'[\mathrm{cont}(F'_0)U']$ for some $F \, \mathcal{S}^{\star}_{N'} \, F'$, $F_0 \, \mathcal{S}^{\star}_{N'} \, F'_0$, and $U \, \mathcal{S}^{\star}_{N'} \, U'$, then $N \overset{\text{top}}{\to} F_0[U]$ and $N' \overset{\text{top}}{\to} F'_0[U']$, so we are done by the first part with $F_0[U] \, \mathcal{S}^{\star}_{F'_0[U']} \, F'_0[U']$.
  - The other cases are routine.
- In the second part,
  - If $N = F[VW_2]$ and $N' = F'[V'W'_2]$ for some $F \, \mathcal{S}^{\star}_{E'[N';W'\langle\rangle]} \, F'$ and $W_2 \, \mathcal{S}^{\star}_{E'[N';W'\langle\rangle]} \, W'_2$, then $E[N] \overset{\text{top}}{\to} E[F[W_2\langle\rangle]]$ and $E'[N'; W'\langle\rangle] \overset{\text{top}}{\to} E'[F'[W'_2\langle\rangle; W'_2\langle\rangle]; W'\langle\rangle]$.
    - * If $E'[F'[W'_2\langle\rangle; W'_2\langle\rangle]; W'\langle\rangle] \overset{\text{top}}{\to} E'[F'[W'_2\langle\rangle]; W'\langle\rangle] (= L')$, then we are done by the second part with $F[W_2\langle\rangle] \, \mathcal{S}^{\star}_{L'} \, F'[W'_2\langle\rangle]$.
    - * Otherwise, let $E_2 = E[F]$ and $E'_2 = E'[F'; W'\langle\rangle]$. We are done by the second part with $E'_2[W'_2\langle\rangle; W'_2\langle\rangle] \overset{\text{top}}{\not\to} E'_2[W'_2\langle\rangle]$ and $W_2\langle\rangle \, \mathcal{S}^{\star}_{E'_2[W'_2\langle\rangle;W'_2\langle\rangle]} \, W'_2\langle\rangle$.

- If $N = E_0[\texttt{callcc } k. N_0]$ and $N' = E_0'[\texttt{callcc } k. N_0']$ for some $E_0 \, \mathcal{S}_{N'}^{\star} \, E_0'$
  and $\texttt{callcc } k. N_0 \, \mathcal{S}_{N'}^{\star} \, \texttt{callcc } k. N_0'$, then $E[N] \overset{\text{top}}{\rightsquigarrow} E[E_0[[\texttt{cont}(E[E_0])/k]$
  $N_0]]$
  and $E'[N'; W'\langle\rangle] \overset{\text{top}}{\rightsquigarrow} E'[E_0'[[\texttt{cont}(E'[E_0'; W'\langle\rangle])/k]N_0']; W'\langle\rangle] \ (= L')$, so
  we are done by the second part with $\texttt{cont}(E[E_0])\mathcal{S}_{L'} \texttt{cont}(E'[E_0'; W'\langle\rangle])$
  by the second inductive rule above and therefore $E_0[[\texttt{cont}(E[E_0])/k]N_0]$
  $\mathcal{S}_{L'}^{\star} \, E_0'[[\texttt{cont}(E'[E_0'; W'\langle\rangle])/k]N_0']$.
- If N and N' are values, then the assumption $E'[N'; W'\langle\rangle] \overset{\text{top}}{\not\rightsquigarrow} E'[W'\langle\rangle]$
  does not hold.
- The other cases are similar to the first part.

Example 6.4 (Call/cc in a loop, taken from Sect. 5.3 of [10]). Let $V = \lambda x. \texttt{callcc } k. V_k x$ for $V_k = \texttt{recfun}(f(x) = f(xk))$ and $V' = \texttt{recfun}(f(x) = \texttt{callcc } k. f(xk))$. Intuitively, V captures a continuation outside a loop, while V' repeatedly captures essentially the same continuation inside the loop. We show the contextual equivalence of V and V'. Let $\mathcal{R} = \{(V, V')\}$. It suffices to show $E[VW] \sim_{\mathcal{R}} E'[V'W']$ for arbitrary $E \, \mathcal{R}^{\star} \, E'$ and $W \, \mathcal{R}^{\star} \, W'$. Let us define

$$\frac{}{V \, \mathcal{S} \, V'} \qquad \frac{}{\texttt{cont}([\,]) \, \mathcal{S} \, \texttt{cont}([\,])}$$

$$\frac{\texttt{cont}(F) \, \mathcal{S} \, \texttt{cont}(F') \quad F_0 \, \mathcal{S}^{\star} \, F_0'}{\texttt{cont}(F[F_0]) \, \mathcal{S} \, \texttt{cont}(F'[F_0'])} \qquad \frac{\texttt{cont}(F) \, \mathcal{S} \, \texttt{cont}(F')}{\texttt{cont}(F[V_{\texttt{cont}(F)}[\,]]) \, \mathcal{S} \, \texttt{cont}(F'[V'[\,]])}$$

and $\mathcal{X} = \{(F[N], F'[N']) \mid \texttt{cont}(F) \, \mathcal{S} \, \texttt{cont}(F'), \, N \, \mathcal{S}^{\star} \, N'\}$. We show that $\mathcal{X}$ is a termination bisimulation up-to reduction (and $\mathcal{R}$-context) by case analysis on the reductions of $F[N]$ and $F'[N']$.

Again, once the definitions above have been set up, the following details are routine and may be skipped.

- When $N = F_0[VW_2]$ and $N' = F_0'[V'W_2']$ for some $F_0 \, \mathcal{S}^{\star} \, F_0'$ and $W_2 \, \mathcal{S}^{\star}$
  W_2', we have $F[N] \overset{\text{top}}{\rightarrow} F[F_0[V_{\texttt{cont}(F[F_0])}(W_2 \texttt{cont}(F[F_0]))]]$ and $F'[N'] \overset{\text{top}}{\rightarrow}$
  $F'[F_0'[V'(W_2' \texttt{cont}(F'[F_0']))]]$, and apply the third and fourth inductive rules
  above to obtain $\texttt{cont}(F[F_0[V_{\texttt{cont}(F[F_0])}[\,]]]) \, \mathcal{S} \, \texttt{cont}(F'[F_0'[V'[\,]]])$ and therefore
  $W_2 \texttt{cont}(F[F_0]) \, \mathcal{S}^{\star} \, W_2' \texttt{cont}(F'[F_0'])$.
- When $N = F_0[\texttt{cont}(F_1)W_2]$ and $N' = F_0'[\texttt{cont}(F_1')W_2']$ for some $F_0 \, \mathcal{S}^{\star} \, F_0'$,
  $\texttt{cont}(F_1) \, \mathcal{S}^{\star} \, \texttt{cont}(F_1')$, and $W_2 \, \mathcal{S}^{\star} \, W_2'$, we have $F[N] \overset{\text{top}}{\rightsquigarrow} F_1[W_2]$ and $F'[N'] \overset{\text{top}}{\rightsquigarrow}$
  $F_1'[W_2']$.
  - If $\texttt{cont}(F_1) \, \mathcal{S} \, \texttt{cont}(F_1')$, then we are done since $W_2 \, \mathcal{S}^{\star} \, W_2'$.
  - Otherwise $F_1 \, \mathcal{S}^{\star} \, F_1'$ and we are also done since $\texttt{cont}([\,]) \, \mathcal{S} \, \texttt{cont}([\,])$ and
    $F_1[W_2] \, \mathcal{S}^{\star} \, F_1'[W_2']$.
- When $N = F_0[\texttt{callcc } k. N_0]$ and $N' = F_0'[\texttt{callcc } k. N_0']$ for some $F_0 \, \mathcal{S}^{\star} \, F_0'$
  and $\texttt{callcc } k. N_0 \, \mathcal{S}^{\star} \, \texttt{callcc } k. N_0'$, we have $F[N] \overset{\text{top}}{\rightsquigarrow} F[F_0[[\texttt{cont}(F[F_0])/k]N_0]]$
  and $F'[N'] \overset{\text{top}}{\rightsquigarrow} F'[F_0'[[\texttt{cont}(F'[F_0'])/k]N_0']]$, and apply the third induc-
  tive rule above to obtain $\texttt{cont}(F[F_0]) \, \mathcal{S} \, \texttt{cont}(F'[F_0'])$ and therefore
  $[\texttt{cont}(F[F_0])/k]N_0 \, \mathcal{S}^{\star} \, [\texttt{cont}(F'[F_0'])/k]N_0'$.

- When $N = W_2$ and $N' = W_2'$ for some $W_2\,\mathcal{S}^\star\,W_2'$, we proceed by induction on the derivation of $\mathrm{cont}(F)\,\mathcal{S}\,\mathrm{cont}(F')$.
  - If $F = F' = [\,]$, then $F[N] = W_2$ and $F'[N'] = W_2'$, and we are done trivially.
  - If $F = F_1[F_0]$ and $F' = F_1'[F_0']$ for some $\mathrm{cont}(F_1)\,\mathcal{S}\,\mathrm{cont}(F_1')$ and $F_0\,\mathcal{S}^\star$ F_0', then $F[N] = F_1[F_0[W_2]]$ and $F'[N'] = F_1'[F_0'[W_2']]$ with $\mathrm{cont}(F_1)\,\mathcal{S}$ $\mathrm{cont}(F_1')$ and $F_0[W_2]\,\mathcal{S}^\star\,F_0'[W_2']$. If $F_0 = F_0' = [\,]$, then $F_0[W_2]$ and $F_0'[W_2']$ are values, and we are done by the induction hypothesis. Otherwise $F_0[W_2]$ and $F_0'[W_2']$ are not values and the proof is the same as in the other cases where N and N' are not values.
  - If $F = F_0[V_{\mathrm{cont}(F_0)}[\,]]$ and $F' = F_0'[V'[\,]]$ for some $\mathrm{cont}(F_0)\,\mathcal{S}\,\mathrm{cont}(F_0')$, then $F[N] \overset{\mathrm{top}}{\twoheadrightarrow} F_0[V_{\mathrm{cont}(F_0)}(W_2\mathrm{cont}(F_0))]$ and $F'[N'] \overset{\mathrm{top}}{\twoheadrightarrow} F_0'[V'(W_2'\mathrm{cont}(F_0'))]$, and we are done since $W_2\mathrm{cont}(F_0)\,\mathcal{S}^\star\,W_2'\mathrm{cont}(F_0')$ and, by the fourth rule, $\mathrm{cont}(F_0[V_{\mathrm{cont}(F_0)}[\,]])\,\mathcal{S}\,\mathrm{cont}(F_0'[V'[\,]])$.

The other cases are straightforward.

Example 6.5 (adapted from Sect. 4 of [23], a contextual equivalence in the presence of continuations but no exceptions or state). We show that $\mathcal{R} = \{(T, T')\}$ with

$$T = \lambda\_.\, M_W \qquad T' = \lambda\_.\, M_{W'}$$
$$W = \lambda\_.\, V \qquad W' = \lambda\_.\, M_W; V$$

is adequate up-to context and reduction for any M_w with $fv(M_w) = \{w\}$ and closed V. It suffices to show $E[TU] \sim_{\mathcal{R}} E'[T'U']$ for any $E\,\mathcal{R}^\star\,E'$ and $U\,\mathcal{R}^\star\,U'$. Let

$$
\begin{aligned}
\mathcal{X} = &\{(E[TU], E'[T'U'])\}\\
\cup\ &\{(N, N') \mid \forall G'.\ E'[M_{W'}] \overset{\mathrm{top}}{\twoheadrightarrow} G'[M_W; V] \Rightarrow G'[M_W; V] \overset{\mathrm{top}}{\twoheadrightarrow} G'[V],\\
&\qquad E'[M_{W'}] \overset{\mathrm{top}}{\twoheadrightarrow} N',\\
&\qquad N\,\mathcal{R}_2^\star\,N'\text{ for }\mathcal{R}_2 = \mathcal{R} \cup \{(W, W')\}\}\\
\cup\ &\{(E[N], G'[N'; V]) \mid G'[N'; V] \overset{\mathrm{top}}{\not\twoheadrightarrow} G'[V],\\
&\qquad N\,\mathcal{S}_{G'[N';V]}^\star\,N'\}\\
\cup\ &\{(N, N') \mid N\,\mathcal{S}_{N'}^\star\,N'\}
\end{aligned}
$$

where:

$$
\frac{N' \overset{\mathrm{top}}{\not\twoheadrightarrow} G'[V] \quad G_0\,\mathcal{S}_{N'}^\star\,G_0'}{\mathrm{cont}(E[G_0])\,\mathcal{S}_{N'}\,\mathrm{cont}(G'[G_0'; V])}
$$

It is easy to see that $M' \overset{\mathrm{top}}{\twoheadrightarrow} N'$ implies $\mathcal{S}_{M'} \subseteq \mathcal{S}_{N'}$ as in Example 6.3.

We prove that $\mathcal{X}$ is a termination bisimulation up-to reduction.

- In the first part of $\mathcal{X}$, we have $E[TU] \overset{\mathrm{top}}{\twoheadrightarrow} E[M_W]$ and $E'[T'U'] \overset{\mathrm{top}}{\twoheadrightarrow} E'[M_{W'}]$.
  - If, for some G', $E'[M_{W'}] \overset{\mathrm{top}}{\twoheadrightarrow} G'[M_W; V]$ and $G'[M_W; V] \overset{\mathrm{top}}{\not\twoheadrightarrow} G'[V]$, then we are done by the third part with $M_W\,\mathcal{S}_{G'[M_W;V]}^\star\,M_W$.

- Otherwise, for any G', $E'[M_{W'}] \overset{\text{top}}{\twoheadrightarrow} G'[M_W; V]$ implies $G'[M_W; V] \overset{\text{top}}{\twoheadrightarrow}$ $G'[V]$, so we are done by the second part with $E[M_W] \, \mathcal{R}_2^\star \, E'[M_{W'}]$.
- In the second part,
  - If $N = F[WU]$ and $N' = F'[W'U']$ for some $F \, \mathcal{R}_2^\star \, F'$ and $U \, \mathcal{R}_2^\star \, U'$, then $N \overset{\text{top}}{\twoheadrightarrow} F[V]$ and $N' \overset{\text{top}}{\twoheadrightarrow} F'[M_W; V] \overset{\text{top}}{\twoheadrightarrow} F'[V]$, so we are done by the second part with $F[V] \, \mathcal{R}_2^\star \, F'[V]$.
  - If $N = F[TU]$ and $N' = F'[T'U']$ for some $F \, \mathcal{R}_2^\star \, F'$ and $U \, \mathcal{R}_2^\star \, U'$, then $N \overset{\text{top}}{\twoheadrightarrow} F[M_W]$ and $N' \overset{\text{top}}{\twoheadrightarrow} F'[M_{W'}]$, so we are done by the second part with $F[M_W] \, \mathcal{R}_2^\star \, F'[M_{W'}]$.

  Proofs for the other cases are routine.
- In the third part,
  - If $N = G_0[\texttt{callcc } k. N_0]$ and $N' = G_0'[\texttt{callcc } k. N_0']$ for some $G_0 \, \mathcal{S}_{G'[N';V]}^\star \, G_0'$ and $\texttt{callcc } k. N_0 \, \mathcal{S}_{G'[N';V]}^\star \, \texttt{callcc } k. N_0'$, then $E[N] \overset{\text{top}}{\twoheadrightarrow}$ $E[G_0[[\texttt{cont}(E[G_0])/k]N_0]]$ and $G'[N'; V] \overset{\text{top}}{\twoheadrightarrow} G'[G_0'[[\texttt{cont}(G'[G_0'; V])/k]$ $N_0']; V]$ $(= L')$, so we are done by the third part with $\texttt{cont}(E[G_0])$ $\mathcal{S}_{L'} \, \texttt{cont}(G'[G_0'; V])$ by the inductive rule above and therefore $G_0[[\texttt{cont}(E[G_0])/k]N_0] \, \mathcal{S}_{L'}^\star \, G_0'[[\texttt{cont}(G'[G_0'; V])/k]N_0']$.
  - If $N = F[\texttt{cont}(G_1)U]$ and $N' = F'[\texttt{cont}(G_1')U']$ for some $F \, \mathcal{S}_{G'[N';V]}^\star \, F'$, $U \, \mathcal{S}_{G'[N';V]}^\star \, U'$, and $\texttt{cont}(G_1) \, \mathcal{S}_{G'[N';V]} \, \texttt{cont}(G_1')$, then $E[N] \overset{\text{top}}{\twoheadrightarrow} G_1[U]$ and $G'[N'; V] \overset{\text{top}}{\twoheadrightarrow} G_1'[U']$, so we are done by the third part with the inversion of the rule.
  - If $N = F[\texttt{cont}(G_1)U]$ and $N' = F'[\texttt{cont}(G_1')U']$ for some $F \, \mathcal{S}_{G'[N';V]}^\star \, F'$, $U \, \mathcal{S}_{G'[N';V]}^\star \, U'$, and $G_1 \, \mathcal{S}_{G'[N';V]}^\star \, G_1'$, then $E[N] \overset{\text{top}}{\twoheadrightarrow} G_1[U]$ and $G'[N'; V] \overset{\text{top}}{\twoheadrightarrow}$ $G_1'[U']$, so we are done by the fourth part with $G_1[U] \, \mathcal{S}_{G_1'[U']}^\star \, G_1'[U']$.

  - If N and N' are values, then the assumption $G'[N'; V] \overset{\text{top}}{\not\twoheadrightarrow} G'[V]$ does not hold.

  The other cases are routine.
- Proof for the fourth part is similar.

7 Conclusions

As already discussed in Sect. 1, a large amount of work exists on control operators but none of them to our knowledge was (sound and) complete with respect to contextual equivalence in the presence of call/cc (but no state), as they could only be complete (if at all) with respect to CPS conversion (or in the presence of state [10, personal communication]).

Our examples in Sect. 6 are mostly taken from previous work [10,23]. In particular, Thielecke [23] defines a bisimulation theory for *each* of the examples in his paper. Our bisimulations may partly be seen as a generalization of his[3].

---

[3] In fact, we finished most of our proofs *before* discovering his unpublished manuscript [23], often reinventing essential ideas that are specific to each example.

It is sometimes argued [12] that the undelimited continuation operator call/cc is inferior to delimited ones such as **shift** and **reset**. The present work can be seen as an approach to tackling with theoretical difficulties of reasoning about undelimited continuations.

Although our bisimulations generalize "brute-force" contextual equivalence proofs and remove many "boilerplate parts," some of them still remain as one can see via the examples in Sect. 6. It would be interesting future work to consider how to get rid of them without sacrificing completeness (and simplicity). Mechanical verification using proof assistants would also be useful.

Our bisimulations in this paper are non-trivially different from environment bisimulations, as discussed after Definition 3.7. In fact, this difference could also be adapted for languages without call/cc or any control operator. It may also be interesting to investigate the merit of this direction.

Acknowledgments. We thank Oleg Kiselyov for informing us of the problem of contextual equivalence between M and $M; M$, and the anonymous reviewers for useful comments. This research and the authors are partially supported by KAKENHI JP16K12409, JP15H02681, JP25540001, and JP22300005.

References

1. Aristizábal, A., Biernacki, D., Lenglet, S., Polesiuk, P.: Environmental bisimulations for delimited-control operators with dynamic prompt generation. In: Kesner, D., Pientka, B. (eds.) 1st International Conference on Formal Structures for Computation and Deduction, FSCD 2016, 22–26 June 2016, Porto, Portugal. LIPIcs, vol. 52, pp. 9:1–9:17. Schloss Dagstuhl - Leibniz-Zentrum fuer Informatik (2016). http://dx.doi.org/10.4230/LIPIcs.FSCD.2016.9
2. Biernacki, D., Lenglet, S.: Normal form bisimulations for delimited-control operators. In: Schrijvers, T., Thiemann, P. (eds.) FLOPS 2012. LNCS, vol. 7294, pp. 47–61. Springer, Heidelberg (2012). doi:10.1007/978-3-642-29822-6_7
3. Biernacki, D., Lenglet, S.: Environmental bisimulations for delimited-control operators. In: Shan, C. (ed.) APLAS 2013. LNCS, vol. 8301, pp. 333–348. Springer, Heidelberg (2013). doi:10.1007/978-3-319-03542-0_24
4. Danvy, O., Filinski, A.: Abstracting control. In: LISP and Functional Programming, pp. 151–160 (1990). http://doi.acm.org/10.1145/91556.91622
5. Dreyer, D., Neis, G., Birkedal, L.: The impact of higher-order state and control effects on local relational reasoning. J. Funct. Program. **22**(4–5), 477–528 (2012). http://dx.doi.org/10.1017/S095679681200024X
6. Felleisen, M., Friedman, D.P., Kohlbecker, E.E., Duba, B.F.: A syntactic theory of sequential control. Theor. Comput. Sci. **52**, 205–237 (1987). http://dx.doi.org/10.1016/0304-3975(87)90109-5
7. Felleisen, M., Hieb, R.: The revised report on the syntactic theories of sequential control and state. Theor. Comput. Sci. **103**(2), 235–271 (1992). http://dx.doi.org/10.1016/0304-3975(92)90014-7
8. Griffin, T.: A formulae-as-types notion of control. In: Allen, F.E. (ed.) Conference Record of the Seventeenth Annual ACM Symposium on Principles of Programming Languages, San Francisco, California, USA, January 1990, pp. 47–58. ACM Press (1990). http://doi.acm.org/10.1145/96709.96714

9. Hur, C., Dreyer, D., Neis, G., Vafeiadis, V.: The marriage of bisimulations and kripke logical relations. In: Field, J., Hicks, M. (eds.) Proceedings of the 39th ACM SIGPLAN-SIGACT Symposium on Principles of Programming Languages, POPL 2012, Philadelphia, Pennsylvania, USA, 22–28 January 2012, pp. 59–72. ACM (2012). http://doi.acm.org/10.1145/2103656.2103666

10. Hur, C.K., Neis, G., Dreyer, D., Vafeiadis, V.: A logical step forward in parametric bisimulations. Technical report MPI-SWS-2014-003, Max Planck Institute for Software Systems (2014)

11. Kameyama, Y., Hasegawa, M.: A sound and complete axiomatization of delimited continuations. In: Runciman, C., Shivers, O. (eds.) Proceedings of the Eighth ACM SIGPLAN International Conference on Functional Programming, ICFP 2003, Uppsala, Sweden, 25–29 August 2003, pp. 177–188. ACM (2003). http://doi.acm.org/10.1145/944705.944722

12. Kiselyov, O.: An argument against call/cc. http://okmij.org/ftp/continuations/against-callcc.html

13. Koutavas, V.: Reasoning about imperative and higher-order programs. Ph.D. thesis, Northeastern University (2008)

14. Morris Jr., J.H.: Lambda-calculus models of programming languages. Ph.D. thesis, Massachusetts Institute of Technology (1968)

15. Sabry, A.: Note on axiomatizing the semantics of control operators. Technical report CIS-TR-96-03, Department of Computer Science, University of Oregon (1996)

16. Sabry, A., Felleisen, M.: Reasoning about programs in continuation-passing style. LISP Symb. Comput. **6**(3–4), 289–360 (1993)

17. Sangiorgi, D., Kobayashi, N., Sumii, E.: Environmental bisimulations for higher-order languages. In: Twenty-Second Annual IEEE Symposium on Logic in Computer Science, pp. 293–302 (2007)

18. Støvring, K., Lassen, S.B.: A complete, co-inductive syntactic theory of sequential control and state. In: Palsberg, J. (ed.) Semantics and Algebraic Specification, Essays Dedicated to Peter D. Mosses on the Occasion of His 60th Birthday. LNCS, vol. 5700, pp. 329–375. Springer, Heidelberg (2009). doi:10.1007/978-3-642-04164-8_17

19. Sumii, E.: A complete characterization of observational equivalence in polymorphic λ-calculus with general references. In: Grädel, E., Kahle, R. (eds.) CSL 2009. LNCS, vol. 5771, pp. 455–469. Springer, Heidelberg (2009)

20. Sumii, E., Pierce, B.C.: A bisimulation for dynamic sealing. In: Proceedings of the 31st ACM SIGPLAN-SIGACT Symposium on Principles of Programming Languages, pp. 161–172 (2004)

21. Sumii, E., Pierce, B.C.: A bisimulation for type abstraction and recursion. In: Proceedings of the 32nd ACM SIGPLAN-SIGACT Symposium on Principles of Programming Languages, pp. 63–74 (2005)

22. Sumii, E., Pierce, B.C.: A bisimulation for type abstraction and recursion. J. ACM **54**(5–26), 1–43 (2007). Extended abstract appeared in Proceedings of the 32nd ACM SIGPLAN-SIGACT Symposium on Principles of Programming Languages, pp. 63–74 (2005)

23. Thielecke, H.: Contrasting exceptions and continuations (2001). http://www.cs.bham.ac.uk/hxt/research/exncontjournal.pdf

A Realizability Interpretation for Intersection and Union Types

Daniel J. Dougherty[1], Ugo de'Liguoro[2], Luigi Liquori[3(✉)], and Claude Stolze[4]

[1] Worcester Polytechnic Institute, Worcester, USA
dd@cs.wpi.edu
[2] Università di Torino, Torino, Italy
ugo.deliguoro@unito.it
[3] INRIA Sophia Antipolis-Méditerranée, Valbonne, France
Luigi.Liquori@inria.fr
[4] ENS Rennes and UPMC, Bruz, France
Claude.Stolze@ens-rennes.fr

Abstract. *Proof-functional* logical connectives allow reasoning about the structure of logical proofs, in this way giving to the latter the status of *first-class* objects. This is in contrast to classical *truth-functional* connectives where the meaning of a compound formula is dependent only on the truth value of its subformulas.

In this paper we present a typed lambda calculus, enriched with strong products, strong sums, and a related proof-functional logic. This calculus, directly derived from a typed calculus previously defined by two of the current authors, has been proved isomorphic to the well-known Barbanera-Dezani-Ciancaglini-de'Liguoro type assignment system. We present a logic $\mathcal{L}^{\cap\cup}$ featuring two proof-functional connectives, namely strong conjunction and strong disjunction. We prove the typed calculus to be isomorphic to the logic $\mathcal{L}^{\cap\cup}$ and we give a realizability semantics using *Mints' realizers* [Min89] and a completeness theorem. A prototype implementation is also described.

1 Introduction

This paper is a contribution to the study of intersection and union type systems and their role in *logical* investigations.

There are two well-known points of view on type systems: (i) types as specifications and terms as programs, and (ii) types as propositions and terms as evidence. Let us call the former the "computational" perspective, and the latter the "logical" one.

In the logical view a type judgment $t : \sigma$ is taken to mean that t is a construction providing evidence of the proposition σ, reducing to a canonical element of σ. Typed λ-calculi defined in this way are at the core of proof assistants and logical frameworks. On the other hand, in the computational view a judgment

---

Work supported by the COST Action CA15123 EUTYPES "The European research network on types for programming and verification".

A. Igarashi (Ed.): APLAS 2016, LNCS 10017, pp. 187–205, 2016.
DOI: 10.1007/978-3-319-47958-3_11

$t : \sigma$ is taken to mean that t denotes an element of the datatype σ, which may in fact be defined in a way external to the system for making type-judgments.

Within the computational tradition itself there are two approaches: explicitly-typed calculi ("Church-style") and type assignment systems ("Curry-style"). These represent more than a difference in presentation: in type assignment systems types provide a means for making assertions about the semantics of raw terms, while in explicitly typed calculi types are a method of insuring that only well-behaved terms are considered at all.

The logical view resides naturally in a system of Church-style explicit typing. Existing logical frameworks and proof assistants take such explicitly-typed calculi for their foundation.

Intersection types originated within the computational perspective as a tool for analyzing the functional behavior of λ-terms: intersection type systems give characterizations of each of the sets of strongly normalizing, weakly normalizing, and head-normalizing terms [Pot80, CDC80, BCDC83]. From a programming languages perspective, intersection types support (finitary) *overloading*. Subtyping arises naturally in the study of intersection types.

Later, union types were introduced, as a foundational study [BDCd95] and also from programming languages motivation [MPS86, CF93, Dun12]. Union types are somewhat similar to sum types, but as Pierce [Pie02] notes: *"The main formal difference between disjoint and non-disjoint union types is that the latter lack any kind of **case** construct: if we know only that a value v has type $T_1 \cup T_2$ then the only operations we can safely perform on v are ones that make sense for both T_1 and T_2"*.

Naturally, the question arose whether intersection, union, and subtyping can be given a logical explanation. Pottinger [Pot80] already identified this question: *"Since the meaning of $\cap$ is reasonably clear (to claim that $A \cap B$ is to claim that one has a reason for asserting A which is also a reason for asserting B), it would obviously be of interest to figure out how to add $\cap$ to intuitionist logic and then consider the analysis of intuitionist mathematical reasoning in the light of the resulting system"*. A natural logical analogue of computational interpretation of union types is "if we want to reason from an assumption v that $T_1 \cup T_2$ holds, then we may reason separately assuming v is evidence of T_1 and that v is evidence of T_2 as long as we use that evidence *in the same way*."

There has subsequently been a lot of work on this question of understanding "proof-functional" connectives [MR72, LE85, Min89, AB91, BM94, DCGV97] where the logical analogue of intersection has come to be called "strong conjunction", with "strong disjunction" corresponding to union of course, and, in [DCGV97] with subtyping associated with "relevant implication", long of interest to philosophers. It became clear that a focus on *realizability* was most fruitful, typically taking untyped terms (from λ-calculus or combinatory logic) as realizers.

Independent of this thread of research, the question arose whether intersection and union type systems could be presented naturally in Church-style, *i.e.* explicitly typed. There are technical obstacles to an explicitly-typed treatment that would inherit the core properties of the type-assignment app-roach: subject reduction, subject expansion, strong normalization, unicity of typing, decidability of type reconstruction and type checking. Several proposals [PT94, Rey96, CLV01] [Ron02, WDMT02, WH02, Dun12] were explored, none of which met all the criteria above. The system presented here derives from the system of $\Lambda_t^\cap$ [LR07] subsequently generalized in the system $\Lambda_t^{\cap\cup}$ [DL10] to include union types. These systems do satisfy the core properties listed above. They do not include subtyping, and left open the question of a logical interpretation of the λ-calculus presented.

All of the work on understanding the logical aspects of intersection, union, and subtyping took place in the Curry-style framework. This was natural given the fact that type assignment was the most natural framework for intersection and union types, because the typing rules are not *syntax directed*. But the fact that most uses of λ-calculi in logical systems use explicitly-typed terms poses a compelling question, the main topic of the current paper:

> *Can a logical investigation of intersection and union types, with/without subtyping, take place in the context of an explicitly-typed λ-calculus?*

The motivation is that success here should point the way towards applications of intersection and union types in proof assistants and logical frameworks. The hope is that they can provide as much insight into logical systems as they have in the computational arena.

1.1   Contributions

Our results can be thought of as exploring the relationships between the following four formal systems:

- the original system $\Lambda_u^{\cap\cup}$ for type assignment with intersection and union types from [BDCd95],
- the typed calculus $\Lambda_t^{\cap\cup}$ for type assignment with intersection and union types defined in [DL10],
- the proof-functional logic $\mathcal{L}^{\cap\cup}$, defined in this paper, and
- a natural deduction system NJ(β) for derivations in first-order intuitionistic logic with untyped λ-terms.

Judgements in these systems take the following four forms below. On the right-hand sides of the turnstiles, M is an untyped λ-term, Δ is a simply-typed λ-term with strong products and strong sums, and σ is a simple type formed using $\rightarrow, \cap$, and $\cup$. The $r_\sigma[M]$ are typing predicates to be realized.

$$
\begin{array}{lllllll}
\boldsymbol{\Lambda}_u^{\cap\cup} & B, & x_\iota & :\tau & \vdash & M & :\sigma \\
\boldsymbol{\Lambda}_t^{\cap\cup} & \Gamma^@, & x_\iota @\iota & :\tau & \vdash & M @\Delta & :\sigma \\
\mathcal{L}^{\cap\cup} & \Gamma, & \iota & :\tau & \vdash & \Delta & :\sigma \\
\mathsf{NJ}(\beta) & G, & r_\tau[x_\iota] & & \vdash & r_\sigma[M] &
\end{array}
$$

The relationship between $\Lambda_t^{\cap\cup}$ and $\Lambda_u^{\cap\cup}$ was explored in [DL10], and is recalled in Sect. 2. The first contribution of this paper is the definition of a new notion, the *essence* $\langle\Delta\rangle$ of a typed term Δ, used to connect $\Lambda_t^{\cap\cup}$ and $\mathcal{L}^{\cap\cup}$. Specifically, we prove, as Theorem 6,

$$\Gamma^{@} \vdash M@\Delta : \sigma \text{ if and only if } \Gamma \vdash \Delta : \sigma \text{ and } \langle\Delta\rangle \sqsubseteq M. \tag{1}$$

Here Γ is obtained from $\Gamma^{@}$ by erasing all the "$x@$", and $\sqsubseteq$ is a suitable syntactic preorder on untyped λ-terms. This justifies thinking of $\mathcal{L}^{\cap\cup}$ as a proof-functional logic. We think of the $\Lambda_t^{\cap\cup}$ as a bridge between the intersection and union type assignment system and the logic $\mathcal{L}^{\cap\cup}$.

Our second contribution is to show how $\Lambda_t^{\cap\cup}$ supports a *realizability* analysis of $\mathcal{L}^{\cap\cup}$. In particular, Sect. 3 shows that

$$\Gamma^{@} \vdash M@\Delta : \sigma \text{ and only if } \Delta \text{ realizes } G_\Gamma \vdash r_\sigma[M]. \tag{2}$$

Together with the equivalence in (1) this represents a complete analysis of the relationship between Curry-style and Church-style typing and the associated logic for intersection and union.

Section 4 presents further theoretical and pragmatic developments. Subsect. 4.1 extends the typed system and the logic by adding a natural notion of subtyping. This is represented in the type assignment system as a non-syntax-directed substitution rule, in the typed calculus as an explicit coercion, and in the logic calculus as another well-known proof-functional connective called *relevant implication*. In Subsect. 4.2 we briefly describe our prototype implementation of the type checking and proof inhabitation for the system with intersection/strong conjunction and union/strong disjunction and coercions as relevant implication.

1.2 Related Work

There are far too many studies of type systems featuring intersection, union, and subtyping to identify individually here. We have tried to outline the main currents of research in the introduction; here we will mention some work that is directly related to the contributions of this paper.

The formal investigation of soundness and completeness for a notion of realizability was initiated by Lopez-Escobar [LE85] and subsequently refined by Mints [Min89]. It is Mints' approach that we build on here.

The connection between intersection types and relevant implication was noticed by Alessi and Barbanera in [AB91]. Barbanera and Martini [BM94] studied three proof-functional operators, namely the *strong conjunction*, the *relevant implication* (see Meyer-Routley's [MR72] system B^+), and the *strong equivalence* connective for double implication, relating those connectives with suitable type assignments system, a realizability semantics and a completeness theorem.

Dezani-Ciancaglini, Ghilezan, and Venneri [DCGV97], investigated a *Curry-Howard* interpretation of intersection and union types (for Combinatory Logic). Using the well understood relation between *combinatory logic* and λ-calculus, they encode type-free λ-terms in suitable combinatoric logic formulas and then type them using intersection and union types. As they put it, their goal is *"... to set out a logical system... such that the intersection and union type constructors are interpreted as propositional connectives and then their derivability is completely represented by derivability in a logical Hilbert-style, axiomatization."* This is a complementary approach to the realizability-based one here.

Barbanera, Dezani-Ciancaglini, and de'Liguoro [BDCd95] presented an untyped λ-calculus with related type assignment system featuring intersection and union types. The previous work [DL10] presented a typed calculus that explored the relationship between the proof-functional intersections and unions and the truth-functional (strong) products and (strong) sums; the intersection and union aspect of the system was isomorphic, after erasure, to the Barbanera-Dezani-Ciancaglini-de'Liguoro [BDCd95] type assignment system. The type system we consider is built out of an infinitely enumerable set of type variables $\phi_0, \phi_1, \ldots$ and the constant type ω, by means of the arrow ("$\rightarrow$"), union ("$\cup$"), and intersection ("$\cap$") constructors. Therefore, types have the following syntax:

$$\sigma ::= \phi \mid \omega \mid \sigma \rightarrow \sigma \mid \sigma \cup \sigma \mid \sigma \cap \sigma.$$

Let $B \triangleq \{x_1{:}\sigma_1, \ldots, x_n{:}\sigma_n\}$ ($i \neq j$ implies $x_i \not\equiv x_j$), and $B, x{:}\sigma \triangleq B \cup \{x{:}\sigma\}$

$$\frac{}{B \vdash M : \omega} \ (\omega) \qquad\qquad\qquad \frac{x{:}\sigma \in B}{B \vdash x : \sigma} \ (Var)$$

$$\frac{B, x{:}\sigma_1 \vdash M : \sigma_2}{B \vdash \lambda x.M : \sigma_1 \rightarrow \sigma_2} \ (\rightarrow I) \qquad\qquad \frac{B \vdash M : \sigma_1 \rightarrow \sigma_2 \quad B \vdash N : \sigma_1}{B \vdash M N : \sigma_2} \ (\rightarrow E)$$

$$\frac{B \vdash M : \sigma_1 \quad B \vdash M : \sigma_2}{B \vdash M : \sigma_1 \cap \sigma_2} \ (\cap I) \qquad\qquad \frac{B \vdash M : \sigma_1 \cap \sigma_2 \quad i = 1,2}{B \vdash M : \sigma_i} \ (\cap E_i)$$

$$\frac{B \vdash M : \sigma_i \quad i = 1,2}{B \vdash M : \sigma_1 \cup \sigma_2} \ (\cup I_i) \qquad \frac{\begin{array}{c} B, x{:}\sigma_1 \vdash M : \sigma_3 \\ B, x{:}\sigma_2 \vdash M : \sigma_3 \quad B \vdash N : \sigma_1 \cup \sigma_2 \end{array}}{B \vdash M[N/x] : \sigma_3} \ (\cup E)$$

Fig. 1. The Intersection and Union Type Assignment System $\Lambda_u^{\cap\cup}$ [BDCd95].

2 Type Assignment $\Lambda_u^{\cap\cup}$ and the Typed Calculus $\Lambda_t^{\cap\cup}$

The type assignment system $\Lambda_u^{\cap\cup}$ is the set of inference rules for assigning intersection and union types to terms of the pure λ-calculus. The presentation here, in Fig. 1, is taken from [BDCd95]: the terms are standard raw λ-terms, and the types are generated from a set of base types by the constructors $\rightarrow, \cap$, and $\cup$.

$\Gamma^@ \triangleq \{x_{\iota_1}@\iota_1{:}\sigma_1, \ldots, x_{\iota_n}@\iota_n{:}\sigma_n\}$, where $\iota_i \neq \iota_j$ implies $x_{\iota_i} \neq x_{\iota_j}$, and
$\Gamma^@, x_\iota@\iota{:}\sigma \triangleq \Gamma^@ \cup \{x_\iota@\iota{:}\sigma\}$

$$\frac{}{\Gamma^@ \vdash M@* : \omega} \ (\omega) \qquad\qquad \frac{x_\iota@\iota{:}\sigma \in \Gamma^@}{\Gamma^@ \vdash x_\iota@\iota : \sigma} \ (Var)$$

$$\frac{\Gamma^@, x_\iota@\iota{:}\sigma_1 \vdash M@\Delta : \sigma_2}{\Gamma^@ \vdash \lambda x_\iota.M@\lambda\iota{:}\sigma_1.\Delta : \sigma_1 \to \sigma_2} \ (\to I) \qquad \frac{\begin{array}{c}\Gamma^@ \vdash M@\Delta_1 : \sigma_1 \to \sigma_2\\ \Gamma^@ \vdash N@\Delta_2 : \sigma_1\end{array}}{\Gamma^@ \vdash M\,N@\Delta_1\,\Delta_2 : \sigma_2} \ (\to E)$$

$$\frac{\Gamma^@ \vdash M@\Delta_1 : \sigma_1 \quad \Gamma^@ \vdash M@\Delta_2 : \sigma_2}{\Gamma^@ \vdash M@\langle\Delta_1, \Delta_2\rangle : \sigma_1 \cap \sigma_2} \ (\cap I) \qquad \frac{\Gamma^@ \vdash M@\Delta : \sigma_1 \cap \sigma_2 \quad i \in \{1,2\}}{\Gamma^@ \vdash M@\mathsf{pr}_i\Delta : \sigma_i} \ (\cap E_i)$$

$$\frac{\Gamma^@ \vdash M@\Delta : \sigma_i \quad i \in \{1,2\}}{\Gamma^@ \vdash M@\mathsf{in}_i\Delta : \sigma_1 \cup \sigma_2} \ (\cup I_i)$$

$$\frac{\Gamma^@, x_\iota@\iota{:}\sigma_1 \vdash M@\Delta_1 : \sigma_3 \quad \Gamma^@, x_\iota@\iota{:}\sigma_2 \vdash M@\Delta_2 : \sigma_3 \quad \Gamma^@ \vdash N@\Delta_3 : \sigma_1 \cup \sigma_2}{\Gamma^@ \vdash M\{N/x_\iota\}@[\overline{\lambda}\iota{:}\sigma_1.\Delta_1, \overline{\lambda}\iota{:}\sigma_2.\Delta_2] \cdot \Delta_3 : \sigma_3} \ (\cup E)$$

Fig. 2. The Typed Calculus $\Lambda_\mathsf{t}^{\cap\cup}$ [DL10].

Theorem 1 (Main properties of $\Lambda_\mathsf{u}^{\cap\cup}$ [BDCd95]).

Characterization. *The terms typable without use of the ω rule are precisely the strongly normalizing terms.* □

Parallel reduction. *If $B \vdash M : \sigma$ and $M \to_{gk} N$ then $B \vdash N : \sigma$. Here $\to_{gk}$ is the "Gross-Knuth" reduction, where all residuals of redexes in M are contracted (Def. 13.2.7 in [Bar84]).* □

In [DL10] a typed λ-calculus $\Lambda_\mathsf{t}^{\cap\cup}$ was defined, whose goal was to capture a decidable and Church-style version of the Curry-style $\Lambda_\mathsf{u}^{\cap\cup}$. The pseudo-terms of the $\Lambda_\mathsf{t}^{\cap\cup}$ calculus have the form $M@\Delta$, where M and Δ have the following syntax:

$$M ::= x_\iota \mid \lambda x_\iota.M \mid M\,M$$

$$\Delta ::= \iota \mid * \mid \lambda\iota{:}\sigma.\Delta \mid \Delta\,\Delta \mid \langle\Delta, \Delta\rangle \mid [\overline{\lambda}\iota{:}\sigma.\Delta, \overline{\lambda}\iota{:}\sigma.\Delta] \cdot \Delta \mid \mathsf{pr}_i\Delta \mid \mathsf{in}_i\Delta \quad i = 1, 2$$

Note that the metasymbols $\overline{\lambda}$ and $\cdot$ are *per se* nothing but parts of the strong sum construction. The typed judgments are of the shape $\Gamma^@ \vdash M@\Delta : \sigma$, where in a nutshell M is a type-free λ-term, Δ is a typed λ-term enriched with strong product, strong sum, projections, and injections to faithfully "memorize" every step of a type assignment derivation, and $\Gamma^@$ contains declarations of the shape $x_\iota@\iota{:}\sigma$, where x_ι and ι are free-variables of M and Δ, respectively. The inference rules are presented in Fig. 2. The main feature of the system was to keep M to be "synchronized" with Δ. As an example, we can derive the judgement $\vdash \lambda x_\iota . x_\iota @ \langle \lambda \iota : \sigma_1 . \iota, \ \lambda \iota : \sigma_2 . \iota \rangle : (\sigma_1 \to \sigma_1) \cap (\sigma_2 \to \sigma_2)$. As another example, the term $[\overline{\lambda} \iota_1 : \sigma_1 . \Delta_1, \ \overline{\lambda} \iota_2 : \sigma_2 . \Delta_1] \cdot \Delta_3$ corresponds to the familiar case statement. The type ω plays the role of a terminal object, that is to say it is an object with a single element. The connection with type-assignment is this: every term can be assigned type ω so all proofs of that judgment have no content: all these proofs are considered identical ([Rey98], p. 372). As is typical we name the unique element of the terminal object as $*$.

The relation between untyped and typed reductions is subtle because of the presence of the "Gross-Knuth" parallel reduction in the untyped calculus and a fairly complex notion of synchronization of M and Δ, via synchronized β- and Δ-reductions in the typed calculus. In a nutshell, for a given term $M@\Delta$, the computational part (M) and the logical part (Δ) grow up together while they are built through application of rules (Var), $(\to I)$, and $(\to E)$, but they *get disconnected* when we apply the $(\cap I)$, $(\cup I)$ or $(\cap E)$ rules, which change the Δ but not the M. This disconnection is "logged" in the Δ via occurrences of $\langle -, - \rangle$, $[-, -]$, pr_i, and in_i. In order to correctly identify the reductions that need to be performed in parallel in order to preserve the correct syntax of the term, an *ad hoc* notion of *"overlapping"* that helps to define a redex taking into account the surrounding context was defined in [DL10]. Therefore, we define $\Rightarrow$ as the union of two reductions: $\Rightarrow_\beta$ dealing with β-reduction occurring in both M and Δ, and $\Rightarrow_\Delta$ dealing with reductions arising from reduction only in Δ. We refer to the complete reduction definition in [DL10]. Here are some main properties of the system $\Lambda_t^{\cap\cup}$. Since the system is explicitly typed, properties such as type checking and type reconstruction are immediate.

Theorem 2 (Main properties of $\Lambda_t^{\cap\cup}$ [DL10]).

Subject reduction. *If $\Gamma^@ \vdash M@\Delta : \sigma$ and $M@\Delta \Rightarrow M'@\Delta'$, then*
 $\Gamma^@ \vdash M'@\Delta' : \sigma$.   □

Church-Rosser. *The reduction relation $\Rightarrow$ is confluent.*   □

Strong normalization. *If $M@\Delta$ is typable without using rule (ω) then M is strongly normalizing.*   □

Type reconstruction algorithm. *There is an algorithm* Type *satisfying*
 Soundness. *If* $\mathsf{Type}(\Gamma^@, M@\Delta) = \sigma$, *then $\Gamma^@ \vdash M@\Delta : \sigma$.*   □
 Completeness. *If $\Gamma^@ \vdash M@\Delta : \sigma$, then* $\mathsf{Type}(\Gamma^@, M@\Delta) = \sigma$.   □

Type checking algorithm. *There is an algorithm* Typecheck *satisfying*
 $\Gamma^@ \vdash M@\Delta : \sigma$ *if and only if* $\mathsf{Typecheck}(\Gamma^@, M@\Delta, \sigma) = \mathsf{true}$.

Judgment decidability. *It is decidable whether $\Gamma^@ \vdash M@\Delta : \sigma$ is derivable.* □

Isomorphism of typed-untyped derivations. *Let $\mathcal{D}er\Lambda_u^{\cap\cup}$ and $\mathcal{D}er\Lambda_t^{\cap\cup}$ be the sets of all (un)typed derivations. There are functions $\mathcal{F} : \mathcal{D}er\Lambda_u^{\cap\cup} \Rightarrow \mathcal{D}er\Lambda_u^{\cap\cup}$ and $\mathcal{G} : \mathcal{D}er\Lambda_u^{\cap\cup} \Rightarrow \mathcal{D}er\Lambda_t^{\cap\cup}$ showing the systems $\Lambda_u^{\cap\cup}$ and $\Lambda_u^{\cap\cup}$ to be isomorphic in the following sense: $\mathcal{F} \circ \mathcal{G}$ is the identity in $\mathcal{D}er\Lambda_u^{\cap\cup}$ and $\mathcal{G} \circ \mathcal{F}$ is the identity in $\mathcal{D}er\Lambda_u^{\cap\cup}$ modulo uniform naming of variable-marks, i.e., $\mathcal{G}(\mathcal{F}(\Gamma^@ \vdash M@\Delta : \sigma)) = \mathsf{ren}(\Gamma^@) \vdash \mathsf{ren}(M@\Delta) : \sigma$, where ren is a simple function renaming the free occurrences of variable-marks.*   □

$$
\begin{array}{lll}
\mathsf{Type}(\Gamma^{@}, M@\Delta) & \triangleq & \text{match } M@\Delta \text{ with} \\
\_@* & \Rightarrow & \omega \\
\_@\mathsf{pr}_i\Delta_1 & \Rightarrow & \sigma_i \quad i=1,2 \quad \text{if } \mathsf{Type}(\Gamma^{@}, M@\Delta_1) = \sigma_1 \cap \sigma_2 \\
\_@\langle \Delta_1, \Delta_2 \rangle & \Rightarrow & \sigma_1 \cap \sigma_2 \quad \text{if} \quad \mathsf{Type}(\Gamma^{@}, M@\Delta_1) = \sigma_1 \\
& & \qquad\qquad \text{and } \mathsf{Type}(\Gamma^{@}, M@\Delta_2) = \sigma_2 \\
\_@\mathsf{in}_i\Delta_1 & \Rightarrow & \sigma_1 \cup \sigma_2 \quad \text{if } \mathsf{Type}(\Gamma^{@}, M@\Delta_1) = \sigma_i \quad i=1,2
\end{array}
$$

$$
\_@\begin{bmatrix} \overline{\lambda\iota{:}\sigma_1}.\Delta_1, \\ \overline{\lambda\iota{:}\sigma_2}.\Delta_2 \end{bmatrix} \cdot \Delta_3 \Rightarrow \sigma_3 \quad
\begin{aligned}
&\text{if} \quad \mathsf{Type}((\Gamma^{@}, x_\iota@\iota{:}\sigma_1), M'@\Delta_1) = \sigma_3 \\
&\text{and } \mathsf{Type}((\Gamma^{@}, x_\iota@\iota{:}\sigma_2), M'@\Delta_2) = \sigma_3 \\
&\text{and } \mathsf{Type}(\Gamma^{@}, N@\Delta_3) = \sigma_1 \cup \sigma_3 \text{ and} \\
&\text{and } M \equiv M'[N/x]
\end{aligned}
$$

$$
\begin{array}{lll}
x_\iota & \Rightarrow & \sigma \quad \text{if } x_\iota@\iota{:}\sigma \in \Gamma^{@} \\
\lambda x_\iota.M_1@\lambda\iota{:}\sigma_1.\Delta_1 & \Rightarrow & \sigma_1 \to \sigma_2 \quad \text{if } \mathsf{Type}((\Gamma^{@}, x_\iota@\iota{:}\sigma_1), M_1@\Delta_1) = \sigma_2 \\
M_1\, M_2@\Delta_1\, \Delta_2 & \Rightarrow & \sigma_2 \quad \text{if} \quad \mathsf{Type}(\Gamma^{@}, M_1@\Delta_1) = \sigma_1 \to \sigma_2 \\
& & \qquad\quad \text{and } \mathsf{Type}(\Gamma^{@}, M_2@\Delta_2) = \sigma_1 \\
\_@\_ & \Rightarrow & \text{false} \quad \text{otherwise}
\end{array}
$$

$$
\mathsf{Typecheck}(\Gamma^{@}, M@\Delta, \sigma) \triangleq \mathsf{Type}(\Gamma^{@}, M@\Delta) \stackrel{?}{=} \sigma
$$

Fig. 3. The Type Reconstruction and Type Checking Algorithms for $\Lambda_t^{\cap\cup}$.

The algorithms Type and $\mathsf{Typecheck}$ in Fig. 3 are exactly the ones from [DL10].

2.1 The Proof Essence Partial Function

We start with a simple question: assuming $M@\Delta$ is derivable, can we *extract* the computational part M from a proof-term Δ? Luckily the answer is positive. To do that, let us extend the pure λ-calculus syntax by a constant Ω, typable by ω only, and consider the following pre-order join (partial) operation:

Definition 3. *Let $\sqsubseteq$ be the least pre-congruence over untyped λ-terms extended with the constant Ω such that:*

1. *$\Omega \sqsubseteq M$ for any M*
2. *if $M =_\alpha M'$ and $M' \sqsubseteq N$ then $M \sqsubseteq N$*
3. *if $M =_\eta M'$ and $M' \sqsubseteq N$ then $M \sqsubseteq N$*

By identifying η-convertible terms, the relation $\sqsubseteq$ is a partial order; next we show that the set of extended λ-terms is closed under join of compatible terms: M and N are compatible, written $M \uparrow N$, if $M \sqsubseteq P \sqsupseteq N$, for some P. Although the next lemma is intuitively clear its proof rather technical. We include the proof because existence of join of compatible terms is necessary for the subsequent definition of "essence" to make sense; it also provides a decision method for compatibility and a method to compute the join.

$$\Omega \vee M = M \vee \Omega = M$$

$$\lambda x.M \vee \lambda y.N = \lambda z.M[z/x] \vee N[z/y] \quad z \text{ fresh}$$

$$M\,M' \vee N\,N' = (M \vee N)\,(M' \vee N')$$

$$M \vee N = \text{fail, else}$$

Fig. 4. Syntactical join

Lemma 4. *For any pair M, N of extended λ-terms it is decidable whether they are compatible. Moreover, if $M \uparrow N$ then there exists a term $M \sqcup N$ which is the join of M and N w.r.t. $\sqsubseteq$ that is unique up to η-equality.*

Proof. First observe that if $M \sqsubseteq P =_\eta Q$ then $P \sqsubseteq Q$, as $\sqsubseteq$ includes $=_\eta$ and $M \sqsubseteq Q$, by transitivity of $\sqsubseteq$.

Let $\leq$ be the last pre-congruence such that $\Omega \leq M$, for any M. Then the relation $\sqsubseteq$ coincides with the transitive closure of $(=_\eta \leq) \cup (\leq =_\eta)$, where $M(=_\eta \leq)N$ if $M =_\eta P \leq N$ for some P, and similarly $M(\leq =_\eta)N$. Now suppose that

$$M =_\eta M' \leq P \geq N =_\eta N'$$

Since η-reduction is Church-Rosser and strongly normalizing, there exist the unique η-normal forms M'' of M, M', and P'' of P and N'' of N, N', respectively. By definition and the above remark we have $M'' \sqsubseteq P'' \sqsupseteq N''$; we claim that $M'' \leq P'' \geq N''$.

If $M' \leq P$, then for some context with n holes $C[\cdot]_1 \cdots [\cdot]_n$ we have $M' \equiv C[\Omega]_1 \cdots [\Omega]_n$ and $P \equiv C[P_1]_1 \cdots [P_n]_n$ for some P_i's. Assuming for simplicity $n = 1$ and that $M' \to_\eta M''$ in one step by contracting the η-redex $\lambda x.R\,x$, we either have that the hole filled by Ω does not occur in R or that R contains it. In the first case $\lambda x.R\,x$ is (the only) η-redex of P and we trivially obtain $P \to_\eta P'' \geq M''$ by contracting the same redex. In the second case Ω is a subterm of R which is such that $R \leq R'$ and $P \equiv C[\lambda x.R'\,x]$ for some R': then we have $M'' \equiv C[R] \leq C[R'] \equiv P''$ with $P \to_\eta P''$. The case of $n > 1$ or $M' \to_\eta^+ M''$ in several steps is a straightforward generalization thereof. By a similar reasoning we conclude that $P'' \geq N''$ as well. Also the proof that if

$$M \leq Q =_\eta Q' \geq N$$

then $M'' \leq Q'' \geq N''$, where M'', Q'' and N'' are the respective η-normal forms of M, Q and Q', N is analogous.

From this it follows that if $M \sqsubseteq P \sqsupseteq N$, then $M'' \leq P'' \geq N''$ for their respective η-normal forms; as the inverse implication holds by definition, we can decide whether $M \uparrow N$ by reducing both M and N to their η-normal forms M'' and N'', and then deciding whether they are compatible w.r.t. the simpler relation $\leq$. In such a case we have that $M \sqcup N = M'' \vee N''$, where $\vee$ is defined in Fig. 4, namely the lub w.r.t. $\leq$. $\qquad\square$

Let us define the *essence* of a Δ, written $\wr\Delta\wr$, as a partial mapping as follows:

Definition 5 (Proof essence). *The type-free essence M of a typed proof Δ is:*

$$\wr * \wr \triangleq \Omega \qquad\qquad \wr\iota\wr \triangleq x_\iota$$

$$\wr\lambda\iota{:}\sigma_1.\Delta\wr \triangleq \lambda x_\iota.\wr\Delta\wr \qquad\qquad \wr\Delta_1\,\Delta_2\wr \triangleq \wr\Delta_1\wr\wr\Delta_2\wr$$

$$\wr[\overline{\lambda}\iota{:}\sigma_1.\Delta_1\,,\,\overline{\lambda}\iota{:}\sigma_2.\Delta_2]\cdot\Delta_3\wr \triangleq (\wr\Delta_1\wr\sqcup\wr\Delta_2\wr)\{\wr\Delta_3\wr/x_\iota\} \qquad \wr\mathsf{in}_i\Delta\wr \triangleq \wr\Delta\wr$$

$$\wr\langle\Delta_1\,,\,\Delta_2\rangle\wr \triangleq \wr\Delta_1\wr\sqcup\wr\Delta_2\wr \qquad\qquad \wr\mathsf{pr}_i\Delta\wr \triangleq \wr\Delta\wr$$

The *"essence"* map is partial because join is such; it is however always defined when applied to a typed proof-term Δ in the typed calculus $\Lambda_t^{\cap\cup}$ of [DL10] (see Theorem 6 below) and it produces a type-free λ-term M. Note that M and Δ are both typable with σ using the type assignment and the type system, respectively. Summarizing, the signature of the essence is as follows:

$$\wr - \wr : \text{proof-terms } (\Delta\text{'s}) \to \text{untyped } \lambda\text{-terms } (M\text{'s}).$$

2.2 The Proof-Functional Logic $\mathcal{L}^{\cap\cup}$

Indeed, for a given typable Δ, the left-hand side of the @, namely M, can be omitted since it represents just the essence of Δ, i.e. $\wr\Delta\wr \sqsubseteq M$. Thus we can introduce the proof-functional logic, called $\mathcal{L}^{\cap\cup}$ and presented in Fig. 5. The following theorem holds:

Theorem 6 (Equivalence). *Let Γ be obtained by $\Gamma^@$, simply by erasing all the "$x@$". Then $\Gamma^@\vdash M@\Delta : \sigma$ if and only if $\Gamma \vdash \Delta : \sigma$ and $\wr\Delta\wr \sqsubseteq M$.*   □

Let $\Gamma \triangleq \{\iota_1{:}\sigma_1,\ldots,\iota_n{:}\sigma_n\}$, where $i \neq j$ implies $\iota_i \neq \iota_j$, and $\Gamma,\iota{:}\sigma \triangleq \Gamma \cup \{\iota{:}\sigma\}$

$$\frac{}{\Gamma \vdash * : \omega}\ (\omega) \qquad\qquad \frac{\iota{:}\sigma \in \Gamma}{\Gamma \vdash \iota : \sigma}\ (Var)$$

$$\frac{\Gamma,\iota{:}\sigma_1 \vdash \Delta : \sigma_2}{\Gamma \vdash \lambda\iota{:}\sigma_1.\Delta : \sigma_1 \to \sigma_2}\ (\to\!I) \qquad \frac{\Gamma \vdash \Delta_1 : \sigma_1 \to \sigma_2 \quad \Gamma \vdash \Delta_2 : \sigma_1}{\Gamma \vdash \Delta_1\,\Delta_2 : \sigma_2}\ (\to\!E)$$

$$\frac{\begin{array}{l}\Gamma \vdash \Delta_1 : \sigma_1 \\ \Gamma \vdash \Delta_2 : \sigma_2 \quad \wr\Delta_1\wr\!\uparrow\!\wr\Delta_2\wr\end{array}}{\Gamma \vdash \langle\Delta_1\,,\,\Delta_2\rangle : \sigma_1 \cap \sigma_2}\ (\cap I) \qquad \frac{\Gamma \vdash \Delta : \sigma_1 \cap \sigma_2 \quad i \in \{1,2\}}{\Gamma \vdash \mathsf{pr}_i\Delta : \sigma_i}\ (\cap E_i)$$

$$\frac{\Gamma \vdash \Delta : \sigma_i \quad i \in \{1,2\}}{\Gamma \vdash \mathsf{in}_i\Delta : \sigma_1 \cup \sigma_2}\ (\cup I_i) \qquad \frac{\begin{array}{c}\Gamma,\iota{:}\sigma_1 \vdash \Delta_1 : \sigma_3 \quad \wr\Delta_1\wr\!\uparrow\!\wr\Delta_2\wr \\ \Gamma,\iota{:}\sigma_2 \vdash \Delta_2 : \sigma_3 \quad \Gamma \vdash \Delta_3 : \sigma_1 \cup \sigma_2\end{array}}{\Gamma \vdash [\overline{\lambda}\iota{:}\sigma_1.\Delta_1\,,\,\overline{\lambda}\iota{:}\sigma_2.\Delta_2]\cdot\Delta_3 : \sigma_3}\ (\cup E)$$

Fig. 5. The proof-functional logic $\mathcal{L}^{\cap\cup}$.

Proof. The left-to-right is by induction over the the derivation of $\Gamma^@ \vdash M@\Delta : \sigma$. First observe that if the derivation consists of axiom (ω) then $\Delta \equiv *$ and $\sigma = \omega$ and $\wr * \wr = \Omega \sqsubseteq M$. If the derivation ends by

$$\frac{\Gamma^@ \vdash M@\Delta_1 : \sigma_1 \quad \Gamma^@ \vdash M@\Delta_2 : \sigma_2}{\Gamma^@ \vdash M@\langle \Delta_1, \Delta_2 \rangle : \sigma_1 \cap \sigma_2} \; (\cap I)$$

then by induction we have that both $\wr \Delta_1 \wr$ and $\wr \Delta_2 \wr$ are defined and that $\wr \Delta_1 \wr \sqsubseteq M \sqsupseteq \wr \Delta_2 \wr$, therefore $\wr \langle \Delta_1, \Delta_2 \rangle \wr = \wr \Delta_1 \wr \sqcup \wr \Delta_2 \wr$ is defined and $\wr \Delta_1 \wr \sqcup \wr \Delta_2 \wr \sqsubseteq M$ as desired.

If the derivation ends by $(\cup E)$ we reason in the same way as in case $(\cap I)$, while all other cases are immediate by induction and the fact that $\sqsubseteq$ is a pre-congruence.

The converse direction is is a straightforward induction over the derivation of $\Gamma \vdash \Delta : \sigma$. $\qquad\square$

Since $\mathcal{L}^{\cap\cup}$ is a proof-functional logic it is natural to consider the pair "$\Delta : \sigma$" as a logical formula. Pictorially speaking, we could say that the type assignment system of [BDCd95] and the logic $\mathcal{L}^{\cap\cup}$ are "bridged" by the typed system $\Lambda_t^{\cap\cup}$, and the above. We prove this fact by means of the concept of essence. This is, to the best of our knowledge, the first attempt to interpret union as a proof-functional connective.

3   Realizability Interpretation of Union Types

In contrast to the system of intersection types, the type assignment system $\Lambda_u^{\cap\cup}$ has no simple set-theoretic interpretation (see [BDCd95]). On the other hand system $\Lambda_t^{\cap\cup}$ is grounded on the proof-functional logic $\mathcal{L}^{\cap\cup}$, though this is hardly standard. In this section we provide both a natural semantics for union types and a foundation for the logic $\mathcal{L}^{\cap\cup}$. We do this by interpreting the union type assignment system into the intuitionistic first order theory $\mathsf{NJ}(\beta)$, Mint's provable realizability of intersection types extended with union. Then we prove that the Δ's terms of system $\Lambda_t^{\cap\cup}$ are just proof-terms in $\mathsf{NJ}(\beta)$.

From Theorem 6 we know that if $\Gamma^@ \vdash M@\Delta : \sigma$, then there is a tight relation among Δ and M, which is captured by the essence mapping. Comparing system $\Lambda_t^{\cap\cup}$ to the original $\Lambda_u^{\cap\cup}$ it is easily seen that Δ is a proof-term of the statement $M : \sigma$ in system $\Lambda_u^{\cap\cup}$. But Δ is a simply typed term: in fact if we drop the restriction concerning the "essence" in rules $(\cap I)$ and $(\cup E)$ in system $\mathcal{L}^{\cap\cup}$ replacing $\sigma \cap \tau$ by $\sigma \times \tau$ and $\sigma \cup \tau$ by $\sigma + \tau$ then we get a simply typed λ-calculus with product and sums, namely the intuitionistic propositional logic with implication, conjunction, and disjunction in disguise.

We will provide a foundation for the proof-functional logic $\mathcal{L}^{\cap\cup}$ by interpreting the $\mathcal{L}^{\cap\cup}$ into an extension of Mints' provable realizability. However when proving a formula $r_\sigma[M]$ we have *two kinds* of realizers: the former is the untyped λ-term M, that we propose to call just a "method" borrowing terminology from

Barbanera-Martini, the latter kind are Δ's that turn out to be realizers in the ordinary sense of intuitionistic logic.

Therefore, we prove a completeness proof that this is the case, namely that $\Gamma \vdash \Delta : \sigma$ is derivable in $\mathcal{L}^{\cap \cup}$ if and only if Δ realizes $G_\Gamma \vdash r_\sigma[M]$ for some M related to Δ by the essence mapping.

For this aim we use and extend Mints' approach of Provable Realizability [Min89, AB91, BM94]. We interpret the statement $\vdash M@\Delta : \sigma$ as "Δ is a construction of $M : \sigma$"; on the other hand $M : \sigma$ is the meaning of the formula $r_\sigma[M]$, provided that we extend the notion to cope with union types; the latter formula reads as "M is a method to assess σ" in terms of [LE85, BM94]; now the meaning of Δ is that of a constructive proof of $r_\sigma[M]$, and hence it is a "realizer" of this formula. In short we have "two kinds" of realizers on two levels: the M, which is a Mints' realizer of σ, and the Δ which is an ordinary realizer, in the sense of standard Brouwer–Heyting–Kolmogorov interpretation of intuitionistic logic, of the statement $r_\sigma[M]$.

To avoid confusion, in the following we shall reserve the word "realizer" for the Δ-terms, and we will use the word "method" referring to the untyped λ-term M.

Definition 7. *Let* $\mathbf{P}_\phi(x)$ *be a unary predicate for each atomic type* ϕ. *Then we define the predicates* $r_\sigma[M]$ *for types* σ *and terms* M *by induction over* σ, *as the first order logical formulae:*

$$r_\phi[x] \equiv \mathbf{P}_\phi(x)$$

$$r_{\sigma_1 \to \sigma_2}[x] \equiv \forall y.r_{\sigma_1}[y] \supset r_{\sigma_2}[x\,y]$$

$$r_{\sigma_1 \cap \sigma_2}[x] \equiv r_{\sigma_1}[x] \wedge r_{\sigma_2}[x]$$

$$r_{\sigma_1 \cup \sigma_2}[x] \equiv r_{\sigma_1}[x] \vee r_{\sigma_2}[x]$$

In the above $\supset$, $\wedge$ and $\vee$ are the logical connectives for implication, conjunction and disjunction respectively, that must be kept distinct from $\cap$ and $\cup$. In the first order language whose terms are type-free λ-terms, we have formulas of the shape $r_\sigma[M]$, whose intended meaning is that M is a method for σ in the intersection-union type discipline. Note that in $r_\sigma[x]$ the term-variable x is the only free-variable; in particular in $r_{\sigma_1 \to \sigma_2}[M] \equiv \forall y.r_{\sigma_1}[y] \supset r_{\sigma_2}[M\,y]$ we assume that $y \notin \mathsf{Fv}(M)$.

By NJ we mean the natural-deduction presentation of the intuitionistic first-order predicate calculus. Derivations in NJ are trees of judgments $G \vdash A$, where G is the set of undischarged assumptions, rather than trees of formulas as in Gentzen's original formulation.

Definition 8 (The system NJ(β)). *The system* NJ(β) *is the natural deduction system for first order intuitionistic logic with untyped* λ-*terms and predicates* $\mathbf{P}_\phi(x)$, *the latter being axiomatized via the Post rules:*

$$\frac{G_\Gamma \vdash_{\mathsf{NJ}(\beta)} \mathbf{P}_\phi(M) \quad M =_{\beta\eta} N}{G_\Gamma \vdash_{\mathsf{NJ}(\beta)} \mathbf{P}_\phi(N)} \ (Ax\beta\eta) \qquad \frac{}{G_\Gamma \vdash_{\mathsf{NJ}(\beta)} \mathbf{P}_\omega(M)} \ (Ax\omega)$$

If A is a formula of $\mathsf{NJ}(\beta)$ and $G \triangleq \{A_1, \ldots, A_n\}$ is a set of formulæ (a context), then we write $G \vdash_{\mathsf{NJ}(\beta)} A$ to mean that A is derivable in G. To the context $\Gamma \triangleq \{\iota_1{:}\sigma_1, \ldots, \iota_n{:}\sigma_n\}$ of the logic $\mathcal{L}^{\cap\cup}$ we associate the $\mathsf{NJ}(\beta)$ context $G_\Gamma \triangleq r_{\sigma_1}[x_{\iota_1}], \ldots, r_{\sigma_n}[x_{\iota_n}]$. Note that $G_{\Gamma,\iota:\sigma} \triangleq G_\Gamma, r_\sigma[x_\iota]$ and $x_\iota \notin \mathsf{Fv}(G_\Gamma)$, since $\iota \notin Dom(\Gamma)$, by context definition.

The following lemmas are useful to eliminate some of the intricacies of using derivations in the full system $\mathsf{NJ}(\beta)$, involving the universal quantifier in the definition of $r_{\sigma\to\tau}[M]$.

Lemma 9. *The following rule is admissible in* $\mathsf{NJ}(\beta)$*:*

$$\frac{G_\Gamma \vdash_{\mathsf{NJ}(\beta)} A\{M/x\} \quad M =_{\beta\eta} N}{G_\Gamma \vdash_{\mathsf{NJ}(\beta)} A\{N/x\}} \; (Eq\beta\eta)$$

Proof. By induction over the proof of $G_\Gamma \vdash_{\mathsf{NJ}(\beta)} A\{M/x\}$. $\square$

Lemma 10. *The following rules are admissible in* $\mathsf{NJ}(\beta)$*:*

$$\frac{G_\Gamma, r_{\sigma_1}[x] \vdash_{\mathsf{NJ}(\beta)} r_{\sigma_2}[M]}{G_\Gamma \vdash_{\mathsf{NJ}(\beta)} r_{\sigma_1\to\sigma_2}[\lambda x.M]} \qquad \frac{G_\Gamma \vdash_{\mathsf{NJ}(\beta)} r_{\sigma_1\to\sigma_2}[M] \quad G_\Gamma \vdash_{\mathsf{NJ}(\beta)} r_{\sigma_1}[N]}{G_\Gamma \vdash_{\mathsf{NJ}(\beta)} r_{\sigma_2}[M\,N]}$$

$$\frac{G_\Gamma \vdash_{\mathsf{NJ}(\beta)} r_{\sigma_1}[M] \quad G_\Gamma \vdash_{\mathsf{NJ}(\beta)} r_{\sigma_2}[M]}{G_\Gamma \vdash_{\mathsf{NJ}(\beta)} r_{\sigma_1\cap\sigma_2}[M]} \qquad \frac{G_\Gamma \vdash_{\mathsf{NJ}(\beta)} r_{\sigma_1\cap\sigma_2}[M] \quad i \in \{1,2\}}{G_\Gamma \vdash_{\mathsf{NJ}(\beta)} r_{\sigma_i}[M]}$$

$$\frac{G_\Gamma \vdash_{\mathsf{NJ}(\beta)} r_{\sigma_i}[M] \quad i \in \{1,2\}}{G_\Gamma \vdash_{\mathsf{NJ}(\beta)} r_{\sigma_1\cup\sigma_2}[M]} \qquad \frac{G_\Gamma, r_{\sigma_1}[x] \vdash_{\mathsf{NJ}(\beta)} r_{\sigma_3}[M]}{G_\Gamma, r_{\sigma_2}[x] \vdash_{\mathsf{NJ}(\beta)} r_{\sigma_3}[M] \quad G_\Gamma \vdash_{\mathsf{NJ}(\beta)} r_{\sigma_1\cup\sigma_2}[N]}{G_\Gamma \vdash_{\mathsf{NJ}(\beta)} r_{\sigma_3}[M\{N/x\}]}$$

Proof. In each case, use induction over the proof of the indicated premisses. $\square$

In spite of the similarity of the rules in Lemma 9 with those of system $\mathcal{L}^{\cap\cup}$ there are no restrictions on the shape of the derivations of the $r_\sigma[M]$. This is due to the fact the last lemma is about derivations of the predicate $r_\sigma[M]$ and not just of the proof-functional "formula" σ. Nonetheless we have:

Lemma 11. *If* $\Gamma^@ \vdash M@\Delta : \sigma$ *in system* $\Lambda_{\mathsf{t}}^{\cap\cup}$ *then* $G_\Gamma \vdash_{\mathsf{NJ}(\beta)} r_\sigma[M]$*.*

Proof. By induction over the derivation of $\Gamma^@ \vdash M@\Delta : \sigma$ using Lemmas 9, and 10 $\square$

Theorem 12 (Soundness). *If* $\Gamma \vdash \Delta : \sigma$ *is derivable in* $\mathcal{L}^{\cap\cup}$ *then there exists* M *such that* $G_\Gamma \vdash_{\mathsf{NJ}(\beta)} r_\sigma[M]$*.*

Proof. By Theorem 6 if $\Gamma \vdash \Delta : \sigma$ is derivable then $\Gamma^@ \vdash M@\Delta : \sigma$ for some $M \sqsupseteq \wr\Delta\wr$. The thesis follows by Lemma 11. $\square$

We say that the derivation of $G_\Gamma \vdash r_\sigma[M]$ is *standard* if it uses only the rules of the Post system, rule $(Eq\beta\eta)$ and the rules from Lemmas 9 and 10; then we write $G_\Gamma \vdash_S r_\sigma[M]$.

Recall that $\mathsf{NJ}(\beta)$ is a particular case of systems called $\mathbf{I(S)}$ in [Pra71], which enjoys the property of being strongly normalizable. The normal form of a derivation, called "fully normal derivation" by Prawitz, is split into a topmost "analytical part" consisting of elimination rules, an intermediate "minimum part" consisting of rules of the Post system, and a final "synthetical part" (ending with the very conclusion of the derivation) only consisting of introduction rules. This implies the subformula property.

Lemma 13. *If* $G_\Gamma \vdash_{\mathsf{NJ}(\beta)} r_\sigma[M]$ *then* $G_\Gamma \vdash_S r_\sigma[M]$.

Proof. By induction over the fully-normal derivation of $G_\Gamma \vdash r_\sigma[M]$, and then by cases of σ. If σ is ϕ or ω then both the analytic and the synthetic parts are empty, and the thesis is immediate. Otherwise:

Case $\sigma \equiv \sigma_1 \cap \sigma_2$. Since $r_{\sigma_1 \cap \sigma_2}[M] \equiv r_{\sigma_1}[M] \wedge r_{\sigma_2}[M]$, the fully-normal derivation of $G_\Gamma \vdash r_{\sigma_1}[M] \wedge r_{\sigma_2}[M]$ must end with $(\wedge I)$, whose premises are $G_\Gamma \vdash r_{\sigma_i}[M]$, $i \in \{1, 2\}$ and the thesis follows by induction.

Case $\sigma = \sigma_1 \to \sigma_2$. We have $r_{\sigma_1 \to \sigma_2}[M] \equiv \forall y. r_{\sigma_1}[y] \supset r_{\sigma_2}[M\,y]$, so that the synthetic part ends by:

$$\frac{\dfrac{G_\Gamma, r_{\sigma_1}[y] \vdash r_{\sigma_2}[M\,y]}{G_\Gamma \vdash r_{\sigma_1}[y] \supset r_{\sigma_2}[M\,y]}\,(\supset I)}{G_\Gamma \vdash \forall y. r_{\sigma_1}[y] \supset r_{\sigma_2}[M\,y]}\,(\forall I)$$

where $y \notin \mathsf{Fv}(G_\Gamma) \cup \mathsf{Fv}(M)$ because of the side condition of rule $(\forall I)$ and the definition of $r_{\sigma_1 \to \sigma_2}[M]$. By induction $G_\Gamma, r_{\sigma_1}[y] \vdash_S r_{\sigma_2}[M\,y]$, from which we obtain the standard derivation:

$$\frac{\dfrac{G_\Gamma, r_{\sigma_1}[y] \vdash_S r_{\sigma_2}[M\,y]}{G_\Gamma \vdash_S r_{\sigma_1 \to \sigma_2}[\lambda y.M\,y]} \quad \lambda y.M\,y =_\eta M}{G_\Gamma \vdash_S r_{\sigma_1 \to \sigma_2}[M]}$$

Case $\sigma = \sigma_1 \cup \sigma_2$. Then $r_{\sigma_1 \cup \sigma_2}[M] \equiv r_{\sigma_1}[M] \vee r_{\sigma_2}[M]$ and the fully-normal derivation of $G_\Gamma \vdash r_{\sigma_1}[M] \vee r_{\sigma_2}[M]$ ends by $(\vee I)$, therefore by induction $G_\Gamma \vdash_S r_{\sigma_i}[M]$ with $i \in \{1, 2\}$ and the thesis follows. $\qquad\square$

Definition 14 (Δ-realizability). *We say that a closed* Δ *realizes the formula* $r_\sigma[M]$, *written* $\Delta \Vdash r_\sigma[M]$, *if* $\wr \Delta \wr \sqsubseteq M$ *and:*

$$\Delta \Vdash r_\phi[M] \quad always$$
$$\Delta \Vdash r_\omega[M] \Leftrightarrow \Delta \equiv *$$
$$\Delta \Vdash r_{\sigma \to \tau}[M] \Leftrightarrow \exists M' =_{\beta\eta} M. \forall \Delta', N.\ \Delta' \Vdash r_\sigma[N] \Rightarrow (\Delta\,\Delta') \Vdash r_\tau[M'N]$$
$$\Delta \Vdash r_{\sigma \cap \tau}[M] \Leftrightarrow \Delta \equiv \langle \Delta_1, \Delta_2 \rangle \wedge \Delta_1 \Vdash r_\sigma[M] \wedge \Delta_2 \Vdash r_\tau[M]$$
$$\Delta \Vdash r_{\sigma \cup \tau}[M] \Leftrightarrow (\Delta \xrightarrow{*} \mathsf{in}_1 \Delta_1 \wedge \Delta_1 \Vdash r_\sigma[M]) \vee (\Delta \xrightarrow{*} \mathsf{in}_2 \Delta_2 \wedge \Delta_2 \Vdash r_\tau[M])$$

We then define $\Delta \Vdash G_\Gamma \vdash r_\sigma[M]$ where Δ is a possibly open term such that $\mathsf{Fv}(\Delta) = \{\iota_1, \ldots, \iota_k\} \subseteq \mathsf{Fv}(\Gamma)$, if and only if for all closed $\Delta_1, \ldots, \Delta_k$ and terms $N_1, \ldots, N_k$ such that $\Delta_i \Vdash r_{\Gamma(\iota_i)}[N_i]$ for all $i = 1, \ldots, k$ it is the case that (writing $x_i \equiv x_{\iota_i}$):

$$\Delta\{\Delta_1/\iota_1\} \cdots \{\Delta_k/\iota_k\} \Vdash r_\sigma[M\{N_1/x_1\} \cdots \{N_k/x_k\}].$$

Lemma 15. *If $G_\Gamma \vdash_{\mathsf{NJ}(\beta)} r_\sigma[M]$ then there exists Δ such that $\Delta \Vdash G_\Gamma \vdash r_\sigma[M]$.*

Proof. By Lemma 13 we can argue by induction over the standard derivation of $G_\Gamma \vdash r_\sigma[M]$. If it ends by a Post rule, then the thesis is trivial. Suppose that it ends by the inference

$$\frac{G_\Gamma \vdash r_{\sigma_1}[M] \quad G_\Gamma \vdash r_{\sigma_2}[M]}{G_\Gamma \vdash r_{\sigma_1 \cap \sigma_2}[M]}$$

Then by induction there are Δ_1, Δ_2 such that $\wr \Delta_i \wr \sqsubseteq M$ and $\Delta_i \Vdash G_\Gamma \vdash r_{\sigma_i}[M]$. Taking $\Delta \equiv \langle \Delta_1, \Delta_2 \rangle$ we have that $\wr \Delta_1 \wr \sqsubseteq M \sqsupseteq \wr \Delta_2 \wr$ and $\wr \Delta \wr = \wr \Delta_1 \wr \sqcup \wr \Delta_2 \wr \sqsubseteq M$ hence $\Delta \Vdash G_\Gamma \vdash r_{\sigma_1 \cap \sigma_2}[M]$. All other cases are similar. $\square$

Lemma 16. *If $\Delta \Vdash G_\Gamma \vdash r_\sigma[M]$ then there exists N and Δ' such that $M =_{\beta\eta} N$ and $\Gamma^@ \vdash N @ \Delta' : \sigma$.*

Proof. By induction over σ. $\square$

Theorem 17 (Completeness). *If $G_\Gamma \vdash_{\mathsf{NJ}(\beta)} r_\sigma[M]$ then there exists $N =_{\beta\eta} M$ and Δ such that $\Gamma^@ \vdash N @ \Delta : \sigma$ and therefore $\Gamma \vdash \Delta : \sigma$.*

Proof. By the hypothesis and Lemma 15 we know that there is a Δ' such that $\Delta' \Vdash G_\Gamma \vdash r_\sigma[M]$. By Lemma 16 this implies that $\Gamma^@ \vdash N @ \Delta : \sigma$ for some Δ and $N =_{\beta\eta} M$, and we conclude by Theorem 6. $\square$

4 Further Logical Developments and Implementation

There is active ongoing work on both the theoretical and practical directions of this project.

4.1 Implicit Subtyping as Explicit Coercions

The logic $\mathcal{L}^{\cap\cup}$ does not encompass the subtyping relation treated in [BDCd95], which extends the subtyping relation among intersection types introduced in [BCDC83]. Given such a relation $\leq$, the subsumption rule takes the form:

$$\frac{B \vdash M : \sigma \quad \sigma \leq \tau}{B \vdash M : \tau} \; (Sub)$$

This rule has a character similar to the intersection and union introduction rules because the subject M of the conclusion is the same as in the premise. This calls for a consistent treatment on the side of the Δ's that are typed terms.

In [DL10] it was hinted that the subtyping as coercion should be the proper approach, in the sense that whenever $\sigma \leq \tau$ there should exist a coercion λ-term $coe_{\sigma \leq \tau} : \sigma \to \tau$ such that the following rule is sound:

$$\frac{\Gamma \vdash \Delta : \sigma \quad \sigma \leq \tau}{\Gamma \vdash (coe_{\sigma \leq \tau} \Delta) : \tau} \ (coe)$$

According to the logic $\mathcal{L}^{\cap \cup}$ this rule is sound if $\wr coe_{\sigma \leq \tau}(\Delta) \wr \sqsubseteq M$, while according to the realizability interpretation this is the case if realizers of $r_\sigma[M]$ are sent to realizers of $r_\tau[M]$. We argue that this is the case by showing that, at least for the type theory Ξ from [BDCd95], we could establish the following:

Conjecture 18. If $\sigma \leq \tau \in \Xi$ then there exists a combinator $coe_{\sigma \leq \tau}$ such that $\vdash coe_{\sigma \leq \tau} : \sigma \to \tau$ is a theorem of $\mathcal{L}^{\cap \cup}$ and $\wr coe_{\sigma \leq \tau} \wr \sqsubseteq \lambda x.x$.

We end this subsection by observing that Conjecture 18 is in accordance with the logical interpretation of intersection types proposed in [BM94]. In fact from the logical point of view, subtyping of intersection (and union) types corresponds to inject concepts and rules proper to the *Minimal Relevant Logical* system B^+ introduced by Meyer-Routley in'72. As nicely explained in the Barbanera-Martini paper, the *relevant implication*, denoted by $\supset_r$ from the logic side and $\to_r$ from the type side, captures the behavior of the coercion function $coe_{\sigma \leq \tau}$ as follows:

> "To assert $\sigma \to_r \tau$ (read also $\sigma \leq \tau$) is to assert that any proof-inhabitant of σ is also a proof-inhabitant of τ".

Our system then meets the latter requirement because any coercion is "essentially" the identity.

4.2 Logical Frameworks

The results presented here are part of a larger project to build a small logical framework, *à la* the Edinburgh Logical Framework [HHP93], featuring proof-functional logical connectives like strong conjunction (intersection) and strong sum (union), and allowing reasoning about the structure of logical proofs, in this way giving to the latter the status of *first-class objects*. We could also mention the high expressivity of *ad hoc* (intersection) polymorphism, since it allows to typecheck the untyped λ-term abstraction $\lambda x.x\,x$ (self-application), essence of a suitable Δ term, with the intersection type $(\sigma \cap (\sigma \to \sigma)) \to \sigma$. Other insights could come in studying **case** constructs typechecked with union types.

Another positive outcome of this research line would be the introduction of proof-functional types into existing interactive theorem provers such as Coq [Coq16] or Isabelle [Isa16], and dependently typed programming languages such as Agda [Agd16], Epigram [Epi16], or Idris [Idr16].

Finally, other advances in research line could come in studying other proof-functional logical connectives, like *relevant implication* (where the implication is established by an identity map) and *strong equivalence* (where the two directions of the equivalence are established by mutually inverse maps), the two being proof-functional interpretations of subtyping and provable type isomorphism, respectively.

4.3   Prototype Implementation

Our current implementation experiments with a small kernel for a logical framework featuring union and intersection types satisfying the *De Brujin Principle* saying *"Keep the framework as weak as possible (A plea for weaker frameworks")*.

The prototype is written in the functional language ML. Its *Read-Eval-Print-Loop* (REPL) can read a file containing some signatures, and process it using a lexer, then a parser. Then it can do the following actions:

– type-check the proof
– normalize the proof using strong reduction
– add some definitions in the global context
– perform a (human interactive) type inhabitation algorithm

We are putting our current efforts into make the REPL to consider proofs (Δ terms) as a genuine first-class objects.

We implemented the $\Lambda_t^{\cap\cup}$ calculus and the proof-functional logic $\mathcal{L}^{\cap\cup}$ as presented here. We have added a wildcard type called "?" to deal with union introduction, and we added an unification algorithm to apply eliminations rule for implication and union types. The actual type system also features a first implementation of dependent-types *à la* LF: explicit coercions and strong equivalence are on the top of our implementation' todo list. The aim of the prototype is to check the expressiveness of the proof-functional nature of the logical engine in the sense that when the user must prove *e.g.* a strong conjunction formula $\sigma_1 \cap \sigma_2$ obtaining (mostly interactively) a witness Δ_1 for σ_1, the prototype can "squeeze" the essence M of Δ_1 to accelerate, and in some case automatize, the construction of a witness Δ_2 proof for the formula σ_2 having the same essence M of Δ_1. Existing proof assistants could get some benefit if extended with a proof-functional logic. We are also started an encoding of the proof-functional operators of intersection and union in Coq. The actual state of the prototype can be retrieved at https://github.com/cstolze/Bull.

Acknowledgment. We are grateful to the anonymous reviewers for their useful remarks.

References

[AB91]   Alessi, F., Barbanera, F.: Strong conjunction and intersection types. In: Tarlecki, A. (ed.) MFCS 1991. LNCS, vol. 520, pp. 64–73. Springer, Heidelberg (1991). doi:10.1007/3-540-54345-7_49

[Agd16] The Agda Programming Language (2016). http://wiki.portal.chalmers.se/agda/pmwiki.php. Accessed 2 Sept 2016

[Bar84] Barendregt, H.: The Lambda Calculus: Its Syntax and Semantics, vol. 103 of Studies in Logic and the Foundations of Mathematics. revised edition (1984)

[BCDC83] Barendregt, H., Coppo, M., Dezani-Ciancaglini, M.: A filter lambda model and the completeness of type assignment. J. Symbolic Logic **48**(4), 931–940 (1983)

[BDCd95] Barbanera, F., Dezani-Ciancaglini, M., de'Liguoro, U.: Intersection and union types: syntax and semantics. Inf. Comput. **119**(2), 202–230 (1995)

[BM94] Barbanera, F., Martini, S.: Proof-functional connectives and realizability. Arch. Math. Logic **33**, 189–211 (1994)

[CDC80] Coppo, M., Dezani-Ciancaglini, M.: An extension of the basic functionality theory for the λ-calculus. Notre Dame J. Formal Logic **21**(4), 685–693 (1980)

[CF93] Coppo, M., Ferrari, A.: Type inference, abstract interpretation and strictness analysis. Theoret. Comput. Sci. **121**(1), 113–143 (1993)

[CLV01] Capitani, B., Loreti, M., Venneri, B.: Hyperformulae, parallel deductions and intersection types. Electr. Notes Theor. Comput. Sci. **50**(2), 180–198 (2001)

[Coq16] The Coq Proof Assistant (2016). https://coq.inria.fr/. Accessed 2 Sept 2016

[DCGV97] Dezani-Ciancaglini, M., Ghilezan, S., Venneri, B.: The relevance of intersection and union types. Notre Dame J. Formal Logic **38**(2), 246–269 (1997)

[DL10] Dougherty, D.J., Liquori, L.: Logic and computation in a lambda calculus with intersection and union types. In: Clarke, E.M., Voronkov, A. (eds.) LPAR 2010. LNCS (LNAI), vol. 6355, pp. 173–191. Springer, Heidelberg (2010). doi:10.1007/978-3-642-17511-4_11

[Dun12] Dunfield, J.: Elaborating intersection and union types. In: Proceedings of the 17th ACM SIGPLAN International Conference on Functional Programming, ICFP 2012, pp. 17–28. ACM (2012)

[Epi16] The Epigram Programming Language (2016). https://code.google.com/archive/p/epigram/. Accessed 2 Sept 2016

[HHP93] Harper, R., Honsell, F., Plotkin, G.: A framework for defining logics. J. ACM **40**(1), 143–184 (1993)

[Idr16] The Idris Programming Language (2016). http://www.idris-lang.org/. Accessed 2 Sept 2016

[Isa16] The Isabelle Proof Assistant (2016). https://isabelle.in.tum.de/. Accessed 2 Sept 2016

[LE85] Lopez-Escobar, E.G.K.: Proof functional connectives. In: Prisco, C.A. (ed.) Methods in Mathematical Logic. LNM, vol. 1130, pp. 208–221. Springer, Heidelberg (1985). doi:10.1007/BFb0075313

[LR07] Liquori, L., Della Rocca, S.R.: Intersection typed system à la Church. Inf. Comput. **9**(205), 1371–1386 (2007)

[Min89] Mints, G.: The completeness of provable realizability. Notre Dame J. Formal Logic **30**(3), 420–441 (1989)

[MPS86] MacQueen, D., Plotkin, G., Sethi, R.: An ideal model for recursive polymorphic types. Inf. Control **71**, 95–130 (1986)

[MR72] Meyer, R.K., Routley, R.: Algebraic analysis of entailment I. Logique et Anal. **15**, 407–428 (1972)

[Pie02] Pierce, B.C.: Types and Programming Languages. MIT Press, Cambridge (2002)

[Pot80] Pottinger, G.: A type assignment for the strongly normalizable λ-terms. In: To Curry, H.B. (ed.) Essays on Combinatory Logic, Lambda Calculus and Formalism, pp. 561–577. Academic Press (1980)

[Pra71] Prawitz, D.: Ideas and results in proof theory. In: Proceedings of the Second Scandinavian Logic Symposium, North-Holland (1971)

[PT94] Pierce, B.C., Turner, D.N.: Simple type-theoretic foundations for object-oriented programming. J. Funct. Programm. 4(2), 207–247 (1994)

[Rey96] Reynolds, J.C.: Design of the programming language Forsythe. Algol-like Languages. Progress in Theoretical Computer Science, pp. 173–233. Birkhäuser, Boston (1997)

[Rey98] Reynolds, J.C.: Theories of Programming Languages. Cambridge University Press, New York (1998)

[Ron02] Della Rocca, S.R.: Intersection typed lambda-calculus. Electr. Notes. Theor. Comput. Sci. 70(1), 163–181 (2003)

[WDMT02] Wells, J.B., Dimock, A., Muller, R., Turbak, F.: A calculus with polymorphic and polyvariant flow types. J. Funct. Program. 12(3), 183–227 (2002)

[WH02] Wells, J.B., Haack, C.: Branching types. In: Métayer, D. (ed.) ESOP 2002. LNCS, vol. 2305, pp. 115–132. Springer, Heidelberg (2002). doi:10.1007/3-540-45927-8_9

Open Call-by-Value

Beniamino Accattoli[1([⊠])] and Giulio Guerrieri[2]

[1] Inria, UMR 7161, LIX, École Polytechnique, Palaiseau, France
beniamino.accattoli@inria.fr
[2] Aix Marseille Univ, CNRS, Centrale Marseille, I2M, Marseille, France
giulio.guerrieri@univ-amu.fr

Abstract. The elegant theory of the call-by-value lambda-calculus relies on weak evaluation and closed terms, that are natural hypotheses in the study of programming languages. To model proof assistants, however, strong evaluation and open terms are required, and it is well known that the operational semantics of call-by-value becomes problematic in this case. Here we study the intermediate setting—that we call Open Call-by-Value—of weak evaluation with open terms, on top of which Grégoire and Leroy designed the abstract machine of Coq. Various calculi for Open Call-by-Value already exist, each one with its pros and cons. This paper presents a detailed comparative study of the operational semantics of four of them, coming from different areas such as the study of abstract machines, denotational semantics, linear logic proof nets, and sequent calculus. We show that these calculi are all equivalent from a termination point of view, justifying the slogan Open Call-by-Value.

1 Introduction

Plotkin's call-by-value λ-calculus [26] is at the heart of programming languages such as OCaml and proof assistants such as Coq. In the study of programming languages, call-by-value (CBV) evaluation is usually *weak*, *i.e.* it does not reduce under abstractions, and terms are assumed to be *closed*. These constraints give rise to a beautiful theory—let us call it *Closed CBV*—having the following *harmony property*, that relates rewriting and normal forms:

Closed normal forms are values (and values are normal forms)

where *values* are variables and abstractions. Harmony expresses a form of internal completeness with respect to unconstrained β-reduction: the restriction to CBV β-reduction (referred to as β_v-*reduction*, according to which a β-redex can be fired only when the argument is a value) has an impact on the order in which redexes are evaluated, but evaluation never gets stuck, as every β-redex will eventually become a β_v-redex and be fired, unless evaluation diverges.

It often happens, however, that one needs to go beyond the perfect setting of Closed CBV by considering *Strong CBV*, where reduction under abstractions is allowed and terms may be open, or the intermediate setting of *Open CBV*, where evaluation is weak but terms are not necessarily closed. The need arises,

© Springer International Publishing AG 2016
A. Igarashi (Ed.): APLAS 2016, LNCS 10017, pp. 206–226, 2016.
DOI: 10.1007/978-3-319-47958-3_12

most notably, when trying to describe the implementation model of Coq [13], but also from other motivations, such as denotational semantics [4,8,25,28], monad and CPS translations and the associated equational theories [12,16,21,29,30], bisimulations [18], partial evaluation [17], linear logic proof nets [2], or cost models [1].

Naïve Open CBV. In call-by-name (CBN) turning to open terms or strong evaluation is harmless because CBN does not impose any special form to the argument of a β-redex. On the contrary, turning to Open or Strong CBV is delicate. If one simply considers Plotkin's weak β_v-reduction on open terms—let us call it *Naïve Open CBV*—then harmony does no longer hold, as there are open β-normal forms that are not values, *e.g.* xx, $x(\lambda y.y)$, $x(yz)$ or xyz. As a consequence, there are *stuck β-redexes* such as $(\lambda y.t)(xx)$, *i.e.* β-redexes that will never be fired because their argument is normal, but it is not a value, nor will it ever become one. Such stuck β-redexes are a disease typical of (Naïve) Open CBV, but they spread to Strong CBV as well (also in the closed case), because evaluating under abstraction forces to deal with locally open terms: *e.g.* the variable x is locally open with respect to $(\lambda y.t)(xx)$ in $s = \lambda x.((\lambda y.t)(xx))$.

The real issue with stuck β-redexes is that they prevent the creation of other redexes, and provide *premature β_v-normal forms*. The issue is serious, as it can affect termination, and thus impact on notions of observational equivalence. Let $\delta := \lambda x.(xx)$. The problem is exemplified by the terms t and u in Eq. (1) below.

$$t := ((\lambda y.\delta)(zz))\delta \qquad\qquad u := \delta((\lambda y.\delta)(zz)) \qquad\qquad (1)$$

In Naïve Open CBV, t and u are premature β_v-normal forms because they both have a stuck β-redex forbidding evaluation to keep going, while one would expect them to behave like the divergent term $\Omega := \delta\delta$ (see [2,4,8,15,25,28] and pp. 7–12).

Open CBV. In his seminal work [26], Plotkin already pointed out an asymmetry between CBN and CBV: his CPS translation is sound and complete for CBN, but only sound for CBV. This fact led to a number of studies about monad, CPS, and logical translations [12,16,20,21,29,30] that introduced many proposals of improved calculi for CBV. Starting with the seminal work of Paolini and Ronchi Della Rocca [23,25,28], the dissonance between open terms and CBV has been repeatedly pointed out and studied *per se* via various calculi [1,2,4,8,13–15]. A further point of view on CBV comes from the computational interpretation of sequent calculus due to Curien and Herbelin [9]. An important point is that the focus of most of these works is on Strong CBV.

These solutions inevitably extend β_v-reduction with some other rewriting rule(s) or constructor (as let-expressions) to deal with stuck β-redexes, or even go as far as changing the applicative structure of terms, as in the sequent calculus approach. They arise from different perspectives and each one has its pros and cons. By design, these calculi (when looked at in the context of Open CBV) are never observationally equivalent to Naïve Open CBV, as they all manage to (re)move stuck β-redexes and may diverge when Naïve Open CBV is instead stuck. Each one of these calculi, however, has its own notion of evaluation and normal form, and their mutual relationships are not evident.

The aim of this paper is to draw the attention of the community on Open CBV. We believe that it is somewhat deceiving that the mainstream operational theory of CBV, however elegant, has to rely on closed terms, because it restricts the modularity of the framework, and raises the suspicion that the true essence of CBV has yet to be found. There is a real gap, indeed, between Closed and Strong CBV, as Strong CBV cannot be seen as an iteration of Closed CBV under abstractions because such an iteration has to deal with open terms. To improve the implementation of Coq [13], Grégoire and Leroy see Strong CBV as the iteration of the intermediate case of Open CBV, but they do not explore its theory. Here we exalt their point of view, providing a thorough operational study of Open CBV. We insist on Open CBV rather than Strong CBV because:

1. Stuck β-redexes and premature β_v-normal forms already affect Open CBV;
2. Open CBV has a simpler rewriting theory than Strong CBV;
3. Our previous studies of Strong CBV in [4,8] naturally organized themselves as properties of Open CBV that were lifted to Strong CBV by a simple iteration under abstractions.

Our contributions are along two axes:

1. *Termination Equivalence of the Proposals:* we show that the proposed generalizations of Naïve Open CBV are all equivalent, in the sense that they have exactly the same sets of normalizing and diverging terms. So, *there is just one notion of Open CBV*, independently of its specific syntactic incarnation.
2. *Quantitative Analyses and Cost Models:* the termination results are complemented with quantitative analyses establishing precise relationships between the number of steps needed to evaluate a given term in the various calculi. In particular, we relate the cost models of the various proposals.

The Fab Four. We focus on four proposals for Open CBV, as other solutions, *e.g.* Moggi's [21] or Herbelin and Zimmerman's [16], are already known to be equivalent to these ones (see the end of Sect. 2):

1. *The Fireball Calculus* λ_{fire}, that extends values to *fireballs* by adding so-called *inert terms* in order to restore harmony—it was introduced without a name by Paolini and Ronchi Della Rocca [25,28], then rediscovered independently first by Leroy and Grégoire [13] to improve the implementation of Coq, and then by Accattoli and Sacerdoti Coen [1] to study cost models;
2. *The Value Substitution Calculus* λ_{vsub}, coming from the linear logic interpretation of CBV and using explicit substitutions and contextual rewriting rules to circumvent stuck β-redexes—it was introduced by Accattoli and Paolini [4] and it is a graph-free presentation of proof nets for the CBV λ-calculus [2];

3. *The Shuffling Calculus* λ_{shuf}, that has rules to shuffle constructors, similar to Regnier's σ-rules for CBN [27], as an alternative to explicit substitutions—it was introduced by Carraro and Guerrieri [8] (and further analyzed in [14, 15]) to study the adequacy of Open/Strong CBV with respect to denotational semantics related to linear logic.

4. *The Value Sequent Calculus* λ_{vseq}, *i.e.* the intuitionistic fragment of Curien and Herbelin's $\bar{\lambda}\tilde{\mu}$-calculus [9], that is a CBV calculus for classical logic providing a computational interpretation of sequent calculus rather than natural deduction (in turn a fragment of the $\bar{\lambda}\mu\tilde{\mu}$-calculus [9], further studied in *e.g.* [6, 10]).

A Robust Cost Model for Open CBV. The number of β_v-steps is the canonical time cost model of Closed CBV, as first proved by Blelloch and Greiner [7, 11, 31]. In [1], Accattoli and Sacerdoti Coen generalized this result: the number of steps in λ_{fire} is a reasonable cost model for Open CBV. Here we show that the number of steps in λ_{vsub} and λ_{vseq} are *linearly* related to the steps in λ_{fire}, thus providing reasonable cost models for these incarnations of Open CBV. As a consequence, complexity analyses can now be smoothly transferred between λ_{fire}, λ_{vsub}, and λ_{vseq}. Said differently, our results guarantee that the number of steps is a *robust* cost model for Open CBV, in the sense that it does not depend on the chosen incarnation. For λ_{shuf} we obtain a similar but strictly weaker result, due to some structural difficulties suggesting that λ_{shuf} is less apt to complexity analyses.

On the Value of the Paper. While the equivalences showed here are new, they might not be terribly surprising. Nonetheless, we think they are interesting, for the following reasons:

1. *Quantitative Relationships:* λ-calculi are usually related only *qualitatively*, while our relationships are *quantitative* and thus stronger: not only we show simulations, but we also relate the number of steps.
2. *Uniform View:* we provide a new uniform view on a known problem, that will hopefully avoid further proliferations of CBV calculi for open/strong settings.
3. *Expected but Non-Trivial:* while the equivalences are more or less expected, establishing them is informative, because it forces to reformulate and connect concepts among the different settings, and often tricky.
4. *Simple Rewriting Theory:* the relationships between the systems are developed using basic rewriting concepts. The technical development is simple, according to the best tradition of the CBV λ-calculus, and yet it provides a sharp and detailed decomposition of Open CBV evaluation.
5. *Connecting Different Worlds:* while λ_{fire} is related to Coq and implementations, λ_{vsub} and λ_{shuf} have a linear logic background, and λ_{vseq} is rooted in sequent calculus. With respect to linear logic, λ_{vsub} has been used for syntactical studies while λ_{shuf} for semantical ones. Our results therefore establish bridges between these different (sub)communities.

Finally, an essential contribution of this work is the recognition of Open CBV as a simple and yet rich framework in between Closed and Strong CBV.

Road Map. Section 2 provides an overview of the different presentations of Open CBV. Section 3 proves the termination equivalences for λ_{vsub}, λ_{fire} and λ_{shuf}, enriched with quantitative information. Section 4 proves the quantitative termination equivalence of λ_{vsub} and λ_{vseq}, via an intermediate calculus λ_{vsub_k}.

A longer version of this paper is available on Arxiv [3]. It contains two Appendices, one with a glossary of rewriting theory and one with omitted proofs.

Terms	$t, u, s, r ::= v \mid tu$
Values	$v, v' ::= x \mid \lambda x.t$
Evaluation Contexts	$E ::= \langle \cdot \rangle \mid tE \mid Et$

Rule at Top Level	Contextual closure
$(\lambda x.t)\lambda y.u \mapsto_{\beta_\lambda} t\{x \leftarrow \lambda y.u\}$	$E\langle t \rangle \to_{\beta_\lambda} E\langle u \rangle$ if $t \mapsto_{\beta_\lambda} u$
$(\lambda x.t)y \mapsto_{\beta_y} t\{x \leftarrow y\}$	$E\langle t \rangle \to_{\beta_y} E\langle u \rangle$ if $t \mapsto_{\beta_y} u$

Reduction	$\to_{\beta_v} := \to_{\beta_\lambda} \cup \to_{\beta_y}$

Fig. 1. Naïve Open CBV λ_{Plot}

2 Incarnations of Open Call-by-Value

Here we recall Naïve Open CBV, noted λ_{Plot}, and introduce the four forms of Open CBV that will be compared (λ_{fire}, λ_{vsub}, λ_{shuf}, and λ_{vseq}) together with a semantic notion (*potential valuability*) reducing Open CBV to Closed CBV. In this paper terms are always possibly open. Moreover, we focus on Open CBV and avoid on purpose to study Strong CBV (we hint at how to define it, though).

Naïve Open CBV: Plotkin's Calculus. λ_{Plot} [26]. Naïve Open CBV is Plotkin's weak CBV λ-calculus λ_{Plot} on possibly open terms, defined in Fig. 1. Our presentation of the rewriting is unorthodox because we split β_v-reduction into two rules, according to the kind of value (abstraction or variable). The set of terms is denoted by Λ. Terms (in Λ) are always identified up to α-equivalence and the set of the free variables of a term t is denoted by $\text{fv}(t)$. We use $t\{x \leftarrow u\}$ for the term obtained by the capture-avoiding substitution of u for each free occurrence of x in t. Evaluation $\to_{\beta_v}$ is weak and non-deterministic, since in the case of an application there is no fixed order in the evaluation of the left and right subterms. As it is well-known, non-determinism is only apparent: the system is strongly confluent (see the appendix in [3] for a glossary of rewriting theory).

Proposition 1. $\to_{\beta_y}$, $\to_{\beta_\lambda}$ and $\to_{\beta_v}$ are strongly confluent.

Strong confluence is a remarkable property, much stronger than plain confluence. It implies that, given a term, *all* derivations to its normal form (if any) have the *same length*, and that *normalization and strong normalization coincide*, *i.e.* if there is a normalizing derivation then there are no diverging derivations. Strong confluence will also hold for λ_{fire}, λ_{vsub} and λ_{vseq}, not for λ_{shuf}.

Let us come back to the splitting of $\to_{\beta_v}$. In Closed CBV it is well-known that $\to_{\beta_v}$ is superfluous, at least as long as small-step evaluation is considered, see [5]. For Open CBV, $\to_{\beta_v}$ is instead necessary, but—as we explained in the introduction—it is not enough, which is why we shall consider extensions of λ_{Plot}. The main problem of Naïve Open CBV is that there are stuck β-redexes breaking the harmony of the system. There are three kinds of solution: those *restoring a form of harmony* (λ_{fire}), to be thought as more semantical approaches; those *removing stuck β-redexes* (λ_{vsub} and λ_{shuf}), that are more syntactical in nature; those *changing the applicative structure of terms* (λ_{vseq}), inspired by sequent calculus.

Terms and Values	As in Plotkin's Open CBV (Fig. 1)
Fireballs	$f, f', f'' ::= \lambda x.t \mid i$
Inert Terms	$i, i', i'' ::= x f_1 \dots f_n \quad n \geq 0$
Evaluation Contexts	$E ::= \langle \cdot \rangle \mid tE \mid Et$

RULE AT TOP LEVEL	CONTEXTUAL CLOSURE
$(\lambda x.t)(\lambda y.u) \mapsto_{\beta_\lambda} t\{x \leftarrow \lambda y.u\}$	$E\langle t \rangle \to_{\beta_\lambda} E\langle u \rangle \quad$ if $t \mapsto_{\beta_\lambda} u$
$(\lambda x.t)i \mapsto_{\beta_i} t\{x \leftarrow i\}$	$E\langle t \rangle \to_{\beta_i} E\langle u \rangle \quad$ if $t \mapsto_{\beta_i} u$

Reduction	$\to_{\beta_f} := \to_{\beta_\lambda} \cup \to_{\beta_i}$

Fig. 2. The Fireball Calculus λ_{fire}

2.1   Open Call-by-Value 1: The Fireball Calculus λ_{fire}

The Fireball Calculus λ_{fire}, defined in Fig. 2, was introduced without a name by Paolini and Ronchi Della Rocca in [25] and [28, Definition 3.1.4, p. 36] where its basic properties are also proved. We give here a presentation inspired by Accattoli and Sacerdoti Coen's [1], departing from it only for inessential, cosmetic details. Terms, values and evaluation contexts are the same as in λ_{Plot}.

The idea is to restore harmony by generalizing $\to_{\beta_v}$ to fire when the argument is a more general *inert term*—the new rule is noted $\to_{\beta_i}$. The generalization of values as to include inert terms is called *fireballs*. Actually fireballs and inert terms are defined by mutual induction (in Fig. 2). For instance, $\lambda x.y$ is a fireball as an abstraction, while x, $y(\lambda x.x)$, xy, and $(z(\lambda x.x))(zz)(\lambda y.(zy))$ are fireballs as inert terms. Note that ii' is an inert term for all inert terms i and i'. Inert terms can be equivalently defined as $i := x \mid if$. The main feature of an inert term is that it is open, normal and that when plugged in a context it cannot create a redex, hence the name (it is not a so-called *neutral term* because it might have redexes under abstractions). In Grégoire and Leroy's presentation [13], inert terms are called *accumulators* and fireballs are simply called *values*.

Evaluation is given by the fireball rule $\to_{\beta_f}$, that is the union of $\to_{\beta_\lambda}$ and $\to_{\beta_i}$. For instance, consider $t := ((\lambda y.\delta)(zz))\delta$ and $u := \delta((\lambda y.\delta)(zz))$ as in Eq. (1), p. 2: t and u are β_v-normal but they diverge when evaluated in λ_{fire}, as desired: $t \to_{\beta_i} \delta\delta \to_{\beta_\lambda} \delta\delta \to_{\beta_\lambda} \dots$ and $u \to_{\beta_i} \delta\delta \to_{\beta_\lambda} \delta\delta \to_{\beta_\lambda} \dots$.

The distinguished, key property of λ_{fire} is (for any $t \in \Lambda$):

Proposition 2 (Open Harmony). *t is β_f-normal iff t is a fireball.*

The advantage of λ_{fire} is its simple notion of normal form, *i.e.* fireballs, that have a clean syntactic description akin to that for call-by-name. The other calculi will lack a nice, natural notion of normal form. The drawback of the fireball calculus—and probably the reason why its importance did not emerge before—is the fact that as a strong calculus it is not confluent: this is due to the fact that fireballs are not closed by substitution (see [28, p. 37]). Indeed, if evaluation is strong, the following critical pair cannot be joined, where $t := (\lambda y.I)(\delta\delta)$ and $I := \lambda z.z$ is the identity combinator:

$$I \;_{\beta_\lambda}\!\leftarrow (\lambda x.I)\delta \;_{\beta_i}\!\leftarrow (\lambda x.(\lambda y.I)(xx))\delta \to_{\beta_\lambda} t \to_{\beta_\lambda} t \to_{\beta_\lambda}\dots \qquad (2)$$

On the other hand, as long as evaluation is weak (that is the case we consider) everything works fine—the strong case can then be caught by repeatedly iterating the weak one under abstraction, once a weak normal form has been obtained (thus forbidding the left part of (2)). In fact, the weak evaluation of λ_{fire} has a simple rewriting theory, as next proposition shows. In particular it is strongly confluent.

Proposition 3 (Basic Properties of λ_{fire}).

1. $\to_{\beta_i}$ *is strongly normalizing and strongly confluent.*
2. $\to_{\beta_\lambda}$ *and* $\to_{\beta_i}$ *strongly commute.*
3. $\to_{\beta_f}$ *is strongly confluent, and all β_f-normalizing derivations d from $t \in \Lambda$ (if any) have the same length $|d|_{\beta_f}$, the same number $|d|_{\beta_\lambda}$ of β_λ-steps, and the same number $|d|_{\beta_i}$ of β_i-steps.*

2.2   Open Call-by-Value 2: The Value Substitution Calculus λ_{vsub}

Rewriting Preamble: Creations of Type 1 and 4. The problem with stuck β-redexes can be easily understood at the rewriting level as an issue about creations. According to Lévy [19], in the ordinary CBN λ-calculus redexes can be created in 3 ways. Creations of type 1 take the following form

$$((\lambda x.\lambda y.t)r)s \to_\beta (\lambda y.t\{x\leftarrow r\})s$$

where the redex involving λy and s has been created by the β-step. In Naïve Open CBV if r is β_v-normal and not a value then the creation cannot take place, blocking evaluation. This is the problem concerning the term t in Eq. (1), p. 2. In CBV there is another form of creation—of *type 4*—not considered by Lévy:

$$(\lambda x.t)((\lambda y.v)v') \to_{\beta_v} (\lambda x.t)(v\{y\leftarrow v'\})$$

i.e. a reduction in the argument turns the argument itself into a value, creating a β_v-redex. As before, in an open setting v' may be replaced by a normal form that is not a value, blocking the creation of type 4. This is exactly the problem concerning the term u in Eq. (1), p. 2.

The proposals of this and the next sections introduce some way to enable creations of type 1 and 4, without substituting stuck β-redexes nor inert terms.

The *value substitution calculus* λ_{vsub} of Accattoli and Paolini [2,4] was introduced as a calculus for Strong CBV inspired by linear logic proof nets. In Fig. 3 we present its adaptation to Open CBV, obtained by simply removing abstractions from evaluation contexts. It extends the syntax of terms with the constructor $[x{\leftarrow}u]$, called *explicit substitution* (shortened ES, to not be confused with the meta-level substitution $\{x{\leftarrow}u\}$). A vsub-term $t[x{\leftarrow}u]$ represents the delayed substitution of u for x in t, *i.e.* stands for let $x = u$ in t. So, $t[x{\leftarrow}u]$ binds the free occurrences of x in t. The set of vsub-terms—identified up to α-equivalence—is denoted by Λ_{vsub} (clearly $\Lambda \subsetneq \Lambda_{\mathsf{vsub}}$).

vsub-Terms	$t, u, s ::= v \mid tu \mid t[x{\leftarrow}u]$
vsub-Values	$v ::= x \mid \lambda x.t$
Evaluation Contexts	$E ::= \langle \cdot \rangle \mid tE \mid Et \mid E[x{\leftarrow}u] \mid t[x{\leftarrow}E]$
Substitution Contexts	$L ::= \langle \cdot \rangle \mid L[x{\leftarrow}u]$

RULE AT TOP LEVEL	CONTEXTUAL CLOSURE	
$L\langle \lambda x.t \rangle u \mapsto_{\mathsf{m}} L\langle t[x{\leftarrow}u] \rangle$	$E\langle t \rangle \to_{\mathsf{m}} E\langle u \rangle$	if $t \mapsto_{\mathsf{m}} u$
$t[x{\leftarrow}L\langle \lambda y.u \rangle] \mapsto_{\mathsf{e}_\lambda} L\langle t\{x{\leftarrow}\lambda y.u\} \rangle$	$E\langle t \rangle \to_{\mathsf{e}_\lambda} E\langle u \rangle$	if $t \mapsto_{\mathsf{e}_\lambda} u$
$t[x{\leftarrow}L\langle y \rangle] \mapsto_{\mathsf{e}_y} L\langle t\{x{\leftarrow}y\} \rangle$	$E\langle t \rangle \to_{\mathsf{e}_y} E\langle u \rangle$	if $t \mapsto_{\mathsf{e}_y} u$

Reductions $\to_{\mathsf{e}} := \to_{\mathsf{e}_\lambda} \cup \to_{\mathsf{e}_y}, \quad \to_{\mathsf{vsub}} := \to_{\mathsf{m}} \cup \to_{\mathsf{e}}$

Fig. 3. The Value Substitution Calculus λ_{vsub}

ES are used to remove stuck β-redexes: the idea is that β-redexes can be fired whenever—even if the argument is not a (vsub-)value—by means of the *multiplicative rule* $\to_{\mathsf{m}}$; however the argument is not substituted but placed in a ES. The actual substitution is done only when the content of the ES is a vsub-value, by means of the *exponential rule* $\to_{\mathsf{e}}$. These two rules are sometimes noted $\to_{\mathsf{dB}}$ (β at a distance) and $\to_{\mathsf{vs}}$ (substitution by value)—the names we use here are due to the interpretation of the calculus into linear logic proof-nets, see [2]. A characteristic feature coming from such an interpretation is that the rewriting rules are contextual, or *at a distance*: they are generalized as to act up to a list of substitutions (noted L, from *List*). Essentially, stuck β-redexes are turned into ES and then ignored by the rewriting rules—this is how creations of type 1 and 4 are enabled. For instance, the terms $t := ((\lambda y.\delta)(zz))\delta$ and $u := \delta((\lambda y.\delta)(zz))$ (as in Eq. (1), p. 2) are e-normal but $t \to_{\mathsf{m}} \delta[y{\leftarrow}zz]\delta \to_{\mathsf{m}} (xx)[x{\leftarrow}\delta][y{\leftarrow}zz] \to_{\mathsf{e}} (\delta\delta)[y{\leftarrow}zz] \to_{\mathsf{m}} (xx)[x{\leftarrow}\delta][y{\leftarrow}zz] \to_{\mathsf{e}} (\delta\delta)[y{\leftarrow}zz] \to_{\mathsf{m}} \ldots$ and similarly for u.

The drawback of λ_{vsub} is that it requires explicit substitutions. The advantage of λ_{vsub} is its simple and well-behaved rewriting theory, even simpler than the rewriting for λ_{fire}, since every rule terminates separately (while β_λ does not)—in particular strong confluence holds. Moreover, the theory has a sort of flexible second level given by a notion of structural equivalence, coming up next.

Proposition 4 (Basic Properties of λ_{vsub}, [4]).

1. $\to_{\mathsf{m}}$ and $\to_{\mathsf{e}}$ are strongly normalizing and strongly confluent (separately).
2. $\to_{\mathsf{m}}$ and $\to_{\mathsf{e}}$ strongly commute.
3. $\to_{\mathsf{vsub}}$ is strongly confluent, and all vsub-normalizing derivations d from $t \in \Lambda_{\mathsf{vsub}}$ (if any) have the same length $|d|_{\mathsf{vsub}}$, the same number $|d|_{\mathsf{e}}$ of e-steps, and the same number $|d|_{\mathsf{m}}$ of m-steps
4. Let $t \in \Lambda$. For any vsub-derivation d from t, $|d|_{\mathsf{e}} \leq |d|_{\mathsf{m}}$.

Structural Equivalence. The theory of λ_{vsub} comes with a notion of structural equivalence $\equiv$, that equates vsub-terms that differ only for the position of ES. The basic idea is that the action of an ES via the exponential rule depends on the position of the ES itself only for inessential details (as long as the scope of binders is respected), namely the position of other ES, and thus can be abstracted away. A strong justification for the equivalence comes from the linear logic interpretation of λ_{vsub}, in which structurally equivalent vsub-terms translate to the same (recursively typed) proof net, see [2].

Structural equivalence $\equiv$ is defined as the least equivalence relation on Λ_{vsub} closed by evaluation contexts (see Fig. 3) and generated by the following axioms:

$$t[y\!\leftarrow\!s][x\!\leftarrow\!u] \equiv_{\mathsf{com}} t[x\!\leftarrow\!u][y\!\leftarrow\!s] \qquad \text{if } y \notin \mathtt{fv}(u) \text{ and } x \notin \mathtt{fv}(s)$$
$$t\, s[x\!\leftarrow\!u] \equiv_{\mathsf{@r}} (ts)[x\!\leftarrow\!u] \qquad \text{if } x \notin \mathtt{fv}(t)$$
$$t[x\!\leftarrow\!u]s \equiv_{\mathsf{@l}} (ts)[x\!\leftarrow\!u] \qquad \text{if } x \notin \mathtt{fv}(s)$$
$$t[x\!\leftarrow\!u[y\!\leftarrow\!s]] \equiv_{[\cdot]} t[x\!\leftarrow\!u][y\!\leftarrow\!s] \qquad \text{if } y \notin \mathtt{fv}(t)$$

We set $\to_{\mathsf{vsub}_\equiv} := \equiv\to_{\mathsf{vsub}}\equiv$ (i.e. for all $t, r \in \Lambda_{\mathsf{vsub}}$: $t \to_{\mathsf{vsub}_\equiv} r$ iff $t \equiv u \to_{\mathsf{vsub}} s \equiv r$ for some $u, s \in \Lambda_{\mathsf{vsub}}$). The notation $\to_{\mathsf{vsub}_\equiv}^+$ keeps its usual meaning, while $\to_{\mathsf{vsub}_\equiv}^*$ stands for $\equiv \cup \to_{\mathsf{vsub}_\equiv}^+$, i.e. a $\mathsf{vsub}_\equiv$-derivation of length zero can apply $\equiv$ and is not just the identity. As $\equiv$ is reflexive, $\to_{\mathsf{vsub}} \subsetneq \to_{\mathsf{vsub}_\equiv}$.

The rewriting theory of λ_{vsub} enriched with structural equivalence $\equiv$ is remarkably simple, as next lemma shows. In fact, $\equiv$ commutes with evaluation, and can thus be postponed. Additionally, the commutation is *strong*, as it preserves the number and kind of steps—one says that it is a *strong bisimulation* (with respect to $\to_{\mathsf{vsub}}$). In particular, the equivalence is not needed to compute and it does not break, or make more complex, any property of λ_{vsub}. On the contrary, it enhances the flexibility of the system: it will be essential to establish simple and clean relationships with the other calculi for Open CBV.

Lemma 5 (Basic Properties of Structural Equivalence $\equiv$, [4]). *Let $t, u \in \Lambda_{\mathsf{vsub}}$ and $\mathsf{x} \in \{\mathsf{m}, \mathsf{e}_\lambda, \mathsf{e}_y, \mathsf{e}, \mathsf{vsub}\}$.*

1. *Strong Bisimulation of $\equiv$ wrt $\to_{\mathsf{vsub}}$: if $t \equiv u$ and $t \to_{\mathsf{x}} t'$ then there exists $u' \in \Lambda_{\mathsf{vsub}}$ such that $u \to_{\mathsf{x}} u'$ and $t' \equiv u'$.*
2. *Postponement of $\equiv$ wrt $\to_{\mathsf{vsub}}$: if $d : t \to_{\mathsf{vsub}_\equiv}^* u$ then there are $s \equiv u$ and $e : t \to_{\mathsf{vsub}}^* s$ such that $|d| = |e|$, $|d|_{\mathsf{e}_\lambda} = |e|_{\mathsf{e}_\lambda}$, $|d|_{\mathsf{e}_y} = |e|_{\mathsf{e}_y}$ and $|d|_{\mathsf{m}} = |e|_{\mathsf{m}}$.*
3. *Normal Forms: if $t \equiv u$ then t is x-normal iff u is x-normal.*
4. *Strong confluence: $\to_{\mathsf{vsub}_\equiv}$ is strongly confluent.*

2.3   Open Call-by-Value 3: The Shuffling Calculus λ_{shuf}

The calculus introduced by Carraro and Guerrieri in [8], and here deemed *Shuffling Calculus*, has the same syntax of terms as Plotkin's calculus. Two additional commutation rules help $\to_{\beta_v}$ to deal with stuck β-redexes, by shuffling constructors so as to enable creations of type 1 and 4. As for λ_{vsub}, λ_{shuf} was actually introduced, and then used in [8,14,15], to study Strong CBV. In Fig. 4 we present its adaptation to Open CBV, based on *balanced contexts*, a special notion of evaluation contexts. The reductions $\to_{\sigma^\flat}$ and $\to_{\beta_v^\flat}$ are non-deterministic and—because of balanced contexts—can reduce under abstractions, but they are *morally* weak: they reduce under a λ only when the λ is applied to an argument. Note that the condition $x \notin \mathtt{fv}(s)$ (resp. $x \notin \mathtt{fv}(v)$) in the definition of the shuffling rule $\mapsto_{\sigma_1}$ (resp. $\mapsto_{\sigma_3}$) can always be fulfilled by α-conversion.

Terms and Values   As in Plotkin's Open CBV (Fig. 1)
Balanced Contexts $B ::= \langle \cdot \rangle \mid tB \mid Bt \mid (\lambda x.B)t$

RULE AT TOP LEVEL	CONTEXTUAL CLOSURE
$((\lambda x.t)u)s \mapsto_{\sigma_1} (\lambda x.ts)u, \ x \notin \mathtt{fv}(s)$	$B\langle t \rangle \to_{\sigma_1^\flat} B\langle u \rangle \quad \text{if } t \mapsto_{\sigma_1} u$
$v((\lambda x.s)u) \mapsto_{\sigma_3} (\lambda x.vs)u, \ x \notin \mathtt{fv}(v)$	$B\langle t \rangle \to_{\sigma_3^\flat} B\langle u \rangle \quad \text{if } t \mapsto_{\sigma_3} u$
$(\lambda x.t)v \mapsto_{\beta_v} t\{x \leftarrow v\}$	$B\langle t \rangle \to_{\beta_v^\flat} B\langle u \rangle \quad \text{if } t \mapsto_{\beta_v} u$

Reductions $\to_{\sigma^\flat} := \to_{\sigma_1^\flat} \cup \to_{\sigma_3^\flat}, \quad \to_{\mathsf{shuf}} := \to_{\beta_v^\flat} \cup \to_{\sigma^\flat}$

Fig. 4. The Shuffling Calculus λ_{shuf}

The rewriting (shuffling) rules $\to_{\sigma_1^\flat}$ and $\to_{\sigma_3^\flat}$ unblock stuck β-redexes. For instance, consider the terms $t := ((\lambda y.\delta)(zz))\delta$ and $u := \delta((\lambda y.\delta)(zz))$ where $\delta := \lambda x.xx$ (as in Eq. (1), p. 2): t and u are $\beta_v^\flat$-normal but $t \to_{\sigma_1^\flat} (\lambda y.\delta\delta)(zz) \to_{\beta_v^\flat} (\lambda y.\delta\delta)(zz) \to_{\beta_v^\flat} \ldots$ and $u \to_{\sigma_3^\flat} (\lambda y.\delta\delta)(zz) \to_{\beta_v^\flat} (\lambda x.\delta\delta)(zz) \to_{\beta_v^\flat} \ldots$.

The similar shuffling rules in CBN, better known as Regnier's σ-rules [27], are *contained* in CBN β-equivalence, while in Open (and Strong) CBV they are more interesting because they are not contained into (*i.e.* they enrich) β_v-equivalence.

The advantage of λ_{shuf} is with respect to denotational investigations. In [8], λ_{shuf} is indeed used to prove various semantical results in connection to linear logic, resource calculi, and the notion of Taylor expansion due to Ehrhard. In particular, in [8] it has been proved the adequacy of λ_{shuf} with respect to the relational model induced by linear logic: a by-product of our paper is the extension of this adequacy result to all incarnations of Open CBV. The drawback of λ_{shuf} is its technical rewriting theory. We summarize some properties of λ_{shuf}:

Proposition 6 (Basic Properties of λ_{shuf}, [8]).

1. *Let $t, u, s \in \Lambda$. If $t \to_{\beta_v^\flat} u$ and $t \to_{\sigma^\flat} s$ then $u \neq s$.*
2. *$\to_{\sigma^\flat}$ is strongly normalizing and (not strongly) confluent.*
3. *$\to_{\mathsf{shuf}}$ is (not strongly) confluent.*
4. *Let $t \in \Lambda$: t is strongly shuf-normalizable iff t is shuf-normalizable.*

In contrast to λ_{fire} and λ_{vsub}, λ_{shuf} is not strongly confluent and not all shuf-normalizing derivations (if any) from a given term have the same length (consider, for instance, all shuf-normalizing derivations from $(\lambda y.z)(\delta(zz))\delta$). Nonetheless, normalization and strong normalization still coincide in λ_{shuf} (Proposition 6.4), and Corollary 18 in Sect. 3 will show that the discrepancy is encapsulated inside the additional shuffling rules, since all shuf-normalizing derivations (if any) from a given term have the same number of β_v^b-steps.

2.4   Open Call-by-Value 4: The Value Sequent Calculus λ_{vseq}

A more radical approach to the removal of stuck β-redexes is provided by what is here called the *Value Sequent Calculus* λ_{vseq}, defined in Fig. 5. In λ_{vseq}, it is the applicative structure of terms that is altered, by replacing the application constructor with more constructs, namely commands c and environments e. Morally, λ_{vseq} looks at a sequence of applications from the head, that is the value on the left of a command $\langle v \,|\, e \rangle$ rather than from the tail as in natural deduction. In fact, λ_{vseq} is a handy presentation of the intuitionistic fragment of $\bar{\lambda}\tilde{\mu}$, that in turn is the CBV fragment of $\bar{\lambda}\mu\tilde{\mu}$, a calculus obtained as the computational interpretation of a sequent calculus for classical logic. Both $\bar{\lambda}\tilde{\mu}$ and $\bar{\lambda}\mu\tilde{\mu}$ are due to Curien and Herbelin [9], see [6,10] for further investigations about these systems.

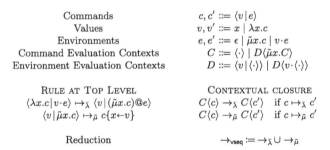

Fig. 5. The Value Sequent Calculus λ_{vseq}

A peculiar trait of the sequent calculus approach is the environment constructor $\tilde{\mu}x.c$, that is a binder for the free occurrences of x in c. It is often said that it is a sort of explicit substitution—we will see exactly in which sense, in Sect. 4.

The change of the intuitionistic variant λ_{vseq} with respect to $\bar{\lambda}\tilde{\mu}$ is that λ_{vseq} does not need the syntactic category of co-variables α, as there can be only one of them, denoted here by ϵ. From a logical viewpoint, this is due to the fact that in intuitionistic sequent calculus the right-hand-side of $\vdash$ has exactly one formula, that is, neither contraction nor weakening are allowed on the right. Consequently, the binary abstraction $\lambda(x,\alpha).c$ of $\bar{\lambda}\tilde{\mu}$ is replaced by a more traditional unary one $\lambda x.c$, and substitution on co-variables is replaced by a notion of *appending of environments*, defined by mutual induction on commands and environments as follows:

$$\langle v \,|\, e'\rangle @e := \langle v \,|\, e'@e\rangle \qquad \epsilon @e := e$$

$$(v\cdot e')@e := v\cdot(e'@e) \qquad (\tilde{\mu}x.c)@e := \tilde{\mu}y.(c\{x{\leftarrow}y\}@e) \text{ with } y \notin \mathtt{fv}(c) \cup \mathtt{fv}(e)$$

Essentially, $c@e$ is a capture-avoiding substitution of e for the only occurrence of ϵ in c that is out of all abstractions, standing for the output of the term. The append operation is used in the rewrite rule $\to_{\bar{\lambda}}$ of λ_{vseq} (Fig. 5). Strong CBV can be obtained by simply extending the grammar of evaluation contexts to commands under abstractions.

We will provide a translation from λ_{vsub} to λ_{vseq} that, beyond termination equivalence, will show that switching to a sequent calculus representation is equivalent to a transformation in administrative normal form [29].

The advantage of λ_{vseq} is that it avoids both rules at a distance and shuffling rules. The drawback of λ_{vseq} is that, syntactically, it requires to step out of the λ-calculus. We will show in Sect. 4 how to reformulate it as a fragment of λ_{vsub}, *i.e.* in natural deduction. However, it will still be necessary to restrict the application constructor, thus preventing the natural way of writing terms.

The rewriting of λ_{vseq} is very well-behaved, in particular it is strongly confluent and every rewriting rule terminates separately.

Proposition 7 (Basic properties of λ_{vseq})

1. $\to_{\bar{\lambda}}$ and $\to_{\tilde{\mu}}$ *are strongly normalizing and strongly confluent (separately).*
2. $\to_{\bar{\lambda}}$ and $\to_{\tilde{\mu}}$ *strongly commute.*
3. $\to_{\mathsf{vseq}}$ *is strongly confluent, and all* vseq*-normalizing derivations d from a command c (if any) have the same length $|d|$, the same number $|d|_{\tilde{\mu}}$ of $\tilde{\mu}$-steps, and the same number $|d|_{\bar{\lambda}}$ of $\bar{\lambda}$-steps.*

2.5   Variations on a Theme

Reducing Open to Closed Call-by-Value: Potential Valuability. Potential valuability relates Naïve Open CBV to Closed CBV via a meta-level substitution closing open terms: a (possibly open) term t is *potentially valuable* if there is a substitution of (closed) *values* for its free variables, for which it β_v-evaluates to a (closed) *value*. In Naïve Open CBV, potentially valuable terms do not coincide with normalizable terms because of premature β_v-normal forms—such as t and u in Eq. (1) at p. 2—which are not potentially valuable.

Paolini, Ronchi Della Rocca and, later, Pimentel [22–25,28] gave several operational, logical, and semantical characterizations of potentially valuable terms in Naïve Open CBV. In particular, in [25,28] it is proved that a term is potentially valuable in Plotkin's Naïve Open CBV iff its normalizable in λ_{fire}.

Potentially valuable terms can be defined for every incarnation of Open CBV: it is enough to update the notions of evaluation and values in the above definition to the considered calculus. This has been done for λ_{shuf} in [8], and for λ_{vsub} in [4]. For both calculi it has been proved that, in the weak setting, potentially valuable terms coincides with normalizable terms. In [15], it has been proved that Plotkin's potentially valuable terms coincide with shuf-potentially valuable terms (which coincide in turn with shuf-normalizable terms). Our paper makes a further step: proving that termination coincides for λ_{fire}, λ_{vsub}, λ_{shuf}, and λ_{vseq} it implies that all their notions of potential valuability coincide with Plotkin's, *i.e.* there is just one notion of potential valuability for Open (and Strong) CBV.

Open CBV 5, 6, 7, ... The literature contains many other calculi for CBV, usually presented for Strong CBV and easily adaptable to Open CBV. Some of them have let-expressions (avatars of ES) and all of them have rules permuting constructors, therefore they lie somewhere in between λ_{vsub} and λ_{shuf}. Often, they have been developed for other purposes, usually to investigate the relationship with monad or CPS translations. Moggi's equational theory [21] is a classic standard of reference, known to coincide with that of Sabry and Felleisen [29], Sabry and Wadler [30], Dychoff and Lengrand [12], Herbelin and Zimmerman [16] and Maraist et al.'s λ_{let} in [20]. In [4], λ_{vsub} modulo $\equiv$ is shown to be termination equivalent to Herbelin and Zimmerman's calculus, and to strictly contain its equational theory, and thus Moggi's. At the level of rewriting these presentations of Open CBV are all more involved than those that we consider here. Their equivalence to our calculi can be shown along the lines of that of λ_{shuf} with λ_{vsub}.

3   Quantitative Equivalence of λ_{fire}, λ_{vsub}, and λ_{shuf}

Here we show the equivalence with respect to termination of λ_{fire}, λ_{vsub}, and λ_{shuf}, enriched with quantitative information on the number of steps.

On the Proof Technique. We show that termination in λ_{vsub} implies termination in λ_{fire} and λ_{shuf} by studying simulations of λ_{fire} and λ_{shuf} into λ_{vsub}. To prove the converse implications we do not use inverse simulations. Alternatively, we show that β_f- and shuf-normal forms are essentially projected into vsub-normal forms, so that if evaluation terminates in λ_{fire} or λ_{shuf} then it also terminates on λ_{vsub}.

Such a simple technique works because in the systems under study *normalization and strong normalization coincide*: if there is a normalizing derivation from a given term t then there are no diverging derivations from t (for λ_{vsub} and λ_{fire} it follows from strong confluence, for λ_{shuf} is given by Proposition 6.4). This fact is also the reason why the statements of our equivalences (forthcoming Corollaries 13 and 17) address a single derivation from t rather than considering *all* derivations from t. Moreover, for any calculus, all normalizing derivations from t have the same number of steps (in λ_{shuf} it holds for $\beta_v^\flat$-steps, see Corollary 18), hence also the quantitative claims of Corollary 13 and Corollary 17 hold actually for *all* normalizing derivations from t.

In both simulations, the structural equivalence $\equiv$ of λ_{vsub} plays a role.

3.1   Equivalence of λ_{fire} and λ_{vsub}

A single β_v-step $(\lambda x.t)v \to_{\beta_v} t\{x\leftarrow v\}$ is simulated in λ_{vsub} by two steps: $(\lambda x.t)v$ $\to_m t[x\leftarrow v] \to_e t\{x\leftarrow v\}$, *i.e.* a m-step that creates a ES, and a e-step that turns the ES into the meta-level substitution performed by the β_v-step. The simulation of an inert step of λ_{fire} is instead trickier, because in λ_{vsub} there is no rule to substitute an inert term, if it is not a variable. The idea is that an inert step $(\lambda x.t)i \to_{\beta_i} t\{x\leftarrow i\}$ is simulated only by $(\lambda x.t)i \to_m t[x\leftarrow i]$, *i.e.* only by the m-step that creates the ES, and such a ES will never be fired—so the simulation is up to the unfolding of substitutions containing inert terms (defined right next). Everything works because of the key property of inert terms: they are normal and their substitution cannot create redexes, so it is useless to substitute them.

The *unfolding* of a vsub-term t is the term $t\!\downarrow$ obtained from t by turning ES into meta-level substitutions; it is defined by:

$$x\!\downarrow := x \quad (tu)\!\downarrow := t\!\downarrow u\!\downarrow \quad (\lambda x.t)\!\downarrow := \lambda x.t\!\downarrow \quad (t[x\leftarrow u])\!\downarrow := t\!\downarrow\{x\leftarrow u\!\downarrow\}$$

For all $t, u \in \Lambda_{\text{vsub}}$, $t \equiv u$ implies $t\!\downarrow = u\!\downarrow$. Also, $t\!\downarrow = t$ iff $t \in \Lambda$.

In the simulation we are going to show, structural equivalence $\equiv$ plays a role. It is used to *clean* the vsub-terms (with ES) obtained by simulation, putting them in a canonical form where ES do not appear among other constructors.

A vsub-term is *clean* if it has the form $u[x_1\leftarrow i_1]\ldots[x_n\leftarrow i_n]$ (with $n \in \mathbb{N}$), $u \in \Lambda$ is called the *body*, and $i_1, \ldots, i_n \in \Lambda$ are inert terms. Clearly, any term (as it is without ES) is clean. We first show how to simulate a single fireball step.

Lemma 8 (Simulation of a β_f-Step in λ_{vsub}). *Let $t, u \in \Lambda$.*

1. *If $t \to_{\beta_\lambda} u$ then $t \to_m \to_{e_\lambda} u$.*
2. *If $t \to_{\beta_i} u$ then $t \to_m \equiv s$, with $s \in \Lambda_{\text{vsub}}$ clean and $s\!\downarrow = u$.*

We cannot simulate derivations by iterating Lemma 8, because the starting term t has no ES but the simulation of inert steps introduces ES. Hence, we have to generalize Lemma 8 up to the unfolding of ES. In general, unfolding ES is a dangerous operation with respect to (non-)termination, as it may erase a diverging subterm (*e.g.* $t := x[y\leftarrow\delta\delta]$ is vsub-divergent and $t\!\downarrow = x$ is normal). In our case, however, the simulation yields clean vsub-terms, so the unfolding is safe since it can erase only inert terms that cannot create, erase, nor carry redexes.

By means of a technical lemma (see the appendix in [3]) we obtain:

Lemma 9 (Projection of a β_f-Step on $\to_{\text{vsub}}$ via Unfolding). *Let t be a clean vsub-term and u be a term.*

1. *If $t\!\downarrow \to_{\beta_\lambda} u$ then $t \to_m \to_{e_\lambda} s$, with $s \in \Lambda_{\text{vsub}}$ clean and $s\!\downarrow = u$.*
2. *If $t\!\downarrow \to_{\beta_i} u$ then $t \to_m \equiv s$, with $s \in \Lambda_{\text{vsub}}$ clean and $s\!\downarrow = u$.*

Via Lemma 9 we can now simulate whole derivations (in forthcoming Theorem 12).

Simulation and Normal Forms. The next step towards the equivalence is to relate normal forms in λ_{fire} (aka fireballs) to those in λ_{vsub}. The relationship is not perfect, since the simulation does not directly map the former to the latter— we have to work a little bit more. First of all, let us characterize the terms in λ_{vsub} obtained by projecting normalizing derivations (that always produce a fireball).

Lemma 10. *Let t be a clean vsub-term. If $t{\downarrow}$ is a fireball, then t is $\{\text{m}, \text{e}_\lambda\}$-normal and its body is a fireball.*

Now, a $\{\text{m}, \text{e}_\lambda\}$-normal form t morally is vsub-normal, as $\to_{\text{e}_y}$ terminates (Proposition 4.1) and it cannot create $\{\text{m}, \text{e}_\lambda\}$-redexes. The part about creations is better expressed as a postponement property.

Lemma 11 (Linear Postponement of $\to_{\text{e}_y}$). *Let $t, u \in \Lambda_{\text{vsub}}$. If $d: t \to^*_{\text{vsub}} u$ then $e: t \to^*_{\text{m}, \text{e}_\lambda} \to^*_{\text{e}_y} u$ with $|e|_{\text{vsub}} = |d|_{\text{vsub}}$, $|e|_{\text{m}} = |d|_{\text{m}}$, $|e|_{\text{e}} = |d|_{\text{e}}$ and $|e|_{\text{e}_\lambda} \geq |d|_{\text{e}_\lambda}$.*

The next theorem puts all the pieces together.

Theorem 12 (Quantitative Simulation of λ_{fire} in λ_{vsub}). *Let $t, u \in \Lambda$. If $d: t \to^*_{\beta_f} u$ then there are $s, r \in \Lambda_{\text{vsub}}$ and $e: t \to^*_{\text{vsub}} r$ such that*

1. *Qualitative Relationship: $r \equiv s$, $u = s{\downarrow} = r{\downarrow}$ and s is clean;*
2. *Quantitative Relationship:*
   1. *Multiplicative Steps: $|d|_{\beta_f} = |e|_{\text{m}}$;*
   2. *Exponential (Abstraction) Steps: $|d|_{\beta_\lambda} = |e|_{\text{e}_\lambda} = |e|_{\text{e}}$.*
3. *Normal Forms: if u is β_f-normal then there exists $g: r \to^*_{\text{e}_y} q$ such that q is a vsub-normal form and $|g|_{\text{e}_y} \leq |e|_{\text{m}} - |e|_{\text{e}_\lambda}$.*

Corollary 13 (Linear Termination Equivalence of λ_{vsub} and λ_{fire}). *Let $t \in \Lambda$. There is a β_f-normalizing derivation d from t iff there is a vsub-normalizing derivation e from t. Moreover, $|d|_{\beta_f} \leq |e|_{\text{vsub}} \leq 2|d|_{\beta_f}$, i.e. they are linearly related.*

The number of β_f-steps in λ_{fire} is a reasonable cost model for Open CBV [1]. Our result implies that also *the number of m-steps in λ_{vsub} is a reasonable cost model*, since the number of m-steps is *exactly* the number of β_f-steps. This fact is quite surprising: in λ_{fire} arguments of β_f-redexes are required to be fireballs, while for m-redexes there are no restrictions on arguments, and yet in any normalizing derivation their number coincide. Note, moreover, that e-steps are linear in m-steps, but only because the initial term has no ES: in general, this is not true.

3.2   Equivalence of λ_{shuf} and λ_{vsub}

A derivation $d: t \to^*_{\text{shuf}} u$ in λ_{shuf} is simulated via a projection on multiplicative normal forms in λ_{vsub}, *i.e.* as a derivation $\text{m}(t) \to^*_{\text{vsub}_\equiv} \text{m}(u)$ (for any vsub-term t, its multiplicative and exponential normal forms, denoted by $\text{m}(t)$ and $\text{e}(t)$ respectively, exist and are unique by Proposition 4). Indeed, a β_v^b-step of λ_{shuf} is simulated in λ_{vsub} by a e-step followed by some m-steps to reach the m-normal form. Shuffling rules $\to_{\sigma^\flat}$ of λ_{shuf} are simulated by structural equivalence $\equiv$ in λ_{vsub}: applying $\mathtt{m}(\cdot)$ to $((\lambda x.t)u)s \to_{\sigma_1^\flat} (\lambda x.(ts))u$ we obtain exactly an instance of the axiom $\equiv_{@l}$ defining $\equiv$: $\mathtt{m}(t)[x\!\leftarrow\!\mathtt{m}(u)]\mathtt{m}(s) \equiv_{@l} (\mathtt{m}(t)\mathtt{m}(s))[x\!\leftarrow\!\mathtt{m}(u)]$ (with the side conditions matching exactly). Similarly, $\to_{\sigma_3^\flat}$ projects to $\equiv_{@r}$ or $\equiv_{[\cdot]}$ (depending on whether v in $\to_{\sigma_3^\flat}$ is a variable or an abstraction). Therefore,

Lemma 14 (Projecting a shuf-Step on $\to_{\mathsf{vsub}_\equiv}$ via m-NF). *Let $t, u \in \Lambda$.*

1. *If $t \to_{\sigma^\flat} u$ then $\mathtt{m}(t) \equiv \mathtt{m}(u)$.*
2. *If $t \to_{\beta_v^\flat} u$ then $\mathtt{m}(t) \to_e \to_m^* \mathtt{m}(u)$.*

In contrast to the simulation of λ_{fire} in λ_{vsub}, here the projection of a single step can be extended to derivations without problems, obtaining that the number of $\beta_v^\flat$-steps in λ_{shuf} matches exactly the number of e-steps in λ_{vsub}. Additionally, we apply the postponement of $\equiv$ (Lemma 5.2), factoring out the use of $\equiv$ (*i.e.* of shuffling rules) without affecting the number of e-steps.

To obtain the termination equivalence we also need to study normal forms. Luckily, the case of λ_{shuf} is simpler than that of λ_{fire}, as next lemma shows.

Lemma 15 (Projection Preserves Normal Forms). *Let $t \in \Lambda$. If t is shuf-normal then $\mathtt{m}(t)$ is vsub-normal.*

The next theorem puts all the pieces together (for any shuf-derivation d, $|d|_{\beta_v^\flat}$ is the number of $\beta_v^\flat$-steps in d: this notion is well defined by Proposition 6.1).

Theorem 16 (Quantitative Simulation of λ_{shuf} in λ_{vsub}). *Let $t, u \in \Lambda$. If $d: t \to_{\mathsf{shuf}}^* u$ then there are $s \in \Lambda_{\mathsf{vsub}}$ and $e: t \to_{\mathsf{vsub}}^* s$ such that*

1. *Qualitative Relationship: $s \equiv \mathtt{m}(u)$;*
2. *Quantitative Relationship (Exponential Steps): $|d|_{\beta_v^\flat} = |e|_e$;*
3. *Normal Form: if u is shuf-normal then s and $\mathtt{m}(u)$ are vsub-normal.*

Corollary 17 (Termination Equivalence of λ_{vsub} and λ_{shuf}). *Let $t \in \Lambda$. There is a shuf-normalizing derivation d from t iff there is a vsub-normalizing derivation e from t. Moreover, $|d|_{\beta_v^\flat} = |e|_e$.*

The obtained quantitative equivalence has an interesting corollary that shows some light on why λ_{shuf} is not strongly confluent. Our simulation maps $\beta_v^\flat$-steps in λ_{shuf} to exponential steps in λ_{vsub}, that are strongly confluent, and thus in equal number in all normalizing derivations (if any) from a given term. Therefore,

Corollary 18 (Number of $\beta_v^\flat$-Steps is Invariant). *All shuf-normalizing derivations from $t \in \Lambda$ (if any) have the same number of $\beta_v^\flat$-steps.*

Said differently, in λ_{shuf} normalizing derivations may have different lengths but the difference is encapsulated inside the shuffling rules $\to_{\sigma_1^\flat}$ and $\to_{\sigma_3^\flat}$.

Concerning the cost model, things are subtler for λ_{shuf}. Note that the relationship between λ_{shuf} and λ_{vsub} uses the number of e-steps, while the cost model (inherited from λ_{fire}) is the number of m-steps. Do e-steps provide a reasonable cost model? Probably not, because there is a family of terms that evaluate in exponentially more m-steps than e-steps. Details are left to a longer version.

4   Quantitative Equivalence of λ_{vsub} and λ_{vseq}, via $\lambda_{\mathsf{vsub}_k}$

The quantitative termination equivalence of λ_{vsub} and λ_{vseq} is shown in two steps: first, we identify a sub-calculus $\lambda_{\mathsf{vsub}_k}$ of λ_{vsub} equivalent to the whole of λ_{vsub}, and then show that $\lambda_{\mathsf{vsub}_k}$ and λ_{vseq} are equivalent (actually isomorphic). Both steps reuse the technique of Sect. 3, *i.e.* simulation plus study of normal forms.

4.1   Equivalence of $\lambda_{\mathsf{vsub}_k}$ and λ_{vsub}

The kernel $\lambda_{\mathsf{vsub}_k}$ of λ_{vsub} is the sublanguage of λ_{vsub} obtained by replacing the application constructor tu with the restricted form tv where the right subterm can only be a value v—i.e., $\lambda_{\mathsf{vsub}_k}$ is the language of so-called *administrative normal forms* [29] of λ_{vsub}. The rewriting rules are the same of λ_{vsub}. It is easy to see that $\lambda_{\mathsf{vsub}_k}$ is stable by vsub-reduction. For lack of space, more details about $\lambda_{\mathsf{vsub}_k}$ are in the appendix of [3].

The translation $(\cdot)^+$ of λ_{vsub} into $\lambda_{\mathsf{vsub}_k}$, which simply places the argument of an application into an ES, is defined by (note that $\mathtt{fv}(t) = \mathtt{fv}(t^+)$ for all $t \in \Lambda_{\mathsf{vsub}}$):

$$x^+ := x \qquad\qquad (tu)^+ := (t^+x)[x{\leftarrow}u^+] \text{ where } x \text{ is fresh}$$
$$(\lambda x.t)^+ := \lambda x.t^+ \qquad t[x{\leftarrow}u]^+ := t^+[x{\leftarrow}u^+]$$

Lemma 19 (Simulation). *Let* $t, u \in \Lambda_{\mathsf{vsub}}$.

1. *Multiplicative: if* $t \to_{\mathsf{m}} u$ *then* $t^+ \to_{\mathsf{m}} \to_{\mathsf{e}_y} \equiv u^+$;
2. *Exponential: if* $t \to_{\mathsf{e}_\lambda} u$ *then* $t^+ \to_{\mathsf{e}_\lambda} u^+$, *and if* $t \to_{\mathsf{e}_y} u$ *then* $t^+ \to_{\mathsf{e}_y} u^+$.
3. *Structural Equivalence:* $t \equiv u$ *implies* $t^+ \equiv u^+$.

The translation of a vsub-normal form is not vsub_k-normal (*e.g.* $(xy)^+ = (xz)[z{\leftarrow}y])$ but a further exponential normalization provides a vsub_k-normal form.

Theorem 20 (Quantitative Simulation of λ_{vsub} in $\lambda_{\mathsf{vsub}_k}$). *Let* $t, u \in \Lambda_{\mathsf{vsub}}$. *If* $d\colon t \to^*_{\mathsf{vsub}} u$ *then there are* $s \in \Lambda_{\mathsf{vsub}_k}$ *and* $e\colon t^+ \to^*_{\mathsf{vsub}_k} s$ *such that*

1. *Qualitative Relationship:* $s \equiv u^+$;
2. *Quantitative Relationship:*
    1. *Multiplicative Steps:* $|e|_{\mathsf{m}} = |d|_{\mathsf{m}}$;
    2. *Exponential Steps:* $|e|_{\mathsf{e}_\lambda} = |d|_{\mathsf{e}_\lambda}$ *and* $|e|_{\mathsf{e}_y} = |d|_{\mathsf{e}_y} + |d|_{\mathsf{m}}$;
3. *Normal Form: if* u *is* vsub-*normal then* s *is* m-*normal and* $e(s)$ *is* vsub_k-*normal*.

Unfortunately, the length of the exponential normalization in Theorem 20.3 cannot be easily bounded, forbidding a precise quantitative equivalence. Note however that turning from λ_{vsub} to its kernel $\lambda_{\mathsf{vsub}_k}$ does not change the number of multiplicative steps: the transformation preserves the cost model.

Corollary 21 (Termination and Cost Equivalence of λ_{vsub} and $\lambda_{\mathsf{vsub}_k}$). *Let* $t \in \Lambda_{\mathsf{vsub}}$. *There exists a* vsub-*normalizing derivation* d *from* t *iff there exists a* vsub_k-*normalizing derivation* e *from* t^+. *Moreover,* $|d|_{\mathsf{m}} = |e|_{\mathsf{m}}$.

4.2   Equivalence of $\lambda_{\mathsf{vsub}_k}$ and λ_{vseq}

The translation $\underline{\cdot}$ of $\lambda_{\mathsf{vsub}_k}$ into λ_{vseq} relies on an auxiliary translation $(\cdot)^{\bullet}$ of values and it is defined as follows:

$$x^{\bullet} := x \qquad (\lambda x.t)^{\bullet} := \lambda x.\underline{t}$$
$$\underline{v} := \langle v \,|\, \epsilon \rangle \qquad \underline{tv} := \underline{t}@(v^{\bullet} \cdot \epsilon) \qquad \underline{t[x \leftarrow u]} := \underline{u}@\tilde{\mu}x.\underline{t}$$

Note the subtle mapping of ES to $\tilde{\mu}$: ES correspond to appendings of $\tilde{\mu}$ to the output of the term u to be substituted, and not of the term t where to substitute.

It is not hard to see that $\lambda_{\mathsf{vsub}_k}$ and λ_{vseq} are actually isomorphic, where the converse translation $(\cdot)^{\circ}$, that maps values and commands to terms, and environments to evaluation contexts, is given by:

$$x^{\circ} := x \qquad \epsilon^{\circ} := \langle \cdot \rangle \qquad \langle v \,|\, e \rangle^{\circ} := e^{\circ} \langle v^{\circ} \rangle$$
$$(\lambda x.c)^{\circ} := \lambda x.c^{\circ} \qquad (v \cdot e)^{\circ} := e^{\circ} \langle \langle \cdot \rangle v^{\circ} \rangle \qquad (\tilde{\mu}x.c)^{\circ} := c^{\circ}[x \leftarrow \langle \cdot \rangle]$$

For the sake of uniformity, we follow the same structure of the other weaker equivalences (*i.e.* simulation plus mapping of normal forms, here working smoothly) rather than proving the isomorphism formally. The simulation maps multiplicative steps to $\overline{\lambda}$ steps, whose number, then, is a reasonable cost model for λ_{vseq}.

Lemma 22 (Simulation of $\rightarrow_{\mathsf{vsub}_k}$ by $\rightarrow_{\mathsf{vseq}}$). *Let t and u be vsub_k-terms.*

1. *Multiplicative: if $t \rightarrow_{\mathsf{m}} u$ then $\underline{t} \rightarrow_{\overline{\lambda}} \underline{u}$.*
2. *Exponential: if $t \rightarrow_{\mathsf{e}} u$ then $\underline{t} \rightarrow_{\tilde{\mu}} \underline{u}$.*

Theorem 23 (Quantitative Simulation of $\lambda_{\mathsf{vsub}_k}$ in λ_{vseq}). *Let t and u be vsub_k-terms. If $d \colon t \rightarrow^{*}_{\mathsf{vsub}_k} u$ then there is $e \colon \underline{t} \rightarrow^{*}_{\mathsf{vseq}} \underline{u}$ such that*

1. *Multiplicative Steps: $|d|_{\mathsf{m}} = |e|_{\overline{\lambda}}$ (the number $\overline{\lambda}$-steps in e);*
2. *Exponential Steps: $|d|_{\mathsf{e}} = |e|_{\tilde{\mu}}$ (the number $\tilde{\mu}$-steps in e), so $|d|_{\mathsf{vsub}_k} = |e|_{\mathsf{vseq}}$;*
3. *Normal Form: if u is vsub_k-normal then $\underline{u}$ is vseq-normal.*

Corollary 24 (Linear Termination Equivalence of $\lambda_{\mathsf{vsub}_k}$ and λ_{vseq}). *Let t be a vsub_k-term. There is a vsub_k-normalizing derivation d from t iff there is a vseq-normalizing derivation e from $\underline{t}$. Moreover, $|d|_{\mathsf{vsub}_k} = |e|_{\mathsf{vseq}}$, $|d|_{\mathsf{e}} = |e|_{\tilde{\mu}}$ and $|d|_{\mathsf{m}} = |e|_{\overline{\lambda}}$.*

Structural Equivalence for λ_{vseq}. The equivalence of λ_{vsub} and $\lambda_{\mathsf{vsub}_k}$ relies on the structural equivalence $\equiv$ of λ_{vsub}, so it is natural to wonder how does $\equiv$ look on λ_{vseq}. The structural equivalence $\simeq$ of λ_{vseq} is defined as the closure by evaluation contexts of the following axiom

$$D\langle \tilde{\mu}x.D'\langle \tilde{\mu}y.c \rangle \rangle \simeq_{\tilde{\mu}\tilde{\mu}} D'\langle \tilde{\mu}y.D\langle \tilde{\mu}x.c \rangle \rangle \quad \text{where } x \notin \mathtt{fv}(D') \text{ and } y \notin \mathtt{fv}(D).$$

As expected, $\simeq$ has, with respect to λ_{vseq}, all the properties of $\equiv$ (see Lemma 5). They are formally stated in the appendix of [3], for lack of space.

5   Conclusions and Future Work

This paper proposes Open CBV as a setting halfway between Closed CBV, the simple framework used to model programming languages such as OCaml, and Strong CBV, the less simple setting underling proof assistants such as Coq. Open CBV is a good balance: its rewriting theory is simple—in particular it is strongly confluent, as the one of Closed CBV—and it can be iterated under abstractions to recover Strong CBV, which is not possible with Closed CBV.

We compared four representative calculi for Open CBV, developed with different motivations, and showed that they share the same qualitative (termination/divergence) and quantitative (number of steps) properties with respect to termination. Therefore, they can be considered as different incarnations of the same immaterial setting, justifying the slogan *Open CBV*.

The qualitative equivalences carry semantical consequences: *the adequacy of relational semantics* for the shuffling calculus proved in [8] actually gives a semantic (and type-theoretical, since the relational model can be seen as a non-idempotent intersection type system) characterization of normalizable terms for Open CBV, *i.e.* it extends to the other three calculi. Similarly, the notion of *potential valuability* for Plotkin's CBV λ-calculus, well-studied in [22–25, 28] and recalled at the end of Sect. 2, becomes a robust notion characterizing the same terms in Open (and Strong) CBV.

Quantitatively, we showed that in three out of four calculi for Open CBV, namely λ_{fire}, λ_{vsub} and λ_{vseq}, evaluation takes exactly the same number of β_f-steps, m-steps and $\bar{\lambda}$-steps, respectively. Since such a number is known to be a reasonable time cost model for λ_{fire} [1], the cost model lifts to λ_{vsub} and λ_{vseq}, showing that the cost model is robust, *i.e.* incarnation-independent. For the shuffling calculus λ_{shuf} we obtain a weaker quantitative relationship that does not allow to transfer the cost model. The $\beta_v^{\flat}$-steps in λ_{shuf}, indeed, match e-steps in λ_{vsub}, but not m-steps. Unfortunately, the two quantities are not necessarily polynomially related, since there is a family of terms that evaluate in exponentially more m-steps than e-steps (details are left to a longer version). Consequently, λ_{shuf} is an incarnation more apt to semantical investigations rather than complexity analyses.

Future Work. This paper is just the first step towards a new, finer understanding of CBV. We plan to purse at the least the following research directions:

1. *Equational Theories.* The four incarnations are termination equivalent but their rewriting rules do not induce the same equational theory. In particular, λ_{fire} equates more than the others, and probably too much because its theory is not a congruence, *i.e.* it is not stable by context closure. The goal is to establish the relationships between the theories and understand how to smooth the calculi as to make them both *equational* and *termination* equivalent.
2. *Abstract Machines.* Accattoli and Sacerdoti Coen introduce in [1] *reasonable* abstract machines for Open CBV, that is, implementation schemas whose overhead is proven to be polynomial, and even linear. Such machines are

quite complex, especially the linear one. Starting from a fine analysis of the overhead, we are currently working on a simpler approach providing cost equivalent but much simpler abstract machines.

3. *From Open CBV to Strong CBV.* We repeatedly said that Strong CBV can be seen as an iteration of Open CBV under abstractions. This is strictly true for λ_{vsub}, λ_{shuf}, and λ_{vseq}, for which the simulations studied here lift to the strong setting. On the contrary, the definition of a good strong λ_{fire} is a subtle open issue. The natural candidate, indeed, is not confluent (but enjoys uniqueness of normal forms) and normalizes more terms than the other calculi for Strong CBV. Another delicate point is the design and the analysis of abstract machines for Strong CBV, of which there are no examples in the literature (both Grégoire and Leroy's [13] and Accattoli and Sacerdoti Coen's [1] study machines for Open CBV only).

4. *Open Bisimulations.* In [18] Lassen studies open (or normal form) bisimulations for CBV. He points out that his bisimilarity is not fully abstract with respect to contextual equivalence, and his counterexamples are all based on stuck β-redexes in Naïve Open CBV. An interesting research direction is to recast his study in Open CBV and see whether full abstraction holds or not.

Acknowledgment. Work partially supported by the A*MIDEX project ANR-11-IDEX-0001-02 funded by the "Investissements d'Avenir" French Government program, managed by the French National Research Agency (ANR), and by ANR projects ANR-12-JS02-006-01 (CoQuaS) and ANR-11-IS02-0002 (Locali).

References

1. Accattoli, B., Sacerdoti Coen, C.: On the relative usefulness of fireballs. In: LICS 2015, pp. 141–155 (2015)
2. Accattoli, B.: Proof nets and the call-by-value λ-calculus. Theor. Comput. Sci. **606**, 2–24 (2015)
3. Accattoli, B., Guerrieri, G.: Open call-by-value (Extended Version). CoRR abs/1609.00322 (2016). http://arxiv.org/abs/1609.00322
4. Accattoli, B., Paolini, L.: Call-by-value solvability, revisited. In: Schrijvers, T., Thiemann, P. (eds.) FLOPS 2012. LNCS, vol. 7294, pp. 4–16. Springer, Heidelberg (2012). doi:10.1007/978-3-642-29822-6_4
5. Accattoli, B., Sacerdoti Coen, C.: On the value of variables. In: WoLLIC 2014, pp. 36–50 (2014)
6. Ariola, Z.M., Bohannon, A., Sabry, A.: Sequent calculi and abstract machines. ACM Trans. Program. Lang. Syst. **31**(4), 13:1–13:48 (2009)
7. Blelloch, G.E., Greiner, J.: Parallelism in sequential functional languages. In: FPCA, pp. 226–237 (1995)
8. Carraro, A., Guerrieri, G.: A semantical and operational account of call-by-value solvability. In: Muscholl, A. (ed.) FoSSaCS 2014. LNCS, vol. 8412, pp. 103–118. Springer, Heidelberg (2014). doi:10.1007/978-3-642-54830-7_7
9. Curien, P.L., Herbelin, H.: The duality of computation. In: ICFP, pp. 233–243 (2000)

10. Curien, P.-L., Munch-Maccagnoni, G.: The duality of computation under focus. In: Calude, C.S., Sassone, V. (eds.) TCS 2010. IAICT, vol. 323, pp. 165–181. Springer, Heidelberg (2010). doi:10.1007/978-3-642-15240-5_13
11. Dal Lago, U., Martini, S.: The weak lambda calculus as a reasonable machine. Theor. Comput. Sci. **398**(1–3), 32–50 (2008)
12. Dyckhoff, R., Lengrand, S.: Call-by-value lambda-calculus and LJQ. J. Log. Comput. **17**(6), 1109–1134 (2007)
13. Grégoire, B., Leroy, X.: A compiled implementation of strong reduction. In: ICFP 2002, pp. 235–246 (2002)
14. Guerrieri, G.: Head reduction and normalization in a call-by-value lambda-calculus. In: WPTE 2015, pp. 3–17 (2015)
15. Guerrieri, G., Paolini, L., Ronchi Della Rocca, S.: Standardization of a call-by-value lambda-calculus. In: TLCA 2015, pp. 211–225 (2015)
16. Herbelin, H., Zimmermann, S.: An operational account of call-by-value minimal and classical λ-calculus in natural deduction form. In: TLCA, pp. 142–156 (2009)
17. Jones, N.D., Gomard, C.K., Sestoft, P.: Partial Evaluation and Automatic Program Generation. Prentice-Hall Inc., Upper Saddle River (1993)
18. Lassen, S.: Eager normal form bisimulation. In: LICS 2005, pp. 345–354 (2005)
19. Lévy, J.J.: Réductions correctes et optimales dans le lambda-calcul. Thèse d'Etat, Univ. Paris VII, France (1978)
20. Maraist, J., Odersky, M., Turner, D.N., Wadler, P.: Call-by-name, call-by-value, call-by-need and the linear λ-calculus. TCS **228**(1–2), 175–210 (1999)
21. Moggi, E.: Computational λ-calculus and Monads. In: LICS 1989, pp. 14–23 (1989)
22. Paolini, L., Pimentel, E., Ronchi Della Rocca, S.: Strong normalization from an unusual point of view. Theor. Comput. Sci. **412**(20), 1903–1915 (2011)
23. Paolini, L.: Call-by-value separability and computability. In: ICTCS, pp. 74–89 (2002)
24. Paolini, L., Pimentel, E., Ronchi Della Rocca, S.: Lazy strong normalization. In: ITRS 2004. Electronic Notes in Theoretical Computer Science, vol. 136C, pp. 103–116 (2005)
25. Paolini, L., Ronchi Della Rocca, S.: Call-by-value solvability. ITA **33**(6), 507–534 (1999)
26. Plotkin, G.D.: Call-by-name, call-by-value and the lambda-calculus. Theor. Comput. Sci. **1**(2), 125–159 (1975)
27. Regnier, L.: Une équivalence sur les lambda-termes. TCS **2**(126), 281–292 (1994)
28. Ronchi Della Rocca, S., Paolini, L.: The Parametric λ-Calculus. Springer, Heidelberg (2004)
29. Sabry, A., Felleisen, M.: Reasoning about programs in continuation-passing style. Lisp Symbolic Comput. **6**(3–4), 289–360 (1993)
30. Sabry, A., Wadler, P.: A reflection on call-by-value. ACM Trans. Program. Lang. Syst. **19**(6), 916–941 (1997)
31. Sands, D., Gustavsson, J., Moran, A.: Lambda calculi and linear speedups. In: The Essence of Computation, Complexity, Analysis, Transformation. Essays Dedicated to Neil D. Jones, pp. 60–84 (2002)

Type Theory

Implementing Cantor's Paradise

Furio Honsell[1], Marina Lenisa[1], Luigi Liquori[2], and Ivan Scagnetto[1(✉)]

[1] Università di Udine, Udine, Italy
{furio.honsell,marina.lenisa,ivan.scagnetto}@uniud.it
[2] INRIA, Sophia Antipolis Méditerranée, Valbonne, France
Luigi.Liquori@inria.fr

Dedicated to Marco Forti for his 70th birthday
Aus dem Paradies, das Cantor uns geschaffen hat,
soll uns niemand vertreiben können.
David Hilbert

Abstract. Set-theoretic paradoxes have made all-inclusive self-referential Foundational Theories almost a taboo. The few daring attempts in the literature to break this taboo avoid paradoxes by restricting the class of formulæ allowed in Cantor's naïve *Comprehension Principle*. A different, more intensional approach was taken by Fitch, reformulated by Prawitz, by restricting, instead, the shape of deductions, namely allowing only normal(izable) deductions. The resulting theory is quite powerful, and *consistent by design*. However, *modus ponens* and Scotus *ex contradictione quodlibet* principles fail. We discuss Fitch-Prawitz Set Theory (FP) and implement it in a Logical Framework with so-called *locked types*, thereby providing a "Computer-assisted Cantor's Paradise": an interactive framework that, unlike the familiar Coq and Agda, is closer to the familiar informal way of doing mathematics by delaying and consolidating the required normality tests. We prove a *Fixed Point Theorem*, whereby all partial recursive functions are definable in FP. We establish an intriguing connection between an extension of FP and the Theory of Hyperuniverses: the bisimilarity quotient of the coalgebra of closed terms of FP satisfies the Comprehension Principle for Hyperuniverses.

Keywords: Fitch-Prawitz set theory · Logical frameworks · Paradoxes · Coalgebras · Hyperuniverses

1 Introduction

The discovery of set-theoretic paradoxes at the turn of last century, such as Russell's, Burali-Forti's and Curry's, inhibited mainstream foundational research from exploring self-referential, all-inclusive Foundational Theories. There are a

---

Work supported by the COST Action IC1201 BETTY "Behavioural Types for Reliable Large-Scale Software Systems" and by the COST Action CA15123 EUTYPES "The European research network on types for programming and verification".

A. Igarashi (Ed.): APLAS 2016, LNCS 10017, pp. 229–250, 2016.
DOI: 10.1007/978-3-319-47958-3_13

very few exceptions in the literature. Quine's NF and the Theory of *Hyperuniverses* by Forti and Honsell [FH96] avoid paradoxes while preserving *extensionality*, by restricting the class of formulæ allowed in Cantor's Comprehension Principle to *stratified* or to *generalized positive formulæ*, respectively.

In 1952, Frederic Brenton Fitch [Fit52] introduced a Foundational Set-Theory, consistent by design, which has a more *intensional* flavour. It compensates the potentially paradoxical effects of an un-constrained *naïve* Comprehension Principle by restricting the class of deductions. Fitch introduced two possible conditions which are rather idiosyncratic and unnecessarily restrictive, see [Fit52]. It was not until Prawitz in 1966 [Pra06], who gave a *natural deduction* presentation of Fitch's Theory, that a more principled restriction on deductions was introduced, namely that the deduction *be normal*.

Apart from the restriction on the shape of deductions, Fitch-Prawitz Set Theory, FP, is otherwise a standard first order theory with classical negation. Sets, *i.e.* abstractions, are introduced and eliminated in the natural way, and equality is expressed by *Leibniz equality*. FP subsumes higher-order logic for all orders. Fitch himself showed how a considerable part of the theory of Real Numbers can be developed in FP. The theory however is only *paraconsistent*, in that Scotus principle *ex contradictione quodlibet* fails. Moreover the standard rules, such as *modus ponens* or *extensionality* are not admissible.

In this paper, we discuss FP and give a *Fixed Point Theorem*, whereby all partial recursive functions are definable in FP as one would in *functional programming languages*.

Furthermore we show how to encode the highly unorthodox *side condition* of FP in a Logical Framework based on Constructive Set Theory featuring *locked types*, [HLMS16]. This allows to build an extremely flexible, *all-inclusive* interactive foundational environment for developing Mathematics and its foundations. This is indeed an interactive, computer-assisted *Cantor's Paradise*, where one can *optimistically* use the unrestricted Comprehension Principle, in the style of [CSW14,DHJG06] and of *optimistic concurrency* control in distributed systems. I.e., the nuisance of checking consistency is done automatically at the end!

Finally, we provide an intriguing set-theoretic connection between an extension of FP and the Theory of Hyperuniverses, [FHL94]. Namely we show that the *strongly extensional* quotient, *i.e.* the *bisimilarity quotient*, of the coalgebra of closed terms of Fitch-Prawitz Theory satisfies the restricted Comprehension Principle of Hyperuniverses. The relevance of this result is twofold. It provides a purely proof-theoretic consistency proof for the Theory of Hyperuniverses. Moreover, it shows that, if we insist on extensionality, a consistent Comprehension Principle cannot be broadened much beyond *positive formulæ*.

Synopsis. In Sect. 2, we present the theory FP, and in Sect. 3 we discuss it. In Sect. 4, we show how Mathematics can be developed in FP, in particular we prove the Fixed Point Theorem. In Sect. 5, we show how to encode FP in a Logical Framework featuring locked types. In Sect. 6, we study the connection between FP and the extensional Theory of Hyperuniverses. In Sect. 7 we discuss

FP as a logical framework and compare it to other "optimistic" frameworks. Final remarks appear in Sect. 8.

2   The Theory of Fitch-Prawitz, FP

We present a classical version of the logical theory of Fitch-Prawitz, which we call FP. We follow essentially [Pra06]. The theory FP includes the usual logical connectives $\wedge, \vee, \rightarrow$, and the $\forall, \exists$ quantifiers, the logical constant $\perp$, together with an unrestricted set constructor. Negation is not a primitive connective, $\neg A$ being expressed as $A \rightarrow \perp$. The crucial non-standard restriction is that only *normal* deductions are allowed in Fitch-Prawitz theory.

2.1   The Language of FP

Definition 1 (Symbols). *The* symbols *consist of the binary constant* $\in$, *the constant* λ *for set abstraction, the logical constant* $\perp$, *the logical connectives* $\neg, \wedge, \vee, \rightarrow$, *the universal and existential quantifiers* $\forall$ *and* $\exists$. *We assume a denumerable set of variables, denoted by lower-case letters* $x, y, z, \ldots$

Definition 2 (Terms and Formulæ). Terms *and* formulæ *are defined by mutual induction:*
$(\mathcal{T} \ni)\ t, u ::= x \mid \lambda x.A$
$(\mathcal{F} \ni)\ A, B, \ldots, P, \ldots ::= \perp \mid \neg A \mid A \wedge A \mid A \vee A \mid A \rightarrow A \mid \forall x.A \mid \exists x.A \mid t \in u,$
where $\neg A$ *is an abbreviation for* $A \rightarrow \perp$.

We use standard conventions concerning free and bound occurrences of variables, and, of course, *Barendregt's hygiene condition*. Open and closed terms and formulæ are defined as usual. The set of free variables of a term t or a formula A will be denoted by $\mathsf{Fv}(t)/\mathsf{Fv}(A)$. The set of closed terms/formulæ is denoted by $\mathcal{T}^0/\mathcal{F}^0$. Formula contexts $A[\ ]$, where $A[\ ]$ is an incomplete formula with a hole, are defined as usual. We denote by $t[u/x]$, $A[u/x]$ the (capture-avoiding) substitution of the term u for the variable x in the term t or in the formula A.

2.2   Inference Rules and Deductions

We present inference rules in natural deduction style (see Fig. 1). The inference rules consist of an introduction and an elimination rule for each logical connective, for $\forall, \exists$ quantifiers, and for λ, and of a rule for $\perp$.

   The rules of FP appear in Fig. 1. In the rules $\forall$I) and $\exists$E), the variable y does not belong to free variables of $A \backslash \{x\}$ and it must not occur free in any hypothesis or undischarged assumptions.

   Notice that in FP the rule of *negation introduction* is absorbed by $\rightarrow$I).

   We call *quasi-deduction* the standard notion of deduction in Natural Deduction. In FP, not all quasi-deductions are allowed, but only those which essentially correspond to *normal deductions* in Natural Deduction.

$\wedge$I) $\dfrac{A\quad B}{A\wedge B}$

$\wedge$E) $\dfrac{A\wedge B}{A}\qquad \dfrac{A\wedge B}{B}$

$$\begin{array}{cc} (A) & (B) \\ \vdots & \vdots \end{array}$$

$\vee$I) $\dfrac{A}{A\vee B}\qquad \dfrac{B}{A\vee B}$

$\vee$E) $\dfrac{A\vee B\quad C\quad C}{C}$

(A)
$\vdots$

$\rightarrow$I) $\dfrac{B}{A\rightarrow B}$

$\rightarrow$E) $\dfrac{A\quad A\rightarrow B}{B}$

$\forall$I) $\dfrac{A[y/x]}{\forall x.A}$

$\forall$E) $\dfrac{\forall x.A}{A[t/x]}$

$(A[y/x])$
$\vdots$

$\exists$I) $\dfrac{A[t/x]}{\exists x.A}$

$\exists$E) $\dfrac{\exists x.A\quad B}{B}$

$(\neg A)$
$\vdots$

λI) $\dfrac{A[t/x]}{t\in\lambda x.A}$

λE) $\dfrac{t\in\lambda x.A}{A[t/x]}$

$\bot$) $\dfrac{\bot}{A}$

Fig. 1. FP rules in natural deduction style

Definition 3. *The premisses A in the rule* $\rightarrow$*E), C in the rule* $\vee$*E), B in the rule* $\exists$*E) are called* minor premisses. *A premiss that is not minor is called a* major premiss.

Definition 4 (Deductions).

- *We call* quasi-deduction *in* FP *a standard deduction in the system* FP, *i.e. a formula tree obtained by applying the inference rules.*
- *A formula occurrence in a deduction that is both the consequence of an application of a I-rule or of the* $\bot$*-rule, and major premiss of an application of a (correspondent) E-rule is said to be a* maximum formula *in the deduction.*
- *A deduction in* FP *is a quasi-deduction with no maximum formulæ, i.e. a* normal *deduction.*
- *We write* $\Gamma\vdash_{FP} A$, *for* Γ *set of formulæ, when there is a deduction of the formula A from the set of formulæ in* Γ.
- *A deduction from no assumptions is called a* proof.

The shape of *normal deductions* manifestly accounts for the fact that no *information* can be logically extracted from a formula which had not been already available at the outset. Normal Deductions apparently satisfy a sort of *nihil fit ex nihilo*. Namely in a main branch β of a deduction Π, the formula occurrences in β that are major premisses of E-rules precede all formula occurrences in β

which are premisses of I-rules or the $\perp$-rule. In the *proposition-as-types* analogy, normal proofs correspond to normal forms of λ-calculus. In most popular logics, all deductions can be normalized, although non normal proofs are usually more concise and more natural. The use of *lemmata*, or *cuts*, produces non-normal proofs. Normalization then amounts to proving all lemmata from first principles within each proof. But cuts, as in FP can lead to circularities. In Sect. 3.1 we give examples of deductions which cannot be normalized. These arise from the unrestricted use of elimination rules, and therefore might yield deductions of $\perp$.

If we consider the fragment of the system FP where we omit the λ-rules, we obtain a system for classical logic with the property that each derivation is normalizable, *i.e.* for each derivation there exists a corresponding derivation in normal form (see [Pra06], Ch. III, Theorems 1 and 2). In the full system FP this property fails. In derivations, it is still possible to remove any given maximum formula, but in general it is impossible to remove all maximum formulæ.

Nevertheless, FP is consistent, namely, there is at least a formula which is not derivable, *i.e.* $\perp$. If this were the case, the $\perp$-rule would make the system *trivial*. This is essentially Theorem 3 of [Pra06], but since consistency does not require a tight control on the shape of subformulæ, we shortcircuit some of the arguments.

Proposition 1. *The system* FP *is consistent.*

Proof. We proceed by contradiction. Assume that there is a proof Π (*i.e.*, a deduction in normal form depending on the empty set) of $\perp$. Consider a main branch β of Π. One can easily see that the formula occurrences in β that are major premisses of E-rules precede all formula occurrences in β which are premisses of I-rules or the $\perp$-rule. Otherwise there would be a first formula occurrence in β which is a major premiss of an E-rule but succeeds a premiss of an I-rule or the $\perp$-rule, and such a formula would be a maximum formula contrary to the hypothesis that β is normal. But there are no I-rules for $\perp$ hence there are no premisses of I-rules in β. Hence the first formula in β must be an undischarged assumption, and this contradicts the initial hypothesis that Π is a proof.   □

3   The Theory FP: Pros and Cons

Why Normal Deductions? Restricting the class of legitimate deductions in FP to normal deductions yields consistency *by design*, see Proposition 1. Alternately, one could have brutally accepted only deductions which do not derive $\perp$, but then huge complications would arise because we do need *subdeductions* which yield $\perp$, in dealing with negation.

Moreover, since Classical Logic is normalizing, FP is a *conservative extension* with respect to classical theorems which *do not mention* simultaneously both λ and $\in$. This allows to develop in FP a considerable portion of standard Mathematics, see [Fit52].

In [Fit52], Fitch did not introduce the *normal deduction* proviso to qualify proper deductions. He discussed instead two alternate conditions which appear rather idiosyncratic and unnecessarily restrictive, which he called the *simple* and the *special restrictions*. The simple restriction does not allow to derive *e.g.* $A \to (B \to ((A \land B) \to C) \to C)$, while the special restriction does not allow to derive $(P \leftrightarrow (P \to Q)) \to Q$ or $((A \to (A \to B) \to B) \to A) \to A$.

Negation. We have already pointed out that *negation* is not a primitive logical operator, but it is encoded using $\bot$, namely $\neg A \overset{\Delta}{=} A \to \bot$. The $\bot$)-rule enforces *classical* negation. It clearly subsumes the intuitionistic rule *ex falso sequitur quodlibet*, namely $\dfrac{\bot}{A}$.

Moreover, applying the $\to$E)-rule and provided the overall deduction normalizes, it encompasses also the *double negation* rule, namely $\dfrac{\neg\neg A}{A}$, and hence it proves also *tertium non datur*, *i.e.* $((A \to \bot) \to \bot) \to A$.

Full Elimination Rules Are Not Admissible. The choice of allowing only normal deductions makes standard elimination rules "unsafe", *i.e.* not admissible. *E.g. Modus Ponens*, *i.e.* the $\to$E)-rule, cannot be applied naïvely, in that if we have normal deductions of $A \to B$ and of A, it is not true in general that the extended deduction obtained by an application of the $\to$E)-rule is still normal.

Normalizable Quasi-deductions. FP$^{\#}$. The constraint of considering quasi-deductions to be legal only if already in *normal form* can be weakened to allow for *normalizable* quasi-derivations. In order to define *normalizable* deductions we need to introduce a *calculus of deductions*, a sort of λ-calculus as in the *propositions-as-types* paradigm, and define an appropriate notion of *reduction* which reflects the *inversion principle* underpinning the normalization procedure. One can easily see that this can be done and that the deduction calculus is strongly normalizing. Then, consistency of FP$^{\#}$ follows from that of FP. This extension of FP, called FP$^{\#}$ has been recently discussed in [HLMS16], where a type system for characterizing the strongly normalizable λ-terms has been introduced, see Subsect. 4.1 below.

Paraconsistency. In FP Duns Scotus rule *ex absurdis sequitur quodlibet*, namely: $\dfrac{A \quad \neg A}{\bot}$ is not admissible, let alone derivable. Since $\neg A$ is encoded as $A \to \bot$, the derivability of *Scotus rule* would require an application of the $\to$E)-rule, which is subject to restrictions on the subdeductions, and hence is not safe in general. In Subsect. 3.1 we will see that also Aristotle's *non-contradiction* principle fails, namely we have that for suitable A's $\vdash_{\mathsf{FP}} A \land \neg A$. Thus FP is paraconsistent. This is inevitable since, in FP a strong fixed point theorem (Theorem 1) holds.

In the original system of Fitch [Fit52], *negation* is a primitive unary connective which behaves differently from our encoding of $\neg$ and satisfies Scotus rule. In [Pra06], Prawitz calls it *constructive negation*. To allow for this notion of negation, Fitch has to give up *excluded middle* and *negation introduction* (which he calls *reductio ad absurdum*). Both restrictions, introduced by Fitch in [Fit52] on quasi-deductions to qualify them as deductions, ensure that the system is consistent but *not* paraconsistent.

3.1   The Taming of Russell's and Curry's Paradoxes

The interest in the theory of Fitch-Prawitz FP lies in its power of taming the naïve *Comprehension Principle*, namely permitting to reason on the set of elements satisfying any formula P.

Thus, in particular, Russell's and Curry's classes are definable in FP, but the deductions, involving these classes, which would allow to derive $\bot$ in classical logic are not normalizable.

Russell's Paradox. Let us define $t \overset{\Delta}{=} \lambda x.(x \not\in x)$, where $t \not\in t$ denotes the formula $\neg(t \in t)$, *i.e.* $t \in t \to \bot$. Then we have the following quasi-deduction:

$$\cfrac{\cfrac{\cfrac{\cfrac{t \in t^{(1)}}{t \not\in t} \quad t \in t^{(1)}}{\bot}}{\cfrac{t \not\in t^{(1)}}{t \in t}} \quad \cfrac{\cfrac{\cfrac{t \in t^{(1)}}{t \not\in t} \quad t \in t^{(1)}}{\bot}}{t \not\in t^{(1)}}}{\bot}$$

the index (1) above indicates where hypotheses are discharged. Notice that we have both $\vdash_{\mathsf{FP}} t \in t$ and $\vdash_{\mathsf{FP}} t \not\in t$, since the two subderivations are legal in FP. However $\bot$ is not derivable, since the overall quasi-deduction cannot be transformed into a normal deduction. If we perform a step of $\to$-reduction we end up introducing a *new* λ-reduction, indefinitely. We can derive legally instead $\vdash_{\mathsf{FP}} (t \in t) \land (t \not\in t)$. This amounts to the failure of Aristotle's *Principle of non-contradiction*. However, Scotus rule does not apply, and hence this contradiction does not trivialize the theory, but just makes it paraconsistent.

Curry's Paradox. Let P be any formula, and let $Y \overset{\Delta}{=} \lambda x.(x \in x \to P)$. Then we have the following quasi-deduction:

$$\cfrac{\cfrac{\cfrac{Y \in Y^{(1)}}{Y \in Y \to P} \quad Y \in Y^{(1)}}{P}}{Y \in Y \to P^{(1)}} \quad \cfrac{\cfrac{\cfrac{Y \in Y^{(1)}}{Y \in Y \to P} \quad Y \in Y^{(1)}}{P}}{\cfrac{Y \in Y \to P^{(1)}}{Y \in Y}}}{P}$$

Clearly, the above quasi-deduction cannot be transformed into a normal deduction, because the same infinite reduction-chain that occurs in Russell's paradox above would be generated here. Notice that the two quasi-derivations obtained by just dropping the last application of the $\to$E)-rule are in normal form.

Moreover, from the very definition of Y, by applying the λI)-rule, we obtain $(Y \in Y \to P) \to (Y \in Y)$, and by applying the λE)-rule, we obtain $(Y \in Y) \to (Y \in Y \to P)$. Hence we have $\vdash_{\mathsf{FP}} (Y \in Y) \leftrightarrow (Y \in Y \to P)$. This is related to the *Fixed Point Theorem* of Sect. 4.1, which takes us very close to a paradox but not quite. Russell's class is a special case of Curry's Paradox, if the formula P is taken to be $\bot$.

The Role of Structural Rules in the Paradoxes. In deriving both Russell's and Curry's Paradoxes, we have used the structural rule of *contraction*. In each branch we have discharged two instances of the same assumption. Grishin [Gri82] was the first to show that Naïve Set Theory without contraction is consistent, albeit very weak. To see this it is enough to realize that it amounts to a Set Theory whose logic is Girard's Linear Logic without exponentials, and therefore all deductions are normalizable even in the presence of λ and $\in$. Hence the "murderer" who chases us away from Cantor's Paradise, namely the "root cause" of the set-theoretic paradoxes, is not *extensionality* or *tertium non datur*, it is not even related to *negation*. It is the structural rule of *contraction* which, via Curry's Paradox, yields inconsistency even in minimal logic.

Incidentally, we point out that the expressive power of J.Y. Girard's Light Linear Logic with abstractions, $LLLs$ (see [Gir98], Appendix A.1) lies in between Grishin's Naïve Set Theory without contraction, and the theory of Fitch-Prawitz.

3.2 Equality and Extensionality

Equality in FP is expressed as *Leibniz Equality*, namely

$$t_1 = t_2 \overset{\Delta}{=} \forall x.\, t_1 \in x \leftrightarrow t_2 \in x.$$

In Set Theory, it is natural to consider a much stronger version of equality, namely *Extensional Equality*

$$t_1 \simeq t_2 \overset{\Delta}{=} \forall x.\, x \in t_1 \leftrightarrow x \in t_2.$$

In FP we can derive $t_1 \simeq t_2 \to t_1 = t_2$. The converse implication amounts to the *Extensionality Axiom* $t_1 = t_2 \to t_1 \simeq t_2$.

Grishin [Gri82] showed in 1982 that, adding Extensionality, the contraction rule becomes derivable. Hence it allows to derive Russell's Paradox already in a Naïve Set Theory based on Linear Logic without exponentials.

Extensionality has a similar impact also on FP. First we need to extend the notion of *normal deduction* to deductions which make use of *axioms*. This is done simply by stipulating that axioms behave as undischarged *assumptions*. Hence, the analogue of Grishin's result for FP is that one can derive a normal deduction of $\bot$ whose only assumptions are instances of Extensionality. Thus, the Extensionality Axiom makes FP inconsistent. We give a direct proof of this:

Proposition 2. Ext $\vdash_{\mathsf{FP}} \bot$.

Proof. Let $Y \stackrel{\Delta}{=} \{x \mid x \in x\}$, $\emptyset \stackrel{\Delta}{=} \{x \mid \bot\}$, $R \stackrel{\Delta}{=} \{x \mid x \in x \rightarrow \bot\}$, $X \stackrel{\Delta}{=} \{x \mid R \in R\}$. Then $R \in R \vdash_{\mathsf{FP}} \forall x. x \in \emptyset \leftrightarrow x \in X$. Namely,

$$
\dfrac{R \in R \quad \dfrac{\dfrac{\dfrac{x \in X^{(1)}}{R \in R}}{R \in R \rightarrow \bot}}{\dfrac{\bot}{\dfrac{x \in \emptyset}{x \in X \rightarrow x \in \emptyset}}}}{}
\qquad
\dfrac{\dfrac{\dfrac{\dfrac{x \in \emptyset^{(1)} \quad R \in R^{(2)}}{\bot}}{R \in R \rightarrow \bot}}{R \in R}}{\dfrac{x \in X}{x \in \emptyset \rightarrow x \in X}}
$$

Using Ext, we have $R \in R \vdash_{\mathsf{FP}} \forall x. \emptyset \in x \leftrightarrow X \in x$. By instantiating x to Y we get $R \in R \vdash_{\mathsf{FP}} \emptyset \in Y \leftrightarrow X \in Y$, hence using $\lambda\mathrm{E}$), we obtain $R \in R \vdash_{\mathsf{FP}} \emptyset \in \emptyset \leftrightarrow X \in X$. Since, by $\lambda\mathrm{I}$) $R \in R \vdash_{\mathsf{FP}} X \in X$, by $\rightarrow\mathrm{E}$) we get $R \in R \vdash_{\mathsf{FP}} \emptyset \in \emptyset$ and by $\lambda\mathrm{E}$) $R \in R \vdash_{\mathsf{FP}} \bot$. Finally, since $\vdash_{\mathsf{FP}} R \in R$ (see Russell's Paradox at the beginning of Sect. 3.1), we get a contradiction. One can easily check that all the above arguments are indeed normal deductions. □

Sect. 6 is devoted to show how Extensionality can be recovered in a weak FP.

4   Developing Mathematics in FP

In this Section we show that even if Extensionality is inconsistent with FP, nevertheless Leibniz Equality allows us to derive a considerable part of Mathematics and Logic in FP. Similar developments can be carried out also in Fitch original Theory [Fit52] and in Girard's *LLLs* [Gir98], Appendix A.1.

First we need to introduce the following fundamental abbreviations:

$$
\emptyset \stackrel{\Delta}{=} \lambda x.\bot \quad V \stackrel{\Delta}{=} \lambda x.(x = x) \quad \{x \mid A\} \stackrel{\Delta}{=} \lambda x.A \quad \{t\} \stackrel{\Delta}{=} \lambda x.(x = t)
$$
$$
\{t_1, \ldots, t_n\} \stackrel{\Delta}{=} \lambda x.(x = t_1 \vee \ldots x = t_n) \quad \langle t_1, t_2 \rangle \stackrel{\Delta}{=} \{t_1, \{t_2\}\}
$$
$$
\langle t_1, \ldots, t_n \rangle \stackrel{\Delta}{=} t \stackrel{\Delta}{=} \langle \ldots \langle t_1, t_2 \rangle, \ldots, t_n \rangle \quad \lambda x_1 \ldots x_n.A \stackrel{\Delta}{=} \lambda z.(z = \langle x_1, \ldots, x_n \rangle \wedge A).
$$

One can easily see that when any such abbreviation is taken as the definition in FP of the intended notion, it satisfies in FP the standard properties of this notion. *E.g.* two t-ple's are equal if and only if all their components are equal.

4.1   The Fixed Point Theorem

The outstanding expressive power of FP derives from the following logical *Fixed Point Theorem*, which allows us to define entities in FP following a sort of *functional programming paradigm*.

Theorem 1 (Fixed Point (FPT)). *Let A be a formula with free variables $x, z_1, \ldots, z_n$, $n > 0$. Then there exists a term u such that $\vdash_{\mathsf{FP}} z \in u \longleftrightarrow A[u/x]$, where z is a shorthand for $\langle z_1, \ldots, z_n \rangle$.*

Proof. Let $u \stackrel{\Delta}{=} \{z \mid \langle z,t \rangle \in t\}$, where $t \stackrel{\Delta}{=} \{\langle z,y \rangle \mid A[\{w \mid \langle w,y \rangle \in y\}/x]\}$. Then the implication $z \in u \longrightarrow A[u/x]$ and its converse can be derived via two applications, respectively, of the λE-rule, and of the λI-rule.   □

Paraconsistency follows immediately from Theorem 1, just take the formula A to be $z \notin x$. Notice that the contradiction, $\bot$, arises from $z \in u \longleftrightarrow z \notin u$, only if we can either use freely the structural rule of *contraction* or a *non-normalizable* proof. The former is precisely what is not allowed in Girard's *LLLs*, while non-normalizable proofs are precisely what are ruled out by FP.

Curry's paradoxical Y as defined in Sect. 3 is closely related to the fixed point construction but it is not an instance of it. In fact, an alternative Y can be obtained using the Fixed Point Theorem. Namely, consider the formula $A \stackrel{\Delta}{=} z \in x \to P$. Then, by the Fixed Point Theorem, there exists a term u such that $\vdash_{\mathsf{FP}} z \in u \longleftrightarrow (z \in u \to P)$. Now, by substituting u for z, we get $u \in u \longleftrightarrow (u \in u \to P)$. By the proof of the Fixed Point Theorem, u can be taken to be $\{z \mid \langle z,t \rangle \in t\}$. Of course, the Fixed Point Theorem above admits a straightforward generalization to the n-ary case, *i.e.* the case of n formulæ. We will illustrate the power of the Fixed Point Theorem in the following examples.

Selfsingleton Construction. Using the Fixed Point Theorem, one can build the selfsingleton set in FP. Namely, let A be the formula $z = x$. Then, by the Fixed Point Theorem, there exists a term u such that $\vdash_{\mathsf{FP}} z \in u \longleftrightarrow z = u$. By the proof of the Fixed Point Theorem, u can be defined by $u \stackrel{\Delta}{=} \{z \mid \langle z,t \rangle \in t\}$, where $t \stackrel{\Delta}{=} \{\langle z,y \rangle \mid z = \{w \mid \langle w,y \rangle \in y\}\}$.

The natural question arises as to whether there exist more than one selfsingleton. The answer is positive, since any fixed point operator induces a different one. For instance, in the proof of the Fixed Point Theorem, one can take $u \stackrel{\Delta}{=} \{z \mid \langle z,a,t \rangle \in t\}$ and $t \stackrel{\Delta}{=} \{\langle z,a,y \rangle \mid A[\{w \mid \langle w,a,y \rangle \in y\}/x]\}$, for any a, thus getting a different fixed point operator, which thus yields a different selfsingleton.

Recursive Definitions of Functions and Sets. The Fixed Point Theorem, *FPT*, allows us to define *recursive* sets and functions in FP as in *functional programming* using general recursion, see also [Gir98], Appendix A.1.

Numerals. To define numerals, consider two fixed conventional sets/terms, which we denote by 0 and S, to represent zero and successor. *E.g.* take $\emptyset$ and V. Then apply *FPT* to the formula A_{Nat}:

$$A_{\mathsf{Nat}}[z,x] \stackrel{\Delta}{=} (\forall A.\ (0 \in A \ \wedge \ \forall y \in A.\ < S, y > \in A)) \longrightarrow z \in A) \longrightarrow z \in x.$$

By *FPT* there exists a term Nat such that

$$\vdash_{\mathsf{FP}} z \in \mathsf{Nat} \longleftrightarrow A_{\mathsf{Nat}}[z, \mathsf{Nat}].$$

We have enforced *Induction* on Nat by means of *minimality*. In what follows, we use the standard notation 0,1, ... to denote numerals.

Subtraction. To define the subtraction function, consider the following formula:

$$A_{\mathsf{Subt}}[z, x] \overset{\Delta}{=} (\forall A.$$

$$\forall y_1, y_2, y_3 \in \mathsf{Nat}. \left\{ \begin{array}{c} \langle\langle 0, y_2\rangle, 0\rangle \in A \wedge \\ \langle\langle y_1, 0\rangle, y_1\rangle \in A \wedge \\ \langle\langle y_1, y_2\rangle, y_3\rangle \in A \rightarrow \langle\langle y_1 + 1, y_2 + 1\rangle, y_3\rangle \in A \end{array} \right\} \rightarrow z \in A)$$

$$\longrightarrow z \in x.$$

Then, by the FPT, there exists a term Subt such that
$$\vdash_{\mathsf{FP}} \langle\langle z_1, z_2\rangle, z_3\rangle \in \mathsf{Subt} \longleftrightarrow A_{\mathsf{Subt}}[z, \mathsf{Subt}].$$

Lambda Terms. The set of closed λ-terms Λ^0 is definable starting from three conventional sets, var the variable marker, app, the application marker, and lam the λ-abstraction marker. For simplicity we omit the "minimality" conditions. Consider the following formula A_{Λ^0}:

$$A_{\Lambda^0} \overset{\Delta}{=} (\exists n \in \mathsf{Nat}.\ z = \langle\mathsf{var}, n\rangle) \vee (\exists y_1, y_2 \in x.\ z = \langle\mathsf{app}, y_1, y_2\rangle) \vee$$
$$(\exists y \in x.\ \exists n \in \mathsf{Nat}.\ z = \langle\mathsf{lam}, n, y\rangle).$$

Then, by the FPT, there exists a term Λ^0 such that

$$\vdash_{\mathsf{FP}} z \in A_{\Lambda^0} \longleftrightarrow (\exists n \in \mathsf{Nat}.\ z = \langle\mathsf{var}, n\rangle) \vee (\exists y_1, y_2 \in \Lambda^0.\ z = \langle\mathsf{app}, y_1, y_2\rangle) \vee$$
$$(\exists y \in \Lambda^0.\ \exists n \in \mathsf{Nat}.\ z = \langle\mathsf{lam}, n, y\rangle).$$

Given a term N of λ-calculus we denote by $\widetilde{N}$ its FP representation.

Normal λ-terms. Using Theorem 1 and the set Λ^0 defined above, we can define the relation R_β consisting of the pairs of terms in Λ^0 such that $\langle\widetilde{M}, \widetilde{N}\rangle \in R_\beta$ iff the λ-terms M and N are β-convertible. Again applying Theorem 1 we can now define a predicate Λ^+ such that $x \in \Lambda^+$ is equivalent in FP to $x \in \Lambda^0 \wedge \forall y.y \in \Lambda^+ \rightarrow \exists u.\langle u, \langle app, x, y\rangle\rangle \in R_\beta \wedge u \in \Lambda^+$. Then, there is a normal proof in FP of $\widetilde{M} \in \Lambda^+$ only if M is a *closed strongly normalizing term*.

In Sect. 3, we introduced $\mathsf{FP}^\#$, the extension of FP where *normalizable* deductions are legal. In [HLMS16], a type system was suggested for characterizing the strongly normalizable λ-terms. That construction amounts to carrying out the above argument in $\mathsf{FP}^\#$ instead of FP. A legal deduction in $\mathsf{FP}^\#$ of $\widetilde{M} \in \Lambda^+$ would then amount to *typing* M with the type Λ^+. There is indeed a natural reflection of the metatheoretic normalizability of the $\mathsf{FP}^\#$ deduction of the typing judgement $\widetilde{M} \in \Lambda^+$, and the fact that M is indeed strongly normalizable!

Partial Recursive Functions. The above examples can be generalized. Relying on the FPT, we can define objects as in Functional Programming provided we enforce the "minimality" condition, thereby showing that FP is a *Universal Model of Computation*:

Theorem 2. *For any* partial recursive *function* h *on natural numbers of arity* k, *there exists a formula* P_h *with free variables* $x_1, \ldots, x_k, y$ *such that*

$$h(n_1, \ldots, n_k) \simeq m \iff \vdash_{\mathsf{FP}} P_h[\tilde{n}_1/x_1, \ldots, \tilde{n}_k/x_k, \tilde{m}/y],$$

where $n_1, \ldots n_k, m$ *are natural numbers and* $\tilde{n}_1, \ldots, \tilde{n}_k, \tilde{m}$ *denote the corresponding numerals in* FP.

Notice that if we do not enforce the "minimality" condition in the formulæ used in FPT, then we might end up with a lot of "junk". This might be a feature, whereby one can include also infinite and circular objects, *i.e.* introduce co-inductive datatypes.

5   Encoding FP in a Type Theoretic Logical Framework

An implementation of FP in a computer-assisted proof development environment, such as LF, see [HHP93, PS99, WCPW03, COQ], would take us as close as consistently possible to Cantor's Paradise. However, FP is a formal system whose encoding in standard Logical Frameworks is not straightforward. It is indeed very awkward to capture the side-condition which allows only normal deductions.

In this section, we assume the reader familiar with Logical Frameworks and we present the encoding of FP in LLF$_\mathcal{P}$ [HLMS16], a recent extension of the Edinburgh LF which features *lock types*. This encoding provides, in effect, a paramount example of the power of *locks*.

In LLF$_\mathcal{P}$, a new type constructor is introduced and, as costumary in Constructive Type Theory, it is explained through appropriate Introduction, Elimination, and Equality rules. More precisely, in LLF$_\mathcal{P}$ we define objects using a new constructor of the form $\mathcal{L}^{\mathcal{P}}_{N,\sigma}[M]$, whose type $\mathcal{L}^{\mathcal{P}}_{N,\sigma}[\rho]$ is assigned via the type-checking *introduction rule* ($O \cdot Lock$). Correspondingly, also an *unlock destructor*, $\mathcal{U}^{\mathcal{P}}_{N,\sigma}[M]$, is introduced whose type is given by the *elimination rule* ($O \cdot Top \cdot Unlock$). This latter rule allows for the elimination of the lock-type constructor, under the condition that a specific predicate $\mathcal{P}$ is verified, possibly *externally*, on a judgement. The rules mentioned above are:

$$\frac{\Gamma \vdash_\Sigma M : \rho \quad \Gamma \vdash_\Sigma N : \sigma}{\Gamma \vdash_\Sigma \mathcal{L}^{\mathcal{P}}_{N,\sigma}[M] : \mathcal{L}^{\mathcal{P}}_{N,\sigma}[\rho]} \; (O \cdot Lock) \qquad \frac{\begin{array}{c}\Gamma \vdash_\Sigma M : \mathcal{L}^{\mathcal{P}}_{N,\sigma}[\rho] \\ \mathcal{P}(\Gamma \vdash_\Sigma N : \sigma)\end{array}}{\Gamma \vdash_\Sigma \mathcal{U}^{\mathcal{P}}_{N,\sigma}[M] : \rho} \; (O \cdot Top \cdot Unlock)$$

The *equality rule* for lock types amounts to a new form of reduction called *lock reduction* ($\mathcal{L}$-reduction), $\mathcal{U}^{\mathcal{P}}_{N,\sigma}[\mathcal{L}^{\mathcal{P}}_{N,\sigma}[M]] \to_{\mathcal{L}} M$, which allows for the removing of a *lock*, in the presence of an *unlock* with the same superscripts and subscripts. The $\mathcal{L}$-reduction combines with standard β-reduction into $\beta\mathcal{L}$-reduction.

Capitalizing on the monadic nature of the lock constructor [HLMS16], one can use locked terms without necessarily establishing the predicate, provided an *outermost* lock is present. This increases the expressivity of the system, and allows for reasoning under the assumption that the verification is successful, as well as for postponing and reducing the number of verifications. The rules which make all this work are:

$$\frac{\Gamma, x{:}\tau \vdash_{\Sigma} \mathcal{L}^{\mathcal{P}}_{S,\sigma}[\rho] : \mathsf{type} \quad \Gamma \vdash_{\Sigma} N : \mathcal{L}^{\mathcal{P}}_{S',\sigma'}[\tau] \quad \sigma =_{\beta\mathcal{L}} \sigma' \quad S =_{\beta\mathcal{L}} S'}{\Gamma \vdash_{\Sigma} \mathcal{L}^{\mathcal{P}}_{S,\sigma}[\rho[\mathcal{U}^{\mathcal{P}}_{S',\sigma'}[N]/x]] : \mathsf{type}} \; (F\text{-}Guarded\text{-}Unlock)$$

$$\frac{\Gamma, x{:}\tau \vdash_{\Sigma} \mathcal{L}^{\mathcal{P}}_{S,\sigma}[M] : \mathcal{L}^{\mathcal{P}}_{S,\sigma}[\rho] \quad \Gamma \vdash_{\Sigma} N : \mathcal{L}^{\mathcal{P}}_{S',\sigma'}[\tau] \quad \sigma =_{\beta\mathcal{L}} \sigma' \quad S =_{\beta\mathcal{L}} S'}{\Gamma \vdash_{\Sigma} \mathcal{L}^{\mathcal{P}}_{S,\sigma}[M[\mathcal{U}^{\mathcal{P}}_{S',\sigma'}[N]/x]] : \mathcal{L}^{\mathcal{P}}_{S,\sigma}[\rho[\mathcal{U}^{\mathcal{P}}_{S',\sigma'}[N]/x]]} \; (O\text{-}Guarded\text{-}Unlock)$$

The second rule is the counterpart of the elimination rule for monads, once we realize that the standard destructor of monads $let_{T_{\mathcal{P}(\Gamma \vdash S:\sigma)}} x = A \; in \; N$ can be replaced in this setting by $N[\mathcal{U}^{\mathcal{P}}_{S,\sigma}[A]/x]$. This is the case since the $\mathcal{L}^{\mathcal{P}}_{S,\sigma}[\cdot]$-monad satisfies the property $let_{T_{\mathcal{P}}} x = M \; in \; N \to N$ if $x \notin \mathsf{Fv}(N)$, provided x occurs *guarded* in N, *i.e.* within subterms of the appropriate lock-type. The first rule takes care of elimination at the level of types.

The system LLF$_{\mathcal{P}}$ can smoothly enforce the *global* normalization constraint of FP *locally* by enforcing a suitable lock on the proof-object. The crucial step is the definition of the predicate involved in the lock, because it needs to be *well-behaved*, see [HLMS16], Definition 2.1. Namely it must be closed under substitution as well as signature and context extension, and this is problematic when dealing with open terms. To overcome these difficulties we need to introduce the notion of *skeleton* of a term in a given signature Σ:

Definition 5. *Given a signature Σ, let Λ_{Σ} (respectively Λ^{o}_{Σ}) be the set of LLF$_{\mathcal{P}}$ terms (respectively closed LLF$_{\mathcal{P}}$ terms) definable using constants from Σ. A term M has a skeleton in Λ_{Σ} if there exists a context $N[\,,\ldots,\,] \in \Lambda_{\Sigma}$ with n holes such that $M \equiv N[M_1, \ldots, M_n]$ for suitable terms $M_1, \ldots, M_n$.*

Furthermore we need to introduce two basic judgements to deal with variables. Namely we make the distinction between *generic* judgements, which cannot be directly utilized in arguments, but which can be assumed, and *apodictic* judgements, which are directly involved in proof rules. In order to make use of generic judgements, one has to downgrade them to an apodictic one, and this is achieved by a suitable coercion function.

The encoding in LLF$_{\mathcal{P}}$ of the system of Fitch as presented in Sect. 2.1 is given in the following definition, where (due to lack of space) we focus on the crucial connectives and rules of FP:

Definition 6 (LLF$_{\mathcal{P}}$ signature Σ_{FP} for Fitch Prawitz Set Theory FP). *The following constants are introduced:*

o	: Type	ι :	Type
T	: o -> Type	δ :	ΠA:o.(V(A) -> T(A))

```
V    : o -> Type                    ⊃ : o -> o -> o              false : o
lam : (ι -> o)-> ι                  ε : ι -> ι -> o              not: o -> o
⊃_intro: ΠA,B:o.(V(A) -> T(B)) -> (T(A ⊃B))
⊃_elim : ΠA,B:o.Πx:T(A).Πy:T(A⊃B) -> L^Fitch_⟨x,y⟩,T(A)×T(A⊃B)[T(B)]
λ_intro : ΠA:ι ->o.Πt:ι.T(A t) -> T(ε t (lam A))
λ_elim : ΠA:ι ->o.Πt:ι.T(ε t (lam A))->T(A t)
bot : ΠA:o.(V(not A) -> T(false)) -> T(A)
```

where o *is the type of propositions,* ⊃ *is the implication connective,* ε *is the "membership" predicate,* not *is the negation,* lam *is the "abstraction" operator for building "sets",* T *is the apodictic judgement,* V *is the generic judgement,* δ *is the coercion function, and* ⟨x, y⟩ *denotes the encoding of pairs, whose type is denoted by* σ×τ, *e.g.* λu:σ → τ → ρ. u x y : (σ → τ → ρ) → ρ. *The predicate in the lock is defined as follows:* Fitch(Γ ⊢_{Σ_{FP}} ⟨x, y⟩ : T(A)×T(A ⊃ B)) *holds iff* x *and* y *have skeletons in* Λ_{Σ_{FP}}, *all the holes of which have either type* o *or are guarded by a* δ, *and hence have type* V(A), *and, moreover, the proof derived by combining the skeletons of* x *and* y *is normal in the natural sense.*

The notion of *normal* deduction is the standard notion of Definition 4. The predicate Fitch is well-behaved because it considers terms only up-to holes in the skeleton, which can have type o or are generic judgements. Adequacy for this signature can be achieved in the format of [HLLMS13]:

Theorem 3 (Adequacy for FP). *If* $A_1, \ldots, A_n$ *are the atomic formulæ occurring in* $B_1, \ldots, B_m, A$, *then* $B_1 \ldots B_m \vdash_{\mathsf{FP}} A$ *iff there exists a normalizable* M *such that* $A_1{:}o, \ldots, A_n{:}o, \; x_1{:}V(B_1), \ldots, x_m{:}V(B_m) \vdash_{\Sigma_{\mathsf{FP}}} M{:}T(A)$ *(where* A, *and* B_i *represent the encodings of, respectively,* A *and* B_i *in* $\mathsf{LLF}_{\mathcal{P}}$, *for* $1 \le i \le m$).

If in the definition of the well-behaved predicate Fitch we enforce that the deduction is normalizable, we obtain a signature for FP#. The predicate would then be only semi-decidable.

In the spirit of $\mathsf{LLF}_{\mathcal{P}}$, we do not specify how to enforce the verification of the constraint in the locks. This is left for optimization. The idea underpinning $\mathsf{LLF}_{\mathcal{P}}$ is to specify neatly the interface that this, possibly external, module needs to satisfy in order to be safely plugged in the Logical Framework.

6   The Extensional Quotient of FP

In this section, we relate Fitch-Prawitz Set Theory, FP, to the Theory of Hyperuniverses, TH. Namely, we show that the *extensional quotient* of the closed term model of a suitable extension of FP, called FP+, is a hyperuniverse.

6.1   The Theory of Hyperuniverses TH

The naïve Comprehension Principle can be consistently approximated, by restricting the class of admissible formulæ. In [FH89, FH89a], the *Generalized Positive Comprehension Scheme* has been introduced, namely:

Axiom 1 (Generalized Positive Comprehension Scheme (GPC)). $\{x \mid A\}$ *is a set, if* A *is a* Generalized Positive Formula, *where* Generalized Positive Formulæ (GPF) *are the smallest class of formulæ*

- *including* $u \in t$, $u = t$;
- *closed under the logical connectives* $\wedge, \vee$;
- *closed under the quantifiers* $\forall x, \exists x, \forall x \in y, \exists x \in y$, *where* $\forall x \in y.A$ ($\exists x \in y.A$) *is an abbreviation for* $\forall x.(x \in y \to A)$ ($\exists x.(x \in y \to A)$);
- *closed under the formula* $\forall x.(B \to A)$, *where* A *is a generalized positive formula and* B *is any formula such that* $\mathsf{Fv}(B) \subseteq \{x\}$.

In [FH89,FH89a], the Theory of Hyperuniverses TH, namely $\mathsf{GPC} +$ Extensionality, was introduced and proved consistent, together with many extensions which include arbitrary models of Zermelo-Frænkel Set Theory.

The theory TH is a rather expressive Set Theory, in which one can show the existence of many large sets, *e.g.*:

- the universe V, the empty set $\emptyset$;
- $\langle x, y \rangle$, $\{t\}$, $\{t, u\}$, $t \cup u$, $t \cap u$, $t \times u$, $t \circ u$, $\bigcup t$, $\bigcap t$, $\mathsf{dom}(t)$, $\mathsf{cod}(t)$, t^{-1}, $\mathcal{P}(t)$, $\diamond(t) = \{x \mid t \cap x \neq \emptyset\}$, $\widehat{t}(u) = \{z \mid \exists w \in u. \langle w, z \rangle \in t\}$, $\mathcal{F}(t) = \{y \mid t \in y\}$, $t_1 \star t_2 = \{\langle u, v, w \rangle \mid \langle u, v \rangle \in t_1 \wedge \langle u, w \rangle \in t_2\}$;
- the equality $\Delta \stackrel{\Delta}{=} \{\langle x, y \rangle | x = y\}$, the membership relation $\in \stackrel{\Delta}{=} \{\langle x, y \rangle | x \in y\}$, the graph of the projection functions π_1, π_2, $\pi_1 \stackrel{\Delta}{=} \{z \mid \exists x, y.\ z = \langle \langle x, y \rangle, x \rangle\}$, the inclusion relation $\subseteq \stackrel{\Delta}{=} \{z \mid \exists x, y.\ (z = \langle x, y \rangle \wedge \forall w.\ y \in w \longrightarrow x \in w)\}$, the graph of the singleton function $\lambda x.\{x\} \stackrel{\Delta}{=} \{z \mid z = \langle x, \{x\} \rangle\}$.

We call *hyperuniverses* the set-theoretic structures which are models of TH, following the terminology of [FH89,FH89a], where many such structures were defined using topological and categorical tools.

6.2   The Extensional Quotient of the Fitch-Prawitz Coalgebra

In this section we study the *extensional quotient*, or *extensional collapse*, of the Fitch-Prawitz coalgebra of closed terms. In particular, we show that a suitable extension of FP, called FP^+, yields an extensional collapse which is (strongly) extensional, and satisfies the GPC scheme, *i.e.* it is a hyperuniverse. This result establishes a connection between FP and TH. For basic definitions and results on coalgebras, we refer to [JR11]. The theory FP^+ is the extension of FP with the following ω-rule:

$$\text{(Bounded-}\omega) \quad \frac{A[w/x] \text{ for all closed } w \text{ s.t. } B[w/x], \ \mathsf{Fv}(B) \subseteq \{x\}}{\forall x.(B[w/x] \to A)}$$

Even if the (Bounded-ω)-rule has infinitely many premises, once it is taken as an introduction rule, the notions of quasi-deduction and deduction for FP can be naturally extended to FP^+. Consistency of FP^+ is proved then as for FP.

Notice that in our setting the conclusion of the (Bounded-ω)-rule really amounts to a restricted quantification w.r.t. a closed term. Given that $\mathsf{Fv}(B) \subseteq \{x\}$, the formula $\forall x.(B[w/x] \rightarrow A)$ amounts to $\forall x \in \{z \mid B[z]\}.A$, where $\{z \mid B[z]\}$ is a closed term. Notice that the *Induction Rule* is subsumed by the (Bounded-ω)-rule. Before defining the coalgebra of closed FP^+-terms, we recall the notion of *set-theoretic structure*:

Definition 7 (Set-theoretic Structure). *A set-theoretic structure* $(X, \in)$ *is a first-order structure X together with a binary predicate $\in$ on $X \times X$, denoting the membership relation.*

Notice that set-theoretic structures are coalgebras for the powerset functor $\mathcal{P}(\ )$ on the category *Set*. The following definition will be useful in the sequel.

Definition 8 ((Strongly) Extensional Coalgebra)

– *A $\mathcal{P}(\ )$-coalgebra (X, f_X) is extensional if f is injective.*
– *A $\mathcal{P}(\ )$-coalgebra (X, f_X) is strongly extensional if the unique coalgebra morphism from (X, f_X) into the final coalgebra is injective.*

Clearly, strong extensionality implies extensionality.

The provable instances of the $\in$-relation on the set of closed FP^+-terms, $\mathcal{T}^0$, naturally induce a coalgebra structure for the powerset functor.

Definition 9 (Fitch-Prawitz Coalgebra). *Let $f_{\mathcal{T}^0} : \mathcal{T}^0 \longrightarrow \mathcal{P}(\mathcal{T}^0)$ be the $\mathcal{P}(\ )$-coalgebra defined by $f_{\mathcal{T}^0}(t) = \{s \mid \vdash_{\mathsf{FP}^+} s \in t\}$, where $\mathcal{P}(\ )$ denotes the standard powerset functor on the category* Set.

Given a $\mathcal{P}(\ )$-coalgebra (X, f_X), there is a unique mapping into the *final coalgebra*, $g : (X, f_X) \rightarrow (\Omega, f_\Omega)$, where (Ω, f_Ω) denotes the final coalgebra. This latter is clearly extensional, actually it is strongly extensional. The image via g of (X, f_X) into the final coalgebra (Ω, f_Ω) is called the *extensional quotient* of (X, f_X). The extensional quotient is given by the equivalence classes under bisimilarity. In FP^+ (actually already in FP), the notion of bisimilarity can be defined in the theory itself.

Definition 10 (Bisimilarity)

– *Let A_{Bis} be the FP^+ formula with free variable x defined by*
$$A_{\mathsf{Bis}} \triangleq \forall t, t' \ (\langle t, t' \rangle \in x \longrightarrow \forall s(s \in t \longrightarrow \exists s'(s' \in t' \wedge \langle s, s' \rangle \in x)) \wedge \forall s'(s' \in t' \longrightarrow \exists s.(s \in t \wedge \langle s, s' \rangle \in x))).$$

A bisimulation is a binary relation R such that $\vdash_{\mathsf{FP}^+} A_{\mathsf{Bis}}[R/x]$.
– *The bisimilarity relation $\sim$ is defined by the following FP^+-term:*

$$\sim \ \triangleq \{\langle t, t' \rangle \mid \exists R. \ (\langle t, t' \rangle \in R \ \wedge \ A_{\mathsf{Bis}}[R/x])\}.$$

In the following lemma we show that bisimilarity is a maximal bisimulation equivalence:

Lemma 1. *(a) Bisimilarity is an equivalence on* $\mathsf{FP^+}$.
(b) $\vdash_{\mathsf{FP+}} t \sim t' \longleftrightarrow \forall s(s \in t \longrightarrow \exists s'(s' \in t' \wedge s \sim s')) \wedge$
$$\forall s'(s' \in t' \longrightarrow \exists s.(s \in t \wedge s \sim s')).$$

Proof. (a) Straightforward.
(b) ($\Rightarrow$) This amounts to $\vdash_{\mathsf{FP+}} A_{\mathsf{Bis}}[\sim /x]$, which can be easily proved.
($\Leftarrow$) This follows by defining $R \stackrel{\Delta}{=} \{(t, t') \mid \forall s(s \in t \longrightarrow \exists s'(s' \in t' \wedge s \sim s')) \wedge \forall s'(s' \in t' \longrightarrow \exists s.(s \in t \wedge s \sim s'))\}$ and $R' \stackrel{\Delta}{=} R \cup \sim$, and proving $\vdash_{\mathsf{FP+}} A_{\mathsf{Bis}}[R'/x]$. $\qquad\square$

We can now quotient the $\mathsf{FP^+}$-coalgebra by the bisimilarity $\sim$.

Definition 11 ($\sim$-quotient of the $\mathsf{FP^+}$-coalgebra). *Let* $\mathcal{M} = \mathcal{T}^0 / \sim$ *be the quotient of* $\mathcal{T}^0$ *by the bisimilarity* $\sim$ *on* $\mathsf{FP^+}$, *i.e., for any* $t \in \mathcal{T}^0$, *we define* $\underline{t} \in \mathcal{M}$ *by* $\underline{t} \stackrel{\Delta}{=} \{t' \mid \vdash_{\mathsf{FP+}} t \sim t'\}$.
$\mathcal{M}$ *can be endowed with a structure of* $\mathcal{P}(\ )$-*coalgebra as follows. Let* $f_{\mathcal{M}} : \mathcal{M} \to \mathcal{P}(\mathcal{M})$ *be defined by* $f_{\mathcal{M}}(\underline{t}) = \{\underline{s} \mid \vdash_{\mathsf{FP+}} s \in t\}$. *Then the projection* $\pi : \mathcal{T}^0 \to \mathcal{M}$, *defined by* $\pi(t) = \underline{t}$, *is a coalgebra-morphism from* $(\mathcal{T}^0, f_{\mathcal{T}^0})$ *to* $(\mathcal{M}, f_{\mathcal{M}})$, *i.e.*

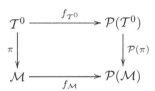

Finally we prove strong extensionality of $\mathcal{M}$ w.r.t. $\mathsf{FP^+}$, notice the role of the (Bounded-ω)-rule.

Proposition 3. *The quotient* $\mathcal{M}$ *is extensional, i.e. for all* $\underline{t}, \underline{t'} \in \mathcal{M}$,

$$\underline{t} = \underline{t'} \iff f_{\mathcal{M}}(\underline{t}) = f_{\mathcal{M}}(\underline{t'}).$$

Proof. If $f_{\mathcal{M}}(\underline{t}) = f_{\mathcal{M}}(\underline{t'})$, i.e. $\{\underline{s} \mid \vdash_{\mathsf{FP+}} s \in t\} = \{\underline{s'} \mid \vdash_{\mathsf{FP+}} s' \in t'\}$, then for all s, $(\vdash_{\mathsf{FP+}} s \in t \implies \exists s' \ (\vdash_{\mathsf{FP+}} s' \in t' \wedge \vdash_{\mathsf{FP+}} s \sim s'))$, and vice versa, hence, for all s, $(\vdash_{\mathsf{FP+}} s \in t \implies \vdash_{\mathsf{FP+}} \exists s' \ (s' \in t' \wedge \vdash_{\mathsf{FP+}} s \sim s'))$, and vice versa. Therefore, by applying the bounded-ω-rule, we get
$\vdash_{\mathsf{FP+}} \forall s(s \in t \longrightarrow \exists s'(s' \in t' \wedge s \sim s')) \wedge \forall s'(s' \in t' \longrightarrow \exists s.(s \in t \wedge s \sim s'))$,
hence by Lemma 1, $\vdash_{\mathsf{FP+}} t \sim t'$, i.e. $\underline{t} = \underline{t'}$. $\qquad\square$

Corollary 1. *The quotient* $\mathcal{M}$ *is strongly extensional.*

We prove now that $\mathcal{M}$ satisfies the Generalized Positive Comprehension Scheme, namely it is a hyperuniverse. We start with the following definition, which actually defines an *inner model* of TH in $\mathsf{FP^\#}$:

Definition 12. *Let A be a formula with constants in $\mathcal{M}$. We define a corresponding formula $\widehat{A}$ by induction on A as follows:*

$$A \overset{\triangle}{=} \bot \implies \widehat{A} \overset{\triangle}{=} \bot$$
$$A \overset{\triangle}{=} \underline{u} \in \underline{t} \implies \widehat{A} \overset{\triangle}{=} \exists u'.u' \sim u \wedge u' \in t$$
$$A \overset{\triangle}{=} \underline{u} = \underline{t} \implies \widehat{A} \overset{\triangle}{=} u \sim t$$
$$A \overset{\triangle}{=} \neg A_1 \implies \widehat{A} \overset{\triangle}{=} \neg \widehat{A}_1$$

$$A \overset{\triangle}{=} A_1 \wedge A_2 \implies \widehat{A} \overset{\triangle}{=} \widehat{A}_1 \wedge \widehat{A}_2$$
$$A \overset{\triangle}{=} A_1 \vee A_2 \implies \widehat{A} \overset{\triangle}{=} \widehat{A}_1 \vee \widehat{A}_2$$
$$A \overset{\triangle}{=} A_1 \to A_2 \implies \widehat{A} \overset{\triangle}{=} \widehat{A}_1 \to \widehat{A}_2$$
$$A \overset{\triangle}{=} \forall x.A_1 \implies \widehat{A} \overset{\triangle}{=} \forall x.\widehat{A}_1$$
$$A \overset{\triangle}{=} \exists x.A_1 \implies \widehat{A} \overset{\triangle}{=} \exists x.\widehat{A}_1$$

Lemma 2. *For all A, u, t, x, $\widehat{A[t/x]} \equiv \widehat{A}[t/x]$ and $\widehat{u[t/x]} \equiv u[t/x]$.*

The following lemma, whose proof which uses (Bounded-ω-rule), is crucial.

Lemma 3. *For all GPF A with free variables $x_1, \ldots, x_n$, for all $t_1, \ldots, t_m \in T^0$, $m \leq n$, we have: $\mathcal{M} \models A[t_1/x_1, \ldots, t_m/x_m] \iff \vdash_{\mathsf{FP+}} \widehat{A}[t_1/x_1, \ldots, t_m/x_m]$.*

Proof. By induction on A, using Lemma 2, and the (Bounded-ω)-rule for dealing with the restricted $\forall$-case.
Base cases. $A \overset{\triangle}{=} \underline{u} = \underline{v}$. Let $\mathcal{M} \models (\underline{u} = \underline{v})[t/x]$, i.e., using Lemma 2, this holds if and only if $\mathcal{M} \models (u[t/x] = v[t/x])$, and this amounts to $\vdash_{\mathsf{FP+}} u[t/x] \sim v[t/x]$.
$A \overset{\triangle}{=} \underline{u} \in \underline{v}$. Let $\mathcal{M} \models (\underline{u} \in \underline{v})[t/x]$, i.e., using Lemma 2, this amounts to $\vdash_{\mathsf{FP+}} \exists u' (u' \sim u[t/x] \wedge u' \in v[t/x])$.
Induction step. We only deal with two cases: the remaining are similar.
$A \overset{\triangle}{=} A_1 \wedge A_2$. Let $\mathcal{M} \models (A_1 \wedge A_2)[t/x]$, then $\mathcal{M} \models A_1[t/x]$ and $\mathcal{M} \models A_2[t/x]$. By induction hypothesis, $\vdash_{\mathsf{FP+}} \widehat{A}_1[t/x]$ and $\vdash_{\mathsf{FP+}} \widehat{A}_2[t/x]$, hence $\vdash_{\mathsf{FP+}} (\widehat{A}_1 \wedge \widehat{A}_2)[t/x]$. The converse implication follows from the standard definition of the interpretation of $\wedge$ in a first-order structure.
$A \overset{\triangle}{=} \forall y \in z.A_1$. Unrestricted quantification is clearly a special case of this one, and by our earlier remark the case where $A \overset{\triangle}{=} \forall y.(B \to A_1)$, with $\mathsf{Fv}(B) \subseteq \{y\}$, amounts to restricted quantification. So if $\mathcal{M} \models \forall y \in z. A_1[t/x, u/z]$ then for all t' such that $\mathcal{M} \models t' \in u$, we have that $\mathcal{M} \models A_1[t/x, u/z, t'/y]$. Then by induction hypothesis we have that for all t and for all t', such that $\vdash_{\mathsf{FP+}} \exists y'.y' \sim t' \wedge y' \in u$ we have that $\vdash_{\mathsf{FP+}} \widehat{A}[t/x, u/z, t'/y]$, hence applying the (Bounded-ω)-rule, we have that $\vdash_{\mathsf{FP+}} \forall y.\exists y'.y' \sim u \wedge y' \in z \to \widehat{A}[t/x, u/z]$. The reverse implication follows from the interpretation of first-order formulæ in a structure. □

Now we are in the position to establish the main theorem of this section.

Theorem 4 ($\mathcal{M}$ satisfies GPC). *For any formula A in GPF with free variable x, $\mathcal{M} \models \underline{t} \in \underline{v} \iff \mathcal{M} \models A[\underline{t}/x]$, where $\underline{v} \overset{\triangle}{=} \{x \mid \widehat{A}\}$. Hence $\mathcal{M}$ is a hyperuniverse.*

Proof. ($\Rightarrow$) From $\mathcal{M} \models \underline{t} \in \{x \mid \widehat{A}\}$ we have $\vdash_{\mathsf{FP+}} \exists t'.t' \sim t \wedge t' \in \{x \mid \widehat{A}\}$. Hence $\vdash_{\mathsf{FP+}} \exists t'.t' \sim t \wedge \widehat{A}[t'/x]$, which, by Lemma 3, implies $\mathcal{M} \models A[t'/x]$, for $t' \sim t$. Hence $\mathcal{M} \models A[\underline{t}/x]$. ($\Leftarrow$) By Lemma 3, from $\mathcal{M} \models A[\underline{t}/x]$ it follows $\vdash_{\mathsf{FP+}} \widehat{A}[t/x]$. Hence $\vdash_{\mathsf{FP+}} t \in \{x \mid \widehat{A}\}$, which implies $\mathcal{M} \models \underline{t} \in \{x \mid \widehat{A}\}$. □

7   FP as a Logical Framework

FP is essentially Naïve Set-Theory, probably the most natural and straightforward of all Logical Frameworks, which we are familiar with since our schooldays. The reason for considering FP is twofold. The first reason is pragmatic, i.e., to explore how to use it for *fast and loose formal reasoning* on general recursion and datatypes, *i.e.*, as a proper Logical Framework (we borrow from [DHJG06] this felicitous expression). The second reason is foundational. FP allows for a fine-tuned analysis of paradoxes arising from *diagonal arguments*.

Recently, in the formal methods community, there has been growing interest in logical systems which support convenient and fast, but logically unsound or even invalid features and heuristics [Cap05, CSW14, DHJG06]. Those arise especially in program transformation and program synthesis in non-terminating functional languages when dealing with general recursion. Albeit invalid, these methods are nonetheless extremely useful pragmatically. Furthermore, they can be justified. But this can be done only at the end, once there is a good reason for going through the often daunting overhead of checking all the totality and predicativity preconditions [DHJG06, CSW14]. Oleg Kiselyov has remarked that the principled but cautious approach of Coq and Agda is akin to pessimistic concurrency: assuming that shared resources are likely to be contended and hence have to be proactively protected with (often numerous) locks. An alternative is optimistic concurrency, proceeding as if there were no contention – checking for consistency only at the end of a transaction. Optimistic concurrency is akin to *loose and fast programming* and the approach to termination checking, which can be carried out in Twelf and LF [Twelf, WN13].

Using FP as a Logical Framework goes precisely in the direction of *optimistic reasoning*, actually at two different levels. The first is that of using Lock types in the implementation to check the normalizability of deductions. Locks do not amount merely to the postponement of the checks. They rather allow for aggregating and simplifying the checks, so that the final check can be done possibly at some other level, rather than delegated to the metalanguage as in Coq or Agda.

Somewhat more ambitious, and not completely explored yet, is the *pragmatic* value of using a *paraconsistent* system. It was De Bruijn the founding author of AUTOMATH, himself, who first raised the challenging and provocative question: *do we really need a terminating metalanguage?* Of course if we use Scotus rule, then our reasoning is empty. But otherwise we still have plenty of useful arguments to carry out which can make visible *truly* false or missing requirements. So, even paraconsistent systems can increase our confidence in the outcome. After all, absolute certainty cannot be achieved, even with terminating systems.

A sharper understanding of which statements have a paraconsistent cognate is still missing. These arise usually in connection with *diagonal arguments*. Reasoning with small sets or, as we have shown, *generalized positive formulæ* does not lead to *paraconsistencies*. But there are probably many more classes of sentences, for instance in connection with the foundations of Category Theory.

8   Conclusions and Final Remarks

We have discussed the Naïve Set Theory of Fitch-Prawitz [Fit52, Pra06], FP, which is consistent by design, but nevertheless is expressive enough to define all partial recursive functions. Furthermore we have related it to the Theory of Hyperuniverses [FH89a, FHL94]. Foundationally, FP allows for a deeper understanding of the limitations implied by set theoretic paradoxes. In particular, we have that even if $\vdash_{\mathsf{FP+}} u \notin v$, then not necessarily $\mathcal{M} \models \underline{u} \notin \underline{v}$. This hints to the fact that, while retaining *Extensionality*, we cannot hope to go significantly beyond GPC in approximating the naïve Comprehension Principle, *e.g.* to include some *negative formulæ*. Pragmatically, FP offers a natural mathematical framework where to develop "optimistically" [CSW14, DHJG06] important branches of Mathematics from Real Numbers [Fit50] to Category Theory. We have encoded FP in the type-theoretic Logical Framework $\mathsf{LLF}_{\mathcal{P}}$, [HLMS16], which is currently under implementation, thereby providing what we called a "Computer Assisted Cantor's Paradise". Further lines of research on FP are the following.

Alternate Inner Models. In Sect. 6.2 we have proved that in FP^+ we can define an *Inner Model* for TH, namely, the model $\mathcal{M}$. But there are also *inner models* which have more than one *selfsingleton* and hence satisfy only Extensionality. E.g., the extensional quotient w.r.t. a bisimulation, which is an equivalence but does not equate the two selfsingletons defined in Subsect. 4.1, would be an example of a hyperuniverse which is not strongly extensional.

Propositions as Types for FP. So far we have based FP on *classical logic*. But we can replace the $\bot$-rule by its intuitionistic version, namely *ex falso quodlibet*, to get an intuitionistic version of FP. One can then extend the λ-calculus language of proofs with new constructs to account for the rules concerning $\in$ and λ in FP. A simple solution is to extend a typed λ-calculus for intuitionistic proofs with a *1-ple* constructor $< M >$ to account for λI), and correspondingly introduce a π elimination constructor to account for λE):

$$\frac{\Gamma \vdash_{\mathsf{FP}} M : P(t)}{\Gamma \vdash_{\mathsf{FP}} < M > : t \in \lambda x.P(x)} \; \lambda\mathsf{Intro} \qquad \frac{\Gamma \vdash_{\mathsf{FP}} N : t \in \lambda x.P(x)}{\Gamma \vdash_{\mathsf{FP}} \pi(N) : P(t)} \; \lambda\mathsf{Elim}$$

The two constructors are related by the obvious reduction $\pi(\langle N \rangle) \longrightarrow N$. We can then prove that all proof terms corresponding to a contraction-free intuitionistic deduction are *normalizing*, thereby recovering Grishin's result. Notice that in normal deductions, where introduction constructs appear outermost w.r.t. elimination constructs, one can apply π only to variables, *i.e. generic* proof terms.

Escaping Gödel's Second Incompleteness Theorem. Since FP is a *cut free* Set Theory, *i.e.* it is *consistent by design*, within FP one can prove that there is a model of FP. This does not contradict Gödel's second Incompleteness Theorem, since FP is not closed under *modus ponens* which is the, so-called, Hilbert-Bernays third condition necessary for Gödel's result to go through.

FP *and Higher-Order Logics.* The Theory FP, being a *theory of sets*, subsumes higher order logics for any order. For instance $\forall P.Q[P]$ can be expressed as $\forall x.\ Pred(x) \to Q[x]$, for a suitable definition of *Pred*.

The Ubiquitous Hyperuniverse. $\mathcal{N}_\omega(\emptyset)$. In [FH89a,FHL94], many hyperuniverses have been introduced. One of these, $\mathcal{N}_\omega(\emptyset)$, arises in many conceptually independent contexts, nicely described by Abramsky in [Abr11]. Namely, $\mathcal{N}_\omega(\emptyset)$ is *Cantor-1* space, the union of Cantor's space (obtained removing the middle thirds of the unit interval) with the centres of the removed intervals. $\mathcal{N}_\omega(\emptyset)$ is the unique solution of the metric domain equation $X \cong \mathcal{P}_{cl}(X_{\frac{1}{2}})$ in the category of *complete metric spaces.* $\mathcal{N}_\omega(\emptyset)$ is the space of *maximal* points of the solution in Plotkin's category of *SFP domains* of the domain equation $X \cong \mathcal{P}_P(X_\perp) \oplus_\perp 1$, see [ABH03]. $\mathcal{N}_\omega(\emptyset)$ is the free *Stone modal Algebra* over 0 generators. By Theorem 4 we can add a new item to the list, namely: $\mathcal{N}_\omega(\emptyset)$ is the *extensional quotient* of Fitch-Prawitz coalgebra.

Acknowledgments. The authors are grateful to the anonymous referees, and to Oleg Kiselyov, for many useful remarks and intriguing questions.

References

[ABH03] Alessi, F., Baldan, P., Honsell, F.: A category of compositional domain-models for separable Stone spaces. Theor. Comput. Sci. **2901**, 599–635 (2003)

[Abr11] Abramsky, S.: A Cook's Tour of the Finitary Non-Well-Founded Sets. CoRR, abs/1111.7148 (2011). http://arXiv.org/abs/1111.7148

[Cap05] Capretta, V.: General recursion via coinductive types. Log. Meth. Comput. Sci. **1**(2), 1–18 (2005)

[CSW14] Casinghino, C., Sjöberg, V., Weirich, S.: Combining proofs and programs in a dependently typed language. In: POPL 2014, pp. 33–45. ACM (2014)

[COQ] Development Team: Assistant, The Coq Proof Documentation, system download. http://coq.inria.fr/

[DHJG06] Danielsson, N.A., Hughes, J., Jansson, P., Gibbons, J.: Fast and loose reasoning is morally correct. In: POPL 2006, pp. 206–217. ACM (2006)

[FH89] Forti, M., Hinnion, R.: The consistency problem for positive comprehension principles. J. Symb. Log. **54**, 1401–1418 (1989)

[FH89a] Forti, M., Honsell, F.: Models of self-descriptive set theories. In: Colombini, F., Marino, A., Modica, L., Spagnolo, S. (eds.) Partial Differential Equations and the Calculus of Variations. Birkhäuser, Boston (1989). Dedicated to Ennio De Giorgi on his sixtieth birthday

[FHL94] Forti, M., Honsell, F., Lenisa, M.: Processes and hyperuniverses. In: Prívara, I., Rovan, B., Ruzička, P. (eds.) MFCS 1994. LNCS, vol. 841, pp. 352–363. Springer, Heidelberg (1994). doi:10.1007/3-540-58338-6_82

[FH96] Forti, M., Honsell, F.: A general construction of hyperuniverses. Theor. Comput. Sci. **156**(1&2), 203–215 (1996)

[Fit50] Fitch, F.B.: A demonstrably consistent mathematics. J. Symb. Log. **15**(1), 17–24 (1950)

[Fit52]   Fitch, F.B.: Symbolic Logic - An Introduction. The Ronald Press, New York (1952)

[Gir98]   Girard, J.-Y.: Light linear logic. Inf. Comput. **143**(2), 175–204 (1998). doi:10.1006/inco.1998.2700

[Gri82]   Grishin, V.N.: Predicate and set-theoretic calculi based on logics without contractions. Math. USSR Izv. **18**, 41–59 (1982)

[HHP93]   Harper, R., Honsell, F., Plotkin, G.: A framework for defining logics. J. ACM (JACM) **40**(1), 143–184 (1993). ACM

[HLLMS13] Honsell, F., Lenisa, M., Liquori, L., Maksimovic, P., Scagnetto, I.: An open logical framework. JLC **26**(1), 293–335 (2016). (First pub. in 2013)

[HLMS16] Honsell, F., Liquori, L., Maksimovic, P., Scagnetto, I.: A logical framework for modeling external evidence, side conditions, and proof irrelevance using monads. In: LMCS (2016, to appear)

[JR11]   Jacobs, B., Rutten, J.: An introduction to (co)algebras and (co)induction. In: Sangiorgi, D., Rutten, J. (eds.) Advanced Topics in Bisimulation and Coinduction, pp. 38–99. Cambridge University Press, Cambridge (2011)

[PS99]   Pfenning, F., Schürmann, C.: System description: twelf—a meta-logical framework. In: Pfenning, F., Schürmann, C. (eds.) CADE 1999. LNCS (LNAI), vol. 1632, pp. 202–206. Springer, Heidelberg (1999). doi:10.1007/3-540-48660-7_14

[Pra06]   Prawitz, D.: Natural Deduction – A proof-theoretical Study. Dover Publications, New York (2006)

[Twelf]   The Twelf Project. http://twelf.org/wiki/Totality_assertion

[WN13]   Wang, Y., Nadathur, G.: Towards extracting explicit proofs from totality checking in twelf. In: LFMTP 2013, pp. 55–66. ACM (2013)

[WCPW03] Watkins, K., Cervesato, I., Pfenning, F., Walker, D.: A concurrent logical framework: the propositional fragment. In: Berardi, S., Coppo, M., Damiani, F. (eds.) TYPES 2003. LNCS, vol. 3085, pp. 355–377. Springer, Heidelberg (2004). doi:10.1007/978-3-540-24849-1_23

Unified Syntax with Iso-types

Yanpeng Yang$^{(\boxtimes)}$, Xuan Bi, and Bruno C.d.S. Oliveira

The University of Hong Kong, Pokfulam, Hong Kong, China
{ypyang,xbi,bruno}@cs.hku.hk

Abstract. Traditional designs for functional languages (such as Haskell or ML) have separate sorts of syntax for terms and types. In contrast, many dependently typed languages use a unified syntax that accounts for both terms and types. Unified syntax has some interesting advantages over separate syntax, including less duplication of concepts, and added expressiveness. However, integrating *unrestricted* general recursion in calculi with unified syntax is challenging when some level of type-level computation is present, as *decidable type-checking* is easily lost.

This paper argues that the advantages of unified syntax also apply to traditional functional languages, and there is no need to give up decidable type-checking. We present a dependently typed calculus that uses unified syntax, supports general recursion and has decidable type-checking. The key to retain decidable type-checking is a generalization of *iso-recursive types* called *iso-types*. Iso-types replace the conversion rule typically used in dependently typed calculus, and make every computation explicit via cast operators. We study two variants of the calculus that differ on the reduction strategy employed by the cast operators, and give different trade-offs in terms of simplicity and expressiveness.

1 Introduction

We live exciting times in the design of functional programming languages. In recent years, dependent types have inspired novel designs for new programming languages, such as Agda [19] or Idris [6], as well as numerous programming language research [2,3,8,23–25,28]. Dependently typed languages bring additional expressiveness to type systems, and they can also support different forms of assurances, such as strong normalization and logical consistency, not typically present in traditional programming languages. Nevertheless, traditional designs for functional languages still have some benefits. While strong normalization and logical consistency are certainly nice properties to have, and can be valuable to have in many domains, they can also impose restrictions on how programs are written. For example, the termination checking algorithms typically employed by dependently typed languages such as Agda or Idris can only automatically ensure termination of programs that follow certain patterns. In contrast Haskell or ML programmers can write their programs much more freely, since they do not need to worry about retaining strong normalization and logical consistency. Thus there is still plenty of space for both types of designs.

© Springer International Publishing AG 2016
A. Igarashi (Ed.): APLAS 2016, LNCS 10017, pp. 251–270, 2016.
DOI: 10.1007/978-3-319-47958-3_14

From an implementation and foundational point-of-view, dependently typed languages and traditional functional languages also have important differences. Languages like Haskell or ML have a strong separation between terms and types (and also kinds). This separation often leads to duplication of constructs. For example, when the type language provides some sort of type level computation, constructs such as type application (mimicking value level application) may be needed. In contrast many dependently typed languages unify types and terms. There are benefits in unifying types and terms. In addition to the extra expressiveness afforded, for example, by dependent types, only one syntactic level is needed. Thus duplication can be avoided. Having less language constructs simplifies the language, making it easier to study (from the meta-theoretical point of view) and maintain (from the implementation point of view).

In principle having unified syntax would be beneficial even for more traditional designs of functional languages, which have no strong normalization or logical consistency. Not surprisingly, researchers have in the past considered such an option for implementing functional languages [3,7,21], by using some variant of *pure type systems* (PTS) [5] (normally extended with general recursion). Thus, with a simple and tiny calculus, they showed that powerful and quite expressive functional languages could be built with unified syntax.

However having unified syntax for types and terms brings challenges. One pressing problem is that integrating (unrestricted) general recursion in dependently typed calculi with unified syntax, while retaining logical consistency, strong normalization and *decidable type-checking* is difficult. Indeed, many early designs using unified syntax and unrestricted general recursion [3,7] lose all three properties. For pragmatic reasons languages like Agda or Idris also allow turning off the termination checker, which allows for added expressiveness, but loses the three properties as well. More recently, various researchers [8,24,27] have been investigating how to combine those properties, general recursion and dependent types. However, this is usually done by having the type system carefully control the total and partial parts of computation, adding significant complexity to those calculi when compared to systems based on pure type systems.

Nevertheless, if we are interested in traditional languages, only the loss of decidable type-checking is problematie. Unlike strong normalization and logical consistency, decidable type-checking is normally one property that is expected from a traditional programming language design.

This paper proposes λI: a simple call-by-name variant of the calculus of constructions. The key challenge solved in this work is how to define a calculus comparable in simplicity to the calculus of constructions, while featuring both general recursion and decidable type checking. The main idea, is to recover decidable type-checking by making each type-level computation step explicit. In essence, each type-level reduction or expansion is controlled by a *type-safe* cast. Since single computation steps are trivially terminating, decidability of type checking is possible even in the presence of non-terminating programs at the type level. At the same time term-level programs using general recursion work as in any conventional functional languages, and can be non-terminating.

Our design generalizes *iso-recursive types* [22], which are our main source of inspiration. In λI, not only folding/unfolding of recursion at the type level is explicitly controlled by term level constructs, but also any other type level computation (including beta reduction/expansion). There is an analogy to language designs with *equi-recursive* types and *iso-recursive* types, which are normally the two options for adding recursive types to languages. With equi-recursive types, type-level recursion is implicitly folded/unfolded, which makes establishing decidability of type-checking much more difficult. In iso-recursive designs, the idea is to trade some convenience by a simple way to ensure decidability. Similarly, we view the design of traditional dependently typed calculi, such as the calculus of constructions as analogous to systems with equi-recursive types. In the calculus of constructions it is the *conversion rule* that allows type-level computation to by implicitly triggered. However, the proof of decidability of type checking for the *calculus of constructions* [10] (and other normalizing PTS) is non-trivial, as it depends on strong normalization [16]. Moreover decidability is lost when adding general recursion. In contrast, the cast operators in λI have to be used to *explicitly* trigger each step of type-level computation, but it is easy to ensure decidable type-checking, even with general recursion.

We study two variants of the calculus that differ on the reduction strategy employed by the cast operators, and give different trade-offs in terms of simplicity and expressiveness. The first variant λI_w uses weak-head reduction in the cast operators. This allows for a very simple calculus, but loses some expressiveness in terms of type level computation. Nevertheless in this variant it is still possible to encode useful language constructs such as algebraic datatypes. The second variant λI_p uses *parallel reduction* for casts and is more expressive. It allows equating terms such as *Vec* $(1 + 1)$ and *Vec* 2 as equal. The price to pay for this more expressive design is some additional complexity. For both designs type soundness and decidability of type-checking are proved.

It is worth emphasizing that λI does sacrifice some convenience when performing type-level computations in order to gain the ability of doing arbitrary general recursion at the term level. The goal of this work is to show the benefits of unified syntax in terms of economy of concepts for programming language design, and not use unified syntax to express computationally intensive type-level programs. Investigating how to express computationally intensive type-level programs (as in dependently typed programming) in λI is left for future work.

In summary, the contributions of this work are:

- **The λI calculus:** A simple calculus for functional programming, that collapses terms, types and kinds into the same hierarchy and supports general recursion. λI is type-safe and the type system is decidable. Full proofs are provided in the extended version of this paper [29].
- **Iso-types:** λI generalizes iso-recursive types by making all type-level computation steps explicit via *casts operators*. In λI the combination of casts and recursion subsumes iso-recursive types.
- **A prototype implementation:** The prototype of λI is available online[1].

---

[1] https://bitbucket.org/ypyang/aplas16.

2   Overview

In this section, we informally introduce the main features of λI. In particular, we show how the casts in λI can be used instead of the typical conversion rule present in calculi such as the calculus of constructions. The formal details of λI are presented in Sects. 3 and 4.

2.1   The Calculus of Constructions and the Conversion Rule

The calculus of constructions (λC) [10] is a higher-order typed lambda calculus supporting dependent types (among various other features). A crucial feature of λC is the *conversion rule*:

$$\frac{\Gamma \vdash e : \tau_1 \qquad \Gamma \vdash \tau_2 : s \qquad \tau_1 =_\beta \tau_2}{\Gamma \vdash e : \tau_2}$$

It allows one to derive $e : \tau_2$ from the derivation of $e : \tau_1$ and the beta equality of τ_1 and τ_2. This rule is important to *automatically* allow terms with beta equivalent types to be considered type-compatible. For example, consider the following identity function:

$$f = \lambda y : (\lambda x : \star.\ x)\, Int.\ y$$

The type of y is a *type-level* identity function applied to *Int*. Without the conversion rule, f cannot be applied to 3 for example, since the type of 3 (*Int*) differs from the type of y (($\lambda x : \star.\ x$) *Int*). Note that the beta equivalence ($\lambda x : \star.\ x$) *Int* $=_\beta$ *Int* holds. The conversion rule allows the application of f to 3 by converting the type of y to *Int*.

Decidability of Type Checking and Strong Normalization. While the conversion rule in λC brings a lot of convenience, an unfortunate consequence is that it couples decidability of type checking with strong normalization of the calculus [16]. Therefore adding general recursion to λC becomes difficult, since strong normalization is lost. Due to the conversion rule, any non-terminating term would force the type checker to go into an infinite loop (by constantly applying the conversion rule without termination), thus rendering the type system undecidable. For example, assume a term z that has type loop, where loop stands for any diverging computation. If we type check ($\lambda x : Int.\ x$) z under the normal typing rules of λC, the type checker would get stuck as it tries to do beta equality on two terms: *Int* and loop, where the latter is non-terminating.

2.2   An Alternative to the Conversion Rule: Iso-types

In contrast to the conversion rule of λC, λI features *iso-types*, making it explicit as to when and where to convert one type to another. Type conversions are explicitly controlled by two language constructs: cast$_\downarrow$ (one-step reduction) and cast$_\uparrow$ (one-step expansion). The benefit of this approach is that decidability of type checking is no longer coupled with strong normalization of the calculus.

Reduction. The cast$_\downarrow$ operator allows a type conversion provided that the resulting type is a *reduction* of the original type of the term. To explain the use of cast$_\downarrow$, assume an identity function g defined by $g = \lambda y : Int.\ y$ and a term e such that $e : (\lambda x : \star.\ x)\ Int$. In contrast to λC, we cannot directly apply g to e in λI since the type of e $((\lambda x : \star.\ x)\ Int)$ is not *syntactically equal* to Int. However, note that the reduction relation $(\lambda x : \star.\ x)\ Int \longrightarrow Int$ holds. We can use cast$_\downarrow$ for the explicit (type-level) reduction:

$$\text{cast}_\downarrow\ e : Int$$

Then the application $g\ (\text{cast}_\downarrow\ e)$ type checks.

Expansion. The dual operation of cast$_\downarrow$ is cast$_\uparrow$, which allows a type conversion provided that the resulting type is an *expansion* of the original type of the term. To explain the use of cast$_\uparrow$, let us revisit the example from Sect. 2.1. We cannot apply f to 3 without the conversion rule. Instead, we can use cast$_\uparrow$ to expand the type of 3:

$$(\text{cast}_\uparrow\ [(\lambda x : \star.\ x)\ Int]\ 3) : (\lambda x : \star.\ x)\ Int$$

Thus, the application $f\ (\text{cast}_\uparrow\ [(\lambda x : \star.\ x)\ Int]\ 3)$ becomes well-typed. Intuitively, cast$_\uparrow$ performs expansion, as the type of 3 is Int, and $(\lambda x : \star.\ x)\ Int$ is the expansion of Int witnessed by $(\lambda x : \star.\ x)\ Int \longrightarrow Int$. Notice that for cast$_\uparrow$ to work, we need to provide the resulting type as argument. This is because for the same term, there may be more than one choice for expansion. For example, $1+2$ and $2+1$ are both the expansions of 3.

One-Step. The cast rules allow only *one-step* reduction or expansion. If two type-level terms require more than one step of reductions or expansions for normalization, then multiple casts must be used. Consider a variant of the example such that $e : (\lambda x : \star.\ \lambda y : \star.\ x)\ Int\ Bool$. Given $g = \lambda y : Int.\ y$, the expression $g\ (\text{cast}_\downarrow\ e)$ is ill-typed because cast$_\downarrow$ e has type $(\lambda y : \star.\ Int)\ Bool$, which is not syntactically equal to Int. Thus, we need another cast$_\downarrow$:

$$\text{cast}_\downarrow\ (\text{cast}_\downarrow\ e) : Int$$

to further reduce the type and allow the program $g\ (\text{cast}_\downarrow\ (\text{cast}_\downarrow\ e))$ to type check.

Decidability Without Strong Normalization. With explicit type conversion rules the decidability of type checking no longer depends on the strong normalization property. Thus the type system remains decidable even in the presence of non-termination at type level. Consider the same example using the term z from Sect. 2.1. This time the type checker will not get stuck when type checking $(\lambda x : Int.\ x)\ z$. This is because in λI, the type checker only performs syntactic comparison between Int and loop, instead of beta equality. Thus it rejects the above application as ill-typed. Indeed it is impossible to type check such application even with the use of cast$_\uparrow$ and/or cast$_\downarrow$: one would need to write infinite number of cast$_\downarrow$'s to make the type checker loop forever (e.g., $(\lambda x : Int.\ x)(\text{cast}_\downarrow(\text{cast}_\downarrow \dots z)))$. But it is impossible to write such program in practice.

Variants of Casts. A reduction relation is used in cast operators to convert types. We study two possible reduction relations: call-by-name *weak-head reduction* and *full reduction*. Weak-head reduction cannot reduce sub-terms at certain positions (e.g., inside λ or $\varPi$ binders), while full reduction can reduce sub-terms at any position. We define two variants of casts, namely *weak* and *full* casts, by employing weak-head and full reduction respectively. We also create two variants of λI, namely λI_w and λI_p. The only difference is that λI_w uses weak-head reduction in weak cast operators $\mathsf{cast}_\uparrow$ and $\mathsf{cast}_\downarrow$, while λI_p uses full reduction, specifically *parallel reduction*, in full cast operators $\mathsf{cast}_\Uparrow$ and $\mathsf{cast}_\Downarrow$. Both variants reflect the idea of iso-types, but have trade-offs between simplicity and expressiveness: λI_w uses the same call-by-name reduction for both casts and evaluation to keep the system and metatheory simple, but loses some expressiveness, e.g. cannot convert *Vec* $(1+1)$ to *Vec* 2. λI_p is more expressive but results in a more complicated metatheory (see Sect. 4.2). Note that when generally referring to λI, we do not specify the reduction strategy, which could be either variant.

2.3   General Recursion

λI supports general recursion and allows writing unrestricted recursive programs at term level. The recursive construct is also used to model recursive types at type level. Recursive terms and types are represented by the same μ primitive.

Recursive Terms. The primitive $\mu x : \tau. \ e$ can be used to define recursive functions. For example, the factorial function would be written as:

$$fact = \mu f : Int \to Int. \ \lambda x : Int. \ \textbf{if } x == 0 \ \textbf{then } 1 \ \textbf{else } x \times f \ (x-1)$$

We treat the μ operator as a *fixpoint*, which evaluates $\mu x : \tau. \ e$ to its recursive unfolding $e[x \mapsto \mu x : \tau. \ e]$. Term-level recursion in λI works as in any standard functional language, e.g., *fact* 3 produces 6 as expected (see Sect. 3.4).

Recursive Types. The same μ primitive is used at the type level to represent iso-recursive types [11]. In the *iso-recursive* approach a recursive type and its unfolding are different, but isomorphic. The isomorphism is witnessed by two operations, typically called fold and unfold. In λI, such isomorphism is witnessed by $\mathsf{cast}_\uparrow$ and $\mathsf{cast}_\downarrow$. In fact, $\mathsf{cast}_\uparrow$ and $\mathsf{cast}_\downarrow$ *generalize* fold and unfold: they can convert any types, not just recursive types, as we shall see in the example of encoding parametrized datatypes in Sect. 5.

3   Dependent Types with Iso-types

In this section, we present the λI_w calculus, which uses a (call-by-name) weak-head reduction strategy in casts. This calculus is very close to the calculus of constructions, except for three key differences: (1) the absence of the $\square$ constant (due to use of the "type-in-type" axiom); (2) the existence of two cast operators; (3) general recursion on both term and type level. Unlike λC the proof of decidability of type checking for λI_w does not require the strong normalization of the calculus. Thus, the addition of general recursion does not break decidable type checking. In the rest of this section, we demonstrate the syntax, operational semantics, typing rules and metatheory of λI_w. Full proofs of the meta-theory can be found in the extended version of this paper [29].

3.1 Syntax

Figure 1 shows the syntax of λI_w, including expressions, contexts and values. λI_w uses a unified representation for different syntactic levels by following the *pure type system* (PTS) representation of λC [5]. There is no syntactic distinction between terms, types or kinds. We further merge types and kinds together by including only a single sort $\star$ instead of two distinct sorts $\star$ and $\square$ of λC. This design brings economy for type checking, since one set of rules can cover all syntactic levels. We use metavariables τ and σ for an expression on the type-level position and e for one on the term level. We use $\tau_1 \to \tau_2$ as a syntactic sugar for $\Pi x : \tau_1 . \tau_2$ if x does not occur free in τ_2.

Explicit Type Conversion. We introduce two new primitives $\mathsf{cast}_\uparrow$ and $\mathsf{cast}_\downarrow$ (pronounced as "cast up" and "cast down") to replace the implicit conversion rule of λC with *one-step* explicit type conversions. The type-conversions perform two directions of conversion: $\mathsf{cast}_\downarrow$ is for the *one-step reduction* of types, and $\mathsf{cast}_\uparrow$ is for the *one-step expansion*. The $\mathsf{cast}_\uparrow$ construct takes a type parameter τ as the result type of one-step expansion for disambiguation (see also Sect. 2.2). The $\mathsf{cast}_\downarrow$ construct does not need a type parameter, because the result type of one-step reduction is uniquely determined, as we shall see in Sect. 3.5.

We use syntactic sugar $\mathsf{cast}_\uparrow^n$ and $\mathsf{cast}_\downarrow^n$ to denote n consecutive cast operators (see Fig. 1). Alternatively, we can introduce them as built-in operators but treat one-step casts as syntactic sugar instead. Making n-step casts built-in can reduce the number of individual cast constructs, but makes cast operators less fundamental in the discussion of meta-theory. Thus, in the paper, we treat n-step casts as syntactic sugar but make them built-in in the implementation for better performance. Note that $\mathsf{cast}_\uparrow^n$ is simplified to take just one type parameter, i.e., the last type τ_1 of the n cast operations. Due to the determinacy of one-step reduction (see Lemma 1), the intermediate types can be uniquely determined, thus can be left out from the $\mathsf{cast}_\uparrow^n$ operator.

General Recursion. We add one primitive μ to represent general recursion. It has a uniform representation on both term level and type level: the same construct works both as a term-level fixpoint and a recursive type. The recursive expression $\mu x : \tau . e$ is *polymorphic*, in the sense that τ is not restricted to $\star$ but can be any type, such as a function type $Int \to Int$ or a kind $\star \to \star$.

3.2 Operational Semantics

Figure 2 shows the small-step, *call-by-name* operational semantics. Three base cases include S_BETA for beta reduction, S_MU for recursion unrolling and

Expressions $e, \tau, \sigma \quad ::= \quad x \mid \star \mid e_1\, e_2 \mid \lambda x : \tau.\ e \mid \Pi x : \tau_1.\ \tau_2$
$\mid \quad \mu x : \tau.\ e \mid \mathsf{cast}_\uparrow [\tau]\, e \mid \mathsf{cast}_\downarrow\, e$

Contexts $\Gamma \quad ::= \quad \varnothing \mid \Gamma, x : \tau$

Values $v \quad ::= \quad \star \mid \lambda x : \tau.\ e \mid \Pi x : \tau_1.\ \tau_2 \mid \mathsf{cast}_\uparrow [\tau]\, v$

Syntactic Sugar

$$\tau_1 \rightarrow \tau_2 \quad \triangleq \quad \Pi x : \tau_1.\ \tau_2, \text{ where } x \notin \mathsf{FV}(\tau_2)$$

$$\mathsf{cast}_\uparrow^n [\tau_1]\, e \quad \triangleq \quad \mathsf{cast}_\uparrow [\tau_1](\mathsf{cast}_\uparrow [\tau_2](\dots(\mathsf{cast}_\uparrow [\tau_n]\, e)\dots))$$
$$, \text{ where } \tau_1 \longrightarrow \tau_2 \longrightarrow \cdots \longrightarrow \tau_n$$

$$\mathsf{cast}_\downarrow^n\, e \quad \triangleq \quad \underbrace{\mathsf{cast}_\downarrow(\mathsf{cast}_\downarrow(\dots(\mathsf{cast}_\downarrow\, e)\dots))}_{n}$$

Fig. 1. Syntax of λI_w

$\boxed{e \longrightarrow e'}$ One-step Weak-head Reduction

$$\frac{}{(\lambda x : \tau.\ e_1)\, e_2 \longrightarrow e_1[x \mapsto e_2]}\ \text{S\_Beta} \qquad \frac{e_1 \longrightarrow e_1'}{e_1\, e_2 \longrightarrow e_1'\, e_2}\ \text{S\_App}$$

$$\frac{}{\mu x : \tau.\ e \longrightarrow e[x \mapsto \mu x : \tau.\ e]}\ \text{S\_Mu} \qquad \frac{e \longrightarrow e'}{\mathsf{cast}_\downarrow\, e \longrightarrow \mathsf{cast}_\downarrow\, e'}\ \text{S\_CastDown}$$

$$\frac{e \longrightarrow e'}{\mathsf{cast}_\uparrow [\tau]\, e \longrightarrow \mathsf{cast}_\uparrow [\tau]\, e'}\ \text{S\_CastUp} \qquad \frac{}{\mathsf{cast}_\downarrow (\mathsf{cast}_\uparrow [\tau]\, v) \longrightarrow v}\ \text{S\_CastElim}$$

Fig. 2. Operational semantics of λI_w

S_CastElim for cast canceling. Three inductive cases, S_App, S_CastDown and S_CastUp, define reduction at the head position of an application, and the inner expression of $\mathsf{cast}_\downarrow$ and $\mathsf{cast}_\uparrow$ terms, respectively. Note that S_CastElim and S_CastDown do not overlap because in the former rule, the inner term of $\mathsf{cast}_\downarrow$ is a value (see Fig. 1), i.e., $\mathsf{cast}_\uparrow [\tau]\, v$, but not a value in the latter rule.

The reduction rules are called *weak-head* because only the head term of an application can be reduced, as indicated by the rule S_App. Reduction is also not allowed inside the λ-term and Π-term which are both defined as values. Weak-head reduction rules are used for both type conversion and term evaluation. Thus, we refer to cast operators in λI_w as *weak* casts. To evaluate the value of a term-level expression, we apply the one-step (weak-head) reduction multiple times, i.e., multi-step reduction, the transitive and reflexive closure of the one-step reduction.

3.3 Typing

Figure 3 gives the *syntax-directed* typing rules of λI_w, including rules of context well-formedness $\vdash \Gamma$ and expression typing $\Gamma \vdash e : \tau$. Note that there is only a single set of rules for expression typing, because there is no distinction of different syntactic levels.

Most typing rules are quite standard. We write $\vdash \Gamma$ if a context Γ is well-formed. We use $\Gamma \vdash \tau : \star$ to check if τ is a well-formed type. Rule T_Ax is the "type-in-type" axiom. Rule T_VAR checks the type of variable x from the valid context. Rules T_APP and T_LAM check the validity of application and abstraction respectively. Rule T_PI checks the type well-formedness of the dependent function. Rule T_MU checks the validity of a recursive term. It ensures that the recursion $\mu x : \tau.\ e$ should have the same type τ as the binder x and also the inner expression e.

The Cast Rules. We focus on the rules T_CASTUP and T_CASTDOWN that define the semantics of cast operators and replace the conversion rule of λC. The relation between the original and converted type is defined by one-step weak-head reduction (see Fig. 2). For example, given a judgment $\Gamma \vdash e : \tau_2$ and relation $\tau_1 \longrightarrow \tau_2 \longrightarrow \tau_3$, $\mathsf{cast}_\uparrow [\tau_1]\ e$ expands the type of e from τ_2 to τ_1, while $\mathsf{cast}_\downarrow e$ reduces the type of e from τ_2 to τ_3. We can formally give the typing derivations of the examples in Sect. 2.2:

$$\frac{\Gamma \vdash e : (\lambda x : \star.\ x)\ Int \quad (\lambda x : \star.\ x)\ Int \longrightarrow Int}{\Gamma \vdash (\mathsf{cast}_\downarrow e) : Int} \qquad \frac{\Gamma \vdash 3 : Int \quad \Gamma \vdash (\lambda x : \star.\ x)\ Int : \star \quad (\lambda x : \star.\ x)\ Int \longrightarrow Int}{\Gamma \vdash (\mathsf{cast}_\uparrow [(\lambda x : \star.\ x)\ Int]\ 3) : (\lambda x : \star.\ x)\ Int}$$

Importantly, in λI_w term-level and type-level computation are treated differently. Term-level computation is dealt in the usual way, by using multi-step reduction until a value is finally obtained. Type-level computation, on the other hand, is controlled by the program: each step of the computation is induced by a cast. If a type-level program requires n steps of computation to reach the normal form, then it will require n casts to compute a type-level value.

Pros and Cons of Type in Type. The "type-in-type" axiom is well-known to give rise to logical inconsistency [14]. However, since our goal is to investigate core languages for languages that are logically inconsistent anyway (due to general recursion), we do not view "type-in-type" as a problematic rule. On the other hand the rule T_AX brings additional expressiveness and benefits: for example *kind polymorphism* [30] is supported in λI_w.

Syntactic Equality. Finally, the definition of type equality in λI_w differs from λC. Without λC's conversion rule, the type of a term cannot be converted freely against beta equality, unless using cast operators. Thus, types of expressions are equal only if they are syntactically equal (up to alpha renaming).

3.4   The Two Faces of Recursion

Term-Level Recursion. In λI_w, the μ-operator works as a *fixpoint* on the term level. By rule S_MU, evaluating a term $\mu x : \tau.\ e$ will substitute all x's in e with the whole μ-term itself, resulting in the unrolling $e[x \mapsto \mu x : \tau.\ e]$. The μ-term is equivalent to a recursive function that should be allowed to unroll without restriction. Recall the factorial function example in Sect. 2.3. By rule T_MU, the type of *fact* is $Int \to Int$. Thus we can apply *fact* to an integer. Note that by

$\boxed{\vdash \Gamma}$ Well-formed Context

$$\frac{}{\vdash \varnothing} \text{ENV\_EMPTY} \qquad \frac{\vdash \Gamma \qquad \Gamma \vdash \tau : \star}{\vdash \Gamma, x : \tau} \text{ENV\_VAR}$$

$\boxed{\Gamma \vdash e : \tau}$ Typing

$$\frac{\vdash \Gamma}{\Gamma \vdash \star : \star} \text{T\_AX} \qquad \frac{\vdash \Gamma \qquad x : \tau \in \Gamma}{\Gamma \vdash x : \tau} \text{T\_VAR}$$

$$\frac{\Gamma \vdash e_1 : \Pi x : \tau_2. \, \tau_1 \qquad \Gamma \vdash e_2 : \tau_2}{\Gamma \vdash e_1 \, e_2 : \tau_1[x \mapsto e_2]} \text{T\_APP} \qquad \frac{\Gamma, x : \tau_1 \vdash e : \tau_2 \qquad \Gamma \vdash \Pi x : \tau_1. \, \tau_2 : \star}{\Gamma \vdash \lambda x : \tau_1. \, e : \Pi x : \tau_1. \, \tau_2} \text{T\_LAM}$$

$$\frac{\Gamma \vdash \tau_1 : \star \qquad \Gamma, x : \tau_1 \vdash \tau_2 : \star}{\Gamma \vdash \Pi x : \tau_1. \, \tau_2 : \star} \text{T\_PI} \qquad \frac{\Gamma, x : \tau \vdash e : \tau \qquad \Gamma \vdash \tau : \star}{\Gamma \vdash \mu x : \tau. \, e : \tau} \text{T\_MU}$$

$$\frac{\Gamma \vdash e : \tau_2 \qquad \Gamma \vdash \tau_1 : \star \qquad \tau_1 \longrightarrow \tau_2}{\Gamma \vdash \mathsf{cast}_\uparrow [\tau_1] \, e : \tau_1} \text{T\_CASTUP} \qquad \frac{\Gamma \vdash e : \tau_1 \qquad \tau_1 \longrightarrow \tau_2}{\Gamma \vdash \mathsf{cast}_\downarrow e : \tau_2} \text{T\_CASTDOWN}$$

Fig. 3. Typing rules of λI_w

rule S_MU, *fact* will be unrolled to a λ-term. Assuming the evaluation of **if-then-else** construct and arithmetic expressions follows the one-step reduction, we can evaluate the term *fact* 3 as follows:

$$
\begin{aligned}
&fact \ 3 \\
\longrightarrow \ &(\lambda x : Int. \ \textbf{if } x == 0 \textbf{ then } 1 \textbf{ else } x \times fact \ (x-1)) \ 3 \quad \text{-- by S\_APP} \\
\longrightarrow \ &\textbf{if } 3 == 0 \textbf{ then } 1 \textbf{ else } 3 \times fact \ (3-1) \qquad \text{-- by S\_BETA} \\
\longrightarrow \ &\ldots \longrightarrow 6
\end{aligned}
$$

Note that we never check if a μ-term can terminate or not, which is an undecidable problem for general recursive terms. The factorial function example above can stop, while there exist some terms that will loop forever. However, term-level non-termination is only a runtime concern and does not block the type checker. In Sect. 3.5 we show type checking λI_w is still decidable in the presence of general recursion.

Type-Level Recursion. On the type level, $\mu x : \tau. \, e$ works as a *iso-recursive* type [11], a kind of recursive type that is not equal but only *isomorphic* to its unrolling. Normally, we need to add two more primitives fold and unfold for the iso-recursive type to map back and forth between the original and unrolled form. Assuming there exist expressions e_1 and e_2 such that $e_1 : \mu x : \tau. \, \sigma$ and $e_2 : \sigma[x \mapsto \mu x : \tau. \, \sigma]$, we have the following typing results:

$$
\begin{aligned}
&\mathsf{unfold} \ e_1 &&: \sigma[x \mapsto \mu x : \tau. \, \sigma] \\
&\mathsf{fold} \ [\mu x : \tau. \, \sigma] \ e_2 : \mu x : \tau. \, \sigma
\end{aligned}
$$

by applying standard typing rules of iso-recursive types [22]:

$$\frac{\Gamma \vdash e_1 : \mu x : \tau. \, \sigma}{\Gamma \vdash \mathsf{unfold} \ e_1 : \sigma[x \mapsto \mu x : \tau. \, \sigma]} \qquad \frac{\Gamma \vdash \mu x : \tau. \, \sigma : \star \qquad \Gamma \vdash e_2 : \sigma[x \mapsto \mu x : \tau. \, \sigma]}{\Gamma \vdash \mathsf{fold} \ [\mu x : \tau. \, \sigma] \ e_2 : \mu x : \tau. \, \sigma}$$

However, in λI_w we do not need to introduce fold and unfold operators, because with the rule S_Mu, $cast_\uparrow$ and $cast_\downarrow$ *generalize* fold and unfold. Consider the same expressions e_1 and e_2 above. The type of e_2 is the unrolling of e_1's type, which follows the one-step reduction relation by rule S_Mu: $\mu x : \tau.\ \sigma \longrightarrow \sigma[x \mapsto \mu x : \tau.\ \sigma]$. By applying rules T_CastUp and T_CastDown, we can obtain the following typing results:

$$cast_\downarrow e_1 \qquad\qquad : \sigma[x \mapsto \mu x : \tau.\ \sigma]$$
$$cast_\uparrow [\mu x : \tau.\ \sigma]\, e_2 : \mu x : \tau.\ \sigma$$

Thus, $cast_\uparrow$ and $cast_\downarrow$ witness the isomorphism between the original recursive type and its unrolling, behaving in the same way as fold and unfold in iso-recursive types.

An important remark is that casts are necessary, not only for controlling the unrolling of recursive types, but also for type conversion of other constructs, which is essential for encoding parametrized algebraic datatypes (see Sect. 5). Also, the "type-in-type" axiom [7] makes it possible to encode fixpoints even without a fixpoint primitive, i.e., the μ-operator. Thus if no casts would be performed on terms without recursive types, it would still be possible to build a term with a non-terminating type and make type-checking non-terminating.

3.5   Metatheory

We now discuss the metatheory of λI_w. We focus on two properties: the decidability of type checking and the type safety of the language. First, we show that type checking λI_w is decidable without requiring strong normalization. Second, the language is type-safe, proven by subject reduction and progress theorems.

Decidability of Type Checking. The proof for decidability of type checking is by induction on the structure of e. The non-trivial case is for cast-terms with typing rules T_CastUp and T_CastDown. Both rules contain a premise that needs to judge if two types τ_1 and τ_2 follow the one-step reduction, i.e., if $\tau_1 \longrightarrow \tau_2$ holds. We show that τ_2 is *unique* with respect to the one-step reduction, or equivalently, reducing τ_1 by one step will get only a sole result τ_2. Such property is given by the following lemma:

Lemma 1 (Determinacy of One-step Weak-head Reduction). *If $e \longrightarrow e_1$ and $e \longrightarrow e_2$, then $e_1 \equiv e_2$.*

We use the notation $\equiv$ to denote the *alpha* equivalence of e_1 and e_2. Note that the presence of recursion does not affect this lemma: given a recursive term $\mu x : \tau.\ e$, by rule S_Mu, there always exists a unique term $e' \equiv e[x \mapsto \mu x : \tau.\ e]$ such that $\mu x : \tau.\ e \longrightarrow e'$. With this result, we show it is decidable to check whether the one-step relation $\tau_1 \longrightarrow \tau_2$ holds. We first reduce τ_1 by one step to obtain τ_1' (which is unique by Lemma 1), and compare if τ_1' and τ_2 are syntactically equal. Thus, we can further show type checking cast-terms is decidable.

For other forms of terms, the typing rules only contain typing judgments in the premises. Thus, type checking is decidable by the induction hypothesis and the following lemma which ensures the typing result is unique:

Lemma 2 (Uniqueness of Typing for λI_w). *If $\Gamma \vdash e : \tau_1$ and $\Gamma \vdash e : \tau_2$, then $\tau_1 \equiv \tau_2$.*

Thus, we can conclude the decidability of type checking:

Theorem 1 (Decidability of Type Checking for λI_w). *Given a well-formed context Γ and a term e, it is decidable to determine if there exists τ such that $\Gamma \vdash e : \tau$.*

We emphasize that when proving the decidability of type checking, we do not rely on strong normalization. Intuitively, explicit type conversion rules use one-step weak-head reduction, which already has a decidable checking algorithm according to Lemma 1. We do not need to further require the normalization of terms. This is different from the proof for λC which requires the language to be strongly normalizing [16]. In λC the conversion rule needs to examine the beta equivalence of terms, which is decidable only if every term has a normal form.

Type Safety. The proof of the type safety of λI_w is by showing subject reduction and progress theorems:

Theorem 2 (Subject Reduction of λI_w). *If $\Gamma \vdash e : \sigma$ and $e \longrightarrow e'$ then $\Gamma \vdash e' : \sigma$.*

Theorem 3 (Progress of λI_w). *If $\varnothing \vdash e : \sigma$ then either e is a value v or there exists e' such that $e \longrightarrow e'$.*

The proof of subject reduction is straightforward by induction on the derivation of $e \longrightarrow e'$. Some cases need supporting lemmas: S_CastElim requires Lemma 1; S_Beta and S_Mu require the following substitution lemma:

Lemma 3 (Substitution of λI_w). *If $\Gamma_1, x : \sigma, \Gamma_2 \vdash e_1 : \tau$ and $\Gamma_1 \vdash e_2 : \sigma$, then $\Gamma_1, \Gamma_2[x \mapsto e_2] \vdash e_1[x \mapsto e_2] : \tau[x \mapsto e_2]$.*

The proof of progress is also standard by induction on $\varnothing \vdash e : \sigma$. Notice that $\mathsf{cast}_\uparrow [\tau] v$ is a value, while $\mathsf{cast}_\downarrow e_1$ is not: by rule S_CastDown, e_1 will be constantly reduced until it becomes a value that could only be in the form $\mathsf{cast}_\uparrow [\tau] v$ by typing rule T_CastDown. Then rule S_CastElim can be further applied and the evaluation does not get stuck. Another notable remark is that when proving the case for application $e_1 e_2$, if e_1 is a value, it could only be a λ-term but not a $\mathsf{cast}_\uparrow$-term. Otherwise, suppose e_1 has the form $\mathsf{cast}_\uparrow [\Pi x : \tau_1. \tau_2] e_1'$. By inversion, we have $\varnothing \vdash e_1' : \tau_1'$ and $\Pi x : \tau_1. \tau_2 \longrightarrow \tau_1'$. But such τ_1' does not exist because $\Pi x : \tau_1. \tau_2$ is a value which is not reducible.

4 Iso-types with Full Casts

In Sect. 3, casts use one-step *weak-head* reduction, which is also used by term evaluation and simplifies the design. To gain extra expressiveness, we take one step further to generalize casts with *full* reduction. In this section, we present a variant of λI called λI_p, where casts use *parallel reduction* for type conversion. Full specification and proofs can be found in the extended version [29].

4.1 Full Casts with Parallel Reduction

Using weak-head reduction in cast operators keeps the simplicity of the language design. However, it lacks the ability to do *full* type-level computation, because reduction cannot occur at certain positions of terms. For example, weak casts cannot convert the type *Vec* $(1+1)$ to *Vec* 2 since the desired reduction is at the non-head position. Thus, we generalize weak casts to *full* casts ($\mathsf{cast}_\Uparrow$ and $\mathsf{cast}_\Downarrow$) utilizing *one-step parallel reduction* ($\longrightarrow_\mathsf{p}$) for type conversion. Figure 4 shows the definition of $\longrightarrow_\mathsf{p}$. It allows to reduce terms at any position, e.g., non-head positions or inside binders $\lambda x : \star.\ 1+1 \longrightarrow_\mathsf{p} \lambda x : \star.\ 2$, thus enables full type-level computation for casts.

$$\boxed{r \longrightarrow_\mathsf{p} r'} \quad \text{One-step Parallel Reduction}$$

$$\frac{}{x \longrightarrow_\mathsf{p} x}\ \text{P\_VAR} \qquad \frac{}{\star \longrightarrow_\mathsf{p} \star}\ \text{P\_STAR} \qquad \frac{}{(\lambda x : \rho.\ r_1)\ r_2 \longrightarrow_\mathsf{p} r_1[x \mapsto r_2]}\ \text{P\_BETA}$$

$$\frac{}{\mu x : \rho.\ r \longrightarrow_\mathsf{p} r[x \mapsto \mu x : \rho.\ r]}\ \text{P\_MuBETA} \qquad \frac{r_1 \longrightarrow_\mathsf{p} r_1' \quad r_2 \longrightarrow_\mathsf{p} r_2'}{r_1\ r_2 \longrightarrow_\mathsf{p} r_1'\ r_2'}\ \text{P\_APP}$$

$$\frac{\rho \longrightarrow_\mathsf{p} \rho' \quad r \longrightarrow_\mathsf{p} r'}{\lambda x : \rho.\ r \longrightarrow_\mathsf{p} \lambda x : \rho'.\ r'}\ \text{P\_LAM} \qquad \frac{\rho_1 \longrightarrow_\mathsf{p} \rho_1' \quad \rho_2 \longrightarrow_\mathsf{p} \rho_2'}{\Pi x : \rho_1.\ \rho_2 \longrightarrow_\mathsf{p} \Pi x : \rho_1'.\ \rho_2'}\ \text{P\_PI}$$

$$\frac{\rho \longrightarrow_\mathsf{p} \rho' \quad r \longrightarrow_\mathsf{p} r'}{\mu x : \rho.\ r \longrightarrow_\mathsf{p} \mu x : \rho'.\ r'}\ \text{P\_Mu}$$

Fig. 4. One-step parallel reduction of erased terms

There are three remarks for parallel reduction worth mentioning. First, parallel reduction is defined up to *erasure*, a process that removes all casts from terms (see Fig. 5). We use metavariable r and ρ to range over erased terms and types, respectively. The only syntactic change of erased terms is that there is no cast. The syntax is omitted here and can be found in the extended version [29]. It is feasible to define parallel reduction only for erased terms because casts in λI_p (also λI_w) are only used to ensure the decidability of type checking and have no effect on dynamic semantics, thus are *computationally irrelevant*.

Second, the definition of parallel reduction in Fig. 4 is slightly different from the standard one for PTS [1]. It is *partially* parallel: rules P_BETA and P_MuBETA do not parallel reduce sub-terms but only do beta reduction and recursion unrolling, respectively. Such definition makes the decidability property (see Lemma 6) easier to prove than the conventional fully parallel version.

Erased Expressions r, ρ

Erasure

$|x|$ $= x$

$|\star|$ $= \star$

$|e_1\ e_2|$ $= |e_1|\ |e_2|$

$|\lambda x : \tau.\ e|$ $= \lambda x : |\tau|.\ |e|$

$|\Pi x : \tau_1.\ \tau_2| = \Pi x : |\tau_1|.\ |\tau_2|$

$|\mu x : \tau.\ e|$ $= \mu x : |\tau|.\ |e|$

$|\mathsf{cast}_\Uparrow [\tau]\ e| = |e|$

$|\mathsf{cast}_\Downarrow [\tau]\ e| = |e|$

Fig. 5. Erasure of casts

Erased Values

$u ::= \star \mid \lambda x : \rho.\ r \mid \Pi x : \rho_1.\ \rho_2$

Evaluation Rules

$$\frac{}{(\lambda x : \rho.\ r_1)\ r_2 \longrightarrow r_1[x \mapsto r_2]}$$

$$\frac{r_1 \longrightarrow r_1'}{r_1\ r_2 \longrightarrow r_1'\ r_2}$$

$$\frac{}{\mu x : \rho.\ r \longrightarrow r[x \mapsto \mu x : \rho.\ r]}$$

Fig. 6. Values and evaluation rules of erased terms

Expressions $e, \tau, \sigma ::= \cdots \mid \mathsf{cast}_\Uparrow [\tau]\ e \mid \mathsf{cast}_\Downarrow [\tau]\ e$

Values $v ::= \cdots \mid \mathsf{cast}_\Uparrow [\tau]\ v \mid \mathsf{cast}_\Downarrow [\tau]\ v$

Typing

$$\frac{\Gamma \vdash e : \tau_2 \qquad \Gamma \vdash \tau_1 : \star \qquad |\tau_1| \longrightarrow_p |\tau_2|}{\Gamma \vdash \mathsf{cast}_\Uparrow [\tau_1]\ e : \tau_1} \ \text{TF\_CastUp}$$

$$\frac{\Gamma \vdash e : \tau_1 \qquad \Gamma \vdash \tau_2 : \star \qquad |\tau_1| \longrightarrow_p |\tau_2|}{\Gamma \vdash \mathsf{cast}_\Downarrow [\tau_2]\ e : \tau_2} \ \text{TF\_CastDown}$$

Fig. 7. Syntactic and typing changes of λI_p

It also requires fewer reduction steps than the non-parallel version, thus correspondingly needs fewer casts.

Third, parallel reduction does *not* have the determinacy property like weak-head reduction (Lemma 1). For example, for term $(\lambda x : \star.\ 1 + 1)\ Int$, we can (parallel) reduce it to either $(\lambda x : \star.\ 2)\ Int$ by rule P_App and P_Lam, or $1 + 1$ by rule P_Beta. Thus, to ensure the decidability, we also need to add the type annotation for $\mathsf{cast}_\Downarrow$ operator to indicate what exact type we want to reduce to. Similar to $\mathsf{cast}_\Uparrow$, $\mathsf{cast}_\Downarrow [\tau]\ v$ is a value, which is different from the weak $\mathsf{cast}_\downarrow$-term.

Figure 7 shows the syntactic and typing changes of λI_p. Notice that in λI_w, reduction rules for type casting and term evaluation are the *same*, i.e., the weak-head call-by-name reduction. But in λI_p, parallel reduction is only used by casts. We define *weak-head* reduction ($\longrightarrow$) for term evaluation individually (see Fig. 6). Note that the relation $\longrightarrow$ is defined only for *erased terms*, which is similar to the treatment of $\longrightarrow_p$. We also define syntactic values for erased terms, ranged over by u (see Fig. 6).

4.2   Metatheory

We show that the two key properties, type safety and decidability of type checking, still hold in λI_p.

Type Safety. Full casts are more expressive but also complicate the metatheory: term evaluation could get stuck by full casts. For example, the following term,

$$(\mathsf{cast}_\Downarrow \,[Int \to Int]\,(\lambda x : ((\lambda y : \star.\ y)\,Int).\ x))\,3$$

cannot be further reduced because the head position is already a value but not a λ-term. Note that weak casts do not have such problem because only $\mathsf{cast}_\uparrow$ is annotated and not legal to have a Π-type in the annotation (see last paragraph of Sect. 3.5). To avoid getting stuck by full casts, one could introduce several *cast push rules* similar to System F_C [26]. For example, the stuck term above can be further evaluated by pushing $\mathsf{cast}_\Downarrow$ into the λ-term:

$$(\mathsf{cast}_\Downarrow \,[Int \to Int]\,(\lambda x : ((\lambda y : \star.\ y)\,Int).\ x))\,3 \longrightarrow (\lambda x : Int.\ x)\,3$$

However, adding "push rules" significantly complicates the reduction relations and metatheory. Instead, we adopt the erasure approach inspired by Zombie [24] and GURU [25] that removes all casts when proving the type safety. We define a type system for erased terms, called *erased system*. Its typing judgment is $\Delta \vdash r : \rho$ where Δ ranges over the erased context. Omitted typing rules are available in the extended version [29].

The erased system is basically calculus of constructions with recursion and "type-in-type". Thus, we follow the standard proof steps for PTS [5]. Notice that term evaluation uses the weak-head reduction $\longrightarrow$. We only need to prove subject reduction and progress theorems for $\longrightarrow$. But we generalize the result for subject reduction, which holds up to the parallel reduction $\longrightarrow_\mathsf{p}$.

Lemma 4 (Substitution of Erased System). *If $\Delta_1, x : \rho', \Delta_2 \vdash r_1 : \rho$ and $\Delta_1 \vdash r_2 : \rho'$, then $\Delta_1, \Delta_2[x \mapsto r_2] \vdash r_1[x \mapsto r_2] : \rho[x \mapsto r_2]$.*

Theorem 4 (Subject Reduction of Erased System). *If $\Delta \vdash r : \rho$ and $r \longrightarrow_\mathsf{p} r'$ then $\Delta \vdash r' : \rho$.*

Theorem 5 (Progress of Erased System). *If $\varnothing \vdash r : \rho$ then either r is a value u or there exists r' such that $r \longrightarrow r'$.*

Given that the erased system is type-safe, if we want to show the type-safety of the original system, it is sufficient to show the typing is preserved after erasure:

Lemma 5 (Soundness of Erasure). *If $\Gamma \vdash e : \tau$ then $|\Gamma| \vdash |e| : |\tau|$.*

Decidability of Type Checking. The proof of decidability of type checking λI_p is similar to λI_w in Sect. 3.5. The only difference is for cast rules TF_CASTUP and TF_CASTDOWN, which use parallel reduction $|\tau_1| \longrightarrow_\mathsf{p} |\tau_2|$ as a premise. We first show the decidability of parallel reduction:

Lemma 6 (Decidability of Parallel Reduction). *If $\Delta \vdash r_1 : \rho_1$ and $\Delta \vdash r_2 : \rho_2$, then whether $r_1 \longrightarrow_\mathsf{p} r_2$ holds is decidable.*

As $\mathsf{cast}_\Uparrow$ and $\mathsf{cast}_\Downarrow$ are annotated, both τ_1 and τ_2 can be determined and the well-typedness is checked in the original system. By Lemma 5, the erased terms keeps the well-typedness. Thus, by Lemma 6, it is decidable to check if $|\tau_1| \longrightarrow_\mathsf{p} |\tau_2|$. We conclude the decidability of type checking by following lemmas:

Lemma 7 (Uniqueness of Typing for λI_p). *If $\Gamma \vdash e : \tau_1$ and $\Gamma \vdash e : \tau_2$, then $\tau_1 \equiv \tau_2$.*

Theorem 6 (Decidability of Type Checking for λI_p). *Given a well-formed context Γ and a term e, it is decidable to determine if there exists τ such that $\Gamma \vdash e : \tau$.*

5   Application of Iso-types

λI is a simple core calculus, but expressive enough to encode useful language constructs. We have implemented a simple functional language **Fun** to show how features of modern functional languages can be encoded in λI. We focus on common features available in traditional functional languages and some interesting type-level features, but not the *full power* of dependent types. Supported features include algebraic datatypes, records, higher-kinded types, kind polymorphism [30] and datatype promotion [30].

Due to lack of space, many examples illustrating the various language features supported in **Fun** are provided only in the extended version [29]. Here we show the essential idea of how to exploit iso-types to encode language constructs.

Encoding Parametrized Algebraic Datatypes with Weak Casts. We give an example of encoding parametrized algebraic datatypes in λI_w via μ-operator and *weak casts*. Importantly we should note that having iso-recursive types alone (and alpha equality) would be insufficient to encode parametrized types: the generalization afforded by iso-types is needed here. In **Fun** we can define *polymorphic list* as:

data $List\ a = Nil \mid Cons\ a\ (List\ a)$;

This **Fun** definition is translated into λI_w using a Scott encoding [18] of datatypes:

$$
\begin{aligned}
List\ &= \mu L : \star \to \star.\, \lambda a : \star.\, \Pi b : \star.\, b \to (a \to L\ a \to b) \to b \\
Nil\ &= \lambda a : \star.\, \mathsf{cast}^2_\downarrow\, [List\ a]\ (\lambda b : \star.\, \lambda n : b.\, \lambda c : (a \to List\ a \to b).\, n) \\
Cons\ &= \lambda a : \star.\, \lambda x : a.\, \lambda(xs : List\ a). \\
&\quad\ \mathsf{cast}^2_\uparrow\, [List\ a]\ (\lambda b : \star.\, \lambda n : b.\, \lambda c : (a \to List\ a \to b).\, c\ x\ xs)
\end{aligned}
$$

The type constructor *List* is encoded as a recursive type. The body is a *type-level function* that takes a type parameter a and returns a dependent function type, i.e., Π-type. The body of Π-type is universally quantified by a type parameter b, which represents the result type instantiated during pattern matching. Following are the types corresponding to data constructors: b for *Nil*, and $a \to L\ a \to b$ for *Cons*, and the result type b at the end. The data constructors *Nil* and *Cons* are encoded as functions. Each of them selects a different function from the parameters (n and c). This provides branching in the process flow, based on the constructors. Note that $\mathsf{cast}_\uparrow$ is used twice here (written as $\mathsf{cast}^2_\uparrow$): one for *one-step expansion* from τ to $(\lambda a : \star.\ \tau)\,a$ and the other for *folding the recursive type* from $(\lambda a : \star.\ \tau)\,a$ to *List a*, where τ is the type of $\mathsf{cast}^2_\uparrow$ body.

We have two notable remarks from the example above. First, iso-types are critical for the encoding and cannot be replaced by iso-recursive types. Since type constructors are parameterized, not only folding/unfolding recursive types, but also type-level reduction/expansion is required, which is only possible with casts. Second, though weak casts are not as powerful as full casts, they are capable of encoding many useful constructs, such as algebraic datatypes and records [29]. Nevertheless full-reduction casts enable other important applications. Some applications of full casts are discussed in the extended version [29].

6 Related Work

Core Calculus for Functional Languages. Girard's System F_ω [14] is a typed lambda calculus with higher-kinded polymorphism. For the well-formedness of type expressions, an extra level of *kinds* is added to the system. In comparison, because of unified syntax, λI is considerably simpler than System F_ω, both in terms of language constructs and complexity of proofs. As for type-level computation, System F_ω differs from λI in that it uses a conversion rule, while λI uses explicit casts. The current core language for GHC Haskell, System F_C [26] is a significant extension of System F_ω, which supports GADTs [20], functional dependencies [15], type families [13], and kind equality [28]. These features use a non-trivial form of type equality, which is currently missing from λI. On the other hand, λI uses unified syntax and has only 8 language constructs, whereas System F_C uses multiple levels of syntax and currently has over 30 language constructs, making it significantly more complex. One direction of our future work is to investigate the addition of such forms of non-trivial type-equality.

Unified Syntax with Decidable Type-Checking. Pure Type Systems [4] show how a whole family of type systems can be implemented using just a single syntactic form. PTSs are an obvious source of inspiration for our work. Although this paper presents a specific system based on λC, it should be easy to generalize λI in the same way as PTSs and further show the applicability of our ideas to other systems. An early attempt of using a PTS-like syntax for an intermediate language for functional programming was Henk [21]. The Henk proposal was to use the *lambda cube* as a typed intermediate language, unifying all three levels. However the authors have not studied the addition of general recursion nor full dependent types.

Zombie [8] is a dependently typed language using a single syntactic category. It is composed of two fragments: a logical fragment where every expression is known to terminate, and a programmatic fragment that allows general recursion. Though Zombie has one syntactic category, it is still fairly complicated (with around 24 language constructs) as it tries to be both consistent as a logic and pragmatic as a programming language. Even if one is only interested in modeling a programmatic fragment, additional mechanisms are required to ensure the validity of proofs, e.g., call-by-value semantics and value restriction [23,24]. In contrast to Zombie, λI takes another point of the design space, giving up logical consistency and reasoning about proofs for simplicity in the language design.

Unified Syntax with General Recursion and Undecidable Type Checking. Cayenne [3] integrates the full power of dependent types with general recursion, which bears some similarities with λI. It uses one syntactic form for both terms and types, allows arbitrary computation at type level and is logically inconsistent because of allowing unrestricted recursion. However, the most crucial difference from λI is that type checking in Cayenne is *undecidable*. From a pragmatic point of view, this design choice simplifies the implementation, but the desirable property of decidable type checking is lost. Cardelli's Type:Type language [7] also features general recursion to implement equi-recursive types. Recursion and recursive types are unified in a single construct. However, both equi-recursive types and the Type:Type axiom make the type system undecidable. $\Pi\Sigma$ [2] is another example of a language that uses one recursion mechanism for both types and functions. The type-level recursion is controlled by lifted types and boxes since definitions are not unfolded inside boxes. However, $\Pi\Sigma$ does not have decidable type checking due to the "type-in-type" axiom. And its metatheory is not formally developed.

Casts for Managed Type-Level Computation. Type-level computation in λI is controlled by explicit casts. Several studies [12,17,23–26] also attempt to use explicit casts for managed type-level computation. However, casts in those approaches are not inspired by iso-recursive types. Instead they require *equality proof terms*, while casts in λI do not. The need for equality proof terms complicates the language design because: (1) building equality proofs requires various other language constructs, adding to the complexity of the language design and metatheory; (2) It is desirable to ensure that the equality proofs are valid. Otherwise, one can easily build bogus equality proofs with non-termination, which could endanger type safety. Guru [25] and Sep3 [17] make *syntactic separation* between proofs and programs to prevent certain programmatic terms turning into invalid proofs. The programmatic part of Zombie [23,24], which has no such separation, employs *value restriction* that restricts proofs to be syntactic values to avoid non-terminating terms. PTS with convertibility proofs (PTS$_f$) [12] extends PTS by replacing the implicit conversion rule with explicit conversion proofs embedded into terms. However, it requires many language constructs to build equality proofs; and it does not allow general recursion, thus does not need to deal with problem 2). Our treatment of full casts in λI_p, using a separate erased system for developing metatheory, is similar to the approach of Zombie or Guru which uses an unannotated system.

Restricted Recursion with Termination Checking. As proof assistants, dependently typed languages such as Coq [9] and Adga [19] are conservative as to what kind of computation is allowed. They require all programs to terminate by means of a termination checker, ensuring recursive calls are decreasing. Decidable type checking and logical consistency are preserved. But the conservative, syntactic criteria is insufficient to support a variety of important programming paradigms. Agda offers an option to disable the termination checker to allow writing arbitrary functions. However, this may endanger both decidable type checking and logical consistency. Idris [6] is a dependently typed language that allows writing unrestricted functions. However, to achieve decidable type checking, it also requires termination checker to ensure only terminating functions are evaluated by the type checker. While logical consistency is an appealing property, it is not a goal of λI. Instead λI aims at retaining (term-level) general recursion as found in languages like Haskell or ML, while benefiting from a unified syntax to simplify the implementation of the core language.

7 Conclusion

This work proposes λI: a minimal dependently typed core language that allows the same syntax for terms and types, supports type-level computation, and preserves decidable type checking under the presence of general recursion. The key idea is to control type-level computation using iso-types via casts. Because each cast can only account for one-step of type-level computation, type checking becomes decidable without requiring strong normalization of the calculus. At the same time one-step casts together with recursion provide a generalization of iso-recursive types. Two variants of λI show trade-offs of employing different reduction strategies in casts. In future work, we hope to investigate surface language mechanisms, such as type families in Haskell, to express intensive type-level computation in a more convenient way.

Acknowledgments. We thank the anonymous reviewers for their helpful comments. This work has been sponsored by the Hong Kong Research Grant Council Early Career Scheme project number 27200514.

References

1. Adams, R.: Pure type systems with judgemental equality. J. Funct. Program. **16**(02), 219–246 (2006)
2. Altenkirch, T., Danielsson, N.A., Löh, A., Oury, N.: $\Pi\Sigma$: dependent types without the sugar. In: Blume, M., Kobayashi, N., Vidal, G. (eds.) Functional and Logic Programming. LNCS, vol. 6009, pp. 40–55. Springer, Heidelberg (2010). doi:10.1007/978-3-642-12251-4_5
3. Augustsson, L.: Cayenne – a language with dependent types. In: ICFP 1998. pp. 239–250 (1998)
4. Barendregt, H.: Introduction to generalized type systems. J. Funct. Program. **1**(2), 125–154 (1991)
5. Barendregt, H.: Lambda Calculi with types. Handbook of Logic in Computer Science **2**, 117–309 (1992)
6. Brady, E.: IDRIS–systems programming meets full dependent types. In: PLPV 2011, pp. 43–54 (2011)
7. Cardelli, L.: A Polymorphic Lambda-Calculus with type: type. Digital Systems Research Center (1986)

8. Casinghino, C., Sjöberg, V., Weirich, S.: Combining proofs and programs in a dependently typed language. In: POPL 2014, pp. 33–45 (2014)

9. Coq development team: The coq proof assistant. http://coq.inria.fr/

10. Coquand, T., Huet, G.: The calculus of constructions. Inf. Comput. **76**, 95–120 (1988)

11. Crary, K., Harper, R., Puri, S.: What is a recursive module?. In: PLDI 1999, pp. 50–63 (1999)

12. van Doorn, F., Geuvers, H., Wiedijk, F.: Explicit convertibility proofs in pure type systems. In: LFMTP 2013, pp. 25–36 (2013)

13. Eisenberg, R.A., Vytiniotis, D., Peyton Jones, S., Weirich, S.: Closed type families with overlapping equations. In: POPL 2014 (2014)

14. Girard, J.Y.: Interprtation fonctionnelle et limination des coupures de l'arithmtique d'ordre suprieur. Ph.D. thesis, Universit Paris VII (1972)

15. Jones, M.P.: Type classes with functional dependencies. In: Proceedings of the 9th European Symposium on Programming Languages and Systems, March 2000

16. Jutting, L.: Typing in pure type systems. Inf. Comput. **105**(1), 30–41 (1993)

17. Kimmell, G., Stump, A., Eades III, H.D., Fu, P., Sheard, T., Weirich, S., Casinghino, C., Sjöberg, V., Collins, N., Ahn, K.Y.: Equational reasoning about programs with general recursion and call-by-value semantics. In: PLPV 2012, pp. 15–26 (2012)

18. Mogensen, T.A.: Theoretical pearls: efficient self-interpretation in Lambda Calculus. J. Funct. Program. **2**(3), 345–364 (1992)

19. Norell, U.: Towards a practical programming language based on dependent type theory. Ph.D. thesis, Chalmers University of Technology (2007)

20. Peyton Jones, S., Washburn, G., Weirich, S.: Wobbly types: type inference for generalised algebraic data types. Technical report, MS-CIS-05-26, University of Pennsylvania, July 2004

21. Jones, S.P., Meijer, E.: Henk: a typed intermediate language. In: Types in Compilation Workshop (1997)

22. Pierce, B.C.: Types and Programming Languages. MIT press, Cambridge (2002)

23. Sjöberg, V., Casinghino, C., Ahn, K.Y., Collins, N., Eades III, H.D., Fu, P., Kimmell, G., Sheard, T., Stump, A., Weirich, S.: Irrelevance, heterogenous equality, and call-by-value dependent type systems. In: MSFP 2012, pp. 112–162 (2012)

24. Sjöberg, V., Weirich, S.: Programming up to congruence. In: POPL 2015, pp. 369–382 (2015)

25. Stump, A., Deters, M., Petcher, A., Schiller, T., Simpson, T.: Verified programming in Guru. In: PLPV 2009, pp. 49–58 (2008)

26. Sulzmann, M., Chakravarty, M.M.T., Jones, S.P., Donnelly, K.: System F with type equality coercions. In: TLDI 2007, pp. 53–66 (2007)

27. Swamy, N., Chen, J., Fournet, C., Strub, P.Y., Bhargavan, K., Yang, J.: Secure distributed programming with value-dependent types. In: ICFP 2011, pp. 266–278 (2011)

28. Weirich, S., Hsu, J., Eisenberg, R.A.: System FC with explicit kind equality. In: ICFP 2013, pp. 275–286 (2013)

29. Yang, Y., Bi, X., Oliveira, B.C.d.S.: Unified syntax with iso-types. Extended Version (2016). https://bitbucket.org/ypyang/aplas16

30. Yorgey, B.A., Weirich, S., Cretin, J., Jones, S.P., Vytiniotis, D., Magalhães, J.P.: Giving Haskell a promotion. In: TLDI 2012, pp. 53–66 (2012)

Refined Environment Classifiers
Type- and Scope-Safe Code Generation with Mutable Cells

Oleg Kiselyov[1]([⊠]), Yukiyoshi Kameyama[2], and Yuto Sudo[2]

[1] Tohoku University, Sendai, Japan
oleg@okmij.org
[2] University of Tsukuba, Tsukuba, Japan
kameyama@acm.org

Abstract. Generating high-performance code and applying typical optimizations within the bodies of loops and functions involves moving or storing open code for later use, often in a different binding environment. There are ample opportunities for variables being left unbound or accidentally captured. It has been a tough challenge to statically ensure that by construction the generated code is nevertheless well-typed and *well-scoped*: all free variables in manipulated and stored code fragments shall eventually be bound, by their intended binders.

We present the calculus for code generation with mutable state that for the first time achieves type-safety and hygiene without ad hoc restrictions. The calculus strongly resembles region-based memory management, but with the orders of magnitude simpler proofs. It employs the rightly abstract representation for free variables, which, like hypothesis in natural deduction, are free from the bureaucracy of syntax imposed by the type environment or numbering conventions.

Although the calculus was designed for the sake of formalization and is deliberately bare-bone, it turns out easily implementable and not too bothersome for writing realistic program.

1 Introduction

Code generation exhibits the all-too-common trade-off: obtaining code with the highest performance; statically ensuring the code quality; being able to use the code-generating system in practice – choose two. Optimizing compilers and many practical code-generating tools do all desired optimizations. The correctness of the result is ensured however only by careful programming. This is not a problem in case of a compiler written by a small team of experts and changed relatively infrequently. The lack of static assurances is worrisome for code transformation and generation libraries written by domain experts, who have less time to devote to proofs and have to continually tune their libraries to the domain knowledge and circumstances. There is the attested danger of generating code with unbound, or worse, unexpectedly bound variables. At the very least, we would like to guarantee that the generated code – at all times, even the code

© Springer International Publishing AG 2016
A. Igarashi (Ed.): APLAS 2016, LNCS 10017, pp. 271–291, 2016.
DOI: 10.1007/978-3-319-47958-3_15

fragments – is well-formed, well-typed, and all of its free variables will eventually be bound by their intended binders. This guarantee should hold before we compile the generated code, which is typically unfit for human reading. Ideally, the guarantee should hold even before we compile the generator.

On the other side of the trade-off are the staged calculi such as λ° and λ^α [4,15] that express code generators with the desired static guarantees. They are called 'staged' because evaluation is stratified: the result of the present, or Level-0, stage is the code to be evaluated at the next, Level-1, or future stage. The calculi have been implemented as full-featured staged languages used in practice [8,17]. Another example is Pouillard's [13] code generation and analysis library with proven correctness. Alas, all these systems restrict the range of safe operations on open code: in particular, they limit or outlaw the operations that move or store open code, retrieving it later in a different binding environment. Such operations are required for many optimizations such as let-insertion, memoization, loop interchange and tiling. There have been general approaches that permit the desired open code motions and provide static guarantees: for example, [12]. Alas, they are too complex to use in practice or even to implement. For more discussion, see Sect. 5 and especially [6].

StagedHaskell [6] overcomes the impasse, but partially. It is the library for code generation that supports code movements, including movements via any computational (monadic) effect. Using a contextual modal type system, the library statically assures that at all times the generated code is well-formed, well-typed and *well-scoped*: all free variables in manipulated and stored code fragments shall eventually be bound by their intended binders. However, the safety properties have been argued only informally. The main reason is that the complexity of the Haskell implementation, specifically, the encoding of the contextual modal type system, make the formal reasoning difficult.

The present paper takes the first step of formalizing StagedHaskell: it distills the staged calculus <NJ> that safely permits open code movements across different binding environments via mutable cells. The calculus can express realistic examples from StagedHaskell, such as the assert-insertion, see Sect. 4.

Although <NJ> was motivated by code generation with safety guarantees, it turned a vantage point to view seemingly unrelated areas. First, there is an uncanny similarity between generating code of functions (or other blocks with local binders) and region-based memory management. Preventing the 'extrusion' of free variables out of the bodies of generated functions is similar to keeping reference cells allocated within a region from leaking out. We have consciously used this similarity, adapting techniques from region calculi [5].

The key to ensuring hygiene and type safety when manipulating open code is reflecting free variables of a code fragment in its type – which evokes contextual modal type theory [10] and, in general, sequent calculus. The structural rules such as weakening now turn up in programs, e.g., as 'shifts' of De Bruijn indices [3]. After all, in metaprogramming, meta-level becomes the object level. 'The bureaucracy of syntax' now worries not only logicians but also programmers.

A particularly elegant method to overcome the complexities and redundancies of concrete name and environment representations is environment classifiers [15] (recalled and discussed in Sect. 3.2). A single classifier represents a set of free variables, abstracting from their order, quantity, or names. Unfortunately, in the presence of effects, the original environment classifiers are too coarse, abstracting away the information needed to ensure the type safety of effectful generators. Inspired by the concept of local assumptions from Natural Deduction NJ, we have identified the minimal necessary refinement of environment classifiers.

Contributions. Our specific contributions are as follows:

- Practical two-stage calculus <NJ> whose type system statically ensures hygiene and the type-safety of the generated code in the presence of mutable reference cells. The calculus distills the design of the practical StagedHaskell library. The calculus itself is easily implementable.
- Refinement of environment classifiers – imposing partial order – that preserves all their simplicity and advantages and is compatible with effects.

<NJ> is close to the current MetaOCaml [8], which permits leaking of variables (scope extrusion) but raises a run-time error at the moment the code with leaked (extruded) variables is about to be used. Our calculus prevents such errors statically.

The calculus has been implemented as a simple embedding in OCaml, whose type checker checks <NJ> types and even infers them. Signatures are only needed for functions that receive code values as arguments *and* use them in distinct binding environments. One is immediately reminded of ML^F [9]; this is not an accident, as we shall see in Sect. 3.3. All examples in the paper are slightly reformatted running code. The implementation, with more examples, is available at http://okmij.org/ftp/tagless-final/TaglessStaged/metaNJ.ml.

This paper is organized as follows: The next section introduces the calculus, using many examples to illustrate its syntax and dynamic semantics. Section 3 describes the type systems and proves its soundness. Section 3.1 specifically demonstrates the obvious and very subtle dangers arising from storing open code in mutable cells, and how <NJ> prevents the dangers but not the free use of reference cells. Responsible for this are refined environment classifiers; Sect. 3.2 discusses what, why and how. Section 4 shows off a complex example: It is used exactly as was explained in [6], deliberately to demonstrate that <NJ> is capable of representing practical StagedHaskell examples.

2   <NJ>, Its Syntax and Semantics

Formally, the syntax of <NJ> is defined in Fig. 1. This section introduces the calculus and its dynamic semantics more accessibly, on a series of small examples.

<NJ> is a lambda-calculus with reference cells and special constants to create and combine code values. Whereas 1 : int is the familiar constant of the base type int, <u>cint</u> 1 is an expression of the code type $\langle\,\mathrm{int}\,\rangle^\gamma$ which evaluates to $\langle 1 \rangle$.

The code types are explained in Sect. 3. Here, $\underline{\text{cint}}$ is a special code-generating constant, also called code combinator[1] [16,18]. We underline all such constants. Likewise, $\underline{\text{cbool}}$ **true** evaluates to $\langle\textbf{true}\rangle$ Since the $\underline{\text{cint}}$ and $\underline{\text{cbool}}$ expressions are common we adopt the abbreviated notation % that stands for either constant, depending on the context.

The bracketed expressions like $\langle 1 \rangle$ cannot appear in source programs; they come only during and as the result of reductions. This is the most visible distinction from stage calculi like λ^α [15] and MetaOCaml. Neither do we have 'splicing' (or, 'escape', unquotation). Bracketed expressions are essentially constants: they cannot be decomposed, inspected, or substituted into. Only a subset of expressions may be bracketed: underlined constants and the brackets themselves are excluded. <NJ> therefore is the two-stage calculus, for generating code but not for generating code generators[2]. We will sometimes use the superscript e^1 to emphasize the distinction between the host language and the generated language. Most of the time the superscript is elided for ease of notation.

Figure 2 defines the constants of <NJ>. They come in different arities. Seen earlier 1 and **true** are zero-ary constants, denoted as c_0 in Fig. 1. On the other hand, $\underline{\text{cint}}$ and $\underline{\text{cbool}}$ have the arity 1, and are not considered expressions per se: only their applications to one argument are expressions, see Fig. 1. Likewise, $+$ is an arity-2 constant, requiring two arguments to be regarded as an expression. We write such an expression in the conventional infix notation $1 + 2$, which evaluates to 3. Besides $\underline{\text{cint}}$ and $\underline{\text{cbool}}$, there are constants that combine already built code values: $\%1 \pm \%1$ of the code type $\langle\,\text{int}\,\rangle^\gamma$ evaluates as follows according to the rules of Figs. 3 and 4.

$$\%1 \pm \%2 \rightsquigarrow \langle 1 \rangle \pm \%2 \rightsquigarrow \langle 1 \rangle \pm \langle 2 \rangle \rightsquigarrow \langle 1+2 \rangle$$

Here, $\pm$ is an arity-2 constant, which we also write in infix. Again, all constants must be fully applied: there are no partial applications, sections, or other sugar.

<NJ> is the lambda-calculus, with the standard abstractions $\lambda x.\ e$ and applications $e_1\ e_2$. We let **let** $x = e_1$ **in** e_2 stand as the abbreviation for $(\lambda x.e_2)\ e_1$, and $e_1; e_2$ for **let** $x = e_1$ **in** e_2 where x does not appear free in e_2. The semantics of <NJ> is the standard small-step left-to-right call-by-value, see Fig. 3. (Heaps will be explained later on and can be ignored for now). <NJ> can also generate the code of functions, using the expression form $\underline{\lambda}x.\ e$ with peculiar semantics, which we explain in detail. For example, the expression $\underline{\lambda}x.\ x \pm \%3$ eventually generates the code of the function that increments its argument by 3:

$$\underline{\lambda}x.\ x \pm \%3 \rightsquigarrow \underline{\lambda}y.\langle y \rangle \pm \%3 \rightsquigarrow \underline{\lambda}y.\langle y \rangle \pm \langle 3 \rangle \rightsquigarrow \underline{\lambda}y.\langle y+3 \rangle \rightsquigarrow \langle \lambda y.y+3 \rangle$$

First, the expression $\underline{\lambda}x.\ x \pm \%3$ reduces by choosing a fresh variable name y, replacing all free occurrences of x in its body with $\langle y \rangle$ and wrapping the result in $\underline{\lambda}y$. (Expressions of the form $\underline{\lambda}y.e$ come up during the evaluation and do not appear in source programs.) Next, the body of thus built $\underline{\lambda}y.\langle y \rangle \pm \%3$ reduces as

---

[1] The StagedHaskell library, the prototype of <NJ>, is a code-combinator library.

[2] This restriction certainly simplifies the formalism. It is also realistic: in all our experience of using MetaOCaml, the multi-stage language, we are yet to come across any real-life example needing more than two stages. Template Haskell is also two-stage.

described earlier. The final reduction in the sequence builds the resulting code. Thus producing the code for functions has two separate phases: generating the name for the bound variable, and generating the binder for that name at the end. In many staged calculi the two phases can be (and are) combined. The effects force them apart however, as we shall see soon.

Variables	$x, y, z, u, f, n, r \ldots$
Classifier	γ
Location	l
Types	$t ::= \mathbf{int} \mid \mathbf{bool} \mid t \to t \mid t\ \mathbf{ref} \mid \langle t \rangle^\gamma$
Level 1 Types	$t^1 ::= \mathbf{int} \mid \mathbf{bool} \mid t^1 \to t^1 \mid t^1\ \mathbf{ref}$
Level 0 Expressions	$e ::= x \mid \mathsf{l} \mid c_0 \mid c_1\ e \mid c_2\ e\ e \mid c_3\ e\ e\ e \mid \lambda x.\ e \mid \underline{\lambda} x.\ e \mid e\ e$ $\mid\ \mathbf{if}\ e\ \mathbf{then}\ e\ \mathbf{else}\ e$
Internal Expressions	$\underline{\lambda} x.\ e \mid \langle e^1 \rangle$
Level 1 Expressions	$e^1 ::= e$ without code combinators, internal expressions, locations
Values	$v ::= c_0 \mid \mathsf{l} \mid \lambda x.\ e \mid \langle e \rangle$

Fig. 1. Syntax of `<NJ>`. The constants c_i with their arities i are defined in Fig. 2.

Arity 0
$1, 2, 3, \ldots\ :\ \mathbf{int}$
$\mathbf{true},\ \mathbf{false} :\ \mathbf{bool}$

Arity 1
$\underline{\text{cint}} :\quad \mathbf{int} \to \langle \mathbf{int} \rangle^\gamma$
$\underline{\text{cbool}} :\ \mathbf{bool} \to \langle \mathbf{bool} \rangle^\gamma$
$\text{fix} :\ ((t_1 \to t_2) \to (t_1 \to t_2)) \to (t_1 \to t_2)$
$\underline{\text{fix}} :\ \langle (t_1 \to t_2) \to (t_1 \to t_2) \rangle^\gamma \to \langle t_1 \to t_2 \rangle^\gamma$
$! :\quad \langle t\ \mathbf{ref} \rangle^\gamma \to \langle t \rangle^\gamma$
$\mathbf{ref} :\ t \to t\ \mathbf{ref}$
$\underline{\mathbf{ref}} :\ \langle t \rangle^\gamma \to \langle t\ \mathbf{ref} \rangle^\gamma$

Arity 2
$+ :\ \mathbf{int} \to \mathbf{int} \to \mathbf{int}$
$\underline{+} :\ \langle \mathbf{int} \rangle^\gamma \to \langle \mathbf{int} \rangle^\gamma \to \langle \mathbf{int} \rangle^\gamma$
$= :\ \mathbf{int} \to \mathbf{int} \to \mathbf{bool}$
$\underline{=} :\ \langle \mathbf{int} \rangle^\gamma \to \langle \mathbf{int} \rangle^\gamma \to \langle \mathbf{bool} \rangle^\gamma$
$\underline{@} :\ \langle t_1 \to t_2 \rangle^\gamma \to \langle t_1 \rangle^\gamma \to \langle t_2 \rangle^\gamma$
$:= :\ t\ \mathbf{ref} \to t \to t$
$\underline{:=} :\ \langle t\ \mathbf{ref} \rangle^\gamma \to \langle t \rangle^\gamma \to \langle t \rangle^\gamma$

Arity 3
$\underline{\text{cif}} :\ \langle \mathbf{bool} \rangle^\gamma \to \langle t \rangle^\gamma \to \langle t \rangle^\gamma \to \langle t \rangle^\gamma$

Fig. 2. The constants c_i of `<NJ>` with their arities i. The underlined constants, whose result type is code type, are code combinators. The shown types are schematic: t denotes any suitable type and γ any suitable classifier. We silently add other arithmetic and comparison constants and code combinators, similar to $+$ and $=$. Although the constants may have function types, they are not expressions, unless applied to the right number of arguments.

For another illustration we take the familiar power example: generating a function that raises its argument to the given power by repeated multiplications.

$\mathbf{let}\ \text{body} = \lambda f\ n\ x.\ \mathbf{if}\ n=0\ \mathbf{then}\ \%1\ \mathbf{else}\ x \underline{*} f\ (n-1)\ x\ \mathbf{in}$
$\lambda n.\ \underline{\lambda} x.\ (\ \text{fix}\ \text{body})\ n\ x$

Applying the result to, say, 3 produces $\langle \lambda y.\ y * y * y * 1 \rangle$.

$\quad$ `<NJ>` has mutable state in the form of the familiar mutable cells, such as those found in ML and many other languages. Correspondingly, the calculus has the

Contexts	$E ::= [] \mid E\ e \mid v\ E \mid c_1\ E \mid c_2\ E\ e \mid c_2\ v\ E$
	$\mid$ **if** E **then** e **else** $e \mid \underline{\lambda}x.\ E$
Heap	$H ::= [] \mid l{:}v,H$
Names	$N ::= [] \mid y,N$
Substitutions	$e_1[x{:}=e_2]$
Reductions	$N_1;H_1;e_1 \rightsquigarrow N_2;H_2;e_2$

$$\frac{N_1;H_1;e_1 \rightsquigarrow N_2;H_2;e_2}{N_1;H_1;E[e_1] \rightsquigarrow N_2;H_2;E[e_2]}$$

Context compatibility

Primitive reductions

$$
\begin{aligned}
N;H;\ (\lambda x.e)\ v &\rightsquigarrow N;H;\ e[x{:}=v] \\
N;H;\ \textbf{if true then } e_1 \textbf{ else } e_2 &\rightsquigarrow N;H;\ e_1 \\
N;H;\ \textbf{if false then } e_1 \textbf{ else } e_2 &\rightsquigarrow N;H;\ e_2 \\
N;H;\ \underline{\lambda}x.\ e &\rightsquigarrow (y,N);H;\ \underline{\lambda}y.\ e[x{:}=\langle y\rangle] \qquad y \notin N \\
N;H;\ \underline{\lambda}y.\langle e\rangle &\rightsquigarrow N;H;\ \langle \lambda y.e\rangle \\
N;H;\ \textbf{ref } v &\rightsquigarrow N;(l{:}v,H);\ l \qquad l \notin \text{dom}H \\
N;(l{:}v,H);\ !\ l &\rightsquigarrow N;(l{:}v,H);\ v \\
N;(l{:}v,H);\ l := v_2 &\rightsquigarrow N;(l{:}v_2,H);\ v_2
\end{aligned}
$$

Fig. 3. Dynamic semantics of <NJ>: reductions $e_1 \rightsquigarrow e_2$. The reductions involving (code-generating) constants are defined in Fig. 4.

$$
\begin{aligned}
\underline{\text{cint}}\ n &\rightsquigarrow \langle n\rangle & \underline{\text{cif}}\ \langle e_1\rangle\ \langle e_2\rangle\ \langle e_3\rangle &\rightsquigarrow \langle \textbf{if } e_1 \textbf{ then } e_2 \textbf{ else } e_3\rangle \\
\underline{\text{cbool}}\ b &\rightsquigarrow \langle b\rangle & \underline{\text{fix}}\ (\lambda f.\ e) &\rightsquigarrow e[f{:}=\text{fix}\ (\lambda f.\ e)] \\
\langle e_1\rangle\ \underline{+}\ \langle e_2\rangle &\rightsquigarrow \langle e_1 + e_2\rangle & \underline{\text{ref}}\ \langle e\rangle &\rightsquigarrow \langle \textbf{ref } e\rangle \\
\langle e_1\rangle\ \underline{\equiv}\ \langle e_2\rangle &\rightsquigarrow \langle e_1 = e_2\rangle & \underline{!}\ \langle e\rangle &\rightsquigarrow \langle !e\rangle \\
\langle e_1\rangle\ \underline{@}\ \langle e_2\rangle &\rightsquigarrow \langle e_1\ e_2\rangle & \langle e_1\rangle\ \underline{:=}\ \langle e_2\rangle &\rightsquigarrow \langle e_1 := e_2\rangle \\
\underline{\text{fix}}\ \langle e\rangle &\rightsquigarrow \langle \text{fix}\ e\rangle
\end{aligned}
$$

Fig. 4. Constant (code-generating) reductions

form **ref** e to create a fresh reference cell holding the value of e, $!e$ to dereference it, obtaining the held value, and $e_1 := e_2$ to replace the value of the cell e_1 with the value of e_2, returning the latter value. The semantics is standard, involving locations l and the heap H, the finite map from locations to values. The empty heap is denoted as $[]$; $(l{:}v,H)$ is the heap that contains the association of l with v plus the associations in H. The domain of the latter does not include l. From λ^U [2] we borrow the heap-like *name heap* N, which is the set of names used for variables in the generated code. As we shall see throughout the paper, there is an uncanny similarity between reference cells and the future-stage variable names.

The full dynamic semantics of <NJ> thus deals with reductions between *configurations*, made of the name and location heaps, and an expression, see Fig. 3. We will often elide the heaps when presenting reductions, especially in examples. As an illustration, the following reductions show the evaluation of a sample imperative code, and the generation of the imperative code:

N;H;**let** r = **ref** (2+3) **in** r := 0; !r ⤳*
    N;(l :5,H); l := 0; !l ⤳* N;(l :0,H);!l ⤳ N;(l :0,H);0
clet r = **ref** (%2 + %3) **in** clet z = r := %0 **in** !r ≡
    (λr. (λz. !r) @ r := %0) @ **ref** (%2 + %3) ⤳*
    (λy. (λu. !⟨y⟩) @ ⟨y⟩ := %0) @ **ref** (%2 + %3) ⤳*
    (λy. ⟨λu. !y⟩ @ ⟨y := 0⟩) @ **ref** (%2 + %3) ⤳*
    ⟨(λy. (λu. !y) (y := 0))⟩ (**ref** (2 + 3))⟩

where we used clet x = e_1 **in** e_2 to stand for (λx. e_2) @ e_1. In the first example,
l denotes a fresh location. We elided the heaps in the second example.

So far, the lambda-calculus fragment of <NJ>, the code generating and the
reference cell fragments looked like orthogonal extensions. There is one part
of the semantics where they interact non-trivially. It has to do with generating functions and using reference cells to store open code. The following is an
example of how *not* to use reference cells to store open code: it is the infamous
scope-extrusion example.

N;H;**let** r = **ref** %0 **in** (λx. r := x); !r ⤳ N;(l :⟨0⟩,H); (λx. l := x); !l ⤳
(y,N);(l :⟨0⟩,H); (λy. l := ⟨y⟩); !l ⤳ (y,N);(l :⟨y⟩,H): (λy. ⟨y⟩); !l ⤳
(y,N);(l :⟨y⟩,H); ⟨λy. y⟩; !l ⤳
(y,N);(l :⟨y⟩,H); !l ⤳ (y,N);(l :⟨y⟩,H); ⟨y⟩

When building the functions's body we store the code with the yet-to-be-bound
variable y in the reference cell. After the function is constructed we retrieve from
the reference cell the code with what is by now the unbound variable y. We have
just seen the most blatant example of scope extrusion; alas, there are also subtle,
and hence far more dangerous cases; we discuss them in Sect. 3.1.

Our dynamic semantics is really non-chalant about unbound future-stage
variables, treating them essentially as constants. To be pedantic, y in the result
of the scope-extrusion example is bound, technically: it occurs in the name heap.
Real staged languages such as MetaOCaml and Scala-Virtualized [14] likewise
allow unbound variables to appear in code values (in case of MetaOCaml, for
a short interval). We will show in the next section that a well-typed <NJ> program never generates code with unbound variables. The scope-extrusion program
above does not type-check.

Storing open code in reference cells has many legitimate uses. Here we show
one simple example. It is again the power function, but now with reference cells.
Merely computing x^n looks in <NJ> as

λn.λx. **let** r = **ref** 1 **in**
    fix (λf.λn. **if** n = 0 **then** 0 **else** (r := !r ∗ x; f (n−1))) n; !r

To obtain the code for computing x^n for a fixed n, we turn the above program
into the generator, in a rather straightforward way:

let body = λn.λx. **let** r = **ref** %1 **in**
    fix (λf.λn. **if** n = 0 **then** 0 **else** (r := !r ∗ x; f (n−1))) n; !r
in λn. λx. body n x

Applying the result to, say, 3 produces, as before, ⟨λy. y ∗ y ∗ y ∗ 1⟩. The reference cell r accumulates progressively longer code for the product, containing

multiple occurrences of the free variable y, to be bound at the end. Section 4 shows more interesting, realistic example of reference cells in code generators, of assertion insertion.

3   Type System

Figure 1 also defines the syntax of types t, which include the standard, base types of int and bool, the arrow (function) type and the reference type t **ref**. Non-standard is the code-type $\langle t \rangle^\gamma$, containing the so-called classifier γ – similar in intent, but more precise than the environment classifier of [15], as mentioned in the Introduction. One may think of the classifier γ as a type-level representation, or 'name', of a Level-1 variable – although strictly speaking a classifier represents a binding environment. We delay the further discussion of classifiers till Sect. 3.2, after we explained the typing rules that govern classifiers, the partial order on classifiers and classifier subtyping. Since <NJ> is a two-level system – the generated code does not contain any code generating expressions – we distinguish level 1 types t^1 from level 0 types t: the former omits code types. To relieve the notation burden, however, we will often use the same meta-variable t for both sorts of types, using t^1 only where necessary for disambiguation.

Figure 5 defines judgements and their components. The main typing judgement – the expression e has the type t at the level L – has the form $\Upsilon;\Theta;\Gamma \vdash^L e : t$. Here, Γ is the standard environment, an ordered sequence associating types with free variables in an expression. Free variables in e^1 expressions (that is, expressions within brackets) are Level-1 free variables; their associations $(y{:}t^1)^\gamma$ in Γ are annotated with the classifier γ. Besides the free variable bindings, Γ also contains classifiers γ and classifier subtyping witnesses $\gamma_1 \succ \gamma_2$ to be explained shortly. Υ and Θ are essentially the typings of the name and location heaps. Θ is indeed a finite map from locations to types; Υ on the other hand, has more structure. It is an ordered sequence. It contains the classifier γ for each name in N. Like Γ, it also contains the types associated with each name (Level-1 variable) and the classifier subtyping witnesses. One may think of Γ as a local type environment and Υ as a 'global' one. The initial Υ contains only the pre-defined classifier γ_0. We use the standard $\in$ notation to assert that Γ or Υ sequences contain a particular element. In addition, we write $l \in \Theta$ to say the location is in the domain of the finite map Θ. The notation $b \in (\Gamma \uplus \Upsilon)$ means that some binding b is an element of Γ, or else it is an element of Υ (note the asymmetry).

Level indication L	either empty or γ
Environment	$\Gamma ::= [] \mid \Gamma, \gamma \mid \Gamma, (\gamma_1 \succ \gamma_2) \mid \Gamma, (x{:}t)^L$
Heap typing	$\Theta ::= [] \mid \Theta, (l{:}t)$
Name heap typing	$\Upsilon ::= [] \mid \Upsilon, \gamma \mid \Upsilon, (\gamma_1 \succ \gamma_2) \mid \Upsilon, (y{:}t^1)^\gamma$
Judgement	$\Upsilon;\Theta;\Gamma \vdash^L e{:} t$

Fig. 5. Judgements, environments, classifiers

$$\frac{}{\vdash [] \text{ ok}}$$

$$\frac{\vdash \varUpsilon \text{ ok} \quad \gamma \notin \varUpsilon}{\vdash \varUpsilon, \gamma \text{ ok}}$$

$$\frac{\vdash \varUpsilon \text{ ok} \quad \gamma_1 \in \varUpsilon \quad \gamma_2 \in \varUpsilon}{\vdash \varUpsilon, \gamma_1 \succ \gamma_2 \text{ ok}}$$

$$\frac{\vdash \varUpsilon \text{ ok} \quad \gamma \in \varUpsilon \quad y \notin \varUpsilon \quad (y':t')^\gamma \notin \varUpsilon \ (\text{i.e., } \varUpsilon \text{ has no other binding marked by } \gamma)}{\vdash \varUpsilon, (y{:}t^1)^\gamma \text{ ok}}$$

$$\forall \ l \in \varTheta \text{ such that } \varTheta(l) \text{ is } \langle t \rangle^\gamma. \ \gamma \in \varUpsilon$$

$$\frac{}{\varUpsilon \vdash [] \text{ ok}}$$

$$\frac{\varUpsilon \vdash \varTheta \text{ ok}}{\varUpsilon \vdash \varGamma \text{ ok}}$$

$$\frac{\varUpsilon \vdash \varGamma \text{ ok} \quad \gamma \notin \varUpsilon \quad \gamma \notin \varGamma}{\varUpsilon \vdash \varGamma, \gamma \text{ ok}}$$

$$\frac{\varUpsilon \vdash \varGamma \text{ ok} \quad \gamma_1 \in (\varGamma \uplus \varUpsilon) \quad \gamma_2 \in (\varGamma \uplus \varUpsilon)}{\varUpsilon \vdash \varGamma, (\gamma_1 \succ \gamma_2) \text{ ok}}$$

$$\frac{\varUpsilon \vdash \varGamma \text{ ok} \quad \gamma \in (\varGamma \uplus \varUpsilon)}{\varUpsilon \vdash \varGamma, (x{:}\langle t^1 \rangle^\gamma) \text{ ok}}$$

$$\frac{\varUpsilon \vdash \varGamma \text{ ok} \quad \gamma \in (\varGamma \uplus \varUpsilon)}{\varUpsilon \vdash \varGamma, (y{:}t^1)^\gamma \text{ ok}}$$

Fig. 6. Well-formedness of environments and heap typings $\vdash \varUpsilon$ ok, $\varUpsilon \vdash \varTheta$ ok, $\varUpsilon \vdash \varGamma$ ok

Some judgements are generic, so we use superscript L that stands for either empty or a classifier. If L is not empty, then, strictly speaking, the judgement should be written as $\varUpsilon ;[]; \varGamma \vdash^\gamma e^1 {:} t^1$, meaning that only a subset of expressions (and types) are allowed at level 1. In particular, locations cannot appear at Level 1[3]: normally locations result from evaluating expressions **ref** e; although such expressions may appear in the generated code, they remain unevaluated. There are no code combinators in <NJ> that could produce the value $\langle l \rangle$. A substitution cannot insert a location either, since the generated code cannot be substituted into. Therefore, the heap typing $\varTheta$ is irrelevant in such judgements. We will almost always drop the superscript in e^1 and t^1 (we keep it in the rule (Code) as reminder).

Figure 6 states the well-formedness constraints on the environments and heap typings, which can be summarized as the absence of duplicates and the classifiers being defined before use. It becomes clear that each Level-1 variable binding recorded in the global $\varUpsilon$ or local $\varGamma$ environment has its own classifier. Indeed, a classifier acts as a type-level 'name' of a Level-1 variable. To ease the notation, hereafter we shall assume well-formedness of all environments and heap typings. We write $\varGamma, \varGamma'$ and $\varUpsilon, \varUpsilon'$ for the concatenation of two sequences such that the result must be well-formed.

The typing of expressions is presented in Fig. 7 whereas Fig. 9 defines the typing of heaps. Most of the type system is standard. The rule (Const) uses the types of constants tc, given in Fig. 2. We abuse the notation and treat, for type-checking purposes, constant expressions such as $c_2 \ e_1 \ e_2$ as applications to c_2, although c_2 is not an expression per se. The rules (Sub0) and (Sub1) rely on the partial order on classifiers specified in Fig. 8 in the straightforward way: $\varUpsilon, \varGamma \models \gamma_1 \succ \gamma_2$ if either $\gamma_1 \succ \gamma_2$ literally occurs in the environments as a witness, or can be derived by reflexivity and transitivity.

---

[3] If we generate code for later use, e.g., as a library of specialized algorithms, it makes no sense for the generated code to contain pointers into the generator's heap. By the time the produced code is run, the generator will be long gone. Although shared heap may be useful in run-time-code specialization, none of the staged calculi to our knowledge consider this case.

$$\frac{}{\Upsilon;\Theta;\Gamma \vdash \text{c}: \text{tc}} \; \text{Const} \qquad \frac{(\text{x}:\text{t})^L \in (\Gamma \uplus \Upsilon)}{\Upsilon;\Theta;\Gamma \vdash^L \text{x}: \text{t}} \; \text{Var} \qquad \frac{\Upsilon;[\,];\Gamma \vdash^\gamma \text{e}^1: \text{t}^1}{\Upsilon;\Theta;\Gamma \vdash \langle \text{e}^1 \rangle: \langle \text{t}^1 \rangle^\gamma} \; \text{Code}$$

$$\frac{(\text{l}:\text{t}) \in \Theta}{\Upsilon;\Theta;\Gamma \vdash \text{l}: \text{t}} \; \text{Loc} \qquad \frac{\Upsilon;\Theta;\Gamma \vdash \text{e}: \langle \text{t} \rangle^{\gamma_1} \quad \Upsilon;\Gamma \models \gamma_2 \succ \gamma_1}{\Upsilon;\Theta;\Gamma \vdash \text{e}: \langle \text{t} \rangle^{\gamma_2}} \; \text{Sub0}$$

$$\frac{\Upsilon;\Theta;\Gamma \vdash^{\gamma_1} \text{e}: \text{t} \quad \Upsilon;\Gamma \models \gamma_2 \succ \gamma_1}{\Upsilon;\Theta;\Gamma \vdash^{\gamma_2} \text{e}: \text{t}} \; \text{Sub1} \qquad \frac{\Upsilon;\Theta;\Gamma \vdash^L \text{e}_1: \text{t}_1 \rightarrow \text{t}_2 \quad \Upsilon;\Theta;\Gamma \vdash^L \text{e}_2: \text{t}_1}{\Upsilon;\Theta;\Gamma \vdash^L \text{e}_1\, \text{e}_2: \text{t}_2} \; \text{App}$$

$$\frac{\Upsilon;\Theta;(\Gamma, (\text{x}:\text{t}_1)^L) \vdash^L \text{e}: \text{t}_2}{\Upsilon;\Theta;\Gamma \vdash^L \lambda \text{x.e}: \text{t}_1 \rightarrow \text{t}_2} \; \text{Abs}$$

$$\frac{\Upsilon;\Theta;\Gamma \vdash^L \text{e}: \text{bool} \quad \Upsilon;\Theta;\Gamma \vdash^L \text{e}_1: \text{t} \quad \Upsilon;\Theta;\Gamma \vdash^L \text{e}_2: \text{t}}{\Upsilon;\Theta;\Gamma \vdash^L \textbf{if } \text{e} \textbf{ then } \text{e}_1 \textbf{ else } \text{e}_2: \text{t}} \; \text{If}$$

$$\frac{\gamma \in (\Gamma \uplus \Upsilon) \quad \gamma_1 \notin (\Gamma \uplus \Upsilon) \quad \Upsilon;\Theta;(\Gamma, \gamma_1, (\gamma_1 \succ \gamma), (\text{x}:\langle \text{t}_1 \rangle^{\gamma_1})) \vdash \text{e}: \langle \text{t}_2 \rangle^{\gamma_1}}{\Upsilon;\Theta;\Gamma \vdash \underline{\lambda}\text{x.e}: \langle \text{t}_1 \rightarrow \text{t}_2 \rangle^\gamma} \; \text{CAbs}$$

$$\frac{\begin{array}{c} \Upsilon = \Upsilon', \gamma_1, (\gamma_1 \succ \gamma), (\text{y}:\text{t}_1)^{\gamma_1}, \Upsilon'' \\ \forall\, \gamma_2.\ \Upsilon \models \gamma_1 \succ \gamma_2 \textbf{ and } \gamma_2 \neq \gamma_1 \textbf{ imply } \Upsilon \models \gamma \succ \gamma_2 \quad \Upsilon;\Theta;[\,] \vdash \text{e}: \langle \text{t}_2 \rangle^{\gamma_1} \end{array}}{\Upsilon;\Theta;[\,] \vdash \underline{\lambda}\text{y.e}: \langle \text{t}_1 \rightarrow \text{t}_2 \rangle^\gamma} \; \text{IAbs}$$

Fig. 7. Type system: typing of expressions

$$\frac{}{\Upsilon;\Gamma \models \gamma \succ \gamma} \qquad \frac{(\gamma_1 \succ \gamma_2) \in (\Gamma \uplus \Upsilon)}{\Upsilon;\Gamma \models \gamma_2 \succ \gamma_1} \qquad \frac{\Upsilon;\Gamma \models \gamma_1 \succ \gamma_2 \quad \Upsilon;\Gamma \models \gamma_2 \succ \gamma_3}{\Upsilon;\Gamma \models \gamma_1 \succ \gamma_3}$$

Fig. 8. Partial order on classifiers $\Upsilon;\Gamma \models \gamma_1 \succ \gamma_2$

$$\frac{\forall\, \text{y} \in \text{N}.\ (\text{y}:\text{t})^\gamma \in \Upsilon}{\Upsilon \vdash \text{N}} \qquad \frac{\forall\, (\text{l}:\text{v}) \in \text{H}.\ \Upsilon;\Theta;[\,] \vdash \text{v}: \Theta(\text{l})}{\Upsilon;\Theta \vdash \text{H}}$$

Fig. 9. Type system: typing of heaps $\Upsilon \vdash \text{N}$ and $\Upsilon;\Theta \vdash \text{H}$

The most interesting are the rules (CAbs) and (IAbs). To explain them and to illustrate the type system, we show two sample typing derivations. The first deals with the term $\underline{\lambda}\text{x}_1.\underline{\lambda}\text{x}_2.\text{x}_1 \pm \text{x}_2$ – generating the curried addition function – in the initial environment, in which Υ contains only the predefined classifier γ_0, and Θ and Γ are empty. In the following derivation, Γ_2 stands for $\gamma_1, (\gamma_1 \succ \gamma_0), (\text{x}_1:\langle \text{int} \rangle^{\gamma_1}), \gamma_2, (\gamma_2 \succ \gamma_1), (\text{x}_2:\langle \text{int} \rangle^{\gamma_2})$.

$$\frac{\dfrac{\dfrac{\Upsilon;\Theta;\Gamma_2 \vdash \text{x}_1: \langle \text{int} \rangle^{\gamma_1} \quad \Upsilon;\Gamma_2 \models \gamma_1 \succ \gamma_2}{\Upsilon;\Theta;\Gamma_2 \vdash \text{x}_1: \langle \text{int} \rangle^{\gamma_2}} \qquad \Upsilon;\Theta;\Gamma_2 \vdash \text{x}_2: \langle \text{int} \rangle^{\gamma_2}}{\dfrac{\Upsilon;\Theta;\Gamma_2 \vdash \text{x}_1 \pm \text{x}_2: \langle \text{int} \rangle^{\gamma_2}}{\Upsilon;\Theta;(\gamma_1, (\gamma_1 \succ \gamma_0), (\text{x}_1:\langle \text{int} \rangle^{\gamma_1})) \vdash \underline{\lambda}\text{x}_2.\, \text{x}_1 \pm \text{x}_2: \langle \text{int} \rightarrow \text{int} \rangle^{\gamma_1}}}}{\Upsilon;\Theta;[\,] \vdash \underline{\lambda}\text{x}_1.\underline{\lambda}\text{x}_2.\, \text{x}_1 \pm \text{x}_2 : \langle \text{int} \rightarrow \text{int} \rightarrow \text{int} \rangle^{\gamma_0}}$$

The side-conditions of (CAbs) tell that the classifiers γ_1 and γ_2 are 'fresh'. Section 3.1 shows another attempted (but not completed) derivation, in case of scope extrusion. The second derivation is for the expression $\underline{\lambda}y_1.\underline{\lambda}x_2.\langle y_1 \rangle \pm x_2$, which results from the one-step reduction of the expression in the previous derivation. Now, Υ_1 stands for $\gamma_0, \gamma_1, \gamma_1 \succ \gamma_0, (y_1{:}int)^{\gamma_1}$ and Γ_2 for $\gamma_2, \gamma_2 \succ \gamma_1, (x_2{:}\langle int \rangle^{\gamma_2})$.

$$\frac{\dfrac{\dfrac{\Upsilon_1;\Theta;\Gamma_2 \vdash^{\gamma_1} y_1 : int}{\Upsilon_1;\Theta;\Gamma_2 \vdash \langle y_1 \rangle : \langle int \rangle^{\gamma_1} \quad \Upsilon_1;\Gamma_2 \models \gamma_2 \succ \gamma_1}}{\dfrac{\Upsilon_1;\Theta;\Gamma_2 \vdash \langle y_1 \rangle : \langle int \rangle^{\gamma_2} \quad \Upsilon_1;\Theta;\Gamma_2 \vdash x_2 : \langle int \rangle^{\gamma_2}}{\dfrac{\Upsilon_1;\Theta;\Gamma_2 \vdash \langle y_1 \rangle \pm x_2 : \langle int \rangle^{\gamma_2}}{\Upsilon_1;\Theta;[] \vdash \underline{\lambda}x_2.\langle y_1 \rangle \pm x_2 : \langle int {\to} int \rangle^{\gamma_1}}}}{\Upsilon_1;\Theta;[] \vdash \underline{\lambda}y_1.\underline{\lambda}x_2.\langle y_1 \rangle \pm x_2 : \langle int {\to} int {\to} int \rangle^{\gamma_0}}$$

It should be clear, already from (IAbs) in fact, that $\underline{\lambda}y.$ is not really a binding form. The environment Γ in (IAbs) is empty since $\underline{\lambda}y.e$ shows up only during evaluation and it is not a value.

Proposition 1 (Canonical Forms). *The only values of base types int and bool are zero-ary constants (numerals and booleans, respectively). Values of reference types t* **ref** *are locations. Values of code types are all bracketed expressions* $\langle e \rangle$ *and of the function types* $t_1 {\to} t_2$ *are abstractions* $\lambda x.e$.

Although constants of arity 1 and above also have function types (see Fig. 2), not applied to the right number of arguments they are not regarded as expressions.

Proposition 2 (Weakening). *If* $\Upsilon;\Theta;\Gamma \vdash^L e{:}t$, $\Upsilon \vdash N$, *and* $\Upsilon;\Theta \vdash H$ *hold, so do* $(\Upsilon,\Upsilon');(\Theta,\Theta');(\Gamma,\Gamma') \vdash^L e{:}t$ *and* $(\Upsilon,\Upsilon') \vdash N$ *and* $(\Upsilon,\Upsilon');(\Theta,\Theta') \vdash H$.

Recall that comma denotes concatenation that preserves well-formedness; which implies Θ and Θ' are disjoint. The proof is straightforward.

Theorem 1 (Subject Reduction). *If* $\Upsilon;\Theta;[] \vdash e{:} t$, $\Upsilon \vdash N$, $\Upsilon;\Theta \vdash H$, *and* $N;H;e \rightsquigarrow N';H';e'$, *then* $\Upsilon';\Theta'';[] \vdash e'{:} t$, $\Upsilon' \vdash N'$, $\Upsilon';\Theta' \vdash H'$, *for some* Υ' *and* Θ' *that are the extensions of the corresponding unprimed things.*

We outline the proof in Appendix A.

Theorem 2 (Progress). *If* $\Upsilon;\Theta;[] \vdash e{:}t$, $\Upsilon \vdash N$ *and* $\Upsilon;\Theta \vdash H$, *then either e is a value or there are* N', H' *and* e' *such that* $N;H;e \rightsquigarrow N';H';e'$.

The proof is the easy consequence of the canonical forms lemma. For example, if the last rule in the derivation of $\Upsilon;\Theta;[] \vdash e{:}t$ is (IAbs), then e must have the form $\underline{\lambda}y.e'$ for some e', where e' must itself be typeable in the same Υ and Θ. By induction hypothesis, e' either reduces, or is a value. In the latter case, by the canonical forms lemma, it should be of the form $\langle e_2 \rangle$ for some e_2 – meaning $\underline{\lambda}y.\langle e_2 \rangle$ can reduce.

Corollary 1. *If $([], \gamma_0);[];[] \vdash e:\langle t\rangle^{\gamma_0}$ and $[];[];$ $e \rightsquigarrow N;H;v$ then v has the form $\langle e_1\rangle$ and $([], \gamma_0);[];[] \vdash^{\gamma_0} e_1:t.$*

That is, if a well-typed program of the type $\langle t\rangle^{\gamma_0}$ terminates it generates the code well-typed in the empty environment. The generated code hence has no unbound variables.

3.1   Scope Extrusion

When generating the body of a function, its formal argument is available as a code value – as the free variable. Scope extrusion occurs when that open code value is used outside the dynamic scope of the function generator and hence the free variable can never be properly bound. Although the error is obvious once we attempt to compile the generated code, it is not at all obvious what part of the generator is responsible. Debugging generated code is very difficult in general. We now demonstrate how <NJ> prevents scope extrusion.

We start with the example of blatant scope extrusion, from Sect. 2:

let r = **ref** %0 **in** (λx. r := x); !r

We have seen that its evaluation indeed produces the code with an unbound variable. The example does not type check however. Specifically, the type error occurs not when the open code is retrieved from the reference cell r at the end. Rather, the generator of the function body, specifically, r := x fails to type-check. Here is the attempt at the derivation, where we assumed $\gamma \in (\Gamma \uplus \Upsilon)$ and so is γ_1 (which may be the same as γ). We take Γ_2 to be $\Gamma,(r:\langle int\rangle^{\gamma_1} \textbf{ref}),\gamma_2,\gamma_2\succ\gamma,(x:\langle int\rangle^{\gamma_2})$ where γ_2 is fresh.

$$\frac{\Upsilon;\Theta;\Gamma_2 \vdash r := x: \langle int\rangle^{\gamma_2}}{\dfrac{\Upsilon;\Theta;(\Gamma,(r:\langle int\rangle^{\gamma_1} \textbf{ref})) \vdash (\lambda x. r := x): \langle int\rightarrow int\rangle^{\gamma}}{\Upsilon;\Theta;\Gamma \vdash \textbf{let } r = \textbf{ref } \underline{cint}\ 0 \textbf{ in } (\lambda x. r := x): \langle int\rightarrow int\rangle^{\gamma}}}$$

The derivation cannot be completed since r has the type $\langle int\rangle^{\gamma_1}$ **ref** but x is of the type $\langle int\rangle^{\gamma_2}$ where γ_2 is specifically chosen by (CAbs) to be different from any other classifiers in Γ and Υ, including γ_1.

If such examples were our only worry, a simpler type system would have sufficed. Instead of named classifiers, we would annotate code types with just a natural number: the nesting level of λ. Our blatant example will likewise fail to type-check. The error will be reported later, however, when type checking the last expression !r retrieving the code with the already leaked variable as the program result. The program result must be closed: be at the 0th nesting level. The type system of [3] (extended with reference cells) likewise rejects the blatant example, as was described in that paper. (After all, their type system annotates code types with the typing environment sequence, which is the refinement of the nesting depth.) MetaOCaml also reports the scope extrusion error – when running the program and executing the !r expression. In contrast, <NJ> rejects r := x, when merely attempting to leak out the free variable.

Alas, scope extrusion can be subtle. Consider a small modification of the earlier example:

let r = **ref** %0 **in** ($\underline{\lambda}$x. r := x); ($\underline{\lambda}$z. !r)

The simpler type system with mere level counting accepts the code: the free variable leaks out of one binder into another, at the same nesting level of λ. Likewise, the calculus of [3] (extended with reference cells as described therein) will type-check and even run the example, producing the code for the identity function. This is not what one may expect from the generator $\underline{\lambda}$z. !r. Our <NJ> rejects r := x in the first part of the example as described earlier: it rejects even an attempt to leak the variable.

Finally, scope extrusion may be harmless, as in the following, yet another variation of the example:

let r = **ref** (λz.z) **in** ($\underline{\lambda}$x. r := (λz. (x; z)); %0); !r

When generating the body of the function, we incorporate the free variable x in the closure λz. (x; z), but in a way that it does not contribute to the result and hence is not reflected in the closure's type, which remains int$\rightarrow$int. Technically, the free variable has leaked – but in a useless way, embedded in dead code.

<NJ> accepts the latter example. When run, it indeed produces the closure with an unbound variable – which remains typeable since the unbound variable is still in the global heap N and its classifier in Υ. Such open code must have been dead, however: it cannot be the result of a well-typed generator, since the type of such result would have contained the classifier γ that is different from γ_0. The well-typed generator program must have the type $\langle t \rangle^{\gamma_0}$. We have seen before that even a fragment, let alone the whole program, that attempts to 'usefully leak' a bound variable will fail to type-check.

Accepting unbound variables in dead code has many precedents. Most region calculi (see [5] and references therein) and their implementations (such as runST monad in Haskell) allow dangling references, provided they are not accessed – that is, remain embedded in essentially dead code.

3.2 Environment Classifiers, Binding Abstractions, and Lexical Scope

As we have seen from Sect. 3.1, the key to preventing scope extrusion is annotating the type of a code value with some representation of free variables that may be contained therein. This section discusses a few choices for the representation and the position of <NJ> among them as the most abstract while still sufficient to prevent scope extrusion. By free variables we always mean Level-1 free variables: all values and terms produced and evaluated in stage calculi are closed with respect to Level-0 variables.

On one end of the spectrum is annotating the type of a code value with the names of the containing free variables, or the typing environment: the set or the sequence listing the free variables and their types. Taha and Nielsen [15, Sect. 1.4] describe many difficulties of this approach (the sheer size of the type being one of them), which makes it hard to implement, and use in practice.

On the other extreme is the most abstract representation of a set of free variables: as a single name (the environment classifier, [15]) or a number, the cardinality of the set. Section 3.1 showed that this is not sufficient to prevent the scope extrusion, of the devious, most harmful sort.

The approach of [3] also annotates the code types with the type environment; however, by using De Bruijn indices, it avoids many difficulties of the nominal approach, such as freshness constraints, α-renaming, etc. The approach is indeed relatively easy to implement, as the authors have demonstrated. Alas, although preventing blatant scope extrusion, it allows the devious one, as we saw in Sect. 3.1.

The representation of [3] is also just too concrete: the code type $\langle int \rangle^{(int,bool,int)}$ tells not only that the value may contain three free variables with the indices 0, 1 and 2. The type also tells that the int and the bool variables will be bound in that order and there is no free variable to be bound in between. There is no need to know with such exactitude when free variables will be bound. In fact, there is no need to even know their number, to prevent scope extrusion. The concreteness of the representation has the price: the system of [3, Sect. 3.3] admits the term, in our notation, $\lambda f.\underline{\lambda}x.\underline{\lambda}y.f\ y$, which may, depending on the argument f, generate either $\langle \lambda x.\lambda y.y \rangle$ or, contrary to any expectation, $\langle \lambda x.\lambda y.x \rangle$.

Such a behavior is just not possible in <NJ>: consider $\underline{\lambda}x.\ f\ x$ where f is some function on code values. The function receives the code of a Level-1 variable and is free to do anything with it: discard it, use it once or several times in the code it is building, store in global reference cells, as well as do any other effects, throw exceptions or diverge. Still, we are positive that whatever f may do, if it eventually returns the code that includes the received Level-1 variable, that variable shall be bound by $\underline{\lambda}x.$ of our expression – regardless of whatever binders f may introduce. This is what we call 'lexical' scope for Level-1 variables: the property, not present in [7] (by choice) or [3].

<NJ> avoids the problematic 'variable conversions' because it does not exposes in types or at run-time any structure of the Level-1 typing environment. The environment classifier in <NJ> is the type-level representation of the variable name. There is a partial order on classifiers, reflecting the nesting order of the corresponding $\underline{\lambda}x$ generators. The relation $\gamma_2 \succ \gamma_1$ tells that the variable corresponding to γ_1 is (to be) introduced earlier than the free variable corresponding to γ_2, with no word on which or how many variables are to be introduced in-between. The code type is annotated not with the set of free variables, not with the set of the corresponding classifiers – but only with the single classifier, the maximal in the set. The type system ensures that there is always the maximal element. To be precise, any free Level-1 variable that may appear within $\underline{\lambda}y.\ \langle e \rangle\ :\ \langle t_1 \rightarrow t_2 \rangle^{\gamma_2}$ is marked by such a classifier γ_1 that $\gamma_2 \succ \gamma_1$. Therefore, any such variable will be bound by an ancestor of $\underline{\lambda}y$. This is another way to state the property of 'lexical scope' for free variables.

3.3 Classifier Polymorphism

The classifier polymorphism and its importance are best explained on examples. The following generator

$$\lambda x.\, \textbf{let}\ f\ =\ \underline{\lambda} z.\ \underline{\text{cint}}\ x\ \underline{+}\ \%1\ \underline{+}\ z\ \textbf{in let}\ f'\ =\ \underline{\lambda} z'.\ (\,\underline{\text{cint}}\ x\ \underline{+}\ \%1)\ \underline{*}\ z'\ \textbf{in}\ e$$

contains the repeated code that we would like to factor out, to make the generators clearer and more modular:

$$\lambda x.\, \textbf{let}\ u\ =\ \underline{\text{cint}}\ x\ \underline{+}\ \%1\ \textbf{in let}\ f\ =\ \underline{\lambda} z.\ u\ \underline{+}\ z\ \textbf{in let}\ f'\ =\ \underline{\lambda} z'.\ u\ \underline{*}\ z'\ \textbf{in}\ e$$

One may worry if the code type-checks: after all, u is used in contexts associated with two distinct classifiers. The example does type-check, thanks to (Sub0) rule: u can be given the type $\langle\, \text{int}\,\rangle^{\gamma_0}$, and although $z\colon \langle\, \text{int}\,\rangle^{\gamma_1}$ and $z'\colon \langle\, \text{int}\,\rangle^{\gamma_2}$ are associated with unrelated classifiers, $\gamma_1 \succ \gamma_0$ and $\gamma_2 \succ \gamma_0$ hold.

Alas, the classifier subtyping gets us only that far. It will not help in the more interesting and common example of functions on code values:

$$\lambda x.\, \textbf{let}\ u\ =\ \underline{\lambda} z.\underline{\text{cint}}\ x\ \underline{+}\ z\ \textbf{in let}\ f\ =\ \underline{\lambda} z.\ u\ z\ \underline{+}\ z\ \textbf{in let}\ f'\ =\ \underline{\lambda} z'.\ u\ z'\ \underline{*}\ z'\ \textbf{in}\ e$$

where the function u is applied to code values associated with unrelated classifiers. To type-check this example we need to give u the type $\forall\, \gamma.\ \langle\, \text{int}\,\rangle^{\gamma} {\rightarrow} \langle \text{int}\rangle^{\gamma}$. Before, γ was used as a (sometimes schematic) constant; now we use it as a classifier variable.

Extending <NJ> with let-bound classifier polymorphism with attendant value restriction is unproblematic and straightforward. In fact, our implementation already does it, inheriting let-polymorphism from the host language, OCaml. Sometimes we may need more extensions, however.

For example, we may write a generator that introduces an arbitrary, statically unknown number of Level-1 variables, e.g., as let-bound variables to share the results of computed expressions. Such pattern occurs, for example, when specializing dynamic programming algorithms. Appendix B demonstrates the let-sharing on the toy example of specializing the Fibonacci-like function, described in [6, Sect. 2.4]. As that paper explains, the generator requires polymorphic recursion – which is well-understood. Both Haskell and OCaml supports it, and hence our implementation of <NJ>. Polymorphic recursion also shows in [3].

There are, however, times (not frequent, in our experience) where even more polymorphism is needed. The poster example is the staged eta-function, the motivating example in [15]: $\lambda f.\ \underline{\lambda} x.\ f\ x$, whose type is, $(\langle t_1\rangle^{\gamma} \rightarrow \langle t_2\rangle^{\gamma}) \rightarrow \langle t_1{\rightarrow} t_2\rangle^{\gamma}$, approximately. The type is not quite right: f accepts the code value that contains a fresh free variable, which comes with a previously unseen classifier. Hence we should assign eta at least the type $(\forall\, \gamma_1.\ \langle t_1\rangle^{\gamma_1} \rightarrow \langle t_2\rangle^{\gamma_1}) \rightarrow \langle t_1{\rightarrow} t_2\rangle^{\gamma}$ – the rank-2 type. This is still not quite right: we would like to use eta in the expression such as $\underline{\lambda} u.\ \text{eta}\ (\underline{\lambda} z.\ u\ \underline{\pm} z)$, where f combines the open code received as argument with some other open code. To type-check this combination we need $\Upsilon, \Gamma \models \gamma_1 \succ \gamma$. Hence the correct type for eta should be

$$\forall\, \gamma.\ (\forall\, \gamma_1 \succ \gamma.\ \langle t_1\rangle^{\gamma_1} \rightarrow \langle t_2\rangle^{\gamma_1}) \rightarrow \langle t_1{\rightarrow} t_2\rangle^{\gamma}$$

with the bounded quantification. One is immediately reminded of ML^F. Such bounded quantification is easy to implement, however, by explicit passing of subtyping witnesses (as done in the implementation of the region calculus [5]) Our implementation of <NJ> supports it too – and how it cannot: eta is just the first-class form of λ. Thus the practical drawback is the need for explicit type signatures for the sake of the rank-2 type (just as signatures are required in ML^F when the polymorphic argument function is used polymorphically). Incidentally, the original environment classifiers calculus of [15] gives eta the ordinary rank-1 type: here the coarseness of the original classifiers is the advantage. The formal treatment of rank-2 classifier polymorphism is the subject of the future research.

4   Complex Example

To demonstrate the expressiveness of <NJ>, we show a realistic example of assert-insertion – exactly the same example that was previously written in Staged-Haskell. The latter is the practical Haskell code-generation library, too complex to reason about formally and prove correctness. The example was explained in detail in [6]; therefore, we elide many explanations here.

For the sake of the example, we add the following constants to <NJ>:

/	: int $\rightarrow$ int $\rightarrow$ int	**assert**	: bool $\rightarrow$ bool
$\underline{/}$	: $\langle$int$\rangle^\gamma \rightarrow \langle$int$\rangle^\gamma \rightarrow \langle$int$\rangle^\gamma$	assertPos	: $\langle$int$\rangle^\gamma \rightarrow \langle$t$\rangle^\gamma \rightarrow \langle$t$\rangle^\gamma$

The first two are the integer division and the corresponding code combinator; **assert** e returns the result of the boolean expression, if it is true. Otherwise, it crashes the program. The constant assertPos is the corresponding combinator, with the reduction rule assertPos $\langle e_1 \rangle \langle e_2 \rangle \rightsquigarrow \langle$**assert** $(e_1 > 0); e_2 \rangle$.

The goal is to implement the guarded division, which makes sure that the divisor is positive before attempting the operation. The naive version

let guarded_div = λx.λy. assertPos y (x $\underline{/}$ y)

to be used as

λy. complexExp $\underline{+}$ guarded_div %10 y

produces $\langle \lambda$x. complexExp + (**assert** (x>0); (10 / x))$\rangle$. The result is hardly satisfactory: we check the divisor right before the division. If it is not positive, the time spent computing complexExp is wasted. If the program is going to end up in error, we had rather it end sooner than much later.

The solution is explained in [6], implemented in StagedHaskell and is reproduced below in <NJ>. Intuitively, we first reserve the place where it is appropriate to place assertions, which is typically right at the beginning of a function. As we go on generating the body of the function, we determine the assertions to insert and accumulate them in a mutable 'locus'. Finally, when the body of the function is generated, we retrieve the accumulated assertion code and prepend it to the body. The function add_assert below accumulates the assertions; assert_locus allocates the locus at the beginning and applies the accumulated assertions at the end.

```
let  assert_locus  = λf.
  let  r = ref (λx.x)   in let  c = f r  in
  let  transformer  = !r in  transformer  c

let  add_assert  locus transformer  =
  locus := (let  oldtr  = !locus in  λx. oldtr  (transformer  x))

let  guarded_div  = λlocus.λx.λy. add_assert  locus (λz. assertPos  y z); (x / y)
```

They are to be used as in the example below:

λy. assert_locus (λlocus. λz. complexExp + guarded_div locus z y)

As we generate the code, the reference cell r within the locus accumulates the transformer (code-to-code function), to be applied to the result. In our example, the code transformer includes open code (embedded within the assertPos expression), which is moved from within the generator of the inner function. The example thus illustrates all the complexities of imperative code generation. The improved generated code

⟨λx. assert (x>0); (λy. complexExp + y / x)⟩

checks the divisor much earlier: before we started on complexExp, before we even apply the function (λy. complexExp + y / x). If we by mistake switch y and z in guarded_div locus z y, we get a type-error message.

5   Related Work

We thoroughly review the large body of related work in [6]. Here we highlight only the closest connections. First is Template Haskell, which either permits effectful generators but then provides no guarantees by construction; or provides guarantees but permits no effects – the common trade-off. We discuss this issue in detail in [6]. BER MetaOCaml [8] permits any effects and ensures well-scopedness, even in open fragments, using dynamic checks. StagedHaskell and <NJ> are designed to prevent scope extrusion even before running the generator.

Safe imperative multi-staged programming has been investigated in [1,17]. Safety comes at the expense of expressiveness: e.g., only closed code is allowed to be stored in mutable cells (in the former approach).

We share with [15] the idea of using an opaque label, the environment classifier, to refer to a typing environment. The main advantage of environment classifiers, their imprecision (they refer to infinite sets of environments), is also their drawback. On one hand, they let us specify staged-eta Sect. 3.3 without any first-class polymorphism. On the other hand, the imprecision is not enough to safely use effects.

Chen and Xi [3] and Nanevski et al. [10] annotate the code type with the type environment of its free variables. The former relies on the first-order syntax with De Bruijn indices whereas the latter uses higher-order abstract syntax. Although internally Chen and Xi use De Bruijn indices, they develop a pleasant surface syntax a la MetaOCaml (or Lisp's antiquotations). The De Bruijn indices are still there, which may lead to unpleasant surprises, which they discuss in [3, Sect. 3.3]. Their type system indeed rejects the blatant example of scope extrusion. Perhaps that is why [3] said that reference cells do not bring in significant complications. However, scope extrusion is much subtler than its well-known example: Sect. 3.1 presented a just slightly modified example, which is accepted in Chen and Xi's system, but produces an unexpected result. We refer to [6] for extensive discussion.

One may think that any suitable staged calculus can support reference cells through a state-passing translation. The elaborate side-conditions of our (CAbs) and (IAbs) rules indicate that a straightforward state-passing translation is not going to be successful to ensure type and scope safety.

Staged-calculi of [3, 15] have a special constant run to run the generated code. Adding it to <NJ> is straightforward.

Our bracketed expressions are the generalization of data constructors of the code data type in the 'single-stage target language' [2, Fig. 2]. Our name heap also comes from the same calculus. The latter, unlike <NJ>, is untyped, and without effects.

6   Conclusions and Future Work

We have described the first staged calculus <NJ> for imperative code generators without ad hoc restrictions – letting us even store open code in reference cells and retrieve it in a different binding environment. Its sound type system statically assures that the generated code is by construction well-typed and well-scoped, free from unbound or surprisingly bound variables. The calculus has been distilled from StagedHaskell, letting us formally prove the soundness of the latter's approach. The distilled calculus is still capable of implementing StagedHaskell's examples that use mutation.

<NJ> has drawn inspiration from such diverse areas as region-based memory management and Natural Deduction. It turns out a vantage point to overview these areas.

<NJ> trivially generalizes to effects such as exceptions or IO. It is also easy to extend with new non-binding language forms. (Binding-forms like for-loops can always be expressed via lambda-forms: see Haskell or Scala, for example.) <NJ> thus serves as the foundation of real staged programming languages. In fact, it is already implemented as an OCaml library. Although the explicit weakening is certainly cumbersome, it turns out, in our experience, not as cumbersome as we had feared. It is not a stretch to recommend the OCaml implementation of <NJ> as a new, safe, staged programming language.

Extension to effects such as delimited control or non-determinism is however non-trivial and is the subject of on-going research. We are also investigating adding first-class bounded polymorphism for classifiers, relating <NJ> more precisely to ML^F.

Acknowledgments. We thank anonymous reviewers for many helpful comments. This work was partially supported by JSPS KAKENHI Grant Numbers 15K12007, 16K12409, 15H02681.

A   Proof Outlines: Subject Reduction Theorem

Lemma 1 (Substitution). *(1) If* $\Upsilon;\Theta;(\Gamma,(x{:}t_1)) \vdash e{:}\ t$ *and* $\Upsilon,\Theta,\Gamma \vdash e_1{:}\ t_1$ *then* $\Upsilon;\Theta;\Gamma \vdash e[x{:=}e_1]{:}\ t.$ *(2) If* $\Upsilon;\Theta;(\Gamma,\gamma_2,\gamma_2 \succ \gamma_1,\Gamma') \vdash^L e{:}\ t$ *and* $\gamma_1 \in \Upsilon$ *and* $\gamma_2' \notin (\Gamma \uplus \Upsilon)$, *then* $(\Upsilon,\gamma_2',\gamma_2' \succ \gamma_1);\Theta,(\Gamma,\Gamma'[\gamma_2{:=}\gamma_2']) \vdash^L e{:}\ t[\gamma_2{:=}\gamma_2']$ *(if* L *was* γ_2 *it is also replaced with* γ_2').

This lemma is proved straightforwardly.

Theorem 3 (Subject Reduction). *If* $\Upsilon;\Theta;[] \vdash e{:}\ t,\ \Upsilon \vdash N,\ \Upsilon;\Theta \vdash H,$ *and* $N;H;e \leadsto N';H';e'$, *then* $\Upsilon';\Theta';[] \vdash e'{:}\ t,\ \Upsilon' \vdash N',\ \Upsilon';\Theta' \vdash H',$ *for some* Υ' *and* Θ' *that are the extensions of the corresponding unprimed things.*

Proof. We consider a few interesting reductions. The first one is

$N;H;\underline{\lambda}x.\ e \leadsto (N,y);H;\underline{\lambda}\ y.\ e[x{:=}\langle y\rangle], \quad y \notin N$

We are given N' is N,y, H' is H, and $\Upsilon;\Theta;[] \vdash \underline{\lambda}x.e : \langle t_1 {\to} t_2\rangle^\gamma$, which means $\gamma \in \Upsilon$ and $\Upsilon;\Theta;(\gamma_2,\gamma_2 \succ \gamma,(x{:}\langle t_1\rangle^{\gamma_2})) \vdash e{:}\langle t_2\rangle^{\gamma_2}$ for a fresh γ_2. We choose Υ' as $\Upsilon,\gamma_1,\gamma_1 \succ \gamma,(y{:}t_1)^{\gamma_1}$ where γ_1 is fresh, and Θ' as Θ. Υ' is well-formed and is an extension of Υ. Furthermore, $\Upsilon' \vdash N,y$. By weakening, $\Upsilon' \vdash \Theta$ ok and $\Upsilon';\Theta \vdash H$ if it was for Υ. We only need to show that $\Upsilon';\Theta;[] \vdash \underline{\lambda}y.\ e[x{:=}\langle y\rangle] : \langle t_1 {\to} t_2\rangle^\gamma$, which follows by (IAbs) from $\Upsilon';\Theta;[] \vdash e[x{:=}\langle y\rangle] : \langle t_2\rangle^{\gamma_1}$, which in turn follows from the fact that $\Upsilon';\Theta;[] \vdash \langle y\rangle : \langle t_1\rangle^{\gamma_1}$ and the substitution lemma.

The next reduction is

$N;H;\underline{\lambda}y.\langle e\rangle \leadsto N;H;\langle \lambda y.e\rangle$

We are given $\Upsilon;\Theta;[] \vdash \underline{\lambda}y.\langle e\rangle : \langle t_1 {\to} t_2\rangle^\gamma$, $\Upsilon \vdash N$ and $\Upsilon,\Theta \vdash H$. Since N and H are unchanged by the reduction, we do not extend Υ and Θ. By inversion of (IAbs) we know that Υ is $\Upsilon',\gamma_1,\gamma_1 \succ \gamma,(y{:}t_1)^{\gamma_1},\Upsilon''$ and $\forall\ \gamma_2.\ \Upsilon \models \gamma_1 \succ \gamma_2$ **and** $\gamma_2 \neq \gamma_1$ imply $\Upsilon \models \gamma \succ \gamma_2$ and $\Upsilon;\Theta;[] \vdash \langle e\rangle : \langle t_2\rangle^{\gamma_1}$, or, by inversion of (Code) $\Upsilon;[];[] \vdash^{\gamma_1} e : t_2$. By weakening, $\Upsilon;[];([],(\ y'{:}t)^\gamma) \vdash^{\gamma_1} e : t_2$. An easy substitution lemma gives us $\Upsilon;[];([],(\ y'{:}t)^\gamma) \vdash^{\gamma_1} e' : t_2$ where e' is $e[y{:=}y']$, keeping in mind that $\Upsilon \models \gamma_1 \succ \gamma$. The crucial step is strengthening. Since we have just substituted away $(y{:}t_1)^{\gamma_1}$, which is the only variable with the classifier γ_1 (the correspondence of variable names and classifiers is the consequence of well-formedness), the derivation $\Upsilon;[];([],(\ y'{:}t)^\gamma) \vdash^{\gamma_1} e' : t_2$ has no occurrence of the rule (Var) with L equal to γ_1. Therefore, any subderivation with L being γ_1 must have the occurrence of the (Sub1) rule, applied to the derivation $\Upsilon;[];([],(\ y'{:}t)^\gamma) \vdash^{\gamma_2} e'{:}t'$ where $\Upsilon \models \gamma_1 \succ \gamma_2$ and γ_2 is different from γ_1. The inversion of (IAbs) gave us $\forall\ \gamma_2.\ \Upsilon \models \gamma_1 \succ \gamma_2$ **and** $\gamma_1 \neq \gamma_2$ imply $\Upsilon \models \gamma \succ \gamma_2$. Therefore, we can always replace each such occurrence of (Sub1) with the one that gives us $\Upsilon;[];([],(\ y'{:}t)^\gamma) \vdash^\gamma e'{:}t'$. All in all, we build the derivation of

Υ ;[];([],(y': t)$^\gamma$) $\vdash^\gamma$ e' : t$_2$, which gives us Υ ;[];[] $\vdash^\gamma$ λy.e : t$_1\rightarrow$t$_2$ and then
Υ ;[];[] $\vdash$ $\langle\lambda$y.e$\rangle$: $\langle$t$_1\rightarrow$t$_2\rangle^\gamma$.

Another interesting case is

N;H;$\underline{\lambda}$y.E[ref $\langle$y$\rangle$] $\rightsquigarrow$ N;(H,I: $\langle$y$\rangle$);$\underline{\lambda}$y.E[I]

Given, Υ;Θ;[] $\vdash$ $\underline{\lambda}$y.E[ref $\langle$y$\rangle$] : $\langle$t$_1\rightarrow$t$_2\rangle^\gamma$ which   means
Υ = Υ', γ_1, $\gamma_1 \succ \gamma$, (y:t$_1$)$^{\overline{\gamma_1}}$, Υ''. Take Θ' = Θ,(I:$\langle$t$_1\rangle^{\gamma_1}$ ref). It is easy to see that
$\Upsilon \vdash \Theta$' ok and Υ,Θ' $\vdash$ H,(I:$\langle$y$\rangle$). The rest follows from the substitution lemma.

B   Generating Code with Arbitrary Many Variables

Our example is the Fibonacci-like function, described in [6, Sect. 2.4]:

```
let gib = fix (λf.λx.λy.λn.
  if n=0 then x else if n=1 then y else f y (x+y) (n−1))
```

For example, gib 1 1 5 returns 8. The naive specialization to the given n

```
let gib_naive =
  let body = fix (λf.λx.λy.λn.
  if n=0 then x else if n=1 then y else f y (x+y) (n−1))
  in λn.λx.λy. body x y n
```

is unsatisfactory: gib_naive 5 generates

λx.λy. (y + (x + y)) + ((x + y) + (y + (x + y)))

with many duplicates, exponentially degrading performance. A slight change

```
let gibs =
  let body : ∀ γ. ⟨int⟩^γ → ⟨int⟩^γ → int → ⟨int⟩^γ = fix (λf.λx.λy.λn.
  if n=0 then x else if n=1 then y else clet z = (x+y) in f y z (n−1))
  in λn.λx.λy. body x y n
```

gives a much better result: gibs 5 produces

λx.λy. (λz. (λu. (λw. (λx$_1$.x$_1$) (u + w)) (z + u)) (y + z)) (x + y)

which runs in linear time. The improved generator relies on polymorphic recursion: that is why the signature is needed.

References

1. Calcagno, C., Moggi, E., Taha, W.: Closed types as a simple approach to safe imperative multi-stage programming. In: Montanari, U., Rolim, J.D.P., Welzl, E. (eds.) ICALP 2000. LNCS, vol. 1853, pp. 25–36. Springer, Heidelberg (2000). doi:10. 1007/3-540-45022-X_4
2. Calcagno, C., Taha, W., Huang, L., Leroy, X.: Implementing multi-stage languages using ASTs, gensym, and reflection. In: Pfenning, F., Smaragdakis, Y. (eds.) GPCE 2003. LNCS, vol. 2830, pp. 57–76. Springer, Heidelberg (2003). doi:10.1007/ 978-3-540-39815-8_4
3. Chen, C., Xi, H.: Meta-programming through typeful code representation. J. Funct. Program. 15(6), 797–835 (2005)

4. Davies, R.: A temporal logic approach to binding-time analysis. In: LICS, pp. 184–195 (1996)
5. Fluet, M., Morrisett, J.G.: Monadic regions. J. Funct. Program. **16**(4–5), 485–545 (2006)
6. Kameyama, Y., Kiselyov, O., Shan, C.: Combinators for impure yet hygienic code generation. Sci. Comput. Program. **112**, 120–144 (2015)
7. Kim, I.S., Yi, K., Calcagno, C.: A polymorphic modal type system for lisp-like multi-staged languages. In: POPL, pp. 257–268 (2006)
8. Kiselyov, O.: The design and implementation of BER MetaOCaml. In: Codish, M., Sumii, E. (eds.) FLOPS 2014. LNCS, vol. 8475, pp. 86–102. Springer, Heidelberg (2014). doi:10.1007/978-3-319-07151-0_6
9. Le Botlan, D., Rémy, D.: ML^F: raising ML to the power of system F. In: ICFP, pp. 27–38 (2003)
10. Nanevski, A., Pfenning, F., Pientka, B.: Contextual modal type theory. Trans. Comput. Logic **9**(3), 1–49 (2008)
11. POPL 2003: Conference Record of the Annual ACM Symposium on Principles of Programming Languages (2003)
12. Pottier, F.: Static name control for FreshML. In: LICS, pp. 356–365. IEEE Computer Society (2007)
13. Pouillard, N., Pottier, F.: A fresh look at programming with names and binders. In: ICFP, pp. 217–228. ACM, New York (2010)
14. Rompf, T., Amin, N., Moors, A., Haller, P., Odersky, M.: Scala-virtualized: linguistic reuse for deep embeddings. High. Order Symbolic Comput. **25**, 165–207 (2013)
15. Taha, W., Nielsen, M.F.: Environment classifiers. In: POPL [11], pp. 26–37
16. Thiemann, P.: Combinators for program generation. J. Funct. Program. **9**(5), 483–525 (1999)
17. Westbrook, E., Ricken, M., Inoue, J., Yao, Y., Abdelatif, T., Taha, W.: Mint: Java multi-stage programming using weak separability. In: PLDI 2010. ACM, New York (2010)
18. Xi, H., Chen, C., Chen, G.: Guarded recursive datatype constructors. In: POPL [11], pp. 224–235

Verification and Analysis II

Higher-Order Model Checking in Direct Style

Taku Terao[1,2(✉)], Takeshi Tsukada[1], and Naoki Kobayashi[1]

[1] The University of Tokyo, Tokyo, Japan
terao1984@is.s.u-tokyo.ac.jp
[2] JSPS Research Fellow, Tokyo, Japan

Abstract. Higher-order model checking, or model checking of higher-order recursion schemes, has been recently applied to fully automated verification of functional programs. The previous approach has been *indirect*, in the sense that higher-order functional programs are first abstracted to (call-by-value) higher-order Boolean programs, and then further translated to higher-order recursion schemes (which are essentially call-by-*name* programs) and model checked. These multi-step transformations caused a number of problems such as code explosion. In this paper, we advocate a more *direct* approach, where higher-order Boolean programs are directly model checked, without transformation to higher-order recursion schemes. To this end, we develop a model checking algorithm for higher-order call-by-value Boolean programs, and prove its correctness. According to experiments, our prototype implementation outperforms the indirect method for large instances.

1   Introduction

Higher-order model checking [14], or model checking of higher-order recursion schemes (HORS), has recently been applied to automated verification of higher-order functional programs [9,11,12,15,17]. A HORS is a higher-order tree grammar for generating a (possibly infinite) tree, and higher-order model checking is concerned about whether the tree generated by a given HORS satisfies a given property. Although the worst-case complexity of higher-order model checking is huge (k-EXPTIME complete for order-k HORS [14]), practical algorithms for higher-order model checking have been developed [4,8,16,18], which do not always suffer from the k-EXPTIME bottleneck.

A typical approach for applying higher-order model checking to program verification [11] is as follows. As illustrated on the left-hand side of Fig. 1, a source program, which is a *call-by-value* higher-order functional program, is first abstracted to a call-by-value, higher-order *Boolean* functional program, using predicate abstraction. The Boolean functional program is further translated to a HORS, which is essentially a call-by-*name* higher-order functional program, and then model checked. We call this approach *indirect*, as it involves many steps of program transformations. This indirect approach has an advantage that, thanks to the CPS transformation used in the translation to HORS, various control

© Springer International Publishing AG 2016
A. Igarashi (Ed.): APLAS 2016, LNCS 10017, pp. 295–313, 2016.
DOI: 10.1007/978-3-319-47958-3_16

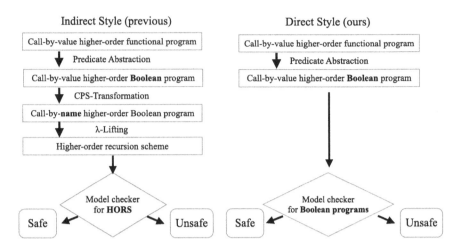

Fig. 1. Overview: indirect vs. direct style

structures (such as exceptions and call/cc) and evaluation strategies (call-by-value and call-by-name) can be uniformly handled. The multi-step transformations, however, incur a number of drawbacks as well, such as code explosion and the increase of the order of programs (where the order of a program is the largest order of functions; a function is first-order if both the input and output are base values, and it is second-order if it can take a first-order function as an argument, etc.). The multi-step transformations also make it difficult to propagate the result of higher-order model checking back to the source program, e.g., for the purpose of counter-example-guided abstraction refinement (CEGAR), and certificate generation.

In view of the drawbacks of the indirect approach mentioned above, we advocate higher-order model checking in a more *direct* style, where call-by-value higher-order Boolean programs are directly model checked, without the translation to HORS, as illustrated on the right-hand side of Fig. 1. That would avoid the increase of the size and order of programs (recall that the complexity of higher-order model checking is k-EXPTIME complete for order-k HORS; thus the order is the most critical parameter for the complexity). In addition, the direct style approach would take an advantage of optimization using the control structure of the original program, which has been lost during the CPS-transformation in indirect style.

Our goal is then to develop an appropriate algorithm that directly solves the model-checking problem for call-by-value higher-order Boolean programs. We focus here on the reachability problem (of checking whether a given program reaches a certain program point); any safety properties can be reduced to the reachability problem in a standard manner.

From a purely theoretical point of view, this goal has been achieved by Tsukada and Kobayashi [20]. They developed an intersection type system for reachability checking of call-by-value higher-order Boolean programs, which gives a better (and exact in a certain sense) upper bound of the worst case complexity of the problem than the naïve indirect approach. However their algorithm, which basically enumerates all the types of subterms, is far from practical since the number of candidate types for a given subterm is hyper-exponential.

Now the challenge is to find an appropriate subset of types to be considered for a given program: this subset has to be large enough to correctly analyze the behaviour of the program and, at the same time, sufficiently small to be manipulated in realistic time. In previous work [4,18] for a call-by-name language, this subset is computed with the help of the control-flow analysis, which gives an over-approximation of the behaviour of the program. The naïve adaptation of this idea to a call-by-value language, however, does not work well. This is because the flow-information tends to be less accurate for call-by-value programs: in an application $t_1 t_2$, one has to over-approximate the evaluation of both t_1 and t_2 in call-by-value, whereas in call-by-name t_2 itself is the accurate actual argument. We propose an algorithm (the *0-Control-Flow-Analysis (CFA) guided saturation algorithm*) that deeply integrates the type system and the 0-CFA. The integration reduces the inaccuracy of the flow analysis and makes the algorithm efficient, although it is technically more complicated.

We have implemented the algorithm, and confirmed through experiments that for large instances, our direct approach for model checking call-by-value Boolean programs outperforms the previous indirect approach of translating a call-by-value program to HORS and then model-checking the HORS.

The contributions of this paper are summarized as follows.

- A practical algorithm for the call-by-value reachability problem in direct style. The way to reduce type candidates using control-flow analysis is quite different from that of previous algorithms [4,18].
- The formalization of the algorithm and a proof of its correctness. The proof is more involved than the corresponding proof of the correctness of Tsukada and Kobayashi's algorithm [20] due to the flow-based optimization, and also than that of the correctness of the HorSat algorithm [4], due to the call-by-value evaluation strategy.
- Implementation and evaluation of the algorithm.

The rest of this paper is structured as follows. Section 2 defines the target language, its semantics, and the reachability problem. Section 3 gives an intersection type system that characterizes the reachability of a program. Section 4 describes the 0-CFA guided saturation algorithm, and proves its correctness. Section 5 describes the experimental results. Section 6 discusses related work, and the final section concludes the paper. Some proofs and figures are omitted in this version and are available in the long version [19].

2 Call-by-Value Reachability Problem

2.1 Target Language

We first introduce notations used in the rest of this paper. We write **Lab**, **Var**, and **Fun**, respectively for the countable sets of *labels*, *variables*, and *function symbols.* We assume that the meta-variable ℓ represents a label, the meta-variables x, y represent variables, and f, g represent function symbols. We write dom(g) for the domain set of a function g, and $\tilde{x}$ for a finite sequence like $x_1, \ldots, x_k$. Let ρ be a map. We denote $\rho[x \mapsto v]$ as the map that maps y to v if $x = y$ and that behaves as the same as ρ otherwise. We denote $\emptyset$ as both the empty set and the empty map, whose domain set is the empty set.

$$
\begin{aligned}
P \text{ (Programs)} &::= \textbf{let rec } D : \mathcal{K} \textbf{ in } t \\
t \text{ (Terms)} &::= e^{\ell} \\
e \text{ (Expressions)} &::= b \mid p \mid x \mid f \mid \text{op}(\tilde{t}) \mid \langle t_1, \ldots, t_k \rangle \mid \pi_i^k t \mid t_1\, t_2 \\
&\quad \mid\ t_1 \oplus t_2 \mid \textbf{fail} \mid \Omega \mid \textbf{let } x = t_1 \textbf{ in } t_2 \mid \textbf{assume } t_1; t_2 \\
p \text{ (Lambda-abstractions)} &::= \lambda x : \kappa.\ t \\
b \text{ (Booleans)} &::= \textbf{true} \mid \textbf{false} \\
\kappa \text{ (Sorts)} &::= \textbf{bool} \mid \langle \kappa_1, \ldots, \kappa_k \rangle \mid \kappa_1 \to \kappa_2 \\
D \text{ (Global definitions)} &::= \{ f_1 \mapsto p_1, \ldots, f_k \mapsto p_k \} \\
\mathcal{K} \text{ (Global sort environments)} &::= \{ f_1 \mapsto \kappa_1, \ldots, f_k \mapsto \kappa_k \} \\
\Sigma \text{ (Local sort environments)} &::= \{ x_1 \mapsto \kappa_1, \ldots, x_k \mapsto \kappa_k \}
\end{aligned}
$$

Fig. 2. Syntax

The target language of the reachability analysis in this paper is a simply-typed, call-by-value lambda calculus with Booleans, tuples and global mutual recursions. The syntax of the language is given in Fig. 2. Each subterm is labeled with **Lab** in this language, for the control-flow analysis described later. We call *terms* for labeled ones, and *expressions* for unlabeled ones. The expression op$(\tilde{t})$ is a Boolean operation, such as $t_1 \wedge t_2$, $t_1 \vee t_2$, and $\neg t$, and $\pi_i^k t$ is the i-th (zero-indexed) projection for the k-tuple t. The expression $t_1 \oplus t_2$ is a non-deterministic choice of t_1 and t_2. The terms Ω and **fail** represent divergence and failure, respectively. The assume-expression **assume** $t_1; t_2$ evaluates t_2 only if t_1 is evaluated to **true** (and diverges if t_1 is evaluated to **false**).

A *sort* is the simple type of a term, which is either Boolean sort **bool**, a tuple sort, or a function sort; we use the word "sort" to distinguish simple types from intersection types introduced later. A *local sort environment* and (resp. *global sort environment*) is a finite map from variables (resp. function symbols) to sorts. A *global definition* is a finite map from function symbols to lambda-expressions. A *program* consists of a global definition D, a global sort environment $\mathcal{K}$, and a term, called the *main term*.

Next, we define *well-sorted* terms. Let $\mathcal{K}$ be a global sort environment, Σ a local sort environment, and κ a sort. A *sort judgment* for a term t (resp. an expression e) is of the form $\mathcal{K}, \Sigma \vdash t : \kappa$ (resp. $\mathcal{K}, \Sigma \vdash e : \kappa$). The sort system of the target language is the standard simple type system with the following primitive types: **fail** $: \kappa$, $\Omega : \kappa$, **assume** $:$ **bool** $\to \kappa$, and $\oplus : \kappa \to \kappa \to \kappa$. The inference rules are given in the long version [19].

The *depth* of a sort κ, written $\mathbf{dep}(\kappa)$, is defined as follows: $\mathbf{dep}(\mathbf{bool}) = 1$, $\mathbf{dep}(\langle \kappa_1, \ldots, \kappa_k \rangle) = \max(\mathbf{dep}(\kappa_1), \ldots, \mathbf{dep}(\kappa_k))$, and $\mathbf{dep}(\kappa_1 \to \kappa_2) = 1 + \max(\mathbf{dep}(\kappa_1), \mathbf{dep}(\kappa_2))$. The *depth of a well-sorted term* t, written $\mathbf{dep}(t)$, is the maximum depth of sorts which appear in the derivation tree of $\mathcal{K}, \Sigma \vdash t : \kappa$. Let D be a global definition, and $\mathcal{K}$ be a global sort environment. We write $\vdash D : \mathcal{K}$ if $\mathrm{dom}(D) = \mathrm{dom}(\mathcal{K})$ and $\forall f \in \mathrm{dom}(D). \mathcal{K}, \emptyset \vdash D(f) : \mathcal{K}(f)$. We say program $P = \mathbf{let\ rec}\ D : \mathcal{K}\ \mathbf{in}\ t_0$ has sort κ if $\vdash D : \mathcal{K}$, and $\mathcal{K}, \emptyset \vdash t_0 : \kappa$. We say P is *well-sorted* if P has some sort κ. The *depth of a well-sorted program* P is the maximum depth of terms in P.

Example 1. Consider the program $P_1 = \mathbf{let\ rec}\ D_1 : \mathcal{K}_1\ \mathbf{in}\ t_1$ where:

$$D_1 = \{ f \mapsto \lambda(y : \mathbf{bool} \to \mathbf{bool}).\ t_f \}\quad \mathcal{K}_1 = \{ f \mapsto (\mathbf{bool} \to \mathbf{bool}) \to \mathbf{bool} \}$$

$$t_f = (\mathbf{assume}\ (y^1\ \mathbf{true}^2)^3; (\mathbf{assume}\ (\neg(y^5\ \mathbf{true}^6)^7)^8; \mathbf{fail}^9)^{10})^{11}$$

$$t_1 = (\mathbf{let}\ z = (\lambda(x : \mathbf{bool}).\ (\mathbf{true}^{12} \oplus \mathbf{false}^{13})^{14})^{15}\ \mathbf{in}\ (f^{16}\ z^{17})^{18})^{19}$$

P_1 is well-sorted and has sort $\mathbf{bool}$.

2.2 Semantics

We define the operational semantics of the language in the style of Nielson et al. [13]; this style of operational semantics is convenient for discussing flow analysis later. First, we define the following auxiliary syntactic objects:

$$e ::= \cdots \mid c \mid \mathbf{bind}\ \rho\ \mathbf{in}\ t$$
$$\rho\ \text{(Environments)} ::= \{ x_1 \mapsto v_1, \ldots, x_n \mapsto v_k \}$$
$$c\ \text{(Closures)} ::= \mathbf{close}\ p\ \mathbf{in}\ \rho$$
$$v\ \text{(Values)} ::= w^\ell$$
$$w\ \text{(Pre-values)} ::= b \mid f \mid c \mid \langle v_1, \ldots, v_k \rangle$$

The term $\mathbf{close}\ p\ \mathbf{in}\ \rho$ represents a closure, and the term $\mathbf{bind}\ \rho\ \mathbf{in}\ t$ evaluates t under the environment ρ. An *environment* is a finite map from variables to values. A value is either a Boolean, a function symbol, a closure, or a tuple of values. We note that values (resp. pre-values) are subclass of terms (resp. expressions). We extend the sort inference rules to support these terms as follows:

$$\frac{\mathcal{K} \vdash \rho : \Sigma' \quad \mathcal{K}, \Sigma' \vdash p : \kappa}{\mathcal{K}, \Sigma \vdash \mathbf{close}\ p\ \mathbf{in}\ \rho : \kappa}\ (\textsc{Close}) \qquad \frac{\mathcal{K} \vdash \rho : \Sigma' \quad \mathcal{K}, \Sigma' \vdash t : \kappa}{\mathcal{K}, \Sigma \vdash \mathbf{bind}\ \rho\ \mathbf{in}\ t : \kappa}\ (\textsc{Bind})$$

$$\frac{\mathrm{dom}(\rho) = \mathrm{dom}(\Sigma) \qquad \forall x \in \mathrm{dom}(\rho).\ \mathcal{K}, \emptyset \vdash \rho(x) : \Sigma(x)}{\mathcal{K} \vdash \rho : \Sigma}\ (\textsc{Env})$$

A sort judgment for environments is of the form $\mathcal{K} \vdash \rho : \Sigma$, which means that for each binding $x \mapsto v$ in ρ, v has type $\Sigma(x)$.

Next, we define reduction relations. We fix some well-sorted program $P = \mathbf{let\ rec}\ D : \mathcal{K}\ \mathbf{in}\ e_0$. Let ρ be an environment, and Σ be a local sort environment such that $\mathcal{K} \vdash \rho : \Sigma$. The reduction relation for terms is of the form $\rho \vdash_D t \longrightarrow t'$, where $\mathcal{K}, \Sigma \vdash t : \kappa$ for some sort κ. The reduction rules are given in Fig. 3. In rule (OP-2), $[\![op]\!]$ denotes the Boolean function that corresponds to each operation op, and $FV(p)$ denotes the set of free variables of p. We write $\rho \vdash_D t \longrightarrow^* t'$ for the reflexive and transitive closure of $\rho \vdash_D t_1 \longrightarrow t_2$.

$$\frac{\rho(x) = w^{\ell_0}}{\rho \vdash_D x^\ell \longrightarrow w^\ell} \text{(VAR)} \qquad \frac{\rho \vdash_D t \longrightarrow t'}{\rho \vdash_D op(\tilde{v}, t, \tilde{t})^\ell \longrightarrow op(\tilde{v}, t', \tilde{t})^\ell} \text{(OP-1)} \qquad \frac{b' = [\![op]\!](\tilde{b})}{\rho \vdash_D op(\tilde{b})^\ell \longrightarrow b'^\ell} \text{(OP-2)}$$

$$\frac{\rho \vdash_D t \longrightarrow t'}{\rho \vdash_D \langle \tilde{v}, t, \tilde{t} \rangle^\ell \longrightarrow \langle \tilde{v}, t', \tilde{t} \rangle^\ell} \text{(TUPLE)} \qquad \frac{\rho \vdash_D t \longrightarrow t'}{\rho \vdash_D (\pi_i^k t)^\ell \longrightarrow (\pi_i^k t')^\ell} \text{(PROJ-1)}$$

$$\frac{v = \langle w_0^{\ell_0}, \ldots, w_{k-1}^{\ell_{k-1}} \rangle^{\ell'}}{\rho \vdash_D (\pi_i^k v)^\ell \longrightarrow w_i^\ell} \text{(PROJ-2)} \qquad \frac{\rho' = \{ x \mapsto \rho(x) \mid x \in \text{FV}(p) \}}{\rho \vdash_D p^\ell \longrightarrow (\textbf{close } p \textbf{ in } \rho')^\ell} \text{(FUN)}$$

$$\frac{\rho \vdash_D t_1 \longrightarrow t_1'}{\rho \vdash_D (t_1\ t_2)^\ell \longrightarrow (t_1'\ t_2)^\ell} \text{(APP-1)} \qquad \frac{c = \textbf{close } \lambda x : \kappa.\ t \textbf{ in } \rho'}{\rho \vdash_D (c^{\ell_1}\ v_2)^\ell \longrightarrow (\textbf{bind } \rho'[x \mapsto v_2] \textbf{ in } t)^\ell} \text{(APP-3)}$$

$$\frac{\rho \vdash_D t_2 \longrightarrow t_2'}{\rho \vdash_D (v_1\ t_2)^\ell \longrightarrow (v_1\ t_2')^\ell} \text{(APP-2)} \qquad \frac{(\lambda x : \kappa.\ t) = D(f)}{\rho \vdash_D (f^{\ell_1}\ v_2)^\ell \longrightarrow (\textbf{bind } [x \mapsto v_2] \textbf{ in } t)^\ell} \text{(APP-4)}$$

$$\frac{\rho \vdash_D t_1 \longrightarrow t_1'}{\rho \vdash_D (\textbf{let } x = t_1 \textbf{ in } t_2)^\ell \longrightarrow (\textbf{let } x = t_1' \textbf{ in } t_2)^\ell} \text{(LET-1)}$$

$$\frac{}{\rho \vdash_D (\textbf{let } x = v_1 \textbf{ in } t_2)^\ell \longrightarrow (\textbf{bind } \rho[x \mapsto v_1] \textbf{ in } t_2)^\ell} \text{(LET-2)}$$

$$\frac{i \in \{1, 2\}}{\rho \vdash_D (e_1^{\ell_1} \oplus e_2^{\ell_2})^\ell \longrightarrow e_i^\ell} \text{(BR)} \qquad \frac{\rho \vdash_D t_1 \longrightarrow t_1'}{\rho \vdash_D (\textbf{assume } t_1; t_2)^\ell \longrightarrow (\textbf{assume } t_1'; t_2)^\ell} \text{(ASSUME-1)}$$

$$\frac{}{\rho \vdash_D (\textbf{assume true}^{\ell_1}; e_2^{\ell_2})^\ell \longrightarrow e_2^\ell} \text{(ASSUME-2)}$$

$$\frac{\rho' \vdash_D t \longrightarrow t'}{\rho \vdash_D (\textbf{bind } \rho' \textbf{ in } t)^\ell \longrightarrow (\textbf{bind } \rho' \textbf{ in } t')^\ell} \text{(BIND-1)} \qquad \frac{}{\rho \vdash_D (\textbf{bind } \rho' \textbf{ in } w^{\ell_1})^\ell \longrightarrow w^\ell} \text{(BIND-2)}$$

Fig. 3. Reduction relation

2.3 Reachability Problem

We are interested in the reachability problem: whether a program P may execute the command **fail** We define the set of *error expressions*, called **Err**, as follows:[1]

---

[1] Note that the terms like **assume false**; t and Ω are not error expressions. They are intended to model divergent terms, although they are treated as stuck terms in the operational semantics for a technical convenience.

ϕ (Error expr.) $::=$ **fail** $|$ **let** $x = \phi^\ell$ **in** t_2 $|$ **bind** ρ **in** ϕ^ℓ $|$ $\langle \tilde{v}, \phi^\ell, \tilde{t} \rangle$ $|$ $\mathrm{op}(\tilde{v}, \phi^\ell, \tilde{t})$
$\qquad\qquad$ $|$ **assume** $\phi^\ell; t$ $|$ $\phi^\ell\, t$ $|$ $v\, \phi^\ell$.

Then, the reachability problem is defined as follows.

Definition 1 (Reachability Problem). *A program $P = $* **let rec** *$D : \mathcal{K}$* **in** *$t_0$ is* unsafe *if $\emptyset \vdash_D t_0 \longrightarrow^* \phi^\ell$ holds for some $\phi \in$ **Err**. A well-sorted program P is called* safe *if P is not unsafe. Given a well-sorted program, the task of the reachability problem is to decide whether the program is safe.*

Example 2 For example, $P_1 = $ **let rec** $D_1 : \mathcal{K}_1$ **in** t_1 in Example 1 is unsafe, and the program $P_2 = $ **let rec** $D_1 : \mathcal{K}_1$ **in** t_2 below is safe.

$$t_2 = (\textbf{let } w = (\textbf{true}^{20} \oplus \textbf{false}^{21})^{22} \textbf{ in } (f^{23}\ (\lambda(x : \textbf{bool}).\ w^{24})^{25})^{26})^{27}$$

3   Intersection Type System

In this section, we present an intersection type system that characterizes the unsafety of programs, which is an extension of Tsukada and Kobayashi's type system [20].

The sets of *value types* σ and *term types* τ are defined by:

$$\sigma ::= \textbf{true} \mid \textbf{false} \mid \langle \sigma_1, \ldots, \sigma_k \rangle \mid \bigwedge_{i \in I}(\sigma_i \to \tau_i) \qquad \tau ::= \sigma \mid \textbf{fail}$$

Value types are those for values, and term types are for terms, as the names suggest. Intuitively the type **true** describes the value **true**. The type of the form $\langle \sigma_1, \ldots, \sigma_k \rangle$ describes a tuple whose i-th element has type σ_i. A type of the form $\bigwedge_{i \in I}(\sigma_i \to \tau_i)$ represents a function that returns a term of type τ_i if the argument has type σ_i for each $i \in I$. Here, we suppose that I be some finite set. We write $\bigwedge \emptyset$ if I is the empty set. A term type is either a value type or the special type **fail**, which represents a term that is evaluated to an error term. We also call a *local type environment* Δ (resp. *a global type environment* Γ) for a finite map from variables (resp. function symbols) to value types.

The *refinement relations* $\sigma :: \kappa$ and $\tau :: \kappa$ for value/term types are defined by the following rules:

$$\frac{}{b :: \textbf{bool}} \qquad\qquad \frac{\sigma_i :: \kappa_1 \qquad \tau_i :: \kappa_2 \qquad \text{for each } i}{(\bigwedge_i \sigma_i \to \tau_i) :: (\kappa_1 \to \kappa_2)}$$

$$\frac{\sigma_i :: \kappa_i \qquad \text{for each } i}{\langle \sigma_1, \ldots, \sigma_k \rangle :: \langle \kappa_1, \ldots, \kappa_k \rangle} \qquad\qquad \frac{}{\textbf{fail} :: \kappa} \qquad \cdot$$

We naturally extend this refinement relation to those for local/global type environments and denote $\Delta :: \Sigma$ and $\Gamma :: \mathcal{K}$.

$$\frac{\Gamma, \Delta \vdash e : \tau}{\Gamma, \Delta \vdash e^\ell : \tau} \ (\text{TERM}) \qquad \frac{\Gamma, \Delta \vdash t_i : \sigma_i \text{ for each } 1 \leq i \leq k}{\Gamma, \Delta \vdash t_1 \ldots t_k : \sigma_1 \ldots \sigma_k} \ (\text{SEQ})$$

$$\frac{\Gamma, \Delta \vdash t_1 \ldots t_{l-1} : \tilde{\sigma} \quad \Gamma, \Delta \vdash t_l : \mathbf{fail} \quad \text{for some } 0 \leq l \leq k}{\Gamma, \Delta \vdash t_1 \ldots t_k : \mathbf{fail}} \ (\text{SEQ-F})$$

$$\frac{}{\Gamma, \Delta \vdash x : \Delta(x)} \ (\text{VAR}) \qquad \frac{}{\Gamma, \Delta \vdash b : b} \ (\text{BOOL}) \qquad \frac{\Gamma, \Delta \vdash \tilde{t} : \tilde{b}}{\Gamma, \Delta \vdash op(\tilde{t}) : [\![op]\!](\tilde{b})} \ (\text{OP})$$

$$\frac{\Gamma, \Delta \vdash \tilde{t} : \tilde{\sigma}}{\Gamma, \Delta \vdash \langle \tilde{t} \rangle : \langle \tilde{\sigma} \rangle} \ (\text{TUPLE}) \qquad \frac{\Gamma, \Delta \vdash t : \langle \sigma_0, \ldots, \sigma_{k-1} \rangle}{\Gamma, \Delta \vdash \pi_i^k t : \sigma_i} \ (\text{PROJ})$$

$$\frac{\Gamma, \Delta \vdash \tilde{t} : \mathbf{fail}}{\Gamma, \Delta \vdash op(\tilde{t}) : \mathbf{fail}} \qquad \frac{\Gamma, \Delta \vdash \tilde{t} : \mathbf{fail}}{\Gamma, \Delta \vdash \langle \tilde{t} \rangle : \mathbf{fail}} \qquad \frac{\Gamma, \Delta \vdash t : \mathbf{fail}}{\Gamma, \Delta \vdash \pi_i^k t : \mathbf{fail}}$$
$$(\text{OP-F}) \qquad\qquad (\text{TUPLE-F}) \qquad\qquad (\text{PROJ-F})$$

$$\frac{\Gamma, \Delta[x \mapsto \sigma_i] \vdash t : \tau_i \quad \sigma_i :: \kappa \quad \text{for each } i \in I}{\Gamma, \Delta \vdash \lambda x : \kappa.\ t : \bigwedge_{i \in I}(\sigma_i \to \tau_i)} \ (\text{FUN}) \qquad \frac{\Gamma, \Delta \vdash t_1, t_2 : \mathbf{fail}}{\Gamma, \Delta \vdash t_1\ t_2 : \mathbf{fail}} \ (\text{APP-F})$$

$$\frac{\Gamma, \Delta \vdash t_1 : \tau}{\Gamma, \Delta \vdash t_1 \oplus t_2 : \tau} \ (\text{BR-1}) \quad \frac{\Gamma, \Delta \vdash t_2 : \tau}{\Gamma, \Delta \vdash t_1 \oplus t_2 : \tau} \ (\text{BR-2}) \quad \frac{}{\Gamma, \Delta \vdash \mathbf{fail} : \mathbf{fail}} \ (\text{FAIL})$$

$$\frac{\Gamma, \Delta \vdash t_1 : \bigwedge_{i \in I}(\sigma_i \to \tau_i) \quad \Gamma, \Delta \vdash t_2 : \sigma_j \text{ for some } j \in I}{\Gamma, \Delta \vdash t_1\ t_2 : \tau_j} \ (\text{APP})$$

$$\frac{\Gamma, \Delta \vdash t_1 : \sigma_1 \quad \Gamma, \Delta[x \mapsto \sigma_1] \vdash t_2 : \tau}{\Gamma, \Delta \vdash \mathbf{let}\ x = t_1\ \mathbf{in}\ t_2 : \tau} \ (\text{LET}) \quad \frac{\Gamma, \Delta \vdash t_1 : \mathbf{fail}}{\Gamma, \Delta \vdash \mathbf{let}\ x = t_1\ \mathbf{in}\ t_2 : \mathbf{fail}}$$
$$(\text{LET-F})$$

$$\frac{\Gamma, \Delta \vdash t_1 : \mathbf{true} \quad \Delta \vdash t_2 : \tau}{\Gamma, \Delta \vdash \mathbf{assume}\ t_1 ; t_2 : \tau} \ (\text{ASSUME}) \quad \frac{\Gamma, \Delta \vdash t_1 : \mathbf{fail}}{\Gamma, \Delta \vdash \mathbf{assume}\ t_1 ; t_2 : \mathbf{fail}}$$
$$(\text{ASSUME-F})$$

$$\frac{\Gamma \vdash \rho : \Delta' \quad \Gamma, \Delta' \vdash p : \sigma}{\Gamma, \Delta \vdash \mathbf{close}\ p\ \mathbf{in}\ \rho : \sigma} \ (\text{CLOSE}) \quad \frac{\Gamma \vdash \rho : \Delta' \quad \Gamma, \Delta' \vdash t : \tau}{\Delta \vdash \mathbf{bind}\ \rho\ \mathbf{in}\ t : \tau} \ (\text{BIND})$$

$$\frac{\mathrm{dom}(\Delta) = \mathrm{dom}(\rho) \quad \Gamma \vdash \rho(x) : \Delta(x) \text{ for each } x \in \mathrm{dom}(\Delta)}{\Gamma \vdash \rho : \Delta} \ (\text{ENV})$$

Fig. 4. Typing rules

There are four kinds of type judgments in the intersection type system;

- $\Gamma, \Delta \vdash t : \tau$ for term t;
- $\Gamma, \Delta \vdash e : \tau$ for expression e;
- $\Gamma, \Delta \vdash \tilde{t} : \tilde{\sigma}$ or $\Gamma, \Delta \vdash \tilde{t} : \mathbf{fail}$ for sequence $\tilde{t}$; and
- $\Gamma \vdash \rho : \Delta$ for environment ρ.

The typing rules for those judgments are given in Fig. 4. Intuitively, the type judgment for terms represents "under-approximation" of the evaluation of the term. The judgment $\Gamma, \Delta \vdash t : \sigma$ intuitively means that there is a reduction $\rho \vdash_D t \longrightarrow^* v$ for some value v of type σ, and $\Gamma, \Delta \vdash t : \mathbf{fail}$ means that $\rho \vdash_D t \longrightarrow^* \phi^\ell$ for some error expression ϕ. For example, for the term $t_1 = \langle \mathbf{true} \oplus \mathbf{false}, \mathbf{true} \rangle^\ell$, the judgments $\Gamma, \Delta \vdash t_1 : \langle \mathbf{true}, \mathbf{true} \rangle$ and $\Gamma, \Delta \vdash t_1 : \langle \mathbf{false}, \mathbf{true} \rangle$ should hold because there are reductions $\rho \vdash_D t_1 \longrightarrow^* \langle \mathbf{true}, \mathbf{true} \rangle^\ell$ and $\rho \vdash_D t_1 \longrightarrow^* \langle \mathbf{false}, \mathbf{true} \rangle^\ell$. Furthermore, for the term $t_2 = ($**let** $x = $ **true** $\oplus$ **false in assume** $x;$**fail**$)^{\ell}$, $\Gamma, \Delta \vdash t_2 : $ **fail** because $\rho \vdash_D t_2 \longrightarrow^*$ (**bind** $\rho[x \mapsto$ **true**$]$ **in fail**$)^{\ell}$. We remark that a term that always diverges (e.g. Ω and **assume false**; t) does not have any types. The judgments $\Gamma, \Delta \vdash \tilde{t} : \tilde{\sigma}$ and $\Gamma, \Delta \vdash \tilde{t} : $ **fail** are auxiliary judgments, which correspond to the evaluation strategy that evaluates $\tilde{t}$ from left to right. For example, the rule (SEQ-F) means that the evaluation $\tilde{t} = t_1 \dots t_k$ fails (e.g. $\Gamma, \Delta \vdash \tilde{t} : $ **fail**) if and only if some t_i fails (e.g. $\Gamma, \Delta \vdash t_i : $ **fail**), and $t_0, \dots, t_{i-1}$ are evaluated to some values $\tilde{v}$ (e.g. $\Gamma, \Delta \vdash t_1, \dots, t_{i-1} : \tilde{\sigma}$). The judgment for environments $\Gamma, \Delta \vdash \rho : \Delta$ represents that for each binding $[x \mapsto v]$ in ρ, v has type $\Delta(x)$.

The type system above is an extension of Tsukada and Kobayashi's one [20]. The main differences are:

- Our target language supports tuples as first-class values, while tuples may occur only as function arguments in their language. By supporting them, we avoid hyper-exponential explosion of the number of types caused by the CPS-transformation to eliminate first-class tuples.
- Our target language also supports let-expressions. Although it is possible to define them as syntactic sugar, supporting them as primitives makes our type inference algorithm more efficient.

We define some operators used in the rest of this section. Let σ and σ' be value types that are refinements of some function sort. The intersection of σ and σ', written as $\sigma \wedge \sigma'$, is defined by:

$$\bigwedge_{i \in I} (\sigma_i \rightarrow \tau_i) \wedge \bigwedge_{j \in J} (\sigma_j \rightarrow \tau_j) = \bigwedge_{k \in (I \cup J)} (\sigma_k \rightarrow \tau_k),$$

where $\sigma = \bigwedge_{i \in I}(\sigma_i \rightarrow \tau_i)$ and $\sigma' = \bigwedge_{j \in J}(\sigma_j \rightarrow \tau_j)$. Let D be a global definition, and Γ and Γ' be global type environments. We say Γ' is a D-expansion of Γ, written as $\Gamma \lhd_D \Gamma'$, if the following condition holds:

$$\Gamma \lhd_D \Gamma' \iff \begin{array}{l} \text{dom}(\Gamma) = \text{dom}(\Gamma'), \\ \forall f \in \text{dom}(\Gamma).\exists \sigma. \; \Gamma, \emptyset \vdash D(f) : \sigma \text{ and } \Gamma'(f) = (\Gamma(f) \wedge \sigma) \end{array}$$

This expansion soundly computes types of each recursive function. Intuitively, $\Gamma \lhd_D \Gamma'$ means that, assuming Γ is a sound type environment for D, $\Gamma'(f)$ is a sound type of f because $\Gamma'(f)$ is obtained from $\Gamma(f)$ by adding a valid type of $D(f)$. We write $\Gamma_D^{\top}$ for the environment $\{f \mapsto \bigwedge \emptyset \mid f \in \text{dom}(D)\}$, which corresponds to approximating D as $D^{\top} = \{f \mapsto \lambda x : \kappa. \; \Omega \mid f \in \text{dom}(D)\}$. It is always safe to approximate the behaviour of D with $\Gamma_D^{\top}$. We write $\lhd_D^*$ for the reflexive and transitive closure of $\lhd_D$. We say Γ is *sound for* D if $\Gamma_D^{\top} \lhd_D^* \Gamma$.

Theorem 1 indicates that the intersection type system characterizes the reachability of Boolean programs. The proof is similar to the proof of the corresponding theorem for Tsukada and Kobayashi's type system [20]: see the long version [19].

Theorem 1. *Let* $P = $ **let rec** $D : \mathcal{K}$ **in** t_0 *be a well-sorted program. P is unsafe if and only if there is a global type environment Γ that is sound for D, and that $\Gamma, \emptyset \vdash t_0 : $ **fail**.*

According to this theorem, the reachability checking problem is solved by saturation-based algorithms. For example, it is easily shown that the following naïve saturation function $\mathcal{F}_D$ is sufficient for deciding the reachability.

$$\mathcal{F}_D(\Gamma)(f) = \Gamma(f) \wedge \bigwedge \left\{ \sigma \to \tau \; \middle| \; \begin{array}{l} D(f) = \lambda x : \kappa.\, t, \sigma :: \kappa, \\ \Gamma, [x \mapsto \sigma] \vdash t : \tau \end{array} \right\}$$

The saturation function is effectively computable. To compute the second operand of $\wedge$ in the definition of $\mathcal{F}_D(\Gamma)(f)$, it suffices to pick each σ such that $\sigma :: \kappa$, and computes τ such that $\Gamma, [x \mapsto \sigma] \vdash t : \tau$. Note that there are only finitely many σ such that $\sigma :: \kappa$. Given a well-sorted program **let rec** $D : \mathcal{K}$ **in** t_0, let $\Gamma_0 = \Gamma_D^\top$ and $\Gamma_{i+1} = \mathcal{F}_D(\Gamma_i)$. The sequence $\Gamma_0, \Gamma_1, \ldots, \Gamma_m, \ldots$ converges for some m, because $\Gamma_i \lhd_D \Gamma_{i+1}$ for each i, and $\lhd_D$ is a partial order on the (finite) set of type environments. Thus, the reachability is decided by checking whether $\Gamma_m, \emptyset \vdash t_0 : \mathbf{fail}$ holds.

4   The 0-CFA Guided Saturation Algorithm

In the following discussion, we fix some well-sorted program $P = \mathbf{let\ rec}\ D : \mathcal{K}\ \mathbf{in}\ t_0$. We assume that all variables bound in lambda-expressions or let-expressions in P are distinct from each other, and that all the labels in P are also distinct from each other. Therefore, we assume each variable x has the corresponding sort, and we write $\mathrm{sort}(x)$ for it.

This section presents an efficient algorithm for deciding the reachability problem, based on the type system in the previous section. Unfortunately, the naïve algorithm presented in Sect. 3 is impractical, mainly due to the (FUN) rule:

$$\frac{\Gamma, \Delta[x \mapsto \sigma_i] \vdash t : \tau_i \qquad \sigma_i :: \kappa \qquad \text{for each } i \in I}{\Gamma, \Delta \vdash \lambda x : \kappa.\, t : \bigwedge_{i \in I}(\sigma_i \to \tau_i)} \tag{FUN}$$

The rule tells us how to enumerate the type judgments for $\lambda x : \kappa.\, t$ from those for t, but there are a huge number of candidate types of the argument x because they are only restricted to have a certain sort κ; when the depth of κ is k, the number of candidate types is k-fold exponential. Therefore, we modify the type system to reduce irrelevant type candidates.

4.1   The $\hat{\delta}$-Guided Type System

A *flow type environment* is a function that maps a variable x to a set of value types that are refinement of $\mathrm{sort}(x)$. Let Γ be a global type environment, $\hat{\delta}$ be a flow type environment, and Δ be a local type environment. We define the $\hat{\delta}$-guided type judgment of the form either $\Gamma, \Delta \vdash_{\hat{\delta}} t : \tau$ or $\Gamma, \Delta \vdash_{\hat{\delta}} e : \tau$. The typing rules for this judgment are the same as that of $\Gamma, \Delta \vdash t : \tau$, except for (FUN), which is replaced by the following rule:

$$S = \left\{ (\sigma, \tau) \,\middle|\, \sigma \in \hat{\delta}(x), \Gamma, \Delta[x \mapsto \sigma] \vdash_{\hat{\delta}} t : \tau \right\} \tag{Fun'}$$
$$\overline{\Gamma, \Delta \vdash_{\hat{\delta}} \lambda x : \kappa.\ t : \bigwedge_{(\sigma, \tau) \in S} (\sigma \to \tau)}$$

This modified rule derives the "strongest" type of the lambda-abstraction, assuming $\hat{\delta}(x)$ is an over-approximation of the set of types bound to x. This type system, named *the $\hat{\delta}$-guided type system*, is built so that the type judgments are deterministic for values, lambda-abstractions and environments.

Proposition 1. *Suppose $\Gamma :: \mathcal{K}$. Then,*

- $\mathcal{K}, \emptyset \vdash v : \kappa$ *implies* $\exists! \sigma. \sigma :: \kappa \wedge \Gamma, \emptyset \vdash_{\hat{\delta}} v : \sigma$,
- $\mathcal{K}, \emptyset \vdash p : \kappa$ *implies* $\exists! \sigma. \sigma :: \kappa \wedge \Gamma, \emptyset \vdash_{\hat{\delta}} p : \sigma$, *and*
- $\mathcal{K} \vdash \rho : \Sigma$ *implies* $\exists! \Delta. \Delta :: \Sigma \wedge \Gamma \vdash_{\hat{\delta}} \rho : \Delta$.

Thereby, we write $[\![v]\!]_{\Gamma, \hat{\delta}}$, $[\![p]\!]_{\Gamma, \hat{\delta}}$ and $[\![\rho]\!]_{\Gamma, \hat{\delta}}$ for the value type of value v, lambda-abstraction p, and environment ρ, respectively.

We define the $\hat{\delta}$-guided saturation function $\mathcal{G}_D(\hat{\delta}, \Gamma)$ as follows:

$$\mathcal{G}_D(\hat{\delta}, \Gamma)(f) = \Gamma(f) \wedge [\![D(f)]\!]_{\Gamma, \hat{\delta}}$$

It is easily shown that the soundness theorem of $\hat{\delta}$-guided type system holds.

Theorem 2 (Soundness). *Let $P = \mathbf{let\ rec}\ D : \mathcal{K}\ \mathbf{in}\ t_0$ be a well-sorted program. Let $\hat{\delta}_0, \hat{\delta}_1, \ldots$ be a sequence of flow type environments. We define a sequence of global type environments $\Gamma_0, \Gamma_1, \ldots$ as follows: (i) $\Gamma_0 = \Gamma_D^\top$, and (ii) $\Gamma_{i+1} = \mathcal{G}_D(\hat{\delta}_i, \Gamma_i)$ for each $i \geq 0$. The program P is unsafe if there is some m such that $\Gamma_m, \emptyset \vdash_{\hat{\delta}_m} t_0 : \mathbf{fail}$.*

However, the completeness of the $\hat{\delta}$-guided type system depends on the flow environments used during saturation. For example, if we use the largest flow type environment, that is, $\hat{\delta}(x) = \{\, \sigma \mid \sigma :: \mathrm{sort}(x)\,\}$, we have the completeness, but we lose the efficiency. We have to find a method to compute a sufficiently large flow type environment $\hat{\delta}$ such that the $\hat{\delta}$-guided type system achieves both the completeness and the efficiency.

In the call-by-name case, a sufficient condition on $\hat{\delta}$ to guarantee the completeness can be formalized in terms of flow information [4]. For each function call $t_1\ t_2$, we just need to require that $\hat{\delta}(x) \supseteq \{\, \sigma \mid \Gamma, \Delta \vdash_{\hat{\delta}} t_2 : \sigma\,\}$ for each possible value $\lambda x.\ t$ of t_1.

However, in the call-by-value case, the condition on $\hat{\delta}$ is more subtle because the actual value bound to argument x is not t_2 itself but an evaluation result of t_2. In order to prove that the $\hat{\delta}$-guided type system is complete, it is required that $\hat{\delta}(x)$ contains all the types of the values bound to x during the evaluation,[2] i.e. $\hat{\delta}(x) \supseteq \{\, [\![v]\!]_{\Gamma, \hat{\delta}} \mid \rho \vdash_D t_2 \longrightarrow^* v\,\}$. Therefore, we have to prove that

---

[2] In the call-by-name case, this property immediately follows from the condition $\hat{\delta}(x) \supseteq \{\, \sigma \mid \Gamma, \Delta \vdash_{\hat{\delta}} t_2 : \sigma\,\}$ because t_2 is not evaluated before the function call.

$\{\, [\![v]\!]_{\Gamma,\hat{\delta}} \mid \rho \vdash_D t_2 \longrightarrow^* v \,\} \supseteq \{\, \sigma \mid \Gamma, \Delta \vdash_{\hat{\delta}} t_2 : \sigma \,\}$, but this fact follows from the completeness of the $\hat{\delta}$-guided type system, which causes a circular reasoning.

In the rest of this section, we first formalize 0-CFA for our target language, propose our 0-CFA guided saturation algorithm, and prove the correctness of the algorithm.

4.2   0-CFA

We adopt the formalization of 0-CFA by Nielson et al. [13].

An *abstract value* is defined by:

$$av \text{ (abstract values)} ::= \texttt{bool} \mid p \mid f \mid \langle av_1, \ldots, av_k \rangle.$$

The set of abstract values is denoted as $\widehat{\mathbf{Value}}$. An abstract value is regarded as a value without environments. The abstract value of a value v, written $\hat{v}$, is defined by:

$$\widehat{w^\ell} = \hat{w} \qquad\qquad \hat{b} = \texttt{bool} \qquad\qquad \hat{f} = f$$

$$\widehat{\textbf{close } p \textbf{ in } \rho} = p \qquad\qquad \widehat{\langle v_1, \ldots, v_k \rangle} = \langle \hat{v_1}, \ldots, \hat{v_k} \rangle.$$

An *abstract cache* is a function from $\mathbf{Lab}$ to $\mathcal{P}(\widehat{\mathbf{Value}})$, and an *abstract environment* is a function from $\mathbf{Var}$ to $\mathcal{P}(\widehat{\mathbf{Value}})$. Let $\hat{C}$ be an abstract cache, and $\hat{\rho}$ be an abstract environment. We define the relations $(\hat{C}, \hat{\rho}) \models_D e^\ell$ and $(\hat{C}, \hat{\rho}) \models_D \rho$, which represents $(\hat{C}, \hat{\rho})$ is an *acceptable* CFA result of the term e^ℓ and the environment ρ, respectively.

The relations are co-inductively defined by the rules given in Fig. 5. In the (TUPLE) rule, $\hat{C}(\ell_1) \otimes \cdots \otimes \hat{C}(\ell_k)$ means the set $\{\, \langle \hat{v}_1, \ldots, \hat{v}_k \rangle \mid \forall i.\hat{v}_i \in \hat{C}(\ell_i) \,\}$. In the (PROJ) rule, $\pi_i^k(\hat{C}(\ell_1)) = \{\, \hat{v}_i \mid \langle \hat{v}_0, \ldots, \hat{v}_{k-1} \rangle \in \hat{C}(\ell_1) \,\}$. The relation $(\hat{C}, \hat{\rho}) \models_D e^\ell$ is defined so that if e^ℓ is evaluated to a value v, then the abstract value of v is in $\hat{C}(\ell)$. The relation $(\hat{C}, \hat{\rho}) \models_D \rho$ means that for each binding $x \mapsto v$ in ρ, $\hat{\rho}(x)$ contains the abstract value of v.

4.3   The 0-CFA Guided Saturation Algorithm

We propose a method to compute a sufficiently large $\hat{\delta}$ so that the $\hat{\delta}$-guided type system would be complete. Let $\hat{C}$ be an abstract cache. We define two relations $(\hat{C}, \hat{\delta}) \models_{D,\Gamma} (t, \Delta)$, and $(\hat{C}, \hat{\delta}) \models_{D,\Gamma} \rho$. The relation $(\hat{C}, \hat{\delta}) \models_\Gamma (t, \Delta)$ means intuitively that, during any evaluations of t under an environment ρ such that $\Gamma \vdash \rho : \Delta$, the type of values bound to variable x is approximated by $\hat{\delta}(x)$. The derivation rules for those relations are given in Fig. 6. We regard these rules as an algorithm to saturate $\hat{\delta}$, given $\hat{C}$, Δ and t. The algorithm basically traverses the term t with possible Δ using $\hat{\delta}$-guided type system as dataflow, and propagates types to $\hat{\delta}$ using the rule (APP): if t is an function call $e_1^\ell t_2$, the algorithm enumerates each lambda abstraction $\lambda x : \kappa. t_0$ that e_1^ℓ may be evaluated to by using $\hat{C}$, and propagates each type σ of t_2 (i.e. $\Gamma, \Delta \vdash_{\hat{\delta}} t : \sigma$) to $\hat{\delta}(x)$.

$$\frac{\hat{C}(\ell) \ni \mathbf{bool}}{(\hat{C}, \hat{\rho}) \models_D b^\ell} \quad \frac{\hat{C}(\ell) \supseteq \hat{\rho}(x)}{(\hat{C}, \hat{\rho}) \models_D x^\ell} \quad \frac{}{(\hat{C}, \hat{\rho}) \models_D \mathbf{fail}^\ell} \quad \frac{}{(\hat{C}, \hat{\rho}) \models_D \Omega^\ell}$$
$$\quad\quad\quad (\textsc{Bool}) \quad\quad\quad\quad (\textsc{Var}) \quad\quad\quad\quad\quad (\textsc{Fail}) \quad\quad\quad (\textsc{Omega})$$

$$\frac{\hat{C}(\ell) \ni f \quad \begin{matrix} D(f) = \lambda x : \kappa.\ t \\ (\hat{C}, \hat{\rho}) \models_D t \end{matrix}}{(\hat{C}, \hat{\rho}) \models_D f^\ell} \ (\textsc{Tfun}) \quad \frac{(\hat{C}, \hat{\rho}) \models_D e^{\ell_1} \quad \hat{C}(\ell) \supseteq \pi_i^k(\hat{C}(\ell_1))}{(\hat{C}, \hat{\rho}) \models_D (\pi_i^k e^{\ell_1})^\ell} \ (\textsc{Proj})$$

$$\frac{(\hat{C}, \hat{\rho}) \models_D \rho \quad (\hat{C}, \hat{\rho}) \models_D p}{(\hat{C}, \hat{\rho}) \models_D (\mathbf{close}\ p\ \mathbf{in}\ \rho)^\ell} \ (\textsc{Close}) \quad \frac{\hat{C}(\ell) \ni (\lambda x : \kappa.\ t) \quad (\hat{C}, \hat{\rho}) \models_D t}{(\hat{C}, \hat{\rho}) \models_D (\lambda x : \kappa.\ t)^\ell} \ (\textsc{Fun})$$

$$\frac{(\hat{C}, \hat{\rho}) \models_D t_i \text{ for each } i \quad \hat{C}(\ell) \ni \mathbf{bool}}{(\hat{C}, \hat{\rho}) \models_D op(t_1, \ldots, t_k)^\ell} \ (\textsc{Op}) \quad \frac{(\hat{C}, \hat{\rho}) \models_D e_i^{\ell_i} \text{ for each } i \quad \hat{C}(\ell) \supseteq \hat{C}(\ell_1) \otimes \cdots \otimes \hat{C}(\ell_k)}{(\hat{C}, \hat{\rho}) \models_D \langle e_1^{\ell_1}, \ldots, e_k^{\ell_k}\rangle^\ell} \ (\textsc{Tuple})$$

$$\frac{\begin{matrix} (\hat{C}, \hat{\rho}) \models_D e_1^{\ell_1} & \forall (\lambda x : \kappa.\ e^{\ell_0}) \in (\hat{C}(\ell_1) \cup \{\, D(f) \mid f \in \hat{C}(\ell_1) \,\}). \\ (\hat{C}, \hat{\rho}) \models_D e_2^{\ell_2} & \hat{\rho}(x) \supseteq \hat{C}(\ell_2) \wedge \hat{C}(\ell) \supseteq \hat{C}(\ell_0) \end{matrix}}{(\hat{C}, \hat{\rho}) \models_D (e_1^{\ell_1}\ e_2^{\ell_2})^\ell} \ (\textsc{App})$$

$$\frac{\begin{matrix} (\hat{C}, \hat{\rho}) \models_D e_1^{\ell_1} & \hat{C}(\ell) \supseteq \hat{C}(\ell_1) \\ (\hat{C}, \hat{\rho}) \models_D \rho \end{matrix}}{(\hat{C}, \hat{\rho}) \models_D (\mathbf{bind}\ \rho\ \mathbf{in}\ e_1^{\ell_1})^\ell} \ (\textsc{Bind}) \quad \frac{\begin{matrix} (\hat{C}, \hat{\rho}) \models_D e_1^{\ell_1} & \hat{C}(\ell) \supseteq \hat{C}(\ell_1) \\ (\hat{C}, \hat{\rho}) \models_D e_2^{\ell_2} & \hat{C}(\ell) \supseteq \hat{C}(\ell_2) \end{matrix}}{(\hat{C}, \hat{\rho}) \models_D (e_1^{\ell_1} \oplus e_2^{\ell_2})^\ell} \ (\textsc{Br})$$

$$\frac{\begin{matrix} (\hat{C}, \hat{\rho}) \models_D e_1^{\ell_1}\ (\hat{C}, \hat{\rho}) \models_D e_2^{\ell_2} \\ \hat{\rho}(x) \supseteq \hat{C}(\ell_1)\ \hat{C}(\ell) \supseteq \hat{C}(\ell_2) \end{matrix}}{(\hat{C}, \hat{\rho}) \models_D \mathbf{let}\ x = e_1^{\ell_1}\ \mathbf{in}\ e_2^{\ell_2}} \ (\textsc{Let}) \quad \frac{\begin{matrix} (\hat{C}, \hat{\rho}) \models_D t_1 \\ (\hat{C}, \hat{\rho}) \models_D e_2^{\ell_2} \end{matrix} \quad \hat{C}(\ell) \supseteq \hat{C}(\ell_2)}{(\hat{C}, \hat{\rho}) \models_D (\mathbf{assume}\ t_1; e_2^{\ell_2})^\ell} \ (\textsc{Assume})$$

$$\frac{(\hat{C}, \hat{\rho}) \models_D w^\ell \quad \hat{\rho}(x) \supseteq \hat{C}(\ell) \quad \text{for each binding } x \mapsto w^\ell \text{ in } \rho}{(\hat{C}, \hat{\rho}) \models_D \rho} \ (\textsc{Env})$$

Fig. 5. 0-CFA rules

Algorithm 1 shows our algorithm for the reachability problem, named *the 0-CFA guided saturation algorithm*. Given a well-sorted program $P = \mathbf{let\ rec}\ D : \mathcal{K}\ \mathbf{in}\ t_0$, the algorithm initializes Γ_0 with $\Gamma_D^\top$, computes a 0-CFA result $(\hat{C}, \hat{\rho})$ such that $(\hat{C}, \hat{\rho}) \models_D t$, sets $i = 0$, and enters the main loop. In the main loop, it computes $\hat{\delta}_i$ such that $(\hat{C}, \hat{\delta}_i) \models_{D,\Gamma_i} t_0$, and then, sets Γ_{i+1} with $\mathcal{G}_D(\hat{\delta}_i, \Gamma_i)$ and increments i. The algorithm outputs "UNSAFE" if $\Gamma_i \vdash_{\hat{\delta}_i} t_0 : \mathbf{fail}$ holds for some i. Otherwise, the main loop eventually breaks when $\Gamma_i = \Gamma_{i-1}$ holds, and then, the algorithm outputs "SAFE".

We explain how the saturation algorithm runs for the program P_1 in Example 1. Let ℓ_1 and ℓ_2 be the labels of the first application of y and the second application of y in function f. A result of 0-CFA would be $\hat{C}(\ell_1) = \hat{C}(\ell_2) = \lambda(x : \mathbf{bool}).\ \mathbf{true} \oplus \mathbf{false}$. Let $\Gamma_0 = \{\, f \mapsto \bigwedge \emptyset \,\}$. Then, $\hat{\delta}_0$ would be

$$\hat{\delta}_0(y) = \{\, \textstyle\bigwedge \emptyset, (\mathbf{true} \to \mathbf{true}) \wedge (\mathbf{true} \to \mathbf{false}) \,\} \qquad \hat{\delta}_0(x) = \{\, \mathbf{true} \,\}.$$

Therefore, $\Gamma_0, \emptyset \vdash_{\hat{\delta}_0} D_1(f) : (\mathbf{true} \to \mathbf{true}) \wedge (\mathbf{true} \to \mathbf{false}) \to \mathbf{fail}$ holds, and it would be $\Gamma_1 = \{\, f : (\mathbf{true} \to \mathbf{true}) \wedge (\mathbf{true} \to \mathbf{false}) \to \mathbf{fail} \,\}$. In the next

$$\frac{}{(\hat{C},\hat{\delta}) \models_{D,\Gamma} (b^\ell, \Delta)} \text{ (Bool)} \qquad \frac{}{(\hat{C},\hat{\delta}) \models_{D,\Gamma} (x^\ell, \Delta)} \text{ (Var)} \qquad \frac{(\hat{C},\hat{\delta}) \models_{D,\Gamma} (t, \Delta)}{(\hat{C},\hat{\delta}) \models_{D,\Gamma} ((\pi_i^k t)^\ell, \Delta)} \text{ (Proj)}$$

$$\frac{}{(\hat{C},\hat{\delta}) \models_{D,\Gamma} (\mathbf{fail}^\ell, \Delta)} \text{ (Fail)} \qquad \frac{D(f) = \lambda x : \kappa.\ t \quad (\hat{C},\hat{\delta}) \models_{D,\Gamma} (t, [x \mapsto \sigma]) \text{ for each } \sigma \in \hat{\delta}(x)}{(\hat{C},\hat{\delta}) \models_{D,\Gamma} (f^\ell, \Delta)} \text{ (Tfun)}$$

$$\frac{}{(\hat{C},\hat{\delta}) \models_{D,\Gamma} (\Omega^\ell, \Delta)} \text{ (Omega)} \qquad \frac{(\hat{C},\hat{\delta}) \models_{D,\Gamma} (t, \Delta[x \mapsto \sigma]) \text{ for each } \sigma \in \hat{\delta}(x)}{(\hat{C},\hat{\rho}) \models_{D,\Gamma} ((\lambda x : \kappa.\ t)^\ell, \Delta)} \text{ (Fun)}$$

$$\frac{(\hat{C},\hat{\delta}) \models_{D,\Gamma} (t_i, \Delta) \text{ for each } i}{(\hat{C},\hat{\delta}) \models_{D,\Gamma} (\mathrm{op}(t_1,\ldots,t_k)^\ell, \Delta)} \text{ (Op)} \qquad \frac{(\hat{C},\hat{\delta}) \models_{D,\Gamma} (t_i, \Delta) \text{ for each } i}{(\hat{C},\hat{\delta}) \models_{D,\Gamma} (\langle t_1,\ldots,t_k\rangle^\ell, \Delta)} \text{ (Tuple)}$$

$$\frac{\begin{array}{ll} (\hat{C},\hat{\delta}) \models_{D,\Gamma} (e_1^{\ell_1}, \Delta), & \forall(\lambda x : \kappa.\ t) \in (\hat{C}(\ell_1) \cup \{ D(f) \mid f \in \hat{C}(\ell_1) \}) \\ (\hat{C},\hat{\delta}) \models_{D,\Gamma} (t_2, \Delta) & \hat{\delta}(x) \supseteq \{ \sigma \mid \Gamma, \Delta \vdash_{\hat{\delta}} t_2 : \sigma \} \end{array}}{(\hat{C},\hat{\delta}) \models_{D,\Gamma} ((e_1^{\ell_1}\ t_2)^\ell, \Delta)} \text{ (App)}$$

$$\frac{(\hat{C},\hat{\delta}) \models_{D,\Gamma} (t_1, \Delta) \qquad (\hat{C},\hat{\delta}) \models_{D,\Gamma} (t_2, \Delta[x \mapsto \sigma]) \text{ for each } \Gamma, \Delta \vdash_{\hat{\delta}} t_1 : \sigma}{(\hat{C},\hat{\delta}) \models_{D,\Gamma} ((\mathbf{let}\ x = t_1 \ \mathbf{in}\ t_2)^\ell, \Delta)} \text{ (Let)}$$

$$\frac{(\hat{C},\hat{\delta}) \models_{D,\Gamma} (t_1, \Delta) \qquad \Gamma, \Delta \vdash_{\hat{\delta}} t_1 : \mathbf{true} \implies (\hat{C},\hat{\delta}) \models_{D,\Gamma} (t_2, \Delta)}{(\hat{C},\hat{\delta}) \models_{D,\Gamma} ((\mathbf{assume}\ t_1; t_2)^\ell, \Delta)} \text{ (Assume)}$$

$$\frac{(\hat{C},\hat{\delta}) \models_{D,\Gamma} (t, [\![\rho]\!]_{\Gamma,\hat{\delta}}) \qquad (\hat{C},\hat{\delta}) \models_{D,\Gamma} \rho}{(\hat{C},\hat{\delta}) \models_{D,\Gamma} ((\mathbf{bind}\ \rho\ \mathbf{in}\ t)^\ell, \Delta)} \text{ (Bind)} \qquad \frac{(\hat{C},\hat{\delta}) \models_{D,\Gamma} \rho \qquad (\hat{C},\hat{\delta}) \models_{\Gamma} (p^\ell, [\![\rho]\!]_{\Gamma,\hat{\delta}})}{(\hat{C},\hat{\delta}) \models_{D,\Gamma} ((\mathbf{close}\ p\ \mathbf{in}\ \rho)^\ell, \Delta)} \text{ (Close)}$$

$$\frac{\begin{array}{l}(\hat{C},\hat{\delta}) \models_{D,\Gamma} (t_1, \Delta) \\ (\hat{C},\hat{\delta}) \models_{D,\Gamma} (t_2, \Delta)\end{array}}{(\hat{C},\hat{\delta}) \models_{D,\Gamma} ((t_1 \oplus t_2)^\ell, \Delta)} \text{ (Br)} \qquad \frac{\forall x \in \mathrm{dom}(\rho).\ (\hat{C},\hat{\delta}) \models_{D,\Gamma} (\rho(x), \emptyset)}{(\hat{C},\hat{\delta}) \models_{D,\Gamma} \rho} \text{ (Env)}$$

Fig. 6. Derivation rules for $(\hat{C},\hat{\delta}) \models_{D,\Gamma} (t, \Delta)$ and $(\hat{C},\hat{\delta}) \models_{D,\Gamma} \rho$

Algorithm 1. The 0-CFA guided saturation algorithm

---

function IsSafe($P = \mathbf{let\ rec}\ D : \mathcal{K}\ \mathbf{in}\ t_0$)
   $\Gamma_0 := \Gamma_D^\top$
   Compute $(\hat{C}, \hat{\rho})$ such that $(\hat{C}, \hat{\rho}) \models_D t_0$
   $i := 0$
   repeat
      Compute $\hat{\delta}_i$ such that $(\hat{C}, \hat{\delta}_i) \models_{D,\Gamma_i} (t_0, \emptyset)$
      $\Gamma_{i+1} = \mathcal{G}_D(\hat{\delta}_i, \Gamma_i)$
      $i := i + 1$
      if $\Gamma_{i-1}, \emptyset \vdash_{\hat{\delta}_{i-1}} t_0 : \mathbf{fail}$ **then**
         return Unsafe
      end if
   until $\Gamma_{i-1} = \Gamma_i$
   return Safe
end function

iteration, there are no updates, i.e. $\hat{\delta}_1 = \hat{\delta}_0$ and $\Gamma_1 = \Gamma_0$. Because $\Gamma_1, \emptyset \vdash_{\hat{\delta}_1} t_1 :$ **fail** holds, the algorithm outputs "UNSAFE".

4.4 Correctness of the 0-CFA Guided Saturation Algorithm

We prove the correctness of Algorithm 1. If the algorithm outputs "UNSAFE", the given program is unsafe by using Theorem 2. In order to justify the case that the algorithm outputs "SAFE", we prove the completeness of the $\hat{\delta}$-guided type system.

First, the following lemma indicates that $(\hat{C}, \hat{\rho}) \models_D t$ and $(\hat{C}, \hat{\delta}) \models_{D,\Gamma} (t, \Delta)$ satisfy subject reduction, and also that the $\hat{\delta}$-guided type system satisfies subject expansion. This lemma solves the problem of circular reasoning discussed at the end of Sect. 4.1.

Lemma 1. *Let Γ be a global type environment such that $\Gamma = \mathcal{G}_D(\hat{\delta}, \Gamma)$. Suppose that $(\hat{C}, \hat{\rho}) \models_D t_1$, $(\hat{C}, \hat{\rho}) \models_D \rho$, $\rho \vdash_D t_1 \longrightarrow t_2$, $(\hat{C}, \hat{\delta}) \models_{D,\Gamma} \rho$, and $(\hat{C}, \hat{\delta}) \models_{D,\Gamma} (t_1, \Delta)$, where $\Delta = [\![\rho]\!]_{\Gamma, \hat{\delta}}$. Then, (i) $(\hat{C}, \hat{\delta}) \models_D t_2$, (ii) $(\hat{C}, \hat{\delta}) \models_{D,\Gamma} (t_2, \Delta)$, and (iii) for any term type τ, $\Gamma, \Delta \vdash_{\hat{\delta}} t_2 : \tau$ implies $\Gamma, \Delta \vdash_{\hat{\delta}} t_1 : \tau$.*

We use the fact that $\hat{\delta}$-guided type system derives **fail** for error terms.

Lemma 2. *Let ϕ be a well-sorted error expression. Then, $\Gamma, \emptyset \vdash_{\hat{\delta}} \phi : $ **fail**.*

Then, we have the following completeness theorem, which justifies the correctness of Algorithm 1.

Theorem 3. *Let $P = $ **let rec** $D : \mathcal{K}$ **in** t_0 be a well-sorted program, Γ be a global type environment such that $\Gamma :: \mathcal{K}$ and $\Gamma = \mathcal{G}_D(\hat{\delta}, \Gamma)$. Suppose that $(\hat{C}, \hat{\rho}) \models_D t_0$, and $(\hat{C}, \hat{\delta}) \models_{D,\Gamma} (t_0, \emptyset)$. If $\Gamma, \emptyset \nvdash_{\hat{\delta}} t_0 : $ **fail** then P is safe.*

Proof. We prove the contraposition. Assume that P is unsafe, i.e., that there is a sequence $e_0 \ldots e_n$ such that $e_0^\ell = t_0$, $\emptyset \vdash_D e_i^\ell \longrightarrow e_{i+1}^\ell$ for each $0 \leq i \leq n-1$, and that e_n^ℓ is an error term. We have $\forall \tau. \Gamma, \emptyset \vdash_{\hat{\delta}} e_n^\ell : \tau \implies \Gamma, \emptyset \vdash_{\hat{\delta}} t_0 : \tau$ by induction on n and using Lemma 1. By Lemma 2, $\Gamma, \emptyset \vdash_{\hat{\delta}} e_n^\ell : $ **fail**. Therefore, we have $\Gamma, \emptyset \vdash_{\hat{\delta}} t_0 : $ **fail**. $\square$

5   Implementation and Experiments

5.1   Benchmarks and Environment

We have implemented a reachability checker named HIBOCH for call-by-value Boolean programs. In order to evaluate the performance of our algorithm, we prepared two benchmarks. The first benchmark consists of Boolean programs generated by a CEGAR-based verification system for ML programs. More precisely, we prepared fourteen instances of verification problems for ML programs, which have been manually converted from the MoCHi benchmark [17], and passed them to our prototype CEGAR-based verification system, which uses

HiBoch as a backend reachability checker. During each CEGAR cycle, the system generates an instance of the reachability problem for Boolean programs by predicate abstraction, and we used these problem instances for the first benchmark.

The second benchmark consists of a series of Boolean programs generated by a template named "Flow", which was manually designed to clarify the differences between the direct and indirect styles. More details on this benchmark are given in the long version [19].

We compared our direct method with the previous indirect method, which converts Boolean programs to HORS and checks the reachability with a higher-order model checker. We use HorSat [4] as the main higher-order model checker in the indirect method; since HorSat also uses a 0-CFA-based saturation algorithm (but for HORS, not for Boolean programs), we believe that HorSat is the most appropriate target of comparison for evaluating the difference between the direct/indirect approaches. We also report the results of the indirect method using the other state-of-the-art higher-order model checkers HorSat2 [10] and Preface [16], but one should note that the difference of the performance may not properly reflect that between the direct/indirect approaches, because HorSat2 uses a different flow analysis and Preface is not based on saturation.

The experimental environment was as follows. The machine spec is 2.3 GHz Intel Core i7 CPU, 16 GB RAM. Our implementation was compiled with the Glasgow Haskell Compiler, version 7.10.3, HorSat and HorSat2 were compiled with the OCaml native-code compiler, version 4.02.1, and Preface was run on Mono JIT compiler version 3.2.4. The running times of each model checker were limited to 200 s.

5.2 Experimental Result

Figures 7 and 8 show the experimental results. The horizontal axis is the size of Boolean programs, measured on the size of the abstract syntax trees, and the vertical axis is the elapsed time of each model checker, excluding the elapsed times for converting the reachability problem instances to the higher-order model checking instances.

For the first benchmark, HiBoch solves all the test cases in a few seconds. For the instances of size within 5000, HorSat2 is the fastest, and HiBoch is the second fastest, which is 4–7 times faster than HorSat (and also Preface). For the instances of size over 5000, HiBoch is the fastest[3] by an order of magnitude. We regard the reason of this result as the fact that these instances have larger arity (where the arity means the number of function arguments). The indirect style approach suffers from huge numbers of combinations between argument types. Our direct approach reduces many irrelevant combinations using the structure of call-by-value programs, which is lost during the CPS-transformation.

For the second benchmark, as we expected, HiBoch clearly outperforms the indirect approaches, even the one using HorSat2.

---

[3] Unfortunately, we could not measure the elapsed time of HorSat2 for some large instances because it raised stack-overflow exceptions.

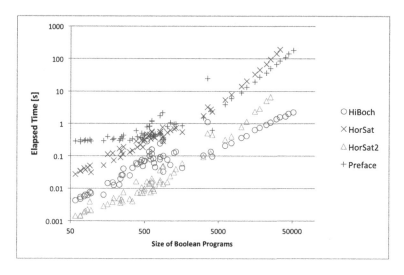

Fig. 7. Experimental result for MoCHi benchmark

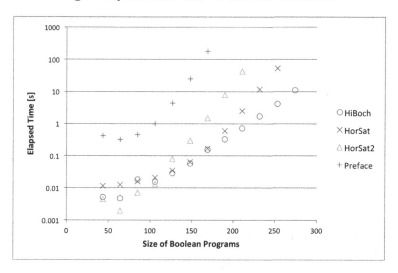

Fig. 8. Experimental result for flow benchmark

6   Related Work

As mentioned already, the reachability of higher-order call-by-value Boolean programs has been analyzed by a combination of CPS-transformation and higher-order model checking [11,17]. Because the naïve CPS-transformation algorithm often generates too complex HORS, Sato et al. [17] proposed a method called *selected CPS transformation*, in which insertion of some redundant continuations is avoided. The experiments reported in Sect. 5 adapt this selective

CPS transformation, but the indirect method still suffers from the complexity due to the CPS transformation.

Tsukada and Kobayashi [20] studied the complexity of the reachability problem, and showed that the problem is k-EXPTIME complete for *depth-k* programs. They also introduced an intersection type system and a type inference algorithm, which are the basis of our work. However, their algorithm has been designed just for proving an upper-bound of the complexity; the algorithm is impractical in the sense that it always suffers from the k-EXPTIME bottleneck, while our 0-CFA guided algorithm does not.

For *first-order* Boolean programs, Ball and Rajamani [2] proposed a path-sensitive, dataflow algorithm and implemented `Bebop` tool, which is used as a backend of SLAM [1]. It is not clear whether and how their algorithm can be extended to deal with *higher-order* Boolean programs.

Flow-based optimizations have been used in recent model checking algorithms for higher-order recursion schemes [3,4,16,18]. However, naïve application of such optimizations to call-by-value language would be less accurate because we need to estimate the evaluation result of not only functions but also their arguments. Our method employs the intersection type system to precisely represent the evaluation results.

Some of the recent higher-order model checkers [10,16] use more accurate flow information. For example, PREFACE [16] dynamically refines flow information using type-based abstraction. We believe it is possible to integrate more accurate flow analysis [5–7] also into our algorithm.

7   Conclusion

We have proposed a direct algorithm for the reachability problem of higher-order Boolean programs, and proved its correctness. We have confirmed through experiments that our direct approach improves the performance of the reachability analysis.

We are now developing a direct-style version of MoCHi, a fully automated software model checker for OCaml programs, on top of our reachability checker for Boolean programs, and plan to compare the overall performance with the indirect style. We expect that avoiding CPS transformations also benefits the predicate discovery phase.

Acknowledgment. This work was supported by JSPS KAKENHI Grant Numbers JP16J01038 and JP15H05706.

References

1. Ball, T., Cook, B., Levin, V., Rajamani, S.K.: SLAM and static driver verifier: technology transfer of formal methods inside microsoft. In: Boiten, E.A., Derrick, J., Smith, G. (eds.) IFM 2004. LNCS, vol. 2999, pp. 1–20. Springer, Heidelberg (2004). doi:10.1007/978-3-540-24756-2_1

2. Ball, T., Rajamani, S.K.: Bebop: a path-sensitive interprocedural dataflow engine. In: Proceedings of PASTE 2001, pp. 97–103. ACM (2001)
3. Broadbent, C.H., Carayol, A., Hague, M., Serre, O.: C-SHORe: acollapsible approach to higher-order verification. In: Proceedings of ICFP 2013, pp. 13–24 (2013)
4. Broadbent, C.H., Kobayashi, N.: Saturation-based model checking of higher-order recursion schemes. In: Proceedings of CSL 2013, LIPIcs, vol. 23, pp. 129–148 (2013)
5. Gilray, T., Lyde, S., Adams, M.D., Might, M., Horn, D.V.: Pushdown control-flow analysis for free. In: Proceedings of POPL 2016, pp. 691–704. ACM (2016)
6. Horn, D.V., Might, M.: Abstracting abstract machines. In: Proceedings of ICFP 2010, pp. 51–62. ACM (2010)
7. Johnson, J.I., Horn, D.V.: Abstracting abstract control. In: Proceedings of DLS 2014, pp. 11–22. ACM (2014)
8. Kobayashi, N.: Model-checking higher-order functions. In: Proceedings of PPDP 2009, pp. 25–36. ACM (2009)
9. Kobayashi, N.: Model checking higher-order programs. J. ACM **60**(3) (2013)
10. Kobayashi, N.: HorSat2: a saturation-based higher-order model checker. A toolpaper under submission (2015). http://www-kb.is.s.u-tokyo.ac.jp/~koba/horsat2
11. Kobayashi, N., Sato, R., Unno, H.: Predicate abstraction and CEGAR for higher-order model checking. In: Proceedings of PLDI 2011, pp. 222–233. ACM (2011)
12. Kuwahara, T., Terauchi, T., Unno, H., Kobayashi, N.: Automatic termination verification for higher-order functional programs. In: Shao, Z. (ed.) ESOP 2014. LNCS, vol. 8410, pp. 392–411. Springer, Heidelberg (2014). doi:10.1007/978-3-642-54833-8_21
13. Nielson, F., Nielson, H.R., Hankin, C.: Principles of Program Analysis. Springer, New York (1999)
14. Ong, C.H.L.: On model-checking trees generated by higher-order recursion schemes. In: Proceedings of LICS 2006, pp. 81–90. IEEE Computer Society Press (2006)
15. Ong, C.H.L., Ramsay, S.: Verifying higher-order programs with pattern-matching algebraic data types. In: Proceedings of POPL 2011, pp. 587–598. ACM (2011)
16. Ramsay, S.J., Neatherway, R.P., Ong, C.L.: A type-directed abstraction refinement approach to higher-order model checking. In: Proceedings of POPL 2014, pp. 61–72. ACM (2014)
17. Sato, R., Unno, H., Kobayashi, N.: Towards a scalable software model checker for higher-order programs. In: Proceedings of PEPM 2013, pp. 53–62. ACM (2013)
18. Terao, T., Kobayashi, N.: A ZDD-based efficient higher-order model checking algorithm. In: Garrigue, J. (ed.) APLAS 2014. LNCS, vol. 8858, pp. 354–371. Springer, Heidelberg (2014). doi:10.1007/978-3-319-12736-1_19
19. Terao, T., Tsukada, T., Kobayashi, N.: Higher-order model checking in direct style (2016). http://www-kb.is.s.u-tokyo.ac.jp/~terao/papers/aplas16.pdf
20. Tsukada, T., Kobayashi, N.: Complexity of model-checking call-by-value programs. In: Muscholl, A. (ed.) FoSSaCS 2014. LNCS, vol. 8412, pp. 180–194. Springer, Heidelberg (2014). doi:10.1007/978-3-642-54830-7_12

Verifying Concurrent Graph Algorithms

Azalea Raad[1(✉)], Aquinas Hobor[2], Jules Villard[1], and Philippa Gardner[1]

[1] Imperial College, London, UK
azalea@doc.ic.ac.uk
[2] Yale-NUS College and School of Computing,
National University of Singapore, Singapore, Singapore

Abstract. We show how to verify four challenging concurrent fine-grained graph-manipulating algorithms, including graph copy, a speculatively parallel Dijkstra, graph marking and spanning tree. We develop a reasoning method for such algorithms that dynamically tracks the contributions and responsibilities of each thread operating on a graph, even in cases of arbitrary recursive thread creation. We demonstrate how to use a logic without abstraction (CoLoSL) to carry out abstract reasoning in the style of iCAP, by building the abstraction into the proof structure rather than incorporating it into the semantic model of the logic.

1 Introduction

The verification of fine-grained concurrent algorithms is nontrivial. There has been much recent progress verifying such algorithms modularly using variants of concurrent separation logic [4,6,9,12,15,16]. One area of particular difficulty has been verifying such algorithms that manipulate graphs. This is only to be expected: even in a semi-formal "algorithmic" sense, the correctness arguments of concurrent graph algorithms can be dauntingly subtle [2].

To verify such algorithms, we must not only understand these algorithmic arguments, but must also determine a precise way to express them in a suitable formal system. Even sequential graph algorithms are challenging to verify due to the overlapping nature of the graph structures, preventing e.g. easy use of the frame rule of separation logic [8]. Concurrent graph algorithms pose a number of additional challenges, such as reasoning how the actions of each thread advance the overall goal despite the possible interference from other threads.Unsurprisingly, verifications of such algorithms are rare in the literature.

We verify the functional correctness of four nontrivial concurrent fine-grained graph algorithms. We study a structure-preserving copy, a speculatively-parallel version of Dijkstra's shortest-path algorithm, a graph marking, and a spanning tree algorithm. We have found common "proof patterns" for tackling these algorithms, principally reasoning about the functional correctness of the algorithm on abstract *mathematical* graphs γ, defined as sets of vertices and edges. We use such abstractions to state and prove key invariants. Another pattern is that we track the progress of each thread using a notion of *tokens* to record each thread's

© Springer International Publishing AG 2016
A. Igarashi (Ed.): APLAS 2016, LNCS 10017, pp. 314–334, 2016.
DOI: 10.1007/978-3-319-47958-3_17

portion of the computation. Informally, if the token of thread t is on vertex v, then t is responsible for some work on/around v. Our tokens are sufficiently general to handle sophisticated parallelism. (e.g. dynamic thread creation/destruction).

We then reason about the memory safety of the algorithm by connecting our reasoning on mathematical graphs to *spatial* graphs (sets of memory cells in the heap) by defining spatial predicates that implement mathematical structures in the heap e.g. $\mathsf{graph}(\gamma) \overset{\text{def}}{=} \ldots$. We define our spatial predicates in such a way that simplifies many of the proof obligations (e.g. when parallel computations join).

This pattern of doing the algorithmic reasoning on abstract states is similar to the style of reasoning used in logics such as CaReSL [16] and iCAP [15]. CaReSL introduced the idea of reasoning on abstract states. Later, iCAP extended the program logic of CAP [4] to reason about higher-order code and adopted CaReSL's abstract states. Just as with these logics, we carry out our reasoning on abstract states, which enables simpler proofs and lessens the burden of side conditions such as establishing stability. With these logics, this abstract style of reasoning has been "baked in" to the semantic models. Here, we demonstrate that this baking is unnecessary by using a logic (CoLoSL [12]) without such built-in support. We do not use any of the unique features of CoLoSL. As such, we believe that our proofs and style of abstract reasoning port to other program logics without difficulty.

Related Work. There has been much work on reasoning about graph algorithms using separation logic. For *sequential* graph algorithms, Bornat et al. presented preliminary work on dags in [1], Yang studied the Schorr-Waite graph algorithm [17], Reynolds conjectured how to reason about dags [13], and Hobor and Villard showed how to reason about dags and graphs [8]. We make critical use of some of Hobor and Villard's graph-related verification infrastructure.

Many *concurrent* program logics have been proposed in recent years; both iCAP and CaReSL encourage the kind of abstract reasoning we employ in our verifications. However, published examples in these logics focus heavily on verifying concurrent data structures, whereas we focus on verifying concurrent graph algorithms. Moreover, the semantic models for both of these logics incorporate significant machinery to enable this kind of abstract reasoning, whereas we are able to use it without built-in support.

There has hardly been any work on *concurrent* graph algorithms. Raad et al. [12] and Sergey et al. [14] have verified a concurrent spanning tree algorithm, one of our examples. In [12], Raad et al. introduced CoLoSL and gave a shaped-based proof of spanning tree to demonstrate CoLoSL reasoning. A full functional correctness proof in CoLoSL was available at the time, although not using the proof pattern presented here. Later in [14], Sergey et al. gave a full functional correctness proof in Coq, but only that single example. We believe we are the first to verify `copy_dag`, which is known to be difficult, and `parrellel_dijkstra`, which we believe is the first verification of an algorithm that uses speculative parallel decomposition [7].

Outline. The rest of this paper is organised as follows. In Sect. 2 we give an overview of the CoLoSL program logic and outline our proof pattern. We then use our proof pattern to verify the concurrent `copy_dag` (Sect. 3) and `parallel_dijkstra` (Sect. 4) algorithms, and finish with concluding remarks. We refer the reader to [10, 11] for the verification of two further concurrent graph algorithms for graph marking and computing the spanning tree of a graph.

2   Background

2.1   CoLoSL: Concurrent Local Subjective Logic

In the program logic of CoLoSL [12], the program state is modelled as a pair comprising a *thread-local* state, and a *global shared* state accessible by all threads. For instance, a shared counter at location x can be specified as:

$$\mathsf{C} \stackrel{\text{def}}{=} \iota * \boxed{\exists v \leq max.\, x \mapsto v * x{+}1 \mapsto max}_I, \qquad I \stackrel{\text{def}}{=} \{ \iota : x \mapsto v \wedge v{<}max \,\rightsquigarrow\, x \mapsto v{+}1$$

The assertion C states that the counter at location x is a *shared* resource (denoted by the $\boxed{\text{box}}$) with some value $v \leq max$, that the maximum value permitted for the counter (max) is also a shared resource stored at location $x{+}1$, and that the current thread holds some *capability* ι in its *local* state. The *interference* relation, I, describes how the shared state may be updated and is specified through actions indexed by capabilities. A thread can perform an action if it holds the capability for that action in its local state. Here, I declares one action for incrementing the value of x, indexed by the increment capability ι. As such, this thread (or any other that also holds some ι capability in its local state) may increment x by one, provided that the incremented value does not exceed max.

Shared state assertions can be freely duplicated using the COPY principle in Fig. 1. This allows us to duplicate and pass on the knowledge about the shared state to new threads, using the standard parallel composition rule PAR. To allow local reasoning, a thread may weaken its view of the shared state to obtain a partial *subjective* view of it using the FORGET principle. For instance given the counter specification C above, if this thread is not interested in location $x{+}1$ where max is stored, it may *forget* it and obtain $\boxed{\exists v \leq max.\, x \mapsto v}_I$. That is, each (subjective) shared state assertion describes (potentially) only parts of the shared global resources. As such, subjective views may arbitrarily overlap with each other. For instance, while this thread chooses to forget the $x{+}1$ location in C, a second thread may choose to observe both x and $x{+}1$, and a third thread may choose to observe $x{+}1$ only. CoLoSL also allows for weakening (framing) of the interference relation using the SHIFT principle: $\boxed{P}_{I \cup I'} \wedge [\text{side-condition-omitted}] \stackrel{\text{SHIFT}}{\Longrightarrow} \boxed{P}_I$. Hence, subjective views may also arbitrarily overlap in their interference relations. Due to space constraints we have omitted this rule from Fig. 1 as we do not use it in this paper. Different subjective views of the shared state can be combined using the MERGE principle.

$$\boxed{P}_I \overset{\text{COPY}}{\Longrightarrow} \boxed{P}_I * \boxed{P}_I \qquad \boxed{P * Q}_I \overset{\text{FORGET}}{\Longrightarrow} \boxed{P}_I \qquad \boxed{P}_{I_1} * \boxed{Q}_{I_2} \overset{\text{MERGE}}{\Longrightarrow} \boxed{P \uplus Q}_{I_1 \cup I_2}$$

$$\frac{\{P_1\} \ \text{C1} \ \{Q_1\} \quad \{P_2\} \ \text{C2} \ \{Q_2\}}{\{P_1 * P_2\} \ \text{C1} \ || \ \text{C2} \ \{Q_1 * Q_2\}} \ \text{PAR} \qquad \frac{P \Rrightarrow P' \quad \{P'\} \ \text{C} \ \{Q'\} \quad Q' \Rrightarrow Q}{\{P\} \ \text{C} \ \{Q\}} \ \text{CON}$$

Fig. 1. An excerpt of the reasoning principles and proof rules in CoLoSL

Since subjective views may overlap both in their resources and interference relations, we use the *overlapping conjunction* [8], $\uplus$, to combine the resources, and set union $\cup$ to combine their interference relations. Intuitively, $P \uplus Q$ describes a state comprising two (potentially) overlapping parts satisfying P and Q, respectively.

CoLoSL is parametric in the model of its resources and may be instantiated with any PCM (partial commutative monoid).[1] In the example above (counter), our resource PCM is that of ordinary concrete heaps, $\mathbb{H} \overset{\text{def}}{=} (\mathcal{H}, \uplus, \varnothing)$, with the composition operator as the disjoint function union, and the function with empty domain ($\varnothing$) as the single unit element. In the remainder of this paper, we take our PCM elements as pairs (h_c, h_g) in the PCM $\mathbb{H}^2 \overset{\text{def}}{=} (\mathcal{H}^2, (\uplus, \uplus), (\varnothing, \varnothing))$ where h_c is the concrete heap, and h_g is the ghost heap. CoLoSL is also parametric in its capability model and may be instantiated with any PCM. In the following sections, we choose the capability PCM on a per-example basis (see Footnote 1).

CoLoSL borrows the consequence rule (CON) of the Views framework [3], with $\Rrightarrow$ denoting the *semantic consequence* relation (semantic implication). That is, we write $P \Rrightarrow Q$ when the set of low-level machine states described by P are contained in that of Q. This way ghost heaps may be manipulated by an application of CON rather than explicit ghost instructions.

2.2 Proof Pattern: Combining Mathematical and Spatial Reasoning

Our graph verifications follow a common pattern which we outline as follows. First, we select an appropriate abstract model for *mathematical graphs*, which is typically sets of vertices and edges together with labels. Second, we choose a *token* model. We use tokens to identify each thread uniquely and to track the contribution of each thread to the global computation. For instance, for an algorithm with only two threads this might be as simple as the set {red, blue}, identifying each thread as a distinct colour.

Third, we define *mathematical actions* to capture the operations performed by threads. These actions model both *concrete* updates to the graph (e.g. removing an edge), as well as *ghost* updates used solely for reasoning (e.g. adding or removing tokens to track the computation progress). Fourth, we define *mathematical assertions* to describe program invariants and pre-/postconditions. These assertions are on mathematical graphs and involve abstract concepts

---

[1] CoLoSL stipulates that PCMs satisfy the cross-split property [8], which ours do.

(e.g. reachability along a path). As a key proof obligation, we must prove that our mathematical assertions are *stable* with respect to our mathematical actions, i.e. they remain true under the actions of other threads in the environment.

Fifth, we define *spatial predicates* (e.g. graph(γ)) that describe how mathematical graphs are implemented in the heap. For instance, a graph may be implemented as a set of heap-linked nodes or as an adjacency matrix. We then combine these spatial predicates with our mathematical actions to define *spatial actions*. Intuitively, if a mathematical action transforms γ to γ', then the corresponding spatial action transforms graph(γ) to graph(γ').

3   Copying Heap-Represented Dags Concurrently

The copy_dag(x) program in Fig. 4 makes a deep structure-preserving copy of the dag (directed acyclic graph) rooted at x concurrently. To do this, each node x in the source dag records in its copy field (x->c) the location of its copy when it exists, or 0 otherwise. Our language is C with a few cosmetic differences. Line 1 gives the data type of heap-represented dags. The statements between angle brackets <.> (e.g. lines 5–7) denote atomic instructions that cannot be interrupted by other threads. We write C1 || C2 (e.g. line 9) for the parallel computation of C1 and C2. This corresponds to the standard fork-join parallelism.

A thread running copy_dag(x) first checks atomically (lines 5–7) if x has already been copied. If so, the address of the copy is returned. Otherwise, the thread allocates a new node y to serve as the copy of x and updates x->c accordingly; it then proceeds to copy the left and right subdags in parallel by spawning two new threads (line 9). At the beginning of the initial call, none of the nodes have been copied and all copy fields are 0; at the end of this call, all nodes are copied to a new dag whose root is returned by the algorithm. In the intermediate recursive calls, only parts of the dag rooted at the argument are copied. Note that the atomic block of lines 5–7 corresponds to a CAS (compare and set) operation. We have unwrapped the definition for better readability.

Although the code is short, its correctness argument is rather subtle as we need to reason simultaneously about both deep unspecified sharing inside the dag as well as the parallel behaviour. This is not surprising since the unspecified sharing makes verifying even the sequential version of similar algorithms nontrivial [8]. However, the non-deterministic behaviour of parallel computation makes even *specifying* the behaviour of copy_dag challenging. Observe that each node x of the source dag may be in one of the following three stages:

1. x is not visited by any thread (not copied yet), and thus its copy field is 0.
2. x has already been visited by a thread π, a copy node x' has been allocated, and the copy field of x has been accordingly updated to x'. However, the edges of x' have not been directed correctly. That is, the thread copying x has not yet finished executing line 10.
3. x has been copied and the edges of its copy have been updated accordingly.

Note that in stage 2 when x has already been visited by a thread π, if another thread π' visits x, it simply returns even though x and its children may not have been fully copied yet. How do we then specify the postcondition of thread π' since we cannot promise that the subdag at x is fully copied when it returns? Intuitively, thread π' can safely return because another thread (π) has copied x and has made a *promise* to visit its children and ensure that they are also copied (by which time the said children may have been copied by other threads, incurring further promises). More concretely, to reason about `copy_dag` we associate each node with a *promise set* identifying those threads that must visit it.

Consider the dags in Fig. 2 where a node x is depicted as (i) a white circle when in stage 1, e.g. ⬭$(x,0)$ in Fig. 2a; (ii) a grey ellipse when in stage 2, e.g. $\overset{x,x'}{\underset{\pi}{⬭}}$ in Fig. 2b where thread π has copied x to x'; and (iii) a black circle when in stage 3, e.g. ⚫$_{x,x'}$ in Fig. 2g. Initially no node is copied and as such all copy fields are 0. Let us assume that the top thread (the thread running the very first call to `copy_dag`) is identified as π. That is, thread π has made a promise to visit the top node x and as such the promise set of x comprises π. This is depicted in the initial snapshot of the graph in Fig. 2a by the $\{\pi\}$ promise set next to x. Thread π proceeds with copying x to x', and transforming the dag to that of Fig. 2b. In doing so, thread π fulfils its promise to x and π is thus removed from the promise set of x. Recall that if another thread now visits x it simply returns, relinquishing the responsibility of copying the descendants of x. This is because the responsibility to copy the left and right subdags of x lies with the left and right sub-threads of π (spawned at line 9), respectively. As such, in transforming the dag from Fig. 2a to b, thread π extends the promise sets of l and r, where $\pi.l$ (resp. $\pi.r$) denotes the left (resp. right) sub-thread spawned by π at line 9. Subsequently, the $\pi.l$ and $\pi.r$ sub-threads copy l and r as illustrated in Fig. 2c, each incurring a promise to visit y via their sub-threads. That is, since both l and r have an edge to y, they race to copy the subdag at y. In the trace detailed in Fig. 2, the $\pi.r.l$ sub-thread wins the race and transforms the dag to that of Fig. 2d by removing $\pi.r.l$ from the promise set of y, and incurring a promise at z. Since the $\pi.l.r$ sub-thread lost the race for copying y, it simply returns (line 3). That is, $\pi.l.r$ needs not proceed to copy y as it has already been copied. As such, the promise of $\pi.l.r$ to y is trivially fulfilled and the copying of l is finalised. This is captured in the transition from Fig. 2d to e where $\pi.l.r$ is removed from the promise set of y, and l is taken to stage 3. Thread $\pi.r.l.l$ then proceeds to copy z, transforming the dag to that of Fig. 2f. Since z has no descendants, the copying of the subdag at z is now at an end; thread $\pi.r.l.l$ thus returns, taking z to stage 3. In doing so, the copying of the entire dag is completed; sub-threads join and the effect of copying is propagated to the parent threads, taking the dag to that depicted in Fig. 2g.

Note that in order to track the contribution of each thread and record the overall copying progress, we must identify each thread uniquely. To this end, we appeal to a *token* (identification) mechanism that can (1) distinguish one token (thread) from another; (2) identify two distinct sub-tokens given any token, to

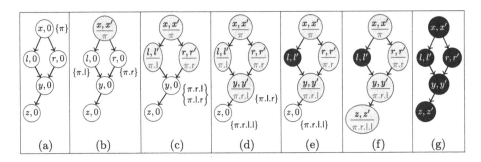

Fig. 2. An example trace of `copy_dag`

reflect the new threads spawned at recursive call points; and (3) model a parent-child relationship to discern the spawner thread from its sub-threads. We model our tokens as a variation of the tree share algebra in [5] as described below.

Trees as Tokens. A tree token (henceforth a token), $\pi \in \Pi$, is defined by the grammar below as a binary tree with boolean leaves $(\circ, \bullet)$, exactly one $\bullet$ leaf, and unlabelled internal nodes.

$$\Pi \ni \pi ::= \bullet \mid \widehat{\circ\ \pi} \mid \widehat{\pi\ \circ}$$

We refer to the thread associated with π as thread π. To model the parent-child relation between thread π and its two sub-threads (left and right), we define a mechanism for creating two distinct sibling tokens $\pi.\mathsf{l}$ and $\pi.\mathsf{r}$ defined below. Intuitively, $\pi.\mathsf{l}$ and $\pi.\mathsf{r}$ denote replacing the $\bullet$ leaf of π with $\widehat{\circ\ \bullet}$ and $\widehat{\bullet\ \circ}$, respectively. We model the ancestor-descendant relation between threads by the $\sqsubseteq$ ordering defined below where $+$ denotes the transitive closure of the relation.

$$
\begin{aligned}
\bullet.\mathsf{l} &= \widehat{\circ\ \bullet} & (\widehat{\circ\ \pi}).\mathsf{l} &= \widehat{\circ\ \pi.\mathsf{l}} & (\widehat{\pi\ \circ}).\mathsf{l} &= \widehat{\pi.\mathsf{l}\ \circ} \\
\bullet.\mathsf{r} &= \widehat{\bullet\ \circ} & (\widehat{\circ\ \pi}).\mathsf{r} &= \widehat{\circ\ \pi.\mathsf{r}} & (\widehat{\pi\ \circ}).\mathsf{r} &= \widehat{\pi.\mathsf{r}\ \circ}
\end{aligned}
\qquad \sqsubseteq \overset{\text{def}}{=} \{(\pi.\mathsf{l}, \pi), (\pi.\mathsf{r}, \pi) \mid \pi \in \Pi\}^+
$$

We write $\pi \sqsubseteq \pi'$ for $\pi = \pi' \vee \pi \sqsubset \pi'$, and write $\pi \not\sqsubset \pi'$ (resp. $\pi \not\sqsubseteq \pi'$) for $\neg(\pi \sqsubset \pi')$ (resp. $neg(\pi \sqsubseteq \pi')$). Observe that $\bullet$ is the maximal token, i.e. $\forall \pi \in \Pi. \pi \sqsubseteq \bullet$. As such, the top-level thread is associated with the $\bullet$ token, since all other threads are its sub-threads and are subsequently spawned by it or its descendants (i.e. $\pi = \bullet$ in Fig. 2a–g). In what follows we write $\overline{\pi}$ to denote the token set comprising the descendants of π, i.e. $\overline{\pi} \overset{\text{def}}{=} \{\pi' \mid \pi' \sqsubseteq \pi\}$.

As discussed in Sect. 2.2, we carry out most of our reasoning abstractly by appealing to *mathematical objects*. To this end, we define *mathematical dags* as an abstraction of the dag structure in `copy_dag`.

Mathematical Dags. A mathematical dag, $\delta \in \Delta$, is a triple of the form (V, E, L) where V is the vertex set; $E : V \rightarrow V_0 \times V_0$, is the edge function with $V_0 = V \uplus \{0\}$, where 0 denotes the absence of an edge (e.g. a null pointer); and

$L = V \to D$, is the vertex labelling function with the label set D defined shortly. We write δ^V, δ^E and δ^L, to project the various components of δ. Moreover, we write $\delta^l(x)$ and $\delta^r(x)$ for the first and second projections of $E(x)$; and write $\delta(x)$ for $(L(x), \delta^l(x), \delta^r(x))$ when $x \in V$. Given a function f (e.g. E, L), we write $f[x \mapsto v]$ for updating $f(x)$ to v, and write $f \uplus [x \mapsto v]$ for extending f with x and value v. Two dags are *congruent* if they have the same vertices and edges, i.e. $\delta_1 \cong \delta_2 \overset{\text{def}}{=} \delta_1^V = \delta_2^V \wedge \delta_1^E = \delta_2^E$. We define our mathematical objects as pairs of dags $(\delta, \delta') \in (\mathcal{W}_\delta \times \mathcal{W}_\delta)$, where δ and δ' denote the source dag and its copy, respectively.

To capture the stages a node goes through, we define the node labels as $D = (V_0 \times (\Pi \uplus \{0\}) \times \mathcal{P}(\Pi))$. The first component records the *copy* information (the address of the copy when in stage 2 or 3; 0 when in stage 1). This corresponds to the second components in the nodes of the dags in Fig. 2, e.g. 0 in $(x,0)$. The second component tracks the node *stage* as described on page 5: 0 in stage 1 (white nodes in Fig. 2), some π in stage 2 (grey nodes in Fig. 2), and 0 in stage 3 (black nodes in Fig. 2). That is, when the node is being *processed* by thread π, this component reflects the thread's token. Note that this is a *ghost* component in that it is used purely for reasoning and does not appear in the physical memory. The third (ghost) component denotes the *promise* set of the node and tracks the tokens of those threads that are yet to visit it. This corresponds to the sets adjacent to nodes in the dags of Fig. 2, e.g. $\{\pi.l\}$ in Fig. 2b. We write $\delta^c(x)$, $\delta^s(x)$ and $\delta^p(x)$ for the first, second, and third projections of x's label, respectively. We define the *path* relation, $x \overset{\delta}{\rightsquigarrow} y$, and the *unprocessed path* relation, $x \overset{\delta}{\rightsquigarrow}_0 y$, as follows and write $\overset{\delta}{\rightsquigarrow}{}^*$ and $\overset{\delta}{\rightsquigarrow}{}^*_0$ for their reflexive transitive closure, respectively.

$$x \overset{\delta}{\rightsquigarrow} y \overset{\text{def}}{=} \delta^l(x) = y \vee \delta^r(x) = y \qquad x \overset{\delta}{\rightsquigarrow}_0 y \overset{\text{def}}{=} x \overset{\delta}{\rightsquigarrow} y \wedge \delta^c(x) = 0 \wedge \delta^c(y) = 0$$

The lifetime of a node x with label (c, s, P) can be described as follows. Initially, x is in stage 1 ($c=0$, $s=0$). When thread π visits x, it creates a copy node x' and takes x to stage 2 ($c=x'$, $s=\pi$). In doing so, it removes its token π from the promise set P, and adds $\pi.l$ and $\pi.r$ to the promise sets of its left and right children, respectively. Once π finishes executing line 10, it takes x to stage 3 ($c=x'$, $s=0$). If another thread π' then visits x when it is in stage 2 or 3, it removes its token π' from the promise set P, leaving the node stage unchanged.

As discussed in Sect. 2.2, to model the interactions of each thread π with the shared data structure, we define mathematical *actions* as relations on mathematical objects. We thus define several families of actions, each indexed by a token π.

Actions. The mathematical actions of `copy_dag` are given in Fig. 3. The A_π^1 describes taking a node x from stage 1 to 2 by thread π. In doing so, it removes its token π from the promise set of x, and adds $\pi.l$ and $\pi.r$ to the promise sets of its left and right children respectively, indicating that they will be visited by its sub-threads, $\pi.l$ and $\pi.r$. It then updates the copy field of x to y, and extends the copy graph with y. This action captures the atomic block of lines 5–7 when

$$A_\pi^1 \stackrel{def}{=} \left\{ \begin{array}{l} ((\delta_1,\delta_2), \\ (\delta_1',\delta_2')) \end{array} \middle| \begin{array}{l} \delta_1(x){=}((0,0,P{\uplus}\{\pi\}),l,r) \ \wedge\ \delta_1^{\text{L}}(l){=}(c_l,s_l,P_l)\ \wedge\ \delta_1^{\text{L}}(r){=}(c_r,s_r,P_r) \\ \wedge\delta_1' = (\delta_1^{\text{Y}},\delta_1^{\text{E}},L_1')\ \wedge\ \delta_2' = (V_2',E_2',L_2') \\ \wedge L_1'{=}\delta_1^{\text{L}}[x \mapsto (y,\pi,P)][l \mapsto c_l,s_l,P_l \uplus \{\pi.l\}][r \mapsto c_r,s_r,P_r{\uplus}\{\pi.r\}] \\ \wedge V_2'{=}\delta_2^{\text{Y}}{\uplus}\{y\}\ \wedge\ E_2'{=}\delta_2^{\text{E}}{\uplus}[y \mapsto (0,0)]\ \wedge\ L_2'{=}\delta_2^{\text{L}}{\uplus}[y \mapsto (0,\pi,\varnothing)]) \end{array} \right\}$$

$$A_\pi^2 \stackrel{def}{=} \left\{ \begin{array}{l} ((\delta_1,\delta_2), \\ (\delta_1,\delta_2')) \end{array} \middle| \begin{array}{l} \delta_1(x){=}((y,\pi,P),l,-)\ \wedge\ ((l{=}0\wedge c_l{=}0)\ \vee\ (\delta_1^{\text{c}}(l){=}c_l \wedge c_l{\neq}0)) \\ \wedge\ \delta_2(y){=}((0,\pi,\varnothing),0,r)\ \wedge\ \delta_2'{=}(\delta_2^{\text{Y}},E_2',\delta_2^{\text{L}})\ \wedge\ E_2'{=}\delta_2^{\text{E}}[y \mapsto (c_l,r)] \end{array} \right\}$$

$$A_\pi^3 \stackrel{def}{=} \left\{ \begin{array}{l} ((\delta_1,\delta_2), \\ (\delta_1,\delta_2')) \end{array} \middle| \begin{array}{l} \delta_1(x){=}((y,\pi,P),-,r)\ \wedge\ ((r{=}0\wedge c_r{=}0)\ \vee\ (\delta_1^{\text{c}}(r){=}c_r \wedge c_r{\neq}0)) \\ \wedge \delta_2(y){=}((0,\pi,\varnothing),l,0)\ \wedge\ \delta_2'{=}(\delta_2^{\text{Y}},E_2',\delta_2^{\text{L}})\ \wedge\ E_2'{=}\delta_2^{\text{E}}[y \mapsto (l,c_r)] \end{array} \right\}$$

$$A_\pi^4 \stackrel{def}{=} \left\{ \begin{array}{l} ((\delta_1,\delta_2), \\ (\delta_1',\delta_2')) \end{array} \middle| \begin{array}{l} \delta_1(x){=}((y,\pi,P),l,r)\ \wedge\ \delta_2(y){=}((0,\pi,\varnothing),c_l,c_r) \\ \wedge (l{=}0\wedge c_l{=}0\ \vee\ \delta_1^{\text{c}}(l){=}c_l \wedge c_l{\neq}0)\ \wedge\ (r{=}0\wedge c_r{=}0\ \vee\ \delta_1^{\text{c}}(r){=}c_r \wedge c_r{\neq}0) \\ \wedge\ \delta_1'{=}(\delta_1^{\text{Y}},\delta_1^{\text{E}},\delta_1^{\text{L}}[x \mapsto (y,0,P)])\ \wedge\ \delta_2'{=}(\delta_2^{\text{Y}},\delta_2^{\text{E}},\delta_2^{\text{L}}[y \mapsto (0,0,\varnothing)]) \end{array} \right\}$$

$$A_\pi^5 \stackrel{def}{=} \left\{ ((\delta_1,\delta_2),(\delta_1',\delta_2))\ \middle|\ \delta_1^{\text{L}}(x){=}(y,s,P{\uplus}\{\pi\})\ \wedge\ y{\neq}0\ \wedge\ \delta_1'{=}(\delta_1^{\text{Y}},\delta_1^{\text{E}},\delta_1^{\text{L}}[x \mapsto (y,s,P)]) \right\}$$

Fig. 3. The mathematical actions of `copy_dag`

successful. The next two sets capture the execution of atomic commands in line 10 by thread π where A_π^2 and A_π^3 respectively describe updating the left and right edges of the copy node. Once thread π has finished executing line 10 (and has updated the edges of y), it takes x to stage 3 by updating the relevant ghost values. This is described by A_π^4. The A_π^5 set describes the case where node x has already been visited by another thread (it is in stage 2 or 3 and thus its copy field is non-zero). Thread π then proceeds by removing its token from x's promise set. We write A_π to denote the actions of thread π: $A_\pi \stackrel{def}{=} A_\pi^1 \cup A_\pi^2 \cup A_\pi^3 \cup A_\pi^4 \cup A_\pi^5$.

We can now specify the behaviour of `copy_dag` mathematically.

Mathematical Specification. Throughout the execution of `copy_dag`, the source dag and its copy (δ,δ'), satisfy the invariant Inv below.

$$\text{Inv}(\delta,\delta') \stackrel{def}{=} \text{acyc}(\delta)\wedge\text{acyc}(\delta')\wedge(\forall x' \in \delta'.\ \exists! x \in \delta.\ \delta^{\text{c}}(x){=}x')\wedge(\forall x \in \delta.\ \exists x'.\ \text{ic}(x,x',\delta,\delta'))$$
$$\text{ic}(x,x',\delta,\delta') \stackrel{def}{=} (x{=}0 \wedge x'{=}0)\ \vee$$
$$\Big(x{\neq}0\wedge\big[(x'{=}0\wedge\ \delta^{\text{c}}(x){=}x' \wedge \exists y.\ \delta^{\text{P}}(y){\neq}\emptyset \wedge y \stackrel{\delta}{\leadsto}_0^* x\big)$$
$$\vee\big(x'{\neq}0\wedge x' \in \delta'\wedge\exists\pi,l,r,l',r'.\ \delta(x){=}((x',\pi,-),l,r)\wedge\delta'(x'){=}(-,l',r')$$
$$\wedge(l'{\neq}0 \Rightarrow \text{ic}(l,l',\delta,\delta'))\ \wedge\ (r'{\neq}0 \Rightarrow \text{ic}(r,r',\delta,\delta')))$$
$$\vee\big(x'{\neq}0\wedge x' \in \delta'\wedge\exists l,r,l',r'.\ \delta(x){=}((x',0,-),l,r)\wedge\delta'(x'){=}(-,l',r')$$
$$\wedge\ \text{ic}(l,l',\delta,\delta')\ \wedge\ \text{ic}(r,r',\delta,\delta'))\big]\Big)$$

with $\text{acyc}(\delta) \stackrel{def}{=} \neg\exists x.\ x \stackrel{\delta}{\leadsto}^+ x$, where $\stackrel{\delta}{\leadsto}^+$ denotes the transitive closure of $\stackrel{\delta}{\leadsto}$.

Informally, the invariant asserts that δ and δ' are acyclic (first two conjuncts), and that each node x' of the copy dag δ' corresponds to a unique node x of the source dag δ (third conjunct). The last conjunct states that each node x of the source dag (i.e. $x{\neq}0$) is in one of the three stages described above, via the second disjunct of the ic predicate: (i) x is not copied yet (stage 1), in which case there is an unprocessed path from a node y with a non-empty promise set to x, ensuring that it will eventually be visited (first disjunct); (ii) x is currently being processed (stage 2) by thread π (second disjunct), and if its children have been copied they also satisfy the invariant; (iii) x has been processed completely (stage 3) and thus its children also satisfy the invariant (last disjunct).

The mathematical precondition of `copy_dag`, $P^\pi(x, \delta)$, is defined below where x identifies the top node being copied (the argument to `copy_dag`), π denotes the thread identifier, and δ is the source dag. It asserts that π is in the promise set of x, i.e. thread π has an obligation to visit x (first conjunct). Recall that each token uniquely identifies a thread and thus the descendants of π correspond to the sub-threads subsequently spawned by π. As such, prior to spawning new threads the precondition asserts that none of the strict descendants of π can be found anywhere in the promise sets (second conjunct), and π itself is only in the promise set of x (third conjunct). Similarly, neither π nor its descendants have yet processed any nodes (last conjunct). The mathematical postcondition, $Q^\pi(x, y, \delta, \delta')$, is as defined below and asserts that x (in δ) has been copied to y (in δ'); that π and all its descendants have fulfilled their promises and thus cannot be found in promise sets; and that π and all its descendants have finished processing their charges and thus cannot correspond to the stage field of a node.

$$P^\pi(x, \delta) \stackrel{\text{def}}{=} (x{=}0 \vee \pi \in \delta^P(x)) \wedge \forall \pi'. \forall y \in \delta.$$
$$(\pi' \in \delta^P(y) \Rightarrow \pi' \sqsubset \pi) \wedge (x{\neq}y \Rightarrow \pi \notin \delta^P(y)) \wedge (\delta^s(y){=}\pi' \Rightarrow \pi' \sqsubset \pi)$$
$$Q^\pi(x, y, \delta, \delta') \stackrel{\text{def}}{=} (x{=}0 \vee (\delta^c(x){=}y \wedge y \in \delta')) \wedge \forall \pi'. \forall z \in \delta.$$
$$\pi' \in \delta^P(z) \vee \delta^s(z){=}\pi' \Rightarrow \pi' \not\sqsubseteq \pi$$

Observe that when the top level thread (associated with $\bullet$) executing `copy_dag(x)` terminates, since $\bullet$ is the maximal token and all other tokens are its descendants (i.e. $\forall \pi. \pi \sqsubseteq \bullet$), the second conjunct of $Q^\bullet(x, \text{ret}, \delta, \delta')$ entails that no tokens can be found anywhere in δ, i.e. $\forall y. \delta^P(y){=}\emptyset \wedge \delta^s(y){=}0$. As such, $Q^\bullet(x, \text{ret}, \delta, \delta')$ together with Inv entails that all nodes in δ have been correctly copied into δ', i.e. only the third disjunct of ic($x, \text{ret}, \delta, \delta'$) in Inv applies.

Recall from Sect. 2.2 that as a key proof obligation we must prove that our mathematical assertions are stable with respect to our mathematical actions. This is captured by Lemma 1 below. Part (1) states that the invariant Inv is stable with respect to the actions of all threads. That is, if the invariant holds for (δ_1, δ_2), and a thread π updates (δ_1, δ_2) to (δ_3, δ_4), then the invariant holds for (δ_3, δ_4). Parts (2) and (3) state that the pre- and postconditions of thread π' ($P^{\pi'}$ and $Q^{\pi'}$) are stable with respect to the actions of all threads π, but those of its descendants ($\pi \not\sqsubseteq \pi'$). Observe that despite this latter stipulation, the actions of π are irrelevant and do not affect the stability of $P^{\pi'}$ and $Q^{\pi'}$. More concretely, the precondition $P^{\pi'}$ only holds at the beginning of the program *before* new descendants are spawned (line 9). As such, at these program points $P^{\pi'}$ is trivially stable with respect to the actions of its (non-existing) descendants. Analogously, the postcondition $Q^{\pi'}$ only holds at the end of the program *after* the descendant threads have completed their execution and joined. Therefore, at these program points $Q^{\pi'}$ is trivially stable with respect to the actions of its descendants.

Lemma 1. *For all mathematical objects* $(\delta_1, \delta_2), (\delta_3, \delta_4)$, *and all tokens* π, π',

$$\mathsf{Inv}(\delta_1, \delta_2) \wedge (\delta_1, \delta_2) \, A_\pi \, (\delta_3, \delta_4) \Rightarrow \mathsf{Inv}(\delta_3, \delta_4) \tag{1}$$

$$\mathsf{P}^{\pi'}(x, \delta_1) \wedge (\delta_1, \delta_2) \, A_\pi \, (\delta_3, \delta_4) \wedge \pi \notin \overline{\pi'} \Rightarrow \mathsf{P}^{\pi'}(x, \delta_3) \tag{2}$$

$$\mathsf{Q}^{\pi'}(x, y, \delta_1, \delta_2) \wedge (\delta_1, \delta_2) \, A_\pi \, (\delta_3, \delta_4) \wedge \pi \notin \overline{\pi'} \Rightarrow \mathsf{Q}^{\pi'}(x, y, \delta_3, \delta_4) \tag{3}$$

Proof. Follows from the definitions of A_π, Inv, P, and Q. The full proof is given in [10].

We are almost in a position to verify `copy_dag`. As discussed in Sect. 2.2, in order to verify `copy_dag` we integrate our mathematical correctness argument with a machine-level memory safety argument by linking our abstract mathematical objects to concrete structures in the heap. We proceed with the spatial representation of our mathematical dags in the heap.

Spatial Representation. We represent a mathematical object (δ, δ') in the heap through the icdag (in-copy) predicate below as two disjoint (∗-separated) dags, as well as a ghost location (d) in the ghost heap tracking the current abstract state of each dag. Observe that this way of tracking the abstract state of dags in the ghost heap eliminates the need for baking in the abstract state into the model. That is, rather than incorporating the abstract state into the model as in [15,16], we encode it as an additional resource in the ghost heap. We use $\Rightarrow$ for ghost heap cells to differentiate them from concrete heap cells indicated by $\mapsto$. We implement each dag as a collection of nodes in the heap. A node is represented as three adjacent cells in the heap together with two additional cells in the ghost heap. The cells in the heap track the addresses of the copy (c), and the left (l) and right (r) children, respectively. The ghost locations are used to track the node state (s) and the promise set (P). It is also possible (and perhaps more pleasing) to implement a dag via a *recursive* predicate using the overlapping conjunction $\uplus$ (see [10]). Here, we choose the implementation below for simplicity.

$$\mathsf{icdag}(\delta_1, \delta_2) \overset{\text{def}}{=} d \Rightarrow (\delta_1, \delta_2) \ast \mathsf{dag}(\delta_1) \ast \mathsf{dag}(\delta_2) \qquad \mathsf{dag}(\delta) \overset{\text{def}}{=} \bigstar_{x \in \delta} \mathsf{node}(x, \delta)$$

$$\mathsf{node}(x, \delta) \overset{\text{def}}{=} \exists l, r, c, s, P. \, \delta(x) {=} (c, s, P), l, r \wedge x \mapsto c, l, r \ast x \Rightarrow s, P$$

We can now specify the spatial precondition of `copy_dag`, $\mathsf{Pre}(x, \pi, \delta)$, as a CoLoSL assertion defined below where x is the top node being copied (the argument of `copy_dag`), π identifies the running thread, and δ denotes the initial top-level dag (where none of the nodes are copied yet). Recall that the spatial actions in CoLoSL are indexed by *capabilities*; that is, a CoLoSL action may be performed by a thread only when it holds the necessary capabilities. Since CoLoSL is parametric in its capability model, to verify `copy_dag` we take our capabilities to be the same as our tokens. The precondition Pre states that the current thread π holds the capabilities associated with itself and all its descendants $(\overline{\pi}^*)$. Thread π will subsequently pass on the descendant capabilities when spawning new sub-threads and reclaim them as the sub-threads return and join. The Pre further asserts that the initial dag δ and its copy currently correspond to δ_1 and δ_2, respectively. That is, since the dags are concurrently manipulated by several threads, to ensure the stability of the shared state assertion to the actions of the environment, Pre states that the initial dag δ may have evolved to another congruent dag δ_1 (captured by the existential quantifier). The Pre also states that the shared state contains the spatial resources of the dags ($\mathsf{icdag}(\delta_1, \delta_2)$), that (δ_1, δ_2) satisfies the invariant Inv, and that the source dag δ_1 satisfies the mathematical precondition P^π. The spatial actions on the shared state are declared in I where mathematical actions are simply lifted to spatial ones indexed by the associated capability. That is, if thread π holds the π capability, and the actions of π (A_π) admit the update of the mathematical object (δ_1, δ_2) to (δ_1', δ_2'), then thread π may update the spatial resources $\mathsf{icdag}(\delta_1, \delta_2)$ to $\mathsf{icdag}(\delta_1', \delta_2')$. Finally, the spatial postcondition Post is analogous to Pre and further states that node x has been copied to y.

$$\mathsf{Pre}(x, \pi, \delta) \stackrel{\text{def}}{=} \overline{\pi}^* * \boxed{\exists \delta_1, \delta_2.\, \mathsf{icdag}(\delta_1, \delta_2) * (\delta \stackrel{.}{\cong} \delta_1 \wedge \mathsf{Inv}(\delta_1, \delta_2) \wedge \mathsf{P}^\pi(x, \delta_1))}_I$$

$$\mathsf{Post}(x, y, \pi, \delta) \stackrel{\text{def}}{=} \overline{\pi}^* * \boxed{\exists \delta_1, \delta_2.\, \mathsf{icdag}(\delta_1, \delta_2) * (\delta \stackrel{.}{\cong} \delta_1 \wedge \mathsf{Inv}(\delta_1, \delta_2) \wedge \mathsf{Q}^\pi(x, y, \delta_1, \delta_2))}_I$$

$$\overline{\pi}^* \stackrel{\text{def}}{=} \bigstar_{\pi \in \overline{\pi}} \pi \qquad I \stackrel{\text{def}}{=} \left\{ \pi : \mathsf{icdag}(\delta_1, \delta_2) \wedge (\delta_1, \delta_2) A_\pi(\delta_1', \delta_2') \rightsquigarrow \mathsf{icdag}(\delta_1', \delta_2') \right.$$

Verifying `copy_dag`. We give a proof sketch of `copy_dag` in Fig. 4. At each proof point, we have highlighted the effect of the preceding command, where applicable. For instance, after line 4 we allocate a new node in the heap at y as well as two consecutive cells in the ghost heap at y. One thing jumps out when looking at the assertions at each program point: they have *identical* spatial parts in the shared state: $\mathsf{icdag}(\delta_1, \delta_2)$. Indeed, the spatial graph in the heap is changing constantly, due both to the actions of this thread and the environment. Nevertheless, the spatial graph in the heap remains in sync with the mathematical object (δ_1, δ_2), however (δ_1, δ_2) may be changing. Whenever this thread interacts with the shared state, the mathematical object (δ_1, δ_2) changes, reflected by the changes to the pure mathematical facts. Changes to (δ_1, δ_2) due to other threads in the environment are handled by the existential quantification of δ_1 and δ_2.

On line 3 we check if x is 0. If so the program returns and the postcondition, $\mathsf{Post}(x, 0, \delta, \pi)$, follows trivially from the definition of the precondition $\mathsf{Pre}(x, \delta, \pi)$. If $x \neq 0$, then the atomic block of lines 5–7 is executed. We first check if x is copied; if so we set b to false, perform action A_π^5 (i.e. remove π from the promise set of x) and thus arrive at the desired postcondition $\mathsf{Post}(x, \delta_1^c(x), \pi, \delta)$. On the other hand, if x is not copied, we set b to true and perform A_π^1. That is, we remove π from the promise set of x, and add $\pi.\mathsf{l}$ and $\pi.\mathsf{r}$ to the left and right children of x, respectively. In doing so, we obtain the mathematical preconditions $\mathsf{P}^{\delta_1}(l, \pi.\mathsf{l})$ and $\mathsf{P}^{\delta_1}(r, \pi.\mathsf{r})$. On line 8 we check whether the thread did copy

```
1. struct node {struct node *c, *l, *r};
```
$\left\{\mathsf{Pre}(x, \pi, \delta)\right\}$

```
2. copy_dag(struct node *x) {struct node *l,*r, *ll,*rr,*y; bool b;
```
$\left\{\overline{\pi}^* * \left(\exists \delta_1, \delta_2.\, \mathsf{icdag}(\delta_1, \delta_2) * (\delta \cong \delta_1 \wedge \mathsf{Inv}(\delta_1, \delta_2) \wedge \mathsf{P}^\pi(x, \delta_1))\right)_I \right\}$

```
3.   if(!x){ return 0; }
```
$\left\{\overline{\pi}^* * \mathsf{ret} \doteq 0 * \left(\exists \delta_1, \delta_2.\mathsf{icdag}(\delta_1, \delta_2) * (\delta \cong \delta_1 \wedge \mathsf{Inv}(\delta_1, \delta_2) \wedge \mathsf{Q}^\pi(x, \mathsf{ret}, \delta_1, \delta_2))\right)_I \right\}$

```
4.   y = malloc(sizeof(struct node));
```
$\left\{\overline{\pi}^* * \left(\exists \delta_1, \delta_2.\, \mathsf{icdag}(\delta_1, \delta_2) * (\delta \cong \delta_1 \wedge \mathsf{Inv}(\delta_1, \delta_2) \wedge \mathsf{P}^\pi(x, \delta_1))\right)_I * y \mapsto 0, 0, 0 * y \Rightarrow \pi, \varnothing \right\}$

```
5.   <if(x->c){ b = false;        //Perform the action A_π^5
```
$\left\{\begin{array}{l}\overline{\pi}^* * \left(\exists \delta_1, \delta_2.\, \mathsf{icdag}(\delta_1, \delta_2) * (\delta \cong \delta_1 \wedge \mathsf{Inv}(\delta_1, \delta_2) \wedge \mathsf{Q}^\pi(x, \delta_1^c(x), \delta_1, \delta_2) \wedge \delta_1^c(x) \neq 0)\right)_I \\ * y \mapsto 0, -, - * y \Rightarrow \pi, \varnothing * b \doteq 0 \end{array}\right\}$

```
6.   }else{ x->c = y; b = true;    //Perform the action A_π^1
```
$\left\{\overline{\pi}^* * \left(\begin{array}{l}\exists \delta_1, \delta_2.\, \mathsf{icdag}(\delta_1, \delta_2) * (\delta \cong \delta_1 \wedge \mathsf{Inv}(\delta_1, \delta_2) \wedge \forall u \in \delta_1.\, \pi \notin \delta_1^p(u) \wedge \\ (x \neq y \Rightarrow \pi \neq \delta_1^s(y)) \wedge \exists l, r.\, \delta_1(x) = (y, \pi, -, l, r) \wedge y \dot{\in} \delta_2 \wedge \mathsf{P}^{\pi.l}(l, \delta_1) \wedge \mathsf{P}^{\pi.r}(r, \delta_1)\end{array}\right)_I * b \doteq 1 \right\}$

```
7.   }>
8.   if(b){ l = x->l; r = x->r;
```
$\left\{\overline{\pi}^* * \left(\begin{array}{l}\exists \delta_1, \delta_2.\, \mathsf{icdag}(\delta_1, \delta_2) * (\delta \cong \delta_1 \wedge \mathsf{Inv}(\delta_1, \delta_2) \wedge \forall y \in \delta_1.\, \pi \neq \delta_1^p(y) \wedge \\ (x \neq y \Rightarrow \pi \neq \delta_1^s(y)) \wedge \delta_1(x) = (y, \pi, -, l, r) \wedge y \dot{\in} \delta_2 \wedge \mathsf{P}^{\pi.l}(l, \delta_1) \wedge \mathsf{P}^{\pi.r}(r, \delta_1)\end{array}\right)_I \right\}$

$\left\{\begin{array}{l}\pi * \left(\begin{array}{l}\exists \delta_1, \delta_2.\mathsf{icdag}(\delta_1, \delta_2) * (\delta \cong \delta_1 \wedge \mathsf{Inv}(\delta_1, \delta_2) \wedge \forall y \in \delta_1.\, \pi \neq \delta_1^p(y) \wedge \\ (x \neq y \Rightarrow \pi \neq \delta_1^s(y)) \wedge \delta_1(x) = (y, -, \pi, l, r) \wedge y \dot{\in} \delta_2)\end{array}\right)_I \\ * \overline{\pi.l}^* * \left(\exists \delta_1, \delta_2.\, \mathsf{icdag}(\delta_1, \delta_2) * (\delta \cong \delta_1 \wedge \mathsf{Inv}(\delta_1, \delta_2) \wedge \mathsf{P}^{\pi.l}(l, \delta_1))\right)_I \\ * \overline{\pi.r}^* * \left(\exists \delta_1, \delta_2.\, \mathsf{icdag}(\delta_1, \delta_2) * (\delta \cong \delta_1 \wedge \mathsf{Inv}(\delta_1, \delta_2) \wedge \mathsf{P}^{\pi.r}(r, \delta_1))\right)_I\end{array}\right\}$

$\left\{\begin{array}{ll}\pi * \left(\begin{array}{l}\exists \delta_1, \delta_2.\mathsf{icdag}(\delta_1, \delta_2) * (\delta \cong \delta_1 \wedge \mathsf{Inv}(\delta_1, \delta_2) \wedge \forall y \in \delta_1.\, \pi \neq \delta_1^p(y) \\ \wedge (x \neq y \Rightarrow \pi \neq \delta_1^s(y)) \wedge \delta_1(x) = (y, -, \pi, l, r) \wedge y \dot{\in} \delta_2)\end{array}\right)_I & * \mathsf{Pre}(l, \pi.l, \delta) \\ & * \mathsf{Pre}(r, \pi.r, \delta)\end{array}\right\}$

	$\{\mathsf{Pre}(l, \pi.l, \delta)\}$	$\{\mathsf{Pre}(r, \pi.r, \delta)\}$
9.	ll = copy_dag(l)	rr = copy_dag(r)
	$\{\mathsf{Post}(l, ll, \pi.l, \delta)\}$	$\{\mathsf{Post}(r, rr, \pi.r, \delta)\}$

$\left\{\begin{array}{ll}\pi * \left(\begin{array}{l}\exists \delta_1, \delta_2.\mathsf{icdag}(\delta_1, \delta_2) * (\delta \cong \delta_1 \wedge \mathsf{Inv}(\delta_1, \delta_2) \wedge \forall y \in \delta_1.\, \pi \neq \delta_1^p(y) \\ \wedge (x \neq y \Rightarrow \pi \neq \delta_1^s(y)) \wedge \delta_1(x) = (y, -, \pi, l, r) \wedge y \dot{\in} \delta_2)\end{array}\right)_I & * \mathsf{Post}(l, ll, \pi.l, \delta) \\ & * \mathsf{Post}(r, rr, \pi.r, \delta)\end{array}\right\}$

$\left\{\overline{\pi}^* * \left(\begin{array}{l}\exists \delta_1, \delta_2.\mathsf{icdag}(\delta_1, \delta_2) * (\delta \cong \delta_1 \wedge \mathsf{Inv}(\delta_1, \delta_2) \wedge \forall y \in \delta_1.\, \pi \neq \delta_1^p(y) \wedge \\ (x \neq y \Rightarrow \pi \neq \delta_1^s(y)) \wedge \delta_1(x) = (y, -, \pi, l, r) \wedge y \dot{\in} \delta_2 \wedge \mathsf{Q}^{\pi.l}(l, ll, \delta_1, \delta_2) \wedge \mathsf{Q}^{\pi.r}(r, rr, \delta_1, \delta_2))\end{array}\right)_I \right\}$

```
10.   <y->l = ll>; <y->r = rr>;  //Perform A_π^2, A_π^3 and A_π^4 in order.
```
$\left\{\overline{\pi}^* * \left(\exists \delta_1, \delta_2.\, \mathsf{icdag}(\delta_1, \delta_2) * (\delta \cong \delta_1 \wedge \mathsf{Inv}(\delta_1, \delta_2) \wedge \mathsf{Q}^\pi(x, y, \delta_1, \delta_2))\right)_I \right\}$

```
11.   return y;
```
$\left\{\overline{\pi}^* * \left(\exists \delta_1, \delta_2.\, \mathsf{icdag}(\delta_1, \delta_2) * (\delta \cong \delta_1 \wedge \mathsf{Inv}(\delta_1, \delta_2) \wedge \mathsf{Q}^\pi(x, \mathsf{ret}, \delta_1, \delta_2))\right)_I \right\}$

```
12.   }else{
```
$\left\{\overline{\pi}^* * \left(\exists \delta_1, \delta_2.\, \mathsf{icdag}(\delta_1, \delta_2) * (\delta \cong \delta_1 \wedge \mathsf{Inv}(\delta_1, \delta_2) \wedge \mathsf{Q}^\pi(x, \delta_1^c(x), \delta_1, \delta_2) \wedge \delta_1^c(x) \neq 0)\right)_I \begin{array}{l} * y \mapsto 0, -, - \\ * y \Rightarrow \pi, \varnothing \end{array}\right\}$

```
13.   free(y, sizeof(struct node)) ; return x->c;
```
$\left\{\overline{\pi}^* * \left(\exists \delta_1, \delta_2.\, \mathsf{icdag}(\delta_1, \delta_2) * (\delta \cong \delta_1 \wedge \mathsf{Inv}(\delta_1, \delta_2) \wedge \mathsf{Q}^\pi(x, \mathsf{ret}, \delta_1, \delta_2))\right)_I \right\}$

```
14. } }
```
$\left\{\mathsf{Post}(x, \mathsf{ret}, \pi, \delta)\right\}$

Fig. 4. The code and a proof sketch of copy_dag

x and has thus incurred an obligation to call `copy_dag` on x's children. If this is the case, we load the left and right children of x into l and r, and subsequently call `copy_dag` on them (line 9). To obtain the preconditions of the recursive calls, we duplicate the shared state twice ($\boxed{P}_I \overset{\text{COPY} \times 2}{\Longrightarrow} \boxed{P}_I * \boxed{P}_I * \boxed{P}_I$), drop the irrelevant pure assertions, and unwrap the definition of π^*. We then use the PAR rule (Fig. 1) to distribute the resources between the sub-threads and collect them back when they join. Subsequently, we combine multiple copies of the shared states into one using MERGE. Finally, on line 10 we perform actions A_π^2, A_π^3 and A_π^4 in order to update the edges of y, and arrive at the postcondition $\mathsf{Post}(x, y, \pi, \delta)$.

Copying Graphs. Recall that a dag is a directed graph that is *acyclic*. However, the `copy_dag` program does not depend on the acyclicity of the dag at x and thus `copy_dag` may be used to copy *both* dags and cyclic graphs. The specification of `copy_dag` for cyclic graphs is rather similar to that of dags. More concretely, the spatial pre- and postcondition (Pre and Post), as well as the mathematical pre- and postcondition (P and Q) remain unchanged, while the invariant Inv is weakened to allow for cyclic graphs. That is, the Inv for cyclic graphs does not include the first two conjuncts asserting that δ and δ' are acyclic. As such, when verifying `copy_dag` for cyclic graphs, the proof obligation for establishing the Inv stability (i.e. Lemma 1(1)) is somewhat simpler. The other stability proofs (Lemma 1(2) and (3)) and the proof sketch in Fig. 4 are essentially unchanged.

4   Parallel Speculative Shortest Path (Dijkstra)

Given a graph with `size` vertices, the weighted adjacency matrix a, and a designated source node `src`, Dijkstra's sequential algorithm calculates the shortest path from `src` to all other nodes incrementally. To do this, it maintains a cost array c, and two sets of vertices: those processed thus far (`done`), and those yet to be processed (`work`). The cost for each node (bar `src` itself) is initialised with the value of the adjacency matrix (i.e. c[src]=0; c[i]=a[src][i] for i≠src). Initially, all vertices are in `work` and the algorithm proceeds by iterating over `work` performing the following two steps at each iteration. First, it extracts a node i with the *cheapest* cost from `work` and inserts it to `done`. Second, for each vertex j, it updates its cost (c[j]) to $min\{$c[j], c[i]+a[i][j]$\}$. This greedy strategy ensures that at any one point the cost associated with the nodes in `done` is minimal. Once the `work` set is exhausted, c holds the minimal cost for all vertices.

We study a *parallel non-greedy* variant of Dijkstra's shortest path algorithm, `parallel_dijkstra` in Fig. 5, with `work` and `done` implemented as bit arrays. We initialize the c, `work` and `done` arrays as described above (lines 2–5), and find the shortest path from the source `src` concurrently, by spawning multiple threads, each executing the non-greedy `dijkstra` (line 6). The code for `dijkstra` is given in Fig. 5. In this non-greedy implementation, at each iteration an *arbitrary* node from the `work` set is selected rather than one with minimal cost. Unlike the greedy variant, when a node is processed and inserted into `done`, its associated cost is

```
1 void parallel_dijkstra(int[][] a, int[] c, int size, src){
2  bitarray work[size], done[size];
3   for (i=0; i<size; i++){
4    c[i] = a[src][i]; work[i] = 1; done[i] = 0;
5   }; c[src] = 0;
6   dijkstra(a,c,size,work,done) || ... || dijkstra(a,c,size,work,done)
7   return c;
8 }
```

```
1 void dijkstra(int[][] a, int[] c, int size, bitarray work, done){ i = 0;
2   while(done != 2^size-1){ b = <CAS(work[i], 1, 0)>;
3    if(b){ cost = c[i];
4      for(j=0; j<size; j++){ newcost = cost + a[i][j];  b = true;
5        do{ oldcost = c[j];
6          if(newcost < oldcost){
7            b = <CAS(work[j], 1, 0)>;
8            if(b){ b = <CAS(c[j], oldcost, newcost)>; <work[j] = 1>; }
9            else { b = <CAS(done[j], 1, 0)>;
10             if(b){ b = <CAS(c[j], oldcost, newcost)>;
11               if(b){ < work[j] = 1 > } else { < done[j] = 1 > }
12           } } }
13         } while(!b)
14       } < done[i] = 1 >;
15     } i = (i+1) mod size;
16 } }
```

Fig. 5. A parallel non-greedy variant of Dijkstra's algorithm

not necessarily the cheapest. As such, during the second step of each iteration, when updating the cost of node j to $min\{c[j], c[i]+a[i][j]\}$ (as described above), we must further check if j is already processed. This is because if the cost of j goes down, the cost of its adjacent siblings may go down too and thus j needs to be *reprocessed*. When this is the case, j is removed from **done** and reinserted into **work** (lines 9–11). If on the other hand j is unprocessed (and is in **work**), we can safely decrease its cost (lines 7–8). Lastly, if j is currently being processed by another thread, we must wait until it is processed (loop back and try again).

The algorithm of **parallel_dijkstra** is an instance of *speculative parallelism* [7]: each thread running **dijkstra** assumes that the costs of the nodes in **done** will not change as a result of processing the nodes in **work** and proceeds with its computation. However, if at a later point it detects that its assumption was wrong, it reinserts the affected nodes into **work** and recomputes their costs.

Mathematical Graphs. Similar to dags in Sect. 3, we define our mathematical graphs, $\gamma \in \Gamma$, as tuples of the form (V, E, L) where V is the set of vertices, $E : V \to (V \to \mathcal{W})$ is the weighted adjacency function with weights $\mathcal{W} \stackrel{\text{def}}{=} \mathbb{N} \uplus \{\infty\}$, and $L : V \to D$ is the label function, with the labels D defined shortly. We use the matrix notation for adjacency functions and write $E[i][j]$ for $E(i)(j)$.

Unlike `copy_dag` in Sect. 3 where a new thread is spawned at every recursive call point, in `parallel_dijkstra` the number of threads to run concurrently is decided at the beginning (line 7) and remains unchanged thereafter. This allows for a simpler token mechanism. We define our tokens as elements of the (countably) infinite set $t \in \Theta \overset{\text{def}}{=} \mathbb{N}\setminus\{0,1\}$. We refer to the thread with token t simply as thread t. Recall that each node x in the graph can be either: unprocessed (in `work`); processed (in `done`); or under process by a thread (neither in `work` nor in `done`). We define our labels as $D \overset{\text{def}}{=} \mathcal{W} \times (\{0,1\} \uplus \Theta) \times (V \rightarrow \{\circ, \bullet\} \uplus \mathcal{W})$. The first component denotes the cost of the shortest path from the source (so far) to the node. The second component describes the node state (0 for unprocessed, 1 for processed, and t when under process by thread t). The last component denotes the *responsibility* function. Recall that when a thread is processing a node, it iterates over all vertices examining whether their cost can be improved. To do this, at each iteration the thread records the current cost of node j under inspection in `oldcost` (line 5). If the cost may be improved (i.e. the conditional of line 6 succeeds), it then *attempts* to update the cost of j with the improved value (lines 8, 10). Note that since the cost associated with j may have changed from the initial cost recorded (`oldcost`), the update operation may fail and thus the thread needs to re-examine j. To track the iteration progress, for each node the responsibility function records whether (i) its cost is yet to be examined ($\circ$); (ii) its cost has been examined ($\bullet$); or (iii) its cost is currently being examined ($c \in \mathcal{W}$) with its initial cost recorded as c (`oldcost`$=c$). We use the string notation for responsibility functions and write e.g. $\bullet^n.c.\circ^m$, when the first n nodes are mapped to $\bullet$, the (n+1)st node is mapped to c, and the last m nodes are mapped to $\circ$. We write $\bigcirc$ (resp. $\bullet$) for a function that maps all elements to $\circ$ (resp. $\bullet$).

Given a graph $\gamma = (V, E, L)$, we write $\gamma^{\vee}$ for V, γ^{E} for E, and γ^{L} for L. We write $\gamma^c(x)$, $\gamma^s(x)$ and $\gamma^r(x)$, for the first, second and third projections of $L(x)$, respectively. Two graphs are *congruent* if they have equal vertices and edges: $\gamma_1 \cong \gamma_2 \overset{\text{def}}{=} \gamma_1^{\vee} = \gamma_2^{\vee} \wedge \gamma_1^{\text{E}} = \gamma_2^{\text{E}}$. We define the weighted path relation ($\overset{\gamma}{\leadsto}_c$), and its reflexive transitive closure as:

$$x \overset{\gamma}{\leadsto}_c y \overset{\text{def}}{=} (\gamma^{\text{E}})[x][y] = c \qquad x \overset{\gamma}{\leadsto^*_c} y \overset{\text{def}}{=} (x = y \wedge c = 0) \vee (\exists c_1, c_2, z.\, c = c_1 + c_2 \wedge x \overset{\gamma}{\leadsto^*_{c_1}} z \wedge z \overset{\gamma}{\leadsto^*_{c_2}} y)$$

Actions. We define several families of actions in Fig. 6, each of which indexed by a token t. The A_t^1 describes the CAS operation of line 2 in the algorithm: the state of a node is changed from unprocessed to being processed by thread t (i is removed from `work`). The A_t^2 describes a *ghost* action at line 5 for iteration j when storing the current cost of j in `oldcost`. The thread has not yet examined the cost of node j ($R[j]=\circ$). It then reads the current cost (c') of j and (ghostly) updates the responsibility function. The A_t^3 describes the CAS operations of lines 7 and 9 when successful: when processing i, we discovered that the cost of j may be improved ($c + E[i][j] \leq c'$). In the former case, j is currently

$$A_t^1 \overset{\text{def}}{=} \left\{ ((V,E,L),(V,E,L')) \mid L(i)=(c,0,\bigcirc) \wedge L'=L[i \mapsto (c,t,\bigcirc)] \right\}$$

$$A_t^2 \overset{\text{def}}{=} \left\{ ((V,E,L),(V,E,L')) \,\middle|\, \begin{array}{l} L(i)=(c,t,R) \wedge \forall k<j.\, R[k]= \bullet \wedge R[j]=\circ \\ \wedge L(j)=(c',-,-) \wedge R'=R[j \mapsto c'] \wedge L'=L[i \mapsto (c,t,R')] \end{array} \right\}$$

$$A_t^3 \overset{\text{def}}{=} \left\{ ((V,E,L),(V,E,L')) \,\middle|\, \begin{array}{l} L(i)=(-,t,R) \wedge R[j]=c' \wedge c+E[i][j] \leq c' \\ \wedge L(j)=(c,s,R') \wedge s \in \{0,1\} \wedge L'=L[j \mapsto (c,t,R')] \end{array} \right\}$$

$$A_t^4 \overset{\text{def}}{=} \left\{ ((V,E,L),(V,E,L')) \,\middle|\, \begin{array}{l} L(i)=(c,t,R) \wedge R[j]=c' \wedge L(j)=(c',t,R'') \\ \wedge c''=c+E[i][j] \wedge c''<c' \\ \wedge R'=R[j \mapsto \bullet] \wedge L'=L[i \mapsto (c,t,R')][j \mapsto (c'',t,R'')] \end{array} \right\}$$

$$A_t^5 \overset{\text{def}}{=} \left\{ ((V,E,L),(V,E,L')) \,\middle|\, \begin{array}{l} L(i)=(c,t,R) \wedge R[j]= \bullet \wedge L(j)=(c',t,-) \\ \wedge L'=L[j \mapsto (c',0,\bigcirc)] \end{array} \right\}$$

$$A_t^6 \overset{\text{def}}{=} \left\{ ((V,E,L),(V,E,L')) \,\middle|\, \begin{array}{l} L(i)=(c,t,R) \wedge R[j]=c'' \wedge L(j)=(c',t,\bigcirc) \wedge c' \neq c'' \\ \wedge R'=R[j \mapsto \circ] \wedge L'=L[i \mapsto (c,t,R')][j \mapsto (c',0,\bigcirc)] \end{array} \right\}$$

$$A_t^7 \overset{\text{def}}{=} \left\{ ((V,E,L),(V,E,L')) \,\middle|\, \begin{array}{l} L(i)=(c,t,R) \wedge R[j]=c'' \wedge L(j)=(c',t,\bullet) \wedge c' \neq c'' \\ \wedge R'=R[j \mapsto \circ] \wedge L'=L[i \mapsto (c,t,R')][j \mapsto (c',1,\bullet)] \end{array} \right\}$$

$$A_t^8 \overset{\text{def}}{=} \left\{ ((V,E,L),(V,E,L')) \,\middle|\, \begin{array}{l} L(i)=(c,t,R) \wedge R[j]=c' \wedge c+E[i][j] \geq c' \\ \wedge R'=[j \mapsto \bullet]R \wedge L'=[i \mapsto (c,t,R')]L \end{array} \right\}$$

$$A_t^9 \overset{\text{def}}{=} \left\{ ((V,E,L),(V,E,L')) \mid L(x)=(c,t,\bullet) \wedge L'=L[x \mapsto (c,1,\bullet)] \right\}$$

Fig. 6. The mathematical actions of `dijkstra`

unprocessed (in `work`, $s=0$), while in the latter j is processed (in `done`, $s=1$). In both cases, we remove j from the respective set and temporarily change its state to under process by t until its cost is updated and it is reinserted into the relevant set. The A_t^4 describes the CAS operations in lines 8 and 10 when successful. The cost of j has not changed since we first read it ($R[j]=c'$) and we discovered that this cost may be improved ($c'' \leq c'$). The responsibility of i towards j is then marked as fulfilled ($R'[j]=\bullet$) and the cost of j is updated until it is subsequently reinserted into `work` via A_t^5. The A_t^5 denotes the reinsertion of j into `work` in lines 8 and 11 following *successful* CAS operations at lines 8 and 10. The state of j is changed to 0 to reflect its insertion to `work`. The A_t^6 and A_t^7 sets respectively describe the reinsertion of j into `work` and `done` in lines 8 and 10, following *failed* CAS operations at lines 8 and 10. When attempting to update the cost of j, we discovered that the cost of j has changed since we first read it ($c' \neq c''$). We thus reinsert j into the relevant set and (ghostly) update the responsibility function to reflect that j is to be re-examined ($R'[j]=\circ$). The A_t^8 describes a ghost action in line 6 when the conditional fails: examining j yielded no cost improvement and thus the responsibility of i towards j is marked as fulfilled. Lastly, the A_t^9 captures the atomic operation in line 14: processing of i is at an end since all nodes have been examined. The state of i is thus changed to processed (i is inserted into `done`). We write A_t for actions of t, i.e. $A_t \overset{\text{def}}{=} \bigcup_{i \in \{1...9\}} A_t^i$.

Mathematical Invariant. Throughout the execution of `dijkstra` for a source node src, the graph γ satisfies the invariant $\mathsf{Inv}(src, \gamma)$ described below.

$$\mathsf{Inv}(\gamma, src) \stackrel{\text{def}}{=} \forall x \in \gamma.\ \min_{\gamma}^{src}(x, \gamma^c(x))$$
$$\vee \left(\exists y, z, c.\ \min_{\gamma}^{src}(y, \gamma^c(y)) \wedge \gamma(y) \neq 1 \wedge \gamma^r[y][z] = 0\right.$$
$$\left.\wedge\ y \overset{\gamma}{\leadsto}_c z \wedge \mathsf{wit}_{\gamma}^{src}(\gamma^c(y) + c, z, x)\right)$$

$$\min_{\gamma}^{src}(x, c) \stackrel{\text{def}}{=} \min\{c' \mid s \overset{\gamma}{\leadsto}^{*}_{c'} x\} = c$$

$$\mathsf{wit}_{\gamma}^{src}(c, z, x) \stackrel{\text{def}}{=} \min_{\gamma}^{src}(z, c) \wedge \gamma^c(z) > c$$
$$\wedge\ (z = x \vee (\exists c', w.\ z \overset{\gamma}{\leadsto}_{c'} w \wedge \mathsf{wit}_{\gamma}^{src}(c + c', w, x)))$$

The $\mathsf{Inv}(\gamma, src)$ asserts that for any node x, either its associated cost from src is minimal; or there is a minimal path to x from a node y (via z), such that the cost of y is minimal and y is either unprocessed or is being processed. Moreover, none of the nodes along this path (except y) are yet associated with their correct (minimal) cost. As such, when y is finally processed, its effect will be propagated down this path, correcting the costs of the nodes along the way. Observe that when `dijkstra` terminates, since all nodes are processed (i.e. $\forall x.\ \gamma^s(x) = 1$), the $\mathsf{Inv}(\gamma, src)$ entails that the cost associated with all nodes is minimal.

Lemma 2. *For all mathematical graphs γ, γ', source nodes src, and tokens t, the $\mathsf{Inv}(\gamma, src)$ invariant is stable with respect to A_t:*

$$\mathsf{Inv}(\gamma, src) \wedge \gamma\, A_t\, \gamma' \Rightarrow \mathsf{Inv}(\gamma', src)$$

Proof. Follows from the definitions of A_t and Inv. The full proof is given in [10].

Spatial Representation. Using the $g(\gamma)$ predicate below, we represent a mathematical graph γ in the heap as multiple $*$-separated arrays: two bit-arrays for the `work` and `done` sets, a two-dimensional array for the adjacency matrix, a one dimensional array for the cost function, and finally two ghost arrays for the label function (one for the responsibility function, another for the node states).

$$g(\gamma) \stackrel{\text{def}}{=} \mathsf{work}(\gamma) * \mathsf{done}(\gamma) * \mathsf{adj}(\gamma) * \mathsf{cost}(\gamma) * \mathsf{resp}(\gamma) * \mathsf{state}(\gamma)$$

$$\mathsf{work}(\gamma) \stackrel{\text{def}}{=} \underset{i \in \{i \mid \gamma^{\bullet}(i) = 0\}}{\bigstar} \left(\mathsf{work}[i] \mapsto 1\right) * \underset{i \in \{i \mid \gamma^{\bullet}(i) \neq 0\}}{\bigstar} \left(\mathsf{work}[i] \mapsto 0\right)$$

$$\mathsf{done}(\gamma) \stackrel{\text{def}}{=} \underset{i \in \{i \mid \gamma^{\bullet}(i) = 1\}}{\bigstar} \left(\mathsf{done}[i] \mapsto 1\right) * \underset{i \in \{i \mid \gamma^{\bullet}(i) \neq 1\}}{\bigstar} \left(\mathsf{done}[i] \mapsto 0\right)$$

$$\mathsf{adj}(\gamma) \stackrel{\text{def}}{=} \underset{i \in \gamma}{\bigstar} \left(\underset{j \in \gamma}{\bigstar}\ a[i][j] \mapsto \gamma^E[i][j]\right) \qquad \mathsf{cost}(\gamma) \stackrel{\text{def}}{=} \underset{i \in \gamma}{\bigstar}\ (c[i] \mapsto \gamma^c(i))$$

$$\mathsf{resp}(\gamma) \stackrel{\text{def}}{=} \underset{i \in \gamma}{\bigstar} \left(\underset{j \in \gamma}{\bigstar}\ r[i][j] \Rrightarrow \gamma^r[i][j]\right) \qquad \mathsf{state}(\gamma) \stackrel{\text{def}}{=} \underset{i \in \gamma}{\bigstar}\ (s[i] \Rrightarrow \gamma^s(i))$$

We specify the spatial precondition of `dijkstra`, $\mathsf{Pre}(t, \gamma_0)$, as a CoLoSL assertion defined below where t identifies the running thread, and γ_0 denotes the original graph (at the beginning of `parallel_dijkstra`, before spawning new

---

$\{\mathsf{Pre}(t,\gamma_0)\}$

```
1. void dijkstra(int[][] a, int[] c, int size, bitarray work, done){ i=0;
2.   while(done != 2^size-1){ b=<CAS(work[i],1,0)>;  //perform A_t^1 if possible
3.     if(b){
```
$\left\{t * \left(\boxed{\exists \gamma.\, g(\gamma) * (\gamma_0 \stackrel{\cdot}{\cong} \gamma \wedge \mathsf{Inv}(\gamma,\mathsf{src}) \wedge \gamma^s(i)=t \wedge \gamma^r(i)=\bullet)}\right)_I\right\}$

```
       cost = c[i];
```
$\left\{t * \left(\boxed{\exists \gamma.\, g(\gamma)*(\gamma_0 \stackrel{\cdot}{\cong} \gamma \wedge \mathsf{Inv}(\gamma,\mathsf{src}) \wedge \gamma^s(i)=t \wedge \gamma^r(i)=\bullet \wedge \mathsf{cost}=\gamma^c(i))}\right)_I\right\}$

```
4.     for(j=0;j<size;j++){
```
$\left\{t * \left(\boxed{\exists \gamma.\, g(\gamma)*(\gamma_0 \stackrel{\cdot}{\cong} \gamma \wedge \mathsf{Inv}(\gamma,\mathsf{src}) \wedge \gamma^s(i)=t \wedge \gamma^r(i)=1^j.0^{size-j} \wedge \mathsf{cost}=\gamma^c(i))}\right)_I\right\}$

```
       newcost = cost + a[i][j]; b = 1;
```
$\left\{t * \left(\boxed{\begin{array}{l}\exists \gamma.\, g(\gamma)*(\gamma_0 \stackrel{\cdot}{\cong} \gamma \wedge \mathsf{Inv}(\gamma,\mathsf{src}) \wedge \gamma^s(i)=t \wedge \gamma^r(i)=1^j.0^{size-j} \\ \wedge\, \mathsf{cost}=\gamma^c(i) \wedge \mathsf{newcost}=\mathsf{cost}+\gamma^E[i][j] \wedge b=1)\end{array}}\right)_I\right\}$

```
5.       do{ oldcost=c[j];  //perform A_t^2
```
$\left\{t * \left(\boxed{\begin{array}{l}\exists \gamma, c.\, g(\gamma)*(\gamma_0 \stackrel{\cdot}{\cong} \gamma \wedge \mathsf{Inv}(\gamma,\mathsf{src}) \wedge \gamma^s(i)=t \wedge \gamma^r(i)=1^j.c.0^{size-j-1} \\ \wedge\, \mathsf{cost}=\gamma^c(i) \wedge \mathsf{newcost}=\mathsf{cost}+\gamma^E[i][j] \wedge b=1 \wedge \mathsf{oldcost}=c)\end{array}}\right)_I\right\}$

```
6.         if(newcost<oldcost){
```
$\left\{t * \left(\boxed{\begin{array}{l}\exists \gamma, c.\, g(\gamma)*(\gamma_0 \stackrel{\cdot}{\cong} \gamma \wedge \mathsf{Inv}(\gamma,\mathsf{src}) \wedge \gamma^s(i)=t \wedge \gamma^r(i)=1^j.c.0^{size-j-1} \\ \wedge\, \mathsf{cost}=\gamma^c(i) \wedge \mathsf{newcost}=\mathsf{cost}+\gamma^E[i][j] \wedge \mathsf{oldcost}=c \wedge \mathsf{newcost}<\mathsf{oldcost})\end{array}}\right)_I\right\}$

```
7.           b=<CAS(work[j],1,0)>;  //perform A_t^3 if possible
8.           if(b){
```
$\left\{t * \left(\boxed{\begin{array}{l}\exists \gamma, c.\, g(\gamma)*(\gamma_0 \stackrel{\cdot}{\cong} \gamma \wedge \mathsf{Inv}(\gamma,\mathsf{src}) \wedge \gamma^s(i)=t \wedge \gamma^r(i)=1^j.c.0^{size-j-1} \wedge \mathsf{cost}=\gamma^c(i) \\ \wedge\, \mathsf{newcost}=\mathsf{cost}+\gamma^E[i][j] \wedge \mathsf{oldcost}=c \wedge \mathsf{newcost}<\mathsf{oldcost} \wedge \gamma^s(j)=t \wedge \gamma^r(j)=\circ)\end{array}}\right)_I\right\}$

```
             b=<CAS(c[j],oldcost,newcost)>;  //perform A_t^4 if possible
```
$\left\{t * \left(\boxed{\begin{array}{l}\exists \gamma, c.\, g(\gamma)*(\gamma_0 \stackrel{\cdot}{\cong} \gamma \wedge \mathsf{Inv}(\gamma,\mathsf{src}) \wedge \gamma^s(i)=t \wedge \mathsf{cost}=\gamma^c(i) \wedge \mathsf{newcost}<\mathsf{oldcost} \\ \wedge\, ((b=1 \wedge \gamma^r(i)=1^{j+1}.0^{size-j-1}) \vee (b=0 \wedge \gamma^r(i)=1^j.c.0^{size-j-1})) \wedge \gamma^s(j)=t \wedge \gamma^r(j)=\circ)\end{array}}\right)_I\right\}$

```
             <work[j] = 1>; }  //perform A_t^5 or A_t^6 depending on the value of b
```
$\left\{t * \left(\boxed{\begin{array}{l}\exists \gamma.\, g(\gamma)*(\gamma_0 \stackrel{\cdot}{\cong} \gamma \wedge \mathsf{Inv}(\gamma,\mathsf{src}) \wedge \gamma^s(i)=t \wedge \mathsf{cost}=\gamma^c(i) \wedge \mathsf{newcost}<\mathsf{oldcost} \\ \wedge\, ((b=1 \wedge \gamma^r(i)=1^{j+1}.0^{size-j-1}) \vee (b=0 \wedge \gamma^r(i)=1^j.0^{size-j})))\end{array}}\right)_I\right\}$

Fig. 7. A proof sketch of the `dijkstra` algorithm (continued in Fig. 8)

threads). We instantiate the CoLoSL capabilities to be the same as our tokens. The precondition Pre states that the current thread t holds the t capability, that the original graph γ_0 may have evolved to another congruent graph γ (captured by the existential quantifier) satisfying the invariant Inv, and that the shared state contains the spatial resources of the graph $g(\gamma)$. As before, the spatial actions on the shared state are declared in I by lifting mathematical actions to spatial ones indexed by the corresponding capability. Finally, the spatial post-condition Post is analogous to Pre and further states that all nodes in γ are processed (in `done`).

$$\mathsf{Pre}(t,\gamma_0) \stackrel{\text{def}}{=} t * \left(\boxed{\exists \gamma.\, g(\gamma)*(\gamma_0 \stackrel{\cdot}{\cong} \gamma \wedge \mathsf{Inv}(\gamma,\mathsf{src}))}\right)_I \qquad I \stackrel{\text{def}}{=} \left\{t: g(\gamma) \wedge \gamma\; A_t\; \gamma' \rightsquigarrow g(\gamma')\right.$$

$$\mathsf{Post}(t,\gamma_0) \stackrel{\text{def}}{=} t * \left(\boxed{\exists \gamma.\, g(\gamma)*(\gamma_0 \stackrel{\cdot}{\cong} \gamma \wedge \mathsf{Inv}(\gamma,\mathsf{src}) \wedge \forall x \in \gamma.\, \gamma^s(x) \stackrel{\cdot}{=} 1)}\right)_I$$

Verifying parallel_dijkstra. A proof sketch of `dijkstra` is given in Figs. 7 and 8. As before, in all proof points the spatial part $(g(\gamma))$ remains unchanged,

9.   `else {`

$$\left\{ t * \left(\begin{array}{l} \exists \gamma, c. \, g(\gamma) * (\gamma_0 \stackrel{.}{=} \gamma \wedge \mathsf{Inv}(\gamma, \mathsf{src}) \wedge \gamma^s(\mathtt{i}){=}t \wedge \gamma^r(\mathtt{i}){=}1^\mathtt{j}.c.0^{\mathtt{size}\text{-}\mathtt{j}\text{-}1} \wedge \mathtt{cost}{=}\gamma^c(\mathtt{i})) \\ \wedge \, \mathtt{newcost}{=}\mathtt{cost}{+}\gamma^E[\mathtt{i}][\mathtt{j}] \wedge \mathtt{oldcost}{=}c \wedge \mathtt{newcost}{<}\mathtt{oldcost}) \end{array} \right)_I \right\}$$

          `b=<CAS(done[j],1,0)>;`   //perform A^3_t if possible

10.   `if(b){`

$$\left\{ t * \left(\begin{array}{l} \exists \gamma, c. \, g(\gamma) * (\gamma_0 \stackrel{.}{=} \gamma \wedge \mathsf{Inv}(\gamma, \mathsf{src}) \wedge \gamma^s(\mathtt{i}){=}t \wedge \gamma^r(\mathtt{i}){=}1^\mathtt{j}.c.0^{\mathtt{size}\text{-}\mathtt{j}\text{-}1} \wedge \mathtt{cost}{=}\gamma^c(\mathtt{i}) \\ \wedge \, \mathtt{newcost}{=}\mathtt{cost}{+}\gamma^E[\mathtt{i}][\mathtt{j}] \wedge \mathtt{oldcost}{=}c \wedge \mathtt{newcost}{<}\mathtt{oldcost} \wedge \gamma^s(\mathtt{j}){=}t \wedge \gamma^r(\mathtt{j}){=}\bullet) \end{array} \right)_I \right\}$$

          `b=<CAS(c[j],oldcost,newcost)>;`   //perform A^4_t if possible

$$\left\{ t * \left(\begin{array}{l} \exists \gamma, c. \, g(\gamma) * (\gamma_0 \stackrel{.}{=} \gamma \wedge \mathsf{Inv}(\gamma, \mathsf{src}) \wedge \gamma^s(\mathtt{i}){=}t \wedge \mathtt{cost}{=}\gamma^c(\mathtt{i}) \wedge \mathtt{newcost}{<}\mathtt{oldcost} \\ \wedge \, ((b{=}1 \wedge \gamma^r(\mathtt{i}){=}1^{\mathtt{j}+1}.0^{\mathtt{size}\text{-}\mathtt{j}\text{-}1}) \vee (b{=}0 \wedge \gamma^r(\mathtt{i}){=}1^\mathtt{j}.c.0^{\mathtt{size}\text{-}\mathtt{j}\text{-}1})) \\ \wedge \, \mathtt{newcost}{=}\mathtt{cost}{+}\gamma^E[\mathtt{i}][\mathtt{j}] \wedge \gamma^s(\mathtt{j}){=}t \wedge \gamma^r(\mathtt{j}){=}\bullet) \end{array} \right)_I \right\}$$

11.   `if(b){<work[j]=1>}else{<done[j]=1>}` //A^5_t or A^7_t based on b

$$\left\{ t * \left(\begin{array}{l} \exists \gamma. \, g(\gamma) * (\gamma_0 \stackrel{.}{=} \gamma \wedge \mathsf{Inv}(\gamma, \mathsf{src}) \wedge \gamma^s(\mathtt{i}){=}t \wedge \mathtt{cost}{=}\gamma^c(\mathtt{i}) \wedge \mathtt{newcost}{<}\mathtt{oldcost} \\ \wedge \, ((b{=}1 \wedge \gamma^r(\mathtt{i}){=}1^{\mathtt{j}+1}.0^{\mathtt{size}\text{-}\mathtt{j}\text{-}1}) \vee (b{=}0 \wedge \gamma^r(\mathtt{i}){=}1^\mathtt{j}.0^{\mathtt{size}\text{-}\mathtt{j}}))) \end{array} \right)_I \right\}$$

12.   `}}}`

$$\left\{ t * \left(\begin{array}{l} \exists \gamma. g(\gamma) * (\gamma_0 \stackrel{.}{=} \gamma \wedge \mathsf{Inv}(\gamma, \mathsf{src}) \wedge \gamma^s(\mathtt{i}){=}t \\ ((\mathtt{newcost}{<}\mathtt{oldcost} \wedge b{=}1 \wedge \gamma^r(\mathtt{i}){=}1^{\mathtt{j}+1}.0^{\mathtt{size}\text{-}\mathtt{j}\text{-}1}) \\ \vee (\mathtt{newcost}{<}\mathtt{oldcost} \wedge b{=}0 \wedge \gamma^r(\mathtt{i}){=}1^\mathtt{j}.0^{\mathtt{size}\text{-}\mathtt{j}}) \\ \vee (\mathtt{newcost}{\geq}\mathtt{oldcost} \wedge b{=}1 \wedge \gamma^r(\mathtt{i}){=}1^\mathtt{j}.{-}.0^{\mathtt{size}\text{-}\mathtt{j}\text{-}1}))) \end{array} \right)_I \right\}$$ //perform A^8_t on 3rd disjunct

$$\left\{ t * \left(\begin{array}{l} \exists \gamma. \, g(\gamma) * (\gamma_0 \stackrel{.}{=} \gamma \wedge \mathsf{Inv}(\gamma, \mathsf{src}) \wedge \gamma^s(\mathtt{i}){=}t \\ ((b{=}1 \wedge \gamma^r(\mathtt{i}){=}1^{\mathtt{j}+1}.0^{\mathtt{size}\text{-}\mathtt{j}\text{-}1}) \vee (b{=}0 \wedge \gamma^r(\mathtt{i}){=}1^\mathtt{j}.0^{\mathtt{size}\text{-}\mathtt{j}}))) \end{array} \right)_I \right\}$$

13.   `} while(!b)` $\left\{ t * \left(\exists \gamma. \, g(\gamma) * (\gamma_0 \stackrel{.}{=} \gamma \wedge \mathsf{Inv}(\gamma, \mathsf{src}) \wedge \gamma^s(\mathtt{i}){=}t \wedge \gamma^r(\mathtt{i}){=}1^{\mathtt{j}+1}.0^{\mathtt{size}\text{-}\mathtt{j}\text{-}1}) \right)_I \right\}$

14.   `}` $\left\{ t * \left(\exists \gamma. g(\gamma) * (\gamma_0 \stackrel{.}{=} \gamma \wedge \mathsf{Inv}(\gamma, \mathsf{src}) \wedge \gamma^s(\mathtt{i}){=}t \wedge \gamma^r(\mathtt{i}){=}\bullet) \right)_I \right\}$

      `<done[i]=1>;` //perform A^9_t $\left\{ t * \left(\exists \gamma. g(\gamma) * (\gamma_0 \stackrel{.}{=} \gamma \wedge \mathsf{Inv}(\gamma, \mathsf{src}) \wedge \gamma^s(\mathtt{i}){=}1) \right)_I \right\}$

15.   `} i = (i+1) mod size;`

16. `} }` $\left\{ t * \left(\exists \gamma. g(\gamma) * (\gamma_0 \stackrel{.}{=} \gamma \wedge \mathsf{Inv}(\gamma, \mathsf{src}) \wedge \forall x. \gamma^s(x){=}1) \right)_I \right\}$

$\{ \mathsf{Post}(t, \gamma_0) \}$

Fig. 8. A proof sketch of the `dijkstra` algorithm (continued from Fig. 7)

and the changes to the graph are reflected in the changes to the pure mathematical assertions. Observe that when all threads return, the pure part of the postcondition ($\mathsf{Inv}(\gamma, \mathsf{src}) \wedge \forall x \in \gamma. \gamma^s(x) \stackrel{.}{=} 1$) entails that all costs in `cost` are minimal as per the first (and the only applicable) disjunct in $\mathsf{Inv}(\gamma, \mathsf{src})$. As such, the proof of `parallel_dijkstra` is immediate from the parallel rule (PAR).

Concluding Remarks. We have verified two sophisticated concurrent graph algorithms, `copy_dag` and `parallel_dijkstra`, neither of which has been verified previously. We used several proof patterns, such as doing the tricky reasoning on mathematical abstractions and using tokens to track the progress of cooperating threads. We used an "iCAP-like" abstract proof style despite using CoLoSL which does not support this proof style natively. In [10, 11] we verify two further graph algorithms using our proof pattern: graph marking, which is the simplest nontrivial concurrent algorithm and which accordingly enjoys the cleanest proof; and spanning tree, which has been done previously but with different invariants.

Acknowledgements. This research was supported by EPSRC programme grants EP/H008373/1 and EP/K008528/1, Yale-NUS College and R-607-265-045-121.

References

1. Bornat, R., Calcagno, C., O'Hearn, P.: Local reasoning, separation and aliasing. In: SPACE, vol. 4 (2004)
2. Dijkstra, E.W., Lamport, L., Martin, A.J., Scholten, C.S., Steffens, E.F.M.: On-the-fly darbage collection: an exercise in cooeration. In: Bauer, F.L., Dijkstra, E.W., Ershov, A., Griffiths, M., Hoare, C.A.R., Wulf, W.A., Samelson, K. (eds.) Language Hierarchies and Interfaces. LNCS, vol. 46, pp. 43–56. Springer, Heidelberg (1976). doi:10.1007/3-540-07994-7_48
3. Dinsdale-Young, T., Birkedal, L., Gardner, P., Parkinson, M., Yang, H.: Views: compositional reasoning for concurrent programs. In: POPL, pp. 287–300 (2013)
4. Dinsdale-Young, T., Dodds, M., Gardner, P., Parkinson, M., Vafeiadis, V.: Concurrent abstract predicates. In: ECOOP, pp. 504–528 (2010)
5. Dockins, R., Hobor, A., Appel, A.: A fresh look at separation algebras and share accounting. In: APLAS (2009)
6. Feng, X.: Local rely-guarantee reasoning. In: POPL, pp. 315–327 (2009)
7. Grama, A., Anshul, G., Karypis, G., Kumar, V.: Introduction to Parallel Computing, 2nd edn. Addison Wesley, Boston (2003)
8. Hobor, A., Villard, J.: The ramifications of sharing in data structures. In: Giacobazzi, R., Cousot, R. (eds.) POPL, pp. 523–536. ACM (2013)
9. Nanevski, A., Ley-Wild, R., Sergey, I., Delbianco, G.: Communicating state transition systems for fine-grained concurrent resources. In: ESOP, pp. 290–310 (2014)
10. Raad, A.: Ph.D. thesis, Imperial College London (2016, to appear)
11. Raad, A., Hobor, A., Villard, J., Gardner, P.: Verifying concurrent graph algorithms (extended) (2016)
12. Raad, A., Villard, J., Gardner, P.: CoLoSL: concurrent local subjective logic. In: ESOP, pp. 710–735 (2015)
13. Reynolds, J.: A short course on separation logic (2003). http://www.cs.cmu.edu/afs/cs.cmu.edu/project/fox-19/member/jcr/wwwaac2003/notes7.ps
14. Sergey, I., Nanevski, A., Banerjee, A.: Mechanized verification of fine-grained concurrent programs. In: PLDI (2015)
15. Svendsen, K., Birkedal, L.: Impredicative concurrent abstract predicates. In: ESOP (2014)
16. Turon, A., Dreyer, D., Birkedal, L.: Unifying refinement and Hoare-style reasoning in a logic for higher-order concurrency. In: ICFP, pp. 377–390 (2013)
17. Yang, H.: Local reasoning for stateful programs. Ph.D. thesis, University of Illinois (2001)

Verification of Higher-Order Concurrent Programs with Dynamic Resource Creation

Kazuhide Yasukata, Takeshi Tsukada[✉], and Naoki Kobayashi

The University of Tokyo, Tokyo, Japan
{yasukata,tsukada,koba}@kb.is.s.u-tokyo.ac.jp

Abstract. We propose a sound and complete static verification method for (higher-order) concurrent programs with *dynamic creation* of resources, such as locks and thread identifiers. To deal with (possibly infinite) resource creation, we prepare a finite set of abstract resource names and introduce the notion of *scope-safety* as a sufficient condition for avoiding the confusion of different concrete resources mapped to the same abstract name. We say that a program is *scope-safe* if no resource is used after the creation of another resource of the same abstract name. We prove that the pairwise-reachability problem is decidable for scope-safe programs with nested locking. We also propose a method for checking that a given program is scope-safe and with nested locking.

1 Introduction

Verification of concurrent programs is important but fundamentally difficult. Ramalingam [11] has proved that the reachability problem for two-thread programs is undecidable in the presence of rendezvous-style synchronization and recursive procedures. To deal with this limitation, several restricted models of concurrent computation have been studied. Kahlon et al. [2] have shown that the pairwise-reachability problem ("Given a program and their control locations, can the locations be reached simultaneously") for multi-threaded programs (without dynamic thread creation) is decidable if only nested locking with a finite number of locks is allowed as synchronization primitives. The result has later been extended to allow dynamic thread creation [7], joins (to wait for the termination of all the child threads) [1], and higher-order functions [13].

One of the important limitations in the programming models in the above line of work is that the dynamic creation of locks is not allowed; the number of locks must be finite and they must be statically allocated. In real programs, dynamic creation of locks is common; for example, in Java, every object may be used as a lock. Another, related limitation is that, although dynamic thread creation is supported [1,7,13], there is no way to refer to each thread, e.g., to specify the target of a join; the models in [1,13] support join operations, but they can only be used for synchronizing with *all* the child threads. Again, this deviates from real concurrent programming models.

To address the limitation above, we propose a method for checking the pairwise reachability of higher-order concurrent programs with primitives for

© Springer International Publishing AG 2016
A. Igarashi (Ed.): APLAS 2016, LNCS 10017, pp. 335–353, 2016.
DOI: 10.1007/978-3-319-47958-3_18

dynamic creation of locks and thread identifiers. To keep the verification problem decidable, however, we introduce the notion of *scope safety*. We consider a map from concrete resources (such as locks and thread identifiers) to *abstract resources*, and say that a program is scope-safe if, intuitively, at most one concrete resource per each abstract resource is accessible to each thread at each run-time state. For example, consider the following program:

```
main() {
  l = newlock();              /* create a new lock */
  spawn{acq(l);L:rel(l);};    /* spawn a child thread */
  acq(l);L:rel(l);            /* acquire and release l */
  main();    }               /* repeat */
```

The main function repeatedly creates a new lock, spawns a child process, and synchronizes with it through the lock. Although infinitely many locks are created, only one lock is visible to each thread; thus, the program is scope-safe. We show that for the class of scope-safe programs with nested locking, the pairwise reachability problem is decidable. Our method is an extension of Yasukata et al.'s one [13], based on higher-order model checking. We also present a method for deciding whether a given program satisfies the required condition: scope safety and nested locking. The latter method is also based on a reduction to higher-order model checking. We have implemented our verification method and confirmed its effectiveness.

The rest of the paper is structured as follows. Section 2 introduces the target language with dynamic lock creation and gives the formal definitions of pairwise reachability and scope safety. Section 3 describes our method for checking the pairwise-reachability of a given program under the assumption that the program is scope-safe and has nested locking. Section 4 describes a method for checking whether a given program is scope-safe and has nested locking. Section 5 briefly describes how to extend our method for pairwise reachability to support join operations. Section 6 reports the experimental reports. Section 7 discusses related work and Sect. 8 concludes the paper.

Due to the space limitation, we omit some proofs and formal definitions, which can be found in the full version available at the last author's web page.

2   Pairwise Reachability Problem and Scope Safety

This section formally defines the problem that we address in this paper, namely, the pairwise reachability problem of higher-order concurrent programs with dynamic lock creation. We also introduce the notion of *scope safety*, which is a condition on programs that is crucial for the soundness and completeness of our verification method.

2.1   Language

The target of our analysis is a simply-typed, call-by-name, non-deterministic, higher-order language with primitives for nested locking and dynamic creation of threads and locks. An extension with join primitives shall be introduced later in Sect. 5.

Definition 1 (Programs). A *program* p is a finite set of function definitions:

$$p = \{F_1 \, \tilde{x}_1 = e_1, \ldots, F_n \, \tilde{x}_n = e_n\}.$$

Here, F_i and $\tilde{x}_i$ denote a function symbol and a sequence of variables respectively. We allow more than one definition for each function symbol (so that a program has non-determinism), and assume that $F_i = S$ and $\tilde{x}_i$ is an empty sequence for some i; S serves as the "main" function. The meta-variable e ranges over the set Exp of *expressions*, defined by:

$$e ::= (\,) \mid x \mid F \mid e_1 \, e_2 \mid \mathbf{new}_\kappa \, e \mid \mathbf{acq}(e_1);\ e_2 \mid \mathbf{rel}(e_1);\ e_2 \mid \mathbf{spawn}(e_c);\ e_p \mid e^\ell.$$

Here, ℓ and κ range over a finite set Label of program point labels and a finite set $\mathcal{K}$ of identifiers (called *abstract lock names*, or *abstract locks*).

The intuitive meaning of each expression is as follows; the formal operational semantics will be given later. The expression $(\,)$ denotes the unit value, and $e_1 e_2$ applies the function e_1 to e_2. The expression $\mathbf{new}_\kappa \, e$ creates a new (concrete) lock with abstract name κ, and passes it to the function e. The expression $\mathbf{acq}(e_1);\ e_2$ waits to acquire the lock e_1, and executes e_2 after the acquisition. The expression $\mathbf{rel}(e_1);\ e_2$ releases the lock e_1 and then executes e_2. The expression $\mathbf{spawn}(e_c);\ e_p$ spawns a child thread that executes e_c, and then the parent thread itself executes e_p. The labeled expression e^ℓ just behaves like e; ℓ is used to specify the pairwise reachability problem, and does not affect the operational semantics.

We require that all the programs must be simply-typed. The set of *types* is defined by:

$$\tau ::= \star \mid \mathbf{lock} \mid \tau_1 \to \tau_2,$$

where $\star$ and $\mathbf{lock}$ describe the unit value and locks respectively. The type $\tau_1 \to \tau_2$ describes functions from τ_1 to τ_2. The typing rules are standard ones (see the full version). The only point deserving attention is that in each function definition $F \, \tilde{x} = e$, the type of e must be $\star$; this condition can be ensured by applying CPS transformation [9].

Remark 1. The language has only the unit value and locks as primitive data. Boolean values can be expressed by using Church encoding. Infinite data domains such as integers and lists can also be handled by using predicate abstraction [6] (though the completeness of the analysis will be lost by the abstraction).

Example 1. Consider the following program p.

$$p = \left\{ \begin{array}{l} S = \mathbf{new}_\kappa \, F \\ F \, x = \mathbf{spawn}(\mathbf{acq}(x);\ (\mathbf{rel}(x);\ (\,))^\ell);\ (\mathbf{acq}(x);\ (\mathbf{rel}(x);\ S)^\ell) \end{array} \right\}.$$

This program is obtained by CPS-transforming the following C-like code:

```
main() {  x = newlock(); spawn{acq(x);L:rel(x);};
  acq(x);L:rel(x); main(); }
```

In every loop, the root thread and a created child thread enter the program point labeled ℓ by using a created lock x.

Now we define the operational semantics of the language. In the following semantics, we use a sequence ι of natural numbers as a thread identifier and a triple (κ, ι, m) as a lock identifier (also called a *concrete lock name*); that is just for the technical convenience in formalizing our method. Intuitively, (κ, ι, m) represents the m-th lock created by the thread ι at $\mathbf{new}_\kappa$. We write ν for a lock identifier. In presenting the operational semantics below, e ranges over expressions extended with lock identifiers: $e ::= \cdots \mid (\kappa, \iota, m)$. A *thread state* is a quadruple (e, L, s, σ) where e is the (extended) expression to be executed by the thread, $L \in (\mathcal{K} \times \mathbb{N}^* \times \mathbb{N}_+)^*$ describes the lock acquisition history of the thread, $s \in \mathbb{N}$ is the number of children spawned by the thread so far, and σ is a partial map from $\mathcal{K}$ to $\mathbb{N}^* \times \mathbb{N}_+$; intuitively, $\sigma(\kappa) = (\iota, m)$ means that the concrete lock with abstract name κ created most recently by the thread or inherited from the parent thread is (κ, ι, m). A *configuration* is a partial map c from a finite set consisting of sequences of natural numbers (where each sequence serves as a process identifier) to the set of thread states. A transition relation $c_1 \xrightarrow{\iota, a}_p c_2$ on configurations is the least relation closed under the rules given below. We write $\uplus$ for the disjoint union, $\emptyset$ for the empty map, and $f\{x \mapsto v\}$ for the map defined by: $f\{x \mapsto v\}(x) = v$ and $f\{x \mapsto v\}(y) = f(y)$ for $y \neq x$.

$$\frac{F\,\tilde{x} = e' \in p}{c \uplus \{\iota \mapsto (F\,\tilde{e}, L, s, \sigma)\} \xrightarrow{\iota, \bullet}_p c \uplus \{\iota \mapsto ([\tilde{e}/\tilde{x}]e', L, s, \sigma)\}}$$

$$\frac{\sigma(\kappa) = (\iota, m) \qquad \sigma' = \sigma\{\kappa \mapsto (\iota, m+1)\}}{c \uplus \{\iota \mapsto (\mathbf{new}_\kappa\, e, L, s, \sigma)\} \xrightarrow{\iota, \mathsf{new}(\kappa, \iota, m+1)}_p c \uplus \{\iota \mapsto (e\,(\kappa, \iota, m+1), L, s, \sigma')\}}$$

$$\frac{\forall \iota', m.(\sigma(\kappa) = (\iota', m) \Rightarrow \iota \neq \iota') \qquad \sigma' = \sigma\{\kappa \mapsto (\iota, 1)\}}{c \uplus \{\iota \mapsto (\mathbf{new}_\kappa\, e, L, s, \sigma)\} \xrightarrow{\iota, \mathsf{new}(\kappa, \iota, 1)}_p c \uplus \{\iota \mapsto (e\,(\kappa, \iota, 1), L, s, \sigma')\}}$$

$$\frac{(\kappa, \iota', m) \notin \mathbf{locked}(c \uplus \{\iota \mapsto (\mathbf{acq}(\kappa, \iota', m); e, L, s, \sigma)\})}{c \uplus \{\iota \mapsto (\mathbf{acq}(\kappa, \iota', m); e, L, s, \sigma)\} \xrightarrow{\iota, \mathsf{acq}(\kappa, \iota', m)}_p c \uplus \{\iota \mapsto (e, L \cdot (\kappa, \iota', m), s, \sigma)\}}$$

$$\frac{L = L' \cdot (\kappa, \iota', m)}{c \uplus \{\iota \mapsto (\mathbf{rel}(\kappa, \iota', m); e, L, s, \sigma)\} \xrightarrow{\iota, \mathsf{rel}(\kappa, \iota', m)}_p c \uplus \{\iota \mapsto (e, L', s, \sigma)\}}$$

$$\frac{}{c \uplus \{\iota \mapsto (\mathbf{spawn}(e_c); e_p, L, s, \sigma)\} \xrightarrow{\iota, \mathsf{sp}(\iota \cdot s)}_p c \uplus \left\{ \begin{array}{l} \iota \quad\ \mapsto (e_p, L, s+1, \sigma), \\ \iota \cdot s \mapsto (e_c, \epsilon, 0, \sigma) \end{array} \right\}}$$

$$c \uplus \{\iota \mapsto (e^\ell, L, s, \sigma)\} \xrightarrow{\iota, \ell}_p c \uplus \{\iota \mapsto (e, L, s, \sigma)\}$$

$$\frac{L = \epsilon}{c \uplus \{\iota \mapsto ((\,), L, s, \sigma)\} \xrightarrow{\iota, \$}_p c}$$

In the first rule, $[\widetilde{e}/\widetilde{x}]e'$ denotes the expression obtained from e' by simultaneously substituting $\widetilde{e}$ for $\widetilde{x}$. The second and third rules are for lock creations. A lock identifier of the form (κ, ι, m') is allocated to a new lock, where m' is the number of locks created so far (including the new one) by the thread ι at $\mathbf{new}_\kappa$. In the fourth rule, $\mathbf{locked}(c)$ denotes the set of locks acquired by some thread, i.e., the set $\{(\kappa, \iota, m) \mid \exists \iota'.\ c(\iota') = (e, L, s, \sigma) \wedge (\kappa, \iota, m) \in L\}$. The fourth and fifth rules ensure that locks are acquired/released in a nested manner, i.e., that each thread releases locks in the opposite order of acquisition; the execution of a thread violating this condition gets stuck. We write c_0 for the *initial configuration* $\{\epsilon \mapsto (S, \epsilon, 0, \emptyset)\}$. We sometimes omit transition labels and just write $c \rightarrow_p c'$ for $c \xrightarrow{\iota, a}_p c'$ for some ι and a.

Recall that a program has to acquire/release locks in the nested manner; otherwise a thread spawned by the program gets stuck at a release operation. We say that a program *has nested locking* if no release operations get stuck, that is, whenever the program reaches a configuration $c \uplus \{\iota \mapsto (\mathbf{rel}(\kappa, \iota', m); e, L, s, \sigma)\}$, (κ, ι', m) is the last lock acquired by the thread ι, i.e., L is of the form $L' \cdot (\kappa, \iota', m)$.

2.2 Pairwise Reachability

Now we define the goal of our analysis: pairwise reachability.

Definition 2 (Pairwise Reachability). Let p be a program and ℓ_1, ℓ_2 be labels. We say that (ℓ_1, ℓ_2) is *pairwise-reachable* by p, written $p \vDash \ell_1 \| \ell_2$, if

$$c_0 \rightarrow^*_p c \uplus \{\iota_1 \mapsto (e_1^{\ell_1}, L_1, s_1, \sigma_1), \iota_2 \mapsto (e_2^{\ell_2}, L_2, s_2, \sigma_2)\}$$

holds for some $c, \iota_1, \iota_2, L_1, L_2, s_1, s_2, \sigma_1, \sigma_2$ with $\iota_1 \neq \iota_2$. The *pairwise-reachability problem* is the problem of deciding whether $p \vDash \ell_1 \| \ell_2$ holds.

Example 2. Recall the program of Example 1. It has the following transitions:

$$\{\epsilon \mapsto (S, \epsilon, 0, \emptyset)\} \longrightarrow \{\epsilon \mapsto (\mathbf{new}_\kappa\ F, \epsilon, 0, \emptyset)\}$$

$$\longrightarrow \{\epsilon \mapsto (\mathbf{spawn}(\mathbf{acq}(\kappa, \epsilon, 1);\ (\mathbf{rel}(\kappa, \epsilon, 1);\ (\,))^\ell);\ \cdots, \epsilon, 0, \{\kappa \mapsto (\epsilon, 1)\})\}$$

$$\longrightarrow^* \left\{ \begin{array}{l} \epsilon \mapsto (\mathbf{new}_\kappa\ F, \epsilon, 1, \{\kappa \mapsto (\epsilon, 1)\}), \\ 0 \mapsto (\mathbf{acq}(\kappa, \epsilon, 1);\ (\mathbf{rel}(\kappa, \epsilon, 1);\ (\,))^\ell, \epsilon, 0, \{\kappa \mapsto (\epsilon, 1)\} \end{array} \right\}$$

$$\longrightarrow \left\{ \begin{array}{l} \epsilon \mapsto (\mathbf{spawn}(\mathbf{acq}(\kappa, \epsilon, 2);\ (\mathbf{rel}(\kappa, \epsilon, 2);\ (\,))^\ell);\ \cdots, \epsilon, 1, \{\kappa \mapsto (\epsilon, 2)\}), \\ 0 \mapsto (\mathbf{acq}(\kappa, \epsilon, 1);\ (\mathbf{rel}(\kappa, \epsilon, 1);\ (\,))^\ell, \epsilon, 0, \{\kappa \mapsto (\epsilon, 1)\}) \end{array} \right\}$$

$$\longrightarrow^* \left\{ \begin{array}{l} \epsilon \mapsto (S, \epsilon, 2, \{\kappa \mapsto (\epsilon, 2)\}), \\ 0 \mapsto (\mathbf{acq}(\kappa, \epsilon, 1);\ (\mathbf{rel}(\kappa, \epsilon, 1);\ (\,))^\ell, \epsilon, 0, \{\kappa \mapsto (\epsilon, 1)\}), \\ 1 \mapsto (\mathbf{acq}(\kappa, \epsilon, 2);\ (\mathbf{rel}(\kappa, \epsilon, 2);\ (\,))^\ell, \epsilon, 0, \{\kappa \mapsto (\epsilon, 2)\}) \end{array} \right\}$$

$$\longrightarrow^* \left\{ \begin{array}{l} \epsilon \mapsto (S, \epsilon, 2, \{\kappa \mapsto (\epsilon, 2)\}), 0 \mapsto ((\mathbf{rel}(\kappa, \epsilon, 1);\ (\,))^\ell, (\kappa, \epsilon, 1), 0, \{\kappa \mapsto (\epsilon, 1)\}), \\ 1 \mapsto ((\mathbf{rel}(\kappa, \epsilon, 2);\ (\,))^\ell, (\kappa, \epsilon, 2), 0, \{\kappa \mapsto (\epsilon, 2)\}) \end{array} \right\}$$

Thus, the program is pairwise-reachable to (ℓ, ℓ). If the definition of F is replaced by:

$$F\ x = \mathbf{spawn}(\mathbf{acq}(x);\ (\mathbf{rel}(x);\ (\ ))^{\ell});\ (\mathbf{acq}(x);\ (\mathbf{rel}(x);\ F\ x)^{\ell}),$$

then the resulting program is *not* pairwise-reachable to (ℓ, ℓ), since all the program points ℓ are now guarded by the same (concrete) lock.

2.3   Scope Safety

Pairwise reachability is known to be decidable for the language *without* dynamic lock creations [13]. In the presence of dynamic lock creations, the decidability of pairwise reachability is open, to our knowledge. To make the problem tractable, we introduce the notion of *scope safety*: a thread of a scope-safe program can access only the newest lock in the scope for each abstract lock κ.

Definition 3 (Scope-Safety). A program p is *scope-safe* if

$$c_0 \to_p^* c \uplus \{\iota \mapsto (op(\kappa, \iota', m); e, L, s, \sigma)\} \quad\Longrightarrow\quad \sigma(\kappa) = (\iota', m)$$

holds for every $c, \iota, (\kappa, \iota', m), e, L, s, \sigma$ and $op \in \{\,\mathbf{acq}, \mathbf{rel}\,\}$.

For a scope-safe program, the number of locks is locally bounded in the sense that, at each run-time state, the number of locks accessible to each thread is bounded. Note that the number of locks in a configuration is still unbounded.

Example 3. The program in Example 1 is scope-safe. Although infinitely many locks are created with the abstract lock name κ, every thread accesses only the lock that is most recently created by itself or the parent thread.

The following program is *not* scope-safe:

$$S = \mathbf{new}_\kappa\ G \qquad G\ x = \mathbf{new}_\kappa(F\ x)$$
$$F\ x\ y = \mathbf{spawn}(\mathbf{acq}(x);\ (\mathbf{rel}(x);\ (\ ))^{\ell});\ (\mathbf{acq}(y);\ (\mathbf{rel}(y);\ S)^{\ell}).$$

$F\ x\ y$ accesses two locks x and y with the same abstract lock κ simultaneously. If κ in G is renamed to κ', however, the resulting program is scope-safe, since x and y now have different abstract lock names: κ and κ' respectively.

Now we can state the main result of this paper proved in the next section.

Theorem 1. *The pairwise reachability problem for scope-safe programs with nested locking is decidable.*

We think that the scope-safety is a natural assumption, and that there are many programs that create an unbounded number of locks but satisfy the scope safety. Like the program in Example 1, such a program typically spawns an unbounded number of threads, each of which creates a lock (thus; the number of locks is globally unbounded) and uses it locally for synchronizations with child threads.

3 Verification of Pairwise Reachability

This section gives a sound and complete verification method of the pairwise-reachability problem of scope-safe programs with nested locking. We reduce the problem to (a variant of) higher-order model checking, a decision problem whether a language of a given higher-order tree grammar is a subset of a given regular tree language.

1. We use (extended) action trees [1,7], which represent transition sequences in a thread-wise manner. Let $\mathsf{ATrees}(p)$ be the set of all action trees representing possible transitions of the program p. Then $p \vDash \ell_1 \| \ell_2$ if and only if $\mathsf{ATrees}(p)$ contains an action tree with leaves labeled by ℓ_1 and ℓ_2, respectively. Writing R_{ℓ_1,ℓ_2} for the set of action trees with leaves labeled by ℓ_1 and ℓ_2, the pairwise reachability problem is reduced to the emptiness problem of $\mathsf{ATrees}(p) \cap R_{\ell_1,\ell_2}$.

2. If we could represent $\mathsf{ATrees}(p)$ by a higher-order tree grammar, we would be done, since the emptiness problem $\mathsf{ATrees}(p) \cap R_{\ell_1,\ell_2} \overset{?}{=} \emptyset$ is equivalent to the higher-order model checking problem $\mathsf{ATrees}(p) \overset{?}{\subseteq} \overline{R_{\ell_1,\ell_2}}$; note that $\overline{R_{\ell_1,\ell_2}}$ is regular. Unfortunately, however, it is not easy to give a grammar to generate $\mathsf{ATrees}(p)$ because of synchronization by locks. Instead we consider a superset of $\mathsf{ATrees}(p)$, written $\mathsf{RelaxedATrees}(p)$, including action trees that are infeasible because of locks. In other words, an action tree in $\mathsf{RelaxedATrees}(p)$ represents a transition sequence in which the synchronization constraint on locks is ignored. It is easy to construct a grammar generating $\mathsf{RelaxedATrees}(p)$.

3. We give a way to check the feasibility of an action tree (i.e. whether an action tree conforms to the synchronization constraint on locks) by introducing an operational semantics of action trees. Let $\mathsf{LSATrees}$ be the set of feasible action trees. We show that $\mathsf{ATrees}(p) = \mathsf{RelaxedATrees}(p) \cap \mathsf{LSATrees}$ provided that p is a scope-safe program. Thus, the pairwise reachability is reduced to the (non)-emptiness of $\mathsf{RelaxedATrees}(p) \cap \mathsf{LSATrees} \cap R_{\ell_1,\ell_2}$.

4. We show that $\mathsf{LSATrees}$ is a regular tree language.

Now the pairwise reachability problem has been reduced to the emptiness problem $\mathsf{RelaxedATrees}(p) \cap \mathsf{LSATrees} \cap R_{\ell_1,\ell_2} \overset{?}{=} \emptyset$, which is equivalent to the instance of higher-order model checking problem:

$$\mathsf{RelaxedATrees}(p) \overset{?}{\subseteq} \overline{\mathsf{LSATrees} \cap R_{\ell_1,\ell_2}}$$

and thus decidable. In the rest of this section, we first review higher-order model checking [5,8], in Sect. 3.1. We then explain each step in Sects. 3.2, 3.3, 3.4 and 3.5.

3.1 Higher-Order Model Checking

Higher-order model checking is concerned about properties of the trees generated by higher-order tree grammars called *higher-order recursion schemes* (HORS, in short). In the standard definition of higher-order model checking [5,8], a HORS is treated as a generator of a *single*, possibly *infinite* tree. In the present paper, we consider a (non-deterministic) HORS as a generator of a *finite tree language* (i.e., a set of finite trees).

Definition 4 (Non-deterministic HORS). Let Σ be a finite set of symbols called *tree constructors*. We assume that each tree constructor is associated with a non-negative integer called an *arity*. A (non-deterministic) HORS is a set of function definitions: $\{F_1 \widetilde{x}_1 = t_1, \ldots, F_n \widetilde{x}_n = t_n\}$, where t_i ranges over the set of terms given by: $t ::= a \mid x \mid F \mid t_1 t_2$. Here, a ranges over Σ. As in the language in Sect. 2, we allow more than one definition for each function symbol F_i, and require that $F_i = S$ and $\widetilde{x}_i$ is empty for some i. We also require that HORS be simply-typed; in each definition $F \widetilde{x} = t$, t must have the tree type o. Each constructor of arity k is given type $\underbrace{\mathsf{o} \to \cdots \to \mathsf{o}}_{k} \to \mathsf{o}$.

Given a HORS $\mathcal{G}$, the reduction relation $\longrightarrow_{\mathcal{G}}$ on terms is defined by: (i) $F t_1 \cdots t_k \longrightarrow_{\mathcal{G}} [t_1/x_1, \ldots, t_k/x_k]t$ if $F x_1 \cdots x_k = t \in \mathcal{G}$; and (ii) $a t_1 \cdots t_i \cdots t_k \longrightarrow_{\mathcal{G}} a t_1 \cdots t_i' \cdots t_k$ if $t_i \longrightarrow_{\mathcal{G}} t_i'$. We call a term t a (Σ-labeled) *tree* if it consists of only tree constructors, and write **Tree** for the set of trees. The language generated by a HORS $\mathcal{G}$, written $\mathcal{L}(\mathcal{G})$, is $\{t \in \textbf{Tree} \mid S \longrightarrow_{\mathcal{G}}^* t\}$.

Compared with the language in the previous section, we have tree constructors in HORS instead of primitives on locks and treads. The following is an easy corollary of the decidability of (the standard version of) higher-order model checking [8].

Theorem 2. *Given a HORS $\mathcal{G}$ and a regular language R, it is decidable whether $\mathcal{L}(\mathcal{G}) \subseteq R$ holds.*

3.2   Action Trees

Action trees, first introduced by Lammich et al. [7], represent thread-wise action histories of a concurrent program. We extend them to deal with dynamic lock creation.

Definition 5 (Action Trees). The set $\mathcal{T}$ of *action trees*, ranged over by γ, is defined inductively by: $\gamma ::= \perp \mid \$ \mid \ell \gamma \mid \mathsf{new}_\kappa \gamma \mid \mathsf{acq}_\kappa \gamma \mid \mathsf{rel}_\kappa \gamma \mid \mathsf{sp} \, \gamma_p \, \gamma_c$.

Each inner node of γ represents an action performed by a thread. The tree $\ell \gamma$ means that the thread has reached an expression labeled ℓ and then behaved like γ. The tree $\mathsf{new}_\kappa \gamma$ means that the thread has created a new lock of abstract name κ, and then behaved like γ. The tree $\mathsf{acq}_\kappa \gamma$ (resp. $\mathsf{rel}_\kappa \gamma$) means that the thread has acquired (resp. released) a lock of abstract name κ, and then behaved like γ. The tree $\mathsf{sp} \, \gamma_p \, \gamma_c$ means that the thread has spawned a child thread that behaved like γ_c, and the thread itself behaved like γ_p.

A leaf node represents the status of the thread: $\perp$ means that it is alive and $\$$ means that it has terminated.

Example 4. The figure on the righthand side below shows the action tree corresponding to the transition sequence in Example 2. The superscripts 0–12 are the node numbers added for the convenience of explanation; they reflect the order of actions in the transition sequence in Example 2.

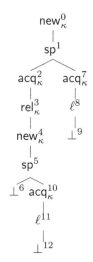

The tree represents the computation in which (i) the root thread creates a new lock with abstract name κ (as shown by node 0), spawns a new thread (node 1), acquires and releases the lock (nodes 2 and 3), creates another lock with the same abstract name κ (node 4) and spawns another thread (node 5), and (ii) the two child threads acquire the locks (nodes 7 and 10) and reaches the program point ℓ (nodes 8 and 11). The leaves of the action tree show that all the threads are still alive (nodes 6, 9 and 12). Note that the locks acquired by the two child threads are different, although nodes 7 and 10 have the same label acq_κ; based on the scope safety assumption, κ refers to the lock created at the closest ancestor node labeled by new_κ. Thus, nodes 7 and 10 refer to the locks created at nodes 0 and 4 respectively.

Note also that the action tree does not specify the order between actions of different threads. For example, the action at node 7 may occur before the one at node 4. Due to the synchronization constraint on locks, however, some order may be implicitly imposed; for example, since nodes 2, 3, and 7 refer to the same lock created at node 0, the action at 3 must precede the one at 7.   □

For a sequence of events $(\iota_1, a_1) \cdots (\iota_n, a_n)$, we write $\mathsf{a}((\iota_1, a_1) \cdots (\iota_n, a_n))$ for the corresponding action tree; see the full version for the formal definition. We write $\mathsf{ATrees}(p)$ for the set

$$\{\mathsf{a}((\iota_1, a_1) \cdots (\iota_n, a_n)) \mid c_0 \xrightarrow{\iota_1, a_1}_p c_1 \xrightarrow{\iota_2, a_2}_p \cdots \xrightarrow{\iota_n, a_n}_p c_n; c_0 \text{ is the initial configuration.}\}$$

of action trees of all the possible transition sequences of the program p.

We write R_{ℓ_1, ℓ_2} for the set of action trees of the form $C[\ell_1 \bot, \ell_2 \bot]$, where C is a tree context with two holes. Note that R_{ℓ_1, ℓ_2} does not depend on the program. Clearly, the set R_{ℓ_1, ℓ_2} is regular. By the definition of $\mathsf{ATrees}(p)$, the pairwise reachability is reduced to the non-emptiness of $\mathsf{ATrees}(p) \cap R_{\ell_1, \ell_2}$, as stated below.

Lemma 1. *For every program p and every pair of labels (ℓ_1, ℓ_2), we have*

$$p \models \ell_1 \| \ell_2 \iff \mathsf{ATrees}(p) \cap R_{\ell_1, \ell_2} \neq \emptyset.$$

3.3   Relaxed Transition of Programs

The next step is to obtain a finitary representation of $\mathsf{ATrees}(p)$. If we were able to represent $\mathsf{ATrees}(p)$ as a HORS, then the (non-)emptiness problem

$\mathsf{ATrees}(p) \cap R_{\ell_1,\ell_2}$ obtained in Lemma 1 can be solved by higher-order model checking. Unfortunately, a direct construction of such a HORS is difficult, due to the synchronization constraint on locks.

Instead, we consider an approximation $\mathsf{RelaxedATrees}(p)$ of $\mathsf{ATrees}(p)$, which are obtained by ignoring the synchronization constraint, and represent it as a HORS. The set $\mathsf{ATrees}(p)$ is then obtained as $\mathsf{RelaxedATrees}(p) \cap \mathsf{LSATrees}$, where $\mathsf{LSATrees}$ is the set of all the action trees that respect the synchronization constraint but are independent of the program p. In this subsection, we define $\mathsf{RelaxedATrees}(p)$ and provide its grammar representation; $\mathsf{LSATrees}$ shall be constructed and proved to be regular in Sects. 3.4 and 3.5.

A *relaxed* transition relation $c_1 \xrightarrow{\iota,a}_p c_2$ on configurations is the least relation closed under the rules in Sect. 2 except that the conditions $(\kappa, \iota', m) \notin \mathbf{locked}(c \uplus \{\iota \mapsto (\mathbf{acq}(\kappa, \iota', m);\ e_2, L, \sigma)\})$ of the fourth rule (for lock acquisition), $L = L'\cdot(\kappa, \iota', m)$ of the fifth rule (for lock release) and $L = \epsilon$ of the last rule (for thread termination) are removed. Similarly to $\mathsf{ATrees}(p)$ we write $\mathsf{RelaxedATrees}(p)$ for the set

$$\{\mathsf{a}((\iota_1,a_1)\ldots(\iota_n,a_n)) \mid c_0 \xrightarrow{\iota_1,a_1}_p \ldots \xrightarrow{\iota_n,a_n}_p c_n\}$$

of action trees of all possible relaxed transition sequence of the program p. Obviously $\mathsf{RelaxedATrees}(p)$ is a superset of $\mathsf{ATrees}(p)$.

We can easily transform a given program p into a HORS $\mathcal{G}_p$ whose language is $\mathsf{RelaxedATrees}(p)$. Each lock is replaced by a pair of tree constructors acq_κ and rel_κ, and each action in the program is replaced by a construction of the corresponding tree node. For example, $\mathbf{spawn}(e_1);\ e_2$ and $\mathbf{new}_\kappa\ e_1$ are respectively transformed to $\mathsf{sp}\ e_1'\ e_2'$, and $\mathsf{new}_\kappa\ (e_1'\ (\mathsf{acq}_\kappa, \mathsf{rel}_\kappa))$, where e_i' is obtained by recursively transforming e_i. (Here, for the sake of simplicity, we have used pairs as primitives; they can be represented as functions using the standard Church encoding.) In addition, since we are interested in intermediate states of a program instead of the final state, we prepare rules to abort reductions and generate leaves $\bot$. We illustrate these points through an example below; the formal definition of $\mathcal{G}_p$ is given in the full version.

Example 5. Recall Example 1. The set $\mathsf{RelaxedATrees}(p)$ is generated by the following HORS $\mathcal{G}_p$:

$$
\begin{aligned}
&S = New_\kappa\ F \\
&F\ x = Spawn\ (Acq\ x\ (Label_\ell\ (Rel\ x\ End)))\ (Acq\ x\ (Label_\ell\ (Rel\ x\ S))) \\
&New_\kappa\ e = \mathsf{new}_\kappa\ (e\ (\mathsf{acq}_\kappa, \mathsf{rel}_\kappa)) \qquad Acq\ (x_a, x_r)\ e = x_a\ e \qquad Rel\ (x_a, x_r)\ e = x_r\ e \\
&Spawn\ e_c\ e_p = \mathsf{sp}\ e_p\ e_c \qquad Label_\ell\ e = \ell\ e \qquad End = \$ \\
&N\ \tilde{x} = \bot \qquad (\text{for each } N \in \{S, F, New_\kappa, Acq, Rel, Spawn, Label_\ell, End\}.)
\end{aligned}
$$

The first two lines correspond to the function definitions in the original programs; we have just replaced each action with the corresponding function symbols. The next two lines define functions for generating a tree node corresponding to each action. The function New_κ represents a new lock as a pair $(\mathsf{acq}_\kappa, \mathsf{rel}_\kappa)$ and passes it to e as an argument. The function Acq extracts the first component acq_κ of lock x, which is a tree constructor acq_κ, and creates a node acq_κ. Similarly the

Rel rule creates a node rel_κ. The last rule is used to stop the thread and generate the symbol $\perp$ meaning that the thread is alive.   □

3.4   Lock Sensitivity of Action Trees

The set $\mathsf{RelaxedATrees}(p)$ may contain action trees for which there are no corresponding transition sequences that respect the synchronization constraint. To exclude them, we introduce a subset $\mathsf{LSATrees}$ of γ, which consists of only action trees that have corresponding transition sequences for *some* program (that satisfies scope safety and well-nested locking), so that the set $\mathsf{ATrees}(p)$ is represented by $\mathsf{RelaxedATrees}(p) \cap \mathsf{LSATrees}$. To this end, we introduce an *abstract* transition relation $\hat{c} \xrightarrow{\iota, a} \hat{c}'$, obtained by replacing expressions with action trees.

Definition 6 (Abstract Configurations). An *abstract thread state* is a quadruple (γ, L, s, σ), obtained by replacing the first component of a thread state in Sect. 2 with an action tree γ. An *abstract configuration* $\hat{c}$ is a partial map from the set of thread identifiers to the set of abstract thread states. The transition relation on abstract configurations is defined by:

$$\hat{c} \uplus \{\iota \mapsto (\gamma, L, s, \sigma)\} \xrightarrow{\iota, \bullet} \hat{c} \uplus \{\iota \mapsto (\gamma, L, s, \sigma)\}$$

$$\frac{\sigma(\kappa) = (\iota, m) \qquad \sigma' = \sigma\{\kappa \mapsto (\iota, m+1)\}}{\hat{c} \uplus \{\iota \mapsto (\mathsf{new}_\kappa \, \gamma, L, s, \sigma)\} \xrightarrow{\iota, \mathsf{new}(\kappa, \iota, m+1)} \hat{c} \uplus \{\iota \mapsto (\gamma, L, s, \sigma')\}}$$

$$\frac{\forall \iota', m.(\sigma(\kappa) = (\iota', m) \Rightarrow \iota \neq \iota') \qquad \sigma' = \sigma\{\kappa \mapsto (\iota, 1)\}}{\hat{c} \uplus \{\iota \mapsto (\mathsf{new}_\kappa \, \gamma, L, s, \sigma)\} \xrightarrow{\iota, \mathsf{new}(\kappa, \iota, 1)} \hat{c} \uplus \{\iota \mapsto (\gamma, L, s, \sigma')\}}$$

$$\frac{\sigma(\kappa) = (\iota', m) \qquad (\kappa, \iota', m) \notin \mathbf{locked}(\hat{c} \uplus \{\iota \mapsto (\mathsf{acq}_\kappa \, \gamma, L, s, \sigma)\})}{\hat{c} \uplus \{\iota \mapsto (\mathsf{acq}_\kappa \, \gamma, L, s, \sigma)\} \xrightarrow{\iota, \mathsf{acq}(\kappa, \iota', m)} \hat{c} \uplus \{\iota \mapsto (\gamma, L \cdot (\kappa, \iota', m), s, \sigma)\}}$$

$$\frac{\sigma(\kappa) = (\iota', m) \qquad L = L' \cdot (\kappa, \iota', m)}{\hat{c} \uplus \{\iota \mapsto (\mathsf{rel}_\kappa \, \gamma, L, s, \sigma)\} \xrightarrow{\iota, \mathsf{rel}(\kappa, \iota', m)} \hat{c} \uplus \{\iota \mapsto (\gamma, L', s, \sigma)\}}$$

$$\hat{c} \uplus \{\iota \mapsto (\mathsf{sp} \, \gamma_p \, \gamma_c, L, s, \sigma)\} \xrightarrow{\iota, \mathsf{sp}(\iota \cdot s)} \hat{c} \uplus \left\{ \begin{array}{l} \iota \quad \mapsto (\gamma_p, L, s+1, \sigma), \\ \iota \cdot s \mapsto (\gamma_c, \epsilon, 0, \sigma) \end{array} \right\}$$

$$\hat{c} \uplus \{\iota \mapsto (\ell \, \gamma, L, s, \sigma)\} \xrightarrow{\iota, \ell} \hat{c} \uplus \{\iota \mapsto (\gamma, L, s, \sigma)\}$$

$$\frac{L = \epsilon}{\hat{c} \uplus \{\iota \mapsto (\$, L, s, \sigma)\} \xrightarrow{\iota, \$} \hat{c}}$$

Here, $\mathbf{locked}(\hat{c})$ is defined similarly to that for (concrete) configurations, by

$$\mathbf{locked}(\hat{c}) = \{(\kappa, \iota', m) \mid \exists \iota.\ \hat{c}(\iota) = (\gamma, L, s, \sigma) \wedge (\kappa, \iota', m) \in L\}.$$

In the rules above for acquiring and releasing locks, we have added the condition $\sigma(\kappa) = (\iota', m)$, which captures the scope safety assumption.

Using the abstract transition relation, the set of lock sensitive action trees is defined as follows.

Definition 7 (Lock Sensitivity). An action tree γ is *lock sensitive* if $\{0 \mapsto (\gamma, \epsilon, 0, \emptyset)\} \overset{*}{\to} \hat{\perp}$, where $\hat{\perp}$ is any abstract configuration such that $\hat{\perp}(\iota) = (\gamma, L, s, \sigma)$ implies $\gamma = \perp$. We write LSATrees for the set of lock-sensitive action trees.

Theorem 3. *Let p be a scope-safe program. Then,*

$$\mathsf{ATrees}(p) = \mathsf{RelaxedATrees}(p) \cap \mathsf{LSATrees}.$$

Intuitively, the theorem above holds because the concrete transition system $c \overset{\iota,a}{\longrightarrow}_p c'$ is obtained as the product of the relaxed transition system and the abstract transition system; see the full version for a proof.

3.5 Regularity of **LSATrees**

We show that LSATrees is a regular tree language. To this end, we adapt the notion of an *acquisition structure* [1,7] to deal with an unbounded number of locks. An acquisition structure is a summary of the usage of locks in an action tree.

Let us first review the idea behind acquisition structures. Let $\hat{c}_i = \{\iota_i \mapsto (\gamma_i, L_i, s_i, \sigma_i)\}$ $(i = 1, \dots, n)$ be abstract configurations that are individually lock-sensitive, i.e. $\hat{c}_i \overset{*}{\to} \hat{\perp}_i$ for some bottom configuration $\hat{\perp}_i$ for each i. We would like to decide if the merged configuration is also lock-sensitive, i.e. whether $\biguplus_{i=1}^{n} \hat{c}_i \overset{*}{\to} \biguplus_{i=1}^{n} \hat{\perp}_i$. In some cases, it is obviously impossible.

- Let $\check{A}^f{}_i$ be the set of (concrete) locks that the final configuration $\hat{\perp}_i$ has. If $\check{A}^f{}_i \cap \check{A}^f{}_j \neq \emptyset$, the merged configuration is not lock-sensitive since $\biguplus_{i=1}^{n} \hat{\perp}_i$ violates the condition that each lock can be assigned to at most one thread.
- Let us call (an occurrence of) an acquire operation in the transition sequence $\pi : \hat{c}_i \overset{*}{\to} \hat{\perp}_i$ *final* if the lock is not released in the following subsequence. Let G_π be the strict preorder[1] on concrete lock names defined by $(\nu, \nu') \in G_\pi$ just if an acquire operation of ν' appears after the final acquisition of ν in π. Let $\check{G}_i$ be the intersection of G_π for all possible transition sequences $\pi : \hat{c}_i \overset{*}{\to} \hat{\perp}_i$. If $\bigcup_{i=1}^{n} \check{G}_i$ is cyclic, the merged configuration is not lock-sensitive. For example, if $(\nu, \nu'), (\nu', \nu) \in \bigcup_{i=1}^{n} \check{G}_i$ and $\pi : \biguplus_{i=1}^{n} \hat{c}_i \overset{*}{\to} \biguplus_{i=1}^{n} \hat{\perp}_i$, then the final acquisition of ν in π must precede that of ν' and vice versa, a contradiction.

---

[1] A strict preorder, often written as $<$, is an irreflexive and transitive relation.

Conversely, provided that $L_i = \epsilon$ for all i, the above conditions are sufficient for the lock-sensitivity of the merged configuration. A transition sequence can be constructed by an eager scheduling as follows. If there is a thread whose next operation is not a final acquisition, run the thread. Furthermore if the thread acquires a lock, run it until the lock is released; then, by nested locking, the thread does not have any lock at that state. If all the threads reach $\bot$ or final acquisition operations, choose a thread acquiring a minimal lock with respect to $\bigcup_{i=1}^{n} \check{G}_i$. Since such a lock is ensured not to appear in the sequel, we can safely forget the lock and regard the thread as having no lock.

Unlike the previous work [1,7], the number of locks is unbounded in our setting. However the above test is concerned only about the locks shared by $\hat{c}_i$ and $\hat{c}_j$ for some $i \neq j$. Thanks to the scope-safety of the program, the locks used by $\hat{c}_i$ are in $\{ (\kappa, \sigma(\kappa)) \mid \kappa \in \mathcal{K} \}$ or those that will be generated by $\hat{c}_i$ in the subsequent computation. Hence the restrictions of $\mathring{A}^f{}_i$ and $\check{G}_i$ to $\{ (\kappa, \sigma_i(\kappa)) \mid \kappa \in \mathcal{K} \}$, which is finite, is sufficient for the purpose. We represent those restrictions as sets and relations on abstract locks $\kappa \in \mathcal{K}$.

The formal definition of the acquisition structure of an action tree is as follows. It has additional fields: A (the set of locks used in the action tree) is used to compute G in an inductive way, and R (the list of dangling release operations) and T (the leaf node of this thread) are used to check if the locks are used in the expected manner (i.e. well-nested, no re-entrant and that a terminating thread have released all the locks). Given a relation G, let G^+ be its transitive closure and $G{\restriction}_A$ be the restriction $\{ (x,y) \in G \mid x, y \in A \}$. Given a set A, we write $A^\circledast$ for the set of all finite sequences on A without repetition.

Definition 8 (Acquisition Structure). The *acquisition structure* $\mathsf{as}(\gamma)$ of an action tree γ is a tuple $(A, A^f, R, T, G) \in \mathcal{P}(\mathcal{K}) \times \mathcal{P}(\mathcal{K}) \times \mathcal{K}^\circledast \times \{ \$, \bot \} \times \mathcal{P}(\mathcal{K} \times \mathcal{K})$, inductively defined as follows (where we write A_γ for the first component of $\mathsf{as}(\gamma)$ and so on, and undef means undefined):

$$\mathsf{as}(\bot) = (\emptyset, \emptyset, \epsilon, \bot, \emptyset) \qquad \mathsf{as}(\$) = (\emptyset, \emptyset, \epsilon, \$, \emptyset) \qquad \mathsf{as}(\ell\,\gamma) = \mathsf{as}(\gamma)$$

$$\mathsf{as}(\mathsf{acq}_\kappa\,\gamma) = \begin{cases} (A_\gamma \cup \{\kappa\}, A_\gamma^f, R', T_\gamma, G_\gamma) \\ \qquad (\text{if } R_\gamma = R' \cdot \kappa) \\ (A_\gamma \cup \{\kappa\}, A_\gamma^f \cup \{\kappa\}, \epsilon, T_\gamma, (G_\gamma \cup (\{\kappa\} \times A_\gamma))^+) \\ \qquad (\text{if } R_\gamma = \epsilon \text{ and } T_\gamma = \bot \text{ and } G_\gamma \cup (\{\kappa\} \times A_\gamma) \text{ is acyclic}) \\ \mathsf{undef} \qquad (\text{otherwise}) \end{cases}$$

$$\mathsf{as}(\mathsf{rel}_\kappa\,\gamma) = \begin{cases} (A_\gamma, A_\gamma^f, R_\gamma \cdot \kappa, T_\gamma, G_\gamma) & (\text{if } \kappa \notin R_\gamma) \\ \mathsf{undef} & (\text{if } \kappa \in R_\gamma) \end{cases}$$

$$\mathsf{as}(\mathsf{sp}\,\gamma_p\,\gamma_c) = \begin{cases} (A_{\gamma_p} \cup A_{\gamma_c}, A_{\gamma_p}^f \cup A_{\gamma_c}^f, R_{\gamma_p}, T_{\gamma_p}, (G_{\gamma_p} \cup G_{\gamma_c})^+) \\ \qquad (\text{if } R_{\gamma_c} = \epsilon \text{ and } A_{\gamma_p}^f \cap A_{\gamma_c}^f = \emptyset \text{ and } G_{\gamma_p} \cup G_{\gamma_c} \text{ is acyclic}) \\ \mathsf{undef} \qquad (\text{if } R_{\gamma_c} \neq \epsilon \text{ or } A_{\gamma_p}^f \cap A_{\gamma_c}^f \neq \emptyset \text{ or } G_{\gamma_p} \cup G_{\gamma_c} \text{ is cyclic}) \end{cases}$$

$$\mathsf{as}(\mathsf{new}_\kappa\,\gamma) = \begin{cases} (A_\gamma \backslash \{\kappa\}, A_\gamma^f \backslash \{\kappa\}, R_\gamma, T_\gamma, G_\gamma {\restriction}_{\mathcal{K} \backslash \{\kappa\}}) & (\text{if } \kappa \notin R) \\ \mathsf{undef} & (\text{if } \kappa \in R). \end{cases}$$

For every action tree γ, no element $\kappa \in \mathcal{K}$ appears twice in the sequence $R_\gamma \in \mathcal{K}^*$ (if defined). Hence the set of all acquisition structures can be seen as finite.

The set of lock-sensitive action trees is characterized by the acquisition structure; see the full version for a proof.

Theorem 4. *An action tree γ is lock sensitive iff* $\mathsf{as}(\gamma) = (\emptyset, \emptyset, \epsilon, T, \emptyset)$.

By the definition of the acquisition structure, it can be obviously computed by a bottom-up tree automaton. Hence:

Theorem 5. LSATrees *is a regular tree language.*

Now we can reduce the pairwise-reachability problem to a higher-order model checking problem as follows. Let p be a scope-safe program and (ℓ_1, ℓ_2) be a pair of labels. Then $p \vDash \ell_1 \| \ell_2$ if and only if $\mathsf{RelaxedATrees}(p) \cap \mathsf{LSATrees} \cap R_{\ell_1, \ell_2} \neq \emptyset$ by Lemma 1 and Theorem 3. This is equivalent to $\mathsf{RelaxedATrees}(p) \not\subseteq \overline{\mathsf{LSATrees} \cap R_{\ell_1, \ell_2}}$. Since $\mathsf{LSATrees}$ is regular (Theorem 5), the right-hand-side is regular. Hence the problem is an instance of higher-order model checking, and thus decidable. This completes the proof of the main theorem, Theorem 1.

4 Checking Scope-Safety and Well-Nested Locking

The verification method for the pairwise reachability in the previous section is sound and complete for the class of scope-safe programs with nested locking. For programs outside the class, our verification method is *unsound.*[2] Thus, it is desirable to have methods for checking that a given program satisfies the conditions of scope-safety and well-nested locking. Fortunately, higher-order model checking can also be used for that purpose, as described below.

4.1 Strong Scope Safety

For ease of explanation, we first present a method for checking a stronger condition called *strong scope-safety*. We call a program *strongly scope-safe* if it satisfies the conditions of Definition 3 where the transition relation $\rightarrow_p$ is replaced with the relaxed transition relation $\dashrightarrow_p$.

It would be quite easy to find a violation of strong scope-safety if one could construct a "concrete action tree", in which lock operations are annotated by concrete lock names, e.g. $\mathsf{new}_\kappa^{(\iota, m)}$. In this setting, what we should do is to check whether the "concrete action tree" has a node $op_\kappa^{(\iota, m)}$ ($op \in \{ \mathsf{acq}, \mathsf{rel} \}$) whose nearest ancestor new_κ-node is annotated with a different concrete name $(\iota', m')(\neq (\iota, m))$. Although the naive application of this idea seems to require infinitely many names, we can do this by using only two names because it suffices to ensure that two chosen concrete lock names are indeed different.

Given a transition sequence, and a subset $\mathcal{X}$ of concrete lock names, its *semi-concrete action tree* is an action tree in which lock operations are annotated with

---

[2] Since the pairwise reachability is usually considered an undesirable behavior (e.g. a race), we say that a pairwise reachability analysis is sound when it does not miss the possibility of pairwise reachability.

A or B, e.g. new_κ^A, where A means that the concrete lock name is in $\mathcal{X}$ and B otherwise. A semi-concrete action tree *violates scope-safety* if there is a node op_κ^B ($op \in \{\, \mathsf{acq}, \mathsf{rel}\,\}$) whose nearest ancestor new_κ node is labeled with A (i.e. it is new_κ^A). This is a regular tree property, which we write as S.

A HORS $\mathcal{G}_p^{A,B}$ generating the set of semi-concrete action trees of a program p can be constructed in the same way as in Sect. 3.3, except that the behaviour of New_κ is now nondeterministic as follows:

$$New_\kappa\, e = \mathsf{new}_\kappa^A\,(e\,(\mathsf{ack}_\kappa^A, \mathsf{rel}_\kappa^A)) \qquad New_\kappa\, e = \mathsf{new}_\kappa^B\,(e\,(\mathsf{ack}_\kappa^B, \mathsf{rel}_\kappa^B)).$$

Intuitively New nondeterministically chooses if the newly created concrete lock name should belong to $\mathcal{X}$ or not.

By the discussion above, it should be clear that a program is strongly scope-safe if and only if $\mathcal{L}(\mathcal{G}_p^{A,B}) \cap \mathsf{S} = \emptyset$. Thus, the problem to check whether a given program is strongly scope-safe is decidable.

4.2   Well-Nested Locking

Here we give a method for conservatively checking whether a given *scope-safe* program has nested locking, ignoring inter-thread synchronization.

We give a sketch of the construction of a top-down tree automaton, which nondeterministically chooses a thread of the action tree and computes acquired locks, and accepts the tree if the chosen thread indeed violates well-nested locking. A state is either $\star$ (meaning that the automaton has not chosen a thread) or a sequence $R \in (\mathcal{K} \cup \{\sharp\})^*$ (meaning that the chosen thread has acquired (and not released) the locks in the order specified in R) such that each $\kappa \in \mathcal{K}$ appears at most once in R. The symbol $\sharp$ is used to express locks that have been shadowed (i.e., those that are no longer visible due to the creation of a lock of the same abstract name). For example, if the current node is $\mathsf{new}(\kappa)$ and the state is $R \cdot \kappa \cdot R'$, then the automaton changes its state to $R \cdot \sharp \cdot R'$ and moves to the child node. If the node is acq_κ and the state is R, then the automaton checks if κ appears in R; if so, the automaton rejects the tree since this thread gets stuck (note that locks are non-reentrant) and does not violate well-nested locking; otherwise, it moves to the child node with the state $R \cdot \kappa$. If the node is $\mathsf{rel}(\kappa)$ and the state is $R \cdot \kappa$, then the automaton goes to the child node with the state R. If the automaton sees $\mathsf{rel}(\kappa)$ at the state $R \cdot \xi$ ($\xi \in \mathcal{K} \cup \{\sharp\}$) with $\kappa \neq \xi$, then it accepts the tree because this release operation violates well-nested locking. In the construction above, R may contain an unbounded number of $\sharp$, so the number of states is infinite. However, only the right-most occurrence of $\sharp$ is meaningful and one can safely forget the other occurrences of $\sharp$. Thus the number of states can be reduced to finite.

Let us write N for the tree language accepted by the above automaton. The following result is obvious.

Lemma 2. *Let p be a scope-safe program. If $\mathcal{L}(\mathcal{G}_p^{A,B}) \cap \mathsf{N} = \emptyset$, then p has nested locking.*

4.3   Scope-Safety and Well-Nested Locking

We have seen above that $\mathcal{L}(\mathcal{G}_p^{A,B}) \cap (\mathsf{N} \cup \mathsf{S}) = \emptyset$ implies p is a scope-safe program with nested locking. The converse does not hold, however. This is because even if $\mathcal{L}(\mathcal{G}_p^{A,B}) \cap (\mathsf{N} \cup \mathsf{S}) \neq \emptyset$, $\gamma \in \mathcal{L}(\mathcal{G}_p^{A,B}) \cap (\mathsf{N} \cup \mathsf{S})$ may be infeasible because of the synchronization through locks.

We can obtain a complete method by taking into account the lock-sensitivity of action trees, in a manner similar to Sect. 3.4. We call a (semi-concrete) action tree γ *almost lock-sensitive* if it is obtained by adding an action to a lock-sensitive action tree (i.e. there exists a pair of a one-hole tree context C and an action tree γ' such that $\gamma = C[\gamma']$, $C[\bot]$ is lock-sensitive and γ' has exactly one node whose label is not $\bot$). Let $\mathsf{LSATrees}'$ be the set of semi-concrete action trees that are almost lock-sensitive.

Lemma 3. $(\mathcal{L}(\mathcal{G}_p^{A,B}) \cap \mathsf{LSATrees}') \cap (\mathsf{N} \cup \mathsf{S}) = \emptyset$ *if and only if p is a scope-safe program with nested locking.*

As a corollary, we obtain:

Theorem 6. *The problem to check whether a given program is scope-safe and has nested locking is decidable.*

5   Extension with Join Operations

We briefly discuss our method for pairwise reachability (described in Sect. 3) to support first-class thread identifiers and join operations. The target language is extended as follows. We introduce a new base type **ID** for thread IDs. Each spawn expression $\mathbf{spawn}(e_c)$; e_p is now annotated with an *abstract thread ID* θ, which does not affect the transition but is used to define the notion of scope safety. The expression spawns a new child thread e_c, and executes $e_p(\iota)$, where ι is the (unique) identifier (ID) of the new thread; thus e_p has type $\mathbf{ID} \to \star$. We add a new expression $\mathbf{join}(e_1)$; e_2, which waits for the termination of the thread with ID e_1, and then executes e_2. A program of the extended language is *scope-safe* if, in addition to the condition on scope-safety on locks, it satisfies the analogous condition on thread identifiers, that each join operation may refer to only the newest thread identifier in the scope for each abstract thread ID θ.

Example 6. The following program is a variation of the program in Example 1.

$$p_2 = \left\{ \begin{array}{ll} S = \mathbf{new}_i \; F & F \; x = \mathbf{spawn}^\theta(\mathbf{acq}(x); \; (\mathbf{rel}(x); \; \$)^\ell); G \; x) \\ G \; x \; t = \mathbf{acq}(x); \; (\mathbf{rel}(x); \; \mathbf{join}(t); \; S). \end{array} \right\}$$

The function F takes a lock as an argument, spawns a new thread, and passes its identifier to $G \; x$. The program is scope-safe. Unlike the program in Example 1, (ℓ, ℓ) is *not* pairwise reachable, because the root thread waits for the termination of a child thread before spawning another thread.

Our pairwise reachability verification method in Sect. 3 can be smoothly extended, except for the regularity of the set of lock-sensitive action trees, which we briefly discuss below. Let $\hat{c}_1 = \{\, \iota \mapsto (\gamma, s+1, L, \sigma)\,\}$ and $\hat{c}'_1 = \{\, \iota \cdot s \mapsto (\gamma', 0, \epsilon, \sigma)\,\}$ be abstract configurations and assume that each of them is schedulable alone, i.e. $\hat{c}_1 \xrightarrow{*}_p \hat{\perp}_1$ and $\hat{c}_2 \xrightarrow{*}_p \hat{\perp}_2$. The question is when $\hat{c}_1 \uplus \hat{c}'_1$ is schedulable. If $\hat{c}_1$ does not do $\mathbf{join}(\iota \cdot s)$, the schedulability of $\hat{c}_1 \uplus \hat{c}'_1$ can be checked in the same way as in Sect. 3.5. If $\hat{c}_1$ does a $\mathbf{join}(\iota \cdot s)$ action, an additional condition is required for schedulability of $\hat{c}_1 \uplus \hat{c}'_1$: if $\nu \in L$ and ν will not be released until the join operator, then $\hat{c}_2$ cannot use this lock. Hence the additionally required piece of data is the set of pairs (ι', ν') of a thread ID and a lock name such that ν' is kept locked from the current state until a $\mathbf{join}(\iota')$ action. Since only the thread IDs and lock names in the scope are relevant, this information can be described in finite states.

6   Experiments

We have implemented a tool for checking the pairwise reachability and strong scope safety based on our methods. The tool uses HORSAT2 [3] as the backend higher-order model checker. We have tested the tool on a machine with an Intel Core i5 CPU with 2.5 GHz and 16 GB memory.

The table on the righthand side shows the result of preliminary experiments. The column "Reachability" shows the answers for the pairwise reachability problems. The columns "SS" and "PR" respectively show the

Program	Reachability	SS	PR
example1	YES	0.002	0.385
example2	NO	0.002	29.5
datarace	NO	0.004	1.04

times spent for checking (strong) scope-safety and pairwise-reachability, measured in seconds. indicates the elapsed time of scope-safety checking and pairwise-reachability checking. The programs example1 and example2 are those given in Examples 1 and 6 respectively. The benchmark program datarace models the following C-like code:

```
main() {  r = newref();  l = newlock();
   spawn{acq(l);write(r);rel(l);}; acq(l);write(r);rel(l); main(); }
```

where the dynamic creation of reference cells is handled in a manner similar to that of locks and thread identifiers. We checked whether two write commands for the *same* reference cell may be reached simultaneously. All the programs are strongly scope-safe. According to the experimental results, the strong scope safety can be checked instantly. The pairwise reachability checking is slower, but reasonably fast, considering the complexity of higher-order model checking [8]. The pairwise reachability checking for example2 took much longer than for the other programs. We think this is due to the use of the join primitive, which probably blowed up the space exploited by the model checker. This suggests that a further improvement of the higher-order model checker is required for handling real-world programs; we leave it for future work.

7   Related Work

There have been several studies on the decidability of pairwise reachability of concurrent programs with nested locking [1,2,7,13]. To our knowledge, however, our result is the first one that allows dynamic creation of an unbounded number of locks, albeit under the condition of scope safety. The notion of scope safety is also new. The idea of reducing pairwise reachability to higher-order model checking has been first proposed by Yasukata et al. [13]; our method described in Sect. 3 is an extension of their method to deal with an unbounded number of locks. There are many other methods for analyzing concurrent programs with dynamic resource creation [4,10,12], but they are either incomplete or unsound (due to over- or under-approximation of reachable states).

The idea of non-deterministically tracking the usage of locks used in Sect. 4 (for checking scope safety and well-nested locking) has been inspired from Kobayashi's work for applying higher-order model checking to resource usage analysis [5]. His method is for sequential (functional) programs, however.

8   Conclusion

We have presented a method for deciding the pairwise reachability of concurrent programs with dynamic creation of resources and thread identifiers. We have introduced the notion of scope safety, and proved that our method is sound and complete for scope-safe programs with nested locking. We have also presented methods for checking whether a given program satisfies the conditions of scope safety and well-nested locking.

Acknowledgment. We would like to thank anonymous referees for useful comments. This work was supported by JSPS KAKENHI Grant Number JP15H05706 and JP16K16004.

References

1. Gawlitza, T.M., Lammich, P., Müller-Olm, M., Seidl, H., Wenner, A.: Join-lock-sensitive forward reachability analysis for concurrent programs with dynamic process creation. In: Jhala, R., Schmidt, D. (eds.) VMCAI 2011. LNCS, vol. 6538, pp. 199–213. Springer, Heidelberg (2011)
2. Kahlon, V., Ivančić, F., Gupta, A.: Reasoning about threads communicating via locks. In: Etessami, K., Rajamani, S.K. (eds.) CAV 2005. LNCS, vol. 3576, pp. 505–518. Springer, Heidelberg (2005)
3. Kobayashi, N.: HorSat2: a saturation-based higher-order model checker. http://www-kb.is.s.u-tokyo.ac.jp/~koba/horsat2/
4. Kobayashi, N.: Type systems for concurrent programs. In: Aichernig, B.K. (ed.) Formal Methods at the Crossroads. From Panacea to Foundational Support. LNCS, vol. 2757, pp. 439–453. Springer, Heidelberg (2003)
5. Kobayashi, N.: Model checking higher-order programs. J. ACM **60**(3), 20 (2013)

6. Kobayashi, N., Sato, R., Unno, H.: Predicate abstraction and CEGAR for higher-order model checking. Proceedings of PLDI 2011, pp. 222–233 (2011)
7. Lammich, P., Müller-Olm, M., Wenner, A.: Predecessor sets of dynamic pushdown networks with tree-regular constraints. In: Bouajjani, A., Maler, O. (eds.) CAV 2009. LNCS, vol. 5643, pp. 525–539. Springer, Heidelberg (2009)
8. Ong, C.H.L.: On model-checking trees generated by higher-order recursion schemes. In: LICS, pp. 81–90 (2006)
9. Plotkin, G.D.: Call-by-name, call-by-value and the lambda-calculus. Theor. Comput. Sci. 1(2), 125–159 (1975)
10. Pratikakis, P., Foster, J.S., Hicks, M.: LOCKSMITH: practical static race detection for C. ACM Trans. Program. Lang. Syst. (TOPLAS) 33(1), Article 3 (2011)
11. Ramalingam, G.: Context-sensitive synchronization-sensitive analysis is undecidable. ACM Trans. Program. Lang. Syst. 22(2), 416–430 (2000)
12. Terauchi, T.: Checking race freedom via linear programming. In: Proceedings of PLDI 2008, pp. 1–10. ACM, New York (2008)
13. Yasukata, K., Kobayashi, N., Matsuda, K.: Pairwise reachability analysis for higher order concurrent programs by higher-order model checking. In: Baldan, P., Gorla, D. (eds.) CONCUR 2014. LNCS, vol. 8704, pp. 312–326. Springer, Heidelberg (2014)

Programming Paradigms

Probabilistic Programming Language and its Incremental Evaluation

Oleg Kiselyov[(✉)]

Tohoku University, Sendai, Japan
oleg@okmij.org

Abstract. This system description paper introduces the probabilistic programming language Hakaru10, for expressing, and performing inference on (general) graphical models. The language supports discrete and continuous distributions, mixture distributions and conditioning. Hakaru10 is a DSL embedded in Haskell and supports Monte-Carlo Markov Chain (MCMC) inference.
Hakaru10 is designed to address two main challenges of probabilistic programming: performance and correctness. It implements the incremental Metropolis-Hastings method, avoiding all redundant computations. In the presence of conditional branches, efficiently maintaining dependencies and correctly computing the acceptance ratio are non-trivial problems, solved in Hakaru10. The implementation is unique in being explicitly designed to satisfy the common equational laws of probabilistic programs. Hakaru10 is typed; specifically, its type system statically prevents meaningless conditioning, enforcing that the values to condition upon must indeed come from outside the model.

1 Introduction

Broadly speaking, probabilistic programming languages are to express computations with degrees of uncertainty, which comes from the imprecision in input data, lack of the complete knowledge or is inherent in the domain. More precisely, the goal of probabilistic programming languages is to represent and automate reasoning about probabilistic models [4,16], which describe uncertain quantities–random variables–and relationships among them. The canonical example is the grass model, with three random variables representing the events of rain, of a switched-on sprinkler and wet grass. The (a priori) probabilities of the first two events are judged to be 30 % and 50 % correspondingly. Probabilities are real numbers from 0 to 1 that may be regarded as weights on non-deterministic choices. Rain almost certainly (90 %) wets the grass. The sprinkler also makes the grass wet, in 80 % of the cases. The grass may also be wet for some other reason. The modeler gives such an unaccounted event 10 % of a chance. This model is often depicted as a directed acyclic graph (DAG)–so-called Bayesian, or belief network [17] (Fig. 1)–with nodes representing random variables and edges conditional dependencies. Associated with each node is a distribution (such as Bernoulli distribution **bern**: the flip of a biased coin), or a function that computes

© Springer International Publishing AG 2016
A. Igarashi (Ed.): APLAS 2016, LNCS 10017, pp. 357–376, 2016.
DOI: 10.1007/978-3-319-47958-3_19

a distribution from the node's inputs (such as the noisy disjunction nor to be described below).

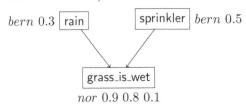

bern 0.3 | rain | | sprinkler | *bern* 0.5

| grass_is_wet |
nor 0.9 0.8 0.1

Fig. 1. Grass model

The sort of reasoning we wish to perform on the model is finding out the probability distribution of some of its random variables. For example, we can work out from Fig. 1 that the probability of the grass being wet is 60.6 %. Such reasoning is called probabilistic *inference*. Often we are interested in the distribution conditioned on the fact that some random variables have been observed to hold a particular value. In our example, having observed in the morning that the grass is wet, we want to find out the chance it was raining overnight. We are thus estimating a hidden parameter–inferring the likelihood of an unseen or unobservable cause–from observations. For background on the statistical modeling and inference, the domain area of the present paper, the reader is referred to Pearl's classic [17] and Getoor and Taskar's collection [4].

In the probabilistic language Hakaru10 to be presented in this paper, the conditional model just described in English can be written as follows:

```
grass = do
  rain          ← dist bern 0.3
  sprinkler     ← dist bern 0.5
  grass_is_wet  ← dist (True `condition` nor 0.9 0.8 0.1) rain  sprinkler
  return  rain

-- noisy-or function
nor strengthX strengthY noise = \x y →
  bern $ 1 − nnot (1−strengthX) x * nnot (1−strengthY) y * (1−noise)

-- noisy not function
type Prob = Double
nnot :: prob → Bool → Prob
nnot p True  = p
nnot p False = 1
```

Even though some words like dist are not yet defined, one can already see the correspondence with Fig. 1. The grass code compactly and, mainly, unambiguously represents the model–for the domain experts and also for the Hakaru10 system. The latter relieves us from working out probabilities by hand, performing the requested inference. Thus probabilistic programming languages let us separate the description of the model from computations on them, making the models declarative and accessible, for domain experts, to discuss and modify.

Probabilistic programming languages are easier to use and develop when they are embedded DSLs, implemented as a library or a macro on top of the existing general-purpose programming language. Hakaru10 is in fact such a DSL, embedded in Haskell. The grass model is the ordinary Haskell function, making use of the library functions bern, dist and condition. The full power of Haskell and all of its libraries is available for expressing deterministic parts of the model (such as the noisy-or probability computation). Embedded DSL let us also take the full advantage of the abstraction facilities of the host language such as functions, module systems, etc. For example, we have defined nor as a particular parameterized Bernoulli distribution conditioned on two inputs x and y. This function can later be re-used in other models. We may hence compose models from simpler components. Starting from the pioneering work of Sato [19], many probabilistic DSL have been proposed [5,8], with host languages been logical [2,19], functional [6,12,20,22], object-functional [18], etc. Wingate et al. [21] deserves special mention for proposing a technique of adding probabilistic programming facilities to just about any language. The authors demonstrated this on the examples of Scheme and Matlab. Wingate's et al. approach has become well-spread and employed in many more probabilistic systems such as [9,22].

There are so many probabilistic languages and we are still writing papers about (more of) them–driven by two main challenges. One is obvious, the other may come as a surprise. The obvious challenge is performance. An expressive, pleasant to use, well abstracted probabilistic programming language may be, it is all for naught if doing inference with realistic models takes unreasonable time or runs out of memory. For example, the probability monad–which adds weights to the well-known List monad for non-determinism–is the straightforward and the easiest to understand example of probabilistic programming in Haskell. It is Haskell folklore, well described in [3]. It is also disastrously inefficient, failing even for toy problems. Therefore, it is all too common in Machine Learning/AI communities to tailor the model to a specific inference method, and tune the inference code for a specific model. However prominent are the drawbacks of such tight coupling, often it is the only way to handle problems of realistic size.

That correctness is still a challenge may be surprising. Given the long history of probabilistic programming, one may think that the basics of the implementation are beyond doubts. Yet we keep finding problems in the published work [11]. The well-known and widely used systems such as STAN [9] turn out to give plain wrong answers even in simple cases, as Hur et al. [10] have clearly demonstrated.

Contributions. Hakaru10 was developed to address both challenges, performance and correctness. It started as a project to improve the implementation of the (original) Hakaru [24] on two points: avoid redundant re-computations and to strengthen the typing discipline. It was discovered [11] along the way that the implementation principles, taken from [21] were flawed. Hakaru10 is the complete re-write, on new principles, to be described in the present paper. Specifically, the paper makes the following contributions.

1. It presents the probabilistic programming language Hakaru10 embedded as a DSL in Haskell.
2. It describes the design of Hakaru10, specifically, its type system, which ensures not only that a model is well-typed, but also that it is well-conditioned. That is, the values used for conditioning really come from the sources external to

the model, rather than being produced from random sources and computations within the model. In [20] that semantic well-conditioning constraint is a mere coding convention, whose violation leads to a run-time exception. We encode the constraint in types, without losing the benefits of the do-notation. Although the original Hakaru [24] enforced well-conditioning statically, it had to give up on the ordinary monads and made the conditioning difficult and error-prone to use: the observed quantities had to be referred to by De Bruijn-like indices. The type system of Hakaru10 improves not only on the static guarantees but also on the 'syntax' of the language: its Haskell embedding.

3. We describe the implementation of the Metropolis-Hastings (MH) probabilistic inference method (one of the Markov Chain Monte Carlo (MCMC) methods, see Sect. 4 for a reminder) that ensures semantic-preserving model transformations such as introduction and elimination of dirac random variables. The implementation is thus guaranteed to obey theoretically justified equational laws of probabilistic programs. The correct MH implementation, in the presence of branching, is quite non-trivial [10].

4. We present the method to improve the efficiency of MH by avoiding redundant re-computations. Although the idea is simple–upon resampling re-compute only those parts of the model that depend on the changed value–the challenge is to minimize the overhead of determining the dependencies and their order. The challenge is acute in the presence of branching: if-then-else statements.

Hakaru10 thus fixes the three problems of the popular Wingate et al. approach [21] that have been pointed out in [11]. First, the implementation is designed to respect the unit law of the Dirac distribution. Second, Hakaru10 by design avoids the accidental sharing of random primitives. In Wingate et al. such sharing, however unjustified theoretically, was justified practically as increasing the performance. Hakaru10 improved the performance by avoiding unnecessary recomputations. The third problem, not able to use conditioning other than 'at the top level' has also been dealt with. This problem is so involved and important that is out of scope here, to be discussed in a separate paper.

We start in Sect. 2 with a Hakaru10 tutorial. Section 3 briefly evaluates the expressiveness and performance of the system. Section 4 describes the implementation in detail. We then review the related work and conclude. The complete code for Hakaru10 with many tests and examples is available at http://okmij.org/ftp/kakuritu/Hakaru10/.

2   Hakaru10 by Example

This section introduces Hakaru10 on a series of many small examples, showing off the features of the language. Incidentally, these simple models are useful regression tests for any probabilistic system. The section also demonstrates equational laws, or valid transformations of Hakaru10 programs.

Hakaru10 is designed for models that are described by a finite directed acyclic graph like Fig. 1, whose nodes represent random variables and edges indicate (typically causal) dependencies. Unlike graphical models in the strict sense [16], we allow dependencies with arbitrary pure computations.

2.1 Model Compositions and Their Laws

The first, elementary program is

    pbern = dist bern 0.4

whose inferred type is Model Bool. The program represents the model consisting of a single Boolean ('Bernoulli') random variable, whose distribution is True with the probability 40 % and False with the probability 60 %. One may think of the function bern :: Double → DistK Bool as creating a distribution given its parameter, and dist :: (a → DistK b) → a → Model b as sampling from it[1]. The types DistK and Model are abstract; the latter has the additional structure to be shown shortly.

The function mcmC, the interpreter of probabilistic programs,

    mcmC :: Integer → Model a → [a]
    pbern_run = mcmC 10 pbern

performs the MH inference on a model and returns the list of samples from the model's distribution. In particular, mcmC 10 pbern produces a list of 10 booleans, which indeed contains 4 True and 6 False values. Hakaru supports not only discrete like bern but also continuous distributions:

    pnorm = dist normal 10 0.5

Here, pnorm, of the inferred type Model Double is a model with the single normally-distributed random variable, with the mean 10 and the standard deviation 0.5. Hakaru10 offers other primitive distributions, such as categorical, uniform, gamma and beta.

Almost all models are more complex, with more random variables, and mainly, with dependencies between random variables. (Hakaru10 intentionally does not support cyclic dependencies, as the semantics of such models is problematic.) The following model has two random variables, normal- and Dirac-distributed[2]. The parameter of the latter depends on the value of the former, for which we re-use the earlier written pnorm:

    −− pdep1 :: Model Double
    pdep1 = do
      x ← pnorm
      diracN (x+1)

To build complex models we use the Haskell do notation. In the example above, we 'name' the submodel (random variable) pnorm as x, which we later use in the expression to compute the parameter of the Dirac distribution. Haskell embedding truly brings modularity: we can name Hakaru10 models (binding them to Haskell variables) and (re)use constructed models as parts of other models, as we have just done with pnorm. Since the Dirac distribution is frequent and special, as we are about to see, there is a shorter syntax for it, just diracN. As expected, the inferred distribution of pdep1 is exactly the same as that of dist normal 11 0.5.

---

[1] These signatures are somewhat simplified. We will later see that dist is overloaded.
[2] Dirac distribution, or Dirac delta, is taken as density of a discrete random variable with the single value.

Likewise, the model

```
pdepR = do
  x ← pnorm
  diracN x
```

is equivalent to just pnorm. This is the general property, not limited to normal distributions: for any model p

do {x ← p; diracN x}

has the distribution identical to that of p. Even the sequences of samples for the two programs are identical. Likewise, for any ˙e,

do {x ← diracN e; p}

is equivalent to let x=e in p. Hence diracN acts as the left and the right unit of the model composition. Not surprisingly, diracN has the alias return. At this point a Haskell programmer may think that Model is a monad. This is not quite true, as we shall soon see.

The joint distribution of pbern and pnorm models is described by

```
pjoin = do
  x ← pbern
  y ← pnorm
  return ( pair x y)
```

Then mcmC 100 pjoin produces a set of (Bool,Double) pairs sampled from the joint distribution, which in this case is the product of pbern and pnorm distributions. That the distributions of x and y are independent can be seen *syntactically*, from the fact that the model named y, namely, pnorm, has no mentioning of x. We can even integrate (that is, 'marginalize') over x:

```
pmarg = do
  x ← pbern
  y ← pnorm
  return y
```

Since x does not appear further in the program, this random variable is irrelevant and is essentially marginalized. Hence the distribution of pmarg is the same as that of pnorm (although the sequences of samples certainly differ). This property is again general, for all models (not using conditioning, see below).

To demonstrate once more the advantage of the Haskell embedding, we borrow the example of a simple hierarchical model from [10, Fig. 3]. In the standalone, C-like imperative probabilistic language of that paper, the example looks as follows:

```
double x;
int i = 0;
x ~ Gaussian(0, 1);
while (i < 10) do {
  x ~ Gaussian(x, 3);
  i = i+1;
}
return x;
```

The graph of this model with 11 variables looks like the straight line. In this C-like code, like in C, x denotes a sample from the model rather than a model.

In Hakaru10, we write the hierarchical model as

```
phier = ( iterate  (\m → do {x←m; dist normal x 3}) $ dist normal 0 1) !! 10
```

taking the advantage of Haskell's standard library: iterate f x produces a list

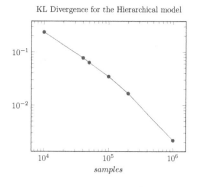

KL Divergence for the Hierarchical model

whose i-th element is the i-th iterate of f over x. The significance of the example is that the popular probabilistic programming systems like STAN infer a wrong distribution for it, as demonstrated in [10]. Hakaru10, like the system of [10], infers the expected normal distribution with the center 0 and the standard deviation $\sqrt{91}$. We can verify the fact by computing the (estimate of the) KullbackLeibler (KL) divergence, a common metric of dissimilarity between distributions:

```
phier_kl  n = kl ( tabulate  0.5  $ mcmC n phier)
 ( tabulate  0.5  $ mcmC n $ dist normal 0 (sqrt 91))
```

Here tabulate computes the histogram with the specified bin size. The above figure plots phier_kl n for the different number of samples n. For the correct sampler, KL is expected to decay as $O(n^{-k})$ for some constant k. Hence, the plot of KL vs. n on the log-log scale should look like a straight line.

2.2 Branching Models

Hakaru10 can express not only 'straight-line' but also branching models. An example is a simple mixture model

```
mixng = do
  x ← dist normal 0 1
  if_ ((>0) <$>  x)
           ( dist  normal 10 2)
           ( dist  gamma 3 (1/3))
```

whose distribution is the mixture of normal and gamma distributions, with the random variable x determining the proportion of the mixture. One can also read this program as sampling either from the normal or the gamma distributions, depending on the sign of x. The mixng program is the first betraying Model being not quite a monad. The variable x is not actually of the type Double, as one might have thought. We have maintained the illusion so far because numbers in Haskell are overloaded. Sadly, booleans are not. As should be apparent from the use of Applicative operator <$>, which is just fmap, Model a is something like M (A a) where M is a monad but A is an applicative. We discuss the representation of Model in Sect. 4.

Just by looking at the mixng code one can tell that what matters for the final distribution is the event of x being positive–which, for the standard normal distribution happens 50 % of the time. Therefore, mixng should be equivalent to the following mixture

```
mixng' = do
   x ← dist bern 0.5
   if_ x
        ( dist  normal 10 2)
        ( dist  gamma  3 (1/3))
```

That is, mcmC 5000 mixng should be roughly the same sequence of samples as mcmC 5000 mixng'–and also as interleave (mcmC 2500 (dist normal 10 2)) (mcmC 2500 (dist gamma (1/3))). Again, we verify the similarity using the KL divergence, which is under 2.3e−2. This example is also borrowed from [10, Fig. 2]. Despite its simplicity, several widely known and used probabilistic programming systems (e.g., STAN) infer wrong distributions for it.

2.3 Conditioning

Finally, Hakaru10 supports conditioning, that is, inferring the conditional distribution of a model where some of its variables have been observed to hold particular values. Conditioning is extraordinarily tricky, especially in case of continuous distributions. The interested reader may look up the Borel paradox. The syntax and the type system of Hakaru10 are specifically designed to steer the programmer (far) away from the pitfalls.

We take as an example the experiment of estimating the bias of a coin, that is, its inherent probability b of coming up as head (that is, True). We toss the coin twice and observe the results as c1 and c2. The following is the model of the experiment, taking the observed values as parameters.

```
biased_coin c1 c2 = do
   b ← dist beta 1 1
   dist (c1 `condition` bern) b
   dist (c2 `condition` bern) b
   return b
```

We do not know the true bias b, but assume a priori that it is distributed as beta 1 1. This is a popular assumption (not in small part due to the fact we can compute the posterior analytically). We toss the coin twice and 'observe the results as c1 and c2': specify that the first toss came in reality as c1 and the second as c2. Then biased_coin c1 c2 gives us the (posterior) distribution of b, letting us estimate the coin's bias. If in the experiment the coin came up first head and then tail, the posterior analytically is beta 2 2, with the average 0.5 and the variance 0.05. Running mcmC 10000 (biased_coin True False) gives the list of 10000 samples, from which we estimate the average as 0.499.

As biased_coin code demonstrates, in Hakaru10 conditioning may only be applied to distributions. One may think that (c1 `condition` bern) creates a new distribution out of bern, with the singular value c1. Conditioning on arbitrary boolean formulas is fraught with peril, both theoretical and practical, degenerating MCMC algorithm into the inefficient rejection sampling. Since repeated conditioning does not make sense, (c1 `condition` (c2 `condition` bern)) is a type error. Hakaru10 is indeed typed, although we have not paid much attention to types, which were all inferred. Types do prevent silly errors like

```
biased_coin_ill_typed   c1 c2 = do
  b ← dist bern 0.5
  dist (c1 `condition` bern) b
  dist (c2 `condition` bern) b
  return b
```

since the parameter of bern, the probability, cannot be a Boolean. Types also prevent less obvious errors like

```
biased_coin_ill_typed_too   c1 c2 = do
  b ← dist bern 0.5
  dist (b `condition` bern) 0.4
  return b
```

Here, we attempted to condition bern on the random choice within the model. This is not allowed: observations must be external to the model. In [20], this semantic condition was a merely a coding convention, whose violation manifested as a run-time exception. In Hakaru10, the violation is a type error.

Previously we have seen that random variables that do not contribute to the result in any way are effectively marginalized. Conditioning changes that. The two condition lines in the biased_coin model are the random variables that do not seem to contribute to the model (therefore, we did not even give them names). However, they had effect. The following model makes that fact clear:

```
post_bias c = do
  coin ← dist bern 0.5
  if_ coin ( dist (c `condition` normal) 0 1)
           ( dist (c `condition` normal) 100 1)
  return coin
```

The result of the model does not overtly depend on the result of the if_ statement. However, it changes the coin's posterior distribution: running mcmC 100 (post_bias 1) gives all True samples.

We conclude the tutorial by looking back at the canonical grass model example described in Sect. 1, repeated below for reference.

```
grass = do
  rain          ← dist bern 0.3
  sprinkler     ← dist bern 0.5
  grass_is_wet  ← dist (True `condition` nor 0.9 0.8 0.1) rain  sprinkler
  return rain
```

This code hopefully has become more understandable. Evaluating mcmC 20000 grass and counting the number of True gives the posterior estimate of rain having observed that the grass is wet: it comes out to 0.468, which matches the analytically determined result.

3 Evaluation

The Hakaru10 tutorial might have given an impression that Hakaru10 tries so hard to preclude problematic behavior, by restricting conditioning and models, that one cannot do much interesting in it. In this section we briefly evaluate the expressiveness of the language on two realistic models.

Bayesian Linear Regression. The first model comes from the small problems collection of challenge problems[3] assembled in the course of DARPA's Probabilistic Programming for Advancing Machine Learning (PPAML) program[4]. It is Problem 4.1, Bayesian linear regression: Given the set of training points $(x_{ij}, y_i), i = 1..N, j = 1..k$ and the generative model $y_i = \sum_j x_{ij} * w_j + noise_i$ find the posterior distribution on w_j. In the conventional linear regression language, we are given N observations of y assumed to be a linear combination of the controlled quantities x with the parameters w; we have to estimate w. The generative model is expressed in Hakaru10 as

```
type RegrDatum = ([Double],Double)   -- Xs and Y
model::[RegrDatum]→ Model [Double]
model xsy = do
  let mu    =  replicate dimK 0
  w_mean    ← normals mu 2
  w         ← normals w_mean 1
  noise_sd ← (1/) <$> dist gamma 0.5 0.5
  let make_cond (xs,y) = dist (y `condition` normal) (dot xs w) noise_sd
  mapM_ make_cond xsy
  return $ collect w
```

Its argument is the list of the training points (x_{ij}, y_i). The model starts by defining the prior for the parameters w and the standard deviation noise_sd for the noise (as specified in the problem description). We then create a random variable for each noisy observation point and condition it to y_i. We are interested in the distribution of the parameter vector w given the conditioning. The Hakaru10 model rather closely matches the problem description (and the RSTAN code given in the problem description document). The model is straightforward but not small: its graph has 511 vertices (there are five hundred observations and five parameters).

The model is naturally expressed in terms of vectors; Hakaru10 however does not provide out of the box any distributions over vectors. Nevertheless, we can express them through Hakaru10 primitives in our host language, Haskell. For example, we can write normals, which produces a list of independently distributed normal random variables of the same standard deviation std whose means are given by the list means:

```
normals means std = mapM (\m → dist normal m std) means
```

Likewise we can write collect (to convert a list of random variables into a random list) in pure Haskell–to say nothing of the dot-product dot.

Population Estimation. We also evaluate Hakaru10 by implementing a realistic model of population estimation, taken from [14, Ex 1.1]: "An urn contains an unknown number of balls–say, a number chosen from a Poisson or a uniform distributions. Balls are equally likely to be blue or green. We draw some balls from the urn, observing the color of each and replacing it. We cannot tell two identically colored balls apart; furthermore, observed colors are wrong with probability

---

[3] http://ppaml.galois.com/wiki/wiki/CP4SmallProblemsCollection.

[4] http://www.darpa.mil/program/probabilistic-programming-for-advancing-machine-Learning.

0.2. How many balls are in the urn? Was the same ball drawn twice?" This example is hard to implement in many probabilistic programming languages. That is why it was used to motivate the language BLOG.

First we define ball colors

```
data Color = Blue | Green deriving (Eq, Show)
opposite_color :: Color→ Color
opposite_color Blue  = Green
opposite_color Green = Blue
```

and introduce the distribution for the observed ball color accounting for the observation error:

```
observed_color color = categorical [( color , 0.8), ( opposite_color color , 0.2)]
```

Although the exact number of balls in unknown, we can reasonably impose an upper bound. We create that many instances of uniformly color-distributed random variables, for each ball. We populate the IntMap data structure, mapping ball's index to the corresponding random variable, for easy retrieval.

```
maxBalls = 8
balls_prior n = do
  balls ← sequence ∘ replicate n $ dist uniformly (pure [Blue,Green])
  return $ M.fromList $ zip [1..] balls
```

Some of these random variables will be unused since the number of balls in the urn is often less than the upper bound. The unused variables will be marginalized[5].

The model is conceptually simple: it takes a list of observations obs as an argument, generates random variables for all possible balls, draws the number of balls from the prior and dispatches to the instance of the model with that number of balls.

```
cballs_model [obs1,obs2 ,...] = do
  balls ← balls_prior maxBalls
  nballs ← dist uniformly (pure [1.. maxBalls])
  if_ ((== 1) <$> nballs) (cballs_model_with_Nballs balls obs 1) $
   if_ ((== 2) <$> nballs) (cballs_model_with_Nballs balls obs 2) $
    ...
    if_ ((== 8) <$> nballs) (cballs_model_with_Nballs balls obs 8) $
     return ()
  return nballs
```

When the number of balls is fixed, the experiment is easy to model: pick one ball b and check its true color balls ! b against the color of the first observed ball; repeat for the second observed ball, etc.

---

[5] Imposing the upper bound on the number of balls may be undesirable, especially for the Poisson distribution. In principle, Hakaru10 could instantiate conditional branches of a model lazily; in which case balls could be an infinite list. We are investigating this possibility.

```
cballs_model_with_Nballs  balls  [obs1,obs2 ,...]  nballs = do
  b ← dist uniformly (pure [1.. nballs ])
  if_ ((= 1) <$> b) (dist (obs1 `condition` observed_color ) ( balls ! 1)) $
    if_ ((= 2) <$> b) (dist (obs1 `condition` observed_color ) ( balls ! 2)) $
      ...
  b ← dist uniformly (pure [1.. nballs ])
  if_ ((= 1) <$> b) (dist (obs2 `condition` observed_color ) ( balls ! 1)) $
    if_ ((= 2) <$> b) (dist (obs2 `condition` observed_color ) ( balls ! 2)) $
      ...

  ...
  return ()
```

The result is a rather large Bayesian network with deeply nested conditional branches with conditioning in the leaves. The fact that the same balls variable is shared among all branches of the complex if-statement corresponds to the intuition that the same ball can be drawn twice since we return the drawn balls into the urn. A ball keeps its true color, no matter how many times it is drawn.

The code outline just shown is not proper Hakaru10 (and is not proper Haskell) because of many ellipses. It is clear however that the code has the regular structure, which can be programmed in Haskell. For example, the (proper, this time, with ellipses filled in) code for cballs_model is as follows:

```
cballs_model :: [Color] → Model Int
cballs_model obs = do
  balls  ← balls_prior maxBalls
  nballs ← dist uniformly (pure [1.. maxBalls])
  let obs_number i = if_ ((= i) <$> nballs) $ cballs_model_with_Nballs balls obs i
  foldr obs_number (return (pure())) [1.. maxBalls]
  return nballs
```

One may think that the huge size of the model makes the inference difficult. However, only small part of the large nest of conditional branches is evaluated on each MH step. Therefore, performance is rather good: on 1.8 GHz Intel Core i3, Hakaru10 running within the GHCi interpreter (bytecode, no optimizations) takes 16 s to do 10,000 samples and reproduce the results of this model programmed in Hansei [12] (running in OCaml bytecode, using importance sampling, taking 5000 samples within 13.4 s) and the results reported in [14, Fig. 1.7], which took 35 s on 3.2 GHz Pentium 4 to obtain.

3.1   Performance

The motivation for Hakaru10 was to improve the performance of the original Hakaru [24], which was the straightforward implementation of the Wingate et al. [21] algorithm. The previous section has already touched upon the Hakaru10 performance. This section evaluates performance directly, against the original Hakaru, on the phier model from Sect. 2. Recall, its expected distribution is normal with the average 0 and variance 91. The table below reports the estimates of the average and variance, as well as the CPU time taken to obtain 1 million samples from the model. The table compares Hakaru10 with the original Hakaru. The platform is Intel Core i3 1.8 GHz; the systems were compiled with GHC 7.8.3 with the −O2 flag.

	Average	Variance	CPU time (sec)
Hakaru original	0.39	87	72 s
Hakaru10	0.22	93	20 s

Hakaru10 indeed significantly improves performance.

4 Implementation

Hakaru10 programs represent directed graphical models. Although we can use state and other effects (e.g., reading various parameters from a file) to build the graph, models themselves are declarative, describing connections between random variables, or their distributions. Having built the model, we want to determine the distribution of some of its random variables, either marginalizing or conditioning on the others. Usually we determine the desired distribution as a sequence of samples form it. If the model is encoded as a program that does the sampling of random variables respecting the dependencies, determining the distribution amounts to repeatedly running the program and collecting its results. Taken literally, this process is rather inefficient however.

Conditioning, especially in the case of continuous distributions, poses a problem. Consider the model

```
do
  tempr ← dist uniform (−20) 50
  (25 `condition` normal) tempr 0.1
  return tempr
```

which represents a simple measurement (of tempr, the air temperature). The measurement has random noise, which is believed to be Gaussian with the standard deviation 0.1. We are interested in the distribution of the true temperature given the observed value 25 °C. The naive procedure will uniformly sample tempr from [−20, 50], then sample from normal tempr 0.1, and, if the latter result differs from 25, reject the tempr sample and repeat. Alas, we will be rejecting almost all samples and produce nothing: mathematically speaking, the event that a value drawn even from the normal distribution centered at 25, is exactly 25 has the zero probability. A more useful question therefore to ask is how likely 25 may come as a sample from the distribution normal tempr 0.1. It becomes clear why Hakaru10 insists the conditioning be applied only to distributions: we have to know what distribution the observation comes from, so we can tell how likely it is. Sampling thus becomes an optimization problem, maximizing the livelihood. One of the multi-dimensional optimization methods is Markov-Chain Monte-Carlo (MCMC).

Hakaru10 supports one of the MCMC methods: Metropolis-Hastings (MH) method of sampling from a model distribution. We remind the algorithm on the following example:

```
mhex = do
  x ← dist normal 0 1
  y ← dist normal x 2
  if_ ((>0.5) <$> x)
      (return x)
      (do {z ← dist beta 1 1; return (y + z)})
```

The algorithm constructs the sequence of Doubles, drawn from the distribution of mhex, that is, the distribution of the values returned by the last statement of the program. To start with, MH "runs" the program, sampling from the distributions of its random variables. For example, x gets a sample from the standard normal distribution, say, 0.1. Then y is sampled from normal 0.1 2, say, as −0.3, and z is sampled as 0.5. The result of the whole program is then 0.2. Along with the samples, MH remembers their probability in the distribution. It is more convenient to work with the logarithms, that is, log likelihoods (LL). For example, the LL of the initial x sample is −0.616. The collection of samples along with their LLs is called the trace of the program. LL of the trace is the sum of the LLs of its samples.

The just constructed trace becomes the initial element in the Markov chain. The next element is obtained by attempting to 'disturb' the current trace. This is the key to the efficiency of Markov Chain Monte Carlo (MCMC) as contrasted to the naive resampling (simple Monte Carlo): rather than resample all of the random variables, we attempt to resample only one/a few at a time. The algorithm picks a subset of random variables and proposes to change them, according to some proposal distribution. Commonly, and currently implemented in Hakaru10, the algorithm selects one random variable and resamples it from its distribution. Suppose we pick x and find another sample from its standard normal distribution. Suppose the result is 0.6. The program is then re-run, while keeping the values of the other random variables. In other words, we re-compute the trace to account for the new value of x. The change in x switches to the first branch of the if statement, and the program result becomes 0.6. Since y was not affected by the change proposal, its old sample, −0.3, is kept. However, it is now drawn from the different distribution, normal 0.6 2, an hence has the different LL. Thus even if a random variable does not contribute to the result of a trace, it may contribute to its LL. From the LLs of the original and the updated trace, MH computes the acceptance ratio (a number between 0 and 1) and accepts the updated trace with that probability. If the trace is accepted, it becomes the new element of the Markov chain. Otherwise, the original trace is retained as current. Running the trace re-computation many times constructs the sequence of samples from the distribution of the trace–or, retaining only the trace result, the sequence of samples from the program distribution.

4.1 Design Overview

We now describe the Hakaru10 implementation in more detail. Hakaru10 represents the trace–random variables of the model and their dependencies–as a directed acyclic graph (DAG). Each node (vertex) in the graph stands for one random variable (whose value can be sampled and resampled) or an observed variable, whose value cannot be resampled. There are also computational nodes, representing 'samples' from the dirac distribution. They cannot be resampled either. Section 4.3 describes the reasons for the special treatment of the dirac distribution. One node in a graph, with no outgoing vertices, is designated as the 'result' node. The graph with the result type a has the type SExp a[6]. For the grass model the trace graph has three nodes and looks exactly like the graphical representation of the model, Fig. 1.

A Hakaru10 model has the type

type Model a = MCMCM (SExp a)

It is a computation that constructs the trace graph. MCMCM is a monad, but SExp is not. It is an applicative [13]: it lets us construct new graph nodes, without looking at their values. The function

mcmC :: Integer → Model a → [a]

first builds the trace graph and then repeatedly runs the trace update algorithm the specified number of times. The fact that SExp is not a monad is significant: the current node values cannot influence the graph construction. Therefore, after the graph is built, its structure does not change. All dependencies among nodes can be computed once and for all.

The type system not only makes the implementation more efficient. It also enforces semantic constraints. Let's recall the code that attempts to condition on the value computed within the model, which is invalid semantically.

```
biased_coin_ill_typed_too    c1 c2 = do
  b ← dist bern 0.5
  dist (b `condition` bern) 0.4
  return b
```

This code does not type-check since the first argument of condition should be Bool, since bern is the distribution over booleans. However, b is not Bool, it is of the type SExp Bool. In the original Hakaru [24], the semantic constraint was enforced via a parameterized monad, which made its syntax (the Haskell embedding) cumbersome. Worse, the values to condition upon could only be referred to indirectly, via De Bruijn-like indices, which were very easy to confuse. The type system of the embedded language thus has significant influence on its 'syntax', its embedding.

4.2 Incremental Recomputation

One of the main features of Hakaru10 is its incremental recomputation algorithm, which avoids the redundant computations during the trace update. Only those nodes that (transitively) depend on the resampled random variable are recomputed. The following example should clarify the meaning of the dependency:

---

[6] The actual implementation has one more level of indirection, but the description given here is a good approximation.

```
pdep = do
    x ← dist normal 0 1
    y ← dist normal x 1
    z ← dist normal y 1
    return (x+y+z)
```

Suppose MH proposes to resample x (and only x). Although the y sample keeps its old value, its distribution parameters, x specifically, changed. Therefore, the LL of the old y sample in the new distribution has to be recomputed. The variable z is not affected by the resampling proposal; also, the parameters of its distribution remain the same. Therefore, no update to the z node is needed. The last, Dirac, node of the trace, corresponding to return (x+y+z), is also updated, to account for the new x: the special treatment of Dirac nodes is explained in the next subsection.

Since the type system ensures that the structure of the graph is preserved, the dependency graph can be computed and topologically sorted once and for all. The fact that Hakaru10 models are acyclic and Hakaru10 programs are declarative (with no mutations) lets us avoid the topological sort and rely on the 'creation times' of trace nodes. A node can only depend on those constructed before it.

The update procedure has the obvious correctness requirement: a node is updated only after all the nodes it depends on have been updated. If we consider the trace update as a graph traversal, the correctness property amounts to maintaining the invariant that a visited node has the creation time earlier than any other node in the update queue. This invariant has guided writing the code and remains in the code in the form of assertions (mostly for documentation).

4.3   Special Treatment of the Dirac Distribution

Hakaru10 by design enforces the laws that

do { x ← p; diracN x } ≡ p
do { x ← diracN v; p } ≡ let x = v in p

for all programs p.

The law is tricky to enforce. Moreover, an MH implementation that does not pay attention to it (such as [21], for example) exhibits incorrect behavior, as pointed out in [11]. We recall the latter's argument here.

Let us consider the following program

p2 = do {x ← dist uniform 0 1; diracN x}

Suppose in the initial trace x is sampled to 0.5 and the MH algorithm now proposes to change it to 0.7. When updating the trace, the values of other random variables are kept as their are; only their LL may change. Thus the value of the dirac node will be kept at 0.5; the update procedure will then try to find its LL within the changed distribution dirac 0.7. Clearly the LL of the old sample in the new distribution is − inf. Therefore, the proposal to resample x will be rejected. *Every* proposal to modify x will likewise be rejected and so the Markov chain of p2 will contain the identical samples.

Mathematically, composing with Dirac is the identity transformation, so p2 should be equivalent to just uniform 0 1, whose Markov chain is anything but constant. Without taking precautions, the MH algorithm converges to the wrong distribution for p2.

One may be tempted to dismiss the problem: the chain fails to mix (all proposals are rejected) because of the single-variable update proposals. However, more general proposals require the interface for the user to tell the system how to make correlated multi-variable proposals. Moreover, the user has to know how to make good a proposal, which is a non-trivial skill. Asking the end user for non-trivial extra hints seems especially bothersome for such a simple problem. Once we know which equational laws we have to satisfy, it is quite easy to account for it and make the problems involving dirac go away.

Therefore, Hakaru10 implementation treats dirac nodes specially. They are considered as pure computation nodes, and their value is always updated whenever their dependencies change. In effect, any proposal to change one random variable is automatically extended to the proposal to change all dependent dirac random variables, in a way that the latters' LL stays zero. Hakaru10 thus employs multi-variable correlated proposals, for all dirac variables. Therefore, Hakaru10 satisfies the Dirac laws by construction.

4.4 Branching

Branching models, with if-expressions, bring in quite a bit of complexity. A change in the branch condition effectively causes one part of the model vanish and a new submodel, from the other branch, to appear. Maintaining node dependencies and correctly computing the acceptance ratio in such a dynamic environment is non-trivial.

Hakaru10 avoids any modifications to the graph structure during the trace update. It compiles both if-branches when constructing the initial graph. That is, the model if_ test thModel elModel corresponds to the following DAG:

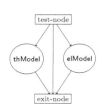

The entry node corresponds to the test condition. The exit node is the result node of the entire if-statement; it holds the value of the thModel or the elModel, depending on the value of the test-node.

Updating the nodes in the inactive branch, whose values will be ultimately ignored, is not good for performance. Therefore, we mark the nodes in the non-current branch as inactive, and delay their updates until they are activated. Thus each node, along with its current value, LL and the distribution also keeps the inactivation count. (The inactivity mark is not a simple boolean because of the nested conditionals and because the same node may appear in several conditionals).

5   Related Work

There are many probabilistic programming languages, with a variety of implementations [7,16]. Closely related to Hakaru10 in its design is Figaro [18], which is also an embedded DSL, in Scala. Like Hakaru10, a Figaro program produces a trace graph, which is then repeatedly updated by the MH algorithm. Figaro does not appear to use the incremental evaluation. Infer.net [15] is also an embedded DSL, for the .NET platform, that first constructs a graph; instead of MH it relies mostly on Expectation Propagation and its variants for inference.

The system of Ścibior et al. [20] is related in its use of Haskell and MCMC. The similarities end here, however. Ścibior et al. use a monad to express models. Therefore, the model construction is "too dynamic" and the semantic constraints on conditioning cannot be statically enforced. On the other hand, Ścibior et al. can express cyclic models (whose semantics, however, may be difficult to determine.) Ścibior et al. implement different MCMC algorithms; none of the implementations are incremental at present.

Although the MH algorithm is the old staple–the original MCMC algorithm–it is not the only one. More advanced MCMC algorithms have been proposed, and recently have been incorporated into probabilistic programming, most prominently in Anglican [22]. It is an interesting challenge to turn these algorithms incremental and implement within Hakaru10, while preserving Hakaru10's features such as conditioning within conditional branches.

Yang et al. [23] propose an incremental evaluation algorithm, using in effect staging, or program generation. They analyze the initial trace and then generate code for the efficient MH update.

Hur et al. [10], whose paper we often used for references and examples, propose the provably correct MH algorithm for the imperative, C-like probabilistic language. It has to deal with the problem of multiple assignments to random variables. The problem does not exist in the declarative Hakaru10, where a random variable, as the name of a model, is immutable.

6   Conclusions and Future Work

We have presented the probabilistic programming language Hakaru10 embedded as a DSL in Haskell. The language features the type system to prevent silly and more subtle mistakes with probabilistic conditioning. We have described the incremental MH evaluation of Hakaru10 programs.

The immediate future work is using the language for more, interesting models. We should consider adding Dirichlet processes. An interesting design challenge is the interface to let the user specify proposals, including proposals to change several random variables in concert.

Although the minimalism of Hakaru10 simplifies the implementation and checking of its correctness, it makes writing interesting models, such as those in Sect. 3, cumbersome. Hakaru10 may hence be viewed as an intermediate language. Fortunately, Haskell proved quite powerful 'macro' language to improve convenience.

Acknowledgments. I am indebted Rob Zinkov and Chung-chieh Shan for many helpful discussions. Comments and suggestions by anonymous reviewers are gratefully acknowledged. The work on Hakaru10 was supported by DARPA grant FA8750-14-2-0007.

References

1. AISTATS, number 33. MIT Press, Cambridge (2014)
2. De Raedt, L., Kimmig, A., Toivonen, H.: ProbLog: a probabilistic Prolog and its application in link discovery. In: Veloso, M.M. (ed.) Proceedings of the 20th International Joint Conference on Artificial Intelligence, pp. 6–12, January 2007
3. Erwig, M., Kollmansberger, S.: Probabilistic functional programming in Haskell. J. Funct. Program. **16**(1), 21–34 (2006)
4. Getoor, L., Taskar, B.: Introduction to Statistical Relational Learning. MIT Press, Cambridge, November 2007
5. Goodman, N.D.: The principles and practice of probabilistic programming. In: POPL 2013: Conference Record of the Annual ACM Symposium on Principles of Programming Languages, pp. 399–402. ACM Press, New York, January 2013
6. Goodman, N.D., Mansinghka, V.K., Roy, D., Bonawitz, K., Tenenbaum, J.B.: Church: a language for generative models. In: McAllester, D.A., Myllymäki, P. (eds.) Proceedings of the 24th Conference on Uncertainty in Artificial Intelligence, pp. 220–229, Corvallis, Oregon, 9–12. AUAI Press, July 2008
7. Goodman, N.D., Stuhlmüller, A.: The design and implementation of probabilistic programming languages (2014). http://dippl.org
8. Gordon, A.D., Henzinger, T.A., Nori, A.V., Rajamani, S.K.: Probabilistic programming. In: FOSE, pp. 167–181. ACM (2014)
9. Hoffman, M.D., Gelman, A.: The No-U-Turn Sampler: Adaptively setting path lengths in Hamiltonian Monte Carlo. e-Print 1111.4246, arXiv.org (2011)
10. Hur, C.K., Nori, A.V., Rajamani, S.K., Samuel, S.: A provably correct sampler for probabilistic programs. In: FSTTCS 2015 (2015)
11. Kiselyov, O.: Problems of the lightweight implementation of probabilistic programming. In: Proceedings of Workshop on Probabilistic Programming Semantics (2016)
12. Kiselyov, O., Shan, C.C.: Monolingual probabilistic programming using generalized coroutines. In: Proceedings of the 25th Conference on Uncertainty in Artificial Intelligence, pp. 285–292, Corvallis, Oregon, 19–21. AUAI Press, June 2009
13. McBride, C., Paterson, R.: Applicative programming with effects. J. Funct. Program. **18**(1), 1–13 (2008)
14. Milch, B., Marthi, B., Russell, S., Sontag, D., Ong, D.L., Kolobov, A.: BLOG: probabilistic models with unknown objects. In: Getoor and Taskar [4], chapter 13, pp. 373–398
15. Minka, T., Winn, J.M., Guiver, J.P., Kannan, A.: Infer.NET 2.2. Microsoft Research Cambridge (2009). http://research.microsoft.com/infernet
16. Murphy, K.: Software for graphical models: a review. Int. Soc. Bayesian Anal. Bull. **14**(4), 13–15 (2007)
17. Pearl, J.: Probabilistic Reasoning in Intelligent Systems: Networks of Plausible Inference, 2nd edn. Morgan Kaufmann, San Francisco (1988)
18. Pfeffer, A., Figaro: an object-oriented probabilistic programming language. Technical report 137, Charles River Analytics (2009)
19. Sato, T.: A glimpse of symbolic-statistical modeling by PRISM. J. Intell. Inf. Syst. **31**(2), 161–176 (2008)
20. Ścibior, A., Ghahramani, Z., Gordon, A.D.: Practical probabilistic programming with monads. In: Proceedings of the 8th ACM SIGPLAN Symposium on Haskell, pp. 165–176. ACM Press, New York (2015)

21. Wingate, D., Stuhlmüller, A., Goodman, N.D.: Lightweight implementations of probabilistic programming languages via transformational compilation. In: AIS-TATS, no. 15, pp. 770–778, Revision 3, February 8, 2014. MIT Press, Cambridge (2011)
22. Wood, F., van de Meent, J.W., Mansinghka, V.: A new approach to probabilistic programming inference. In: AISTATS 2014 [1], pp. 1024–1032 (2014)
23. Yang, L., Hanrahan, P., Goodman, N.D.: Generating efficient MCMC kernels from probabilistic programs. In: AISTATS [1], pp. 1068–1076 (2014)
24. Zinkov, R., Shan, C-C.: Probabilistic programming language Hakaru. v1. DARPA PPAML Report (2014)

ELIOM: A Core ML Language for Tierless Web Programming

Gabriel Radanne[1(⊠)], Jérôme Vouillon[2], and Vincent Balat[2]

[1] Univ Paris Diderot, Sorbonne Paris Cité, IRIF UMR 8243 CNRS, Paris, France
gabriel.radanne@pps.univ-paris-diderot.fr
[2] CNRS, IRIF UMR 8243, Univ Paris Diderot, Sorbonne Paris Cité, BeSport,
Paris, France
jerome.vouillon@pps.univ-paris-diderot.fr,
vincent.balat@univ-paris-diderot.fr

Abstract. ELIOM is a dialect of OCAML for Web programming in which
server and client pieces of code can be mixed in the same file using syntactic annotations. This allows to build a whole application as a single
distributed program, in which it is possible to define in a composable way
reusable widgets with both server and client behaviors. Our language also
enables simple and type-safe communication. ELIOM matches the specificities of the Web by allowing the programmer to interleave client and
server code while maintaining efficient one-way server-to-client communication. The ELIOM language is both sufficiently small to be implemented
on top of an existing language and sufficiently powerful to allow expressing many idioms of Web programming.

In this paper, we present a formalization of the core language of
ELIOM. We provide a type system, the execution model and a compilation scheme.

Keywords: Web · Client-server · OCAML · ML · ELIOM · Functional

1 Introduction

Web programming usually relies on the orchestration of numerous languages and
tools. Web pages are written in HTML and styled in CSS. Their dynamic behavior is controlled through client-side languages such as JAVASCRIPT or ACTION-
SCRIPT. These pages are produced by a server which can be written in about
any language: PHP, Ruby, C++ ... They are produced based on information
stored in databases and retrieved using a query language such as SQL.

Programmers must not only master these tools, but also keep synchronized
the numerous software artifacts involved in a Web site and make them communicate properly. The server must be able to interact with the database, then

---

This work was partially performed at IRILL, center for Free Software Research and
Innovation in Paris, France, http://www.irill.org.

A. Igarashi (Ed.): APLAS 2016, LNCS 10017, pp. 377–397, 2016.
DOI: 10.1007/978-3-319-47958-3_20

send the relevant information to the client. In turn, the client must be able to understand the received data, and interact back properly with the server.

These constraints makes Web programming tedious and prone to numerous errors, such as communication errors. This issue, present in the Web since its inception, has become even more relevant in modern Web applications.

Separation of client and server code also hinders composability, as related pieces of code, that build fragments of a Web page and that define the specific behavior of these fragments, typically have to be placed in different files.

1.1   The Need for Tierless Languages

One goal of a modern client-server Web application framework should be to make it possible to build dynamic Web pages in a *composable* way. One should be able to define on the server a function that creates a fragment of a page together with its associated client-side behavior; this behavior might depend on the function parameters. From this point of view, a DSL for writing HTML documents and serialization libraries are two key ingredients to assemble page fragments and communicate between client and server, but are not enough to associate client behaviors to these page fragments in a composable way.

This is where so-called *tierless* languages come into play. Such languages unify the client and server part of the application in one language with seamless communication. For most of these languages, two parts are extracted from a single program: a part runs on the server while the other part is compiled to JAVASCRIPTand runs on the client.

1.2   ELIOM

We present ELIOM, an extension of OCAML for tierless programming that supports composable and typesafe client-server interactions. ELIOM is part of the larger OCSIGEN [4,12] project, which also includes the compiler JS_OF_OCAML[24], a Web server, and various related libraries to build client-server applications. Besides the language presented here, ELIOM comes with a complete set of modules, for server and/or client side Web programming, such as RPCs; a functional reactive library for Web programming; a GUI toolkit [16]; a powerful session mechanism, to manage the server side state of a Web applications on a per-tab, per-browser, or per-user basis; an advanced *service identification mechanism* [2], providing a way to implement traditional Web interaction (well-specified URLs, back button, bookmarks, forms, ...) in few lines of code. The OCSIGEN project started in 2004, as a research project, with the goal of building a complete framework, usable in the industry. OCSIGEN already has several industrial users, most using the ELIOM language we present in this paper: BeSport [5], NYU gencore [13], Pumgrana [19], ...

1.3   A Core Language for Tierless Web Programming

All of the modules and libraries implemented in OCSIGEN, and in particular in the ELIOM framework, are implemented on top of a core language that allows to express all the features needed for tierless web programming.

Composition. ELIOM encourages the building of independent and reusable components that can be assembled easily. It allows to define and manipulate *on the server*, as first class values, fragments of code which will be executed *on the client*. This gives us the ability to build reusable widgets that capture both the server and the client behaviors transparently. It also makes it possible to define libraries and building blocks without explicit support from the language.

Leveraging the type system. ELIOM introduces a novel type system that allows composition and modularity of client-server programs while preserving type-safety and abstraction. This ensures, via the type-system, that client code is not used inside server code (and conversely) and ensures the correctness of client-server communications.

Explicit communication. Communication between the server and the client in ELIOM is always explicit. This allows the programmer to reason about where the program is executed and the resulting trade-offs. The programmers can ensure that some data stay on the client or on the server, or choose how much communication takes place and where computation is performed.

A simple and efficient execution model. ELIOM relies on a novel and efficient execution model for client-server communication that avoids constant back-and-forth communication. This model is simple and predictable. Having a predictable execution model is essential in the context of an impure language, such as ML.

These four properties lead us to define a core language, ELIOM_ε, that features all these characteristics, while being small enough to be reasoned about in a formal way. Having a small core language into which more complex constructs can be reduced has several advantages. First, it is sufficient to trust the core language. All the desirable properties about the core language will also be valid for the higher-level abstractions introduced later.

A minimal core language also makes the implementation on top of an existing language easier. In the case of ELIOM, it allows us to implement our extension on top of the existing OCAML compiler with a reasonably small amount of changes. By extending an existing language, we gain the ability to use numerous preexisting libraries: cooperative multitasking [23], HTMLmanipulation [22] and database interaction [20] are all provided by libraries implemented in pure OCAML that we can leverage for Web programming, both server and client side.

We present the ELIOM language from a programming point of view in Sect. 2. We then specify ELIOM_ε, an extension of core ML featuring the key points of ELIOM, which allows us to describe the type system and the execution model of ELIOM in Sect. 3 and the compilation model in Sects. 4 and 5.

2   How to: Client-Server Web Programming

An ELIOM application is composed of a single program which is decomposed by the compiler into two parts. The first part runs on a Web server, and is able to manage several connections and sessions at the same time, with the possibility of sharing data between sessions, and to keep state for each browser or tab currently running the application. The client program, compiled statically to JAVASCRIPT, is sent to each client by the server program together with the HTMLpage, in response to the initial HTTP request. It persists until the browser tab is closed or until the user follows an external link.

ELIOM is using manual annotations to determine whether a piece of code is to be executed server or client side [1,3]. This choice of explicit annotations is motivated by the fact that we believe that the programmer must be well aware of where the code is executed, to avoid unnecessary remote interactions. This also avoids ambiguities in the semantics and allows for more flexibility.

In this section, we present the language extension that deals with client-server code and the corresponding communication model. Even though ELIOM is based on OCAML, little knowledge of OCAML is required. We explicitly write some type annotations for illustration purposes but they are not mandatory.

2.1   Sections

The location of code execution is specified by *section* annotations. We can specify that a declaration is performed on the server, or on the client:

```
1 let%server s = ...
2 let%client c = ...
```

A third kind of section, written as shared, is used for code executed on both sides. We use the following color convention: client is in yellow, server is in blue and shared is in green.

2.2   Client Fragments

A client-side expression can be included inside a server section: an expression placed inside [%client ...] will be computed on the client when it receives the page; but the eventual client-side value of the expression can be passed around immediately as a black box on the server.

```
1 let%server x : int fragment = [%client 1 + 3 ]
```

For example, here, the expression 1 + 3 will be evaluated on the client, but it's possible to refer server-side to the future value of this expression (for example, put it in a list). The value of a client fragment cannot be accessed on the server.

2.3   Injections

Values that have been computed on the server can be used on the client by prefixing them with the symbol ~%. We call this an *injection*.

```
1  let%server s : int = 1 + 2
2  let%client c : int = ~%s + 1
```

Here, the expression 1 + 2 is evaluated and bound to variable s on the server. The resulting value 3 is transferred to the client together with the Web page. The expression ~%s + 1 is computed client-side.

An injection makes it possible to access client-side a client fragment which has been defined on the server:

```
1  let%server x : int fragment = [%client 1 + 3 ]
2  let%client c : int = 3 + ~%x
```

The value inside the client fragment is extracted by ~%x, whose value is 4 here.

2.4 Examples

We show how these language features can be used in a natural way to build HTML pages with dynamic behavior in a composable fashion. More detailed examples are available on the OCSIGEN website [12].

Increment Button. We can define a button that increments a client-side counter and invokes a callback each time it is clicked. We use a DSL to specify HTML documents. The callback action is a client function. The state is stored in a client-side reference. The onclick button callback is a client function that modifies the references and then calls action. This illustrates that one can define a function that builds on the server a Web page fragment with a client-side state and a parametrized client-side behavior. It would be straightforward to extend this example with a second button that decrements the counter (sharing the associated state).

```
1  let%server counter (action:(int -> unit) fragment) =
2    let state = [%client ref 0 ] in
3    button ~button_type:'Button
4      ~a:[a_onclick [%client fun _ -> incr ~%state; ~%action !(~%state) ]]
5      [pcdata "Increment"]
```

List of Server Side Buttons with Client Side Actions. We can readily embed client fragments inside server datastructures. Having explicit location annotations really helps here. It would not be possible to achieve this for arbitrary datastructures if the client-server delimitations were implicit.

For instance, one can build an HTML unordered list of buttons from a list composed of pairs of button names and their corresponding client-side actions.

```
1  let%server button_list (l : (string * handler fragment) list) =
2    let aux (name, action) =
3      li [button ~button_type:'Button ~a:[a_onclick action] [pcdata name]]
4    in ul (List.map aux l)
```

2.5   Libraries

These examples show how to build reusable widgets that encapsulate both client and server behavior. They also show some of the libraries that are provided with ELIOM. In contrast to many Web programming languages and frameworks, which provides built-in constructions, all these libraries have been implemented only with the primitives presented in this paper. Using fragments and injections along with converters, which are presented later, we can implement numerous libraries such as remote procedure calls, client-server HTML or reactive programming directly inside the language, without any compiler support.

2.6   Client-Server Communication

In the examples above, we showed complex patterns of interleaved client and server code, including passing client fragments to server functions, and subsequently to client code. This would be costly if the communication between client and server were done naively. Instead, a single communication takes place: from the server to the client, when the Web page is sent. This is made possible by the fact that client fragments are not executed immediately when encountered inside server code. The intuitive semantics is the following: client code is not executed right away; instead, it is registered for later execution, once the Web page has been sent to the client. Then all the client code is executed in the order it was encountered on the server. This intuitive semantics allows the programmer to reason about ELIOM programs, especially in the presence of side effects, while still being unaware of the details of the compilation scheme.

3   A Client-Server Language

We present ELIOM$_\varepsilon$, an extension of core ML containing the key features of ELIOM. It differs from ELIOM as follows. Shared sections are not formalized, as they can be straightforwardly expanded out into a client and a server section by duplicating the code. Additionally, we do not model the interactive behavior of Web servers. Thus, ELIOM$_\varepsilon$ programs compute a single Web page.

3.1   Syntax

In order to clearly distinguish server code from client code, we use subscripts to indicate the location where a piece of syntax belongs: a 's' subscript denotes server code, while a 'c' subscript denotes client code. For instance, e_s is a server expression and τ_c is a client type. We also use 'ς' subscripts for expressions which are location-agnostic: they can stand for either s or c. When the location is clear from the context, we omit the subscripts.

The syntax is presented in Fig. 1. It follows the ML syntax, with two additional constructs for client fragments and injections respectively. [26] was used as a base for the elaboration of ELIOM$_\varepsilon$. The language is parametrized by its

$$p ::= \mathbf{let}_s \ x = e_s \ \mathbf{in} \ p \mid \mathbf{let}_c \ x = e_c \ \mathbf{in} \ p \mid e_c \qquad \text{(Programs)}$$
$$e_s ::= c_s \mid x \mid \mathbf{Y} \mid (e_s \ e_s) \mid \lambda x.e_s \mid \{\{ \ e_c \ \}\} \qquad \text{(Expressions)}$$
$$e_c ::= c_c \mid x \mid \mathbf{Y} \mid (e_c \ e_c) \mid \lambda x.e_c \mid f\%e_s$$
$$f ::= x \mid c_s \qquad\qquad\qquad\qquad\qquad\qquad\qquad \text{(Converter)}$$
$$c_s \in Const_s \qquad\qquad\qquad c_c \in Const_c \qquad \text{(Constants)}$$

Fig. 1. ELIOM$_\varepsilon$'s grammar

constants. There are different sets of constants for the server and for the client: $Const_s$ and $Const_c$. A program is a series of bindings, either client or server ones, ending by a *client* expression. The value of this expression will typically be the Web page rendered on the client's browser.

A *client fragment* $\{\{ \ e_c \ \}\}$ stands for an expression computed by the client but that can be referred from the server. An *injection* $f\%e_s$ is used inside client code to access values defined on the server. This involves a serialization on the server followed by a deserialization on the client, which is explicitly specified by a *converter* f. To simplify the semantics, we syntactically restrict converters to be either a variable x or a server constant c_c. We describe converters more precisely in Sect. 3.2.

Furthermore, we add a validity constraints to our programs: We only consider programs such that variables used under an injection are declared outside of the local client scope, which can be either a client declaration or a client fragment.

3.2   Type System

The type system of ELIOM$_\varepsilon$ is an extension of the regular ML type system. We follow closely [26]. Again, the language is split into a client and a server part.

$$\sigma_\varsigma ::= \forall \alpha^*.\tau_\varsigma \qquad\qquad\qquad\qquad \text{(TypeSchemes)}$$
$$\tau_s ::= \alpha \mid \tau_s \rightarrow \tau_s \mid \{\tau_c\} \mid \tau_s \rightsquigarrow \tau_c \mid \kappa \ \text{for} \ \kappa \in ConstType_s$$
$$\tau_c ::= \alpha \mid \tau_c \rightarrow \tau_c \mid \kappa \ \text{for} \ \kappa \in ConstType_c \qquad \text{(Types)}$$

$ConstType_\varsigma$ is the set of ground types. Two server-side types are added to core ML types: $\{\tau_c\}$ is the type of a client fragment whose content is of type τ_c and $\tau_s \rightsquigarrow \tau_c$ is the type of converters from server type τ_s to client type τ_c. This last type is described in more details below. No client-side constructions are added to core ML types: in particular, the type of a client expression can never contain the type of a client fragment $\{\tau_c\}$.

The typing rules are presented in Fig. 2. There are three distinct judgments: $\blacktriangleright$ is the typing judgment for programs, $\triangleright_c$ for client expressions and $\triangleright_s$ for server expressions. $\triangleright_\varsigma$ is used for rules that are valid both on client and server expressions. An environment Γ contains two kinds of bindings: client and server bindings, marked with the subscripts s and c respectively. The instantiation relation is noted by $\sigma \succ \tau$. It means that the type τ is an instance of the type scheme σ. $Close(\tau, \Gamma)$ is the function that closes a type τ over the environment Γ, hence producing a scheme. $TypeOf_\varsigma$ is a map from constants to their types. Most rules are straightforwardly adapted from regular ML rules. The main rules of interest are FRAGMENT and INJECTION: Rule FRAGMENT is for the construction of client fragments. If e_c is of type τ_c in context Γ, then $\{\{\ e_c\ \}\}$ is of type $\{\tau_c\}$ in the same context. Rule INJECTION is for the communication of server to client. If the server expression e_s is of type τ_s and the converter f is of type $\tau_s \rightsquigarrow \tau_c$, we can use, in a client declaration, the expression $f\%e_s$ with type τ_c. Since no other typing rules involves client fragments, it is impossible to deconstruct them.

Converters. To transmit values from the server to the client, we need a serialization format. We assume the existence of a type `serial` in both $ConstType_s$ and $ConstType_c$, which represents the serialization format. The actual format is irrelevant. For instance, one could use JSON or XML.

Converters are special values that describe how to move a value from the server to the client. A converter can be understood as a pair of functions. A converter f of type $\tau_s \rightsquigarrow \tau_c$ is composed of a server-side encoding function of type $\tau_s \rightarrow$ `serial`, and a client-side decoding function of type `serial` $\rightarrow \tau_c$. We assume the existence of two built-in converters:

- The `serial` converter of type `serial` $\rightsquigarrow$ `serial`. Both sides are the identity.
- The `fragment` converter of type $\forall \alpha.(\{\alpha\} \rightsquigarrow \alpha)$. Note that this type scheme can only be instantiated with client types.

Type Universes. It is important to note that there is no identity converter (of type $\forall \alpha.(\alpha \rightsquigarrow \alpha)$). Indeed the client and server type universes are distinct and we cannot translate arbitrary types from one to the other. Some types are only available on one side: database handles, system types, JAVASCRIPTAPI types. Some types, while available on both sides, are simply not transferable. For example, functions cannot be serialized.Finally, some types may share a semantic meaning, but not their actual representation. This is the case where converters are used. For example, integers are often 64-bit on the server and are 32-bit in JAVASCRIPT. So, there is an int_s and an int_c type, along with a converter of type $int_s \rightsquigarrow int_c$. Another example is an HTTPendpoint. On the server, it is a URL together with a function called when the endpoint is reached. On the client, it is only the URL of the specified endpoint. These two types are distinct but share the same semantic meaning, and a converter relates them.

Implementation of Converters. Specifying which converter to use for which injection is quite tedious in practice. The current implementation of ELIOM uses runtime information to discover which converter to apply. A better implementation would use ad-hoc polymorphism, such as modular implicits [25] or type classes, to define converters.

Common rules

$$\text{VAR} \quad \frac{(x : \sigma)_\varsigma \in \Gamma \qquad \sigma \succ \tau}{\Gamma \triangleright_\varsigma x : \tau}$$

$$\text{LAM} \quad \frac{\Gamma, (x : \tau_1)_\varsigma \triangleright_\varsigma e : \tau_2}{\Gamma \triangleright_\varsigma \lambda x.e : \tau_1 \to \tau_2}$$

$$\text{CONST} \quad \frac{TypeOf_\varsigma(c) \succ \tau}{\Gamma \triangleright_\varsigma c : \tau}$$

$$\text{APP} \quad \frac{\Gamma \triangleright_\varsigma e_1 : \tau_1 \to \tau_2 \qquad \Gamma \triangleright_\varsigma e_2 : \tau_1}{\Gamma \triangleright_\varsigma (e_1 \ e_2) : \tau_2}$$

$$\text{LET} \quad \frac{\Gamma \triangleright_\varsigma e_1 : \tau_1 \qquad \Gamma, (x : Close(\tau_1, \Gamma))_\varsigma \triangleright_\varsigma e_2 : \tau_2}{\Gamma \triangleright_\varsigma \text{let } x = e_1 \text{ in } e_2 : \tau_2}$$

$$\text{Y} \quad \frac{}{\Gamma \triangleright_\varsigma \text{Y} : ((\tau_1 \to \tau_2) \to \tau_1 \to \tau_2) \to \tau_1 \to \tau_2}$$

Server rules

$$\text{FRAGMENT} \quad \frac{\Gamma \triangleright_c e_c : \tau_c}{\Gamma \triangleright_s \{\{ e_c \}\} : \{\tau_c\}}$$

Client rules

$$\text{INJECTION} \quad \frac{\Gamma \triangleright_s f : \tau_s \rightsquigarrow \tau_c \qquad \Gamma \triangleright_s e_s : \tau_s}{\Gamma \triangleright_c f\%e_s : \tau_c}$$

ELIOM$_\varepsilon$'s rules

$$\text{PROG} \quad \frac{\Gamma \triangleright_\varsigma e : \tau_1 \qquad \Gamma, (x : Close(\tau_1, \Gamma))_\varsigma \blacktriangleright p : \tau_2}{\Gamma \blacktriangleright \text{let}_\varsigma x = e \text{ in } p : \tau_2}$$

$$\text{RETURN} \quad \frac{\Gamma \triangleright_c e_c : \tau_c}{\Gamma \blacktriangleright e_c : \tau_c}$$

$$Close(\tau, \Gamma) = \forall \alpha_0 \dots \alpha_n.\tau \text{ where } \{\alpha_0, \dots, \alpha_n\} = FreeTypeVar(\tau) \backslash FreeTypeVar(\Gamma)$$

Fig. 2. Typing rules for ELIOM$_\varepsilon$

3.3 The Semantics

We now define an operational semantics for ELIOM$_\varepsilon$. The goal of this semantics is to provide a good model of how programs behave. It does not model finer details of the execution like network communication. However, the order of execution is the one a programmer using ELIOM should expect. Before defining the semantics, let us provide preliminary definitions. Values are defined in Fig. 3. For the evaluation of constants, we assume the existence of two *partial* functions, δ_c and δ_s that interpret the application of a constant to a closed value in order to yield another closed value: $\delta_\varsigma(c_\varsigma, v_\varsigma) = v'_\varsigma$

A queue ξ accumulates the expressions that will have to be evaluated client-side. It contains bindings $[\mathbf{r} \mapsto e_c]$, where $\mathbf{r}$ is a variable. We adopt the convention that bold letters, like $\mathbf{r}$, denote a variable bound to a client expression. The queue is a first-in, first-out data structure. We note $\mathbin{+\!\!+}$ the concatenation on queues. Substitute of a variable by a value in an expression or a program is noted $e[v/x]$.

ELIOM$_\varepsilon$ is eager and call by value. Evaluation contexts are shown in Fig. 3. Injections are rewritten inside client expressions. The location where this can take place is specified by context $C[e_c]$ below. We write $e_c^\star$ for a client expression containing no injection. Thus, we are forcing a left to right evaluation inside client fragments. The evaluation context for expressions $E_\varsigma[e_\varsigma]$ is standard, except that, we also evaluate server expressions in injections $f\%e_s$ inside client code. Program contexts $F[e_\varsigma]$ specifies that the evaluation can take place either in a server declaration or in server code deep inside injections.

$$v_\varsigma ::= c_\varsigma \mid x \mid \mathsf{Y} \mid \lambda x.e_\varsigma \qquad\qquad\qquad\qquad\qquad \text{(Values)}$$

$$F ::= \mathtt{let}_s\ x = E_s\ \mathtt{in}\ p \mid \mathtt{let}_c\ x = C[f\%E_s]\ \mathtt{in}\ p \qquad\qquad \text{(Program contexts)}$$
$$E_\varsigma ::= [\,]\mid (E_\varsigma\ e_\varsigma) \mid (v_\varsigma\ E_\varsigma) \mid \mathtt{let}\ x = E_\varsigma\ \mathtt{in}\ e_\varsigma \mid \{\!\{\ C[f\%E_\varsigma]\ \}\!\} \quad \text{(Expression ctx.)}$$
$$C ::= [\,] \mid (C\ e_c) \mid (e_c^\star\ C) \mid \lambda x.C \mid \mathtt{let}\ x = C\ \mathtt{in}\ e_c \mid \mathtt{let}\ x = e_c^\star\ \mathtt{in}\ C \text{ (Client ctx.)}$$

Fig. 3. ELIOM$_\varepsilon$'s values and evaluation contexts

The semantics is shown in Fig. 4. We define three single-step reduction relations: two relations $\to$ on expressions indexed by the expression location ς, and the relation $\hookrightarrow$ on programs (or, more precisely on pairs of a program and an environment of execution ξ). We write $\to^*$ and $\hookrightarrow^*$ for the transitive closures of these relations.

Server declarations are executed immediately (rules LET$_s$ and CONTEXT). However client declarations are not. Instead the corresponding expressions are stored in the queue ξ in the order of the program (rule LET$_c$). When encountering a client fragment $\{\!\{\ e_c\ \}\!\}$, the expression e_c is not executed at once. Instead, $\{\!\{\ e_c\ \}\!\}$ is replaced by a fresh variable $\mathbf{r}$ and e_c is stored in ξ (rule CLIENT-FRAGMENT$_s$). When a converter is called inside client code, the encoding part of the converter is executed immediately, while the decoded part is transmitted to the client (rules CONVERTER$_s$ and CONVERTER$_c$, followed by CONTEXT$_\varsigma$). The primitive encode returns the server side encoding function of a converter; the primitive decode returns a reference to a client fragment implementing the client side decoding function of a converter. The **serial** and **fragment** converters are basically the identity, so they are erased once the value to be transferred has been computed (rules SERIAL$_s$ and SERIAL$_c$).

Once all the server declarations have been executed, the expressions in ξ are executed in the same order they were encountered prior in the evaluation (rules EXEC, CONTEXT and BIND). This means that the execution of an ELIOM$_\varepsilon$ program can be split into two phases: server-side execution, then client-side execution. Even though server and client declarations are interleaved in the program, their executions are not. During the first half of the execution, ξ grows as fragments and client code are stored. During the second half of the execution, ξ shrink until it is empty.

This semantics is not equivalent to immediately executing every piece of client code when encountered: the order of execution would be different. The separation of code execution in two stages, the server stage first and the client stage later, allows to properly model common web pattern and to minimize client-server communications. Since execution of stages are clearly separated,

Common semantics

$$\frac{\text{APP}}{(\lambda x.e_\varsigma)\ v_\varsigma\mid \xi \rightarrow e_\varsigma[v_\varsigma/x]\mid \xi}$$

$$\frac{\text{Y}}{\text{Y}\ v_\varsigma\mid \xi \rightarrow v_\varsigma\ (\lambda x.(\text{Y}\ v_\varsigma)\ x)\mid \xi}$$

$$\frac{\text{LET}}{\text{let}\ x = v_\varsigma\ \text{in}\ e_\varsigma\mid \xi \rightarrow e_\varsigma[v_\varsigma/x]\mid \xi}$$

$$\frac{\text{DELTA}\quad \delta_\varsigma(c_\varsigma, v_\varsigma)\ \text{is defined}}{(c_\varsigma\ v_\varsigma)\mid \xi \rightarrow \delta_\varsigma(c_\varsigma, v_\varsigma)\mid \xi}$$

Server semantics

$$\frac{\text{CONVERTER}_s\qquad f \notin \{\text{serial}, \text{fragment}\}}{\{\!\{\ C[f\%e_s]\ \}\!\}\mid \xi \xrightarrow{s} \{\!\{\ C[\text{fragment}\%(\text{decode}\ f)\ \text{serial}\%((\text{encode}\ f)\ e_s)]\ \}\!\}\mid \xi}$$

$$\frac{\text{SERIAL}_s\quad f \in \{\text{serial}, \text{fragment}\}}{\{\!\{\ C[f\%v]\ \}\!\}\mid \xi \xrightarrow{s} \{\!\{\ C[v]\ \}\!\}\mid \xi}$$

$$\frac{\text{CLIENTFRAGMENT}_s\quad \mathbf{r}\ \text{fresh}}{\{\!\{\ e_c^\star\ \}\!\}\mid \xi \xrightarrow{s} \mathbf{r}\mid \xi +\!\!+ [\mathbf{r} \mapsto e_c^\star]}$$

ELIOM$_\varepsilon$'s semantics

$$\frac{\text{CONTEXT}_\varsigma\quad e_\varsigma\mid \xi \xrightarrow{\varsigma} e_\varsigma'\mid \xi'}{F[e_\varsigma]\mid \xi \hookrightarrow F[e_\varsigma']\mid \xi'}$$

$$\frac{\text{FINAL}_c\quad e\mid \emptyset \xrightarrow{c} e'\mid \emptyset}{E_c[e]\mid \emptyset \hookrightarrow E_c[e']\mid \emptyset}$$

$$\frac{\text{EXECVAL}}{e\mid [\mathbf{r} \mapsto v_c] +\!\!+ \xi \hookrightarrow e[v_c/\mathbf{r}]\mid \xi[v_c/\mathbf{r}]}$$

$$\frac{\text{CONVERTER}_c\qquad f \notin \{\text{serial}, \text{fragment}\}}{\begin{array}{l}\text{let}_c\ x = C[f\%e_s]\ \text{in}\ p\mid \xi \hookrightarrow \\ \text{let}_c\ x = C[\text{fragment}\%(\text{decode}\ f)\ \text{serial}\%((\text{encode}\ f)\ e_s)]\ \text{in}\ p\mid \xi\end{array}}$$

$$\frac{\text{SERIAL}_c\quad f \in \{\text{serial}, \text{fragment}\}}{\text{let}_c\ x = C[f\%v]\ \text{in}\ p\mid \xi \hookrightarrow \text{let}_c\ x = C[v]\ \text{in}\ p\mid \xi}$$

$$\frac{\text{LET}_s}{\text{let}_s\ x = v\ \text{in}\ p\mid \xi \hookrightarrow p[v/x]\mid \xi}$$

$$\frac{\text{LET}_c}{\text{let}_c\ x = e_c^\star\ \text{in}\ p\mid \xi \hookrightarrow p\mid \xi +\!\!+ [x \mapsto e_c^\star]}$$

$$\frac{\text{EXEC}\quad e_c\mid \emptyset \xrightarrow{c} e_c'\mid \emptyset}{e\mid [\mathbf{r} \mapsto e_c] +\!\!+ \xi \hookrightarrow e\mid [\mathbf{r} \mapsto e_c'] +\!\!+ \xi}$$

Fig. 4. ELIOM$_\varepsilon$'s operational semantics

only one communication is needed, between the two stage execution. We will see this in more details in the next two sections.

4   Compilation to Client and Server Languages

In a more realistic computation model, different programs are executed on the server and on the client. We thus present a compilation process that separates the server and client parts of ELIOM programs, resulting in purely server-side and client-side programs. We express the output of the compiler in an ML-like language with some specific primitives for both sides. The further compilation of these ML-like languages to machine code for the server, and to JAVASCRIPTfor the client [24] is out of the scope of this paper.

4.1   The Languages

We define ML_s and ML_c, two ML languages extended with specific primitives for client-server communication.

$$
\begin{aligned}
p{::} &= \textbf{let } x = e \textbf{ in } p \mid \textbf{bind } x = e \textbf{ in } p \mid e && \text{(Programs)}\\
e{::} &= v \mid (e\ e) \mid \textbf{let } x = e \textbf{ in } e && \text{(Expressions)}\\
v{::} &= c \mid x \mid \mathbf{Y} \mid \lambda x.e && \text{(Values)}\\
c &\in \textit{Const} && \text{(Constants)}
\end{aligned}
$$

Again, the language is parametrized by a set of constants. We assume a constant () of type **unit**. As previously, we write **r** for a variable referring to a client expression, when we want to emphasize this fact for clarity. The language also contains a **bind** construction. Like a **let** binding, it binds the value of an expression e to a variable x in a program p. However, the variable x is not lexically scoped: you should see it as a global name, that can be shared between the client and the server code.

Primitives. A number of primitives are used to pass information from the server to the client. We use globally scoped variables for communication. In an actual implementation, unique identifiers would be used. We use various meta-variables to make the purpose of these global variables clearer. **x** is a variable that references an injection, **f** references a closure. The server language ML_s provides these primitives:

- "injection **x** e" registers that **x** corresponds to the injection e.
- "fragment **f** $\bar{e}$" registers a client fragment to be executed on the client; the code is expected to be bound to **f** on the clients and the injections values are given by the vector of expressions $\bar{e}$.
- "end ()" signals the end of a server declaration, and hence that there will be no more client fragments from this declaration to execute.

The primitive "exec ()" of the client language ML_cexecutes the client fragments encountered during the evaluation of the last server declaration.

The primitive end () and exec () are used to correctly interleave the evaluation of client fragments (coming from server declarations) and client declarations, since server declarations are not present on the client.

$$E ::= [\,] \mid (E\ e) \mid (v\ E) \mid \texttt{let } x = E \texttt{ in } e \qquad \text{(Evaluation contexts)}$$

Fig. 5. ML_ε's evaluation contexts

4.2   The Semantics

The semantics of ML_ε uses similar tools as the semantics of ELIOM_ε. The rules for ML_s and ML_c are presented in Fig. 6. The rules that are common with ELIOM_ε are omitted. A FIFO queue ξ_c records the client fragments to be executed: it contains bindings $[\mathbf{r} \mapsto e]$ as well as a specific token end that signals the end of a server-side declaration.

Injections are recorded server-side in an environment γ_{inj} which contains a mapping from the injection reference $\mathbf{x}$ to either a reference $\mathbf{r}$ to the corresponding client fragment or a value of type $\texttt{serial}$. Evaluation contexts are shown in Fig. 5.

The semantics for ML_s is given in Fig. 6. It possesses two specific rules, INJECTION_s and CLIENTFRAGMENT_s which queue injections and client fragments inside respectively γ_{inj} and ξ_c. The rule CLIENTFRAGMENT_s generates a fresh reference $\mathbf{r}$ for each client fragment that will eventually be bound client-side to a value by the EXECVAL_c rule.

At the end of the execution of the server program, ξ_c only contains bindings of the shape $[\mathbf{r} \mapsto (\mathbf{f}\ \overline{v})]$. We then transmit the client program and the content of γ_{inj} and ξ_c to the client. Before client execution, we substitute once and for all the injections by their values provided by γ_{inj}: $p'_c = p_c[\gamma_{\text{inj}}]$. We can then execute the client program p'_c.

The execution of client fragments is segmented by server-side declaration, materialized client-side by a call to $\texttt{exec}$. Each client fragment coming from the evaluation of the related server declaration is executed in turn through the rules EXEC_c, EXECVAL_c and BIND. Once no more client fragments coming from this declaration is found in ξ_c, rule EXECEND_c is applied.

4.3   From ELIOM_ε to ML_ε

Before introducing the exact semantics of these primitives, we specify how ELIOM_ε is translated using these primitives, which will make their behavior clearer. A key point is that we adopt a distinct compilation strategy for client declarations and for client fragments. Indeed, client declarations are much simpler than client fragments, as they are executed only once and immediately. Their code can be used directly in the client, instead of relying on a sophisticated mechanism.

The rewriting function ρ from ELIOM_ε to ML_ε can be split into two functions ρ_s and ρ_c, respectively for server and client code. For each case, we first decompose injections $f\%e_s$ into an equivalent expression:

$$\texttt{fragment}\%(\texttt{decode } f)\ \texttt{serial}\%(\texttt{encode } f\ e_s)$$

Server semantics

CLIENTFRAGMENT$_s$

$$\frac{\mathbf{r}\ \text{fresh} \qquad \xi'_c = \xi_c \mathbin{+\!\!+} [\mathbf{r} \mapsto (\mathbf{f}\ \bar{v})]}{\texttt{fragment}\ \mathbf{f}\ \bar{v} \mid \xi_c, \gamma_{\text{inj}} \xrightarrow[s]{} \mathbf{r} \mid \xi'_c, \gamma_{\text{inj}}}$$

INJECTION$_s$

$$\frac{\gamma'_{\text{inj}} = \gamma_{\text{inj}} \cup [\mathbf{x} \mapsto v]}{\texttt{injection}\ \mathbf{x}\ v; p \mid \xi_c, \gamma_{\text{inj}} \xrightarrow[s]{} p \mid \xi_c, \gamma'_{\text{inj}}}$$

END

$$\frac{\xi'_c = \xi_c \mathbin{+\!\!+} \texttt{end}}{\texttt{end}\ (); p \mid \xi_c, \gamma_{\text{inj}} \xrightarrow[s]{} p \mid \xi'_c, \gamma_{\text{inj}}}$$

Client semantics

EXEC$_c$

$$\frac{e \to e'}{\texttt{exec}\ (); p \mid [\mathbf{r} \mapsto e] \mathbin{+\!\!+} \xi \xrightarrow[c]{} \texttt{exec}\ (); p \mid [\mathbf{r} \mapsto e'] \mathbin{+\!\!+} \xi}$$

EXECEND$_c$

$$\frac{}{\texttt{exec}\ (); p \mid \texttt{end} \mathbin{+\!\!+} \xi_c \xrightarrow[c]{} p \mid \xi_c}$$

EXECVAL$_c$

$$\frac{}{\texttt{exec}\ (); p \mid [\mathbf{r} \mapsto v_c] \mathbin{+\!\!+} \xi \xrightarrow[c]{} p[v_c/\mathbf{r}] \mid \xi[v_c/\mathbf{r}]}$$

BIND

$$\frac{}{\texttt{bind}\ \mathbf{f} = v\ \texttt{in}\ p \mid \xi_c \xrightarrow[c]{} p[v/\mathbf{f}] \mid \xi_c[v/\mathbf{f}]}$$

Fig. 6. Semantics for ML$_s$ and ML$_c$

Translating client declarations is done by taking the following steps:

- For each injection `fragment%`e_s or `serial%`e_s, we generate a fresh name $\mathbf{x}$.
- In ML$_s$, the primitive "`injection x` e_s" is called for each injection; it signals that the value of x should be transmitted to the client.
- In ML$_c$, we replace each injection `fragment%`e_s or `serial%`e_s by $\mathbf{x}$.

An example is presented Fig. 7. On the server, the return value of the program is always () since the server program never returns anything. The client program returns the same value as the ELIOM$_\varepsilon$ one. The reference to the client fragment implementing the decoder is associated to variable **conv_int**, to be transmitted and used by the client to decode the value.

ELIOM$_\varepsilon$	ML$_S$	ML$_C$
let$_s$ $x = 1$ in	let $x = 1$ in	let $y =$
let$_c$ $y = \texttt{int}\%x + 1$ in	injection **conv_int** (decode int);	(**conv_int** x) $+ 1$
y	injection **x** ((encode int) x)	in y

Fig. 7. Example: Compilation of injections

Translating server declarations containing client fragments is a bit more involved. We need to take care of executing client fragments on the client.

- For each client fragment {{ e }} containing the injections $f_i\%e_i$, we create a fresh reference **f**.
  - In ML_c, we bind **f** to "$\lambda x_0, x_1, \ldots .(e')$" where e' is the expression where each injection fragment$\%e_i$ or serial$\%e_i$ has been replaced by x_i.
  - In ML_s, we replace the original client fragment by "fragment **f** $[e_0, \ldots]$" which encode the injected values and registers that the closure **f** should be executed on the client.
- In ML_s, we call "end ()" which signals the end of a declaration by sending the end token on the queue.
- In ML_c, we call "exec ()" which executes all the client fragments, until the end token is reached.

An example is presented in Fig. 8. You can see that the computation is prepared on the client (by binding a closure), scheduled by the server (by the fragment primitive) and then executed on the client (thanks to primitive exec). Also note that client fragments without any injection are bound to a closure with a unit argument, in order to preserve side effect order.

A more detailed presentation of the translation rules are given in Appendix A.

$\mathrm{ELIOM}_\varepsilon$	ML_s	ML_c
let$_s$ $x = \{\{ 1 \}\}$ in	let $x =$ fragment f_0 [ ] in	bind $f_0 = \lambda().1$ in
	end ();	exec ();
let$_s$ $y = \{\{$ fragment$\%x + 1 \}\}$ in	let $y =$ fragment f_1 $[x]$ in	bind $f_1 = \lambda x.(x + 1)$ in
	end ();	exec ();
$\ldots$	$\ldots$	$\ldots$

Fig. 8. Example: Compilation of client fragments

5   Relating $\mathrm{ELIOM}_\varepsilon$ and ML_ε

We need to guarantee that the translation from $\mathrm{ELIOM}_\varepsilon$ to the two languages two languages, ML_s and ML_c is faithful.

Since $\mathrm{ELIOM}_\varepsilon$ is parametrized by its constants, the functions δ, *Const* and *TypeOf* must satisfy a typability condition for the language to be sound.

Hypothesis 1 (δ-typability). *For ς in $\{c, s\}$, if $TypeOf_\varsigma(c) \succ \tau' \to \tau$ and $\rhd_\varsigma v : \tau'$ then $\delta_\varsigma(c, v)$ is defined and $\rhd_\varsigma \delta_\varsigma(c, v) : \tau$*

We extend the typing relation to account for the execution queue ξ. The judgment $\xi \vDash p : \tau$ states that, given the execution queue ξ, the program p has type τ. We also introduce an judgment $\Gamma \blacktriangleright \xi : \Gamma'$ to type execution queues, where the environment Γ' extends Γ with the types of the bindings in ξ. We introduce the following typing rules.

$$\text{QUEUE} \quad \frac{\emptyset \blacktriangleright \xi : \Gamma \qquad \Gamma \blacktriangleright p : \tau}{\xi \models p : \tau} \qquad \text{EMPTY} \quad \frac{}{\Gamma \blacktriangleright \emptyset : \Gamma} \qquad \text{APPEND} \quad \frac{\Gamma \rhd_c e : \tau \qquad \Gamma, (\mathbf{r} : \{\tau\})_s, (\mathbf{r} : \tau)_c \blacktriangleright \xi : \Gamma'}{\Gamma \blacktriangleright [\mathbf{r} \mapsto e] + \xi : \Gamma'}$$

The rule QUEUE tells us that if we can type a queue, producing an environment Γ, and we can type a program p in this environment, then we can type the pair of the queue and the program. This allows us to type a program during its evaluation, and in particular when the queue is no longer empty since the rule CLIENTVALUE has been applied.

Assuming the δ-typability hypothesis, we can now give the following two theorem. This guarantees that the semantics of ELIOM$_\varepsilon$ can be used to reason about side effects and evaluation behaviors in compiled ELIOM$_\varepsilon$ programs.

Theorem 1 (Subject Reduction). *If $\xi_1 \models p_1 : \tau$ and $p_1 \mid \xi_1 \hookrightarrow p_2 \mid \xi_2$ then $\xi_2 \models p_2 : \tau$.*

Theorem 2 (Simulation). *Let p be an ELIOM$_\varepsilon$ program with an execution $p \mid \emptyset \hookrightarrow^* v \mid \emptyset$ For an execution of p that terminates, we can exhibit a chained execution of $\rho_s(p)$ and $\rho_c(p)$ such that evaluation is synchronized with p.*

6   Related Work

Unified Client-Server Languages. Various directions have been explored to simplify Web development and to adapt it to current needs. ELIOM places itself in one of these directions, which is to use the same language on the server and the client. Several unified client-server languages have been proposed. They can be split in two categories. JAVASCRIPT can be used on the server, with NODE.JS; it can be used as a compilation target: for instance, GOOGLE WEB TOOLKIT for Java or EMSCRIPTEN for C.

The approach of compiling to JAVASCRIPT was also used to develop new client languages aiming to address the shortcomings of JAVASCRIPT. Some of them are new languages, such as HAXE, ELM or DART. Others are simple JAVASCRIPT extensions, such as TYPESCRIPT or COFFEESCRIPT. These various proposals do not help in solving client-server communication issues: the programmer still writes the client and server code separately and must ensure that messages are written and read in a coherent way.

Tierless Languages and Libraries. Several other languages share with ELIOM the characteristic of mixing client and server code in an almost transparent way. We will first give a high-level comparison of the various trade-offs involved.

In ELIOM, code location is indicated by manual annotations. Several other approaches infer code location using known elements (database access is on the server, dynamic DOM interaction is done on the client, etc.) and control flow analysis [9,17,18]. This approach presents various difficulties and drawbacks: It is extremely difficult to integrate to an existing language; it is difficult to achieve with an effectful language; the slicing cannot be as precise as explicit annotations. For example it will not work if the program builds datastructures that mix client fragments and other data, as shown in Sect. 2.4. We believe that the efficiency of a complex Web application relies a lot on the programmer's ability to know exactly where the computation is going to happen at each point in time. In many cases, both choices are possible, but the result is very different from a user or a security point of view.

ELIOM has two type universes for client and server types (see Sect. 3.2). This allows the type system to check which functions and types are usable on which side. Most other systems do not track such properties at the type level.

ELIOM uses asymmetric communication between client and server (see Sect. 3.3). Most other languages provide only two-way communications. The actual implementation of ELIOM also provides two-way communications as a library, allowing the user to use them when appropriate.

We now provide an in-depth comparison with the most relevant approaches.

UR/WEB [7,8] is a new statically typed language special purposed for Web programming. While similar in scope to ELIOM, it presents a very different approach: UR/WEBuses whole-program compilation and a global automatic slicing to separate client and server code. This makes some examples hard to express, such as the one in Sect. 2.4. Client and server locations are not tracked by the type system and are not immediately visible in the source code, which can make compiler errors hard to understand, and is incompatible with separate compilation. Furthermore and contrary to ELIOM, several primitives such as RPC are hardcoded in the language.

HOP [6,21] is a dialect of Scheme for programming Web applications. Like ELIOM it uses explicit location annotations and provide facilities to write complex client-server applications. However, as a Scheme-based language, it does not provide static typing. In particular, contrary to ELIOM, HOPdoes not enforce statically the separation of client and server universes (such as using database code inside the client).

LINKS [10] is an experimental functional language for client-server Web programming with a syntax close to JAVASCRIPTand an ML-like type system. Its type system is extended with a notion of *effects*, allowing a clean integration of database queries in the language. It does not provide any mechanisms to separate client and server code, so they are shared by default, but uses effects to avoid erroneous uses of client code in server contexts (and conversely). Compared to ELIOM, compilation is not completely available and LINKSdoes not provide an efficient communication mechanism.

HASTE [11] is an extension of HASKELL similar to ELIOM. Instead of using syntactic annotations, it embeds client and server code into monads. This approach works well in the HASKELL ecosystem. However HASTE makes the strong assumption that there exists a universe containing both client and server types, shared by the client and the server. ELIOM, on the contrary, does not make this assumption, so the monadic `bind` operator for client fragments, of type `( 'a -> { 'b })-> { 'a } -> { 'b }`, makes no sense: `'a` would be a type both in the server and the client, which is not generally true.

METEOR.JS [15] is a framework to write both the client and the serve side of an application in JAVASCRIPT. It has no built-in mechanism for sections and fragments but relies on `if` statements on the `Meteor.isClient` and `Meteor.isServer` constants. This means that there are no static guarantees over the respective execution of server and client code. Besides, it provides no facilities for client-server communication such as fragments and injections. Compared to ELIOM, this solution only provides coarse grain composition.

METAOCAML [14] is an extension of OCAML for meta programming, it introduces a quotation annotation for staged expressions for which execution will be delayed. While having a different goal, stage quotations are very similar to ELIOM's client fragments. The main difference is the choice of universes: ELIOM possesses two universes, client and server, that are distinct. METAOCAML possesses a series of universes for each stage, included in one another.

7   Conclusion

We have presented a formalization of the core language ELIOM_ε, a client-server Web application programming language. First, we have given a formal semantics and a type system for a language that contains the key features of ELIOM. This semantics is intuitive and easy to understand. It corresponds to what a programmer needs to know. Then, we have defined a lower level semantics, corresponding to how ELIOM is compiled. We then showed how this compilation is done and that it preserves the semantics.

ELIOM_ε is used as a core language for the larger ELIOM framework and the OCSIGEN ecosystem. ELIOM_ε is sufficiently small to be reasoned about and implemented on top of an existing language, such as OCaml. It is also expressive enough to allow the implementation, without any additional language built-in constructs, to all kinds of widgets and libraries used for Web programming.

The implementation of ELIOM as an extension of an existing language makes it possible to reuse a large set of existing libraries and benefit from an already large community of users. Web programming is never about the Web per se, but almost always related to other fields for which dedicated libraries are necessary.

Explicit annotations indicate at which location the program execution takes place. Adding them is really easy for programmers and is a good way to help them see exactly where computation is going to happen, which is crucial when developing real-size applications. ELIOM makes it impossible to introduce by mistake unwanted communication.

ELIOM makes strong use of static typing to guarantee many properties of the program at compile time. Developing both the client and server parts as a single program allows to guarantee the consistency between the two parts, to check all communications: injections, server push, remote procedure calls, ...

These design choices have always been guided by concrete uses. From the beginning, OCSIGEN has been used for developing real-scale applications. The experience of users has shown that the use of a tierless language is more than a viable alternative to the traditional Web development techniques, and is well suited to the current evolution of the Web into an application platform. The fluidity gained by using a tierless programming style with static typing matches the need of a new style of applications, combining both the advantages of sophisticated user interfaces and the specificities of Web sites (connectivity, traditional Web interaction, with URLs, back button, ...). This is made even more convenient through the use of features such as an advanced service identification model and the integration of reactive functional programming that are provided by ELIOM but have not been covered here.

A   Translation from ELIOM_ε to ML_ε

We define two rewriting functions, ρ_s and ρ_c, which take as input an ELIOM_ε program and output respectively an ML_s and an ML_c program.

We define some preliminaries notations. Brackets [and] are used as meta-syntactic markers for repeated expressions: $[\ldots]_i$ is repeated for all i. The bounds are usually omitted. Lists are denoted with an overline: $\overline{x_i}$ is the list $[x_0, \ldots, x_{n-1}]$. We allow the use of lists inside substitutions to denote simultaneous independent substitutions. For instance $e[\overline{v_i}/\overline{x_i}]$ is equivalent to $e[v_0/x_0] \ldots [v_{n-1}/x_{n-1}]$. We will only consider substitutions where the order is irrelevant.

We also consider two new operations:

– $injections(e_c)$ returns the list of injections in e_c.
– $fragments(e_s)$ returns the list of fragments in e_s.

The order corresponds to the order of execution for our common subset of ML.

As in Sect. 4.3, we assume that fragments are first rewritten in the following manner:

$$f\%e_s \longrightarrow \texttt{fragment}\%(\texttt{decode } f) \ \texttt{serial}\%(\texttt{encode } f \ e_s)$$

We also assume that expressions inside injections are hoisted out of the local client scope. For example $\{\{\ f\%(3{+}x)\ \}\}$ is transformed to $\lambda y.\{\{\ f\%y\ \}\}\ (3{+}x)$. More formally, we apply the following transformations:

$$\{\{\ C[f\%e_s]\ \}\} \longrightarrow (\lambda x.C[f\%x])\ e_s$$
$$\texttt{let}_c\ y = C[f\%e_s] \text{ in } p \longrightarrow \texttt{let}_s\ x = e_s \text{ in } \texttt{let}_c\ y = C[f\%x] \text{ in } p$$
$$\text{Where } x \text{ is fresh.}$$

This transformation preserves the semantics, thanks to the validity constraint on programs presented in Sect. 3.1.

We can now define ρ_s and ρ_c by induction over ELIOM_ε programs. We refer to Sect. 4.3 for a textual explanation.

Since we already translated custom converters, all the converters considered are either `fragment` or `serial`. Here is the definition for client sections:

$$\rho_s(\mathtt{let}_c\ x = e_c\ \mathtt{in}\ p) \equiv \big[\mathtt{injection}\ \mathbf{x}_i\ e_i;\big]_i\ \rho_s(p)$$

$$\rho_c(\mathtt{let}_c\ x = e_c\ \mathtt{in}\ p) \equiv \mathtt{let}\ x = e_c[\overline{\mathbf{x}_i}/\overline{f_i\%e_i}]\ \mathtt{in}\ \rho_c(p)$$

$$\text{Where} \begin{cases} \overline{f_i\%e_i} = injections(e_c) \\ \forall i, e_i \text{ does not contain fragments.} \\ \overline{\mathbf{x}_i} \text{ is a list of fresh variables.} \end{cases}$$

Here is the definition for server sections. Note the presence of lists of lists, to handle injections inside each fragment.

$$\rho_s(\mathtt{let}_s\ x = e_s\ \mathtt{in}\ p) \equiv \mathtt{let}\ x = e_s[\mathtt{fragment}\ \mathbf{f}_i\ \overline{a}_i/\{\!\{\ e_i\ \}\!\}]_i\ \mathtt{in}\ \mathtt{end}();\ \rho_s(p)$$

$$\rho_c(\mathtt{let}_s\ x = e_s\ \mathtt{in}\ p) \equiv \big[\mathtt{bind}\ \mathbf{f}_i = \lambda(\overline{x})_i.(e_i[(\overline{x})_i/\overline{(f\%a)}_i])\ \mathtt{in}\ \big]_i \mathtt{exec}();\ \rho_c(p)$$

$$\text{Where} \begin{cases} \{\!\{\ e_i\ \}\!\} = fragments(e_s) \\ \overline{\mathbf{f}_i} \text{ is a list of fresh variables.} \\ \forall i, \overline{(f\%a)}_i = injections(e_i) \\ \forall i, (\overline{x})_i \text{ is a list of fresh variables;} \end{cases}$$

Finally, the returned expression of an ELIOM$_\varepsilon$ program. The translation is similar to client sections:

$$\rho_s(e_c) \equiv \big[\mathtt{injection}\ \mathbf{x}_i\ e_i;\big]_i\ ()$$

$$\rho_c(e_c) \equiv e_c[\overline{\mathbf{x}_i}/\overline{f_i\%e_i}]$$

$$\text{Where} \begin{cases} \overline{f_i\%e_i} = injections(e_c) \\ \forall i, e_i \text{ does not contain fragments.} \\ \overline{\mathbf{x}_i} \text{ is a list of fresh variables.} \end{cases}$$

References

1. Balat, V.: Client-server web applications widgets. In: WWW 2013 Dev Track (2013)
2. Balat, V.: Rethinking traditional web interaction: theory and implementation. Int. J. Adv. Internet Technol. 63–74 (2014)
3. Balat, V., Chambart, P., Henry, G.: Client-server web applications with Ocsigen. In: WWW 2012 Dev Track, p. 59. Lyon, France, April 2012
4. Balat, V., Vouillon, J., Yakobowski, B.: Experience report: Ocsigen, a web programming framework. In: ICFP, pp. 311–316. ACM (2009)
5. BeSport. http://www.besport.com/
6. Boudol, G., Luo, Z., Rezk, T., Serrano, M.: Reasoning about web applications: an operational semantics for HOP. Trans. Program. Lang. Syst. **34**(2), 10 (2012)
7. Chlipala, A.: An optimizing compiler for a purely functional web-application language. In: ICFP (2015)
8. Chlipala, A.: Ur/Web: a simple model for programming the web. In: POPL (2015)
9. Chong, S., Liu, J., Myers, A.C., Qi, X., Vikram, K., Zheng, L., Zheng, X.: Secure web applications via automatic partitioning. In: SOSP 2007 (2007)

10. Cooper, E., Lindley, S., Wadler, P., Yallop, J.: Links: web programming without tiers. In: Boer, F.S., Bonsangue, M.M., Graf, S., Roever, W.-P. (eds.) FMCO 2006. LNCS, vol. 4709, pp. 266–296. Springer, Heidelberg (2007). doi:10.1007/978-3-540-74792-5_12

11. Ekblad, A., Claessen, K.: A seamless, client-centric programming model for type safe web applications. In: SIGPLAN Symposium on Haskell, Haskell 2014 (2014)

12. Eliom web site. http://ocsigen.org/

13. New York University Gencore. http://gencore.bio.nyu.edu/

14. Kiselyov, O.: The design and implementation of BER MetaOCaml - system description. In: FLOPS (2014)

15. Meteor.js. http://meteor.com

16. Ocsigen toolkit. http://ocsigen.org/ocsigen-toolkit/

17. Opa web site. http://opalang.org/

18. Philips, L., De Roover, C., Van Cutsem, T., De Meuter, W.: Towards tierless web development without tierless languages. In: Onward! 2014 (2014)

19. Pumgrana. http://www.pumgrana.com/

20. Scherer, G., Vouillon, J.: Macaque : Interrogation sûre et flexible de base de données depuis OCaml. In: 21ème journées francophones des langages applicatifs (2010)

21. Serrano, M., Queinnec, C.: A multi-tier semantics for Hop. Higher-Order Symbolic Comput. 23(4), 409–431 (2010)

22. Tyxml. http://ocsigen.org/tyxml/

23. Vouillon, J.: Lwt: a cooperative thread library. In: ACM Workshop on ML (2008)

24. Vouillon, J., Balat, V.: From bytecode to JavaScript: the Js_of_ocaml compiler. Softw. Pract. Experience 44(8), 951–972 (2014)

25. White, L., Bour, F., Yallop, J.: Modular implicits. In: ML workshop (2014)

26. Wright, A.K., Felleisen, M.: A syntactic approach to type soundness. Inf. Comput. 115(1), 38–94 (1994)

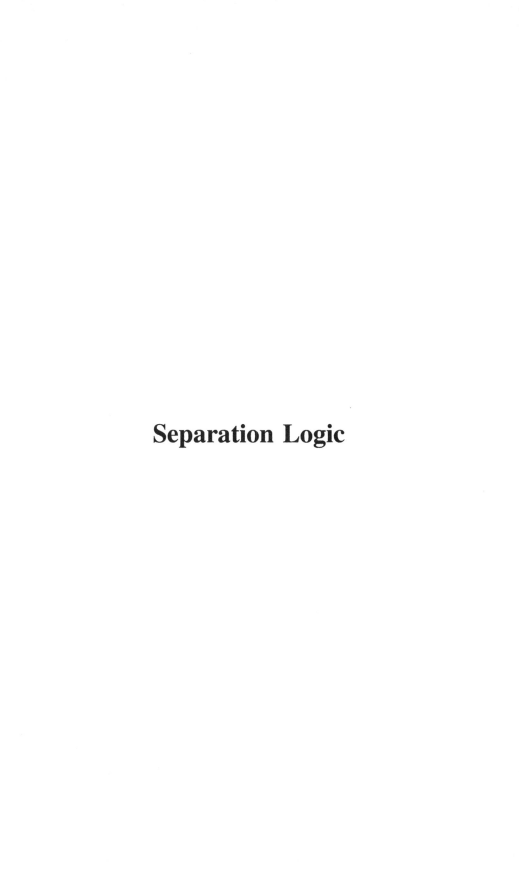

Separation Logic

DOM: Specification and Client Reasoning

Azalea Raad$^{(\boxtimes)}$, José Fragoso Santos, and Philippa Gardner

Imperial College, London, UK
azalea@doc.ic.ac.uk

Abstract. We present an axiomatic specification of a key fragment of DOM using structural separation logic. This specification allows us to develop modular reasoning about client programs that call the DOM.

1 Introduction

The behaviour of JavaScript programs executed in the browser is complex. Such programs manipulate a heap maintained by the browserss and call a wide range of APIs via specific objects in this heap. The most notable of these is the Document Object Model (DOM) API and the DOM document object, which are used to represent and manipulate the web page. JavaScript programs must run uniformly across all browsers. As such, the English standards of JavaScript and DOM are rather rigorous and are followed closely by browser vendors. While there has been work on formal specifications of JavaScript [14], including mechanised specifications [4], and some work on the formal specification of DOM [9,22] and on the verification of JavaScript programs [7], we are not aware of any work on the verification of JavaScript programs that call the DOM.

The W3C DOM standard [1] describes an XML update library used by all browsers. This English standard is written in an axiomatic style that lends itself well to formalisation. The first formal axiomatic DOM specification has been given in [9,22], using context logic (CL) [5,6], which extends ideas from separation logic (SL) [19] to complex data structures. However, this work has several shortcomings. First, it is not simple to integrate SL reasoning about e.g. C [19], Java [16] and JavaScript [7] with the DOM specifications in CL. The work in [9,22] explores the verification of simple client programs manipulating a variable store and calling the DOM. It does not verify clients manipulating a standard program heap. Second, this specification does not always allow *compositional* client-side reasoning. Finally, this specification makes simplifying choices (e.g. with live collections), and does not always remain faithful to the standard.

We present a faithful axiomatic specification of a key fragment of the DOM and verify substantial client programs, using structural separation logic (SSL) introduced in [8,25]. SSL provides fine-grained reasoning about complex data structures. The SSL assertion language contains the commutative separating conjunction (*), as in SL, that serves to split the DOM tree into smaller subtrees. By contrast, the CL assertion language contains the non-commutative separating application (•), that splits the DOM tree into a tree context with

© Springer International Publishing AG 2016
A. Igarashi (Ed.): APLAS 2016, LNCS 10017, pp. 401–422, 2016.
DOI: 10.1007/978-3-319-47958-3_21

a hole applied to a partial DOM tree. These two operators are not compatible with each other. In particular, the integration of the CL DOM specification with an SL-based program logic involves extending the program logic to include a frame rule for the separating application. By contrast, the integration of our SSL DOM specification with an SL-based program logic requires no extensions. We can reason about DOM client programs written in e.g. C, Java and JavaScript, by simply using a combination of the appropriate SL-based program logic for reasoning about the particular programming language and our DOM axioms. We illustrate this by verifying several realistic ad-blocker client programs written in JavaScript, using the program logic of [7]. Our reasoning abstracts the complexities of JavaScript, simply using standard SL assertions, an abstract variable store predicate, and JavaScript heap assertions. It is thus straightforward to transfer our ideas to other languages, as we show in Sect. 3.

As the authors noted in [9,22], CL does not always allow for *local* reasoning. As we demonstrate in Sect. 2, it also does not provide *compositional* reasoning. In contrast, SSL provides both local and compositional client reasoning. We demonstrate this by presenting a simple client program which can be specified using a *single* SSL triple whose precondition captures its intuitive footprint, compared to *six* CL triples, whose preconditions are substantially larger than the footprint.

The DOM English standard [1] is written in an axiomatic style, allowing for a straightforward comparison of our formal axiomatic specification with the standard. A typical way to justify an axiomatic specification of a library is to compare it against an operational semantics, as in [9,22,25] for DOM. However, this approach seems unsuitable as it involves inventing an operational semantics for the library, even though the standard is written in an axiomatic style. Instead, we justify our specification with respect to reference implementations that can be independently tested. In [17] we present two JavaScript implementations of our DOM fragment, and prove them correct with respect to our specifications.

Related Work. There has been much work on simple models of semi-structured data, following the spirit of DOM, such as [2,3,6] (axiomatic, program logic) and [20] (operational, information flow). We do not detail this work here. Instead, we concentrate on axiomatic and operational models, with a primary focus on DOM. Smith et al. developed an axiomatic specification of the DOM [9,22] in CL [5,6], as discussed above. Others have also studied operational models of DOM. Lerner et al. were the first to formalise the DOM event model [13]. This model is executable and can be used as an oracle for testing browser compliance with the standard. Unlike our work, this model was not designed for proving functional properties of client programs, but rather meta-properties of the DOM itself. The main focus of this work is the event dispatch model in DOM. Rajani et al. [18] have developed an operational model for DOM events and live collections, in order to study information flow. We aim to study DOM events in the future.

There has been much work on type analysis for client programs calling the DOM. Thiemann [24] developed a type system for establishing safety properties of DOM client programs written in Java. He extended the Java type system of [10] with recursion and polymorphism, and used this extension to specify the DOM data structures and operations. Later, Jensen et al. added DOM types to JavaScript [11,12,21], developing a flow sensitive type analysis tool TAJS. They used DOM types to reason about control and data flow in JavaScript applications that interact with the DOM. Recently, Park et al. developed a framework for statically analysing JavaScript web applications that interact with the DOM [15]. As with TAJS, this framework uses configurable DOM abstraction models. However, the proposed models are significantly more fine-grained than those of TAJS in that they can precisely describe the structure of DOM trees whereas TAJS simply treats them as black boxes. In [23], Swamy et al. translate JavaScript to a typed language and type the DOM operations. The DOM types are intentionally restrictive to simplify client analysis (e.g. modelling live collections as iterators in [23]). In contrast, there has been little work on the verification of programs calling the DOM. Smith et al. [9,22] look at simple client programs which manipulate the variable store and the DOM. However, their reasoning is not compositional, as previously discussed and formally justified in Sect. 2.

Outline. In Sect. 2, we summarise our contributions. In Sect. 3, we present our DOM specification and describe how our specification may be integrated with an arbitrary SL-based program logic. In Sect. 4, we verify a JavaScript ad-blocker client program which calls the DOM, and we finish with concluding remarks.

2 Overview

2.1 A Formal DOM Specification

The W3C DOM standard [1] is presented in an object-oriented (OO) and language-independent fashion. It consists of a set of interfaces describing the fields and methods exposed by each DOM datatype. A DOM object is a tree comprising a collection of *node* objects. DOM defines twelve specialised node types. As our goal is to present our specification methodology, we focus on an expressive fragment of DOM Core Level 1 (CL1) that allows us to create, update, and traverse DOM documents. We thus model the four most commonly used node types: *document, element, text* and *attribute* nodes. Additionally, we model *live collections of nodes* such as the *NodeList* interface in DOM CL1-4 (discussed in Sect. 3.5). Our fragment underpins DOM Core Levels 1–4. As shown in [22], it is straightforward to extend this fragment to the full DOM CL1 without adding to the complexity of the underlying program logic. It will be necessary to extend the program logic as we consider additional features in the higher levels of the standard (e.g. DOM events). However, these features will not affect the fragment specified here. We proceed with an account of our DOM fragment, hereafter simply called DOM.

DOM Nodes. Each node in DOM is associated with a *type*, a *name*, an optional *value*, and information about its surroundings (e.g. its parent, siblings, etc.). Given the OO spirit of the standard, each node object is uniquely identified by its reference. To capture this more abstractly (and admit non-OO implementations),

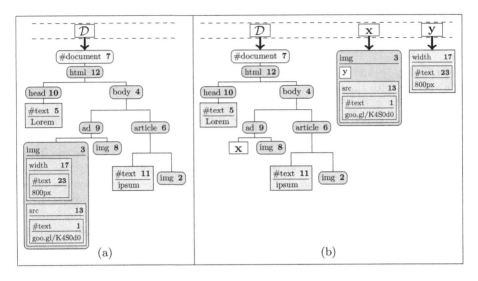

Fig. 1. A complete DOM heap (a); same DOM heap after abstract allocation (b)

we associate each node with a unique *node identifier*. As mentioned earlier, the standard defines twelve different node types of which we model the following four. *Document nodes* represent entire DOM objects. Each DOM object contains exactly one document node, named #document, with no value and at most a single child, referred to as the *document element*. In Fig. 1a, the document node is the node with identifier 7 (with document element 12). *Text nodes* (named #text) represent the textual content of the document. They have no children and may have arbitrary strings as their values. In Fig. 1a, node 5 is a text node with string data "Lorem". *Element nodes* structure the contents of a DOM object. They have arbitrary names (not containing the '#' character), no values and an arbitrary number of text and element nodes as their children. In Fig. 1a, node 12 is an element node with name "html" and two children with identifiers 10 and 4. *Attribute nodes* store information about the element nodes to which they are attached. The attributes of an element must have unique names. Attribute nodes may have arbitrary names (not containing the '#' character) and an arbitrary number of text nodes as their children. The value of an attribute node is given by concatenating the values of its children. In Fig. 1a, the element node with identifier 3 has two attributes: one with name "width", identifier 17, and value "800px" (i.e. the value of text node 23); and another with name "src", identifier 13, and value "goo.gl/K4S0d0" (i.e. the value of text node 1).

DOM Operations. The complete set of DOM operations and their axioms are given in [17]. In Sect. 3, we present the axioms for the operations used in the examples of this paper. Here, we describe the n.getAttribute(s) and n.setAttribute(s,v) operations and their axioms to give an intuitive account of SSL. The n.getAttribute(s) operation inspects the attributes of element node n. It returns the value of the attribute named s if it exists, or the empty string otherwise. For instance, given the DOM tree of Fig. 1a, when variable n holds value 3 (the element node named "img", placed as the left child of node "ad"), and s holds "src", then r = n.getAttribute(s) yields r="goo.gl/K4S0d0".

Intuitively, the footprint of n.getAttribute(s) is limited to the element node n and its "src" attribute. To describe this footprint minimally, we need to split the element node at n away from the larger surrounding DOM tree. To do this, we introduce *abstract DOM heaps* that store abstract tree fragments. For instance, Fig. 1a contains an abstract DOM heap with one cell at address $\mathcal{D}$ and a complete abstract DOM tree as its value. It is abstract in that it hides the details of how a DOM tree might be concretely represented in a machine. Abstract heaps allow for their data to be split by imposing additional instrumentation using *abstract addresses*. Such splitting is illustrated by the transition from Fig. 1a to b. The heap in Fig. 1a contains a complete tree at address $\mathcal{D}$. This tree can be split using *abstract allocation* to obtain the heap in Fig. 1b with the subtree at node 3 at a fresh, fictional *abstract cell* x, and an incomplete tree at $\mathcal{D}$ with a *context hole* x indicating the position to which the subtree will return. Since we are only interested in the attribute named "src", we can use abstract allocation again to split away the other unwanted attribute ("width") and place it at a fresh abstract cell y as illustrated in Fig. 1b. The subtree at node 3 and its "src" attribute correspond to the intuitive footprint of n.getAttribute(s). Once the getAttribute operation is complete, we can join the tree back together through *abstract deallocation*, as in the transition from Fig. 1b to a.

Using SSL [25], we develop *local* specifications of DOM operations that only touch the intuitive footprints of the operations. The assertion language comprises *DOM assertions* that describe abstract DOM heaps. For example, the DOM assertion $\alpha \mapsto \mathrm{img}_3[\beta \odot \mathrm{src}_{13}[\#\mathrm{text}_1[\mathrm{goo.gl/K4S0d0}]], \varnothing]$ describes the abstract heap cell at x in Fig. 1b, where α and β denote logical variables corresponding to abstract addresses x and y, respectively. It states that the heap cell at abstract logical address α holds an "img" element with identifier 3, no children ($\varnothing$) and a set of attributes described by $\beta \odot \mathrm{src}_{13}[\#\mathrm{text}_1[\mathrm{goo.gl/K4S0d0}]]$, which contains a "src" attribute (with identifier 13 and value "goo.gl/K4S0d0") and other attributes to be found at abstract logical address β. The attributes of a node are grouped by the commutative $\odot$ operator. When we are only interested in the value of an attribute, we can write an assertion that is agnostic to the shape of the text content under the attribute. For instance, we can write $\alpha \mapsto \mathrm{img}_3[\beta \odot \mathrm{src}_{13}[\mathrm{T}], \varnothing] * \mathrm{val}(\mathrm{T}, \mathrm{goo.gl/K4S0d0})$ to state that attribute 13 contains some text content described by logical variable T, and that the value of T (i.e. the value of the attribute) is "goo.gl/K4S0d0". Assertion val(T, goo.gl/K4S0d0) is *pure* in that it contains no resources and merely describes the string value of T.

Using SSL triples, we can now locally specify `r = n.getAttribute(s)` as[1]:

$$\left\{\begin{array}{l}\mathsf{store}(\mathsf{n}:\mathrm{N},\mathsf{s}:\mathrm{S},\mathbf{r}:-)\\ *\,\alpha\mapsto\mathsf{s}'_{\mathrm{N}}[\beta\odot\mathsf{s}_{\mathrm{M}}[\mathrm{T}],\gamma]\\ *\,\mathsf{val}(\mathrm{T},\mathrm{S}'')\end{array}\right\}\ \texttt{r = n.getAttribute(s)}\ \left\{\begin{array}{l}\mathsf{store}(\mathsf{n}:\mathrm{N},\mathsf{s}:\mathrm{S},\mathbf{r}:\mathrm{S}'')\\ *\,\alpha\mapsto\mathsf{s}'_{\mathrm{N}}[\beta\odot\mathsf{s}_{\mathrm{M}}[\mathrm{T}],\gamma]\\ *\,\mathsf{val}(\mathrm{T},\mathrm{S}'')\end{array}\right\}\quad(1)$$

$$\left\{\begin{array}{l}\mathsf{store}(\mathsf{n}:\mathrm{N},\mathsf{s}:\mathrm{S},\mathbf{r}:-)\\ *\,\alpha\mapsto\mathsf{s}'_{\mathrm{N}}[\mathrm{A},\gamma]*\mathsf{out}(\mathrm{A},\mathrm{S})\end{array}\right\}\ \texttt{r = n.getAttribute(s)}\ \left\{\begin{array}{l}\mathsf{store}(\mathsf{n}:\mathrm{N},\mathsf{s}:\mathrm{S},\mathbf{r}:\text{``''})\\ *\,\alpha\mapsto\mathsf{s}'_{\mathrm{N}}[\mathrm{A},\gamma]*\mathsf{out}(\mathrm{A},\mathrm{S})\end{array}\right\}\quad(2)$$

SSL triples have a fault-avoiding, partial-correctness interpretation as in other separation logics: if an abstract DOM heap satisfies the precondition then either the operation does not terminate, or the operation terminates and the resulting state will satisfy the postcondition. Axiom (1) captures the case when n contains an attribute named s; axiom (2) when n has no such attribute. The precondition of (1) contains three assertions. Assertion $\mathsf{store}(\mathsf{n}:\mathrm{N},\mathsf{s}:\mathrm{S},\mathbf{r}:-)$ describes a variable store where program variables n, s and $\mathbf{r}$ have logical values N, S and an arbitrary value $(-)$, respectively.[2] Assertion $\alpha\mapsto\mathsf{s}'_{\mathrm{N}}[\beta\odot\mathsf{s}_{\mathrm{M}}[\mathrm{T}],\gamma]$ describes an abstract DOM heap cell at the logical abstract address α containing the subtree described by assertion $\mathsf{s}'_{\mathrm{N}}[\beta\odot\mathsf{s}_{\mathrm{M}}[\mathrm{T}],\gamma]$. This assertion describes a subtree with a single element node with identifier N and name S'. Its children have been framed off, leaving behind the context hole γ (using abstract allocation as in the transition from Fig. 1a to 1b, then framing off the cell at γ). It has an attribute named s with identifier M and text content T, plus (potentially) other attributes that have been framed off, leaving behind the context hole β. This framing off of the children and attributes other than s captures the intuition that the footprint of $\mathsf{n.getAttribute(s)}$ is limited to element n and attribute s. Lastly, assertion $\mathsf{val}(\mathrm{T},\mathrm{S}'')$ states that the value of text content T is S''. The postcondition of (1) declares that the subtree remains the same and that the value of $\mathbf{r}$ in the variable store is updated to S'', i.e. the value of the attribute named s.

The precondition of (2) contains the assertion $\alpha\mapsto\mathsf{s}'_{\mathrm{N}}[\mathrm{A},\gamma]$ where, this time, the attributes of the element node identified by N are described by the logical variable A. With the precondition of (1), all other attributes can be framed off leaving context hole β. With the precondition of (2) however, the attributes are part of the intuitive footprint since we must check the absence of an attribute named s. This is captured by the $\mathsf{out}(\mathrm{A},\mathrm{S})$ assertion. The postcondition of (2) declares that the subtree remains the same and the value of $\mathbf{r}$ in the variable store is updated to the empty string "", as mandated by the English specification.

The $\mathsf{n.setAttribute(s,v)}$ operation inspects the attributes of element node n. It then sets the value of the attribute named s to v if such an attribute exists

---

[1] It is possible to combine multiple cases into one by rewriting the pre- and postconditions as a disjunction of the cases and using logical variables to track each case. For clarity, we opt to write each case separately.

[2] Since DOM may be called by different client programs written in different languages, store denotes a *black-box* predicate that can be instantiated to describe a variable store in the client language. Here, we instantiate it as the JavaScript variable store.

(3). Otherwise, it creates a new attribute named s with value v and attaches it to node n (4). We can specify this English description as (see footnote 1):

$$\left\{\begin{array}{l} \text{store}(n:N,s:S,v:S'') \\ *\,\alpha \mapsto s'_N[\beta \odot s_M[T],\gamma] \\ *\,\delta \mapsto \varnothing_g \end{array}\right\} n.\texttt{setAttribute(s,v)} \left\{\begin{array}{l} \exists R.\ \text{store}(n:N,s:S,v:S'') \\ *\,\alpha \mapsto s'_N[\beta \odot s_M[\#\text{text}_R[S'']],\gamma] \\ *\,\delta \mapsto T \end{array}\right\} (3)$$

$$\left\{\begin{array}{l} \text{store}(n:N,s:S,v:S'') \\ *\,\alpha \mapsto s'_N[A,\gamma]*\text{out}(A,S) \end{array}\right\} n.\texttt{setAttribute(s,v)} \left\{\begin{array}{l} \exists M,R.\,\text{store}(n:N,s:S,v:S'') \\ *\,\alpha \mapsto s'_N[A\odot s_M[\#\text{text}_R[S']],\gamma] \end{array}\right\}(4)$$

Recall that attribute nodes may have an arbitrary number of text nodes as their children where the concatenated values of the text nodes denotes the value of the attribute. As such, when n contains an attribute named s, its value is set to v by removing the existing children (text nodes) of s, creating a new text node with value v and attaching it to s (axiom 3). What is then to happen to the removed children of s? In DOM, nodes are not disposed of: whenever a node is removed, it is no longer a part of the DOM tree but still exists in memory. To model this, we associate the document object with a *grove* designating a space for the removed nodes. The $\delta \mapsto \varnothing_g$ assertion in the precondition of (3) simply reserves an empty spot ($\varnothing_g$) in the grove. In the postcondition the removed children of s (i.e. T) are moved to the grove. Similarly, when n does not contain an attribute named s, a new attribute named s is created and attached to n. The value of s is set to v by creating a new text node with value v and attaching it to s (axiom 4).

Comparison with Existing Work [9,22]. In contrast to the *commutative* separating conjunction $*$ in SSL, context logic (CL) and multi-holed context logic (MCL) use a *non-commutative separating application* $\bullet$ to split the DOM tree structure. For instance, the $C \bullet_\alpha P$ formula describes a tree that can be split into a context tree C with hole α and a subtree P to be applied to the context hole. The application is not commutative; it does not make sense to apply a context to a tree. In [9,22], the authors noted that the appendChild axiom was not *local*, as it required more than the intuitive footprint of the operation. What they did not observe was that CL client reasoning is not *compositional*. Consider a program $\mathbb{C}$ that copies the value of the "src" attribute in element p to that of q:

$$\mathbb{C} \triangleq s = p.\texttt{getAttribute("src");}\ q.\texttt{setAttribute("src",s)}$$

Let us assume that p contains a "src" attribute while q does not. Using SSL, we can specify $\mathbb{C}$ as follows, where $S \triangleq \text{store}(p{:}P,q{:}Q,s{:}-) * \text{val}(T,S_1) * \text{out}(A,S)$, $P \triangleq s_P[\gamma_1 \odot \text{src}_N[T],F_1]$, $Q \triangleq s'_Q[A,F_2]$ and $Q' \triangleq s'_Q[A \odot s_M[\#\text{text}_R[S_1]],F_2]$:

$$\{S * \alpha \mapsto P * \beta \mapsto Q\}\ \mathbb{C}\ \{\exists M,R.\ S * \alpha \mapsto P * \beta \mapsto Q'\} \quad (5)$$

Observe that the P and Q elements may be in one of three orientations with respect to one another: (i) P and Q are not related and describe disjoint subtrees;

(ii) Q is an ancestor of P; and (iii) P is an ancestor of Q. All three orientations are captured by (5). In contrast, using MCL (adapted to our notation) $\mathbb{C}$ is specified as follows where i-iii correspond to the three orientations above.

(i) $\left\{ S * \left((C \bullet_\alpha P) \bullet_\beta Q \right) \right\} \mathbb{C} \left\{ \exists \text{M}, \text{R}.\ S * \left((C \bullet_\alpha P) \bullet_\beta Q' \right) \right\}$
(ii) $\left\{ S * \left(Q \bullet_\alpha P \right) \right\} \mathbb{C} \left\{ \exists \text{M}, \text{R}.\ S * \left(Q' \bullet_\alpha P \right) \right\}$ (iii) $\left\{ S * \left(P \bullet_\alpha Q \right) \right\} \mathbb{C} \left\{ \exists \text{M}, \text{R}.\ S * \left(P \bullet_\alpha Q' \right) \right\}$

When P and Q are not related, the precondition of (i) states that the DOM tree can be split into a subtree with top node Q, and a tree context with hole variable β satisfying the $C \bullet_\alpha P$ formula. This context itself can be split into a subcontext with top node P and a context C with hole α. The postcondition of (i) states that Q is extended with a "src" attribute, and the context $C \bullet_\alpha P$ remains unchanged. This specification is not *local* in that it is larger than the intuitive footprint of $\mathbb{C}$. The only parts of the tree required by $\mathbb{C}$ are the two elements P and Q. However, the precondition in (i) also requires the surrounding *linking* context C: to assert that P and Q are not related (P is not an ancestor of Q and vice versa), we must appeal to a linking context C that is an ancestor of both P and Q. This results in a significant overapproximation of the footprint. As either C or P, but not both, may contain context hole β, (i) includes the behaviour of (iii), which can thus be omitted. We have included it as it is more local.

More significantly however, due to the non-commutativity of $\bullet$ we need to specify (ii) and (iii) separately. Therefore, the number of CL axioms of a client program may grow rapidly as its footprint grows. Consider the program $\mathbb{C}'$ below:

$$\mathbb{C}' \triangleq \texttt{s = p.getAttribute("src"); \ s' = r.getAttribute("src");}$$
$$\texttt{q.setAttribute("src", s+s')}$$

with its larger footprint given by the distinct p, q, r. When p and q contain a "src" attribute and r does not, we can specify $\mathbb{C}'$ in SSL with *one* axiom similar to (5). By contrast, when specifying $\mathbb{C}'$ in MCL, not only is locality compromised in cases analogous to (i) above, but we need *eight* separate specifications. Forgoing locality, as described above, we still require *six* specifications. This example demonstrates that CL reasoning is not compositional for client programs.

2.2 Verifying JavaScript Programs that Call the DOM

We demonstrate how to use our DOM specification to reason about client programs that call the DOM. Our DOM specification is agnostic to the choice of client programming language. In contrast to previous work [9,22], our DOM specification integrates simply with any SL-based program logic such as those for Java [16] and JavaScript [7]. Here, we choose to reason about JavaScript client programs.

We study a JavaScript *image sanitiser* that sanitises the "src" attribute of an element node by replacing its value with a trusted URL if the value is blacklisted. To determine whether or not a value is blacklisted, a remote database

$$st \triangleq \mathsf{store}(\mathsf{img}{:}N,\mathsf{cat}{:}S_2,\mathsf{cache}{:}C,\mathsf{url}{:}{-},\mathsf{isB}{:}{-}) \quad P_{\mathsf{out}} \triangleq \alpha \mapsto s_N[A,\gamma]*\mathsf{out}(A,\text{``src''})$$

$$P \triangleq \alpha \mapsto s_N[\beta \odot \mathsf{src}_M[\mathsf{T}],\gamma]*\mathsf{val}(\mathsf{T},S_1)*\delta \mapsto \varnothing_g \qquad Q \triangleq \exists R.\,\alpha \mapsto s_N[\beta \odot \mathsf{src}_M[\#\mathsf{text}_R[S_2]],\gamma]*\delta \mapsto \mathsf{T}$$

$\{st*P_{\mathsf{out}}\}$	$\mathsf{sanitiseImg(img,cat)}$	$\{st*P_{\mathsf{out}}\}$	(6)
$\{st*P*(\mathsf{C},S_1)\mapsto 1*\mathsf{isB}(S_1)\}$	$\mathsf{sanitiseImg(img,cat)}$	$\{st*Q*(\mathsf{C},S_1)\mapsto 1*\mathsf{isB}(S_1)\}$	(7)
$\{st*P*(\mathsf{C},S_1)\mapsto 0*\mathsf{isB}(S_1)\}$	$\mathsf{sanitiseImg(img,cat)}$	$\{st*Q*(\mathsf{C},S_1)\mapsto 1*\mathsf{isB}(S_1)\}$	(8)
$\{st*P*(\mathsf{C},S_1)\mapsto 0*\neg\mathsf{isB}(S_1)\}$	$\mathsf{sanitiseImg(img,cat)}$	$\{st*P*(\mathsf{C},S_1)\mapsto 0*\neg\mathsf{isB}(S_1)\}$	(9)

$\{\mathsf{store}(\mathsf{url}{:}S_1,\mathsf{isB}{:}{-})*\mathsf{isB}(S_1)\}$	$\mathsf{isB}{=}\mathsf{isBlackListed(url)}$	$\{\mathsf{store}(\mathsf{url}{:}S_1,\mathsf{isB}{:}1)*\mathsf{isB}(S_1)\}$
$\{\mathsf{store}(\mathsf{url}{:}S_1,\mathsf{isB}{:}{-})*\neg\mathsf{isB}(S_1)\}$	$\mathsf{isB}{=}\mathsf{isBlackListed(url)}$	$\{\mathsf{store}(\mathsf{url}{:}S_1,\mathsf{isB}{:}0)*\neg\mathsf{isB}(S_1)\}$

$\{\mathsf{store}(\mathsf{img}{:}N,\mathsf{cat}{:}S_2,\mathsf{cache}{:}C,\mathsf{url}{:}{-},\mathsf{isB}{:}{-})*P*(\mathsf{C},S_1)\mapsto 0*\mathsf{isB}(S_1)\}$

```
1.  sanitiseImg(img,cat) ≜ {
2.    url = img.getAttribute("src");
```
$\{\mathsf{store}(\mathsf{img}{:}N,\mathsf{cat}{:}S_2,\mathsf{cache}{:}C,\mathsf{url}{:}S_1,\mathsf{isB}{:}{-})*P*(\mathsf{C},S_1)\mapsto 0*\mathsf{isB}(S_1)\}$
```
3.    if (url){ // img has an attribute named "src"
4.      isB = cache.url;
```
$\{\mathsf{store}(\mathsf{img}{:}N,\mathsf{cat}{:}S_2,\mathsf{cache}{:}C,\mathsf{url}{:}S_1,\mathsf{isB}{:}0)*P*(\mathsf{C},S_1)\mapsto 0*\mathsf{isB}(S_1)\}$
```
5.      if (isB){ img.setAttribute("src",cat) } // url is in cache (thus blacklisted)
6.      else { // url is not in cache
```
$\{\mathsf{store}(\mathsf{img}{:}N,\mathsf{cat}{:}S_2,\mathsf{cache}{:}C,\mathsf{url}{:}S_1,\mathsf{isB}{:}0)*P*(\mathsf{C},S_1)\mapsto 0*\mathsf{isB}(S_1)\}$
```
7.        isB = isBlackListed(url);
```
$\{\mathsf{store}(\mathsf{img}{:}N,\mathsf{cat}{:}S_2,\mathsf{cache}{:}C,\mathsf{url}{:}S_1,\mathsf{isB}{:}1)*P*(\mathsf{C},S_1)\mapsto 0*\mathsf{isB}(S_1)\}$
```
8.        if (isB){ // url is blacklisted
```
$\{\mathsf{store}(\mathsf{img}{:}N,\mathsf{cat}{:}S_2,\mathsf{cache}{:}C,\mathsf{url}{:}S_1,\mathsf{isB}{:}1)*P*(\mathsf{C},S_1)\mapsto 0*\mathsf{isB}(S_1)\}$
```
9.          img.setAttribute("src",cat);
```
$\{\mathsf{store}(\mathsf{img}{:}N,\mathsf{cat}{:}S_2,\mathsf{cache}{:}C,\mathsf{url}{:}S_1,\mathsf{isB}{:}1)*Q*(\mathsf{C},S_1)\mapsto 0*\mathsf{isB}(S_1)\}$
```
10.         cache.url = 1
```
$\{\mathsf{store}(\mathsf{img}{:}N,\mathsf{cat}{:}S_2,\mathsf{cache}{:}C,\mathsf{url}{:}S_1,\mathsf{isB}{:}1)*Q*(\mathsf{C},S_1)\mapsto 1*\mathsf{isB}(S_1)\}$
```
11. } } } } 
```
$\{\mathsf{store}(\mathsf{img}{:}N,\mathsf{cat}{:}S_2,\mathsf{cache}{:}C,\mathsf{url}{:}{-},\mathsf{isB}{:}{-})*Q*(\mathsf{C},S_1)\mapsto 1*\mathsf{isB}(S_1)\}$

Fig. 2. The specifications of $\mathsf{sanitiseImg}$ (above); a proof sketch of (8) (below)

is queried. The results of successful lookups are stored in a local cache to minimise the number of queries. In Sect. 4, we use this sanitiser to implement an *ad blocker* that filters untrusted contents of a web page. The code of this sanitiser, $\mathsf{sanitiseImg}$, is given in Fig. 2. It inspects the img element node for its "src" attribute (line 2). When such an attribute exists (line 3), it consults the local cache (cache) to check whether its value (url) is blacklisted (line 4). If so, it changes its value to the trusted cat value. If the cache lookup is unsuccessful (line 6), the database is queried by the $\mathsf{isBlackListed}$ call (line 7). If the value is deemed blacklisted (line 8), the value of "src" is set to the trusted cat value (line 9), and the local cache is updated to store the lookup result (line 10). Observe that $\mathsf{sanitiseImg}$ does not use JavaScript-specific constructs (e.g. eval) and simply appeals to the standard language constructs of a while language. As such, it is straightforward to transform this proof to verify $\mathsf{sanitiseImg}$ written in e.g. C and Java.

The behaviour of $\mathsf{sanitiseImg}$ is specified in Fig. 2. The specifications in (6)–(9) capture different cases of the code as follows: in (6) img has no "src" attribute (i.e. the conditional of line 3 fails); in (7) the value of "src" is blacklisted in the local cache (line 5); in (8) the value is blacklisted and the cache has no record of it (lines 9–10); and in (9) the value is not blacklisted and the cache has no record of it (i.e. the conditional of 8 fails). We focus on (8) here; the remaining ones are analogous. The precondition of (8) consists of four assertions: the st captures the values of program variables; the P describes an element with an attribute named "src" and value s_1; the $(c, s_1) \mapsto 0$ asserts that the s_1 field of cache c holds value 0 (i.e. value s_1 may or may not be blacklisted but the cache has no record of it); and $isB(s_1)$ states that s_1 is blacklisted. This last assertion is used in the `isBlackListed` call of line 7 with its behaviour as specified in Fig. 2. A proof sketch of specification (8) is given in Fig. 2. At each proof point, we have highlighted the effect of the preceding command, where applicable.

3   A Formal DOM Specification

We give our formal axiomatic specification of DOM, comprising the DOM model in Sect. 3.1 eliding some details about DOM live collections until Sect. 3.5, the DOM assertions in Sect. 3.2, the framework for reasoning about DOM client programs in Sect. 3.3, the DOM axioms in Sect. 3.4, and DOM live collections in Sect. 3.5.

3.1   DOM Model

We model *DOM heaps* (e.g. Fig. 1) as mappings from addresses to DOM data. To this end, we assume a countably infinite set of *identifiers*, $n \in \text{ID}$, a designated *document identifier* associated with the document object, $d \in \text{ID}$, a countably infinite set of *abstract addresses*, $\mathbf{x} \in \text{AADD}$, and a designated *document address* $\mathcal{D}$, where the sets ID, AADD and $\{\mathcal{D}\}$ are pairwise disjoint.

DOM Data. DOM nodes are the building blocks of DOM data. Formally, we write: (i) $\#\text{text}_n[s]_{fs}$ for the text node with identifier n and text data s; (ii) $s_n[\mathbf{a}, \mathbf{f}]_{fs}^{ts}$ for the element node with identifier n, tag name s, attribute set $\mathbf{a}$, and children $\mathbf{f}$; (iii) $s_n[\mathbf{tf}]_{ts}$ for the attribute node with identifier n, name s, and children $\mathbf{tf}$; and (iv) $\#\text{doc}_d[\mathbf{e}]_{fs}^{ts}$ & $\mathbf{g}$ for the document object with the designated identifier d, document element $\mathbf{e}$ (or $\varnothing_e$ for no document element) and *grove* $\mathbf{g}$, ignoring the fs and ts for now. DOM nodes can be grouped into attribute sets, forests, groves, and text forests, respectively ranged over by $\mathbf{a}$, $\mathbf{f}$, $\mathbf{g}$ and $\mathbf{tf}$. An attribute set represents the attribute nodes associated with an element node and is modelled as an *unordered*, possibly empty collection of attribute nodes. A forest represents the children of an element node, modelled as an *ordered*, possibly empty collection of element and text nodes. A grove is where the orphaned nodes are stored. In DOM, nodes are never disposed of and whenever a node is removed from the document, it is moved to the grove. The grove is also where newly created nodes are placed. The document object is thus associated with a grove, modelled as an *unordered*, possibly empty collection of text, element and attribute nodes. A text forest represents the children of an attribute node, modelled as an *ordered*, possibly empty collection of text nodes. We associate each node with a set of *forest listeners*, fs; we further associate element and document nodes with a set of *tag listeners*, ts. We delay the motivation for these listeners until Sect. 3.5 when we model live collections. DOM data may be either incomplete with context holes (e.g. $\mathbf{x}$), or complete with no context holes. Notationally, data written in **bold** may contain context holes; regular font indicates the absence of context holes.

Definition 1. *The sets of* strings $s \in \mathbb{S}$, texts $t \in \mathbb{T}$, elements $\mathbf{e} \in \mathbb{E}$, documents $\mathbf{doc} \in \mathbb{D}$, attribute sets $\mathbf{a} \in \mathbb{A}$, forests $\mathbf{f} \in \mathbb{F}$, groves $\mathbf{g} \in \mathbb{G}$, and text forests $\mathbf{tf} \in \mathbb{TF}$, *are defined below where* $\mathbf{x} \in \mathrm{AADD}$, $n \in \mathrm{ID}$, $fs \in \mathcal{P}(\mathrm{ID})$ *and* $ts \in \mathcal{P}(\mathbb{S} \times \mathrm{ID})$:

$$s ::= \varnothing_s \mid c \mid s_1.s_2 \quad t ::= \#\mathrm{text}_n[s]_{fs} \quad \mathbf{e} ::= s_n[\mathbf{a}, \mathbf{f}]_{fs}^{ts} \quad \mathbf{a} ::= \varnothing_a \mid \mathbf{x} \mid s_n[\mathbf{tf}]_{fs} \mid \mathbf{a}_1 \odot \mathbf{a}_2$$

$$\mathbf{doc} ::= \#\mathrm{doc}_d[\varnothing_e]_{fs}^{ts} \,\&\, \mathbf{g} \mid \#\mathrm{doc}_d[\mathbf{e}]_{fs}^{ts} \,\&\, \mathbf{g} \mid \#\mathrm{doc}_d[\mathbf{x}]_{fs}^{ts} \,\&\, \mathbf{g}$$

$$\mathbf{f} ::= \varnothing_f \mid \mathbf{x} \mid t \mid \mathbf{e} \mid \mathbf{f}_1 \otimes \mathbf{f}_2 \quad \mathbf{g} ::= \varnothing_g \mid \mathbf{x} \mid t \mid \mathbf{e} \mid s_n[\mathbf{tf}]_{fs} \mid \mathbf{g}_1 \oplus \mathbf{g}_2 \quad \mathbf{tf} ::= \varnothing_{tf} \mid \mathbf{x} \mid t \mid \mathbf{tf}_1 \oslash \mathbf{tf}_2$$

where the operations $.$, $\oslash$, $\otimes$, $\odot$ *and* $\oplus$ *are associative with identities* $\varnothing_s$, $\varnothing_{tf}$, $\varnothing_f$, $\varnothing_a$ *and* $\varnothing_g$, *respectively; the* $\odot$ *and* $\oplus$ *operations are commutative; and all data are equal up to the properties of* $.$, $\oslash$, $\otimes$, $\odot$ *and* $\oplus$. *Data does not contain repeated identifiers and abstract addresses; element nodes contain attributes with distinct names. The set of* DOM *data is* $\mathbf{d} \in \mathrm{DATA} \triangleq \mathbb{E} \cup \mathbb{F} \cup \mathbb{TF} \cup \mathbb{A} \cup \mathbb{G} \cup \mathbb{D}$.

When the type of data is clear from the context, we drop the subscripts for empty data and write e.g. $\varnothing$ for $\varnothing_f$. We drop the forest and tag listeners when not relevant to the discussion and write e.g. $s_n[\mathbf{a}, \mathbf{f}]$ for $s_n[\mathbf{a}, \mathbf{f}]_{fs}^{ts}$. Given the set of DOM data DATA, there is an associated address function, $\mathsf{Adds}(.)$, which returns the set of context holes present in the data. Context application $\mathbf{d}_1 \circ_{\mathbf{x}} \mathbf{d}_2$ denotes the standard substitution of $\mathbf{d}_2$ for $\mathbf{x}$ in $\mathbf{d}_1$ ($\mathbf{d}_1[\mathbf{d}_2/\mathbf{x}]$) provided that $\mathbf{x} \in \mathsf{Adds}(\mathbf{d}_1)$ and the result is well-typed, and is otherwise undefined.

DOM Heaps. A DOM heap is a mapping from addresses, $x \in \mathrm{ADDR} \triangleq \mathrm{AADD} \uplus \{\mathcal{D}\}$, to DOM data. DOM heaps are subject to structural invariants to ensure that they are well-formed. In particular, a context hole $\mathbf{x}$ must not be reachable from the abstract address $\mathbf{x}$ in the domain of the heap. For instance, $\{\mathbf{x} \mapsto s_n[\varnothing, \mathbf{y}], \mathbf{y} \mapsto s'_m[\varnothing, \mathbf{x}]\}$ is not a DOM heap due to the cycle. We capture this by the reachability relation $\rightsquigarrow$ defined as: $x \rightsquigarrow \mathbf{y} \iff \mathbf{y} \in \mathsf{Adds}(\mathbf{h}(x))$, for heap $\mathbf{h}$ and address $x \in \mathrm{ADDR}$. We write $\rightsquigarrow^+$ to denote the transitive closure of $\rightsquigarrow$.

Definition 2. *The set of* DOM *heaps is:* $\mathbf{h} \in \mathrm{DOMHEAP} \subseteq (\{\mathcal{D}\} \rightharpoonup \mathbb{D}) \cup (\mathrm{AADD} \overset{fin}{\rightharpoonup} \mathrm{DATA})$ *provided that for all* $\mathbf{h} \in \mathrm{DOMHEAP}$ *and* $x \in \mathrm{ADDR}$ *the following hold:*

1. *identifiers and context holes are unique across* $\mathbf{h}$;
2. $\neg \exists \mathbf{x}.\ \mathbf{x} \rightsquigarrow^+ \mathbf{x}$;
3. *context holes in* $\mathbf{h}$ *are associated with data of correct type:*
   $$\forall x, \mathbf{y}.\ \mathbf{y} \in \mathsf{Adds}(\mathbf{h}(x)) \wedge \mathbf{y} \in \mathrm{dom}(\mathbf{h}) \Rightarrow \exists \mathbf{d}.\ \mathbf{h}(x) \circ_{\mathbf{y}} \mathbf{h}(\mathbf{y}) = \mathbf{d}$$

DOM Heap composition, $\bullet : \mathrm{DOMHEAP} \times \mathrm{DOMHEAP} \rightharpoonup \mathrm{DOMHEAP}$, *is the standard disjoint function union provided that the resulting heap meets the constraints above. The* empty DOM heap, $\mathbf{0}$, *is a function with an empty domain.*

Definition 3. *The* abstract (de)allocation relation, $\approx:$ DOMHEAP$\times$DOMHEAP, *is defined as follows where* $*$ *denotes the reflexive transitive closure of the set.*

$$\approx \triangleq \big\{(\mathbf{h_1},\mathbf{h_2}), (\mathbf{h_2},\mathbf{h_1}) \,\big|\, \exists x, \mathbf{d_1}, \mathbf{d_2}, \mathbf{x}.\ \mathbf{h_1}(x) = (\mathbf{d_1} \circ_\mathbf{x} \mathbf{d_2}) \wedge \mathbf{h_2} = \mathbf{h_1}[x \mapsto \mathbf{d_1}] \bullet [\mathbf{x} \mapsto \mathbf{d_2}]\big\}^*$$

During abstract allocation (from $\mathbf{h_1}$ to $\mathbf{h_2}$), part of the data $\mathbf{d_2}$ at address x is split and promoted to a fresh abstract address $\mathbf{x}$ in the heap leaving the context hole $\mathbf{x}$ behind in its place. Dually, during abstract deallocation (from $\mathbf{h_2}$ to $\mathbf{h_1}$) the context hole $\mathbf{x}$ in DOM data $\mathbf{d_1}$ is replaced by its associated data $\mathbf{d_2}$ at abstract address $\mathbf{x}$, removing $\mathbf{x}$ from the domain of the heap in doing so.

3.2 DOM Assertions

DOM assertions comprise heap assertions describing DOM heaps such as those in Fig. 1. DOM heap assertions are defined via DOM data assertions describing the underlying DOM structure such as nodes, forests and so forth. As we show later, pure assertions such as $\mathsf{out}(\mathrm{A}, \mathrm{S})$ in Sect. 2 are derived assertions defined in Fig. 4.

Definition 4. *The* DOM assertions, $\psi \in$ DOMASST, *and* DOM data assertions, $\phi \in$ DOMDASST, *are defined as follows where* $\alpha, \mathrm{A}, \mathrm{N}, \cdots$ *denote logical variables.*

$$\begin{aligned}
\psi ::=\ & \mathcal{D} \mapsto \phi \mid \alpha \mapsto \phi && \text{DOM heap assertions}\\
\phi ::=\ & \mathsf{false} \mid \phi_1 \Rightarrow \phi_2 \mid \exists \mathrm{X}.\ \phi \mid \mathrm{V} \mid\ \alpha \mid \phi_1 \circ_\alpha \phi_2 \mid \Diamond\alpha && \text{classical} \mid \text{context hole}\\
& \mid \#\mathrm{text}_\mathrm{N}[\phi]_\mathrm{F} \mid \mathrm{S_N}[\phi_1,\phi_2]_\mathrm{F}^\mathrm{E} \mid \mathrm{S_N}[\phi]_\mathrm{F} \mid \#\mathrm{doc}_\mathrm{N}[\phi_1]_\mathrm{F}^\mathrm{E} \,\&\, \phi_2 \mid \varnothing_e && \text{nodes}\mid\text{empty doc. element}\\
& \mid \varnothing_s \mid \phi_1.\phi_2 \mid \varnothing_a \mid \phi_1 \odot \phi_2 \mid \varnothing_f \mid \phi_1 \otimes \phi_2 && \text{strings}\mid\text{attr. sets}\mid\text{forests}\\
& \mid \varnothing_g \mid \phi_1 \oplus \phi_2 \mid \varnothing_{tf} \mid \phi_1 \oslash \phi_2 && \text{groves}\mid\text{text forests}
\end{aligned}$$

The $\mathcal{D} \mapsto \phi$ assertion describes a single-cell DOM heap at document address $\mathcal{D}$; similarly, the $\alpha \mapsto \phi$ describes a single-cell DOM heap at the abstract address denoted by α. For data assertions, classical assertions are standard. The V is a logical variable describing DOM data. The α is a logical variable denoting a context hole; the $\phi_1 \circ_\alpha \phi_2$ describes data that is the result of replacing the context hole α in ϕ_1 with ϕ_2; $\Diamond\alpha$ describes data that contains the context hole α. The node assertions respectively describe element, text, attribute and document nodes with their data captured by the corresponding sub-assertions. The $\varnothing_e$, $\varnothing_s$, $\varnothing_a$, $\varnothing_f$, $\varnothing_g$ and $\varnothing_{tf}$ describe an empty document element, string, attribute set, forest, grove and text forest, respectively. Similarly, $\phi_1.\phi_2$, $\phi_1 \odot \phi_2$, $\phi_1 \otimes \phi_2$, $\phi_1 \oplus \phi_2$ and $\phi_1 \oslash \phi_2$ respectively describe a string, attribute set, forest, grove and text forest that can be split into two, each satisfying the corresponding sub-assertion.

3.3 PLDOMLogic

We show how to reason about client programs that call the DOM. Our DOM specification is agnostic to the client programming language and we can reason about programs in any language with an SL-based program logic. To this end, given an arbitrary programming language, PL, with an SL-based program logic, PLLOGIC, we show how to extend PLLOGIC to PLDOMLOGIC, in order to enable DOM reasoning. Later in Sect. 4, we present a particular instance of PLDOMLOGIC for JavaScript, and use it to reason about JavaScript clients that call the DOM.

States. We assume the underlying program states of PLLOGIC to be modelled as elements of a *PCM* (partial commutative monoid) (PLSTATES, $\circ$, 0_{PL}), where $\circ$ denotes state composition, and 0_{PL} denotes the unit set. To reason about the DOM operations, in PLDOMLOGIC we extend the states of PLLOGIC to incorporate DOM heaps; that is, we define a program state to be a pair, $(h, \mathbf{h})$, comprising a PL state $h \in$ PLSTATES, and a DOM heap $\mathbf{h} \in$ DOMHeaps.

Definition 5. *Given the PCM of* PL, *the set of* PLDOMLOGIC *program states is* $\Sigma \in$ STATE $\triangleq$ PLSTATES$\times$DOMHEAP. *State composition,* $+$: STATE $\times$ STATE $\rightharpoonup$ STATE, *is defined component-wise as* $+ \triangleq (\circ, \bullet)$ *and is not defined if composition on either component is undefined. The unit set is* $I \triangleq \{(h, \mathbf{0}) \mid h \in 0_{PL}\}$.

Assertions. We assume the PLLOGIC assertions to include: (i) standard classical assertions; (ii) standard boolean assertions; (iii) standard SL assertions; and (iv) an assertion to describe the p variable store as seen in Sect. 2 of the form store($\ldots$). In PLDOMLOGIC we extend the PLLOGIC assertions with those of DOM (Definition 4), *semantic implication* $\Rrightarrow$, and the *semantic magic wand* $\rightsquigarrow\!\!*$, described shortly.

Definition 6. *The set of* PLDOMLOGIC *assertions,* $P \in$ ASST, *is defined as follows in the binding order* $*, \Rightarrow, \Rrightarrow, -\!\!*, \rightsquigarrow\!\!*$, *with* $\ominus \in \{\in, =, <, \leq, \subset, \subseteq\}$:

$$
\begin{array}{llr}
P, Q ::= \text{false} \mid P \Rightarrow Q \mid \exists \text{x}.\, P \mid E_1 \ominus E_2 & \text{Classical} \mid \text{Boolean assertions} \\
\mid \text{emp} \mid P * Q \mid P -\!\!* Q & \text{SL assertions} \\
\mid \text{store}(\overline{\text{x}_i : \text{v}_i}) \mid \Lambda & \text{variable store} \mid \text{PLLOGIC-specific assertions} \\
\mid \psi \mid P \Rrightarrow Q \mid P \rightsquigarrow\!\!* Q & \text{DOM} \mid \text{Structural assertions}
\end{array}
$$

Assertions are interpreted as sets of program states (Definition 5). Classical and boolean assertions are standard. The emp assertion describes an empty program state in the unit set I; the $P * Q$ describes a state that can be split into two substates satisfying P and Q. The $-\!\!*$ connective is the right adjunct of $*$, i.e. $P * (P -\!\!* Q) \Rightarrow Q$. Informally, a state that satisfies $P -\!\!* Q$ is one that is *missing* P, and when combined with P, it satisfies Q. The store($\overline{\text{x}_i : \text{v}_i}$) describes a variable store in PL where variables $\overline{\text{x}_i}$ have values $\overline{\text{v}_i}$, respectively. The Λ describes states of the form $(h, \mathbf{0})$ where h satisfies Λ. Dually, the ψ describes states of the form $(h, \mathbf{h})$ where $h \in 0_{PL}$ and $\mathbf{h}$ satisfies ψ. The $P \Rrightarrow Q$ assertion denotes *semantic implication* and integrates logical implication ($\Rightarrow$) with abstract (de)allocation on DOM heaps (Definition 3). The $\rightsquigarrow\!\!*$ connective is the *semantic right adjunct* of $*$: $P * (P \rightsquigarrow\!\!* Q) \Rrightarrow Q$. It is similar to $-\!\!*$ and incorporates the $\approx$ relation on DOM heaps. Intuitively, a state that satisfies $P \rightsquigarrow\!\!* Q$ is one that is missing P, such that when combined with P *and* undergone a number

$$\left\{\begin{array}{l}\mathsf{store}(n\!:\!N,o\!:\!O,r\!:\!-)\\ *\,\alpha\mapsto S_N[\beta,\gamma]_{F_1}^{E_1}\\ *\,\delta\mapsto S'_o[\zeta,T\wedge\mathsf{isComplete}]_{F_2}^{E_2}\end{array}\right\}\quad r=n.\mathtt{appendChild(o)}\quad\left\{\begin{array}{l}\mathsf{store}(n\!:\!N,o\!:\!O,r\!:\!O)\\ *\,\alpha\mapsto S_N[\beta,\gamma\otimes S'_o[\zeta,T]_{F_2}^{E_2}]_{F_1}^{E_1}\\ *\,\delta\mapsto(\varnothing_f\vee\varnothing_g)\end{array}\right\}$$

$$\left\{\begin{array}{l}\mathsf{store}(n:N,s:S,r:-)\\ *\,\alpha\mapsto\#\mathsf{doc}_N[\beta]_F^E\,\&\,\gamma\\ *\,\mathsf{safeName}(s)\end{array}\right\}\quad r=n.\mathtt{createElement(s)}\quad\left\{\begin{array}{l}\exists R,F',E'.\ \mathsf{store}(n:N,s:S,r:R)\\ *\,\alpha\mapsto\#\mathsf{doc}_N[\beta]_F^E\,\&\,\gamma\oplus S_R[\varnothing_a,\varnothing_f]_{F'}^{E'}\end{array}\right\}$$

$$\left\{\begin{array}{l}\mathsf{store}(n\!:\!N,o\!:\!O,r\!:\!-)\\ *\,\alpha\mapsto\#\mathsf{text}_N[S.S']_F * O\cdot\mid\!\!s\!\!\mid\end{array}\right\}\quad r=n.\mathtt{splitText(o)}\quad\left\{\begin{array}{l}\exists R,F'.\ \mathsf{store}(n\!:\!N,o\!:\!O,r\!:\!R)\\ *\,\alpha\mapsto\#\mathsf{text}_N[S]_F\otimes\#\mathsf{text}_R[S']_{F'}\end{array}\right\}$$

$$\left\{\begin{array}{l}\mathsf{store}(n{:}N,r{:}-)\\ *\,\alpha\mapsto S_N[\beta,T]_F^E * \mathsf{TIDs}(T,L)\end{array}\right\}\quad r=n.\mathtt{childNodes}\quad\left\{\begin{array}{l}\exists F,F'.\ \mathsf{store}(n{:}N,r{:}F)\\ *\,\alpha\mapsto S_N[\beta,T]_{F'}^E *F\dot\subseteq F'*F\dot\in F'\end{array}\right\}$$

$$\left\{\begin{array}{l}\mathsf{store}(n{:}N,s{:}S,r{:}-)\\ *\,\alpha\mapsto S'_N[\beta,T]_F^E *\mathsf{search}(T,S,L)\end{array}\right\}\quad r=n.\mathtt{getElementsByTagName(s)}\quad\left\{\begin{array}{l}\exists R,E'.\ \mathsf{store}(n{:}N,s{:}S,r{:}R)\\ *\,\alpha\mapsto S'_N[\beta,T]_F^E *E\dot\subseteq E'*(S,R)\dot\in E'\end{array}\right\}$$

$$\left\{\begin{array}{l}\mathsf{store}(f{:}F,r{:}-)*\alpha\mapsto S_N[\beta,T]_{F'}^E\\ *\,\mathsf{TIDs}(T,L)*F\dot\in F'\end{array}\right\}\quad r=f.\mathtt{length}\quad\left\{\begin{array}{l}\exists R.\ \mathsf{store}(f{:}F,r{:}R)\\ *\,\alpha\mapsto S_N[\beta,T]_F^E * R\cdot\mid\!\!\models\!\!\mid\end{array}\right\}$$

$$\left\{\begin{array}{l}\mathsf{store}(f:F,i:I,r:-)\\ *\,\alpha\mapsto S'_N[\beta,T]_{F'}^E * (S,F)\dot\in E\\ *\,\mathsf{search}(T,S,L)*0\!\leq\!I\!<\!|L|\end{array}\right\}\quad r=f.\mathtt{item(i)}\quad\left\{\begin{array}{l}\exists R.\ \mathsf{store}(f:F,i:I,r:R)\\ *\,\alpha\mapsto S'_N[\beta,T]_{F'}^E\\ *\,R\cdot\mid\!\!\models\!\!\mid^I\end{array}\right\}$$

Fig. 3. DOM core level 1 axioms (excerpt)

of (possibly zero) abstract (de)allocations, it satisfies Q. We write $E_1\dot\ominus E_2$ for $E_1\ominus E_2\wedge\mathsf{emp}$.

Programming Language, Proof Rules and Soundness. We extend the programming language of PL with the operations of our DOM fragment (e.g. `getAttribute` in Sect. 2.1). The proof rules of PLDOMLOGIC are those of PLLOGIC with the exception of the rule of consequence: we generalise the premise to allow semantic implication ($\Rrightarrow$) between assertions rather than logical implication ($\Rightarrow$). We further extend the proof rules with the axioms of DOM operations, DOMAX, defined shortly in Sect. 3.4 below. The modified rule of consequence and the rule for DOM axioms are given below. We prove PLDOMLOGIC sound in [17].

$$\frac{P\Rrightarrow P'\quad\{P'\}\,\mathsf{C}\,\{Q'\}\quad Q'\Rrightarrow Q}{\{P\}\,\mathsf{C}\,\{Q\}}\ \text{(Con)}\qquad\frac{(P,\mathsf{C},Q)\in\mathrm{DOMAX}}{\{P\}\,\mathsf{C}\,\{Q\}}\ \text{(Ax)}$$

3.4   DOM Operations and Axioms

We formally axiomatise the behaviour of a DOM operations associated with our fragment. In Fig. 3 we give a select number of axioms including those of the operations used in the examples of this paper. The behaviour of some of the operations is captured by several axioms; we have omitted analogous cases. A full list of DOM operations modelled and their axioms, DOMAX, are given in [17].

The assertions in the pre- and postconditions of axioms are of the form $\mathsf{store}(\cdots)*\psi$ where the store predicate states the value associated with each program variable, and ψ is a DOM assertion that describes the operation footprint. Since the DOM library may be called by different client programs written in different programming languages, store denotes a *black-box* predicate that can be instantiated to describe a variable store in the client programming language. In Sect. 4 we reason about JavaScript client programs that call the DOM and thus instantiate store to describe the JavaScript variable store emulated in the heap.

We now describe of the DOM operations in Fig. 3 and their axioms, delaying the description of the last four operations until Sect. 3.5.

n.appendChild(o): when n and o both identify nodes, this operation appends o to the end of n's child list and returns o. It fails if o is an ancestor of n (otherwise it would introduce a cycle and break the DOM structure); or if n is a text node or a document node with a non-empty document element; or if o is an attribute or a document node. Figure 3 shows the axiom for when o is an element node (O). To ensure that O is not an ancestor of n, we require the entire subtree at o to be *separate* from the subtree at n. This is achieved by the isComplete assertion and the separating conjunction *. The isComplete is a derived assertion defined in Fig. 4. It describes DOM data with no context holes. The postcondition leaves $\varnothing_f \vee \varnothing_g$ in place of o once moved since we do not know if o has come from a forest or grove position. The disjunction leaves the choice to the frame.

n.createElement(s): when n identifies a document node, it creates a new element named s, and returns its identifier. The new element has no attributes or children and resides in the grove. The grove in the precondition is thus extended with the new node in the postcondition. The safeName(s) assertion is defined in Fig. 4 ensures that the tag name does not contain the invalid character '#'.

n.splitText(o): when n identifies a text node and o denotes an integer, it breaks the data of n into two text nodes at offset o (indexed from 0), keeping both nodes in the tree as siblings. It fails when o is an invalid offset (i.e. negative or greater than the length). The return value is the identifier of the new node.

Our specifications have smaller footprints than those of [9,22]. In particular, the axiom of appendChild requires a substantial *overapproximation* of the footprint due to the reasons discussed in Sect. 2.1, namely the need for a *linking context* (see page 7). This axiom is given below using MCL [5] (adapted to our notation):

$$\{(C \bullet_\alpha \mathrm{S_N}[\mathrm{A}, \gamma]) \bullet_\beta \mathrm{S'_O}[\mathrm{A',T}]\} \ \texttt{n.appendChild(o)} \ \{(C \bullet_\alpha \mathrm{S_N}[\mathrm{A}, \gamma \otimes \mathrm{S'_O}[\mathrm{A', T}]]) \bullet_\beta \varnothing_f\}$$

This axiom is not small enough: the only parts required by appendChild are the tree at O being moved, and the element N whose children are extended by O. However, as before the precondition above also requires the linking context C.

3.5   Live Collections

The DOM API provides several interfaces for traversing DOM trees based on *live collections* of nodes, such as the *NodeList* interface in DOM CL1-4. DOM

$\mathsf{isComplete} \triangleq \neg \exists \alpha. \; \Diamond \alpha$ $\qquad$ $\mathsf{safeName}(s) \triangleq \neg \exists s_1, s_2. \; s \doteq s_1.`\#`.s_2$

$\mathsf{val}(\mathrm{T}, \mathrm{S}) \triangleq (\mathrm{T} \doteq \varnothing_{tf} * \mathrm{S} \doteq \text{``''}) \vee (\exists \mathrm{N}, s_1, s_2, \mathrm{T}'. \; \mathrm{T} \doteq \#\mathsf{text}_{\mathrm{N}}[s_1] \_ \oslash \mathrm{T}' * \mathsf{val}(\mathrm{T}', s_2) * \mathrm{S} \doteq s_1.s_2)$

$\mathsf{out}(\mathrm{A}, \mathrm{S}) \triangleq (\mathrm{A} \doteq \varnothing_a) \vee (\exists \mathrm{S}', \mathrm{N}, \mathrm{T}, \mathrm{A}'. \; \mathrm{A} \doteq \mathrm{S}'_{\mathrm{N}}[\mathrm{T}] \_ \odot \mathrm{A}' * \mathrm{S} \neq \mathrm{S}' * \mathsf{out}(\mathrm{A}', \mathrm{S}))$

$\mathsf{TIDs}(\mathrm{T}, \mathrm{L}) \triangleq (\mathrm{L} \doteq [\,] * \mathrm{T} \doteq \varnothing_f) \vee (\exists \mathrm{N}, \mathrm{S}, \mathrm{A}, \mathrm{F}, \mathrm{T}', \mathrm{L}'. \; \mathrm{L} \doteq \mathrm{N} : \mathrm{L}'$
$\qquad\qquad\qquad * (\mathrm{T} \doteq \#\mathsf{text}_{\mathrm{N}}[\mathrm{S}] \_ \otimes \mathrm{T}' \vee \mathrm{T} \doteq \mathrm{S}_{\mathrm{N}}[\mathrm{A},\mathrm{F}] \_ \otimes \mathrm{T}') * \mathsf{TIDs}(\mathrm{T}', \mathrm{L}'))$

$\mathsf{search}(\mathrm{T}, \mathrm{S}, \mathrm{L}) \triangleq (\mathrm{T} \doteq \varnothing_f * \mathrm{L} \doteq [\,]) \vee (\exists \mathrm{N}, \mathrm{S}', \mathrm{T}'. \; \mathrm{T} \doteq \#\mathsf{text}_{\mathrm{N}}[\mathrm{S}'] \_ \otimes \mathrm{T}' * \mathsf{search}(\mathrm{T}', \mathrm{S}, \mathrm{L}))$
$\qquad \vee (\exists \mathrm{S}', \mathrm{N}, \mathrm{T}_1, \mathrm{T}_2, \mathrm{L}_1, \mathrm{L}_2. \; \mathrm{T} \doteq \mathrm{S}'_{\mathrm{N}}[-, \mathrm{T}_1] \_ \otimes \mathrm{T}_2 * \mathsf{search}(\mathrm{T}_1, \mathrm{S}, \mathrm{L}_1) * \mathsf{search}(\mathrm{T}_2, \mathrm{S}, \mathrm{L}_2)$
$\qquad * (\mathrm{S} \doteq \mathrm{S}' \vee \mathrm{S} \doteq \text{``*''} \Rightarrow \mathrm{L} \doteq \mathrm{N} : (\mathrm{L}_1 +\!\!+ \mathrm{L}_2)) * (\mathrm{S} \neq \mathrm{S}' \wedge \mathrm{S} \neq \text{``*''} \Rightarrow \mathrm{L} \doteq \mathrm{L}_1 +\!\!+ \mathrm{L}_2))$

Fig. 4. Derived DOM assertions

CL 4 also introduces the *HTMLCollection* interface for live collections of element nodes. We describe our model of live collections in terms of NodeLists. However, our model is abstract and captures the behaviour of both NodeLists and HTMLCollections.

The *NodeList* interface is an ordered collection of nodes. NodeLists are *live* in that they dynamically reflect document changes. Several DOM operations return NodeLists. For example, n.getElementsByTagName(s) returns a NodeList (using depth-first, left-to-right search) containing the identifiers of the elements named s underneath the tree rooted at n. Given the DOM tree of Fig. 1a, when n=4 and s="img", then r = n.getElementsByTagName(s) yields r=[3, 8, 2]. However, since NodeLists are live, if node 8 is later removed from the document, then r=[3, 2]. When s="*" denoting a wildcard, then the resulting NodeList must contain the identifiers of *all* element nodes underneath n. For instance, with the DOM tree of Fig. 1a, when n=4 and s="*", then r = n.getElementsByTagName(s) yields r=[9, 3, 8, 6, 2]. This operation may be called on both document and element nodes. We thus associate each such node with a *set of tag listeners*, *ts*. Each listener is of the form (s, fid) where s denotes the search string (e.g. "img" in the example above) and $fid \in \mathrm{ID}$ denotes the identifier of the resulting NodeList.

The n.childNodes operation also returns a NodeList, containing the identifiers of the immediate children of n. For instance, with the DOM tree of Fig. 1a, when n=4, then r = n.childNodes returns r=[9, 6]. Again, the value of r is live and dynamically reflects the changes to the child forest of n. The n.childNodes operation may be called on *any* DOM node. We therefore associate each DOM node with a *set of forest listeners*, *fs*. Each forest listener, $fid \in \mathrm{ID}$, denotes the identifier of a NodeList. Our specification is the first that faithfully models the behaviour of NodeLists. In particular, both [9] and [22] associate a single forest listener with DOM nodes and consequently admit behaviours that are not guaranteed by the standard. We proceed with the NodeList axioms in Fig. 3.

n.childNodes: when n=N, this operation returns (the identifier of) a forest listener NodeList F associated with N. Figure 3 shows the axiom for when N is an element. When asked for a forest listener NodeList, a node may either return an existing one, or generate a fresh one and extend its set with it. This flexibility is due to an under-specification in the standard. Thus, in the post-condition the original set F is extended to F′ (F$\dot\subseteq$F′) with return value F ∈ F′. The TIDs(T,L) assertion is defined in Fig. 4 and states that list L contains the top-level node identifiers (from left to right) of the forest denoted by T. For instance, TIDs(T, [9, 6]) holds in Fig. 1a when T denotes the child forest of node 4 (named "body"). As such, the TIDs(T,L) in the precondition stipulates that T contain enough resource for compiling a list of the immediate children of N (i.e. the top-level nodes in T).

n.getElementsByTagName(s): when n=N and s=S, this operation returns (the identifier of) a NodeList containing the identifiers of the elements with tag name S in the forest underneath N. The axiom in Fig. 3 describes the case when N is an element node. The original set of tag listeners E is extended to E′ with (S, R) ∈ E′ where R is the return value. The search(T, S, L) assertion is defined in Fig. 4 and describes the search result of getElementsByTag-Name (i.e. the list L contains the identifiers of those element nodes in the forest T whose name matches S). For instance, when T denotes the child forest of node 4 (named "body") in Fig. 1a, then both search(T, "img", [3, 8, 2]) and search(T, " * ", [9, 3, 8, 6, 2]) hold. As such, the search(T, S, L) in the precondition ensures that T contains enough resource for compiling a list of elements named S.

f.length: when f=F identifies a NodeList, its length is returned. The axiom in Fig. 3 describes the case when F is a forest listener NodeList on element N; the return value is the number of N's immediate children. This is captured by TIDs(T,L) stipulating that list L contains the identifiers of those nodes at the top level of child forest T. The return value is thus the length of L (i.e. |L|).

f.item(i): this is analogous to f.length with $|L|^i$ denoting the Ith item of L. The axiom in Fig. 3 describes the case when F is a tag listener NodeList on N.

4 Verifying JavaScript Programs that Call the DOM

We instantiate the method described in Sect. 3.3 to extend the SL-based JavaScript program logic (hereafter JSLogic) in [7], to JSDOMLogic, in order to enable DOM reasoning. We then use JSDOMLogic to reason about a realistic ad blocker program in Sect. 4.1, and a further ad blocker in [17]. These examples are interesting as they combine JavaScript heap reasoning with DOM reasoning.

JSLogic States. The states of JSLogic are *JavaScript heaps*. A JavaScript heap, $h \in$ JSHEAP, is a partial function mapping *references*, which are pairs of memory locations and field names, to values. A heap cell is written $(l, x) \mapsto 7$, stating that the object at l has a field named x and holds value 7. An empty JavaScript heap is denoted by 0_{JS}; JavaScript heap composition, $\circ :$ JSHEAP×JSHEAP $\rightharpoonup$ JSHEAP, is the standard disjoint function union. The PCM of JavaScript heaps is (JSHEAP, $\circ$, $\{0_{JS}\}$). The states of JSDOMLogic are then pairs of the form $(h, \mathbf{h})$, comprising a JavaScript heap h, and a DOM heap $\mathbf{h}$ (see Definition 5).

JSLogic Assertions, Programming Language and Proof Rules. As stipulated by Definition 6, the JSLogic assertions include the standard boolean, classical and SL assertions. JSLogic further includes JavaScript heap assertions of the form $(E_1, E_2) \mapsto E_3$, describing a single-cell JavaScript heap. The variable store in JavaScript is emulated in the heap. As required by Definition 6, JSLogic introduces a derived assertion $\mathsf{store}(\overline{\mathsf{x}_i : \mathsf{v}_i})$, describing the JavaScript variable store in the heap where variables $\overline{\mathsf{x}_i}$ have values $\overline{\mathsf{v}_i}$. The programming language of JSLogic is a broad subset of the JavaScript language [7]. The JSLogic assertions, their semantics, the definition of store, and the JSLogic proof rules are given in [7].

4.1 A JavaScript Ad Blocker

We use JSDOMLogic to reason about an *ad blocker* script used for blocking the images from untrusted sources in a DOM tree. The `adBlocker1(n)` program in Fig. 5 compiles a NodeList containing all "img" elements in the tree rooted at n by calling the `getElementsByTagName` operation. It then iterates over this NodeList, sanitising each image by executing the `sanitiseImg` program in Sect. 2.

At each iteration I, the subtree at node n=N is described by $\mathsf{tree}(\mathsf{I}, \mathsf{E})$ where T_I denotes the child forest of N at iteration I, and E denotes the tag listener set associated with N, and L denotes the list of "img" elements below N.[3]

Since we iterate over the "img" elements in L and inspect their attributes, we need to *partition* them in into three categories: (i) *empty*: without a "src" attribute; (ii) *untrusted*: with a "src" attribute and a blacklisted value; (iii) *trusted*: with a "src" attribute and a trusted value. At each iteration, if the node considered is untrusted, it is sanitised and removed from the untrusted category. We thus define a fourth category, *sanitised*, including those elements whose values were initially blacklisted and are later sanitised. This is captured by $\mathsf{partition}(\mathsf{I})$[3]. The first part states that the list of "img" elements L can be partitioned into the three categories described above where $\mathsf{L} \equiv \mathsf{S}$ states that set S is a permutation of list L. The second part states that list L has been processed up to index I; i.e. the sanitised category S_s includes all the untrusted elements in L up to index I. The last four parts describe the "img" elements according to their category.

The $\mathsf{partition}$ predicate describes the "img" elements in L only and does not include the *remainder* of the subtree at N. At every iteration, this remainder is untouched and the modified parts are in the partitions. We thus describe the remainder for an arbitrary iteration I as $\forall \mathsf{I}.\ \mathsf{partition}(\mathsf{I}) \mathbin{\sim\!\!\ast} \mathsf{tree}(\mathsf{I}, \mathsf{E})$, i.e. the entire tree for that iteration, $\mathsf{tree}(\mathsf{I}, \mathsf{E})$, *minus* its partitions. The *unfolded* tree at iteration I, $\mathsf{unfld}(\mathsf{I}, \mathsf{E})$[3], consists of the partitions at I, plus the remainder.

Note that for NodeList operations such as `item` (line 5), we need the *folded* tree ($\mathsf{tree}(\mathsf{I}, \mathsf{E})$) with the entire subtree containing the "img" list L, as required by

---

[3] All free logical variables on the right-hand side are parameters of the predicate on the left. We omit them for readability as they do not change throughout the execution. By contrast, the iteration number I, and the tag listeners E of node N may change (the latter may grow by `getElementsByTagName`) and are explicitly parameterised.

$$\text{cache}(C) \triangleq \underset{F\in\mathcal{X}}{\circledast}\big((C,F)\mapsto 1 \vee (C,F)\mapsto 0\big) \qquad \text{unfld}(I,E) \triangleq \exists\overline{\alpha,\beta,\gamma}^{L}.\,\text{partition}(I)*(\forall I.\,\text{partition}(I)\rightsquigarrow*\text{tree}(I,E))$$

$$\text{tree}(I,E) \triangleq \alpha\mapsto s_N[A,T_I]_F^E * \text{search}(T_I,\text{``img''},L) \qquad \text{fld}(I,E) \triangleq \text{tree}(I,E)*\big((\forall I,E.\,\text{tree}(I,E)\rightsquigarrow*\text{unfld}(I,E))\wedge \text{emp}\big)$$

$$\text{rem}(I) \triangleq \exists s_s.\,s_s \cdot s_{\overline{u}} \cap \{|L|^J \mid J < I\} * \beta \mapsto \varnothing_g \bigoplus_{J\in s_s} A_J$$

$$\text{partition}(I) \triangleq L \doteq s_e \uplus s_u \uplus s_t * \exists s_s.\,s_s \cdot s_{\overline{u}} \cap \{|L|^J \mid J < I\} * \underset{J\in s_s}{\circledast}\big(\alpha_J \mapsto \text{img}_J[\beta_J\odot\text{src}_{M_J}[\#\text{text}_-[s]_-]_{F'}^{E_J},\gamma_J]_{F_J}^{E_J}\big)$$

$$\underset{J\in s_e}{\circledast}\big(\alpha_J\mapsto\text{img}_J[A_J,\gamma_J]_{F_J}^{E_J} * \text{out}(A_J,\text{src})\big) * \underset{J\in s_t}{\circledast}\big(\alpha_J\mapsto\text{img}_J[\beta_J\odot\text{src}_{M_J}[A_J]_{F'},\gamma_J]_{F_J}^{E_J}*\text{val}(A_J,V_J)*\neg\text{isB}(V_J)\big)$$

$$\underset{J\in s_u\setminus s_s}{\circledast}\big(\alpha_J\mapsto\text{img}_J[\beta_J\odot\text{src}_{M_J}[A_J]_{F'},\gamma_J]_{F_J}^{E_J} * \text{val}(A_J,V_J)*\text{isB}(V_J)\big)$$

$\{\text{store}(n:N,\text{cat}:S,\text{cache}:C,\text{imgs}:-,\text{len}:-,i:-,c:-,\text{isB}:-,\text{url}:-)*\neg\text{isB}(S)*\text{cache}(C)*\text{fld}(0,E)*\text{rem}(0)\}$

1. $\texttt{adBlocker1(n)} \triangleq \{$

2. $\texttt{imgs = n.getElementsByTagName("img");}$

$\left\{\begin{array}{l}\exists R,E'.\,\text{store}(n:N,\text{cat}:S,\text{cache}:C,\text{imgs}:R,\text{len}:-,i:-,c:-,\text{isB}:-,\text{url}:-)*\neg\text{isB}(S)*\text{cache}(C)\\ *\,\text{rem}(0)*\text{fld}(0,E')*E\subseteq E'*(\text{``img''},R)\dot{\in}E'\end{array}\right\}$

3. $\texttt{len = imgs.length; i = 0;}$

$\left\{\begin{array}{l}\exists R,E'.\,\text{store}(n:N,\text{cat}:S,\text{cache}:C,\text{imgs}:R,\text{len}:|L|,i:0,c:-,\text{isB}:-,\text{url}:-)*\neg\text{isB}(S)*\text{cache}(C)\\ *\,\text{rem}(0)*\text{fld}(0,E')*E\subseteq E'*(\text{``img''},R)\dot{\in}E'\end{array}\right\}$

$\left\{\begin{array}{l}\exists R,E',I.\,\text{store}(n:N,\text{cat}:S,\text{cache}:C,\text{imgs}:R,\text{len}:|L|,i:I,c:-,\text{isB}:-,\text{url}:-)*\neg\text{isB}(S)*\text{cache}(C)\\ *\,\text{rem}(I)*\text{fld}(I,E')*E\subseteq E'*(\text{``img''},R)\dot{\in}E'*I\le|L|\end{array}\right\}$

4. $\texttt{while(i<len)\{}$

5. $\texttt{c = imgs.item(i);}$

$\left\{\begin{array}{l}\exists R,E',I.\,\text{store}(n:N,\text{cat}:S,\text{cache}:C,\text{imgs}:R,\text{len}:|L|,i:I,c:|L|^I,\text{isB}:-,\text{url}:-)*\neg\text{isB}(S)*\text{cache}(C)\\ *\,\text{rem}(I)*\text{fld}(I,E')*E\subseteq E'*(\text{``img''},R)\dot{\in}E'*I\le|L|\end{array}\right\}$

//Apply derivation steps in (10)-(12).

$\left\{\begin{array}{l}\exists R,E',I.\,\text{store}(n:N,\text{cat}:S,\text{cache}:C,\text{imgs}:R,\text{len}:|L|,i:I,c:|L|^I,\text{isB}:-,\text{url}:-)*\neg\text{isB}(S)*\text{cache}(C)\\ *\,\text{rem}(I)*E\subseteq E'*(\text{``img''},R)\dot{\in}E'*I<|L|*\text{unfld}(I,E')*((\forall I,E.\,\text{tree}(I,E)\rightsquigarrow*\text{unfld}(I,E))\wedge\text{emp})\end{array}\right\}$

6. $\texttt{sanitiseImg(c,cat);}$

$\left\{\begin{array}{l}\exists R,E',I.\,\text{store}(n:N,\text{cat}:S,\text{cache}:C,\text{imgs}:R,\text{len}:|L|,i:I,c:|L|^I,\text{isB}:-,\text{url}:-)*\neg\text{isB}(S)*\text{cache}(C)\\ *\,\text{rem}(I+1)*E\subseteq E'*(\text{``img''},R)\dot{\in}E'*I<|L|*\text{unfld}(I+1,E')*((\forall I,E.\,\text{tree}(I,E)\rightsquigarrow*\text{unfld}(I,E))\wedge\text{emp})\end{array}\right\}$

// Apply derivation steps in (12)-(14).

$\left\{\begin{array}{l}\exists R,E',I.\,\text{store}(n:N,\text{cat}:S,\text{cache}:C,\text{imgs}:R,\text{len}:|L|,i:I,c:|L|^I,\text{isB}:-,\text{url}:-)*\neg\text{isB}(S)*\text{cache}(C)\\ *\,\text{rem}(I+1)*E\subseteq E'*(\text{``img''},R)\dot{\in}E'*I<|L|*\text{fld}(I+1,E')\end{array}\right\}$

7. $\texttt{i = i+1;}$

$\left\{\begin{array}{l}\exists R,E',I.\,\text{store}(n:N,\text{cat}:S,\text{cache}:C,\text{imgs}:R,\text{len}:|L|,i:I,c:-,\text{isB}:-,\text{url}:-)*\neg\text{isB}(S)*\text{cache}(C)\\ *\,\text{rem}(I)*E\subseteq E'*(\text{``img''},R)\dot{\in}E'*I\le|L|*\text{fld}(I,E')\end{array}\right\}$

8. $\texttt{\}}\ \texttt{\}}$ $\left\{\begin{array}{l}\exists R,E',I.\,\text{store}(n:N,\text{cat}:S,\text{cache}:C,\text{imgs}:-,\text{len}:-,i:-,c:-,\text{isB}:-,\text{url}:-)*\neg\text{isB}(S)\\ *\,\text{cache}(C)*\text{rem}(|L|)*E\subseteq E'*(\text{``img''},R)\dot{\in}E'*I\le|L|*\text{fld}(|L|,E')\end{array}\right\}$

Fig. 5. A proof sketch of the $\texttt{adBlocker1}$ program (see Footnote 3)

their axioms (Fig. 3). Conversely, for the $\texttt{sanitiseImg}$ call (line 6), we need the *unfolded* "img" elements ($\text{partition}(I)$) so that we can access the relevant "img" node at each iteration. We thus need to move between the folded and unfolded tree depending on the operation considered. The $\text{fld}(I,E)$ predicate describes the folded tree at iteration I. The first part, $\text{tree}(I,E)$, describes the resources of the folded tree at iteration I. The second part contains no resources (emp); it simply states that at any iteration I, the folded tree $\text{tree}(I,E)$, can be *exchanged* for the unfolded tree $\text{unfld}(I,E)$. As we show in the derivation below, this second part allows us to move from folded to unfolded resources (10–12) and vice versa (12–14), for any I. The bi-implication of (10) follows from the definition of fld

and that empty resources (emp) can be freely duplicated. In (11) we eliminate the first universal quantifier. We then eliminate the adjunct $(P * (P \leadsto\!\!* Q) \Rrightarrow Q)$ and arrive at (12). The implication of (13) follows from the definition of unfld and the elimination of the first universal quantifier. To get (14), we eliminate the adjunct, eliminate the existential quantifiers and wrap the definition of fld.

$$
\begin{aligned}
\mathsf{fld}(\mathrm{I}, \mathrm{E}) &\Leftrightarrow \mathsf{tree}(\mathrm{I}, \mathrm{E}) * (\forall \mathrm{I}, \mathrm{E}.\ \mathsf{tree}(\mathrm{I}, \mathrm{E}) \leadsto\!\!* \mathsf{unfld}(\mathrm{I}, \mathrm{E}) \wedge \mathsf{emp}) \\
&\qquad * (\forall \mathrm{I}, \mathrm{E}.\ \mathsf{tree}(\mathrm{I}, \mathrm{E}) \leadsto\!\!* \mathsf{unfld}(\mathrm{I}, \mathrm{E}) \wedge \mathsf{emp}) \hspace{3em} (10) \\
&\Rightarrow \mathsf{tree}(\mathrm{I}, \mathrm{E}) * (\mathsf{tree}(\mathrm{I}, \mathrm{E}) \leadsto\!\!* \mathsf{unfld}(\mathrm{I}, \mathrm{E})) * (\forall \mathrm{I}, \mathrm{E}.\ \mathsf{tree}(\mathrm{I}', \mathrm{E}) \leadsto\!\!* \mathsf{unfld}(\mathrm{I}, \mathrm{E}) \wedge \mathsf{emp}) \hspace{0.3em} (11) \\
&\Rrightarrow \mathsf{unfld}(\mathrm{I}, \mathrm{E}) * (\forall \mathrm{I}, \mathrm{E}.\ \mathsf{tree}(\mathrm{I}, \mathrm{E}) \leadsto\!\!* \mathsf{unfld}(\mathrm{I}, \mathrm{E}) \wedge \mathsf{emp}) \hspace{3em} (12) \\
&\Rrightarrow \exists \overline{\alpha, \beta, \gamma}^{\mathsf{L}}.\ \mathsf{partition}(\mathrm{I}) * (\mathsf{partition}(\mathrm{I}) \leadsto\!\!* \mathsf{tree}(\mathrm{I}, \mathrm{E})) \\
&\qquad * (\forall \mathrm{I}, \mathrm{E}.\ \mathsf{tree}(\mathrm{I}, \mathrm{E}) \leadsto\!\!* \mathsf{unfld}(\mathrm{I}, \mathrm{E}) \wedge \mathsf{emp}) \hspace{3em} (13) \\
&\Rrightarrow \mathsf{tree}(\mathrm{I}, \mathrm{E}) * (\forall \mathrm{I}, \mathrm{E}.\ \mathsf{tree}(\mathrm{I}, \mathrm{E}) \leadsto\!\!* \mathsf{unfld}(\mathrm{I}, \mathrm{E}) \wedge \mathsf{emp}) \Leftrightarrow \mathsf{fld}(\mathrm{I}, \mathrm{E}) \hspace{2em} (14)
\end{aligned}
$$

Recall that when the value of an attribute node is updated via the setAttribute operation, its text forest is replaced with a new text node containing the new value, and its old text forest is added to the grove (see axiom (3)). As such, at each iteration if we sanitise the "src" attribute of c (via sanitiseImg in line 6), then the old text forest of the "src" attribute is moved to the grove. This is described by the $\mathsf{rem}(\mathrm{I})$ assertion stating that for each attribute node sanitised so far (i.e. those in S_s), the old text forest A_J has been added to the grove.

Recall that sanitiseImg (Fig. 2) maintains a local cache of blacklisted URLs, implemented as an object at c with one field per URL (where $(\mathrm{C}, \mathrm{F}) \mapsto 1$ asserts the URL f is blacklisted, and $(\mathrm{C}, \mathrm{F}) \mapsto 0$ asserts that there are no cached results associated with f). We thus define the cache as the collection of all fields (denoted by $\mathcal{X}$) on c with value 1 or 0, where $\circledast$ is the iterated analogue of $*$.

We give a proof sketch of adBlocker1 in Fig. 5. The precondition consists of the variable store, the cache and the *unprocessed* (iteration 0) tree. The postcondition comprises the store, the cache and the *fully processed* (iteration $|\mathrm{L}|$) tree with the tag listeners of N extended with a new listener for "img".

Concluding Remarks. We use SSL [25] to formally specify an expressive fragment of DOM Core Level 1, closely following the standard [1]. In comparison to existing work [9,22], our specification (i) allows for *local* and *compositional* client specification and verification; (ii) can be simply *integrated* with SL-based program logics; and (iii) is *faithful* to the standard with respect to the behaviour of live collections. We demonstrate our compositional client reasoning by extending JSLogic [7] to incorporate our DOM specification and verifying functional properties of ad-blocker client programs that call the DOM.

Acknowledgements. This research was supported by EPSRC programme grants EP/H008373/1, EP/K008528/1 and EP/K032089/1.

References

1. W3C DOM standard. www.w3.org/TR/REC-DOM-Level-1/level-one-core.html
2. Biri, N., Galmiche, D.: A separation logic for resource distribution. In: Pandya, P.K., Radhakrishnan, J. (eds.) FSTTCS 2003. LNCS, vol. 2914, pp. 23–37. Springer, Heidelberg (2003)
3. Biri, N., Galmiche, D.: Models and separation logics for resource trees. J. Logic Comput. **17**, 687–726 (2007)
4. Bodin, M., Chargueraud, A., Filaretti, D., Gardner, P., Maffeis, S., Naudžiūnienė, D., Schmitt, A., Smith, G.: A mechanised JavaScript specification. In: POPL (2014)
5. Calcagno, C., Dinsdale-Young, T., Gardner, P.: Adjunct elimination in context logic for trees. In: Shao, Z. (ed.) APLAS 2007. LNCS, vol. 4807, pp. 255–270. Springer, Heidelberg (2007)
6. Calcagno, C., Gardner, P., Zarfaty, U.: Context logic and tree update. In: POPL (2005)
7. Gardner, P., Maffeis, S., Smith, G.: Towards a program logic for JavaScript. In: POPL (2012)
8. Gardner, P., Raad, A., Wheelhouse, M., Wright, A.: Local reasoning for concurrent libraries: mind the gap. In: MFPS (2014)
9. Gardner, P., Smith, G., Wheelhouse, M., Zarfaty, U.: Local Hoare reasoning about DOM. In: PODS (2008)
10. Igarashi, A., Pierce, B.C., Wadler, P.: Featherweight Java: a minimal core calculus for Java and GJ. In: OOPSLA (1999)
11. Jensen, S.H., Møller, A., Thiemann, P.: Type analysis for JavaScript. In: Palsberg, J., Su, Z. (eds.) SAS 2009. LNCS, vol. 5673, pp. 238–255. Springer, Heidelberg (2009). doi:10.1007/978-3-642-03237-0_17
12. Jensen, S.H., Madsen, M., Møller, A.: Modeling the HTML DOM and browser API in static analysis of JavaScript Web applications. In: ESEC/FSE 2011 (2013)
13. Lerner, B.S., Carroll, M., Kimmel, D.P., La Vallee, H.Q., Krishnamurthi, S.: Modeling and reasoning about DOM events. In: WebApps (2012)
14. Maffeis, S., Mitchell, J.C., Taly, A.: An operational semantics for JavaScript. In: Ramalingam, G. (ed.) APLAS 2008. LNCS, vol. 5356, pp. 307–325. Springer, Heidelberg (2008). doi:10.1007/978-3-540-89330-1_22
15. Park, C., Won, S., Jin, J., Ryu, S.: A static analysis of JavaScript web applications in the wild via practical DOM modeling (T). In: ASE (2015)
16. Parkinson, M.: Local reasoning for Java. Ph.D. thesis, Cambridge University (2006)
17. Raad, A.: Ph.D. thesis, Imperial College (2016, to appear)
18. Rajani, V., Bichhawat, A., Garg, D., Hammer, C.: Information flow control for event handling and the DOM in web browsers. In: CSF (2015)
19. Reynolds, J.C.: Separation logic: a logic for shared mutable data structures. In: LICS (2002)
20. Russo, A., Sabelfeld, A., Chudnov, A.: Tracking information flow in dynamic tree structures. In: Backes, M., Ning, P. (eds.) ESORICS 2009. LNCS, vol. 5789, pp. 86–103. Springer, Heidelberg (2009). doi:10.1007/978-3-642-04444-1_6
21. Møller, A., Jensen, S.H., Madsen, M.: Modeling the HTML DOM and browser API in static analysis of JavaScript web applications. In: FSE (2011)
22. Smith, G.: Local reasoning for web programs. Ph.D. thesis, Imperial College (2010)
23. Swamy, N., Weinberger, J., Schlesinger, C., Chen, J., Livshits, B.: Verifying higher-order programs with the Dijkstra Monad. In: PLDI (2013)

24. Thiemann, P.: A type safe DOM API. In: Bierman, G., Koch, C. (eds.) DBPL 2005. LNCS, vol. 3774, pp. 169–183. Springer, Heidelberg (2005). doi:10.1007/11601524_11
25. Wright, A.: Structural separation logic. Ph.D. thesis, Imperial College (2013)

Decision Procedure for Separation Logic with Inductive Definitions and Presburger Arithmetic

Makoto Tatsuta[1](✉), Quang Loc Le[2], and Wei-Ngan Chin[3]

[1] National Institute of Informatics, Sokendai, Tokyo, Japan
tatsuta@nii.ac.jp
[2] Singapore University of Technology and Design, Singapore, Singapore
[3] National University of Singapore, Singapore, Singapore

Abstract. This paper considers the satisfiability problem of symbolic heaps in separation logic with Presburger arithmetic and inductive definitions. First the system without any restrictions is proved to be undecidable. Secondly this paper proposes some syntactic restrictions for decidability. These restrictions are identified based on a new decidable subsystem of Presburger arithmetic with inductive definitions. In the subsystem of arithmetic, every inductively defined predicate represents an eventually periodic set and can be eliminated. The proposed system is quite general as it can handle the satisfiability of the arithmetical parts of fairly complex predicates such as sorted lists and AVL trees. Finally, we prove the decidability by presenting a decision procedure for symbolic heaps with the restricted inductive definitions and arithmetic.

1 Introduction

In the last decade, separation logic has provided an appealing paradigm to support memory safety verification [1,2]. For automated program verification, it is necessary to decide the truth of entailment of symbolic heaps. This paper will examine the decidability of the satisfiability problem for symbolic heaps. Decision procedures for satisfiability are important to support entailment proving [5].

This paper considers the symbolic heaps as the conjunction of equalities and disequalities, and the spatial conjunction of empty heap, points-to predicate, and inductive predicates. Inductive definitions for symbolic-heap systems are important [4,7,8] as they can provide a flexible way to express a wide range of recursive data structures. Recently, various extensions of symbolic heaps with arithmetic have been advocated for verifying both quantitative properties and data contents [5,9–11]. These extensions aim to handle more complex data structures involving arithmetic as well as shape information, such as length of lists, minimum values of lists, sorted lists, and even height-balanced AVL trees.

Our work extends the satisfiability decision procedure for symbolic heaps with inductive definitions [4] to symbolic heaps with inductive definitions and Presburger arithmetic. First we show that the satisfiability of symbolic heaps in

© Springer International Publishing AG 2016
A. Igarashi (Ed.): APLAS 2016, LNCS 10017, pp. 423–443, 2016.
DOI: 10.1007/978-3-319-47958-3_22

the system SLA1 which includes (unrestricted) inductive definitions and Presburger arithmetic is undecidable. The undecidability is proved by simulating multiplication and reducing to it Peano arithmetic which is undecidable.

Next, we propose some restrictions on SLA1 to obtain a decidable subsystem, called SLA2. For this purpose, we will use the three ideas: (1) a decidable subsystem DPI of Presburger arithmetic and inductive definitions, (2) projections and unfolding trees, and (3) a periodic structure in the sequence of base pairs.

Our first idea is to propose the decidable system DPI as a subsystem of Presburger arithmetic and inductive definitions with some restrictions. Although the truth for Presburger arithmetic is known to be decidable [6], the decidability of Presburger arithmetic and inductive definitions is challenging; it is undecidable without any restrictions, since some inductive predicate can simulate multiplication and reduce Peano arithmetic to it. We will choose the restrictions so that inductive predicates exactly represent eventually periodic sets. Our choice is reasonable, since Presburger arithmetic is one of the strongest decidable systems and eventually periodic sets are the same as sets characterized by some Presburger arithmetical formulas [6]. Under this restriction, we can show the decidability by eliminating inductive predicates. Our restriction seems complicated, but it is quite general as it can handle non-trivial data structures, such as arithmetical parts of sorted lists and AVL trees.

Our second idea is to decide the satisfiability of a given symbolic heap in separation logic with inductive definitions and arithmetic by deciding the satisfiability of its spatial part and its numeric part. The former satisfiability always implies the latter satisfiability, but the converse does not necessarily hold. In order to synchronize these two parts and guarantee the converse, we will use unfolding trees, which are described, for example, in [7]. An unfolding tree T of an inductive predicate P specifies how P is unfolded. Thus, P unfolded by T is true in separation logic with inductive definitions and arithmetic iff the spatial projection of P unfolded by T is true in separation logic with inductive definitions and the numeric projection of P unfolded by T is true in arithmetic with inductive definitions.

Our third idea is to use base pairs. Brotherston et al. [4] showed the satisfiability of symbolic heaps is decidable in the system of separation logic with inductive definitions. They introduced base pairs and an inductive predicate is interpreted by a set of base pairs. In this paper, we will use their ideas and interpret a symbolic heap without inductive predicates by a single base pair. One of the key observations is that we can find some periodic structure in a given sequence of the interpretations of symbolic heaps, since the set of base pairs is finite in our setting.

Then we will define the decidable system SLA2 as the system SLA1 with some restrictions to inductive definitions, so that the arithmetical part of inductive definitions are those of the system DPI. When the unfolding trees are linear, we can find some periodic structure in the sequence of base pairs that interpret the inductive predicate unfolded by those trees, which enables us to decide its satisfiability. For any tree-like data structures, the system SLA2 concurrently allows size properties, such as the length of lists and the height of trees, and data information such as the minimum and the maximum of data.

To summarize, we make the following technical contributions in this paper: (1) We prove that SLA1 is undecidable. (2) We propose the decidable subsystem DPI of Presburger arithmetic with inductive definitions, and prove its decidability. (3) We present the decidable subsystem SLA2 of symbolic heaps with Presburger arithmetic and inductive definitions, provide its decision procedure, and prove its decidability.

The decidability results of this paper provide theoretical foundations to advance satisfiability decision procedures in verification systems of heap-manipulating programs, like [5,9–11]. A system of symbolic heaps with inductive definitions and arithmetic adds significantly to the expressivity of our specification logic. However no decidability results for such a system have been achieved prior to our current proposal. For symbolic-heap systems with inductive definitions and without arithmetic, [4] shows the decidability of the satisfiability of symbolic heaps, and [7,8] proves the decidability of the truth of the entailments of symbolic heaps under some restrictions such as bounded treewidth. For symbolic-heaps systems with arithmetic and without inductive definitions, entailment decision procedures for hard-coded predicates and entailment of prenex formulas with some quantification were proposed in [3,9–11]. For symbolic-heaps systems with inductive definitions and arithmetic, [5] provided a semi-decision procedure for the validity of the entailments for symbolic heaps. Our results thus provide an important step towards state-of-the-art research on the decidability of symbolic heaps with inductive definitions and arithmetic.

Section 2 defines the system SLA1 and its semantics, and shows the undecidability. Section 3 proposes the decidable subsystem DPI of Presburger arithmetic with inductive definitions, and proves its decidability. The decidable system SLA2 is presented in Sect. 4. This section also defines unfolding trees and base pairs, and proves the decidability of SLA2 by providing its decision procedure. We conclude in Sect. 5.

2   System SLA1

We start off by defining the system SLA1 of separation logic and Presburger arithmetic with inductive definitions. By combination of separation logic and arithmetic, this system can describe range of complex data structures with pure properties, for example, sorted lists with length information.

2.1   Syntax

We use vector notations $\mathbf{x}$ to denote a sequence $x_1, \ldots, x_k$. $|\mathbf{x}|$ denotes the length of the sequence. For simplicity sometimes we also use a notation of a sequence to denote a set. We also write $\mathbf{x} = \mathbf{y}$ to denote $x_i = y_i$ for all i, and $f(\mathbf{x})$ for the sequence $f(x_1), \ldots, f(x_k)$. We write $\equiv$ for the syntactical equivalence. N denotes the set of natural numbers.

The language of SLA1 is defined in Fig. 1. We assume first-order variables
Vars :: $= x, y, v, \ldots$ and inductive predicate symbols $P :: = P_1, P_2, \ldots$. We assume
variables are implicitly classified into pointer variables and integer variables. NC
is a positive number, which specifies the number of elements in a cell.

Pointer terms t	$::= x \mid$ nil
Pure formulas Π	$::=$ true $\mid$ false $\mid t = t \mid t \neq t \mid \Pi \wedge \Pi$
Integer constants k	$::= \ldots \mid -1 \mid 0 \mid 1 \mid 2 \mid \ldots$
Arithmetical terms a	$::= x \mid k \mid k \times a \mid a + a \mid -a \mid \max(a, a) \mid \min(a, a)$
Arithmetical formulas Λ	$::=$ true $\mid a = a \mid a \leq a \mid \neg \Lambda \mid \Lambda \wedge \Lambda \mid \exists x. \Lambda$
Terms u	$::= a \mid t$
Spatial formulas Σ	$::=$ emp $\mid t \mapsto (u_1, \ldots, u_{NC}) \mid P(\mathbf{t}, \mathbf{a}) \mid \Sigma * \Sigma$
Symbolic Heaps ϕ	$::= \Pi \wedge \Sigma \wedge \Lambda$
Definition Clauses Φ	$::= \exists \mathbf{x}. \phi$
Definition Bodies Ψ	$::= \Phi \mid \Psi \vee \Psi$
Inductive Definitions	**pred** $P(\mathbf{x}) \equiv \Psi$

Fig. 1. Syntax of SLA1

We often omit Π or Λ when they are true. SLA1 has an inductive definition
system, which is a finite set of inductive definitions given by **pred**. The system
SLA1 has symbolic heaps $\Pi \wedge \Sigma$ as well as Presburger arithmetic Λ and inductive
predicates P.

We assume $*$ is more tightly bound than $\wedge$. We sometimes write $*_k A_k$ for a
sequence of separating conjunctions such as $A_1 * A_2 * A_3$. We often write $a_1 a_2$
for $a_1 \times a_2$. We write $\mathrm{FV}(O)$ for the set of free variables in O where O is some
syntactic object.

In the following, we illustrate the expressiveness of SLA1 with two examples
and use them as running examples throughout the paper.

Example 1 (Sorted Lists). The following predicate sortll for sorted lists can be
defined in SLA1.

$$\textbf{pred } \mathtt{sortll}(x, y, z) \equiv x \mapsto (z, \text{nil}) \wedge y = 1$$
$$\vee \; \exists x_1 y_1 z_1. x \mapsto (z, x_1) * \mathtt{sortll}(x_1, y_1, z_1) \wedge y = y_1 + 1 \wedge z \leq z_1.$$

y and z represent the length and the minimum value of the list respectively.

Example 2 (AVL Trees). The following predicate avl for AVL trees can be
defined in SLA1.

$$\textbf{pred } \mathtt{avl}(x, h) \equiv \text{emp} \wedge x = \text{nil} \wedge h = 0 \vee$$
$$\exists x_1 x_2 h_1 h_2. x \mapsto (x_1, x_2) * \mathtt{avl}(x_1, h_1) * \mathtt{avl}(x_2, h_2)$$
$$\wedge h = \max(h_1, h_2) + 1 \wedge -1 \leq h_1 - h_2 \leq 1.$$

h is the height of the tree.

We call a definition clause a *base case* when it does not contain any inductive predicates, and we call a definition clause an *induction case* when some inductive predicates appear in it.

We write $\Psi[x := t]$ for ordinary capture-avoiding substitution. $\Phi_1[P := \lambda\mathbf{x}.\Phi_2]$ is defined as the definition clause obtained for Φ_1 by replacing every $P(\mathbf{t})$ by $\Phi_2[\mathbf{x} := \mathbf{t}]$ and moving existential quantifiers to the head. We often write $\Phi[P, \ldots, P]$ to explicitly show occurrences of an inductive predicate P. When we use $\Phi_1[P]$, we write $\Phi_1[\lambda\mathbf{x}.\Phi_2]$ for $\Phi_1[P][P := \lambda\mathbf{x}.\Phi_2]$.

For an induction case $\Phi[P]$ with one occurrence of P and $n \geq 0$, we define

$$\Phi^0[P] \equiv P(\mathbf{x}),$$
$$\Phi^{n+1}[P] \equiv \Phi[\lambda\mathbf{x}.\Phi^n[P]].$$

2.2 Semantics

We write $\mathbf{Z}$ for the set of integers. We assume the set Val of values and the set Loc of addresses such that $\mathrm{Val} = \mathbf{Z} \cup \{\mathrm{null}\}$ and $\mathrm{Val} \cap \mathrm{Loc} = \emptyset$. We use

$$\mathrm{Heaps} = \mathrm{Locs} \rightarrow_{fin} (\mathrm{Loc} \cup \mathrm{Val})^{\mathrm{NC}},$$
$$\mathrm{Stores} = \mathrm{Vars} \rightarrow \mathrm{Loc} \cup \mathrm{Val}.$$

We assume a cell will be interpreted by $(\mathrm{Loc} \cup \mathrm{Val})^{\mathrm{NC}}$ and $s(\mathrm{nil}) = \mathrm{null}$. We use s and h by assuming $s \in \mathrm{Stores}$ and $h \in \mathrm{Heaps}$. We also assume that $s(k) = k$ for an integer constant k, and $\times, +, -, \max, \min, \leq$ are interpreted for integers by a usual semantics, and the interpretation $s \models \Lambda$ for an arithmetic formula Λ is defined using the standard model of integers $\mathbf{Z}$.

The semantics $s, h \models \exists \mathbf{z}.\phi$ of this logic is defined in a usual way as follows.

$s \models t_1 = t_2$ if $s(t_1) = s(t_2)$,

$s \models t_1 \neq t_2$ if $s(t_1) \neq s(t_2)$,

$s \models \Pi_1 \wedge \Pi_2$ if $s \models \Pi_1$ and $s \models \Pi_2$,

$s, h \models \mathrm{emp}$ if $\mathrm{Dom}(h) = \emptyset$,

$s, h \models t \mapsto (t_1, \ldots, t_n)$ if $\mathrm{Dom}(h) = \{s(t)\}$ and $h(s(t)) = (s(t_1), \ldots, s(t_n))$,

$s, h \models \Sigma_1 * \Sigma_2$ if $s, h_1 \models \Sigma_1$ and $s, h_2 \models \Sigma_2$ for some $h_1 + h_2 = h$,

$s, h \models P_i^0(\mathbf{t})$ does not hold,

$s, h \models P_i^{k+1}(\mathbf{t})$ if $s, h \models \Phi[P_i := P_i^k](\mathbf{t})$ for some definition clause Φ of P_i,

$s, h \models P_i(\mathbf{t})$ if $s, h \models P_i^m(\mathbf{t})$ for some m,

$s, h \models \Pi \wedge \Sigma \wedge \Lambda$ if $s \models \Pi$ and $s, h \models \Sigma$ and $s \models \Lambda$, and

$s, h \models \exists z \mathbf{z} \phi$ if $s[z := b], h \models \exists \mathbf{z} \phi$ for some $b \in \mathrm{Loc} \cup \{\mathrm{null}\}$ with a pointer variable z and some $b \in Z$ with an integer variable z.

2.3 Undecidability in SLA1

This section shows that without any restrictions on the shape of inductive definitions, the satisfiability is undecidable in SLA1.

Theorem 2.1. *The satisfiability of symbolic heaps is undecidable in SLA1.*

Proof. For any primitive recursive function $f(\mathbf{x})$, there is an inductive predicate F such that for any numbers $\mathbf{n}, m$, $f(\mathbf{n}) = m$ iff $s_0, h_0 \models F(\mathbf{n}, m)$ where s_0 is the dummy store such that $s_0(x) = \text{null}$ for all x, and h_0 is the empty heap such that $\text{Dom}(h_0) = \emptyset$. In this case, we say the inductive predicate F *represents* the primitive recursive function f. We can show it by induction on the definition of f. We will show only the following cases, since they are only interesting cases.

Case 1. Assume f is the successor function. We define

$$F(x, y) \equiv y = x + 1 \wedge \text{emp}.$$

Then $m = n + 1$ iff $s_0, h_0 \models F(n, m)$.

Case 2. Assume a primitive recursive function $f(x, y)$ is defined by

$$f(0, y) = g(y),$$
$$f(x + 1, y) = h(x, y, f(x, y)).$$

By induction hypothesis for g and h we have inductive predicates G and H that represent g and h respectively. We define the inductive predicate F by

$$F(x, y, z) \equiv x = 0 \wedge G(y, z) \wedge \text{emp} \vee \exists x_1 . x = x_1 + 1 \wedge F(x_1, y, z_1) * H(x, y, z_1, z).$$

Then F represents f, namely, $f(n, m) = l$ iff $s_0, h_0 \models F(n, m, l)$.

Let $T(x, y, z)$ be Kleene's T predicate, namely, for any numbers n, m, l, $T(n, m, l)$ is true iff the n-th partial recursive function with input m terminates with the computation history coded by l.

Since T is primitive recursive (namely, its characteristic function is a primitive recursive), there is an inductive predicate T' such that $T(n, m, l)$ is true iff $s_0, h_0 \models T'(n, m, l)$.

Hence the n-th partial recursive function with input m terminates iff $T'(n, m, x)$ is satisfiable in SLA1. Hence the satisfiability in SLA1 would solve the halting problem if the satisfiability in SLA1 were decidable. Consequently the satisfiability in SLA1 is undecidable. □

3   Presburger Arithmetic with Inductive Definitions

In this section, we define the system PI of Presburger arithmetic with positive inductive definitions. The truth in this system is undecidable. We will use this system as our starting point for constructing a decidable subsystem.

3.1   Presburger Arithmetic with Positive Inductive Definitions

Definition 3.1 (System PI). We assume the same first-order variables, the same inductive predicate symbols, the same integer constants, the same arithmetical terms, and the same arithmetical formulas as those of SLA1 presented in Fig. 1. For PI, we define the following.

$\phi ::= \Lambda \mid P(\mathbf{a}) \mid \phi \wedge \phi.$
Formulas $\Phi ::= \exists \mathbf{x}.\phi.$
Definition Bodies $\Psi ::= \Phi \mid \Psi \vee \Psi.$
Inductive Definitions $\mathtt{pred}\ P_i(\mathbf{x}) \equiv \Psi.$

a is interpreted in $\mathbf{Z}$. We define the truth of Λ by the standard model of integers. We interpret an inductive predicate by the least fixed point in a usual way.

The truth of formulas in this system is undecidable for the following reason. We can define multiplication as follows:

$$\mathtt{pred}\ P(x, y, z) \equiv x = 0 \wedge z = 0 \vee \exists x_1 z_1.x = x_1 + 1 \wedge P(x_1, y, z_1) \wedge z = z_1 + y.$$

Then $P(x, y, z)$ is true iff $x \times y = z$ is true. Since Presburger arithmetic with multiplication is equivalent to Peano arithmetic, the truth of this system is undecidable.

3.2   Decidable Subsystem DPI

We define a subsystem DPI of Presburger arithmetic with inductive definitions. The idea is that we impose some restrictions on the inductive definitions so that every inductive predicate defines some eventually periodic set. Since the decidability proof of Presburger arithmetic relies on the fact that a definable set is exactly an eventually periodic set, this restriction enables us to use the same proof idea for its extension with inductive definitions.

We explain our ideas of restrictions. (1) We assume we have only single induction (namely we do not use mutual induction). Moreover we assume we have at most one induction case. These restrictions enable us to compute the inductive predicates by iteration of the induction case to the base case. (2) When we have more than one arguments of inductive predicates, the i-th argument uses only the i-th arguments of recursive calls. For example, when the induction case of $P(x, y)$ has recursive calls $P(x_1, y_1)$ and $P(x_2, y_2)$, then x is computed by using only x_1 and x_2, and y is computed by using only y_1 and y_2. (3) We assume the induction case has some shape like $\exists x_1(x = x_1 + c \wedge P(x_1))$. In this case, by letting Q be the set represented by the base case, P represents the set $\{x + nc \mid x \in Q, n \in N\}$, which is eventually periodic. We assume this shape of induction case for some argument, for example, the j-th argument. (4) For the other arguments (the i-th argument where $i \neq j$), we assume we reach the fixed point by applying the induction case once. For example, if the induction case for $P(x)$ is $\exists x_1(x \geq x_1 \wedge P(x_1))$, this restriction is satisfied.

Definition 3.2 (System DPI). The language of DPI is the same as that of PI except inductive definitions. The inductive definitions of DPI are defined as those of PI with the following restriction: every inductive definition has the shape

$$\mathtt{pred}\ P(\mathbf{x}) \equiv \Lambda, \quad \text{or} \quad \mathtt{pred}\ P(\mathbf{x}) \equiv \bigwedge_{1 \leq i \leq m} \Lambda_{0,i} \vee \exists \mathbf{z}. \bigwedge_{1 \leq i \leq m} \Lambda_i \wedge \bigwedge_{1 \leq l \leq L} P(\mathbf{z}^l)$$

where m is the arity of P, $\text{FV}(\Lambda_{0,i}) \subseteq \{x_i\}$, $\mathbf{z} \supseteq \mathbf{z}^l$, there is j such that Λ_i is either of $x_i = f(\mathbf{z}_i)$, $x_i \geq f(\mathbf{z}_i)$, or $x_i \leq f(\mathbf{z}_i)$ for all $i \neq j$, and Λ_j is either of the following:

(1) $x_j = f(\mathbf{z}_j) + c \wedge \Lambda'$,
(2) $x_j \geq f(\mathbf{z}_j) + c \wedge \Lambda'$,
(3) $x_j \leq f(\mathbf{z}_j) + c \wedge \Lambda'$,
(4) a conjunction of the following forms with some integer constant $n > 0$:
$\quad \Lambda', \qquad nx_j = f(\mathbf{z}_j), \qquad nx_j \geq f(\mathbf{z}_j), \qquad$ or $nx_j \leq f(\mathbf{z}_j)$,

where c is some integer constant, $\mathbf{z}_j$ is $z_j^1, \ldots, z_j^L$, Λ' is an arithmetical formula such that $\text{FV}(\Lambda') \subseteq \mathbf{z}_j$ and $\Lambda'[\mathbf{z}_j := z]$ is true for any z, $f(\mathbf{z}_j)$ is a combination of $z_j^1, \ldots, z_j^L$ with max, min, defined by

$$f(\mathbf{z}_j) ::= z_j^l \mid \max(f(\mathbf{z}_j), f(\mathbf{z}_j)) \mid \min(f(\mathbf{z}_j), f(\mathbf{z}_j)),$$

and f's may be different from each other in the conjunction of (4).

Note that in DPI, each inductive definition has at most one induction case, and mutual inductive definitions are not allowed.

Example 3 (Arithmetical Part of Sorted List Predicate). Let $\texttt{sortll}^N$ be an inductive predicate symbol. The arithmetical part $\texttt{sortll}^N$ of the predicate $\texttt{sortll}$ is inductively defined by

$$\texttt{pred sortll}^N(y, z) \equiv y = 1 \vee \exists y_1 z_1.\texttt{sortll}^N(y_1, z_1) \wedge y = y_1 + 1 \wedge z \leq z_1.$$

Example 4 (Arithmetical Part of AVL Tree Predicate). Let $\texttt{avl}^N$ be an inductive predicate symbol. The arithmetical part $\texttt{avl}^N$ of the predicate $\texttt{avl}$ is inductively defined by

$$\texttt{pred avl}^N(h) \equiv h = 0 \vee \exists h_1 h_2.\texttt{avl}^N(h_1) \wedge \texttt{avl}^N(h_2)$$
$$\wedge h = \max(h_1, h_2) + 1 \wedge -1 \leq h_1 - h_2 \leq 1.$$

Definition 3.3. A set S of integers is defined to be *eventually periodic* if there are some $M \geq 0, p_1, p_2 > 0$ such that $n \in S$ iff $n + p_1 \in S$ for all $n \geq M$, and $n \in S$ iff $n - p_2 \in S$ for all $n \leq -M$. Then we call the set (M, p_1, p_2)-periodic.

Lemma 3.4. *If $S \neq \emptyset$ is (M, p_1, p_2)-periodic, then $\{x \mid nx = y, y \in S\}$ is (M, p_1, p_2)-periodic for $n > 0$.*

Proof. Let S' be $\{x \mid nx = y, y \in S\}$. Assume $x \in S'$ and $x \geq M$. There is y such that $nx = y$ and $y \in S$. Since $y = nx \geq x \geq M$ and $n(x + p_1) = nx + np_1 = y + np_1 \in S$, we have $x + p_1 \in S'$.

Assume $x + p_1 \in S'$ and $x \geq M$. There is y such that $n(x + p_1) = y$ and $y \in S$. Since $y - np_1 = nx \geq x \geq M$ and $nx = y - np_1 \in S$, we have $x \in S'$.

Similarly for $x \leq -M$, $x \in S'$ iff $x - p_2 \in S'$.

Hence S' is (M, p_1, p_2)-periodic. $\qquad \square$

Theorem 3.5 (Inductive Predicate Elimination). *For every inductive predicate P, there is a formula Λ equivalent to $P(\mathbf{x})$ such that Λ does not contain any inductive predicates.*

Proof. Let

$$\texttt{pred } P(\mathbf{x}) \equiv \bigwedge_{1 \leq i \leq m} \Lambda_{0,i} \vee \Phi_1,$$

$$\Phi_1 \equiv \exists \mathbf{z}. \bigwedge_{1 \leq i \leq m} \Lambda_i \wedge \bigwedge_l P(\mathbf{z}^l).$$

Let $\mathbf{x}$ be $(x_1, \ldots, x_m)$, S be $\{\mathbf{x} \mid P(\mathbf{x})\}$, Q be $\{\mathbf{x} \mid \bigwedge_i \Lambda_{0,i}\}$, S_i be $\{x_i \mid P(\mathbf{x})\}$, and Q_i be $\{x_i \mid \Lambda_{0,i}\}$. We have $Q = Q_1 \times \ldots \times Q_m$.

Since $\{f(\mathbf{z}_i) \mid \bigwedge_l z_i^l \in X\} = X$, we have the following facts: $\{x_i \mid x_i = f(\mathbf{z}_i) \wedge \bigwedge_l z_i^l \in X\} = X$, $\{x_i \mid x_i \geq f(\mathbf{z}_i) \wedge \bigwedge_l z_i^l \in X\} = X_+$, and $\{x_i \mid x_i \leq f(\mathbf{z}_i) \wedge \bigwedge_l z_i^l \in X\} = X_-$, where X_+ is $\emptyset$ if $X = \emptyset$, $\{z \mid z \geq \min X\}$ if $\min X$ exists, $\mathbf{Z}$ otherwise, and X_- is $\emptyset$ if $X = \emptyset$, $\{z \mid z \leq \max X\}$ if $\max X$ exists, $\mathbf{Z}$ otherwise.

Define $F : p(\mathbf{Z}^m) \to p(\mathbf{Z}^m)$ by $F(X) = Q \cup \{\mathbf{x} \mid \Phi_1[\lambda \mathbf{x}.(\mathbf{x} \in X)]\}$. Then $S = \bigcup_{n=0}^{\infty} F^n(\emptyset)$. We define $F_j : p(\mathbf{Z}) \to p(\mathbf{Z})$ by $F_j(X) = Q_j \cup \{x_j \mid \Lambda_j \wedge \bigwedge_l z_j^l \in X\}$.

By the above facts, the i-th element of $F^n(\emptyset)$ is Q_i, Q_{i+}, or Q_{i-} for all $i \neq j$ and $n > 1$. Hence $S = S_1 \times \ldots \times S_m$ where $S_i = Q_i, Q_{i+}$, or Q_{i-} for all $i \neq j$, and $S_j = \bigcup_{n=0}^{\infty} F_j^n(\emptyset)$, since the j-th value x_j depends on only the previous j-th values $\mathbf{z}_j$ in the definition of P.

It is known that a set definable in Presburger arithmetic is exactly an eventually periodic set [6]. Hence each Q_j is eventually periodic. Let Q_j be (M, p_1, p_2)-periodic.

We show S_j is eventually periodic by considering cases by the cases (1) to (4) in the restriction 2 according to the shape of Λ_j.

We have the fact (a) : $\{f(\mathbf{z}_j) \mid \bigwedge_l z_j^l \in X \wedge \Lambda'\} = X$. We can show it as follows: take a in the righthand side. By taking z_j^l to be a, since $\Lambda'[\mathbf{z}_j := a]$ is true and $f(\mathbf{z}_j) = a$, we have a is in the lefthand side.

The case (1). Λ_j is $x_j = f(\mathbf{z}_j) + c \wedge \Lambda'$. We have $F_j(X) = Q_j \cup \{x + c \mid x \in X\}$ and $S_j = \{x + nc \mid x \in Q_j, n \in N\}$. Let R_i be $\{x \in Q_j \mid x \equiv i \pmod{c}\}$. Assume $c > 0$. Define R_i' as $\emptyset$ if $R_i = \emptyset$, $\{k_i + nc \mid n \in N\}$ if R_i has the minimum k_i, and $\{x \mid x \equiv i \pmod{c}\}$ otherwise. Then $S_j = \bigcup_{0 \leq i < c} R_i'$. Then S_j is (M', c, p_2)-periodic where $M' = \max_{0 \leq i < c}(M, |k_i|)$. Similarly, if $c < 0$ then S_j is $(M', p_1, -c)$-periodic where $M' = \max_{0 \leq i < c}\{M, |k_i| \mid R_i \text{ has the maximum } k_i\}$. If $c = 0$, then $S_j = Q_j$ and S_j is (M, p_1, p_2)-periodic.

The case (2). Λ_j is $x_j \geq f(\mathbf{z}_j) + c \wedge \Lambda'$. We have $F_j(X) = Q_j \cup \{x \mid x \geq x' + c, x' \in X\}$. If $Q_j = \emptyset$, then $S_j = \emptyset$. Assume $Q_j \neq \emptyset$. S_j is $\mathbf{Z}$ if Q_j does not have any minimum. Assume Q_j has the minimum. If $c < 0$ then $Q_j = \mathbf{Z}$. If $c \geq 0$ then S_j is $Q_j \cup \{x \mid x \geq \min Q_j + c\}$. Hence either is eventually periodic.

The case (3). Λ_j is $x_j \leq f(\mathbf{z}_j) + c \wedge \Lambda'$. This case is shown in a similar manner to the case (2).

The case (4). Λ_j is a conjunction of the forms Λ', $nx_j = f_1(\mathbf{z}_j)$, $nx_j \geq f_2(\mathbf{z}_j)$, and $nx_j \leq f_3(\mathbf{z}_j)$. First we show S_j is (M, p_1, p_2)-periodic when Λ_j is either $nx_j = f(\mathbf{z}_j) \wedge \Lambda'$, $nx_j \geq f(\mathbf{z}_j) \wedge \Lambda'$, or $nx_j \leq f(\mathbf{z}_j) \wedge \Lambda'$.

Case (4).1. Λ_j is $nx_j = f(\mathbf{z}_j) \wedge \Lambda'$. If $Q_j = \emptyset$, then $S_j = \emptyset$ and it is (M, p_1, p_2)-periodic. If $Q_j \neq \emptyset$, by Lemma 3.4 and the fact (a), S_j is (M, p_1, p_2)-periodic.

Case (4).2. Λ_j is $nx_j \geq f(\mathbf{z}_j) \wedge \Lambda'$. If $Q_j = \emptyset$, then $S_j = \emptyset$. Assume $Q_j \neq \emptyset$. If Q_j does not have any minimum, $S_j = \mathbf{Z}$. Assume Q_j has the minimum k. If X has the minimum, $F_j(X) = Q_j \cup \{x \mid x \geq \lceil (\min X)/n \rceil\}$. By this, S_j is $\{x \mid x \geq k\}$ if $k > 0$ and $n = 1$, $\{x \mid x > 0\}$ if $k > 0$ and $n > 1$, $\{x \mid x \geq 0\}$ if $k = 0$, $\{x \mid x \geq k\}$ if $k < 0$. Moreover $k \geq -M$. Hence either is (M, p_1, p_2)-periodic.

Case (4).3. Λ_j is $nx_j \leq f(\mathbf{z}_j) \wedge \Lambda'$. In a similar way to the case (4).2, we can show S_j is (M, p_1, p_2)-periodic.

We have shown S_j is (M, p_1, p_2)-periodic when Λ_j is either $nx_j = f(\mathbf{z}_j) \wedge \Lambda'$, $nx_j \geq f(\mathbf{z}_j) \wedge \Lambda'$, or $nx_j \leq f(\mathbf{z}_j) \wedge \Lambda'$.

We show the general case when Λ_j is $\bigwedge_k \Lambda'_k$ where Λ'_k is either $nx_j = f_1(\mathbf{z}_j) \wedge \Lambda'$, $nx_j \geq f_2(\mathbf{z}_j) \wedge \Lambda'$, or $nx_j \leq f_3(\mathbf{z}_j) \wedge \Lambda'$. Let $F'_k(X) = Q_j \cup \{x_j \mid \Lambda'_k \wedge \bigwedge_l z_j^l \in X\}$ and S'_k be the least fixed point of F'_k. Since the least fixed point of $\bigcap_k F'_k(X)$ is the intersection of the least fixed points of $F'_k(X)$ for all k, we have $S_j = \bigcap_k S'_k$. We have the fact: if X_i is (M, p_1, p_2)-periodic for all i, then $\bigcap_i X_i$ is also (M, p_1, p_2)-periodic. By this fact, since S'_k is (M, p_1, p_2)-periodic for all k, S_j is (M, p_1, p_2)-periodic.

We have shown that the truth of $P(x_1, \ldots, x_m)$ is equivalent to $\bigwedge_{1 \leq i \leq m} (x_i \in Q_i) \vee x_j \in (S_j - Q_j) \wedge \bigwedge_{1 \leq i \leq m, j \neq i} (x_i \in S_i)$ and each of Q_i, Q_j, S_i, S_j is eventually periodic. Since an eventually periodic set is definable by a Presburger formula [6], we have a formula that does not contain any inductive predicates and is equivalent to $P(x_1, \ldots, x_m)$. □

The decision procedure for DPI is obtained by computing the above M, p_1, p_2 and S_j according to the decidability proof.

4   Decidable Subsystem SLA2

In this section we define a decidable subsystem SLA2 of the system SLA1.

4.1   Syntax of SLA2

First we define a numeric projection from SLA1 to PI. Next we define a spatial projection from SLA1 to the symbolic-heap system presented in [4] (we call it SL).

We define the system SL. The difference from the system in [4] is that the number of elements in a cell is fixed to be NC in SL and SL has only single induction (namely, it does not have mutual induction).

Definition 4.1 (System SL). Pointer terms $t ::= x \mid$ nil.
  Pure formulas $\Pi ::=$ true $\mid$ false $\mid t = t \mid t \neq t \mid \Pi \wedge \Pi$.
  Spatial formulas $\Sigma ::=$ emp $\mid t \mapsto (t_1, \ldots, t_{NC}) \mid P(\mathbf{t}) \mid \Sigma * \Sigma$.
  Symbolic Heaps $\phi ::= \Pi \wedge \Sigma$.
  Definition Clauses $\Phi ::= \exists \mathbf{x}.\phi$.
  Definition Bodies $\Psi ::= \Phi \mid \Psi \vee \Psi$.
  Inductive Definitions pred $P(\mathbf{x}) \equiv \Psi$.

We assume inductive predicate symbols P^N and P^S for each inductive predicate symbol P. We write $\mathbf{x}^N$ and $\mathbf{x}^S$ for the integer variables and the pointer variables among the variables $\mathbf{x}$ respectively.

Definition 4.2 (Projection). The numeric projection $(\Sigma)^N$ is defined by $(\text{emp})^N \equiv (t \mapsto (\mathbf{u}))^N \equiv$ true, $(P(\mathbf{t}, \mathbf{a}))^N \equiv P^N(\mathbf{a})$, and $(\Sigma_1 * \Sigma_2)^N \equiv (\Sigma_1)^N \wedge (\Sigma_2)^N$.
  $(\phi)^N$ is defined by $(\Pi \wedge \Sigma \wedge \Lambda)^N \equiv (\Sigma)^N \wedge \Lambda$.
  $(\Phi)^N$ is defined by $(\exists \mathbf{x}.\phi)^N \equiv \exists \mathbf{x}^N.(\phi)^N$.
  $(\Psi)^N$ is defined by $(\Psi_1 \vee \Psi_2)^N \equiv (\Psi_1)^N \vee (\Psi_2)^N$.
  The spatial projection $(u)^S$ is defined by $(t)^S \equiv t$ and $(a)^S \equiv$ nil.
  The spatial projection $(\Sigma)^S$ is defined by $(\text{emp})^S \equiv$ emp, $(t \mapsto (\mathbf{u}))^S \equiv t \mapsto ((\mathbf{u})^S)$, $(P(\mathbf{t}, \mathbf{a}))^S \equiv P^S(\mathbf{t})$, and $(\Sigma_1 * \Sigma_2)^S \equiv (\Sigma_1)^S * (\Sigma_2)^S$.
  $(\phi)^S$ is defined by $(\Pi \wedge \Sigma \wedge \Lambda)^S \equiv \Pi \wedge (\Sigma)^S$.
  $(\Phi)^S$ is defined by $(\exists \mathbf{x}.\phi)^S \equiv \exists \mathbf{x}^S.(\phi)^S$.
  $(\Psi)^S$ is defined by $(\Psi_1 \vee \Psi_2)^S \equiv (\Psi_1)^S \vee (\Psi_2)^S$.

We give the spatial projections of the predicates sortll and avl in Sect. 2.1. Their numerical projections are already given in Sect. 3.

Example 5 (Spatial Part of Sorted Lists).

$$\text{pred sortll}^S(x) \equiv x \mapsto (\text{nil}, \text{nil}) \ \vee \ \exists x_1.x \mapsto (\text{nil}, x_1) * \text{sortll}^S(x_1).$$

Example 6 (Spatial Part of AVL Trees).

$$\text{pred avl}^S(x) \equiv \text{emp} \wedge x = \text{nil} \vee \exists x_1 x_2.x \mapsto (x_1, x_2) * \text{avl}^S(x_1) * \text{avl}^S(x_2).$$

Definition 4.3 (System SLA2). The language of SLA2 is the same as that of SLA1 except inductive definitions. The inductive definitions of SLA2 are those of SLA1 with the following two restrictions. Let the inductive definition pred $P(\mathbf{x}) \equiv \Psi$.

(1) Its numeric projection `pred` $P^N(\mathbf{x}^N) \equiv (\Psi)^N$ is an inductive definition of DPI.

(2) If the induction case has more than one occurrences of P, then the spatial projection of Ψ has the following form

$$(\Psi)^S \equiv \psi_0 \vee \exists \mathbf{z}.\Pi \wedge *_{k \in K} w_k \mapsto (\mathbf{t}^k) * *_l P^S(\mathbf{z}^l),$$

where ψ_0 is a disjunction of the base cases, $\mathbf{z}^l \subseteq \mathbf{z}$, the variables in $(\mathbf{z}^l)_l$ are mutually distinct and do not appear in Π or $\{w_k \mid k \in K\}$.

We explain the condition (2). Let the induction case with more than one occurrences of P be Φ. It says the argument $\mathbf{z}^l$ of P are distinct existential variables and they do not appear in Π or $\{w_k \mid k \in K\}$. Hence for the existential variables, we can choose arbitrary values such that $P^S(\mathbf{x})$ is satisfiable by taking $\mathbf{x}$ to these values. In particular, we can choose some values such that the base case is true. Hence $(\Phi)^{S(T')}$ is satisfiable for some unfolding tree T' of height 1, when $(\Phi)^{S(T)}$ is satisfiable for some unfolding tree T of height ≥ 1. Consequently The restriction (2) guarantees that if an unfolding tree T of P is not linear, then the base pair that interprets P unfolded by T is determined to be two possibilities depending on the height 0 or ≥ 1 of T.

Example 7 (Sorted Lists). The predicate `sortll` in Sect. 2.1 can be defined in SLA2 as its spatial projection $\mathtt{sortll}^S(x)$ satisfies the restriction (2) (the condition trivially holds since it does not apply) and its numeric projection $\mathtt{sortll}^N(x)$ is in DPI.

Example 8 (AVL Trees). The predicate `avl` in Sect. 2.1 can be defined in SLA2 as its spatial projection $\mathtt{avl}^S(x)$ satisfies the restriction (2) and its numeric projection $\mathtt{avl}^N(x)$ is in DPI.

4.2   Unfolding Tree

This section defines unfolding trees, introduced in [7], in our notation. We use unfolding trees to synchronize the spatial part and the numeric part of a given symbolic heap in the proof of the decidability for SLA2. In general we can define unfolding trees for any logical system with inductive definitions including SLA1, SLA2, DPI, and SL.

Definition 4.4 (Unfolding Tree). Suppose the inductive definition of P

$$\mathtt{pred}\ P(\mathbf{x}) \equiv \bigvee_{1 \leq i \leq I} \Phi_i \vee \Phi[P, \ldots, P]$$

where Φ_i is a base case and the induction case $\Phi[P, \ldots, P]$ contains n occurrences of P. An unfolding tree T of P is defined by $T ::= i \mid (T_1, \ldots, T_n)$ where $1 \leq i \leq I$.

An unfolding tree T of P specifies how we unfold the inductive predicate P. It is described as follows.

Definition 4.5. Suppose $\text{pred } P(\mathbf{x}) \equiv \bigvee_{1 \le i \le I} \Phi_i \vee \Phi[P, \ldots, P]$.

For an unfolding tree T of P, $P^{(T)}$ is defined by:

$$P^{(i)} \equiv \lambda \mathbf{x}.\Phi_i,$$
$$P^{((T_1, \ldots, T_n))} \equiv \lambda \mathbf{x}.\Phi[P^{(T_1)}, \ldots, P^{(T_n)}].$$

We write $T(i, k)$ for $(\ldots (i) \ldots)$ where $\ldots$ denotes k parentheses. $T(i, k)$ is the unfolding tree of length k with the leaf i and $n = 1$.

The next proposition guarantees the synchronization of the spatial and numeric projections by an unfolding tree.

Proposition 4.6. $s, h \models P^{(T)}(\mathbf{t}, \mathbf{a})$ *in SLA2 for some* h *iff* $s, h \models P^{S(T)}(\mathbf{t})$ *in SL for some* h *and* $s \models P^{N(T)}(\mathbf{a})$ *in DPI.*

Proof. By induction on T. $\qquad\qquad\qquad\qquad\qquad\qquad\qquad\qquad\qquad\qquad\qquad$ $\square$

The next proposition says the truth of P is that of P unfolded by some unfolding tree.

Proposition 4.7. $s, h \models P^{(T)}(\mathbf{x})$ *for some* T *iff* $s, h \models P(\mathbf{x})$.

Proof. The only if part is proved by $P^k(\mathbf{x})$ where k is the height of T. The if part is shown by the definition of the truth. $\qquad\qquad\qquad\qquad\qquad\qquad$ $\square$

4.3 Base Pairs

In this section, we define base pairs adopted from [4]. We use base pairs to characterize unfolding trees T such that $P^{(T)}(\mathbf{x})$ is satisfiable. For this purpose, we define a base pair (B, Π) for $P^{(T)}(\mathbf{t})$ so that (B, Π) is satisfiable iff $P^{(T)}(\mathbf{t})$ is satisfiable.

Compared with the base pairs in [4], [4] interprets a symbolic heap with inductive predicates by a set of base pairs. On the other hand we will interpret a symbolic heap $\check{\phi}$ without any inductive predicates by a single base pair. A single base pair can work since $\check{\phi}$ does not contain disjunction.

Since we want the set of equivalence classes of base pairs to be finite, we have some notational difference with [4]: While [4] uses a multiset V for a base pair (V, Π), we use a set B for a base pair (B, Π). For free variables, [4] uses $\lambda \mathbf{x}.(V, \Pi)$, but we implicitly use $\mathbf{x}$. (V, Π) is satisfiable when Π is satisfiable in [4], but our (B, Π) is satisfiable when $\Pi \wedge \otimes B$ is satisfiable.

Definition 4.8 (Base Pair). We call (B, Π) a *base pair* when Π is a pure formula, and B is a set of pointer variables. For a pure formula Π, Π is defined to be consistent if $\Pi \not\vdash \text{false}$.

For notation of multisets, we write $\{e[x] \mid_M x \in_M V \wedge \ldots\}$ a multiset counting repetition of $e[x]$ where each x is taken from the multiset V counting repetition.

We define $[t]_\Pi$ as $\{u \mid \Pi \vdash u = t\}$. It is an equivalence class containing t by the equality of Π.

For a multiset V of terms and a pure formula Π, we define V/Π as $\{[t]_\Pi \mid_M t \in_M V\}$. It is a multiset of equivalence classes by the equality of Π. V/Π is called sound when V/Π does not have any duplicates and does not have any equivalence class containing nil.

Definition 4.9 (Satisfiable Base Pair). A base pair (B, Π) is defined to be *satisfiable* if Π is consistent and B/Π is sound.

We define $\perp$ as $(\emptyset, \text{false})$. For a multiset V of terms and a pure formula Π, we define $\overline{(V, \Pi)}$ as (V, Π) if Π is consistent and B/Π is sound. Otherwise we define it as $\perp$.

For a multiset V of terms, we define the multiset $V[\mathbf{x} := \mathbf{t}]_M$ by replacing $\mathbf{x}$ by $\mathbf{t}$ counting repetition. We use $\uplus$ for the multiset union.

We define

$$\Pi_1 \wedge (V, \Pi) = (V, \Pi_1 \wedge \Pi),$$
$$(V, \Pi)[\mathbf{x} := \mathbf{t}]_M = (V[\mathbf{x} := \mathbf{t}]_M, \Pi[\mathbf{x} := \mathbf{t}]),$$
$$(V_1, \Pi_1) * (V_2, \Pi_2) = (V_1 \uplus V_2, \Pi_1 \wedge \Pi_2).$$

Definition 4.10. We define $(V_1, \Pi_1) \simeq (V_2, \Pi_2)$ by $\Pi_1 \leftrightarrow \Pi_2$ and $V_1/\Pi_1 = V_2/\Pi_2$. Then we say (V_1, Π_1) and (V_2, Π_2) are equivalent.

We write $\Pi \leftrightarrow_\mathbf{x} \Pi'$ when $\Pi \to \Pi_0$ iff $\Pi' \to \Pi_0$ for every Π_0 such that $\mathrm{FV}(\Pi_0) \subseteq \mathbf{x}$ and Π_0 is either true, false, $t_1 = t_2$, or $t_1 \neq t_2$. We define $\Pi - \mathbf{x}$ as some Π' such that $\mathrm{FV}(\Pi') \subseteq \mathrm{FV}(\Pi) - \mathbf{x}$ and $\Pi' \leftrightarrow_\mathbf{x} \Pi$.

For a set B of variables, we define $\otimes B$ as

$$\bigwedge\{t \neq u \mid t, u \in B, t \not\equiv u\} \wedge \bigwedge\{t \neq \text{nil} \mid t \in B\}.$$

We define a language that contains $P^{(T)}(\mathbf{t})$. Since $P^{(T)}(\mathbf{t})$ is obtained from $P(\mathbf{t})$ by unfolding inductive predicates, it does not contain any inductive predicates but it may have nested existential quantifiers. We use the name with $\check{}$ for the corresponding syntactical category.

Spatial formulas $\check{\Sigma} ::= \text{emp} \mid t \mapsto (t_1, \ldots, t_{\mathrm{NC}}) \mid \exists \mathbf{x}.\check{\phi} \mid \check{\Sigma} * \check{\Sigma}$.

Symbolic Heaps $\check{\phi} ::= \Pi \wedge \check{\Sigma}$.

We define $[\![\ ]\!]$ for this language. We define $[\![\check{\Sigma}]\!]$ by:

$$[\![\text{emp}]\!] = (\emptyset, \text{true}),$$
$$[\![t \mapsto (t_1, \ldots, t_{\mathrm{NC}})]\!] = (\{t\}, \text{true}),$$
$$[\![\exists \mathbf{x}.\check{\phi}]\!] = \overline{(B - \mathbf{x}, (\Pi \wedge \otimes B) - \mathbf{x})},$$
$$[\![\check{\Sigma}_1 * \check{\Sigma}_2]\!] = \overline{[\![\check{\Sigma}_1]\!] * [\![\check{\Sigma}_2]\!]}.$$

We define $[\![\check{\phi}]\!]$ by $[\![\Pi \wedge \check{\Sigma}]\!] = \overline{\Pi \wedge [\![\check{\Sigma}]\!]}$.

Note that $[\![\check{\phi}]\!]$ is (B, Π) such that B is a set of variables, $\mathrm{FV}(B), \mathrm{FV}(\Pi) \subseteq \mathrm{FV}(\check{\phi})$, and (B, Π) is satisfiable if $(B, \Pi) \neq \bot$.

For a set $\mathbf{x}$ of variables, we write $\beta_{\mathbf{x}}$ for the set of equivalence classes of base pairs with its free variables in $\mathbf{x}$ by $\simeq$. We will often write (B, Π) for the equivalence class containing (B, Π). For example, we will write $(B, \Pi) \in X \subseteq \beta_{\mathbf{x}}$ when the equivalence class containing (B, Π) is in X. Note that $[\![\check{\phi}]\!] \in \beta_{\mathrm{FV}(\check{\phi})}$.

The next lemma is useful to calculate $[\![\ ]\!]$ by substitution. We write $\check{\phi}[\check{\phi}_1]$ to explicitly display an occurrence of $\check{\phi}_1$ in $\check{\phi}$.

Lemma 4.11. *(1)* $[\![\check{\phi}[\mathbf{x} := \mathbf{t}]]\!] \simeq \overline{[\![\check{\phi}]\!][\mathbf{x} := \mathbf{t}]_M}$.
(2) If $[\![\check{\phi}_1]\!] \simeq [\![\check{\phi}_2]\!]$, *then* $[\![\check{\phi}[\check{\phi}_1[\mathbf{x} := \mathbf{t}]]]\!] \simeq [\![\check{\phi}[\check{\phi}_2[\mathbf{x} := \mathbf{t}]]]\!]$.

Proof. (1) By induction on $\check{\phi}$.
(2) By induction on $\check{\phi}$ and (1).   □

We have the following lemma similar to Lemmas 3.7 and 3.8 in [4].

Lemma 4.12. *(1) If* $[\![\check{\phi}]\!] = (B, \Pi)$ *and* $s \models \Pi \wedge \otimes B$, *then there is* h *such that* $s, h \models \check{\phi}$ *and* $s(B) \subseteq Dom(h)$, *and moreover we can freely choose values in* $Dom(h) - s(B)$.
(2) If $s, h \models \check{\phi}$ *and* $[\![\check{\phi}]\!] = (B, \Pi)$, *then* $s \models \Pi \wedge \otimes B$ *and* $s(B) \subseteq Dom(h)$.

Proof. Each of (1) and (2) is proved by induction on $\check{\phi}$.   □

The following proposition is an instance of the theorem 3.9 in [4] in our terms. It says a base pair characterizes the satisfiability.

Proposition 4.13. $\check{\phi}$ *is satisfiable iff* $[\![\check{\phi}]\!]$ *is satisfiable.*

Proof. By Lemma 4.12 (1) and (2).   □

4.4   Decidability in SLA2

This section provides the decision procedure of the satisfiability in SLA2 and proves its correctness.

Our ideas of our decision algorithm are as follows. (1) We list up unfolding trees T such that $[\![P^{S(T)}(\mathbf{t})]\!]$ (the spatial part unfolded by T) is satisfiable. (2) The set $\{T \mid [\![P^{S(T)}(\mathbf{t})]\!]$ satisfiable$\}$ has a periodic structure for the following reason. In the case where the induction case has only one occurrence of the inductive predicate, since the set of base pairs is finite, we have a periodic structure. In the case where the induction case has more than one occurrences of the inductive predicate, the satisfiability for T of height ≥ 1 is the same as that for T of height 1 by the restriction (2) of SLA2. (3) In the case where the induction case has only one occurrence of the inductive predicate, according to the set $X = \{T \mid [\![P_1^{S(T)}(\mathbf{t})]\!]$ satisfiable$\}$, we make new inductive definitions for inductive predicates $P_{1,i}$ so that for any unfolding tree T', $P_{1,i}^{(T')}$ is equivalent to $P_1^{N(T)}$ for some $T \in X$. (4) We decide the numeric part of these inductive predicates $P_{1,i}$ by the decidability of DPI.

We will use the next two lemmas to define our decision procedure for SLA2, which can be straightforwardly shown.

Lemma 4.14. *For an induction case $\Phi[P]$ with one occurrence of P in DPI, $\Phi^n[P]$ is an induction case of P in DPI for $n > 0$.*

We write $\widetilde{T}$ to the set of leaves of an unfolding tree T.

Lemma 4.15. *Assume* pred $P_2(x) \equiv \bigvee\limits_{1 \leq i \leq I_2} \Phi_{2,i} \vee \Phi_2[P_2, P_2]$ *in SLA2. If $\Phi_{2,i}^S$ is satisfiable for all $i \in \widetilde{(T_1, T_2)} \cup \widetilde{(T_3, T_4)}$, then $[\![P_2^{S((T_1,T_2))}(x)]\!] = [\![P_2^{S((T_3,T_4))}(x)]\!]$.*

The next theorem is one of our main results.

Theorem 4.16. *The satisfiability of symbolic heaps is decidable in SLA2.*

Proof. For simplicity, we discuss only the case when only P_1 and P_2 are inductive predicates, the induction case of P_1 has one occurrence of P_1, and the induction case of P_2 has two occurrences of P_2. For simplicity, we also assume P_1 and P_2 take one pointer variable and one integer variable.

The decision procedure for the satisfiability of a given symbolic heap in SLA2 is presented in Algorithm 1, where the input is the following symbolic heap:

$$\phi \equiv \Pi \wedge *_{k \in K} w_k \mapsto (\mathbf{u}^k) * *_{1 \leq i \leq I} P_1(t_{1,i}, a_{1,i}) * *_{1 \leq j \leq J} P_2(t_{2,j}, a_{2,j}) \wedge \Lambda,$$

with the inductive definitions

$$\text{pred } P_1(x, y) \equiv \bigvee_{1 \leq i \leq I_1} \Phi_{1,i} \vee \Phi_1[P_1],$$

$$\text{pred } P_2(x, y) \equiv \bigvee_{1 \leq i \leq I_2} \Phi_{2,i} \vee \Phi_2[P_2, P_2],$$

where x is a pointer variable and y is an integer variable.

Note. In the algorithm, for $1 \leq i \leq I$, we use (l_i, n_i) to represent n_i-times application of the induction case to the l_i-th base case. For $1 \leq j \leq J$, we use $1 \leq m_j \leq I_2$ to represent the m_j-th base case and (r, r) to represent the unfolding tree of height 1 with the r-th base case.

First we will show that there exist $p_i < q_i$ in the step 1. By definition,

$$(\Phi_1^{n+1}[\lambda x.\Phi_{1,i}])^S = (\Phi_1[\lambda x.\Phi_1^n[\lambda x.\Phi_{1,i}]])^S.$$

Hence, by Lemma 4.11 (2), if $[\![\Phi_1^n[\lambda x.\Phi_{1,i}]]\!] \simeq [\![\Phi_1^{n'}[\lambda x.\Phi_{1,i}]]\!]$, then $[\![(\Phi_1^{n+1}[\lambda x.\Phi_{1,i}])^S]\!] \simeq [\![(\Phi_1^{n'+1}[\lambda x.\Phi_{1,i}])^S]\!]$. Since the equivalence class containing $[\![(\Phi_1^n[\lambda x.\Phi_{1,i}])^S]\!]$ is in β_x for $n = 0, 1, 2, \ldots$, and β_x is finite, we have the same occurrences of some equivalence class in the sequence. Hence we have some

Algorithm 1. Decision Procedure for SLA2

input : ϕ

output: Yes or No

Step 1. Compute p_i, q_i for each $1 \le i \le I_1$ as follows. Choose i. Compute the sequence $[\![(\Phi_1^n[\lambda x.\Phi_{1,i}])^S]\!]$ for $n = 0, 1, 2, \ldots$. Take the smallest p_i, q_i such that $p_i < q_i$, and the p_i-th occurrence and the q_i-th occurrence are equivalent.
Set I_3 to be $\{i \mid \Phi_{2,i} \text{ satisfiable}\}$. Set C to be
$$\{(l_1, n_1, \ldots, l_I, n_I, m_1, \ldots, m_J) \mid 1 \le l_i \le I_1, 0 \le n_i < q_i, 1 \le m_j \le I_2 \vee (m_j = (r,r) \wedge r \in I_3)\}.$$

Step 2. If C is empty, then return No and stop. Otherwise take some new element in C and go to the next step.

Step 3. Check whether the following formula is satisfiable:
$$[\![\Pi \wedge *_{k \in K} w_k \mapsto ((u^k)^S) * *_{1 \le i \le I} P_1^{S(T(l_i, n_i))}(t_{1,i}) * *_{1 \le j \le J} P_2^{S(m_j)}(t_{2,j})]\!].$$

If it is not satisfiable, then go to the step 2 for the next loop.

Step 4. For each $1 \le i \le I$, by Lemma 4.14 and Theorem 3.5, define $\Lambda_{1,i}$ as some arithmetical formula equivalent to $P_{1,i}(a_{1,i})$ where $P_{1,i}$ is defined by

$$\mathbf{pred}\ P_{1,i}(y) \equiv (\Phi_1^{n_i}[\lambda y.\Phi_{1,l_i}])^N \vee (\Phi_1^{q_i - p_i}[P_1])^N[P_1^N := P_{1,i}].$$

For each $1 \le j \le J$, by Theorem 3.5, define $\Lambda_{2,j}$ as $(\Phi_{2,m_j})^N[y := a_{2,j}]$ if $1 \le m_j \le I_2$, and some arithmetical formula equivalent to $(\Phi_2[P_2, P_2])^N[P_2^N := P_3][y := a_{2,j}]$ where P_3 is defined by
$$\mathbf{pred}\ P_3(y) \equiv \bigvee_{i \in I_3} \Phi_{2,i}^N \vee (\Phi_2[P_2, P_2])^N$$
if $m_j = (r,r)$.

Step 5. Check if the following formula is satisfiable $\bigwedge_{1 \le i \le I} \Lambda_{1,i} \wedge \bigwedge_{1 \le j \le J} \Lambda_{2,j} \wedge \Lambda$

If it is true, then return Yes and stop.

Step 6. Go to the step 2 for the next loop.

$n < n'$ such that $[\![(\Phi_1^n[\lambda x.\Phi_{1,i}])^S]\!]$ and $[\![(\Phi_1^{n'}[\lambda x.\Phi_{1,i}])^S]\!]$ are equivalent. We can take p_i, q_i as the least ones among these n, n'.

Next, by the following (1) and (2), we will show that the algorithm returns Yes iff ϕ is satisfiable.

(1) We will show that the algorithm returns Yes if ϕ is satisfiable. Assume ϕ is satisfiable.

Let $\mathbf{x} = x_{1,1} \ldots x_{1,I_1} x_{2,1} \ldots x_{2,I_2}$, $\mathbf{y} = y_{1,1} \ldots y_{1,I_1} y_{2,1} \ldots y_{2,I_2}$, $\mathbf{t} = t_{1,1} \ldots t_{1,I_1} t_{2,1} \ldots t_{2,I_2}$, and $\mathbf{a} = a_{1,1} \ldots a_{1,I_1} a_{2,1} \ldots a_{2,I_2}$. Define the predicate P by

$$P(\mathbf{x}, \mathbf{y}) \equiv \Pi \wedge *_{k \in K} w_k \mapsto (u^k) * *_{1 \le i \le I} P_1(x_{1,i}, y_{1,i}) * *_{1 \le j \le J} P_2(x_{2,j}, y_{2,j}).$$

Since $P(\mathbf{t}, \mathbf{a})$ and ϕ are equivalent, $P(\mathbf{t}, \mathbf{a})$ is satisfiable. By Proposition 4.7 we have some T such that $P^{(T)}(\mathbf{t}, \mathbf{a})$ is satisfiable. By Proposition 4.6, both $P^{S(T)}(\mathbf{t})$ and $P^{N(T)}(\mathbf{a})$ are satisfiable.

Let T be $(T_{1,1}, ..., T_{1,I}, T_{2,1}, ..., T_{2,J})$. Let

$$\phi' \equiv \Pi \wedge *_{k \in K} w_k \mapsto (\mathbf{u}^k) * *_{1 \leq i \leq I} P_1^{(T_{1,i})}(t_{1,i}, a_{1,i}) * *_{1 \leq j \leq J} P_2^{(T_{2,j})}(t_{2,j}, a_{2,j})$$

Then $P^{(T)}(\mathbf{t}, \mathbf{a})$ is ϕ', $P^{S(T)}(\mathbf{t})$ is ϕ'^S, and $P^{N(T)}(\mathbf{a})$ is ϕ'^N. Hence both ϕ'^S and ϕ'^N are satisfiable. By Proposition 4.13, $[\![\phi'^S]\!]$ is satisfiable.

Let $T_{1,i}$ be $T(l_i, n'_i)$. Take n_i such that $n'_i = n_i + k(q_i - p_i)$ for some $k \geq 0$ and $n_i < q_i - p_i$. Since $[\![P_1^{S(T_{1,i})}(x)]\!] = [\![(\Phi_1^{n_i}[\lambda x.\Phi_{1,l_i}])^S]\!]$, and $[\![(\Phi_1^{p_i}[\lambda x.\Phi_{1,l_i}])^S]\!] \simeq [\![(\Phi_1^{q_i}[\lambda x.\Phi_{1,l_i}])^S]\!]$ by the step 1, we have $[\![P_1^{S(T_{1,i})}(x)]\!] \simeq [\![P_1^{S(T(l_i,n_i))}(x)]\!]$.

Define m_j as $T_{2,j}$ if $1 \leq T_{2,j} \leq I_2$ and (r,r) if $T_{2,j}$ is (T_1, T_2) for some T_1, T_2 and r is arbitrarily chosen from $\widetilde{(T_1, T_2)}$. Since $P_2^{S(T_{2,j})}(t_{2,j})$ is satisfiable, $\Phi_{2,i}^S$ is satisfiable for all $i \in \widetilde{(T_1, T_2)}$. Since $[\![P_2^{S((T_1,T_2))}(x)]\!] = [\![P_2^{S((r,r))}(x)]\!]$ by Lemma 4.15, $[\![P_2^{S(T_{2,j})}(x)]\!] = [\![P_2^{S(m_j)}(x)]\!]$.

Since $[\![P_1^{S(T_{1,i})}(x)]\!] \simeq [\![P_1^{S(T(l_i,n_i))}(x)]\!]$, $[\![P_2^{S(T_{2,j})}(x)]\!] = [\![P_2^{S(m_j)}(x)]\!]$, and $[\![\phi'^S]\!]$ is satisfiable,

$$[\![\Pi \wedge *_{k \in K} w_k \mapsto ((u^k)^S) * *_{1 \leq i \leq I} P_1^{S(T(l_i,n_i))}(t_{1,i}) * *_{1 \leq j \leq J} P_2^{S(m_j)}(t_{2,j})]\!]$$

is satisfiable by Lemma 4.11 (2). Hence we go from the step 3 to the step 4.

Since ϕ'^N is satisfiable, we have s such that $s \models \phi'^N$. Hence $s \models P_1^{N(T_{1,i})}(a_{1,i})$, $s \models P_2^{N(T_{2,j})}(a_{2,j})$, and $s \models \Lambda$. Since $P_1^{N(T(l_i,k(q_i-p_i)))}(y) \equiv P_{1,i}^k(y)$, we have $P_{1,i}^{N(T_{1,i})}(y) \to P_{1,i}(y)$. Therefore $P_1^{N(T_{1,i})}(a_{1,i}) \to \Lambda_{1,i}$ by the step 4. If $0 \leq T_{2,j} \leq I_2$, then $P_2^{N(T_{2,j})} \equiv \Lambda_{2,j}$ by the step 4. If $T_{2,j} = (T_1, T_2)$, then $P_2^{N(T_{2,j})}(a_{2,j}) \to (\Phi_2[P_2, P_2])^N[P_2^N := P_3][y := a_{2,j}]$ and $P_2^{N(T_{2,j})} \to \Lambda_{2,j}$ by the step 4. Hence we have $s \models \Lambda_{1,i}$ and $s \models \Lambda_{2,j}$. Hence $s \models \bigwedge_{1 \leq i \leq I} \Lambda_{1,i} \wedge \bigwedge_{1 \leq j \leq J} \Lambda_{2,j} \wedge \Lambda$. Hence the algorithm returns Yes at the step 5.

(2) We will show that ϕ is satisfiable if the algorithm returns Yes.

We have some $(l_1, n_1, \ldots, l_I, n_I, m_1, \ldots, m_J)$ such that

$$[\![\Pi \wedge *_{k \in K} w_k \mapsto ((u^k)^S) * *_{1 \leq i \leq I} P_1^{S(T(l_i,n_i))}(t_{1,i}) * *_{1 \leq j \leq J} P_2^{S(m_j)}(t_{2,j})]\!]$$

is satisfiable by the step 3, and $\bigwedge_{1 \leq i \leq I} \Lambda_{1,i} \wedge \bigwedge_{1 \leq j \leq J} \Lambda_{2,j} \wedge \Lambda$ is satisfiable by the step 5.

Then we have s such that $s \models \bigwedge_{1 \leq i \leq I} \Lambda_{1,i} \wedge \bigwedge_{1 \leq j \leq J} \Lambda_{2,j} \wedge \Lambda$. Then $s \models \Lambda_{1,i}$.

Since $\Lambda_{1,i} \leftrightarrow P_{1,i}(a_{1,i})$, we have some $k_i \geq 0$ such that $s \models P_1^{N(T(l_i,n_i+k_i(q_i-p_i)))}(a_{1,i})$. Define $T_{1,i}$ as $T(l_i, n_i + k(q_i - p_i))$. Then $s \models P_1^{N(T_{1,i})}(a_{1,i})$.

We define $T_{2,j}$ such that $s \models P_2^{N(T_{2,j})}(a_{2,j})$ by cases according to m_j.

Case 1. $1 \leq m_j \leq I_2$. We define $T_{2,j}$ as m_j. Then $s \models P_2^{N(T_{2,j})}(a_{2,j})$.

Case 2. $m_j = (r, r)$. Since $\Lambda_{2,j} \hookleftarrow (\Phi_2[P_2, P_2])^N[y := a_{2,j}]$, there are $T_{3,j}, T_{4,j}$ such that $\Phi_{2,i}$ is satisfiable for all $i \in (\widetilde{T_{3,j}, T_{4,j}})$, and $s \models (\Phi_2[P, P])^N[P := P_2^{N(T_{3,j})}, P_2^{N(T_{4,j})}][y := a_{2,j}]$, which is $P_2^{N((\widetilde{T_{3,j}, T_{4,j}}))}(a_{2,j})$. Define $T_{2,j}$ as $(T_{3,j}, T_{4,j})$. Then $s \models P_2^{N(T_{2,j})}(a_{2,j})$.

Let

$$\phi' \equiv \Pi \wedge *_{k \in K} w_k \mapsto (\mathbf{u}^k) * *_{1 \leq i \leq I} P_1^{(T_{1,i})}(t_{1,i}, a_{1,i}) * *_{1 \leq j \leq J} P_2^{(T_{2,j})}(t_{2,j}, a_{2,j}) \wedge \Lambda.$$

Then we have $s \models \phi'^N$.

$[\![P_1^{S(T_{1,i})}(x)]\!] \simeq [\![P_1^{S(T(l_i, n_i))}(x)]\!]$ by the step 1.

We can show that $[\![P_2^{S(T_{2,j})}(x)]\!] = [\![P_2^{S(m_j)}(x)]\!]$ as follows. If $1 \leq m_j \leq I_2$, then $T_{2,j} = m_j$ and the claim holds. Assume $m_j = (r, r)$. Then $T_{2,j}$ is $(T_{3,j}, T_{4,j})$. Since $[\![P_2^{S(T_{2,j})}(x)]\!] = [\![P_2^{S((r,r))}(x)]\!]$ by Lemma 4.15, we have the claim.

Since $[\![P_1^{S(T_{1,i})}(x)]\!] \simeq [\![P_1^{S(T(l_i, n_i))}(x)]\!]$, $[\![P_2^{S(T_{2,j})}(x)]\!] = [\![P_2^{S(m_j)}(x)]\!]$, and

$$[\![\Pi \wedge *_{k \in K} w_k \mapsto ((u^k)^S) * *_{1 \leq i \leq I} P_1^{S(T(l_i, n_i))}(t_{1,i}) * *_{1 \leq j \leq J} P_2^{S(m_j)}(t_{2,j})]\!]$$

is satisfiable, by Lemma 4.11 (2),

$$[\![\Pi \wedge *_{k \in K} w_k \mapsto ((u^k)^S) * *_{1 \leq i \leq I} P_1^{S(T_{1,i})}(t_{1,i}) * *_{1 \leq j \leq J} P_2^{S(T_{2,j})}(t_{2,j})]\!]$$

is satisfiable. Namely $[\![\phi'^S]\!]$ is satisfiable. By Proposition 4.13, ϕ'^S is satisfiable. Hence we have s', h such that $s', h \models \phi'^S$.

We define s'' by $s''(x) = s'(x)$ for a pointer variable x and $s''(y) = s(y)$ for an integer variables y. We have $s'', h \models \phi'^S$.

Let $\mathbf{x} = x_{1,1} \ldots x_{1,I_1} x_{2,1} \ldots x_{2,I_2}$, $\mathbf{y} = y_{1,1} \ldots y_{1,I_1} y_{2,1} \ldots y_{2,I_2}$, $\mathbf{t} = t_{1,1} \ldots t_{1,I_1} t_{2,1} \ldots t_{2,I_2}$, and $\mathbf{a} = a_{1,1} \ldots a_{1,I_1} a_{2,1} \ldots a_{2,I_2}$. Define the predicate P by

$$P(\mathbf{x}, \mathbf{y}) \equiv \Pi \wedge *_{k \in K} w_k \mapsto (\mathbf{u}^k) * *_{1 \leq i \leq I} P_1(x_{1,i}, y_{1,i}) * *_{1 \leq j \leq J} P_2(x_{2,j}, y_{2,j}).$$

Define T as $(T_{1,1}, ..., T_{1,I}, T_{2,1}, ..., T_{2,J})$. Then $P^{(T)}(\mathbf{t}, \mathbf{a})$ is ϕ', $P^{S(T)}(\mathbf{t})$ is ϕ'^S, and $P^{N(T)}(\mathbf{a})$ is ϕ'^N.

Since

$$s'', h \models P^{S(T)}(\mathbf{t}),$$
$$s'' \models P^{N(T)}(\mathbf{a}),$$

by Proposition 4.6 we have some h' such that

$$s'', h' \models P^{(T)}(\mathbf{t}, \mathbf{a}).$$

Namely $s'', h' \models \phi'$. Hence $s'', h' \models \phi$. $\square$

5   Conclusion

We have proved that the satisfiability of symbolic heaps in SLA1 system with inductive definitions and Presburger arithmetic without any restrictions is undecidable. We have proposed a decidable symbolic-heap subsystem SLA2 with inductive definitions and Presburger arithmetic with some restrictions, and provided its decision algorithm as well as its correctness proof. To support this result, we have also defined a related decidable subsystem DPI of Presburger arithmetic and inductive definitions with some restrictions.

We have imposed a significant restriction on SLA2 for the case when the unfolding trees becomes non-linear. SLA2 supports AVL trees, but does not support sorted AVL trees because the minimum values and the maximum values interact. Future work could relax the restrictions by using semilinear sets so that it supports a wider class of data structures. We have not investigated pointer arithmetic. An extension of our results to pointer arithmetic could be another future work.

Acknowledgments. This work is partially supported by MoE Tier-2 grant MOE2013-T2-2-146.

References

1. Berdine, J., Calcagno, C., O'Hearn, P.W.: A decidable fragment of separation logic. In: Lodaya, K., Mahajan, M. (eds.) FSTTCS 2004. LNCS, vol. 3328, pp. 97–109. Springer, Heidelberg (2004). doi:10.1007/978-3-540-30538-5_9
2. Berdine, J., Calcagno, C., O'Hearn, P.W.: Symbolic execution with separation logic. In: Yi, K. (ed.) APLAS 2005. LNCS, vol. 3780, pp. 52–68. Springer, Heidelberg (2005). doi:10.1007/11575467_5
3. Bozga, M., Iosif, R., Perarnau, S.: Quantitative separation logic and programs with lists. J. Autom. Reason. **45**(2), 131–156 (2010)
4. Brotherston, J., Fuhs, C., Gorogiannis, N., Perez, J.N.: A decision procedure for satisfiability inseparation logic with inductive predicates. In: Proceedings of CSL-LICS 2014 (2014). Article 25
5. Chin, W.N., David, C., Nguyen, H.H., Qin, S.: Automated verification of shape, size and bag properties viauser-defined predicates in separation logic. Sci. Comput. Program. **77**(9), 1006–1036 (2012)
6. Enderton, H.B.: A Mathematical Introduction to Logic, 2 edn. Academic Press (2000)
7. Iosif, R., Rogalewicz, A., Simacek, J.: The tree width of separation logic with recursive definitions. In: Bonacina, M.P. (ed.) CADE 2013. LNCS (LNAI), vol. 7898, pp. 21–38. Springer, Heidelberg (2013). doi:10.1007/978-3-642-38574-2_2
8. Iosif, R., Rogalewicz, A., Vojnar, T.: Deciding entailments in inductive separation logic with tree automata. In: Cassez, F., Raskin, J.-F. (eds.) ATVA 2014. LNCS, vol. 8837, pp. 201–218. Springer, Heidelberg (2014). doi:10.1007/978-3-319-11936-6_15
9. Piskac, R., Wies, T., Zufferey, D.: Automating separation logic using SMT. In: Sharygina, N., Veith, H. (eds.) CAV 2013. LNCS, vol. 8044, pp. 773–789. Springer, Heidelberg (2013). doi:10.1007/978-3-642-39799-8_54

10. Piskac, R., Wies, T., Zufferey, D.: Automating separation logic with trees and data. In: Biere, A., Bloem, R. (eds.) CAV 2014. LNCS, vol. 8559, pp. 711–728. Springer, Heidelberg (2014). doi:10.1007/978-3-319-08867-9_47

11. Navarro Pérez, J.A., Rybalchenko, A.: Separation logic modulo theories. In: Shan, C. (ed.) APLAS 2013. LNCS, vol. 8301, pp. 90–106. Springer, Heidelberg (2013). doi:10.1007/978-3-319-03542-0_7

12. Reynolds, J.C.: Separation logic: a logic for shared mutable data structures. In: Proceedings of Seventeenth Annual IEEE Symposium on Logic in Computer Science (LICS2002), pp. 55–74 (2002)

13. Brotherston, J., Gorogiannis, N., Kanovich, M., Rowe, R.: Model checking for symbolic-heap separation logic with inductive predicates. In: Proceedings of POPL-43, pp. 84–96 (2016)

Completeness for a First-Order Abstract Separation Logic

Zhé Hóu[(⊠)] and Alwen Tiu

Nanyang Technological University, Singapore, Singapore
{zhe.hou,atiu}@ntu.edu.sg

Abstract. Existing work on theorem proving for the assertion language of separation logic (SL) either focuses on abstract semantics which are not readily available in most applications of program verification, or on concrete models for which completeness is not possible. An important element in concrete SL is the points-to predicate which denotes a singleton heap. SL with the points-to predicate has been shown to be non-recursively enumerable. In this paper, we develop a first-order SL, called FOASL, with an abstracted version of the points-to predicate. We prove that FOASL is sound and complete with respect to an abstract semantics, of which the standard SL semantics is an instance. We also show that some reasoning principles involving the points-to predicate can be approximated as FOASL theories, thus allowing our logic to be used for reasoning about concrete program verification problems. We give some example theories that are sound with respect to different variants of separation logics from the literature, including those that are incompatible with Reynolds's semantics. In the experiment we demonstrate our FOASL based theorem prover which is able to handle a large fragment of separation logic with heap semantics as well as non-standard semantics.

1 Introduction

Separation Logic (SL) is widely used in program verification and reasoning about memory models [29,31]. SL extends the traditional Hoare Logic with logical connectives $*, -\!*$ from the logic of Bunched Implications (BI). These new connectives in BI provide an elegant way to reason about resources locally, enabling analyses of large scale programs. Current work on SL can be divided into two categories: one on the abstract separation logics and the other on the concrete ones. On the abstract side there has been study on BI and its Boolean variant BBI [23,28]. Closely related are abstract separation logic and its neighbours [9,22]. Abstract separation logics lack the interpretation of the points-to predicate $\mapsto$, which represents a single memory cell. In this setting, the semantics is just an extension of commutative monoids with certain properties usually called separation theory [8,13]. On the concrete side there have been developments along several directions, such as proof methods for SL with memory model semantics [15,17,25], and symbolic heaps [1,2,6,27]. There have been numerous modifications of SL, e.g., Fictional Separation Logic [19], Rely/Guarantee [35], Concurrent Separation Logic [4].

© Springer International Publishing AG 2016
A. Igarashi (Ed.): APLAS 2016, LNCS 10017, pp. 444–463, 2016.
DOI: 10.1007/978-3-319-47958-3_23

To support reasoning about Hoare triples, it is essential to have proof methods for the assertion logic. In the reminder of this paper we focus on the assertion logic of separation logic. Although theorem proving for propositional abstract separation logics (PASLs) is undecidable [7,23], there have been semi-decision procedures for those logics [5,8,16,24,30]. However, since PASLs do not impose a concrete semantic model, they usually cannot be directly used in program verification. The situation is more intriguing for separation logic with memory model semantics. Calcagno et al. showed that the full logic is not recursively enumerable [10], thus it is not possible to have a sound and complete finite proof system for the full separation logic. Interestingly, their result uses only an extension of first-order logic, without function symbols, but with a two-field points-to predicate, i.e., predicates of the form $[a \mapsto c, d]$, which represents a memory cell with a record of two fields. Recent study also shows that the points-to predicate $\mapsto$ is a source of undecidability. For example, restricting the record field (i.e., right hand side) of $\mapsto$ to one variable and allowing only one quantified variable reduces the satisfiability of SL to PSPACE-complete [12]. The above work indicates that directly handling the points-to predicate in the logic may not be easy. Section 4 of [17] details related issues on various proof systems for separation logic with memory model. Another complicating factor in designing a proof system for separation logic is the "magic wand" $-\!\!*$ connective. The separation conjunction $*$ can be encoded using $-\!\!*$, but not the other way around [3,11]. Consequently, most proof methods for SL with concrete semantics are restricted to fragments of SL, typically omitting $-\!\!*$. The connective $-\!\!*$, however, has found many applications, such as tail-recursion [26], iterators [20], "septraction" in rely/guarantee [35], amongst other motivating examples discussed in the introduction of [25].

Since completeness with respect to Reynolds's model is not possible, an interesting question arises as to what properties of points-to ($-\!\!*$ is not so crucial in terms of the completeness property) one should formalize in the system, and what kind of semantics the resulting proof system captures. There have been at least a couple of attempts at designing a proof system that features both $-\!\!*$ and points-to; one by Lee and Park [25] and the other by Hou et al. [17]. In [25], Lee and Park claimed incorrectly that their proof system is complete with respect to Reynolds's semantics, though this claim was later retracted.[1] In [17], Hou et al. give a proof system LS_{SL} that is sound with respect to Reynolds's semantics, but no alternative semantics was proposed nor any completeness result stated. It is also not clear in general what proof rules one should include in the proof system such as that in [17]. This has led to the introduction of various ad hoc proof rules in [17], which are often complex and unintuitive, in order to capture specific properties of the underlying concrete separation logic models (e.g., Reynolds's model), resulting in a complex proof system, which is both hard to implement and hard to reason about.

---

[1] See http://pl.postech.ac.kr/SL/ for the revised version of their proof system, which is sound but not complete w.r.t. Reynolds's semantics.

In this paper, we revisit our previous work [17] in order to provide an abstract semantics and a sound and complete proof system with respect to that abstract semantics, that are useful for reasoning about the meta-theory of the proof system, and easy to extend to support reasoning about various concrete models of separation logic. Our point of departure is to try to give a minimal proof system and encode as many properties of points-to as possible using *logical theories*, rather than proof rules, and to formalize as inference rules only those properties that cannot be easily encoded as theories. This led us to keep only two proof rules for the points-to predicate from [17] (see the rules $\rightsquigarrow_1$ and $\rightsquigarrow_2$ in Fig. 1 in Sect. 3). Semantically, these two rules are justified by a new semantics of an abstract version of the points-to predicate (notationally represented by $\rightsquigarrow$ here, to distinguish it from the points-to predicate $\mapsto$ in the concrete SL), that is, it is a function that constructs a heap from a tuple of values. In particular, we do not assume that the constructed heap from a tuple is a singleton heap, so a points-to predicate such as $[a \rightsquigarrow b, c]$ in our semantics denotes a heap, but not necessarily a singleton heap mapping a to a two-field record (b, c). Reasoning in the concrete models, such as Reynolds's SL, which may require properties of singleton heaps, can be approximated by adding theories to restrict the interpretation of points-to (see e.g., Sect. 5.1). Obviously one would not be able to completely restrict the interpretation of $\rightsquigarrow$ to singleton heaps via a finite theory, as one would then run into the same incompleteness problem as shown in [10].

The proof system for the first-order abstract separation logic that we introduce here, called LS_{FOASL}, is based on the proof system LS_{PASL} for propositional abstract separation logic (PASL) [16], which is a labelled sequent calculus. We choose labelled calculi as the framework to formalize our logic since it has been shown to be a good framework for proof search automation for abstract separation logics [17,24]. Formulas in a labelled sequent in LS_{PASL} are interpreted relative to the interpretation of the labels they are attached to, so a labelled formula such as $h : F$, where h is a label and F is a formula, denotes the truth value of F when evaluated against the heap h. In extending PASL to the first-order case, especially when formulating theories for specific concrete models, it turns out that we need to be able to assert that some formulas hold universally for all heaps, or that they hold in some unspecified heap, both of which are not expressible in PASL. To get around this limitation, we introduce modal operators to allow one to state properties that hold globally in all heaps or in some heap. Section 5 shows some examples of uses of these modal operators in theories approximating concrete models of separation logics.

The semantics of FOASL is formally defined in Sect. 2. In Sect. 3 we present the proof system LS_{FOASL}, which is an extension of LS_{PASL} with rules for first-order quantifiers, the points-to predicate and modal operators. In Sect. 4, we prove soundness and completeness of LS_{FOASL} with respect to the semantics described in Sect. 2. The completeness proof is done via a counter-model construction similar to that in [16,21] for the propositional case, but our proof is significantly more complicated as we have to deal with the first-order language and the construction of the model for the points-to predicate, which requires a novel proof technique. We show in Sect. 5 that all the inference rules for points-to in the labelled sequent calculus LS_{SL} [17] can be derived using theories in our logic, except one rule called HC, which is not used in the current program verification tools. Our theories for points-to cover the widely-used symbolic heap fragment of SL, thus our logic can be used in many existing program verification methods. Furthermore, we can also prove many formulae that are valid in SL but which cannot be proved by most existing tools. An implementation is discussed in Sect. 6, we show that our prover can reason about the standard heap semantics and the non-standard ones.

2   First-Order Abstract Separation Logic

This section introduces First-order Abstract Separation Logic (FOASL). The formulae of FOASL are parameterized by a first order signature $\Sigma = (\mathcal{R}, \mathcal{C})$, consisting of a set of predicate symbols $\mathcal{R}$ and a set of constants $\mathcal{C}$. Constants are ranged by a, b and c, and predicate symbols by p and q (possibly with subscripts). We also assume an infinite set $\mathcal{V}$ of first-order variables, ranged over by x, y, z. A *term* is either a constant or a variable, and is denoted by e, s and t. We assume that $\mathcal{R}$ includes a symbol $=$, denoting the equality predicate, and a finite collection of *abstract points-to* predicates. We shall use the notation $\leadsto^n$ to denote an abstract points-to predicate of arity n. We use an infix notation when writing the abstract points-to predicates. For an abstract points-to predicate of arity k, taking arguments $t_1, \ldots, t_k$, we write it in the form:

$$t_1 \leadsto^k t_2, \ldots, t_k.$$

We shall omit the superscript k when the arity of $\leadsto$ is not important or can be inferred from the context of discussion. Note that the abstract points-to $\leadsto$ is not the points-to predicate in SL, but is a weaker version whose properties will be discussed later. To simplify presentation, we do not consider function symbols in our language, but it is straightforward to add them. In any case, the incompleteness result for concrete SL of [10] holds even in the absence of function symbols, so the omission of function symbols from our logic does not make the completeness proof for our logic conceptually easier.

The formulae of FOASL are given by the following grammar:

$$F ::= \top^* \mid \bot \mid p(t_1, \ldots, t_k) \mid s \leadsto t_1, \ldots, t_l \mid s = t \mid F \to F \mid$$
$$F * F \mid F \mathbin{-\!\!*} F \mid \Diamond F \mid \exists x.F$$

The logical constant $\bot$, the connective $\to$ and the quantifer $\exists$ are the usual logical operators from first-order logic. The operator $\Diamond$ is a modal operator (denoting "possibility"). Classical negation $\neg F$ is defined as $F \to \bot$. Other operators, i.e., $\top$, $\vee$, $\wedge$, $\forall$, and $\Box$, can be defined via classical negation, e.g., $\Box A = \Diamond (A \to \bot) \to \bot$. The connectives $*$ and $-\!\!*$ correspond to separation conjunction and the "magic wand" from separation logic [31], and $\top^*$ is the multiplicative truth.

The semantics of FOASL is defined based on a *separation algebra*, i.e., a commutative monoid $(H, \circ, \epsilon)$ where H is a non-empty set, $\circ$ is a partial binary

Table 1. The semantics of FOASL.

$\mathcal{M}, v, h \Vdash p(t_1, \cdots, t_n)$ iff $(t_1^{\mathcal{M}}, \cdots, t_n^{\mathcal{M}}) \in p^I$ $\qquad\qquad \mathcal{M}, v, h \Vdash \top^*$ iff $h = \epsilon$

$\mathcal{M}, v, h \Vdash A \rightarrow B \qquad$ iff $\mathcal{M}, v, h \nVdash A$ or $\mathcal{M}, v, h \Vdash B \qquad \mathcal{M}, v, h \Vdash \bot$ iff never

$\mathcal{M}, v, h \Vdash A * B$ iff $h_1 \circ h_2 = h$ and $\mathcal{M}, v, h_1 \Vdash A$ and $\mathcal{M}, v, h_2 \Vdash B$ for some h_1, h_2

$\mathcal{M}, v, h \Vdash A \mathbin{-\!\!*} B$ iff for all h_1, h_2, if $h \circ h_1 = h_2$ and $\mathcal{M}, v, h_1 \Vdash A$, then $\mathcal{M}, v, h_2 \Vdash B$

$\mathcal{M}, v, h \Vdash \exists x. A(x)$ iff $\exists d \in D. \mathcal{M}, v[d/x], h \Vdash A(x)$

$\mathcal{M}, v, h \Vdash \Diamond A \qquad$ iff $\exists h_1 \in H. \mathcal{M}, v, h_1 \Vdash A$

$\mathcal{M}, v, h \Vdash t_1 = t_2 \qquad$ iff $t_1^{\mathcal{M}}$ and $t_2^{\mathcal{M}}$ are the same element in D.

$\mathcal{M}, v, h \Vdash t_1 \rightsquigarrow t_2, \ldots, t_k$ iff $\mathfrak{f}_k(t_1^{\mathcal{M}}, \ldots, t_k^{\mathcal{M}}) = h$.

function $H \times H \rightharpoonup H$ written infix, and $\epsilon \in H$ is the unit. This separation algebra satisfies the following conditions, where '=' is interpreted as 'both sides undefined, or both sides defined and equal':

identity: $\forall h \in H. h \circ \epsilon = h$.

commutativity: $\forall h_1, h_2 \in H. h_1 \circ h_2 = h_2 \circ h_1$.

associativity: $\forall h_1, h_2, h_3 \in H. h_1 \circ (h_2 \circ h_3) = (h_1 \circ h_2) \circ h_3$.

cancellativity: $\forall h_1, h_2, h_3, h_4 \in H$. if $h_1 \circ h_2 = h_3$ and $h_1 \circ h_4 = h_3$ then $h_2 = h_4$.

indivisible unit: if $h_1 \circ h_2 = \epsilon$ then $h_1 = \epsilon$.

disjointness: $\forall h_1, h_2 \in H$. if $h_1 \circ h_1 = h_2$ then $h_1 = \epsilon$.

cross-split: if $h_1 \circ h_2 = h_0$ and $h_3 \circ h_4 = h_0$, then $\exists h_{13}, h_{14}, h_{23}, h_{24} \in H$ such that $h_{13} \circ h_{14} = h_1$, $h_{23} \circ h_{24} = h_2$, $h_{13} \circ h_{23} = h_3$, and $h_{14} \circ h_{24} = h_4$.

Note that *partial-determinism* is assumed since $\circ$ is a partial function: for any $h_1, h_2, h_3, h_4 \in H$, if $h_1 \circ h_2 = h_3$ and $h_1 \circ h_2 = h_4$ then $h_3 = h_4$.

A FOASL model is a tuple $\mathcal{M} = (D, I, v, \mathcal{F}, H, \circ, \epsilon)$ where D is a non-empty domain, I is an interpretation function mapping constant symbols to elements of D, and predicate symbols, other than $=$ and $\rightsquigarrow$, to relations. The function v is a valuation function mapping variables to D. We use a set $\mathcal{F}$ of functions to interpret the abstract points-to predicates. To each abstract points-to predicate of arity n, we associate an n-argument total function $\mathfrak{f}_n : D \times \cdots \times D \mapsto H \in \mathcal{F}$. The tuple $(H, \circ, \epsilon)$ is a separation algebra. For a predicate symbol p and a constant symbol c, we write p^I and c^I, respectively, for their interpretations under I. We write $t^{\mathcal{M}}$ for the interpretation of term t in the model $\mathcal{M}$. For a variable x, $x^{\mathcal{M}} = v(x)$. A term t is *closed* if it has no variables, and we write t^I for the interpretation of t since it is independent of the valuation function v.

A separation algebra $(H, \circ, \epsilon)$ can be seen as a Kripke frame, where H is the set of worlds and the (ternary) accessibility relation R is defined as: $R(h_1, h_2, h_3)$ iff $h_1 \circ h_2 = h_3$. Modal operators are thus a natural extension to FOASL.

The semantics of FOASL formulae are defined via Kripke style notations in Table 1, where $\mathcal{M} = (D, I, v, \mathcal{F}, H, \circ, \epsilon)$ is a FOASL model, and $h, h_1, h_2 \in H$. In the table, we write $v[c/x]$ to denote the valuation function that may differ from v only in the mapping of x, i.e., $v[c/x](x) = c$ and $v[c/x](y) = v(y)$ if $y \neq x$. A FOASL formula A is true at h in the model $\mathcal{M} = (D, I, v, \mathcal{F}, H, \circ, \epsilon)$

if $\mathcal{M}, v, h \Vdash A$. It is true in $\mathcal{M}$ if it is true at some h in H. A formula is valid if it is true in all models; a formula is satisfiable if it is true in some model. A formula is called a *sentence* if it has no free variables.

Besides the first-order language, FOASL has two main extensions over PASL: the abstract points-to predicate $\rightsquigarrow$ and the modality $\Diamond$. We explain their intuitions here. In the concrete SL models, the points-to predicate $[a \mapsto b]$ is true only in a singleton heap that maps a to b. In our abstract semantics for $[a \rightsquigarrow b]$, we drop the requirement that the heap must be singleton. Instead, we generalize this by parameterizing the semantics with a function (the function $\mathfrak{f}$ discussed earlier) that associates values to (possibily non-singleton) heaps. The predicate $[a \rightsquigarrow b]$ is true in a world h iff h is the image of $\mathfrak{f}_2(a, b)$. As a consequence of this interpretation of $\rightsquigarrow$, we have the following properties where $\vec{t}$ is a list of fields:

- *(Injectivity)* If $s \rightsquigarrow \vec{t}$ holds in both h_1 and h_2, then $h_1 = h_2$.
- *(Totality)* For any s and $\vec{t}$, there is some h such that $s \rightsquigarrow \vec{t}$ holds in h.

The latter in particular is a consequence of the fact that functions in $\mathcal{F}$ are total functions. We do not impose any other properties on $\rightsquigarrow$. For example, we do not assume an invalid address nil such that $nil \mapsto \vec{t}$ must be false. The reason we cannot disprove $nil \rightsquigarrow \vec{t}$ is partly because we do not insist on a fixed interpretation of nil in our logic. This *does not* mean that $nil \rightsquigarrow \vec{t}$ is valid in our logic; it is only satisfiable. We can strengthen $\rightsquigarrow$ by adding more theories to it, including a formula to force $nil \rightsquigarrow \vec{t}$ to be unsatisfiable. See Sects. 5 and 6 for details.

To motivate the need for the modal operators, consider an example to approximate, in our framework, a separation logic where the points-to relation maps an address to a multiset of addresses. In the binary case, one could formalize this as:

$$F = \forall x, y, z.(x \mapsto y, z) \rightarrow (x \mapsto z, y)$$

We can encode this property as a rule in a labelled sequent calculus as shown below left. When generalising this to points-to of $(n+1)$-arities, we will have to consider adding many variants of rules that permute the right hand side of $\mapsto$, which is what we are trying to avoid. Alternatively, we can add the formula F to the antecedent of the sequent, and attach a label l to F, and do a forward-chaining on $l : F$, as shown below right, where Γ, Δ are sets of labelled formulae:

$$\frac{\Gamma; l : (a \mapsto c, b) \vdash \Delta}{\Gamma; l : (a \mapsto b, c) \vdash \Delta} \qquad \frac{\cdots \qquad \Gamma, l : F, l : (a \mapsto c, b) \vdash \Delta}{\Gamma, l : F, l : (a \mapsto b, c) \vdash \Delta}$$

where the $\cdots$ are the instantiation of x, y, z with a, b, c respectively, and the discharge of the assumption $(x \mapsto y, z)$ of F. However, if $(a \mapsto b, c)$ in the conclusion is attached to another label (world) m, we then have to add $m : F$ to the sequent. In effect, we would have to add an infinite set of labelled formulae of the form $k : F$ to the sequent to achieve the same effect of the inference rule. With modalities, we can simply use $l : \Box F$, which would then allow F to be used at any world in the antecedent of the sequent.

Example 1. Consider Reynolds's semantics for separation logic [31], with an abstract points-to predicate of arity two. This can be shown to be an instance of our abstract semantics, where the domain D is the set of integers, H is the set of heaps (i.e., finite partial maps from integers to integers), ϵ denotes the empty heap, and the function f_2 is defined as $f_2(a, b) = [a \mapsto b]$ where $[a \mapsto b]$ is the singleton heap, mapping a to b. The operation $\circ$ on H is defined as heap composition. It can be shown that $(H, \circ, \epsilon)$ forms a separation algebra. Note that if we relax the interpretation of H to allow infinite heaps, $(H, \circ, \epsilon)$ is still a separation algebra, which shows that our semantics may admit non-standard interpretations of separation logic.

3 LS_{FOASL}: A Labelled Calculus for FOASL

Let LVar be an infinite set of *label variables*, the set $\mathcal{L}$ of *labels* is LVar $\cup \{\epsilon\}$, where $\epsilon \notin$ LVar is a label constant. We overload the notation and write h with subscripts as labels. A function $\rho : \mathcal{L} \to H$ from labels to worlds is a *label mapping* iff it satisfies $\rho(\epsilon) = \epsilon$, mapping the label constant ϵ to the identity world of H. A *labelled formula* is a pair consisting of a label and a formula. We write a labelled formula as $h : A$, when h is the label and A is the formula of the labelled formula. A *relational atom* is an expression of the form $(h_1, h_2 \triangleright h_3)$, where h_1, h_2 and h_3 are labels, this corresponds to $h_1 \circ h_2 = h_3$ in the semantics. A relational atom is not a formula; rather it can be thought of as a structural component of a sequent. A *sequent* takes the form $\mathcal{G}; \Gamma \vdash \Delta$ where $\mathcal{G}$ is a set of relational atoms, Γ, Δ are sets of labelled formulae, and ; denotes set union. Thus $\Gamma; h : A$ is the union of Γ and $\{h : A\}$. The left hand side of a sequent is the *antecedent* and the right hand side is the *succedent*.

We call our labelled proof system LS_{FOASL}. The logical rules of LS_{FOASL} are shown in Fig. 1, structural rules are in Fig. 2. To simplify some rules, we introduce the notation $h_1 \sim h_2$ as an abbreviation of $(\epsilon, h_1 \triangleright h_2)$. We use the notation $[t/x]$ to denote a variable substitution, and similarly $[h'/h]$ for a label substitution, where h is a label variable. The equality rules, for terms ($=_1$ and $=_2$) and labels ($\sim_1$ and $\sim_2$), are the usual equality rules (see e.g., [34]). These rules allow one to replace a term (label) with its equal anywhere in the sequent. Note that in those rules, the replacement of terms (labels) need not be done for all occurrences of equal terms; one can replace just one occurrence or more. For example, below left is a valid instance of $=_2$. This is because both the premise and the conclusion of the rules are instances of the sequent below right:

$$\frac{h : s = t; h_1 : p(t, s) \vdash h_2 : q(s, s)}{h : s = t; h_1 : p(s, s) \vdash h_2 : q(s, s)} =_2 \qquad h : s = t; h_1 : p(x, s) \vdash h_2 : q(s, s)$$

i.e., the premise sequent is obtained from the above sequent with substitution $[t/x]$, and the conclusion sequent with $[s/x]$. A similar remark applies for label replacements in sequents affected via $\sim_2$. The rules $\rightsquigarrow_1$ and $\rightsquigarrow_2$ respectively capture the injectivity and the totality properties of the underlying semantic function interpreting $\rightsquigarrow$.

$$\dfrac{}{\mathcal{G};\Gamma;h:A\vdash h:A;\Delta}\;id \qquad \dfrac{}{\mathcal{G};\Gamma;h:\bot\vdash\Delta}\;{\bot}L$$

$$\dfrac{\mathcal{G};h\sim\epsilon;\Gamma\vdash\Delta}{\mathcal{G};\Gamma;h:\top^{*}\vdash\Delta}\;{\top}^{*}L \qquad \dfrac{}{\mathcal{G};\Gamma\vdash\epsilon:\top^{*};\Delta}\;{\top}^{*}R$$

$$\dfrac{\mathcal{G};\Gamma;h:A\vdash h:B;\Delta}{\mathcal{G};\Gamma\vdash h:A\to B;\Delta}\;{\to}R \qquad \dfrac{\mathcal{G};\Gamma\vdash h:A;\Delta \quad \mathcal{G};\Gamma;h:B\vdash\Delta}{\mathcal{G};\Gamma;h:A\to B\vdash\Delta}\;{\to}L$$

$$\dfrac{(h_1,h_2\triangleright h_0);\mathcal{G};\Gamma;h_1:A;h_2:B\vdash\Delta}{\mathcal{G};\Gamma;h_0:A*B\vdash\Delta}\;*L \qquad \dfrac{(h_1,h_0\triangleright h_2);\mathcal{G};\Gamma;h_1:A\vdash h_2:B;\Delta}{\mathcal{G};\Gamma\vdash h_0:A\!-\!\!*\,B;\Delta}\;{-\!\!*}R$$

$$\dfrac{(h_1,h_2\triangleright h_0);\mathcal{G};\Gamma\vdash h_1:A;h_0:A*B;\Delta \quad (h_1,h_2\triangleright h_0);\mathcal{G};\Gamma\vdash h_2:B;h_0:A*B;\Delta}{(h_1,h_2\triangleright h_0);\mathcal{G};\Gamma\vdash h_0:A*B;\Delta}\;*R$$

$$\dfrac{(h_1,h_0\triangleright h_2);\mathcal{G};\Gamma;h_0:A\!-\!\!*\,B\vdash h_1:A;\Delta \quad (h_1,h_0\triangleright h_2);\mathcal{G};\Gamma;h_0:A\!-\!\!*\,B;h_2:B\vdash\Delta}{(h_1,h_0\triangleright h_2);\mathcal{G};\Gamma;h_0:A\!-\!\!*\,B\vdash\Delta}\;{-\!\!*}L$$

$$\dfrac{\mathcal{G};\Gamma;h:A(y)\vdash\Delta}{\mathcal{G};\Gamma;h:\exists x.A(x)\vdash\Delta}\;\exists L \qquad \dfrac{\mathcal{G};\Gamma\vdash h:A(t);h:\exists x.A(x);\Delta}{\mathcal{G};\Gamma\vdash h:\exists x.A(x);\Delta}\;\exists R \qquad \dfrac{\mathcal{G};\Gamma;h':A\vdash\Delta}{\mathcal{G};\Gamma;h:\Diamond A\vdash\Delta}\;\Diamond L$$

$$\dfrac{\mathcal{G};\Gamma;h:t=t\vdash\Delta}{\mathcal{G};\Gamma\vdash\Delta}\;{=}_1 \qquad \dfrac{\mathcal{G};h:s=t;\Gamma[t/x]\vdash\Delta[t/x]}{\mathcal{G};h:s=t;\Gamma[s/x]\vdash\Delta[s/x]}\;{=}_2 \qquad \dfrac{\mathcal{G};\Gamma\vdash h':A;h:\Diamond A;\Delta}{\mathcal{G};\Gamma\vdash h:\Diamond A;\Delta}\;\Diamond R$$

$$\dfrac{\mathcal{G};\Gamma;h:s\rightsquigarrow\vec{t}\vdash\Delta}{\mathcal{G};\Gamma\vdash\Delta}\;\rightsquigarrow_1 \qquad \dfrac{\mathcal{G};h_1\sim h_2;\Gamma;h_1:s\rightsquigarrow\vec{t};h_2:s\rightsquigarrow\vec{t}\vdash\Delta}{\mathcal{G};\Gamma;h_1:s\rightsquigarrow\vec{t};h_2:s\rightsquigarrow\vec{t}\vdash\Delta}\;\rightsquigarrow_2$$

Side conditions:
In $*L$ and $-\!\!*\,R$, the labels h_1 and h_2 do not occur in the conclusion.
In $\exists L$, y is not free in the conclusion.   In $\Diamond L$, h' does not occur in the conclusion.
In $\rightsquigarrow_1$, h does not occur in the conclusion.

Fig. 1. Logical rules in LS_{FOASL}.

$$\dfrac{h\sim h;\mathcal{G};\Gamma\vdash\Delta}{\mathcal{G};\Gamma\vdash\Delta}\;\sim_1 \qquad \dfrac{h_1\sim h_2;\mathcal{G}[h_2/h];\Gamma[h_2/h]\vdash\Delta[h_2/h]}{h_1\sim h_2;\mathcal{G}[h_1/h];\Gamma[h_1/h]\vdash\Delta[h_1/h]}\;\sim_2$$

$$\dfrac{(h_2,h_1\triangleright h_0);(h_1,h_2\triangleright h_0);\mathcal{G};\Gamma\vdash\Delta}{(h_1,h_2\triangleright h_0);\mathcal{G};\Gamma\vdash\Delta}\;E \qquad \dfrac{(h_1,h_1\triangleright h_2);h_1\sim\epsilon;\mathcal{G};\Gamma\vdash\Delta}{(h_1,h_1\triangleright h_2);\mathcal{G};\Gamma\vdash\Delta}\;D$$

$$\dfrac{(h_3,h_5\triangleright h_0);(h_2,h_4\triangleright h_5);(h_1,h_2\triangleright h_0);(h_3,h_4\triangleright h_1);\mathcal{G};\Gamma\vdash\Delta}{(h_1,h_2\triangleright h_0);(h_3,h_4\triangleright h_1);\mathcal{G};\Gamma\vdash\Delta}\;A$$

$$\dfrac{(h_1,h_2\triangleright h_0);h_0\sim h_3;\mathcal{G};\Gamma\vdash\Delta}{(h_1,h_2\triangleright h_0);(h_1,h_2\triangleright h_3);\mathcal{G};\Gamma\vdash\Delta}\;P \qquad \dfrac{(h_1,h_2\triangleright h_0);h_2\sim h_3;\mathcal{G};\Gamma\vdash\Delta}{(h_1,h_2\triangleright h_0);(h_1,h_3\triangleright h_0);\mathcal{G};\Gamma\vdash\Delta}\;C$$

$$\dfrac{(h_5,h_6\triangleright h_1);(h_7,h_8\triangleright h_2);(h_5,h_7\triangleright h_3);(h_6,h_8\triangleright h_4);(h_1,h_2\triangleright h_0);(h_3,h_4\triangleright h_0);\mathcal{G};\Gamma\vdash\Delta}{(h_1,h_2\triangleright h_0);(h_3,h_4\triangleright h_0);\mathcal{G};\Gamma\vdash\Delta}\;CS$$

Side conditions:
In A, the label h_5 does not occur in the conclusion.
In CS, the labels h_5,h_6,h_7,h_8 do not occur in the conclusion.

Fig. 2. Structural rules in LS_{FOASL}.

An *extended model* $(\mathcal{M}, \rho)$ is a FOASL model $\mathcal{M}$ equipped with a label mapping ρ. A sequent $\mathcal{G}; \Gamma \vdash \Delta$ is *falsifiable* in an extended model if: (1) every relational atom $(h_1, h_2 \triangleright h_3) \in \mathcal{G}$ is true, i.e., $\rho(h_1) \circ \rho(h_2) = \rho(h_3)$; (2) every labelled formula $h : A \in \Gamma$ is true, i.e., $\mathcal{M}, v, \rho(h) \Vdash A$; (3) every labelled formula $h' : B \in \Delta$ is false, i.e., $\mathcal{M}, v, \rho(h') \nVdash B$. A sequent is falsifiable if it is falsifiable in some extended model.

To prove a formula F, we start from the sequent $\vdash h : F$ with an arbitrary label $h \neq \epsilon$, and try to derive a closed derivation by applying inference rules backwards from this sequent. A derivation is closed if every branch can be closed by a rule with no premises. The soundness of LS_{FOASL} can be proved by arguing that each rule preserves falsifiability upwards. The proof is given in [18].

Theorem 1 (Soundness). *For every FOASL formula F, if $\vdash h : F$ is derivable in LS_{FOASL} for any label h, then F is a valid FOASL formula.*

4   Counter-Model Construction

We now give a counter-model construction for LS_{FOASL} to show that LS_{FOASL} is complete w.r.t. FOASL. The proof here is motivated by the completeness proof of the labelled sequent calculus and labelled tableaux for PASL [16,21], but this proof is significantly more complex, as can be seen in the definition of Hintikka sequent below, which has almost twice as many cases as the previous work. The constructed model extends the non-classical logic model in the previous work with a Herbrand model as in first-order logic. For space reasons we only set up the stage here and give the full proofs in [18].

We define a notion of *saturated sequent*, i.e., *Hintikka sequent*, on which all possible rule instances in LS_{FOASL} have been applied. In the following, we denote with R a relational atom or a labelled formula.

Definition 1 (Hintikka sequent). *Let L be a FOASL language and let T be the set of closed terms in L. A labelled sequent $\mathcal{G}; \Gamma \vdash \Delta$, where Γ, Δ are sets of labelled sentences, is a Hintikka sequent w.r.t. L if it satisfies the following conditions for any sentences A, B, any terms t, t', and any labels $h, h_0, h_1, h_2, h_3, h_4, h_5, h_6, h_7$:*

1. *If $h_1 : A \in \Gamma$ and $h_2 : A \in \Delta$ then $h_1 \sim h_2 \notin \mathcal{G}$.*
2. *$h : \bot \notin \Gamma$.*
3. *If $h : \top^* \in \Gamma$ then $h \sim \epsilon \in \mathcal{G}$.*
4. *If $h : \top^* \in \Delta$ then $h \sim \epsilon \notin \mathcal{G}$.*
5. *If $h : A \rightarrow B \in \Gamma$ then $h : A \in \Delta$ or $h : B \in \Gamma$.*
6. *If $h : A \rightarrow B \in \Delta$ then $h : A \in \Gamma$ and $h : B \in \Delta$.*
7. *If $h_0 : A * B \in \Gamma$ then $\exists h_1, h_2 \in \mathcal{L}$ s.t. $(h_1, h_2 \triangleright h_0) \in \mathcal{G}$, $h_1 : A \in \Gamma$ and $h_2 : B \in \Gamma$.*
8. *If $h_3 : A * B \in \Delta$ then $\forall h_0, h_1, h_2 \in \mathcal{L}$ if $(h_1, h_2 \triangleright h_0) \in \mathcal{G}$ and $h_0 \sim h_3 \in \mathcal{G}$ then $h_1 : A \in \Delta$ or $h_2 : B \in \Delta$.*
9. *If $h_3 : A \mathbin{-\!*} B \in \Gamma$ then $\forall h_0, h_1, h_2 \in \mathcal{L}$ if $(h_1, h_2 \triangleright h_0) \in \mathcal{G}$ and $h_2 \sim h_3 \in \mathcal{G}$, then $h_1 : A \in \Delta$ or $h_0 : B \in \Gamma$.*
10. *If $h_2 : A \mathbin{-\!*} B \in \Delta$ then $\exists h_0, h_1 \in \mathcal{L}$ s.t. $(h_1, h_2 \triangleright h_0) \in \mathcal{G}$, $h_1 : A \in \Gamma$ and $h_0 : B \in \Delta$.*

11. *If $h : \exists x.A(x) \in \Gamma$ then $h : A(t) \in \Gamma$ for some $t \in T$.*
12. *If $h : \exists x.A(x) \in \Delta$ then $h : A(t) \in \Delta$ for every $t \in T$.*
13. *If $h : \Diamond A \in \Gamma$ then $\exists h_1 \in \mathcal{L}$ s.t. $h_1 : A \in \Gamma$.*
14. *If $h : \Diamond A \in \Delta$ then $\forall h_1 \in \mathcal{L}$, $h_1 : A \in \Delta$.*
15. *For any $t \in T$, $\exists h \in \mathcal{L}$ s.t. $h : t = t \in \Gamma$.*
16. *If $h_1 : t = t' \in \Gamma$ and $h_2 : A[t/x] \in \Gamma$ ($h_2 : A[t/x] \in \Delta$) then $h_2 : A[t'/x] \in \Gamma$
    (resp. $h_2 : A[t'/x] \in \Delta$).*
17. *For any label $h \in \mathcal{L}$, $h \sim h \in \mathcal{G}$.*
18. *If $h_1 \sim h_2 \in \mathcal{G}$ and a relational atom or a labelled formula $R[h_1/h] \in \mathcal{G} \cup \Gamma$ (resp.
    $R[h_1/h] \in \Delta$), then $R[h_2/h] \in \mathcal{G} \cup \Gamma$ (resp. $R[h_2/h] \in \Delta$).*
19. *If $(h_1, h_2 \triangleright h_0) \in \mathcal{G}$ then $(h_2, h_1 \triangleright h_0) \in \mathcal{G}$.*
20. *If $\{(h_1, h_2 \triangleright h_0); (h_3, h_4 \triangleright h_6); h_1 \sim h_6\} \subseteq \mathcal{G}$ then $\exists h_5 \in \mathcal{L}$. $\{(h_3, h_5 \triangleright h_0), (h_2, h_4 \triangleright h_5)\} \subseteq \mathcal{G}$.*
21. *If $\{(h_1, h_2 \triangleright h_0); (h_3, h_4 \triangleright h_9); h_0 \sim h_9\} \subseteq \mathcal{G}$ then $\exists h_5, h_6, h_7, h_8 \in \mathcal{L}$ s.t. $\{(h_5, h_6 \triangleright h_1), (h_7, h_8 \triangleright h_2), (h_5, h_7 \triangleright h_3), (h_6, h_8 \triangleright h_4)\} \subseteq \mathcal{G}$.*
22. *For every abstract points-to predicate $\rightsquigarrow^k$ in the language and for any $t_1, \ldots, t'_k \in T$, $\exists h \in \mathcal{L}$ s.t. $h : t_1 \rightsquigarrow^k t_2, \ldots, t_k \in \Gamma$.*
23. *If $\{h_1 : s \rightsquigarrow \vec{t}, h_2 : s \rightsquigarrow \vec{t}\} \subseteq \Gamma$ then $h_1 \sim h_2 \in \mathcal{G}$.*
24. *If $\{(h_1, h_3 \triangleright h_2), h_1 \sim h_3\} \subseteq \mathcal{G}$ then $h_1 \sim \epsilon \in \mathcal{G}$.*
25. *If $\{(h_1, h_2 \triangleright h_0), (h_4, h_5 \triangleright h_3), h_1 \sim h_4, h_2 \sim h_5\} \subseteq \mathcal{G}$ then $h_0 \sim h_3 \in \mathcal{G}$.*
26. *If $\{(h_1, h_2 \triangleright h_0), (h_4, h_5 \triangleright h_3), h_1 \sim h_4, h_0 \sim h_3\} \subseteq \mathcal{G}$ then $h_2 \sim h_5 \in \mathcal{G}$.*

The next lemma shows that we can build an extended FOASL model $(\mathcal{M}, \rho)$ where $\mathcal{M} = (D, I, v, \mathcal{F}, H, \circ, \epsilon)$ that falsifies the Hintikka sequent $\mathcal{G}; \Gamma \vdash \Delta$. The D, I part is a Herbrand model as in first-order logic. The construction of the monoid $(H, \circ, \epsilon)$ is similar to the one for PASL [16], where H is the set of equivalent classes of labels in the sequent. The interpretation of the predicate $\rightsquigarrow$ is defined based the set of functions $\mathcal{F}$. For each n-ary predicate $\rightsquigarrow^n$, there is a function $\mathfrak{f}_n \in \mathcal{F}$ defined as below:

$$\mathfrak{f}_n(t_1, \cdots, t_n) = [h]_{\mathcal{G}} \text{ iff } h' : t_1 \rightsquigarrow^n t_2, \cdots, t_n \in \Gamma \text{ and } h \sim h' \in \mathcal{G}.$$

where $[h]_{\mathcal{G}}$ is the class of labels equivalent to h in $\mathcal{G}$. $\mathcal{F}$ is the set of all such functions. By Condition 22 and 23 of the Hintikka sequent, each function in $\mathcal{F}$ must be a total function. The full proof is in [18].

Lemma 1 (Hintikka's Lemma). *Suppose L is a FOASL language with a non-empty set of closed terms. Every Hintikka sequent w.r.t. L is falsifiable.*

Then we show how to construct a Hintikka sequent for an unprovable formula using the proof system LS_{FOASL}. Unlike the usual procedure, we have to consider the rules with no (or more than one) principal formulae. To this end, we define a notion of *extended formulae* as in the previous work [16]:

$$ExF ::= F \mid \equiv_1 \mid \equiv_2 \mid \mapsto_1 \mid \mapsto_2 \mid \mathbb{E} \mid \mathbb{A} \mid \mathbb{CS} \mid \approx_1 \mid \approx_2 \mid$$
$$\mathbb{P} \mid \mathbb{C} \mid \mathbb{D}$$

Here, F is a FOASL formula, the other symbols correspond to the special rules in LS_{FOASL}. For example, $\equiv_1$ and $\equiv_2$ correspond to rules $=_1$ and $=_2$; $\mapsto_1$ and $\mapsto_2$ correspond to $\rightsquigarrow_1$ and $\rightsquigarrow_2$; $\approx_1$ and $\approx_2$ correspond to $\sim_1$ and $\sim_2$. The saturation procedure is performed according to a schedule, which is defined below.

Definition 2 (Schedule). *A rule instance is a tuple* (O, h, ExF, R, S, n), *where* O *is either* 0 *(left) or* 1 *(right),* h *is a label,* ExF *is an extended formula,* R *is a set of relational atoms such that* $|R| \leq 2$, S *is a set of labelled formulae with* $|S| \leq 2$, *and* n *is a natural number. Let* $\mathcal{I}$ *denote the set of all rule instances. A schedule is a function from natural numbers* $\mathbb{N}$ *to* $\mathcal{I}$. *A schedule* ϕ *is* fair *if for every rule instance* I, *the set* $\{i \mid \phi(i) = I\}$ *is infinite.*

It is easy to verify that a fair schedule must exist. This is proved by checking that $\mathcal{I}$ is a countable set [21], which follows from the fact that $\mathcal{I}$ is a finite product of countable sets. We fix a fair schedule ϕ for the following proofs. We assume the set $\mathcal{L}$ of labels is totally ordered and can be enumerated as $h_0, h_1, h_2, \cdots$, where $h_0 = \epsilon$. Similarly, we assume an infinite set of closed terms which can be enumerated as $t_0, t_1, t_2, \cdots$, all of which are disjoint from the terms in F. Suppose F is an unprovable formula, we start from the sequent $\vdash h_1 : F$ and construct an underivable sequent as below.

Definition 3. *Let* F *be a formula which is not provable in* LS_{FOASL}. *We assume that every variable in* F *is bounded, otherwise we can rewrite* F *so that unbounded variables are universally quantified. We construct a series of finite sequents* $\langle \mathcal{G}_i; \Gamma_i \vdash \Delta_i \rangle_{i \in \mathcal{N}}$ *from* F *where* $\mathcal{G}_1 = \Gamma_1 = \emptyset$ *and* $\Delta_1 = a_1 : F$. *Suppose* $\mathcal{G}_i; \Gamma_i \vdash \Delta_i$ *has been defined, we define* $\mathcal{G}_{i+1}; \Gamma_{i+1} \vdash \Delta_{i+1}$ *in the sequel. Suppose* $\phi(i) = (O_i, h_i, ExF_i, R_i, S_i, n_i)$. *When we use* n_i *to select a term (resp. label) in a formula (resp. relational atom), we assume the terms (resp. labels) are ordered from left to right. If* n_i *is greater than the number of terms in the formula (labels in the relational atom), then no effect is taken. We only show a few cases here, and display this rather involved construction in the Appendix of [18].*

- *If* $O_i = 0$, ExF_i *is a FOASL formula* $C_i = F_1 * F_2$ *and* $h_i : C_i \in \Gamma_i$, *then* $\mathcal{G}_{i+1} = \mathcal{G}_i \cup \{(h_{4i}, h_{4i+1} \triangleright h_i)\}$, $\Gamma_{i+1} = \Gamma_i \cup \{h_{4i} : F_1, h_{4i+1} : F_2\}$, $\Delta_{i+1} = \Delta_i$.
- *If* ExF_i *is* $\equiv_1$ *and* $S_i = \{h_i : t_n = t_n\}$, *where* $n \leq i + 1$, *then* $\mathcal{G}_{i+1} = \mathcal{G}_i$, $\Gamma_{i+1} = \Gamma_i \cup \{h_i : t_n = t_n\}$, *and* $\Delta_{i+1} = \Delta_i$.
- *If* ExF_i *is* $\equiv_2$ *and* $S_i = \{h : t = t', h' : A[t/x]\} \subseteq \Gamma_i$, *where* x *is the* n_ith *term in* A, *then* $\mathcal{G}_{i+1} = \mathcal{G}_i$, $\Gamma_{i+1} = \Gamma_i \cup \{h' : A[t'/x]\}$, *and* $\Delta_{i+1} = \Delta_i$.
- *If* ExF_i *is* $\equiv_2$ *and* $S_i = \{h : t = t', h' : A[t/x]\}$ *where* $h : t = t' \in \Gamma_i$, $h' : A[t/x] \in \Delta_i$, *and* x *is the* n_ith *term in* A. *Then* $\mathcal{G}_{i+1} = \mathcal{G}_i$, $\Gamma_{i+1} = \Gamma_i$, *and* $\Delta_{i+1} = \Delta_i \cup \{h' : A[t'/x]\}$.

The first rule shows how to use the $*L$ rule and how to deal with fresh variables. The indexing of labels guarantees that the choice of h_{4i}, h_{4i+1}, h_{4i+2}, h_{4i+3} are always fresh for the sequent $\mathcal{G}_i; \Gamma_i \vdash \Delta_i$. Similarly, the term t_{i+1} does not occur in the sequent $\mathcal{G}_i; \Gamma_i \vdash \Delta_i$. The second rule generates an identity equality relation for the term t_n. The last two rules find a formula $h' : A$ in the antecedent and succedent respectively, and replace t with t' in A. The construction in Definition 3 non-trivially extends a similar construction of Hintikka CSS due to Larchey-Wendling [21] and a similar one in [16].

We also borrow the notions of consistency and finite-consistency from Larchey-Wendling's work [21]. We say $\mathcal{G}'; \Gamma' \vdash \Delta' \subseteq \mathcal{G}; \Gamma \vdash \Delta$ iff $\mathcal{G}' \subseteq \mathcal{G}$,

$\Gamma' \subseteq \Gamma$ and $\Delta' \subseteq \Delta$. A sequent $\mathcal{G}; \Gamma \vdash \Delta$ is *finite* if $\mathcal{G}, \Gamma, \Delta$ are finite sets. Define $\mathcal{G}'; \Gamma' \vdash \Delta' \subseteq_f \mathcal{G}; \Gamma \vdash \Delta$ iff $\mathcal{G}'; \Gamma' \vdash \Delta' \subseteq \mathcal{G}; \Gamma \vdash \Delta$ and $\mathcal{G}'; \Gamma' \vdash \Delta'$ is finite. If $\mathcal{G}; \Gamma \vdash \Delta$ is a finite sequent, it is *consistent* iff it does not have a derivation in LS_{FOASL}. A (possibly infinite) sequent $\mathcal{G}; \Gamma \vdash \Delta$ is *finitely-consistent* iff every $\mathcal{G}'; \Gamma' \vdash \Delta' \subseteq_f \mathcal{G}; \Gamma \vdash \Delta$ is consistent.

We write $\mathcal{L}_i$ for the set of labels occurring in the sequent $\mathcal{G}_i; \Gamma_i \vdash \Delta_i$, and write D_i for the set of terms which are disjoint from those in F in that sequent. Thus $\mathcal{L}_1 = \{a_1\}$ and $D_1 = \emptyset$. The following lemma states some properties of the construction of the sequents $\mathcal{G}_i; \Gamma_i \vdash \Delta_i$.

Lemma 2. *For any $i \in \mathcal{N}$, the following properties hold:*

1. $\mathcal{G}_i; \Gamma_i \vdash \Delta_i$ *has no derivation*
2. $\mathcal{L}_i \subseteq \{a_0, a_1, \cdots, a_{4i-1}\}$

3. $D_i \subseteq \{t_0, t_1, \cdots, t_i\}$
4. $\mathcal{G}_i; \Gamma_i \vdash \Delta_i \subseteq_f \mathcal{G}_{i+1}; \Gamma_{i+1} \vdash \Delta_{i+1}$

Given the construction of the series of sequents in Definition 3, we define a notion of a *limit sequent* as the union of every sequent in the series.

Definition 4 (Limit sequent). *Let F be a formula unprovable in LS_{FOASL}. The* limit sequent *for F is the sequent $\mathcal{G}^\omega; \Gamma^\omega \vdash \Delta^\omega$ where $\mathcal{G}^\omega = \bigcup_{i \in \mathcal{N}} \mathcal{G}_i$ and $\Gamma^\omega = \bigcup_{i \in \mathcal{N}} \Gamma_i$ and $\Delta^\omega = \bigcup_{i \in \mathcal{N}} \Delta_i$ and where $\mathcal{G}_i; \Gamma_i \vdash \Delta_i$ is as defined in Definition 3.*

The last step is to show that the limit sequent is a Hintikka sequent, which gives rise to a counter-model of the formula that cannot be proved.

Lemma 3. *If F is a formula unprovable in LS_{FOASL}, then the limit sequent for F is a Hintikka sequent.*

Now we can finish the completeness theorem: whenever a FOASL formula has no derivation in LS_{FOASL}, there is an infinite counter-model. The theorem states the contraposition.

Theorem 2 (Completeness). *If F is valid in FOASL, then F is provable in LS_{FOASL}.*

5   Theories for $\mapsto$ in Separation Logics

Our predicate $\rightsquigarrow$ admits more interpretations than the standard $\mapsto$ predicate in SL heap model semantics. We can, however, approximate the behaviors of $\mapsto$ by formulating additional properties of $\mapsto$ as logical theories. We show next some of the theories for $\mapsto$ arising in various SL semantics.

5.1   Reynolds's Semantics

The $\mapsto$ predicate in Reynolds's semantics can be formalized as follows, where the store s is a total function from variables to values, and the heap h is a finite partial function from addresses to values:

$$s, h \Vdash x \mapsto y \text{ iff } dom(h) = \{s(x)\} \text{ and } h(s(x)) = s(y).$$

Here we tackle the problem indirectly from the abstract separation logic angle. We give the following theories to approximate the semantics of $\mapsto$ in SL:

1. $\Box\forall e_1, e_2.(e_1 \mapsto e_2) \wedge \top^* \to \bot$ 2. $\Box\forall e_1, e_2.(e_1 \mapsto e_2) \to \neg(\neg\top^* * \neg\top^*)$
3. $\Box\forall e_1, e_2, e_3, e_4.(e_1 \mapsto e_2) * (e_3 \mapsto e_4) \to \neg(e_1 = e_3)$
4. $\Box\forall e_1, e_2, e_3, e_4.(e_1 \mapsto e_2) \wedge (e_3 \mapsto e_4) \to (e_1 = e_3) \wedge (e_2 = e_4)$
5. $\Box\exists e_1\forall e_2.\neg((e_1 \mapsto e_2) {-\!\!*} \bot)$ 6. $\Box\forall e_1, e_2.(e_1 \mapsto e_2) \to (e_1 \rightsquigarrow e_2)$

Note that the opposite direction $(e_1 \rightsquigarrow e_2) \to (e_1 \mapsto e_2)$ does not necessarily hold because $\rightsquigarrow$ is weaker than $\mapsto$. The above theories intend to capture the inference rules for $\mapsto$ in LS_{SL} [17], the captured rules are given in Fig. 3. The first five formulae simulate the rules $\mapsto L_1$, $\mapsto L_2$, $\mapsto L_3$, $\mapsto L_4$, and HE respectively. The rule $\mapsto L_5$ can be derived by $\rightsquigarrow_2$ and Formula 6.

$$\frac{}{\mathcal{G}; \Gamma; \epsilon : e_1 \mapsto e_2 \vdash \Delta} \mapsto L_1$$

$$\frac{(\epsilon, h_0 \triangleright h_0); \mathcal{G}[\epsilon/h_1, h_0/h_2]; \Gamma[\epsilon/h_1, h_0/h_2]; h_0 : e_1 \mapsto e_2 \vdash \Delta[\epsilon/h_1, h_0/h_2]}{\quad (h_0, \epsilon \triangleright h_0); \mathcal{G}[\epsilon/h_2, h_0/h_1]; \Gamma[\epsilon/h_2, h_0/h_1]; h_0 : e_1 \mapsto e_2 \vdash \Delta[\epsilon/h_2, h_0/h_1] \quad}{(h_1, h_2 \triangleright h_0); \mathcal{G}; \Gamma; h_0 : e_1 \mapsto e_2 \vdash \Delta} \mapsto L_2$$

$$\frac{}{(h_1, h_2 \triangleright h_0); \mathcal{G}; \Gamma; h_1 : e \mapsto e_1; h_2 : e \mapsto e_2 \vdash \Delta} \mapsto L_3 \qquad \frac{\mathcal{G}; \Gamma\theta; h : e_1\theta \mapsto e_2\theta \vdash \Delta\theta}{\mathcal{G}; \Gamma; h : e_1 \mapsto e_2; h : e_3 \mapsto e_4 \vdash \Delta} \mapsto L_4$$

$$\frac{\mathcal{G}[h_1/h_2]; \Gamma[h_1/h_2]; h_1 : e_1 \mapsto e_2 \vdash \Delta[h_1/h_2]}{\mathcal{G}; \Gamma; h_1 : e_1 \mapsto e_2; h_2 : e_1 \mapsto e_2 \vdash \Delta} \mapsto L_5 \qquad \frac{(h_1, h_0 \triangleright h_2); \mathcal{G}; \Gamma; h_1 : e_1 \mapsto e_2 \vdash \Delta}{\mathcal{G}; \Gamma \vdash \Delta} HE$$

Side conditions:
Each label being substituted cannot be ϵ.   In $\mapsto L_4$, $\theta = mgu(\{(e_1, e_3), (e_2, e_4)\})$.
In HE, h_0 occurs in conclusion, h_1, h_2, e_1 are fresh.

Fig. 3. Points-to rules in LS_{SL}.

Lemma 4. *The inference rules in Fig. 3 are admissible in LS_{FOASL} when Formula 1–6 are assumed true.*

The validity of Formula 1–6 w.r.t. Reynolds's SL model is easy to check, the rationale is similar to the soundness of corresponding rules in LS_{SL} [17]. Therefore Reynolds's SL is an instance of our logic.

Lemma 5. *Formula 1–6 are valid in Reynolds's SL semantics.*

The rules in Fig. 3 cover most of the rules for $\mapsto$ in LS_{SL} [17], but we have not found a way to handle the following rule (with two premises):

$$(h_1, h_2 \rhd h_0); \mathcal{G}; \Gamma \vdash \Delta$$

$$\frac{(h_3, h_4 \rhd h_1); (h_5, h_6 \rhd h_2); \mathcal{G}; \Gamma; h_3 : e_1 \mapsto e_2; h_5 : e_1 \mapsto e_3 \vdash \Delta}{\mathcal{G}; \Gamma \vdash \Delta} \; HC$$

The rule HC effectively picks two arbitrary heaps h_1 and h_2, and does a case split of whether they can be combined or not. This rule seems to require more expressiveness than our logic. However, the above formulae cover most of properties about $\mapsto$ that existing tools for SL can handle, including the treatments in [17] and those for symbolic heaps [2].

5.2 Vafeiadis and Parkinson's SL

Vafeiadis and Parkinson's SL [35] is almost the same as Reynolds's definition, but they only consider values as addresses. This is a common setting in many applications, such as [14]. In this setting, the following formula is valid: $\top^* \to \neg((e_1 \mapsto e_2) \mathbin{-\!\!*} \neg(e_1 \mapsto e_2))$. This formula, however, is invalid in Reynolds's SL. Obviously Formula 1 to 6 are valid in Vafeiadis and Parkinson's SL, thus their logic is also an instance of our abstract logic. To cater for the special feature, we propose a formula for "total addressability":

7. $\forall e_1, e_2. \Diamond(e_1 \mapsto e_2)$

This formula ensures that there must exist a heap $(e_1 \mapsto e_2)$ no matter what values e_1, e_2 have. This is sound because in Vafeiadis and Parkinson's SL, e_1 must denote a valid address, thus h with $dom(h) = \{s(e_1)\}$ and $h(s(e_1)) = s(e_2)$, where s is the store, must be a legitimate function, which by definition is a heap.

5.3 Lee et al.'s SL

Lee et al.'s proof system for SL corresponds to a non-standard semantics (although they used Reynolds's semantics in their paper) [25]. While there is not a reference of a formal definition of their non-standard semantics, their inference rule $\mathbin{-\!\!*} Disj$ suggests that they forbid "incompatible heaps". For example, if there exists a heap $e_1 \mapsto e_2$, then there shall not exist another heap $(e_1 \mapsto e_3)$, where $e_2 \neq e_3$. Their $\mathbin{-\!\!*} Disj$ rule can help derive the following formula, which is invalid in Reynolds's SL:

$$(((e_1 \mapsto e_2) * \top) \mathbin{-\!\!*} \bot) \vee (((e_1 \mapsto e_3) * \top) \mathbin{-\!\!*} \neg((e_1 \mapsto e_2) \mathbin{-\!\!*} \bot)) \vee (e_2 = e_3)$$

If we assume that the above non-standard semantics conform with Reynolds's SL in other aspects (as validated by Formula 1–6), then it can be seen as a special instance of our abstract logic. The compatibility property can then be formulated as follows:

8. $\forall e_1, e_2. \Diamond(e_1 \mapsto e_2) \to \neg(\exists e_3. \neg(e_2 = e_3) \wedge \Diamond(e_1 \mapsto e_3))$

With Formula 8 we can prove the invalid formula above.

5.4   Thakur et al.'s SL

There are SL variants that forbid heaps with cyclic lists, for example, the one defined by Thakur et al. [33]. Consequently, the following two formulae are unsatisfiable in their SL:

$$e_1 \mapsto e_1 \qquad\qquad e_1 \mapsto e_2 * e_2 \mapsto e_1$$

To formulate this property, we first define a notion of a path:

$$\forall e_1, e_2.\Box(path(e_1, e_2) \equiv e_1 \mapsto e_2 \vee (\exists e_3.(e_1 \mapsto e_3) * path(e_3, e_2)))$$

where $\equiv$ denotes logical equivalence (bi-implication). Now the property of "acyclism" can be formulated as

9. $\forall e_1, e_2.\Box(path(e_1, e_2) \rightarrow e_1 \neq e_2)$

which renders cyclic paths unsatisfiable in our logic, too. Note that since our proof system does not support inductive definitions, we cannot force the interpretation of *path* to be the least fixed point of its definition. We leave the incorporation of inductive definitions to future work.

6   Implementation and Experiment

Our theorem prover for FOASL extends our previous prover for Reynolds's SL [17] with the ability to handle (non-inductive) predicates and modalities. To speed up proof search, instead of implementing $=_2$ and $\sim_2$, we use the following rules:

$$\frac{\mathcal{G}; \Gamma[s/t] \vdash \Delta[s/t]}{\mathcal{G}; h : s = t; \Gamma \vdash \Delta} =_2' \qquad\qquad \frac{\mathcal{G}\theta; \Gamma\theta \vdash \Delta\theta}{h_1 \sim h_2; \mathcal{G}; \Gamma \vdash \Delta} \sim_2'$$

where $\theta = [h_1/h_2]$ if $h_2 \neq \epsilon$ and $\theta = [h_2/h_1]$ otherwise.

These two rules can be shown to be interchangeable with $=_2$ and $\sim_2$. One direction, i.e., showing that $=_2'$ and $\sim_2'$ can be derived in FOASL, is straightforward. The other direction requires some further justification. Let LS'_{FOASL} be LS_{FOASL} with $=_2$ and $\sim_2$ replaced by $=_2'$ and $\sim_2'$ respectively, we then need to show that $=_2$ and $\sim_2$ are admissible in LS'_{FOASL}. To prove this, we follow a similar proof for free-equality rules for first-order terms by Schroeder-Heister [32]. The key part in that proof is in showing that provability is closed under substitutions. In our setting, we need to show that LS'_{FOASL} is closed under both term substitutions and label substitutions, which are stated below.

Lemma 6. *If $\mathcal{G}; \Gamma \vdash \Delta$ is derivable in LS'_{FOASL}, then so is $\mathcal{G}; \Gamma[s/t] \vdash \Delta[s/t]$ for any terms s and t.*

Lemma 7. *If $\mathcal{G}; \Gamma \vdash \Delta$ is derivable in LS'_{FOASL}, then so is $\mathcal{G}[h_1/h_2]; \vdash \Gamma[h_1/h_2]\Delta[h_1/h_2]$ for any label h_1 and label variable h_2.*

Note that by restricting h_2 to a label variable, we forbid ϵ to be substituted in the above lemma. These two lemmas require induction on the height of derivations, and routine checks confirm that they both hold. Then it is a corollary that $=_2$ and $\sim_2$ are admissible in LS'_{FOASL}.

Since the heap model is widely used, our prover also includes useful rules to reason in the heap model, such as the derived rules in Fig. 3. But we currently have not included the HC rule in our proof search procedure. Since many applications of SL involve reasoning about invalid addresses, such as nil, we also add a theory to capture a simple aspect of the invalid address nil:

10. $\Box \forall \vec{e}.(nil \mapsto \vec{e}) \to \bot$

Since the current prover is an extension of our previous prover, it builds in the inference rules for linked lists and binary trees for reasoning about the *symbolic heap* fragment of SL. It is also capable of proving theorems used in verification of a tail-recursive append function [26], as shown in [17]. However, we do not exploit these aspects here.

We illustrate a list of formulae provable by our prover in Table 2. Formulae 1–4 are examples drawn from Galmiche and Méry's work on resource graph

Table 2. Experiment on selected formulae.

	Formula	Time
1	$((\top -\!\!* (((k \mapsto c, d) -\!\!* (l \mapsto a, b)) \to (l \mapsto a, b))) \to (l \mapsto a, b))$	< 0.001s
2	$((\exists x_2.((\exists x_1.((x_2 \mapsto x_1, b) \to \bot)) \to \bot)) \to (\exists x_3.(x_3 \mapsto a, b)))$	< 0.001s
3	$(((\top^* \to \bot) \to \bot) \to ((\exists x_1.((x_1 \mapsto a, b) * \top)) \to \bot))$	< 0.001s
4	$((\exists x_3\, x_2\, x_1.(((x_3 \mapsto a, x_2) * (x_1 \mapsto c, d)) \wedge x_2 = x_1)) \to$ $(\exists x_5\, x_4.((x_4 \mapsto c, d) * (x_5 \mapsto a, x_4))))$	< 0.001s
5	$((((e_1 \mapsto e_2) * \top) \wedge (((e_3 \mapsto e_4) * \top) \wedge$ $(((e_5 \mapsto e_6) * \top) \wedge (\neg(e_1 = e_3) \wedge (\neg(e_1 = e_5) \wedge \neg(e_3 = e_5)))))) \to$ $(((e_1 \mapsto e_2) * ((e_3 \mapsto e_4) * (e_5 \mapsto e_6))) * \top))$	0.9s
6	$((((e_1 \mapsto e_2) * \neg((e_3 \mapsto e_4) * \top)) \wedge ((e_3 \mapsto e_4) * \top)) \to e_1 = e_3)$	< 0.001s
7	$\neg((\neg \top^* * \neg \top^*) -\!\!* \bot)$	0.0015s
8	$((\neg(((l_1 \mapsto p) * (l_2 \mapsto q)) -\!\!* (\neg(l_3 \mapsto r)))) \to$ $(\neg((l_1 \mapsto p) -\!\!* (\neg(\neg((l_2 \mapsto q) -\!\!* (\neg(l_3 \mapsto r)))))))))$	< 0.001s
9	$((\neg((l_1 \mapsto p) -\!\!* (\neg(\neg((l_2 \mapsto q) -\!\!* (\neg(l3 \mapsto r))))))) \to$ $(\neg(((l_1 \mapsto p) * (l_2 \mapsto q)) -\!\!* (\neg(l_3 \mapsto r)))))$	< 0.001s
10	$((\neg((lx \mapsto ly) -\!\!* (\neg((l1 \mapsto p) * (l2 \mapsto q))))) \to$ $(\neg((\neg((\neg((\neg((lx \mapsto ly) -\!\!* (\neg(l1 \mapsto p)))) * (l2 \mapsto q) \wedge$ $(\neg(\exists x_1.((lx \mapsto x_1) * \top)))))) \wedge (\neg((\neg((\neg((lx \mapsto ly) -\!\!*$ $(\neg(l2 \mapsto q)))) * ((l1 \mapsto p) \wedge (\neg(\exists x_2.((lx \mapsto x_2) * \top)))))))))))$	< 0.001s
11	$((\forall x_2\, x_1.\Diamond(x_2 \mapsto x_1)) \to (\top^* \to \neg((e_1 \mapsto e_2) -\!\!* \neg(e_1 \mapsto e_2))))$	< 0.001s
12	$((\forall x_3\, x_2.(\Diamond(x_3 \mapsto x_2) \to \neg(\exists x_1.(\neg(x2 = x1) \wedge \Diamond(x_3 \mapsto x_1))))) \to$ $(((((e_1 \mapsto e_2) * \top) -\!\!* \bot) \vee ((((e_1 \mapsto e_3) * \top) -\!\!* \neg((e_1 \mapsto e_2) -\!\!* \bot))$ $\vee e_2 = e_3)))$	0.0025s

tableaux for SL [15]. Formula 5 is a property about overlaid data structures: if the current heap contains $(e_1 \mapsto e_2)$ and $(e_3 \mapsto e_4)$ and $(e_5 \mapsto e_6)$, and they are pairwise distinct, then the current heap contains the combination of the three heaps. Formula 6 says that if the current heap can be split into two parts, one is $(e_1 \mapsto e_2)$ and the other part does not contain $(e_3 \mapsto e_4)$, and the current heap contains $(e_3 \mapsto e_4)$, then we deduce that $(e_3 \mapsto e_4)$ and $(e_1 \mapsto e_2)$ must be the same heap, therefore $e_1 = e_3$. Formula 7 says that any heap can be combined with a composite heap. We give a derivation of formula 7 in Appendix A. Formulae 8–10 are properties of "septraction" in SL with Rely-Guarantee [35]. Finally, formulae 11 and 12 show that our prover can easily support reasoning about Vafeiadis and Parkinson's SL (cf. Sect. 5.2) and Lee et al.'s SL (cf. Sect. 5.3) by simply adding the corresponding theories as assumptions. This is a great advantage over our previous work where new rules have to be implemented to extend the ability of the prover. To our knowledge most existing provers for SL cannot prove the formulae in Table 2. Examples of larger formulae used in program verification can be found in the experiment of our previous prover [17], upon which this prover is built.

7   Conclusion

This paper presents a first-order abstract separation logic with modalities. This logic is rich enough to express formulae in real-world applications such as program verification. We give a sound and complete labelled sequent calculus for this logic. The completeness of the finite calculus implies that our logic is recursively enumerable. To deal with $\mapsto$, we give a set of formulae to approximate the semantics of memory model. Of course, we cannot fully simulate $\mapsto$, but we can handle most properties about $\mapsto$ compared with existing tools for SL. Moreover, we can prove numerous formulae that many existing tools for SL cannot handle. The techniques discussed in this paper are demonstrated in a rather flexible theorem prover which supports automated reasoning in different SL variants without any change to the implementation. With this foundation, one can simply add formulae as "assumption", and prove theorems that cannot be proved in the base logic.

Acknowledgments. This research is supported by the National Research Foundation, Prime Minister's Office, Singapore under its National Cybersecurity R&D Program (Award No. NRF2014NCR-NCR001-30) and administered by the National Cybersecurity R&D Directorate.

A   An Example Derivation

We sometimes write $r \times n$ when it is obvious that the rule r is applied n times. We omit some formulae to save space. The derivation is given in the next page. The sub-derivation Π_1 is similar to Π_2.

$$\cfrac{\cfrac{\cfrac{\cfrac{\cfrac{\cfrac{\cfrac{\cdots;\epsilon:e_3\mapsto e_4\vdash\epsilon:e_3\mapsto e_4;\cdots}{\cdots;\epsilon:e_3\mapsto e_4\vdash\epsilon:(e_3\mapsto e_4)\wedge\top^*;\cdots}\,{}^{id}}{\cdots;\epsilon:((e_3\mapsto e_4)\wedge\top^*)\rightarrow\bot;\epsilon:e_3\mapsto e_4\vdash\cdots}\,{}^{\wedge R}}{\cdots;\epsilon:\forall e_1,e_2.((e_1\mapsto e_2)\wedge\top^*)\rightarrow\bot;\epsilon:e_3\mapsto e_4\vdash\cdots}\,{}^{\vee L\times 2}}{\cdots;\epsilon:e_3\mapsto e_4\vdash\cdots}\,{}^{\Box L\text{ on Formula 1}}}{\cdots}\quad}{\quad}$$

$$\cfrac{\cfrac{\cfrac{\cfrac{\cfrac{(\epsilon,h_3\triangleright\epsilon);\cdots;h_3:e_3\mapsto e_4\vdash\cdots}{\cdots;h_3:e_3\mapsto e_4;h_3:\top^*\vdash\cdots}\,{}^{Eq_1}}{\cdots;h_3:e_3\mapsto e_4\vdash h_3:\neg\top^*;\cdots}\,{}^{\top^*L}}{\cdots}\,{}^{\neg R}}{}\,{}^{*R}}{}$$

$$\cfrac{\cfrac{\cfrac{\cdots;\epsilon:e_3\mapsto e_4\vdash\epsilon:\top^*;\cdots}{\cdots;\epsilon:e_3\mapsto e_4\vdash\epsilon:(e_3\mapsto e_4)\wedge\top^*;\cdots}\,{}^{\top^*R}}{}}{}$$

$$\cfrac{\cfrac{\cdots;\epsilon:\bot;\epsilon:e_3\mapsto e_4\vdash\cdots}{\cdots;\epsilon:e_3\mapsto e_4\vdash\cdots}\,{}^{\bot L}}{}\,{}^{\rightarrow L}$$

$$\Pi_1$$

$$\cfrac{\cfrac{\cfrac{\cfrac{\cfrac{\cfrac{\cfrac{\cfrac{\cfrac{\cfrac{\cfrac{\cfrac{\cfrac{\cfrac{\cfrac{(h_3,h_1\triangleright h_5);\cdots;h_1:e_1\mapsto e_2;h_3:e_3\mapsto e_4\vdash h_5:((\neg\top^*)*(\neg\top^*));\cdots}{\cdots}}{}}{}}{}}{}}{}}{}}{}}{}}{}}{}}{}}{}}{}$$

$$\cfrac{\cfrac{\cfrac{\cfrac{\cfrac{\cfrac{\cfrac{\cfrac{\cfrac{\cfrac{\cfrac{\cfrac{\cfrac{\cfrac{(h_5,h_0\triangleright h_4);(h_3,h_1\triangleright h_5);\cdots;h_0:((\neg\top^*)*(\neg\top^*));\cdots;h_0:(((\neg\top^*)*(\neg\top^*))*(\neg\top^*))\rightarrow\bot;h_1:(e_1\mapsto e_2);h_3:(e_3\mapsto e_4)\vdash h_5:((\neg\top^*)*(\neg\top^*));\cdots}{(h_0,h_5\triangleright h_4);(h_3,h_1\triangleright h_5);\cdots;h_0:(((\neg\top^*)*(\neg\top^*)))\vdash\cdots}\,{}^{Eq_1}}{(h_0,h_1\triangleright h_2);(h_2,h_3\triangleright h_4);\cdots;h_0:(((\neg\top^*)*(\neg\top^*));h_3:(e_3\mapsto e_4)\vdash\cdots}\,{}^{E}}{(h_1,h_0\triangleright h_2);\cdots;h_0:(((\neg\top^*)*(\neg\top^*))*(\neg\top^*));h_1:(e_1\mapsto e_2);h_3:(e_3\mapsto e_4)\vdash h_4:\bot;h_2:\bot}\,{}^{A}}{(h_1,h_0\triangleright h_2);\cdots;h_0:((\neg\top^*)*(\neg\top^*));h_1:(e_1\mapsto e_2)\vdash h_2:(e_3\mapsto e_4)-\!\!*\bot;h_2:\bot}\,{}^{E\times 2}}{(h_1,h_0\triangleright h_2);\cdots;h_2:\neg((e_3\mapsto e_4)-\!\!*\bot);h_0:((\neg\top^*)*(\neg\top^*))-\!\!*\bot;h_1:(e_1\mapsto e_2)\vdash h_2:\bot}\,{}^{-\!\!*R}}{(h_1,h_0\triangleright h_2);\cdots;h_2:\forall e_2.\neg((e_3\mapsto e_2)-\!\!*\bot);h_0:((\neg\top^*)*(\neg\top^*))-\!\!*\bot;h_1:(e_1\mapsto e_2)\vdash h_2:\bot}\,{}^{\neg L}}{(h_1,h_0\triangleright h_2);\cdots;h_2:\exists e_1\forall e_2.\neg((e_1\mapsto e_2)-\!\!*\bot);h_0:((\neg\top^*)*(\neg\top^*))-\!\!*\bot;h_1:(e_1\mapsto e_2)\vdash h_2:\bot}\,{}^{\vee L}}{(h_1,h_0\triangleright h_2);\cdots;h_0:((\neg\top^*)*(\neg\top^*))-\!\!*\bot;h_1:(e_1\mapsto e_2)\vdash h_2:\bot}\,{}^{\exists L}}{(h_1,h_0\triangleright h_2);\cdots;h_0:((\neg\top^*)*(\neg\top^*))-\!\!*\bot;h_1:(e_1\mapsto e_2)\vdash h_2:\bot}\,{}^{\Box L\text{ on Formula 5}}}{\cdots;h_0:((\neg\top^*)*(\neg\top^*))-\!\!*\bot\vdash h_0:(e_1\mapsto e_2)-\!\!*\bot}\,{}^{-\!\!*R}}{\cdots;h_0:\neg((e_1\mapsto e_2)-\!\!*\bot);h_0:(((\neg\top^*)*(\neg\top^*))-\!\!*\bot)}\,{}^{\neg L}}{\cdots;h_0:\forall e_2.\neg((e_1\mapsto e_2)-\!\!*\bot);h_0:(((\neg\top^*)*(\neg\top^*))-\!\!*\bot)}\,{}^{\vee L}}{\cdots;h_0:\exists e_1\forall e_2.\neg((e_1\mapsto e_2)-\!\!*\bot);h_0:(((\neg\top^*)*(\neg\top^*))-\!\!*\bot)}\,{}^{\exists L}}{;h_0:\mathcal{A};h_0:((\neg\top^*)*(\neg\top^*))-\!\!*\bot\vdash}\,{}^{\Box L\text{ on Formula 5}}$$

$$\cfrac{\cfrac{;h_0:\mathcal{A};h_0:((\neg\top^*)*(\neg\top^*))-\!\!*\bot\vdash}{;h_0:\mathcal{A}\vdash h_0:\neg(((\neg\top^*)*(\neg\top^*))-\!\!*\bot)}\,{}^{\neg R}}{;\vdash h_0:\mathcal{A}\rightarrow\neg(((\neg\top^*)*(\neg\top^*))-\!\!*\bot)}\,{}^{\rightarrow R}$$

References

1. Berdine, J., Calcagno, C., O'Hearn, P.W.: Smallfoot: modular automatic assertion checking with separation logic. In: Boer, F.S., Bonsangue, M.M., Graf, S., Roever, W.-P. (eds.) FMCO 2005. LNCS, vol. 4111, pp. 115–137. Springer, Heidelberg (2006). doi:10.1007/11804192_6

2. Berdine, J., Calcagno, C., O'Hearn, P.W.: Symbolic Execution with Separation Logic. In: Yi, K. (ed.) APLAS 2005. LNCS, vol. 3780, pp. 52–68. Springer, Heidelberg (2005). doi:10.1007/11575467_5

3. Brochenin, R., Demri, S., Lozes, E.: On the almighty wand. Inf. Comput. **211**, 106–137 (2012)

4. Brookes, S.: A semantics for concurrent separation logic. Theor. Comput. Sci. **375**(1–3), 227–270 (2007)

5. Brotherston, J.: A unified display proof theory for bunched logic. ENTCS **265**, 197–211 (2010)

6. Brotherston, J., Distefano, D., Petersen, R.L.: Automated cyclic entailment proofs in separation logic. In: Bjørner, N., Sofronie-Stokkermans, V. (eds.) CADE 2011. LNCS (LNAI), vol. 6803, pp. 131–146. Springer, Heidelberg (2011). doi:10.1007/978-3-642-22438-6_12

7. Brotherston, J., Kanovich, M.: Undecidability of propositional separation logic and its neighbours. J. ACM **61**(2), 14:1–14:43 (2014). doi:10.1145/2542667

8. Brotherston, J., Villard, J.: Parametric completeness for separation theories. In: POPL, pp. 453–464. ACM (2014)

9. Calcagno, C., O'Hearn, P.W., Yang, H.: Local action and abstract separation logic. In: LICS, pp. 366–378. IEEE (2007)

10. Calcagno, C., Yang, H., O'Hearn, P.W.: Computability and Complexity Results for a Spatial Assertion Language for Data Structures. In: Hariharan, R., Vinay, V., Mukund, M. (eds.) FSTTCS 2001. LNCS, vol. 2245, pp. 108–119. Springer, Heidelberg (2001). doi:10.1007/3-540-45294-X_10

11. Demri, S., Deters, M.: Expressive completeness of separation logic with two variables and no separating conjunction. In: CSL/LICS (2014)

12. Demri, S., Galmiche, D., Larchey-Wendling, D., Méry, D.: Separation logic with one quantified variable. In: Hirsch, E.A., Kuznetsov, S.O., Pin, J.É., Vereshchagin, N.K. (eds.) CSR 2014. LNCS, vol. 8476, pp. 125–138. Springer, Heidelberg (2014). doi:10.1007/978-3-319-06686-8_10

13. Dockins, R., Hobor, A., Appel, A.W.: A fresh look at separation algebras and share accounting. In: Hu, Z. (ed.) APLAS 2009. LNCS, vol. 5904, pp. 161–177. Springer, Heidelberg (2009). doi:10.1007/978-3-642-10672-9_13

14. Galmiche, D., Méry, D., Pym, D.: The semantics of BI and resource tableaux. MSCS **15**(6), 1033–1088 (2005)

15. Galmiche, D., Méry, D.: Tableaux and resource graphs for separation logic. J. Logic Comput. **20**(1), 189–231 (2010)

16. Hóu, Z., Clouston, R., Goré, R., Tiu, A.: Proof search for propositional abstract separation logics via labelled sequents. In: POPL (2014)

17. Hóu, Z., Goré, R., Tiu, A.: Automated theorem proving for assertions in separation logic with all connectives. In: Felty, A.P., Middeldorp, A. (eds.) CADE 2015. LNCS (LNAI), vol. 9195, pp. 501–516. Springer, Heidelberg (2015). doi:10.1007/978-3-319-21401-6_34

18. Hóu, Z., Tiu, A.: Completeness for a first-order abstract separation logic [cs.LO] (2016). arXiv: 1608.06729

19. Jensen, J.B., Birkedal, L.: Fictional separation logic. In: Seidl, H. (ed.) ESOP 2012. LNCS, vol. 7211, pp. 377–396. Springer, Heidelberg (2012). doi:10.1007/978-3-642-28869-2_19

20. Krishnaswami, N.R.: Reasoning about iterators with separation logic. In: SAVCBS, pp. 83–86. ACM (2006)

21. Larchey-Wendling, D.: The formal strong completeness of partial monoidal Boolean BI. JLC **26**(2), 605–640 (2014)

22. Larchey-Wendling, D., Galmiche, D.: Exploring the relation between intuitionistic BI and Boolean BI: an unexpected embedding. MSCS **19**(3), 435–500 (2009)

23. Larchey-Wendling, D., Galmiche, D.: The undecidability of Boolean BI through phase semantics. In: LICS, pp. 140–149 (2010)

24. Larchey-Wendling, D., Galmiche, D.: Looking at separation algebras with Boolean BI-eyes. In: Diaz, J., Lanese, I., Sangiorgi, D. (eds.) TCS 2014. LNCS, vol. 8705, pp. 326–340. Springer, Heidelberg (2014). doi:10.1007/978-3-662-44602-7_25

25. Lee, W., Park, S.: A proof system for separation logic with magic wand. In: POPL, pp. 477–490. ACM (2014)

26. Maeda, T., Sato, H., Yonezawa, A.: Extended alias type system using separating implication. In: TLDI, pp. 29–42. ACM (2011)

27. Pérez, J.A.N., Rybalchenko, A.: Separation logic + superposition calculus = heap theorem prover. In: PLDI. ACM (2011)

28. O'Hearn, P.W., Pym, D.J.: The logic of bunched implications. BSL **5**(2), 215–244 (1999)

29. O'Hearn, P., Reynolds, J., Yang, H.: Local Reasoning about Programs that Alter Data Structures. In: Fribourg, L. (ed.) CSL 2001. LNCS, vol. 2142, pp. 1–19. Springer, Heidelberg (2001). doi:10.1007/3-540-44802-0_1

30. Park, J., Seo, J., Park, S.: A theorem prover for Boolean BI. In: POPL 2013, New York, NY, USA, pp. 219–232 (2013)

31. Reynolds, J.C.: Separation logic: a logic for shared mutable data structures. In: LICS, pp. 55–74. IEEE (2002)

32. Schroeder-Heister, Peter: Definitional reflection and the completion. In: Dyckhoff, Roy (ed.) ELP 1993. LNCS, vol. 798, pp. 333–347. Springer, Heidelberg (1994). doi:10.1007/3-540-58025-5_65

33. Thakur, A., Breck, J., Reps, T.: Satisfiability modulo abstraction for separation logic with linked lists. In: SPIN 2014, pp. 58–67 (2014)

34. Troelstra, A.S., Schwichtenberg, H.: Basic Proof Theory. Cambridge University Press, New York (1996)

35. Vafeiadis, V., Parkinson, M.: A marriage of rely/guarantee and separation logic. In: Caires, L., Vasconcelos, V.T. (eds.) CONCUR 2007. LNCS, vol. 4703, pp. 256–271. Springer, Heidelberg (2007). doi:10.1007/978-3-540-74407-8_18

Author Index

Abe, Tatsuya 63
Accattoli, Beniamino 206
Arai, Ryoya 148

Balat, Vincent 377
Bi, Xuan 251
Binder, Walter 139

Cha, Sooyoung 25
Chen, Lydia Y. 139
Chin, Wei-Ngan 423

de'Liguoro, Ugo 187
DeYoung, Henry 3
Dougherty, Daniel J. 187

Fragoso Santos, José 401

Gandhi, Rajeev 42
Gardner, Philippa 314, 401
Guerrieri, Giulio 206

Hobor, Aquinas 314
Honsell, Furio 229
Horne, Ross 87
Hóu, Zhé 444
Hüttel, Hans 96

Iwasaki, Hideya 148

Jeong, Sehun 25

Kameyama, Yukiyoshi 271
Kiselyov, Oleg 271, 357
Kobayashi, Naoki 295, 335

Le, Quang Loc 423
Lenisa, Marina 229
Liquori, Luigi 187, 229

Maeda, Toshiyuki 63

Narasimhan, Priya 42
Nguyen, Nam 87

Oh, Hakjoo 25
Oliveira, Bruno C.d.S. 251

Pfenning, Frank 3

Raad, Azalea 314, 401
Radanne, Gabriel 377
Rosà, Andrea 139

Sato, Shigeyuki 148
Scagnetto, Ivan 229
Stadtmüller, Kai 116
Stolze, Claude 187
Sudo, Yuto 271
Sulzmann, Martin 116
Sumii, Eijiro 171

Tan, Jiaqi 42
Tatsuta, Makoto 423
Tay, Hui Jun 42
Terao, Taku 295
Thiemann, Peter 116
Tiu, Alwen 87, 444
Tsukada, Takeshi 295, 335

Villard, Jules 314
Vouillon, Jérôme 377

Yachi, Taichi 171
Yang, Yanpeng 251
Yasukata, Kazuhide 335

Printed in the United States
By Bookmasters